# POLYMERS AND RESINS

## Their Chemistry and Chemical Engineering

*by*

### BRAGE GOLDING, Ph.D.

*Head, School of Chemical Engineering*
*Purdue University*
*Formerly Director of Research, Lilly Varnish Company*

## D. VAN NOSTRAND COMPANY, INC.

### PRINCETON, NEW JERSEY

TORONTO                    LONDON

NEW YORK

## D. VAN NOSTRAND COMPANY, INC.

120 Alexander St., Princeton, New Jersey (*Principal office*)
24 West 40th Street, New York 18, New York

### D. VAN NOSTRAND COMPANY, LTD.
358, Kensington High Street, London, W.14, England

### D. VAN NOSTRAND COMPANY (Canada), LTD.
25 Hollinger Road, Toronto 16, Canada

———————

———————

Published simultaneously in Canada by
D. VAN NOSTRAND COMPANY (Canada), LTD.

———————

Library of Congress Catalogue Card No. 59–8412

———————

07602a25
PRINTED IN THE UNITED STATES OF AMERICA

# PREFACE

This book is the outgrowth of a first course offered in the chemistry and chemical engineering of organic polymeric and resinous substances to seniors and graduate students in chemistry and chemical engineering at Purdue University. For some time, the author has been searching for an up-to-date text, not a treatise, which included the theory, chemistry, fabrication, and applications of polymeric and resinous materials. Needless to say, such a book was not available.

Originally planned to be half the size of the present text, the book grew because there was simply so much to cover in all fields, despite the fact that only products of commercial significance have been included. Because of the rapidity of growth of the polymer field, it has been difficult to resist the temptation to add to or revise portions of the manuscript regularly as new products or discoveries have been announced (almost daily). It is believed, however, that the basic information contained herein is adequate for students for some time to come.

The coverage of the book has not been limited to plastics, but includes fibers and elastomers as well. It was purposely made wide, so that the book could be used as a text regardless of the particular field of interest of the instructor. By a judicious selection of portions of the book, either a one semester or a full year course can be based upon it.

The scope, sequence, and method of treatment of the various subjects will be found to differ appreciably from the conventional text, although the author claims no originality for the contents. Much thought has been given to the sequence, classifications, and terminology, since it has been the author's experience that a student understandably has a natural desire to have new subjects presented in a logical manner. Polymers have been classified by chemical type and similarity, rather than by physical end use, since this can be done logically and avoids the grouping of a series of chemically unrelated substances which happen to be useful in a particular field (elastomers, for example).

The organic chemistry involved in the manufacture of the raw materials needed for polymer production has been given in somewhat greater detail than is usual in a book of this kind. This has been done for two reasons: (1) most students (even organic chemistry majors) apparently do not obtain this information in their usual chemistry courses, and (2) recent commercial reactions are found widely scattered in the literature.

As a result of the extensive coverage of the whole field of commercial polymers, this text should also be of value as a reference work. Because the book was designed primarily as a text, however, extensive reference to the literature has not been made. The reference listings at the end of each chapter will provide a means for obtaining more detailed information and contain many of the original sources of the information for this book, excluding the periodical literature which is much too voluminous to be included. Many of the references given are secondary, rather than primary references. This was done deliberately, since it is believed that the beginning student of this subject will assimilate further discussion of the particular topic under consideration more easily in this way than by a study of original articles. Most secondary references contain references to the original periodical literature if further study is desired.

Items of interest have been included which, although not necessarily in themselves of great importance, should arouse the student's interest and enable him to connect the information gained in a polymer course with processes and products found on the market. Trade names of representative commercial products have been capitalized throughout and included parenthetically at appropriate places; these are by no means inclusive, but were selected rather arbitrarily among those likely to be encountered.

The chapter on physicochemical behavior has deliberately been placed near the end of the book, since it was felt that a fuller understanding of the molecular phenomena responsible for the differing properties of various polymers would come after a study of the products themselves; i.e., a correlation can then be made by the student between the molecular configuration being discussed and the chemical and physical structures of the polymers already studied.

The chapters on fabrication and applications were included, in large part due to the engineering students' strongly expressed desire for such information. Sufficient description is given to enable a student to make an intelligent guess concerning the composition and probable method of fabrication of everyday commercial polymeric products.

It is unfortunate, in one way, that the field of polymers has grown so rapidly. Terms describing a product or a process have been adopted or adapted from other fields, or have been coined, which, by themselves, might have served satisfactorily. However, the same term is often found to be in use for more than one chemical entity, product, or process and, further, the etymology of some of the newer terms appears to be inconsistent with that of many of the longer established ones. The disadvantages of this looseness and inconsistency are simply that it makes the task of a beginner in this field much more arduous and makes even more difficult the accurate transfer of thoughts from a writer to his readers.  An example of this looseness in terminology is found in the recent word "telomer," which has been either implicitly or explicitly defined in at least three different ways.  Other particularly irritating examples of poor terminology will be called to the reader's notice throughout this book.  It is hoped that some qualified group, preferably from the Americal Chemical Society in this country, will give its attention to this problem before such terms become too firmly established in this field.  In the meantime, the author has attempted to follow what is believed to be "popular" usage, and, in cases where this has not yet been made clear, has assumed the prerogative of writing as he sees best.  (Unfortunately, it is feared that most other authors also have done this.)

Acknowledgment is gratefully made to the authors and publishers of the many books and periodicals which have been used for source material and to the many companies which have generously furnished illustrations for this book.  The author is indebted to his colleagues at Purdue University, particularly Professors R. N. Shreve, J. M. Smith, J. M. Woods, L. F. Albright, and L. C. Case, and to Professor R. A. Ragatz, University of Wisconsin, for their encouragement and assistance.  Gratitude is expressed to the late Professor E. A. Hauser, Massachusetts Institute of Technology, Professors L. F. Rahm and Bryce Maxwell of the Plastics Laboratory, Princeton University, Dr. R. W. Ivett, Hercules Powder Company, and Dr. S. G. Weissberg, National Bureau of Standards, for their review and constructive comment on the manuscript during its preparation.  Special acknowledgment is due Professor J. M. Church, Columbia University, for his conscientious and critical review of the completed manuscript.  The assistance of R. S. Bailey and M. E. Evans, Lilly Varnish Company, in searching the literature has been of real value.  Without the patience and perseverance of Jacqueline Bailey, Harriet Hite, and Kathryn Stevens, who typed the many revisions of the manuscript, this book would not have been possible. Loving appreciation is gladly expressed to my wife, Hinda, who patiently and competently proof-read the manuscript many times, and to my children, Brage, Jr., Susan, and Julie, who diligently and not always uncomplainingly sharpened pencils, ran sundry errands, and absented themselves at critical times.  Gratitude is expressed to W. I. Longsworth, Monroe Heath, and H. B. Currens, Lilly Varnish Company, whose assistance and encouragement have helped materially.

BRAGE GOLDING

*Indianapolis, Indiana*
*January, 1959*

To

my wife and children

with whom I hope to become reacquainted

# TABLE OF CONTENTS

*Chapter 1*

# INTRODUCTORY CONCEPTS
# AND DEFINITIONS

High-molecular-weight products have been developing naturally since the early days of the earth's formation. The two most essential and widely distributed kinds of organic matter are composed of very large, high-molecular-weight molecules. These two classes of substances are cellulose (the chief component of the cell walls of plants) and proteins (essential constituents of all living cells). Thus, all plants and animals consist in large measure of what are now called polymers.

It may seem strange, then, that the deliberate synthesis of such compounds by man has occurred only during the past fifty years or so. The principal reason is that an understanding of their composition and formation did not come until recently. Even more recent has been the establishment of a firm, quantitative basis for characterizing such compounds; this has taken place only during the past twenty-five years—a very short time.

This latter brief era has seen the development of a tremendous chemical industry devoted exclusively to the production of a very large and constantly increasing number of high-molecular-weight compounds, most of which do not exist in nature. All fibers, most plastics, and all elastomers which we use today, whether natural, modified, or synthetic, are composed of such substances and, in fact, owe most of their unusual properties to their large-molecule composition.

Within the past thirty years, the hypothesis that organic polymers are ordinary compounds whose atoms are joined by covalent bonds has gained almost complete acceptance. Prior to about 1930, many believed that polymers were small molecules held together as colloidal aggregates by unknown forces. This latter view has been disproved by the large amount of experimental evidence and the theoretical agreement with this evidence which have accumulated. The unusual properties of polymers may now be reconciled and explained on the basis of their great length and internal structure without recourse to unknown forces; the colloidal properties, elasticity, flexibility, and high viscosities of polymers are now explainable in terms of high-molecular-weight, linear, branched, and cross-linked

1

molecules, held together by primary covalent bonds and often associated by weaker secondary valence forces, as will be discussed in detail in Chapter 10.

It is the purpose of this book to present to the student of this subject the development of the theory, chemistry, and engineering which has taken place within the lifetime of almost all readers. In order to describe the building units and their products, some preliminary explanations and definitions are necessary.

High-molecular-weight substances of the kind considered in this book are usually termed *polymers* (*poly-* = many; *meros* = part), since they are composed of many parts of a simpler substance, the *monomer* (*mono-* = single). The term "polymer" is indefinite in the sense that the minimum length or size of the molecules is unspecified. Literally, a molecule made up of as few as three "parts" could be termed a polymer. However, the unqualified use of this term is generally accepted to imply a much larger molecule of such size that the properties associated with long-chain molecules have become evident. It is probably preferable to call the lower-molecular-weight products *oligomers* (*oligo-* = few) to distinguish them from polymers. The term "high-molecular-weight polymer" (and its popular contraction "high polymer") is frequently used in order to call attention to the fact that the particular polymer under consideration is one of unusually high molecular weight. Many organic compounds are of fairly high molecular weight, yet are not considered to be polymers, since it is the complexity of their molecules, not the manifold repetition of simple units, which accounts for their molecular size.

The unique chemical and physical properties of very large molecules formed by the adding together of smaller molecules do not begin to appear at a definite molecular size. In general, however, these properties, described and explained in Chapter 10, begin to appear at molecular weights in the range of, roughly, 1,000 to 1,500, and become more prominent as the size of the molecules increases. Some polymers have molecular weights in the thousands, some in the tens and hundreds of thousands, and some even in the millions. However, most of those which have useful physical properties, technically speaking, range from a molecular weight of a few thousand to a few hundred thousand.

Since a polymer is composed principally of one or more types of repeating unit, its constitution is often described in terms of this structural entity, which is herein termed a *mesomer* (*meso-* = middle). [The term "mer" alone has been used by some authors (e.g., Schmidt and Marlies[1]) to indicate the repeating or middle unit, but exception may be taken to this usage, since mer, etymologically speaking, is a general term referring

[1] Schmidt, A. X. and Marlies, C. A. *Principles of High-Polymer Theory and Practice*, p. 1, McGraw-Hill Book Co., New York, 1948.

to *any* part. D'Alelio[2] has used the term "segmer" but, since the prefix is of unknown origin and meaning, it appears preferable to be consistent in the naming of the various polymer parts.] A mesomer may be defined as a *repeating radical* which, when combined with other mesomers, forms the principal portion of the polymer molecule. (Theoretically speaking, a mesomer may be polyvalent, but in actual practice most mesomers are bivalent.)

Polymer molecules, themselves, may be represented by the two types, *linear* and *cross-linked*. Between these two extremes lies the *branched* type, partaking of linear properties when slightly branched, and becoming more closely allied with cross-linked properties as the complexity of branching increases. Schematic representations of these three types of polymer molecules, where A represents a repeating bivalent mesomer, are given below:

$$—A—A—A—A—A—A—A—A—$$

Linear

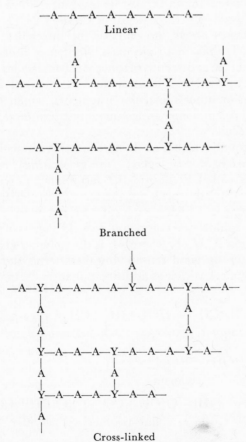

Branched

Cross-linked

² D'Alelio, G. F., *Fundamental Principles of Polymerization*, p. 42, John Wiley and Sons, New York, 1952.

These schematic representations may be more concisely drawn as:

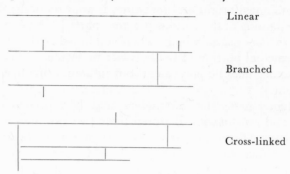

Linear

Branched

Cross-linked

Note that, in the case of nonlinear polymers, some units, Y, must be at least trivalent, whereas all units must be bivalent to form linear polymers. This will be discussed in greater detail in Chapter 2.

In all of the cases above, no ends of the molecules were indicated. Although it is likely that, in a rigid mass of polymer molecules, some may not be terminated (the active ends of some of the molecules being "buried" among their inert neighbors), in most cases the molecules are terminated by radicals, ions, or other molecular fragments, which must, of course, be different from the mesomer, since they must terminate, not propagate, the polymer molecule.

A simple compound which may be split to form monovalent terminating groups is called a *telogen* (*telo-* = end; *-gen* = generating); each terminating ion or radical is called a *telomer*; the terminated polymer is called a *telomerized polymer*. Strictly speaking, the term "telomerization" has been applied to reactions in which a molecule $XY$ reacts with more than one unit of a polymerizable *olefinic* compound to yield a series of products having the general formula $X(M_n)Y$, where $M_n$ is the polymer chain. However, there appears to be no good reason why these terms should not include condensation polymers as well as addition polymers. An example of each type would be:

$$n \text{ CH}_2\text{:CH}_2 + \text{HCl} \rightarrow \text{H}(\text{—CH}_2\text{·CH}_2\text{—})_n\text{Cl}$$
monomer      telogen      telomerized polymer

$$n \text{ HO(CH}_2)_y\text{COOH} + \text{ROH} \rightarrow$$
monomer                telogen

$$\text{H}[\text{—O(CH}_2)_y\text{CO—}]_{n-1}\text{O(CH}_2)_y\text{COOR} + n \text{ H}_2\text{O}$$
half-telomerized polymer

*Polymerization* is the chemical process occurring when simple molecules react to form polymers. Two principal types are recognized: condensation and addition. Carothers,[3] in 1929, defined condensation polymers as those in which the molecular formula of the mesomer lacked certain atoms present in the monomer from which it was formed (or to which it might be chemically degraded); he defined addition polymers as those in which the molecular formula of the mesomer was identical to that of the monomer from which it was derived.

Flory's[4] distinction between a polymerization *process* and a *polymer* also appears to be desirable. A process which occurs by reaction between pairs of functional groups and which forms a type of interunit functional group not present in the reactant(s) is considered to be a *condensation process*. On the other hand, the opening of a bond in a reactant (whether linear or cyclic) and the formation of similar bonds with other reactants without the formation of a by-product is regarded as an *addition process*.

In order to avoid the difficulty which would arise in trying to classify polymers whose structures are identical, yet whose processes of formation may be different, it is desirable to include among the class of condensation *polymers* not only those formed by a condensation process but also those formed by the ring opening of cyclic compounds which, upon chemical degradation (e.g., hydrolysis), yield monomeric end products that are different in composition from their mesomers, regardless of the fact that the *process* may be one of addition polymerization.

What this means is that the relation between the reactant(s) and the mesomer is the basis for the classification of a polymer, regardless of the process involved. This is logical because, in general, the mesomers of condensation polymers are joined by functional groups, such as ether, ester, or amide groups, whereas addition polymers almost always consist of carbon-to-carbon links in the main chain, although side functional groups of the types mentioned above may be present. This difference, as expected, produces appreciable chemical and physical differences between the two types of polymers; for example, hydrolytic cleavage is generally much easier to perform upon condensation polymers than upon addition polymers. Thus, such polymers as the polyoxy(m)ethylenes and poly-urethanes will be included among the condensation *polymers* although the *process* of their formation may be that of addition.

Some examples of condensation polymers are:

$$n \; HO \cdot R \cdot COOH \rightarrow H(-O \cdot R \cdot CO-)_{n-1}O \cdot R \cdot COOH + (n-1) \; H_2O$$

$$n \; H_2N \cdot R \cdot COOH \rightarrow H(-HN \cdot R \cdot CO-)_{n-1}HN \cdot R \cdot COOH + (n-1) \; H_2O$$

$$n \; HO \cdot R' \cdot OH + n \; HOOC \cdot R \cdot COOH \rightarrow$$
$$H(-O \cdot R' \cdot OOC \cdot R \cdot CO-)_{n-1}O \cdot R'OOC \cdot R \cdot COOH + (2n-1) \; H_2O$$

[3] Carothers, W. H., *J. Am. Chem. Soc.*, **51**, 2548 (1929).

[4] Flory, P. J., *Principles of Polymer Chemistry*, pp. 39–40, Cornell University Press, Ithaca, N.Y. 1953.

$n$ HO·R'·OH + $n$ OCN·R·NCO →

$$H(-O·R'·OOC·NH·R·NH·CO-)_{n-1}O·R'·OOC·NH·R·NCO$$

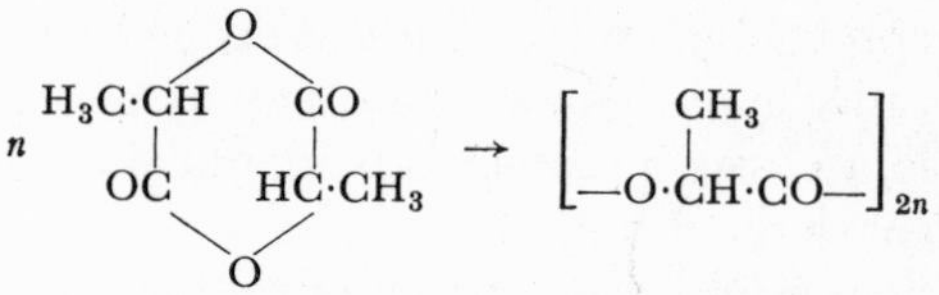

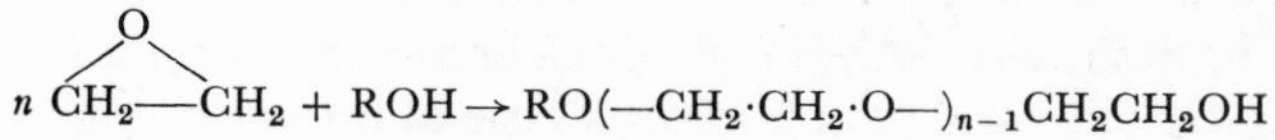

$$n \quad \begin{array}{c} O \\ H_3C·CH \quad CO \\ | \qquad | \\ OC \quad HC·CH_3 \\ O \end{array} \rightarrow \left[ \begin{array}{c} CH_3 \\ | \\ -O·CH·CO- \end{array} \right]_{2n}$$

$$n \ CH_2\!-\!\!-\!CH_2 + ROH \rightarrow RO(-CH_2·CH_2·O-)_{n-1}CH_2CH_2OH$$

where R or R· represents any monovalent radical and ·R· or R< represents any bivalent radical. (This symbolism will be used throughout the book.)

Note that the group in parentheses in all of the cases given represents the repeating radical or mesomer of the polymer molecule. The first three examples illustrate classical condensation reactions; the next two are, formally, addition processes; the last example is sometimes known as a step-addition process and is typical of certain reactions in which *one* initiator molecule is necessary in order for the reaction to occur, regardless of the number of monomer molecules consumed in the polymerization; the initiator molecule also serves as the telogen. Regardless of the mechanism or process occurring in each of the polymerizations illustrated above, each polymer is known as a condensation polymer.

Examples of addition polymers are:

$$n \ CH_2{:}CH_2 \rightarrow (-CH_2·CH_2-)_n$$

$$n \ CH_2{:}CH \rightarrow (-CH_2·CH-)_n$$
$$\phantom{n \ CH_2{:}} | \qquad\qquad\quad | $$
$$\phantom{n \ CH_2{:}CH} \emptyset \qquad\qquad\quad \emptyset$$

$$n \ CH_2{:}CHCl \rightarrow (-CH_2·CHCl-)_n$$

$$n \ CH_2{:}CH·CH{:}CH_2 \rightarrow (-CH_2·CH{:}CH·CH_2-)_n$$

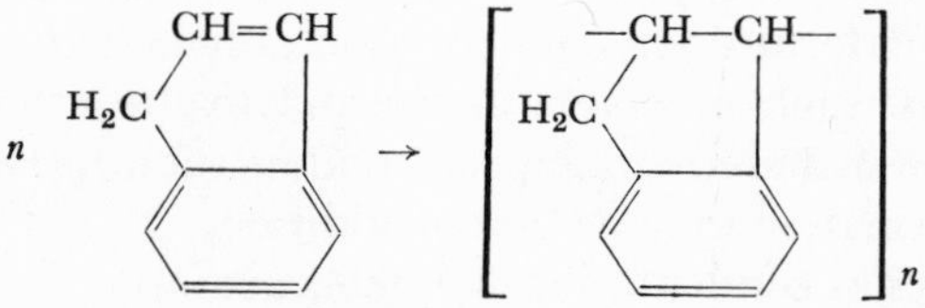

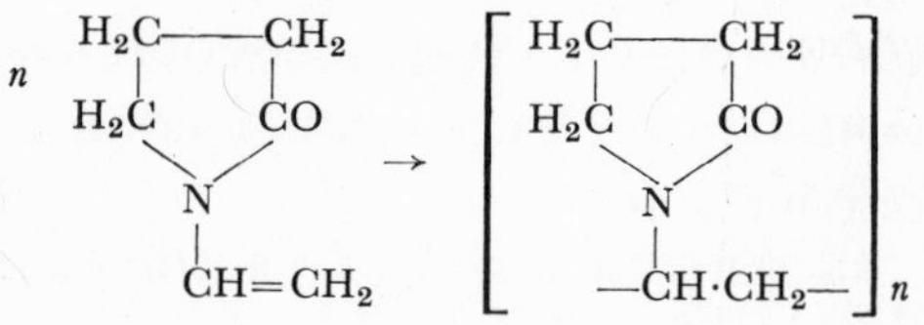

$$n \quad \begin{array}{c} CH\!=\!CH \\ H_2C \diagup \\ \end{array} \rightarrow \left[ \begin{array}{c} -CH\!-\!CH- \\ H_2C \diagup \\ \end{array} \right]_n$$

$$n \quad \begin{array}{c} H_2C\!-\!\!-\!\!-CH_2 \\ | \qquad | \\ H_2C \quad CO \\ N \\ | \\ CH\!=\!CH_2 \end{array} \rightarrow \left[ \begin{array}{c} H_2C\!-\!\!-\!\!-CH_2 \\ | \qquad | \\ H_2C \quad CO \\ N \\ | \\ -CH·CH_2- \end{array} \right]_n$$

The term "monomer" has already been implicitly defined in terms of the polymer. Explicitly, a monomer is a compound (capable of polymerization with others of its species) from which the mesomer is derived. In the case of addition processes, the monomer and mesomer are isomeric, differing from each other only in the arrangement of bonds:

$$n \ CH_2{:}CH_2 \rightarrow n(-CH_2{\cdot}CH_2-) \rightarrow (-CH_2{\cdot}CH_2-)_n$$
$$\text{monomer} \qquad \text{mesomer} \qquad \text{polymer}$$

In condensation processes, the monomer and mesomer are not isomeric, the mesomer having fewer atoms than the monomer:

$$n \ HO(CH_2)_yCOOH \rightarrow n \ [-O(CH_2)_yCO-] \rightarrow$$
$$\text{monomer} \qquad\qquad\qquad \text{mesomer}$$

$$H[-O(CH_2)_yCO-]_{n-1}O(CH_2)_yCOOH + (n-1)H_2O$$
$$\text{polymer}$$

With compounds containing more than one functional group, condensation polymerization does not normally occur unless these groups are dissimilar and can react with one another. For example, a dicarboxylic acid, a diamine, or a glycol will not, under ordinary conditions, react with other molecules of its species to form high-molecular-weight products ("ordinary conditions" excluding such products as anhydrides, ethers, etc.). In such cases, at least two types of functional groups must be present, each of which will react with at least one of the other types of functional groups present:

$$n \ HO(CH_2)_yOH + n \ HOOC(CH_2)_zCOOH \rightarrow n[-O(CH_2)_yOOC(CH_2)_zCO-] \rightarrow$$
$$\text{mesomer}$$

$$H[-O(CH_2)_yOOC(CH_2)_zCO-]_{n-1}O(CH_2)_yOOC(CH_2)_zCOOH + (2n-1) \ H_2O$$
$$\text{polymer}$$

In this and similar cases, neither of the original reactants can be called the monomer, since neither can polymerize with others of its species to form the polymer. Such a substance has been termed a *comer*, since it must react with (*co-* = with) another substance. (Since the Latin *co-* has long been used instead of the Greek *syn-* with such Greek-derived words as monomer and polymer, its use will be retained.) The intermediate reaction product in the above reaction, $HO(CH_2)_yOOC(CH_2)_zCOOH$, is, then, the monomer, since the mesomer must be derived from it. Thus, a comer may be defined as a molecule which will not normally polymerize with others of its species but, in combination with other types of molecules, will form part of a mesomer.

Another case arises when either a self-polymerizable compound or a comer reacts with another self-polymerizable substance to form a polymer. The self-polymerizing compound, if used alone, would properly be termed a monomer, but when it is used to form only a portion of a mesomer it is known as a *comonomer*. The distinction between a comonomer and a comer is that the former *can* polymerize alone, whereas the latter cannot; both form only a portion of the mesomer, however. Examples are:

$$HO(CH_2)_yCOOH + HO(CH_2)_zCOOH \rightarrow -O(CH_2)_yCOO(CH_2)_zCO- \text{ or}$$

comonomer          comonomer                    mesomer

$$-O(CH_2)_zCOO(CH_2)_yCO-$$

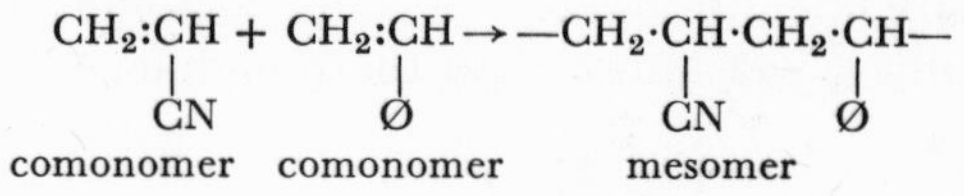

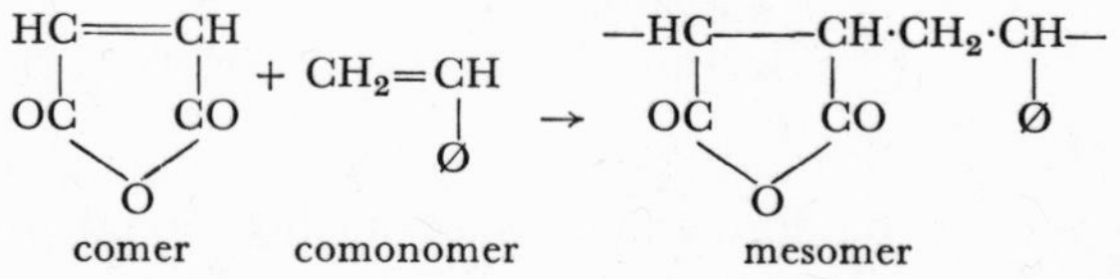

mesomer

In these examples, the hydroxy acids, acrylonitrile ($CH_2:CH \cdot CN$), and styrene ($\emptyset \cdot CH:CH_2$) can polymerize alone, hence are comonomers; maleic anhydride will not polymerize alone, hence is a comer.

It is not necessary that equivalent quantities of comonomers be used to form a mesomer, since any one of them is capable of polymerizing with others of its species. For example:

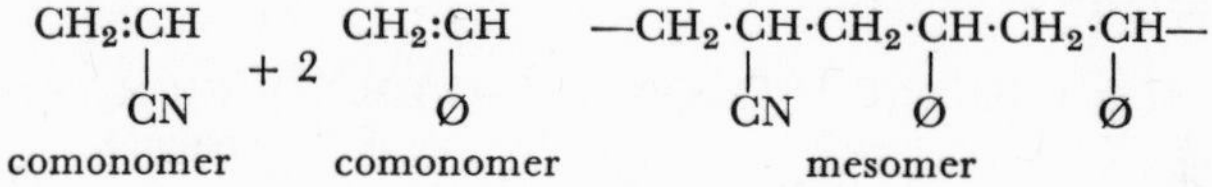

It should be borne in mind, however, that, when one or more of the reactants is a comonomer, the composition of the mesomer becomes indefinite or variable, since there is no assurance that the comonomers will repeat regularly in the chain. Hence, when the mesomer is referred to in such cases, it means the "average" mesomer which, of course, depends upon the ratio of the reactants and their reactivity ratios (see Copolymerization, Chap. 3). Further, when one or more of the reactants is a comer, no more than one equivalent of the comer will react with an equivalent of another comer or comonomer to form a mesomer, although more than one equivalent of a comonomer can react with an equivalent of a comer.

One more point should be made concerning the terminology of reactants. The term "monomer" is used both specifically and generically. The specific meaning has already been given. Generically, "monomer" is a term applied to any of the various types of reactants; i.e., true monomers, comers, and comonomers are all called monomers in the sense that they are the original reactants. "Monomer" will be used in this sense subsequently unless a differentiation is desired.

Polymers formed from the several types of reactants are also often distinguished by specific nomenclature. A *homopolymer* (*homo-* = the same) is a polymer composed of only one type of mesomer; i.e., it is formed from a true monomer, two comers, or from comonomers, provided that, in the latter case, the comonomers react consecutively. A *copolymer* contains more than one type of mesomer; i.e., it is formed from nonequivalent amounts of comonomers or, among the unsaturated compounds, from equivalent amounts of comonomers whose rates of reaction are unequal. [A *heteropolymer* (*hetero-* = different) is a special type of addition polymer and may be either a homopolymer or a copolymer. It is the product obtained from the reaction between a comer and a comonomer and, practically speaking, is rarely encountered. If the comer and comonomer react in equal amounts, the product is a homopolymer; if the comonomer is present in excess, the product is a copolymer.] When the word "polymer" is used without qualification, it, of course, refers to any of the above types. Examples of the different types of polymers are:

$$n \; CH_2{:}CH_2 \rightarrow (-CH_2 \cdot CH_2-)_n$$
monomer    homopolymer

$$n \; H_2N(CH_2)_yCOOH \rightarrow H[-HN(CH_2)_yCO-]_{n-1}HN(CH_2)_yCOOH + (n-1) \; H_2O$$
monomer    homopolymer

$$n \; \begin{matrix} CH_2{:}CH \\ | \\ CN \end{matrix} + m \; \begin{matrix} CH_2{:}CH \\ | \\ \emptyset \end{matrix} \rightarrow \begin{bmatrix} -CH_2 \cdot CH- \\ | \\ CN \end{bmatrix}_n - \begin{bmatrix} -CH_2 \cdot CH- \\ | \\ \emptyset \end{bmatrix}_m$$
comonomer    comonomer    copolymer

$$n \; H_2N(CH_2)_yCOOH + m \; H_2N(CH_2)_zCOOH \rightarrow$$
comonomer    comonomer

$$H\{[-HN(CH_2)_yCO-]_n-[-HN(CH_2)_zCO-]_m\}OH + (n+m-1) \; H_2O$$
copolymer

$$n \; \begin{matrix} HC{=\!=\!=}CH \\ | \quad\quad | \\ OC \quad CO \\ \diagdown\,O\,\diagup \end{matrix} + m \; \begin{matrix} CH_2{=}CH \\ | \\ \emptyset \end{matrix} \rightarrow \begin{bmatrix} -HC\quad\quad CH- \\ | \quad\quad\quad | \\ OC \quad\quad CO \\ \diagdown\,O\,\diagup \end{bmatrix}_n - \begin{bmatrix} -CH_2-CH- \\ | \\ \emptyset \end{bmatrix}_m \quad \text{where } m \geqq n$$
comer    comonomer    heteropolymer

In the third and fourth examples given above, the copolymers as shown are not meant to imply the presence of two blocks of different mesomers, but rather a random distribution of the two comonomer fragments in the chain. This is also true in the last example when $m > n$.

In closing this chapter, it should be pointed out that the nouns "resin" and "plastic" have been avoided, although both are in common use. It is unfortunate that there are no explicit definitions for these words, the meanings being "understood" by most of those who use them. Probably the closest one can come to a definition of a resin is that it is a solid or semisolid, natural or synthetic organic substance of relatively high molecular weight (not necessarily a polymer) which exhibits no sharp melting point, breaks with a conchoidal fracture, and usually (but not always) is predominantly amorphous in structure.  A plastic has been defined in a limited sense as any of a large group of organic substances, whether natural or synthetic, which can be molded (*plastikos* = fit for molding). The noun "plastic" is usually applied to all polymers which are not considered to be elastomers or fibers; i.e., which exhibit neither the long-range elasticity of elastomers nor the very high crystallinity of most fibers. In the engineering sense, however, a plastic is a mixture containing one or more resins compounded with fillers, plasticizers, lubricants, dyes, etc., which has been subsequently fabricated.

The term "resin" originally referred to natural products (particularly of vegetable origin) but now includes the man-made substances.  As will be seen from the physical descriptions of the polymers given in later chapters, the above definitions of both resin and plastic include many of these polymers, and the terms are now often used interchangeably.

### REFERENCES AND RECOMMENDED READING

D'Alelio, G. F., *Fundamental Principles of Polymerization*, John Wiley and Sons, New York, 1952.

Flory, P. J., *Principles of Polymer Chemistry*, Cornell University Press, Ithaca, N.Y., 1953.

Mark, H. and Whitby, G. S., eds., *Collected Papers of Wallace Hume Carothers*, Interscience Publishers, New York, 1946.

Schmidt, A. X. and Marlies, C. A., *Principles of High-Polymer Theory and Practice*, McGraw-Hill Book Co., New York, 1948.

*Chapter 2*

# FUNCTIONALITY AND POLYMER FORMATION

Functionality may be defined as the ability to form primary valence bonds or as the number of positions in a molecule normally available for reaction under the specific conditions of the experiment. The number and kinds of functional groups present in any set of reactants have a simple and fundamental relationship to the types of product obtainable from the reaction and, if polymerization is to occur, certain functionality requirements must be met.

Carothers[1] was the first to emphasize the fact that a molecule must be bi- or polyfunctional in order to be able to take part in a polymerization reaction. A molecule is termed bi- or polyfunctional if it contains two or more than two, respectively, reactive or functional groups. Simple examples of bifunctional molecules are hydroxy or amino acids, dialcohols, diamines, or dicarboxylic acids; polyfunctional molecules would, of course, contain one or more additional functional groups. These molecules react with each other through their chemically active groups, but, since two or more of them are located on each molecule, the reaction continues in two or three directions and linear or three-dimensional molecules are formed.

Another type of bi- or polyfunctionality is exhibited by a large class of molecules containing unsaturated bonds. Once a double bond is opened and a biradical is formed, other monomers collide with its active ends and thus the growth of a chain molecule is started, extending in both directions from the original biradical. It should be noted, also, that bifunctional molecules result from the opening of ring structures, as in the formation of polymer molecules from ethylene oxide or caprolactam.

The chemical interaction between molecules is thus due to their possession of mutually reactive *functional* groups. In the esterification of a monobasic acid with a monohydric alcohol, each molecule has only unit functionality and the interaction of two such molecules produces an ester

[1] Carothers, W. H., *J. Am. Chem. Soc.*, **51**, 2548 (1929); *Chem. Revs.*, **8**, 353 (1931).

molecule no longer containing reactive functional groups; the reaction
cannot proceed further:

$$R \cdot CO_2H + R' \cdot OH \rightarrow R \cdot CO_2 \cdot R' + H_2O$$
$$f = 1 \qquad f = 1 \qquad f = 0$$

If, instead, a dibasic acid is esterified with two equivalents of a monohydric alcohol, the two carboxyl groups of the acid molecule react with
the hydroxyl groups of the alcohol molecules, and the product is again a
neutral ester containing no reactive functional groups:

$$R\!\!\begin{array}{l}{}^{CO_2H}\\{}_{CO_2H}\end{array} + R' \cdot OH + R' \cdot OH \rightarrow R\!\!\begin{array}{l}{}^{CO_2R'}\\{}_{CO_2R'}\end{array} + 2H_2O$$
$$f = 2 \qquad f = 1 \qquad f = 1 \qquad f = 0$$

If, however, a dibasic acid reacts with an equivalent of a dihydric
alcohol, two possibilities for reaction occur. In both cases the first stage
involves the reaction of *one* carboxyl group with *one* hydroxyl group, the
resulting molecule still having *two* unreacted (and different) functional
groups. This product will therefore continue to react, either by *intramolecular* ring closure or by *intermolecular* extension of the open-chain
molecule by further reaction of its functional groups with those in other
molecules in the reaction mixture; thus:

$$R\!\!\begin{array}{l}{}^{CO_2H}\\{}_{CO_2H}\end{array} + HO \cdot R' \cdot OH \longrightarrow R\!\!\begin{array}{l}{}^{CO_2 \cdot R' \cdot OH}\\{}_{CO_2H}\end{array}$$
$$f = 2 \qquad f = 2 \qquad f = 2$$

$$HO \cdot R' \cdot O_2C \cdot R \cdot CO_2 \cdot R' \cdot O_2C \cdot R \cdot CO_2H, \text{ etc.}$$

$$f = 2 \qquad\qquad\qquad\qquad f = 0$$

In one case, the cyclic product has a functionality of zero and no further
reaction can occur; in the other, the open-chain or linear product still has
a functionality of two and can continue to grow if other bifunctional
molecules are present in the reaction mixture.

Where ring formation is impossible or unlikely, long, linear molecules
are likely to be formed. Reactions of this type are known as *polyreactions*.
Where esterification is involved, the process is classed as a *polyesterification*
and the product is called a *linear polyester*. Where amidation is involved,
the process is called a *polyamidation* and the product a *linear polyamide*.

In the foregoing example, two different molecular species were initially
present, each bearing only one type of functional group. However, the
same principles apply where only one species of bifunctional molecule is

present, each molecule bearing two different and mutually reactive functional groups; $\omega$-hydroxy acids and $\omega$-amino acids are of this type. Where linear polymers are formed from compounds of this type, they are sometimes termed *self-polyesters* or *self-polyamides*.

$$H_2N \cdot R \cdot CO_2H \rightarrow H_2N \cdot R \cdot CO \cdot NH \cdot R \cdot CO \cdot NH \cdot R \cdot CO_2H, \text{ etc.}$$
$$f = 2 \qquad\qquad\qquad f = 2$$

Bi- or polyfunctionality can occur in a molecule by its possession of an unsaturated group, as well as of two or more such groups. Such groups are the olefinic (C:C) and acetylenic (C:C), which can react with two or four monovalent groups, respectively, by simple addition. In addition reactions, a molecule, such as $CH_2:CRR'$, has a functionality of two. If it reacts with, say, chlorine or hydrogen atoms, each of which has a functionality of one, the saturated addition product now has a functionality of zero and the reaction ceases. If, however, the molecule above reacts by addition with other similar molecules, again two possible paths of reaction can be expected; i.e., intermolecular addition or intramolecular addition, the latter of which leads to ring formation:

$$3CH_2:CRR' \rightarrow \begin{array}{c} CRR' \\ H_2C \quad CH_2 \\ | \qquad | \\ R'RC \quad CRR' \\ CH_2 \end{array}$$

$$3CH_2:CRR' \rightarrow \; - H_2C \cdot \overset{R}{\underset{R'}{C}} \cdot CH_2 \cdot \overset{R}{\underset{R'}{C}} \cdot CH_2 \cdot \overset{R}{\underset{R'}{C}} -, \text{ etc.}$$

$$f = 2 \qquad\qquad f = 2$$

A brief discussion of the factors determining the relative likelihood of intramolecular and intermolecular condensation or addition reactions will be found in Chapter 3.

In the foregoing discussion the reactions of mono- and bifunctional systems have been covered; this discussion must now be extended to polyfunctional systems. (A polyfunctional system is one in which the average functionality of the reactants is greater than two. For example, when two molecules of glycerol are reacted with three molecules of phthalic anhydride, there are present six functional groups from the three molecules of phthalic anhydride and six more from the two molecules of glycerol. There are, then, twelve functional groups present in the five molecules of reactants or an average of $12/5 = 2 \cdot 4$ functional groups per molecule.)

If addition polymerization be first considered, styrene (bifunctional)

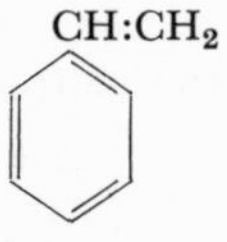

CH:CH$_2$

when polymerized yields a linear polymer of the type

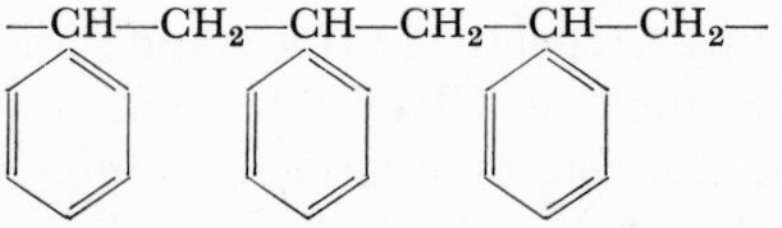

—CH—CH$_2$—CH—CH$_2$—CH—CH$_2$—

This polymer consists of a mass of randomly disposed chains, tangled together mechanically but not attached to one another by primary (covalent) bonds. When heated, the mass becomes soft and is readily distorted by the application of mechanical stress; when cooled, it becomes rigid again and retains the shape impressed upon it while hot. The process is reversible and the substance is said to be *thermoplastic*. Further, upon immersion in a suitable solvent, such as benzene, the small solvent molecules slowly penetrate the chains, thus separating them from one another, and the polymer mass gradually becomes uniformly dispersed in the solvent, forming a viscous, colloidal solution.

If, instead, styrene is polymerized with a small quantity of *p*-divinyl benzene

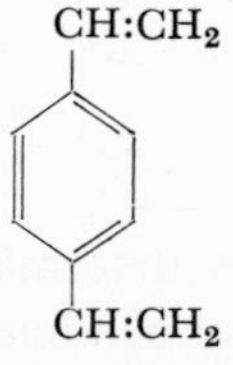

CH:CH$_2$

CH:CH$_2$

which has two vinyl groups instead of one and is therefore tetrafunctional, the growing linear molecules of styrene will incorporate randomly a divinyl benzene molecule by means of one of its vinyl groups, leaving the second vinyl group of the divinyl benzene molecule free to be similarly incorporated in another growing polystyrene chain, thereby linking two chains together. In time, there will be formed a cross-linked and three-dimensional network, which may be expressed by an idealized, two-dimensional diagram:

$$-CH-CH_2-CH-CH_2-CH-CH_2-CH-CH_2-$$

$$-H_2C-HC-H_2C-HC-H_2C-HC-H_2C-HC-$$

$$-CH-CH_2-CH-CH_2-$$

It was found by Staudinger and Heuer that a polymer formed from styrene and as little as 0.002 per cent of $p$-divinyl benzene was no longer soluble in benzene, although it swelled markedly; the linear molecules were now attached to others by an occasional cross-link or bridge and complete dispersion in the solvent was impossible.

By increasing the proportion of $p$-divinyl benzene, the resistance to solvents and heat is steadily increased until, at the extreme, pure poly-($p$-divinyl benzene) is obtained. This polymer is so strongly cross-linked that it is unaffected by solvents and is no longer thermoplastic. A three-dimensional network such as this is often designated as a *space-polymer* or *infinite* network.

The same results are obtainable in condensation polymerizations. Polymerization of a bifunctional system produces linear polymers which are usually fusible and soluble in certain solvents. In a polycondensation, where all reactants have a functionality of at least two and one or more of the reactants has a functionality greater than two, a cross-linked molecule is formed. For example, in the esterification of a dibasic acid with glycerol, each glycerol molecule may be considered, in the early stages of the reaction, as having an *actual* functionality of only *two*, for its primary hydroxyl groups are more readily esterified than its secondary hydroxyl group; chains of the following type will first be formed:

$$-O \cdot CH_2 \cdot CH \cdot CH_2 \cdot O \cdot \overset{O}{\overset{\|}{C}} \cdot R \cdot \overset{O}{\overset{\|}{C}} \cdot O \cdot CH_2 \cdot CH \cdot CH_2 \cdot O \cdot \overset{O}{\overset{\|}{C}} \cdot R \cdot \overset{O}{\overset{\|}{C}} \cdot O \cdot CH_2 \cdot CH \cdot CH_2 \cdot O-$$
$$\underset{OH}{} \qquad\qquad \underset{OH}{} \qquad\qquad \underset{OH}{}$$

Eventually, however, the unreacted secondary hydroxyl groups will enter into the reaction. The glycerol will now exercise its previously *potential* third functionality, and two previously unreacted hydroxyl groups in different chains may form an intermolecular bridge by reaction with a molecule of the dibasic acid. Before this occurs, the reaction mixture exists as a colloidal sol, the degree of polymerization being fairly high but finite; however, at the time when cross-linking begins, the degree of polymerization rises very rapidly, irreversible gelation occurs, and the polyester becomes infusible and insoluble.

It should be pointed out that certain compounds, such as maleic anhydride or acid, can react by an addition and/or a condensation mechanism and may thus exert functionality by either or both types of reaction. Maleic anhydride has a total potential functionality of four, and thermosetting polymers can be obtained if more than two of its functionalities enter into reaction:

$$
\begin{array}{ccc}
& \text{O} & & \text{O} \\
& \parallel & & \parallel \\
\text{HC—C} & & -\text{HC—C—O}- \\
\parallel & \quad\text{O} \rightarrow & \quad | \\
\text{HC—C} & & -\text{HC—C}- \\
& \parallel & & \parallel \\
& \text{O} & & \text{O}
\end{array}
$$

Ideally, networks of the cross-linked type would be regular and continuous, so that $x$ grams of reaction mixture would yield one gigantic molecule weighing $x$ grams. Practically speaking, this seldom, if ever, occurs, except in a few natural inorganic polymers, such as diamond. In almost all cross-linked materials, the network is random and irregular and is broken up into discrete portions by voids, pockets of air or other foreign matter, and volumes where unreacted functional groups still exist.

Further, as Ritchie[2] has pointed out, there are two types of space-polymer networks, which form the ideal limiting cases of a continuous series. In one type, the units in the network are small and irregular and are linked in a random fashion, so that the polymer is isotropic; i.e., it has physical properties which are independent of the direction of measurement. In the other type, the structure of the macromolecule is predominantly linear, pre-existing chains being cross-linked into regularly oriented bundles, giving an anisotropic medium, exhibiting, for example, birefringence. Between these two extremes, many intermediate types can and do exist.

In summary, polymers will result from the *intermolecular* reaction of molecules having a functionality of two or more. Only linear polymers will be formed from the intermolecular reaction of bifunctional molecules; cross-linked or three-dimensional polymers will result from the intermolecular reaction of polyfunctional molecules, provided the reaction is

---

[2] Ritchie, P. D., *A Chemistry of Plastics and High Polymers*, p. 17, Cleaver-Hume Press, London (dist. by Interscience Publishers, New York), 1949.

carried far enough and provided functionalities of three or more are actually operative. With few exceptions, linear polymers are fusible and soluble, whereas cross-linked polymers are infusible and insoluble.

### REFERENCES AND RECOMMENDED READING

Mark, H. and Whitby, G. S., eds., *Collected Papers of Wallace Hume Carothers*, Interscience Publishers, New York, 1940.
Ritchie, P. D., *A Chemistry of Plastics and High Polymers*, Cleaver-Hume Press, London (dist. by Interscience Publishers, New York), 1949.

*Chapter 3*

# MECHANICAL AND CHEMICAL BEHAVIOR

Substances classified under the common term "polymers" can be arranged according to various systems, depending upon the particular characteristic that is to be emphasized. Usually they are grouped together with reference to their mechanical behavior, their chemical structure, their method of preparation, or their technical applications. There is always some overlapping among the various classifications and even between groups of the same system, since often one polymer rightly belongs to two or more subdivisions. For present purposes all polymers will be classified according to their mechanical behavior and their chemical behavior.

## MECHANICAL BEHAVIOR

It is common practice to place all polymers characterized according to mechanical behavior into three overlapping categories. It is thus convenient to speak of polymers as being most useful as one or more of the following: elastomer, plastic, or fiber.

*Elastomers* have relatively low initial moduli of elasticity ranging from $10^1$ to $10^2$ psi. They have a wide range of almost instantaneously reversible extensibility (often greater than 1,000 per cent). Although soft and easily deformable, they stiffen appreciably upon stretching. Within a limited range, their moduli of elasticity increase with temperature; at low temperatures, below the so-called brittle point (see Chap. 10), their extensibilities decrease markedly and eventually they become brittle.

*Plastics* have intermediate moduli of elasticity ranging from about $10^3$ to $10^4$ psi. Unlike elastomers, they possess a marked range of deformability of the order of 100 to 200 per cent, particularly at higher temperatures. This deformation is in part reversible and in part permanent. The extensibility, viscosity, and elastic modulus are direct functions of temperature and are the reasons for the plastic characteristics. Generally speaking, any substance which can be softened by heat and molded in this condition is considered to be a plastic substance. Although the terms "plastic" and "resin" have been defined previously (see Chap. 1), both terms are used rather loosely and often interchangeably in the industry, and, as a result, considerable confusion occurs.

It is also common practice to subdivide plastics into two classes, thermoplastic and thermosetting. *Thermoplastic* materials are those which can be softened with heat and while soft can be molded, cast, or extruded under pressure. However, they must be cooled and, upon cooling below their softening point, become rigid and retain the shape of the mold. Thermoplastic castings or moldings, upon being reheated, again become soft and fusible and can be remolded. *Thermosetting* materials are those which also can be softened with heat and while soft can be molded or cast under heat and pressure. They change chemically, however, during this heat and pressure cycle to become hard, dense, insoluble, and infusible substances. This hardening can also be effected as a straight chemical reaction with heat alone, or heat and catalyst without the use of pressure. In other words, thermoplastic substances are those which can be subjected to a heating and cooling cycle indefinitely, softening under heat and hardening with cooling, whereas thermosetting substances can be heated generally only once, or, at most, only a few times, whereupon they become infusible.

The reasons for the differences in behavior between thermoplastic and thermosetting polymers can usually be traced to their chemical composition and their functionalities. Generally speaking, those substances with functionalities of two remain permanently fusible and hence are of the thermoplastic type. Those with functionalities greater than two generally cross-link upon application of heat and pressure and/or catalysis and no longer are fusible; they fall into the thermosetting class.

The preceding definitions have implied that a thermoplastic polymer is soluble as well as fusible and that a thermosetting polymer is insoluble as well as infusible. Generally, it is true that most thermosetting polymers are insoluble. Copolymers may be made that contain a large amount of monomer with a functionality of two and a trace of a comonomer of a functionality greater than two which are fusible but not soluble. They are swollen, however, in liquids which are normally active solvents for the homopolymers. Such a copolymer is the one made from styrene and a very small quantity of divinyl benzene. If more cross-links are formed by the introduction of larger amounts of divinyl benzene, both insolubility and infusibility will result.

Conversely, if a polymer is infusible or insoluble, the conclusion cannot necessarily be drawn that the polymer is cross-linked, since the substituents in a linear polymer, because of high secondary valence forces, may produce insolubility or infusibility without forming covalent bonds between the polymer chains. Polyacrylonitrile, for example, does not melt without decomposition, yet it is not cross-linked.   Many studies have been carried out on the solubility of polyacrylonitrile and very few substances have been found to be true solvents, among which are $N,N$-dimethyl formamide and $N,N$-dimethyl acetamide.

Up to the present time, no true solvents have been found for the high-molecular-weight polymers of tetrafluoroethylene, while solutions of low concentrations only can be made from polychlorotrifluoroethylene.   At elevated temperatures mesitylene and certain chlorofluorocarbons, such as chlorofluorobutane, $o$-chlorobenzotrifluoride, and 2,5-dichlorobenzo-trifluoride, have been used for solvents for the latter polymer.   Practically speaking, both polymers are considered insoluble, thermoplastic materials, since they are linear and are obtained from bifunctional monomers.   The above solvents are not common ones; nevertheless, such linear polymers must not be considered insoluble without caution.   For a more complete discussion, see Chapter 10.

*Fibers* are characterized by having high initial elastic moduli of about $10^5$ to $10^6$ psi.   Their extensibilities, after orientation, are low—about 10 to 20 per cent.   Part of this extensibility is permanent.   The rest is partly instantaneous, partly delayed.   The mechanical properties change relatively little over the temperature range of about $-50°C$ to about $150°C$, with some variation, of course, depending upon the particular fiber.

It may appear that elastomers, plastics, and fibers are built up by fundamentally different structural designs.   This, however, is not the case; they are all formed according to a common general principle, and the differences in their mechanical and thermal properties are matters of degree rather than the results of fundamentally different molecular structures.

All materials capable of producing elastomers, plastics, and fibers of commercial value must have high molecular weights.   The molecular weights of a large number of these polymers have been determined by various methods and the results have checked fairly satisfactorily.   Table 3-1 contains a series of representative values for the molecular weights and degrees of polymerization of some high-molecular-weight polymers.

It must be borne in mind, however, that for many technical purposes the original material is deliberately degraded and its degree of polymerization is stabilized at a lower level.   Experience has shown that this partial degradation often facilitates the processing of some high-molecular-weight polymers without unduly influencing certain of their mechanical properties.   With synthetic polymers, it is often possible to control the polymerization process in such a way that the approximate degree of polymerization of the product can be predetermined.   When this is the case, different molecular weight ranges of the same polymer may be produced for different industrial purposes, such as for coating, extrusion, and injection molding.

TABLE 3-1. MOLECULAR WEIGHTS AND POLYMERIZATION DEGREES OF SOME POLYMERS[1]

| Material Investigated | Approximate Molecular Weight Range | Corresponding Degree of Polymerization |
|---|---|---|
| Native cellulose in cotton or wood . . . | 1,200,000–1,500,000 | 7,400–9,250 |
| Cellulose in bleached cotton linters . . . | 400,000– 500,000 | 2,500–3,100 |
| Cellulose in purified wood pulp . . . | 300,000– 450,000 | 1,850–2,750 |
| Regenerated cellulose in rayon . . . | 75,000– 100,000 | 460– 620 |
| Regenerated cellulose in staple fiber . . | 60,000– 75,000 | 370– 460 |
| Regenerated cellulose in cellophane. . . | 50,000– 60,000 | 310– 370 |
| Native rubber in Hevea latex . . . | 140,000– 210,000 | 2,050–3,100 |
| Rubber after being milled in air . . | 55,000– 70,000 | 810–1,030 |
| Cellulose nitrate used for molding . . . | 400,000– 700,000 | 1,480–2,600 |
| Cellulose nitrate used for extrusion . . . | 150,000– 300,000 | 550–1,100 |
| Cellulose nitrate used for coatings . . . | 50,000– 100,000 | 185– 370 |
| Polystyrene for injection molding . . . | 120,000– 180,000 | 1,150–1,730 |
| Polystyrene for coatings . . . | 80,000– 120,000 | 770–1,150 |
| Poly(vinyl chloride) . . . . . | 250,000 | 4,000 |
| Polyisobutylene . . . . . . | 120,000– 200,000 | 2,150–3,500 |
| Poly(hexamethylene adipamide) . . . | 16,000– 32,000 | 140– 280 |

[1] Adapted from Mark, H. F., "Molecular Structure and Mechanical Behavior of High Polymers," Table 1, p. 8 in Twiss, S. B., ed., *Advancing Fronts in Chemistry*, Vol. I (High Polymers), Reinhold Publishing Corp., New York, 1945.

The differences among these three classes of polymers are to a large extent caused by the magnitude of the attractive forces among the molecules and by the ease with which their chains fit into crystal lattices. A material exhibiting little tendency to crystallize usually belongs to the class of elastomers; materials of high crystallizability, on the other hand, usually display typical fiber properties.

The tendency to crystallize, as Mark[2] has pointed out, is caused by two factors: the forces among the chains and the geometrical bulkiness of the chains. The inter-chain forces correspond to the $\Delta H$ term in the expression for the free energy change taking place during crystallization: $\Delta F° = \Delta H° - T\Delta S°$. If these forces are great, they will strongly influence the behavior of the polymer and it is likely to behave as a typical fiber.

The influence of the geometrical bulkiness of the chains corresponds to the $T\Delta S$ term. Chains which fit easily into a crystal lattice do so under the influence of relatively weak forces; hence, polymers containing such chains have a tendency to appear more fiberlike than would be expected from a consideration of the forces alone. On the other hand, polymers having very bulky chains do not crystallize, even if the intermolecular forces are quite strong; hence, they will be more rubberlike than expected from taking into account only the intermolecular forces.

A typical elastomer has a specific molar cohesion per 5Å chain length of between 1,000 and 2,000 calories. If this cohesion rises above 5,000

[2] Mark, H., *Ind. Eng. Chem.*, **34**, 1343 (1942).

calories, the substance behaves typically as a fiber, with a high modulus of elasticity and a considerable tensile strength. In the cases where the molar cohesion lies between 2,000 and 5,000 calories, the material behaves as a plastic; i.e., it softens or becomes rubberlike at elevated temperatures but exhibits crystallization at normal temperatures without stretching. Thus, variation of the intermolecular attraction of long-chain molecules and of their geometrical fine structure provides a means of producing an elastomer, a plastic, or a fiber.

It should be remembered that there is considerable overlapping; for example, certain mechanical properties would lead to the classification of polyethylene as both an elastomer and a plastic, a poly (vinyl alcohol) as both a plastic and a fiber, poly(vinyl chloride) as a plastic and an elastomer, and nylon as both a plastic material and a fiber.

Table 3-2 summarizes the gradual change in properties of polymers and the rather arbitrary classification of them into the three groups: elastomers, plastics, and fibers. It should be pointed out that, under the classification of plastics, most of the values given for the properties refer

TABLE 3-2.   MECHANICAL CLASSIFICATION OF POLYMERS

| Property | Elastomers | Plastics | Fibers |
|---|---|---|---|
| Initial modulus of elasticity (psi) | *ca.* 15–150 | *ca.* 1,500–15,000 | *ca.* 150,000–1,500,000 |
| Upper limit of extensibility (%) | *ca.* 100–1,000 | *ca.* 20–100 | < 10 |
| Character of stress deformation | Almost completely and instantaneously elastic | Partly reversible elasticity; little delayed elasticity; some permanent set | Some instantaneously reversible elasticity; some delayed elasticity; some permanent set |
| Effect of temperature upon mechanical properties | Elastic modulus increases with temperature (within a limited range) | Marked temperature dependency (over a wide range) | Little temperature dependency from −50° to +150°C |
| Crystallization tendency | Low (unstressed) | Moderate to high | Very high |
| Molecular cohesion (cal/mole) | *ca.* 1,000–2,000 | *ca.* 2,000–5,000 | *ca.* 5,000–10,000 |
| Representative polymers | Thioplasts Natural rubber<br><br>Polychloroprene Polybutadiene Polyisobutylene | Phenoplasts Poly(vinyl chloride)<br><br>Aminoplasts Polystyrene Poly(vinyl acetate) | Polyamides Poly(vinylidene chloride) Silk Cellulose Poly(ethylene terephthalate) |

particularly to linear polymers, for which considerable information is available correlating the nature of the constituent groups with the physical or mechanical properties. Precise physical knowledge of the properties of cross-linked polymers is still inadequate.

## CHEMICAL BEHAVIOR

Condensations which lead to the formation of polymers progress by the same mechanism as the reaction between two or more simple molecules in classical organic chemistry. Thus, for a polyesterification, the activation energy, heat of reaction, and effective catalysts are similar to those for the esterification of similar small molecules. In fact, experimental results have established the important conclusion that the primary reaction between the various species of molecules is that of reaction between the functional groups and is independent, except early in the reaction, of the nature and length of the chains to which the functional groups are attached. Thus, it appears that the reactivities of the groups involved in a polycondensation reaction remain the same throughout the entire process and the formation of a polyester will occur at the same rate as the formation of a normal ester from a monofunctional alcohol and a monofunctional carboxylic acid. The observed decrease in rate toward the end of such reactions is probably the result of the decreasing number of reactive groups and not of the appreciable increase in the viscosity of the medium, unless the latter becomes extremely high.

Starting with such bifunctional molecules as an amino acid, the average chain length of the linear macromolecules depends upon the extent of reaction. Upon addition of a small amount of a monofunctional compound, the average chain length decreases, since nonreactive terminal groups are quickly formed (telomerization).

Telomerization also occurs if two *different* initial materials, both of which are bifunctional (e.g., a glycol and a dibasic acid), react in the presence of an excess of one component. At some time, all of the molecules will have similar terminal groups and the reaction can proceed no further. By using a large excess of one component, it is even possible to suppress entirely the formation of macromolecular products (see Chap. 4, page 94 f.).

In a condensation polymerization, such as the polyamidification of $\omega$-aminocaproic acid, $H_2N(CH_2)_5COOH$, the first step is the intermolecular reaction $2M \to MM$. The second step will be the reaction of the dimers with another dimer or another monomer:

$$MM \qquad M$$
$$MMMM \longleftarrow MM \longrightarrow MMM$$

At this stage there exist four species of molecules, with the result that the trimers and tetramers of the second step may react with monomers, dimers, or with others of their size. In other words, the synthesis of a given polymer molecule is accomplished by a series of *independent* steps which occur over a definite time period. Thus, the monomers disappear rapidly during the initial part of the polymerization process. Note also that all of the species of polymer chains present may be modified by interruption of the polymerization, since all polymer species still possess reactive terminal groups.

In an addition polymerization, no propagation reaction occurs *between* two growing polymer species, but in a condensation reaction, random reactions among *all* functional groups occur; i.e.,

$$n\text{-mer} + m\text{-mer} \rightarrow (n + m)\text{-mer}$$

occurs equally with

$$n\text{-mer} + \text{monomer} \rightarrow (n + 1)\text{-mer}$$

and both types of reactions have been found to have essentially the same rate constants. Thus, after a short reaction time, nearly all of the monomer disappears, but the mixture consists of low-molecular-weight polymers which continue to grow for as long as they are allowed or until the limit of possible condensation is reached. In order to obtain *any* high-molecular-weight polymer, it is necessary to push the reaction toward completion.

During an addition polymerization, on the other hand, high-molecular-weight polymer and monomer coexist *throughout the reaction* and the average molecular weight of the polymer remains practically constant. Each activation in a chain reaction produces a high-molecular-weight polymer and the amount of monomer decreases slowly throughout the reaction. Increasing the time of the reaction gives an increasing yield of polymer, but does not change the molecular weight of the polymer appreciably.

### Condensation Polymerizations

In the following chapter, the relations between functionality and polymerization are presented, and Carothers' influence on elucidating the nature of condensation polymerizations is shown. From his investigations it has become apparent that, although temperature, concentration, etc., exert their usual influences, the strongest determining factor of the course followed by a polycondensation reaction is the structure of the reacting monomers.

Thus, if the structure is such that five- or six-membered rings can form by *intra*molecular reaction, they do form, and low-molecular-weight cyclic compounds rather than polymers are obtained as the principal product.   The majority of all cyclic compounds that have been isolated and identified contain five- or six-membered rings.   From this, it might be inferred that such structures are more stable than larger rings, that they are easier to form, or both.   Much larger-sized rings have been prepared, and, while it is true that their preparation is usually difficult, it is not true that they are unstable.   The frequent formation of five- and six-membered rings by the intramolecular reaction of two functional groups on the same molecule may be explained, however.   In an aliphatic chain, for example, the groups attached to a single bond are free to rotate, so that in solution or in the liquid state the chains may whip into a great many different positions.   If there is a certain functional group on a particular carbon atom and another functional group of different nature on a nearby carbon atom on the same chain, the geometry between these is such that the two groups will collide frequently and will permit many opportunities for reaction.   This is true for bifunctional compounds containing five or six linear carbon atoms.   As, however, the functional groups become separated by a greater number of carbon atoms, the probability of intramolecular collisions and resultant cyclization becomes greatly reduced.   This means that a large, cyclic structure for a high-molecular-weight polymer is highly improbable.

Since in a melt or solution of a bifunctional compound, there is always the probability of an intermolecular reaction, the intra- and inter-molecular reactions are always competitive.   Consequently, the formation of polymers rather than cyclic compounds depends upon the absence of a tendency toward ring closure in the early stages of reaction; the probability of ring closure will diminish as the length of the chain increases.   These concepts have been substantiated by kinetic studies.

As a matter of fact, cyclic monomers from five-atom carbon chains form almost to the exclusion of linear polymers.   Thus lactones, lactams, and cyclic anhydrides from $\omega$-substituted five-carbon acids are simple to prepare and are quite stable to ring-cleavage reactions.

Bifunctional monomers containing six or seven carbon atoms in the chain normally produce both cyclic and linear products, and, as the length of the chain becomes greater, linear polymers are normally formed exclusively.   It may be mentioned, in passing, that for atoms other than carbon, where the bond lengths and angles are different, a different number of chain-atoms may be necessary to produce the most stable ring configuration; for example, an eight-membered ring is obtained in greatest yield from dimethyl siloxane.   The ease of ring formation will, of course, be different if double bonds or ring structures are present in the monomer since rotation of bonds is then restricted.

Cross-linking will appear if a polyfunctional compound is added to a bifunctional reactant or to a mixture of bifunctional compounds.   The greater the concentration of the polyfunctional material, the sooner cross-linking will begin.    If one of the two initial materials consists entirely of polyfunctional molecules, the polymer will become insoluble long before the reaction is complete.    The mathematical treatment of these situations is covered in the next chapter.    It is possible to control the average size and properties of the macromolecules formed by selecting the proportions of mono-, di-, and polyfunctional molecules before starting.

In his earlier syntheses of linear polyesters, Carothers[3] discovered that the average molecular weight of the final product was always of the same order, roughly, between 2,000 and 5,000.    The polymers did not grow to the great lengths theoretically possible.    The inference from this was that the functional groups on large molecules were less reactive than those on the original monomers and that unexpelled water established equilibrium in the reactions.    Subsequently, however, Flory[4] demonstrated that functional groups on large molecules are just as reactive as those on monomers; that, under the conditions of the earlier experiments, neither the viscosity of the medium nor the rigorousness of expulsion of the water of condensation was the controlling factor for molecular growth; and that Carothers' early polyester products were of low molecular weight because equilibrium had *not* been reached.    In other words, the higher molecular weights of Carothers' *superpolymers* were due to a longer reaction time rather than to displacement of the equilibrium point.    Of course, when the molecular weight and the viscosity become extremely high, the reaction mass may be immobilized to the extent that slow diffusion of the reactants and by-products may actually be rate controlling.

### Kinetics of Condensation Polymerizations

The mechanism of any chemical reaction is best obtained from kinetic data.    In polymerization studies, the kinetic data are concerned with the rate of disappearance of monomer and the extent of polymerization.    The *extent of polymerization* is not to be confused with the *degree of polymerization*. The former refers to the amount of polymer that has been formed in a polymerization reaction in any given time, whereas the latter refers to the number of mesomers in a specific polymer chain.

The determination of the extent to which monomers have been converted to polymers at any particular time is necessary for the determination of polymerization kinetics.    Physical and chemical methods, either alone or together, have been used.    Some of these means are:[5]

[3] Carothers, W. H. and Arvin, G. A., *J. Am. Chem. Soc.*, **51**, 2560 (1929).

[4] See Flory, P. J., *Principles of Polymer Chemistry*, Chap. III, Cornell University Press, Ithaca, N.Y., 1953.

[5] See D'Alelio, G. F., *Fundamental Principles of Polymerization*, Chap. 8, John Wiley and Sons, New York, 1952.

*Physical Methods*                          *Chemical Methods*

Distillation                                End-group analysis

Refractive index measurements               Measurement of residual

Optical rotation measurements                 monomer

Viscosity measurements

Density measurements

Dilatometric measurements

Absorption spectra

Vibrational spectra

Conductance (or resistance) measurements

Diamagnetic susceptibility measurements

Rate-of-reaction studies on homologous series were among the earliest investigations in the field of reaction kinetics. These investigations have shown that any significant change in the rate constant with chain length is confined to the region of low degrees of polymerization. As the chain length increases, the rate constant rapidly approaches an asymptotic (limiting) value. A common impression that larger molecules in an homologous series react more slowly may be caused by the diluting effect of large chains; this effect must be taken into account when any reaction is carried out by mixing the reactants without adjusting to corresponding molar concentrations. It is also possible that limited solubility of higher members of a series may be responsible for an apparently slow reaction rate.

Polyesterification reactions are usually studied under conditions in which the water formed is continuously removed. In the self-esterification of an hydroxy acid to form a linear polymer, every molecule, regardless of its size, will contain one carboxyl group. The rate of reaction can be followed by titration of the unreacted carboxyl groups in samples removed from the mixture at various times. The result is usually expressed in terms of the *extent of reaction*, $p$, which is defined as the fraction of functional groups which has been reacted at the time of removal of the sample. Thus, if $N_o$ is the initial number of reactive groups of one kind and $N_t$ the number of unreacted groups remaining at any time, $t$, then, by definition,

$$p = \frac{N_o - N_t}{N_o} \tag{1}$$

As another example, consider the reaction between equivalent amounts of a dibasic acid and a glycol. As with simple esterifications, the reaction is catalyzed by acid. In the absence of added catalyst, the rate of reaction is proportional to the product of the hydroxyl and the square of the carboxyl concentrations, since under this condition a molecule of the acid undergoing esterification functions as the catalyst. Therefore, if $C$ is the concentration of the reacting groups, the rate of esterification is

$$-\frac{dC}{dt} = k[\text{OH}][\text{COOH}]^2 = kC^3 \tag{2}$$

where $k$ is the reaction rate constant. Integrating and introducing the condition that when $t = 0$, $C = C_o$, the expression for the rate becomes

$$2kt = \frac{1}{C^2} - \frac{1}{C_o^2} \tag{3}$$

If it is assumed that the effect of the by-product (water) formed is negligible —i.e., no appreciable change of concentration occurs due to the volume decrease resulting from the removal of water—then $C$ may be replaced by $C_o(1 - p)$ and the rate expression becomes

$$2ktC_o^2 = \frac{1}{(1-p)^2} - 1 \tag{4}$$

Thus, a plot of $1/(1 - p)^2$ vs. $t$ should increase linearly if $k$ does not vary with change of size of the reacting molecules. This relationship holds for the esterification of a number of glycols with adipic acid and for the polymerization of $\omega$-hydroxy undecanoic acid for the latter portion of the reaction. Failure to follow this third-order relation over the first portion of the reaction has not yet been fully explained. Whatever the exact cause, it is typical of simple esterifications as well as of those which cause polymer formation and is, therefore, not caused by the sizes of the reacting molecules.

In a polyesterification involving bifunctional monomers only, the hydroxyl and carboxyl groups are present in equal numbers, and the number of unreacted carboxyl groups must equal the number of molecules present in the system (provided that no side reactions occur); the number of molecules (in moles per unit volume) is equal, therefore, to $C_o(1 - p)$. If *each* residue from a glycol and from a dibasic acid is regarded as a structural unit, so that the number of structural units equals the total number of bifunctional monomers initially present, the average number of structural units per molecule, or the number-average degree of polymerization, $\overline{DP_n}$, will be given by

$$\overline{DP_n} = \frac{\text{original number of monomer units}}{\text{total number of molecules}} = \sum_{n=1}^{\infty} nN_x = \frac{N_o}{N}$$

$$= \frac{N_o}{N_o(1 - p)} = \frac{C_o}{C} = \frac{C_o}{C_o(1 - p)} = \frac{1}{1 - p} \tag{5}$$

and the weight-average degree of polymerization will be

$$\overline{DP_w} = \sum_{n=1}^{\infty} nW_x = \frac{1 + p}{1 - p} \tag{6}$$

where $n$ is the number of mesomers in an $n$-mer and $N_x$ and $W_x$ are the number- and the weight-fractions of $n$-mer, respectively. The number-average molecular weight (defined as the total weight divided by the total number of molecules) is given by

$$\overline{M_n} = m_o\overline{DP_n} = m_o\left[\frac{1}{1 - p}\right] = \frac{m_o}{1 - p} \tag{7}$$

where $m_o$ is the molecular weight of a mesomer.

By substitution of Eq. 5 in Eq. 4, $\overline{DP_n}$ is found to be almost proportional to the square root of $t$ (for a third-order condensation). This has been found to be generally true experimentally except during the early stages of the reaction. Although low-molecular-weight polymers form rapidly, the rate of increase of molecular weight with time decreases as the third-order reaction proceeds, and the attainment of very high molecular weights requires an extremely long time of reaction. The decrease in the rate of advancement of the degree of polymerization in such poly-esterifications is due to the third-order nature of the esterification reaction, not to low reactivities of large molecules, as has been suggested by early investigators.

Greater success in extending kinetic measurements to higher degrees of polymerization has been achieved with polyesterifications catalyzed by a small amount of a strong acid. The rate of reaction is again proportional to the hydroxyl, carboxyl, and catalyst concentrations, and therefore

$$-\frac{dC}{dt} = k'C_{\text{cat}}C^2 \tag{8}$$

However, since the catalyst concentration is constant, integration gives

$$\frac{1}{C} = k''t + \frac{1}{C_o} \tag{9}$$

where $k'' = k'C_{\text{cat}}$; and, since $C = C_o(1 - p)$,

$$k''tC_o = \frac{1}{1 - p} - 1 \tag{10}$$

and $\overline{DP_n}$ increases *linearly* with time of reaction, a much more favorable situation for obtaining high average molecular weights than that of the "uncatalyzed" third-order reaction. Results reported on acid-catalyzed polyesterifications of certain glycols and dibasic acids have shown that the reactions are of second-order at least up to a degree of polymerization of 90 which corresponds, roughly, to average molecular weights of about 10,000. Despite the great increases in molecular size and the concurrent increases in the viscosities of the medium by factors exceeding 2,000, the rate constants did not decrease in value.

The general conclusion from these and other experimental results is that a polycondensation reaction proceeds in a manner analogous to a mono-functional reaction, and that the reactivities of the functional groups are essentially independent of the sizes of the molecules. This is in agreement with the theory of organic reactions which states that in any hydrocarbon chain the effect of substitution in the molecule does not extend very far along the chain.

In contrast to bifunctional condensations, relatively few kinetic measurements have been made on the technically important polyfunctional reactions which lead to three-dimensional structures. The rate of reaction of glycerol with a series of dibasic acids has been measured by determination of both the carboxyl-group concentration and the water formed, as a function of the extent of the reaction. It has been demonstrated that the reactions occur, as with bifunctional monomers, primarily by inter-esterification, although the course is modified by intra-esterification and anhydride formation. The conclusion has been made that the reactions occur in a stepwise manner and that, when gelation occurs, the average molecular weights correspond to those of tetramers.

The treatment of polyesterification reactions given in the foregoing section may now be generalized.[6] The most probable distribution can be obtained by kinetic methods in much the same way as distributions can be calculated for vinyl polymerizations (see Chap. 4). It is again necessary to assume that each reaction step has the same reaction rate constant, $k$ [which leads to a further equation giving the time dependence of polymer growth (Eq. 15)]. This assumption, as has already been pointed out, is in agreement with the experimental facts.

Starting with a monomer molecule, $M_1$, reaction can occur with other monomer molecules as well as with molecules of all other chain lengths. The rate of disappearance of monomer will therefore be

$$- \frac{dM_1}{dt} = kM_1(M_1 + M_2 + M_3 + \ldots)$$

$$(11)$$

$$= kM_1 \sum_{n=1}^{\infty} M_n$$

[6] Stockmayer, W. H., "Molecular Size Distribution in High Polymers," Chap. 6 in Twiss, S. B., ed., *Advancing Fronts in Chemistry*, Vol. I (High Polymers), Reinhold Publishing Corp., New York, 1945.

(Note that in rate equations, $M$ stands for concentration of the molecules, not for the molecule itself.) Dimers $(M_2)$ are formed only by reaction between monomers, but may be consumed by reacting with molecules of all other lengths. Hence, the net rate of formation of dimers is

$$\frac{dM_2}{dt} = \tfrac{1}{2}kM_1^2 - kM_2 \sum_{n=1}^{\infty} M_n \tag{12}$$

The factor $\tfrac{1}{2}$ is necessary because two monomers must be used to produce a dimer. Similarly, for the formation of trimers,

$$\frac{dM_3}{dt} = kM_1M_2 - kM_3 \sum_{n=1}^{\infty} M_n \tag{13}$$

Thus, in general, there is obtained for the formation and disappearance of $n$-mers

$$\frac{dM_n}{dt} = \tfrac{1}{2}k \sum_{s=1}^{s=n-1} M_s M_{n-s} - kM_n \sum_{n=1}^{\infty} M_n \tag{14}$$

The first term shows that $n$-mers are formed by the combination of two smaller molecules, the indices of which add up to $n$; on carrying out the summation, each molecule with $s$ smaller than $n - 1$ is counted twice; hence the term must be divided by two. The second term describes the disappearance of $n$-mer due to reaction with $s$-mers of any size from $s = 1$ on up. In other words, Eq. 14 defines the rate of formation and disappearance of $n$-mer; i.e., the net rate of formation of $n$-mer.

The solution of the above equations gives the relationship

$$\frac{dp}{dt} = \tfrac{1}{2}N_ok(1 - p)^2 \tag{15}$$

which, upon integration, yields

$$p = \frac{N_okt}{2 + N_okt} \tag{16}$$

This equation defines $p$ in terms of $k$ (or *vice versa*) and is the explicit result of the assumption that $k$ remains constant throughout the reactions.

### ADDITION POLYMERIZATIONS

Addition polymerizations of unsaturated monomers proceed by a chain-reaction mechanism. The tendency to polymerize is a characteristic of molecules which possess a particular type of double or triple bond. However, to be of technical interest, an unsaturated compound must be carefully controlled with regard to purity and reaction conditions; otherwise polymeric products of uniform quality cannot be manufactured. For various reasons, such as cost of raw materials, cost of production, ease of purification and reaction control, monomers containing olefinic bonds are the most important in the commercial production of addition polymers.

The double bond is the site of the initiating reaction that gives rise to an active center which may add on a monomer molecule without loss of activity. The chain grows by successive additions of monomer until, by some means, it becomes stabilized and growth ceases.

It is customary to resolve the chain process into three stages: initiation, propagation, and termination. Activation of a monomer, $M$, (initiation) is followed by the addition of other monomers in rapid succession (propagation)

$$M \xrightarrow{\hspace{2cm}} M^* \xrightarrow{\hspace{1cm}} MM^* \xrightarrow{\hspace{1cm}} MMM^* \xrightarrow{\hspace{2cm}} M_n$$

activation        propagation        deactivation

until the growing chain is deactivated (termination), with the net result that a polymer molecule, $M_n$, has been formed from $n$ monomers. Each growth step consists of reaction with a monomer.

Unlike condensation polymerizations, where polymer-polymer combinations occur very frequently, reaction here between two growing polymer molecules deters the development of large molecules. The center of activation, located at the growing end of a molecule, may be a free radical, a carbonium ion (cationic polymerization), or a carbanion (anionic polymerization). Most polymerizations of unsaturated compounds (usually referred to as vinyl-type polymerizations) which have been investigated in detail proceed by a free-radical mechanism. Free-radical polymerizations are usually induced by radicals released by a decomposing peroxide or other compound; however, the initiating free radicals may also be formed photochemically or thermally.

Regardless of the chain propagation mechanism involved, the entire synthesis of any polymer molecule from unreacted monomer occurs extremely rapidly—usually within a few seconds or less—whereas the conversion of all monomer to polymer may require hours. Thus, at any time during the polymerization process, the reaction mixture consists almost entirely of monomer and high-molecular-weight polymer. Material at intermediate stages of growth (i.e., the portion consisting of actively growing chains) is so small as to be almost immeasurable; however, though small, its concentration is almost constant. As the conversion to polymer increases, the number-average degree of polymerization of the polymerized portion remains approximately the same. Thus, the duration of an addition polymerization process is determined by the *yield* of the polymer desired and not by the molecular weight required.

The above outlined characteristics of vinyl polymerizations are natural consequences of the fact that they are chain reactions in the kinetic sense.

Under proper conditions, they proceed quite rapidly. Unsaturated compounds which react by an ionic mechanism polymerize especially rapidly; the reaction may be violent, even at very low temperatures. Condensation polymerizations generally require a much greater length of time and elevated temperatures if a satisfactorily high molecular weight is to be reached. Molecular weights much above 25,000 are rare for linear condensation polymers, whereas polymers having molecular weights appreciably greater than 100,000 usually are easily obtained in most vinyl polymerizations.

It should be noted that, in addition polymerizations, polar functional groups, such as —COOH, —OH, and —NH$_2$, are not involved. Furthermore, bond rearrangements often take place in more than one way. As a result the course followed by an addition polymerization is more difficult to determine by chemical means and more difficult to control. Undesirable reactions are likely to occur concurrently with the preferred reaction. The structures of the polymeric products are therefore more difficult to establish with certainty.

Nonlinear addition polymers are readily obtained by copolymerizing a polyfunctional compound with a vinyl monomer. These products exhibit the insolubility and other characteristics of space-network structures and are structurally analogous to those formed by the condensation of polyfunctional compounds. Due to the greater length of the chains in vinyl polymerizations, extremely small amounts of a polyfunctional compound may be sufficient to cause gelation and polymer insolubility.

## Ease of Polymerization

Certain guiding principles may be stated which relate the molecular structure of an unsaturated monomer to its ease of polymerization. A compound containing two or more double bonds or having one or more triple bonds polymerizes more readily than a compound with only one double bond. If the double bonds form a conjugated system, as in 1,3-butadiene, CH$_2$:CH·CH:CH$_2$, polymerization occurs more readily than when the double bonds are farther apart. A compound with two conjugated triple bonds would be still more reactive than a compound with two conjugated double bonds. In general, the greater the degree of unsaturation, the greater the ease of polymerization. The same comparisons hold in the case of cyclic unsaturated hydrocarbons; e.g., 1,3-cyclohexadiene polymerizes more readily than cyclohexene.

There is a great difference in the ease with which vinyl compounds form polymers and also in the sizes of polymers which are formed. An examination of the formulas of the ethylene derivatives which have proved to be most satisfactory for the production of commercially useful polymers reveals that every one of these compounds possesses a methylene group linked by a double bond to another carbon atom ($CH_2$:$C<$):

| | |
|---|---|
| $CH_2$:$CH_2$ | ethylene |
| $CH_2$:$CHCl$ | vinyl chloride |
| $CH_2$:$CCl_2$ | vinylidene chloride |
| $CH_2$:$CHCN$ | acrylonitrile |
| $CH_2$:$CHOOCCH_3$ | vinyl acetate |
| $CH_2$:$CHCOOCH_3$ | methyl acrylate |
| $CH_2$:$C(CH_3)COOCH_3$ | methyl methacrylate |
| $CH_2$:$C(CH_3)_2$ | isobutylene |
| $CH_2$:$CHC_6H_5$ | styrene |

Except for certain fluorinated derivatives of ethylene (and cyclic compounds), no useful polymer has been obtained from a derivative of ethylene which does not have this fundamental structure.

Ethylene is the simplest vinyl compound and can be polymerized with some difficulty. The introduction of a negative group greatly increases its reactivity, for vinyl chloride can readily be polymerized. Vinyl bromide polymerizes even more readily, and vinyl iodide polymerizes more readily than any of the other vinyl monohalides. Chloroprene (2-chloro-1,3-butadiene) polymerizes about 700 times as fast as isoprene (2-methyl-1,3-butadiene), whereas bromoprene polymerizes at a somewhat more rapid rate, roughly 1,100 times as rapidly as isoprene. Other negative groups also increase the ease of polymerization, since vinyl acetate and acrylic acid and its esters polymerize easily. The phenyl radical is considered a negative group and phenyl ethylene (styrene) can be polymerized readily. Alkyl groups decrease the tendency to polymerize, and the higher-molecular-weight olefins require stronger conditions to cause polymerization.

When a second group is present, the reactivity varies greatly with the position into which it is introduced. The asymmetrical derivatives polymerize much more readily than the symmetrical. Compounds in which the unsubstituted terminal methylene group is present usually form polymers. If two negative groups are added, polymerization is more rapid than when only one such group is present. Vinylidene chloride polymerizes more readily than does vinyl chloride, which in turn polymerizes more readily than symmetrical dichloroethylene ($CHCl$:$CHCl$); further halogen substitution stabilizes the ethylene molecule. Thus, trichloroethylene is perfectly stable, as is shown by its widespread use as a commercial solvent. Methacrylic esters polymerize readily but not so rapidly as esters of acrylic acid, whereas the symmetrically disubstituted vinyl compounds, the esters of crotonic acid, $CH_3 \cdot CH$:$CH \cdot CO_2R$, may be polymerized only with difficulty.

Generally, the compounds which polymerize readily also form high-molecular-weight polymers and nearly all compounds which polymerize with difficulty form polymers with short chains *under comparable conditions*. For example, isobutylene, in the presence of catalysts, forms polymers of high molecular weight, whereas 2-butene forms only low-molecular-weight polymers under the same conditions.

Cyclic compounds may be considered as symmetrically disubstituted ethylene derivatives but generally polymerize somewhat more readily than the corresponding straight-chain compound.    This is especially true when the ring is five-membered.   Cyclopentadiene polymerizes much more easily than piperylene (1,3-pentadiene).   Indene is readily polymerized in the presence of acid catalysts.

In conjugated dienes, the double bonds are arranged in a 1,3 position and most conjugated dienes polymerize readily.   Such dienes usually polymerize as if only one double bond were present, forming an unsaturated polymer.   Butadiene forms such a polymer.   Most of the doubly unsaturated molecules polymerize in this way but some will polymerize with both vinyl groups polymerizing independently.   Since one vinyl group then forms a mesomer in one chain and the other in a second chain, cross-linked polymers are formed.

If the two double bonds are in the 1,4 position, they may rearrange to the conjugated 1,3 form and polymerize as conjugated dienes, particularly at high temperatures.   If the double bonds are farther apart in the molecule, they usually polymerize independently and react with the formation of cross-linked polymers.

The effects of various substituent groups on the rate of polymerization of diolefin derivatives are much the same as in the case of monovinyl compounds, and negative groups have the same accelerating effect; for example, two halogen atoms in the 1,3-butadiene series still further accelerate the rate of polymerization.

If one of the double bonds is in an aromatic ring, as in styrene, the double bond in the ring does not enter into the polymer, but in alicyclic rings, as in 1-vinyl cyclohexene, 1,4 polymerization occurs as in butadiene.

However, the rate of polymerization cannot always be predicted from compound to compound even when the degree of unsaturation, the conjugation of unsaturated linkages, the alkyl and aryl substitutions, and cyclic structures, even halogen substitutions, are considered, except in the simplest cases.   It is only safe to say that certain structures are associated with most of the rapidly polymerizing compounds.   These structures are (conjugated) unsaturated compounds with hydrogen atoms on one unsaturated carbon (i.e., not substituted) and with one or two substituents on the other carbon atom, preferably aryl groups or halogen atoms (electronegative substituents).

## Mechanisms

*Initiation*

The course of addition polymerizations as previously outlined has been generally accepted. The major points of speculation and controversy have been the specific nature of the activation, indicated simply by *, and the way in which this activation is accomplished. One source of difficulty has been the fact that the activation may be effected in several ways and may even differ in character for polymerizations carried out under varying conditions or with different monomers. In general, it is convenient to classify the types of initiation as follows:

| *Noncatalytic* | *Catalytic* |
|---|---|
| Thermal | Free radical |
| Photochemical | Ionic |
| | Cationic |
| | Anionic |
| | Redox |

The use of the term "catalytic" herein is meant only to imply that a material substance, whether a true catalyst or not, has been added to accelerate the rate of polymerization.

*Thermal Initiation.* The nature of initiation in "uncatalyzed polymerizations" is not well established. Investigators[7] have presented kinetic evidence that initiation is a second-order reaction. An active nucleus is first formed. This reactive nucleus is formed by heat and apparently involves collision between two monomers to give a dimeric biradical:

$$M + M \xrightarrow{\Delta} *MM*$$

Involved in this collision reaction is an energy of activation which is about 25,000 to 35,000 cal per mole.

*Photochemical Initiation.* Studies on the photopolymerization of various vinyl-type compounds indicate that a monomeric biradical is formed:

$$M \xrightarrow{h\nu} *M*$$

Presumably the monomer becomes activated by the absorption of a quantum of light. The amount of energy which can be absorbed by light radiation is very large, in some cases exceeding 100 kcal per mole. The absorption of a quantum of light energy excites an electron in the molecule, which lessens the stability of a bond and causes dissociation to

[7] Schulz, G. V. and Husemann, E., *Z. physik. Chem.*, **B39**, 246 (1938); Mayo, F. R., *J. Am. Chem. Soc.*, **65**, 2324 (1943).

occur unless this energy is transmitted to another molecule by collision (deactivation) or is emitted as light (fluorescence or phosphorescence).

*Free Radical Initiation.* The thermal and photochemical types of initiation differ from the "catalytic" initiations in that, in the latter types, a distinct chemical substance is added. In the normal free-radical type, as, for example, in a vinyl polymerization initiated by an organic peroxide, a free radical, $B\cdot$, is formed by decomposition of the "catalyst." Initiation is caused by its reaction with a monomer molecule to form a new radical. This radical is progressively generated terminally by the further addition of monomer molecules. The radical, $B\cdot$, thus becomes a part of the polymer chain. In the vast majority of commercial vinyl polymerizations, initiation is induced by free radical or ionic agents, rather than by thermal or photochemical means.

The best evidence for the free radical nature of polymerization is obtained by the introduction of free radicals into a monomeric system. Thus, triphenyl methyl readily initiates polymerization of styrene in solution. Further, large numbers of organic and inorganic compounds which are known to form free radicals upon decomposition act as initiators for vinyl polymerizations. These compounds include the acyl and aryl peroxides and hydroperoxides, diazonium compounds, and persulfates. The odd electron in the radical formed by the decomposition of any of these compounds pairs with one of the $\pi$ electrons (of opposite spin) from the double bond of a monomer molecule, at the same time repelling the other electron (with the same spin) to the far end of the monomer molecule, thus reforming a free radical:

$$B\cdot\ +\ CH_2{:}CXY \rightarrow BCH_2{\cdot}\overset{*}{C}XY$$

It is not necessarily true, however, that the introduction of free radicals into a monomer mixture will automatically initiate polymerization and that the process is free of activation energy.

In order to avoid confusion, all initiators or their concentrations in this section on addition polymerization will be designated by $B$ and all active initiator fragments or their concentrations by $B\cdot$. The symbol $M_n^*$ will refer to a monomer ($n = 1$) or polymer ($n = n$) activated by an initiator fragment. For example:

$$B\cdot\ +\ M \rightarrow M_1^*$$

The most commonly employed initiators (often inaccurately referred to as catalysts) are organic peroxides, such as benzoyl peroxide. These decompose slowly at temperatures of $50°$ to $150°C$ with release of free radicals as follows:

$$(ArCOO)_2 \rightarrow 2ArCOO\cdot \rightarrow ArCOO\cdot\ +\ Ar\cdot\ +\ CO_2 \rightarrow 2Ar\cdot\ +\ 2CO_2$$

or

$$B_2 \rightarrow 2B\cdot$$

Both the carboxy and the hydrocarbon free radicals formed by the decomposition of a diacyl or a diaryl peroxide exist, their ratio depending upon the reaction conditions. Higher polymerization temperatures probably favor the formation of the hydrocarbon free radicals.

Organic hydroperoxides, such as *tert*-butyl hydroperoxide, $(CH_3)_3$-$C \cdot O \cdot OH$, also induce polymerization in vinyl monomers by the formation of free radicals formed during their decomposition. There are other classes of compounds which are effective polymerization initiators at temperatures where they undergo slow thermal decomposition by mechanisms which involve the release of free radicals. Of especial interest is the class of substances known as aliphatic azobisnitriles, such as azobis-isobutyronitrile

$$(CH_3)_2 C \cdot N{:}N \cdot C \cdot (CH_3)_2 \rightarrow 2(CH_3)_2 C \cdot \; + \; N_2$$
$$\overset{|}{CN} \quad \overset{|}{CN} \qquad\qquad\qquad \overset{|}{CN}$$

which has been used in many of the recent kinetic investigations because of the freedom of its decomposition from side reactions. It is also useful as a photo-initiator under the influence of near ultraviolet radiation, which upon absorption causes dissociation into radicals. Since organic peroxides have oxygen-oxygen bond energies of about 30 kcal per mole, either heat or light energy is sufficient to cause their dissociation into active free radicals.

Kinetic measurements of the rate of "catalyzed" polymerizations have confirmed the chemical evidence for free-radical initiation. The observed dependence of the consumption of monomer on the concentration of the initiator may be interpreted in terms of a free-radical chain. It appears that the active center of a kinetic chain is retained by a single polymer molecule throughout the course of its growth. A partially polymerized mixture consists of high-molecular-weight polymer and unchanged monomer with virtually no constituents at intermediate stages of growth. In fact, as has also previously been pointed out, polymer molecules formed even during the first fraction of a percentage conversion are comparable in molecular weight to those present at a much later time of reaction. In other words, individual polymer molecules grow to maturity while most of the monomers remain intact. If, on the contrary, the active centers were transferred randomly at every step from one molecule to another, all sizes of molecules would enter into the process of chemical combination with all other species at all stages of the process. All polymer molecules would then grow more or less simultaneously and lower-molecular-weight species, such as dimers, trimers, and tetramers, would be prevalent early in the polymerization process and would increase in size as the process continued. Intermediates of this nature are generally undetectable in addition polymerizations.

These considerations, together with the fact that extremely high-molecular-weight molecules are produced, lead to the conclusion that a given molecule is formed by consecutive steps of a *single* chain process. The active center created is in some way retained by the growing polymer chain during each addition of a monomer molecule. The time for the growth of an individual polymer molecule requires only a fraction of the time required for the over-all conversion, and the final polymer molecule thus produced is not, in general, susceptible to further growth.

*Ionic Initiation.* A different initiation mechanism holds for ionic metal halides, such as stannic chloride, titanium tetrachloride, aluminum chloride, boron trifluoride, etc., for it has been shown that the rate of polymerization is here proportional to the unit power of the initiator concentration (although the degree of polymerization seems to be independent of this factor) and to an unusually high power (e.g., the third) of monomer concentration. All cationic substances which cause ionic polymerization are characterized by a strong affinity for an electron pair and are believed to initiate polymerization by polarization of the double bond of the monomer; i.e., acquire a *pair* of electrons from the monomer double bond. Substituent groups, such as alkyl, aryl, or ether groups, promote the release of electrons, and monomers which contain such groups are most readily polymerized by ionic catalysts; e.g., isobutylene, α-methyl styrene, and vinyl alkyl ethers.

One theory[8] of polymerization of olefins by aluminum chloride postulates that the aluminum chloride combines with the ionic activated state of the olefin (in which two electrons of the unsaturated double bond occupy the same orbit):

$$
\begin{array}{ccc}
\text{R}'\ \text{R}\ \ \text{Cl} & & \text{R}'\ \text{R}\ \text{Cl} \\
\ddot{\phantom{C}}\ \ \ddot{\phantom{C}}\ \ \ddot{\phantom{C}} & & \ddot{\phantom{C}}\ \ \ddot{\phantom{C}}\ \ \ddot{\phantom{C}} \\
\text{C::C} + \text{Al:Cl} & \rightarrow & \text{C}:\text{C}:\text{Al}:\text{Cl} \\
\ddot{\phantom{C}}\ \ \ddot{\phantom{C}}\ \ \ddot{\phantom{C}} & & \ddot{\phantom{C}}\ \ \ddot{\phantom{C}}\ \ \ddot{\phantom{C}} \\
\text{R}'\ \text{R}\ \ \text{Cl} & & \text{R}'\ \text{R}\ \text{Cl}
\end{array}
$$

This complex is highly activated because the terminal structure

$$
\begin{array}{c}
\text{R}' \\
\ddot{\phantom{C}} \\
\text{C}: \\
\ddot{\phantom{C}} \\
\text{R}'
\end{array}
$$

can add to another olefin molecule, again producing a product which would be in an active state.

However, more recent investigations[9] have indicated that halides are

[8] Hunter, W. W. and Yohe, R. V., *J. Am. Chem. Soc.*, **55**, 1248 (1933).
[9] Evans, A. G. and Polanyi, M., *J. Chem. Soc.*, 1947, 252.

ineffective initiators without the presence of small amounts of an activator, such as water or alcohol. Thus, a mechanism proposed for the polymerization of isobutylene in the presence of boron trifluoride and a trace of water is

$$
\mathrm{BF_3\cdot OH_2} + \underset{\substack{|\\ \mathrm{C}}}{\overset{\substack{\mathrm{C}\\ |}}{\mathrm{C}}}\!\!=\!\!\underset{\substack{|\\ \mathrm{C}}}{\overset{\substack{\mathrm{C}\\ |}}{\mathrm{C}}} \rightarrow \underset{\substack{|\\ \mathrm{C}}}{\overset{\substack{\mathrm{C}\\ |}}{\mathrm{C}}}\!\!-\!\!\underset{\substack{|\\ \mathrm{C}}}{\overset{\substack{\mathrm{C}\\ |}}{\mathrm{C}^+}} + \mathrm{BF_3\cdot OH^-} \xrightarrow{\text{monomer}}
$$

$$
\underset{\substack{|\\ \mathrm{C}}}{\overset{\substack{\mathrm{C}\\ |}}{\mathrm{C}}}\!\!-\!\!\underset{\substack{|\\ \mathrm{C}}}{\overset{\substack{\mathrm{C}\\ |}}{\mathrm{C}}}\!\!-\!\!\mathrm{C}\!\!-\!\!\mathrm{C}^+ \rightarrow \rightarrow \mathrm{C}\!\!-\!\!\underset{\substack{|\\ \mathrm{C}}}{\overset{\substack{\mathrm{C}\\ |}}{\mathrm{C}}}\!\!-\!\!\left[\!\!-\!\!\mathrm{C}\!\!-\!\!\underset{\substack{|\\ \mathrm{C}}}{\overset{\substack{\mathrm{C}\\ |}}{\mathrm{C}}}\!\!-\!\!\right]_{n-1}\!\!-\!\!\mathrm{C}\!\!-\!\!\underset{\substack{|\\ \mathrm{C}}}{\overset{\substack{\mathrm{C}\\ |}}{\mathrm{C}^+}}
$$

(a) $\xrightarrow[\mathrm{BF_3\cdot OH^-}]{\text{monomer}}$ 
$$
\mathrm{C}\!\!-\!\!\underset{\substack{|\\ \mathrm{C}}}{\overset{\substack{\mathrm{C}\\ |}}{\mathrm{C}}}\!\!-\!\!\left[\!\!-\!\!\mathrm{C}\!\!-\!\!\underset{\substack{|\\ \mathrm{C}}}{\overset{\substack{\mathrm{C}\\ |}}{\mathrm{C}}}\!\!-\!\!\right]_{n}\!\!-\!\!\mathrm{C}\!\!-\!\!\underset{\substack{|\\ \mathrm{C}}}{\overset{\substack{\mathrm{C}\\ ||}}{\mathrm{C}}} + \mathrm{BF_3\cdot OH_2}
$$
(proton removal)

(b) $\xrightarrow[\mathrm{BF_3\cdot OH^-}]{}$ 
$$
\mathrm{C}\!\!-\!\!\underset{\substack{|\\ \mathrm{C}}}{\overset{\substack{\mathrm{C}\\ |}}{\mathrm{C}}}\!\!-\!\!\left[\!\!-\!\!\mathrm{C}\!\!-\!\!\underset{\substack{|\\ \mathrm{C}}}{\overset{\substack{\mathrm{C}\\ |}}{\mathrm{C}}}\!\!-\!\!\right]_{n-1}\!\!-\!\!\mathrm{C}\!\!-\!\!\underset{\substack{|\\ \mathrm{C}}}{\overset{\substack{\mathrm{C}\\ ||}}{\mathrm{C}}} + \mathrm{C}\!\!-\!\!\underset{\substack{|\\ \mathrm{C}}}{\overset{\substack{\mathrm{C}\\ |}}{\mathrm{C}^+}} + \mathrm{BF_3\cdot OH^-}
$$
(chain transfer)

Reactions of this type are carried out at very low temperatures (down to below $-50°C$) compared with free-radical polymerizations ($+50°C$ to $+150°C$). The formation of polyisobutylene, for example, can occur almost explosively at $-80°C$ in the presence of boron trifluoride. The great speed is a characteristic feature of these reactions and partly accounts for the general lack of knowledge concerning this type of reaction.

Until very recently, less attention has been given to anion-initiated addition polymerization, where an anionic fragment repels the two $\pi$ electrons of the double bond and thus induces a negative charge at the active end of the growing ionic chain, and termination probably occurs by proton capture or some similar mechanism. Common anionic substances used are alkali metal amides, alkyls, and hydrides; alkali metals themselves; Grignard reagents; and Alfin complexes. The recent resurgence of interest in this type of initiation has been in great part due to its successful use in making low-pressure polyethylene.

In the redox (reduction activation) type of initiation, the decomposition of the initiator, normally an oxidizing agent, occurs under the influence of a reducing agent to produce a free radical. In contrast to free radicals initiated by the decomposition of organic compounds, the free radicals generated by a redox system are usually but not always formed by the reaction of *inorganic* materials in *ionic* form in an *aqueous* system. Two of the better-known redox systems are

$$Fe^{++} + H_2O_2 \rightarrow Fe^{+++} + OH^- + HO\cdot$$

and

$$S_2O_8^- + S_2O_3^- \rightarrow SO_4^- + SO_4^-\cdot + S_2O_3^-\cdot$$

In both emulsion and solution polymerizations, the activation energies of redox systems have been reported to be approximately one third those of normal peroxide-induced polymerizations. An explanation of the redox efficiency is based upon the fact that while a small amount of oxygen accelerates polymerizations by the formation of peroxides, larger amounts will compete with monomers for the active nuclei and inhibit the polymerization. The effect of excess oxygen will be overcome by the presence of a reducing agent which reduces the peroxide to an active radical as soon as it is formed.

Ionic-catalyzed systems are frequently characterized by the fact that their rates have a negative temperature coefficient; that is, their rates of reaction increase as the temperature is decreased, in contradistinction to all other initiating systems.

*Inhibition and Retardation*

In common with the more familiar inorganic chain reactions, addition polyreactions are susceptible to both activation and inhibition. The existence of an induction period was noted in many of the early investigations of addition polymerizations. It is now well established that the addition of very small amounts of certain substances to a monomer may inhibit polymerization for a well-defined period of time, after which the reaction follows its normal course. In fact, one of the major problems in studies of addition polymerizations is the purification of monomers from traces of inhibitors.

Inhibitors may act in a number of different ways. One class of these substances completely prevents polymerization. If, as is generally assumed, such a substance acts by combining with and thus inactivating the active centers as soon as they are formed, or by removing adventitious traces of initiators, it will itself be gradually consumed. There will then be an induction period during which substantially no polymerization can be detected, followed by a normal reaction after consumption of the inhibitor. In such cases, the induction period is proportional to the amount of inhibitor initially present, and the rate of consumption of inhibitor is *independent of its concentration*; it depends only on the rate of generation of radicals, whether they are generated by the action of an initiator or by a thermal process which proceeds independently of the presence of inhibitor. Thus, the rate of consumption of inhibitor is of zero order.

The inhibitor, on the other hand, may not be a completely effective one, in which case not all of the active centers will be destroyed, and polymerization will take place without an induction period but at a slower rate than normal.   Strong inhibitors, when nearly consumed, probably produce an effect like this.   Under the latter circumstance, the reaction will occur in three stages: (1) All centers are destroyed and no polymerization occurs, (2) centers are partially destroyed, giving partial polymerization, (3) no centers are destroyed; the inhibitor is completely consumed and normal polymerization follows.

A second process acts by providing an alternative to the normal processes of *propagation* and *termination*.   If the reaction

$$M_n^* + X \rightarrow M_n \cdot X$$

goes much more readily than, say, a normal mutual termination process,

$$M_n^* + M_m^* \rightarrow M_{n+m}$$

then the former can become the main chain-terminating mechanism if enough of $X$ is present.   The net effect is to cut down the over-all rate and also the average chain length, leaving the effective rate of initiation unaltered.   Such a substance is called a *retarder*.   Some apparent retarders are better classified as weak inhibitors; their function as partial deactivators of initiator fragments must be distinguished from that of *true retarders which only interfere with growth and termination*.   Both retarders and inhibitors decrease the over-all rate (but for different reasons), and this is reflected in the kinetics of the reaction.

The exact mechanisms of inhibition and retardation are not clear. Some inhibitors and retarders will act as activator destroyers, but, in many cases, it is known that the best inhibitors can also function as antioxidants in other reactions.   As these molecules prevent oxidation by stopping radical chain growth, it appears likely that, in polymerization reactions, they act similarly by adding to a free-radical chain to form a molecule incapable of further growth.   Such an addition does not necessarily destroy the radical nature of the growing molecule; provided subsequent monomer addition to the adduct is more difficult than to the normal chain, the reaction is effectively inhibited.

If the inhibitor is itself a free radical, the product of reaction with a chain radical will have no unpaired electrons; hence, it will be a stable molecule incapable of adding more monomer.   However, if the free radical chosen to inhibit is not of low reactivity, it may initiate chains as well as terminate them.   Since in such reactions the inhibitor actually reacts with the growing chain, its presence should be detectable in the final polymer; evidence of this exists.

In commercial polymerizations it is important to have as much knowledge as possible about inhibitors and retarders. Their presence for stabilization of monomers is useful, but of more importance is their presence or absence during polymerization. Inhibitors may be of the type which is effective at both storage and polymerization conditions or that which is active at storage conditions but loses its effectiveness at the temperature and other conditions prevailing during polymerization. The second type is usually preferable, as it need not be removed prior to polymerization. Inhibitors of the first type are removed by washing or distillation. Both will affect the average molecular weight and size distribution in the final polymer. Control of these properties is of great importance because various physical properties of the polymer depend on them (Chap. 4).

A number of widely different substances can be employed to inhibit an addition polymerization or to stop the process once it has begun. They include hydroquinone, various quinones, phenols, aromatic nitro compounds, sulfur, free radicals, and oxygen.

Oxygen, a common inhibitor of addition polymerizations, forms a peroxide radical of low reactivity

$$M_n^* + O_2 \rightarrow M_n \cdot O \cdot O*$$

but can also add monomer to regenerate a normal chain radical with the ultimate formation of polymer containing oxygen:

$$M_n \cdot O \cdot O* + M \rightarrow M_n \cdot O \cdot O \cdot M*$$

At the end of the induction period caused by oxygen, polymerization begins at a rate greater than that for pure monomer under the same conditions. It appears that the polymeric peroxides furnish a good source of free radicals. Oxygen therefore sometimes behaves as inhibitor, comonomer, and (indirectly) initiator.

It is generally recognized that the distinction among inhibitors, retarders, and chain-transfer agents (which are discussed later) can be pictured as a continuous sequence, rather than a sharp classification. Classification of a free-radical source as an initiator or an inhibitor depends upon the balance between the rate of addition of these radicals to monomers, rate of growth of the polymer chains, and rates of interaction among radicals.

Fig. 3-1 illustrates graphically the various actions of inhibitors and retarders.

*Propagation*

The chain propagation step consists of free-radical attack at one of the double-bonded carbon atoms of a monomer. One electron of the double bond pairs with the odd electron of the free radical to form a normal covalent bond between the free radical and the carbon atom; the other electron of the double bond shifts to another carbon atom, which then becomes a free radical.  In this way, the active center is transferred to the newly added monomer, which is thereby rendered capable of adding

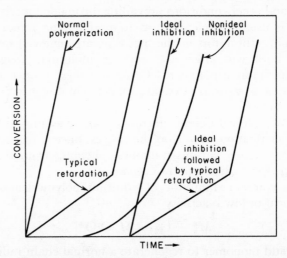

FIG. 3-1.    Typical time-conversion curves for various inhibitory and retarding effects[10]

still another monomer.  The normal chain growth may be represented by the successive series of reactions

$$M_1^* \xrightarrow{M} MM^* \xrightarrow{M} MMM^* \to \to M_n^*$$

The average lifetime of a growing chain has been measured directly in some polymerizations.  For example, in certain photopolymerizations of vinyl acetate, vinyl chloride, methyl acrylate, and styrene, the average lifetime has a value of $10^{-3}$ to $10^{-2}$ second for a chain length of about 1,000.  In these reactions, polymerization ceases almost instantaneously after cessation of illumination.

In an ionic propagation, the fragment is ionic in nature, and growth occurs by a process which retains this ionic character:

$$M^+ \xrightarrow{M} MM^+ \to \to M_n^+$$

These illustrate a general feature of any chain propagation reaction; the addition of monomer does not alter the essential nature of the reaction.

[10] Kolthoff, I. M. and Bovey, F. A., J. Am. Chem. Soc., **70**, 791 (1948).

*Termination*

As has been seen, polymer growth consists of the addition of a monomer to the end of a growing chain, and this requires a collision between the two reactants. As the process of reaction has an activation energy, only a small number of collisions will be effective. Furthermore, since an active molecule can add only at one or both of its ends, collision between a monomer and the middle of the chain will be of no value. Even at the active ends, addition can probably occur only if collision takes place in a specific way and if the energy requirements are adequate; it has been estimated that only about one in $10^6$ collisions are successful. Since polymers of a finite size are produced, most radical-monomer collisions must neither add on to nor deactivate the growing chain. Of the operative collisions, some will not add on to but will *deactivate* the chain to form a dead species; this type of reaction is known as termination, and one type may be written

$$M_n^* + M_m^* \to M_{n+m}$$

The number of deactivating collisions of this type must be very small and, since finite chains are formed, much less than the already small number of successful additions. Such reactions, however, probably are the principal means by which activity is lost.

A number of mechanisms have been proposed whereby an active molecule may become a dead one. It sometimes appears likely that an active molecule may die spontaneously in the bulk phase or may be deactivated by collision with the walls of the container. In ionic polymerizations, what may appear to be spontaneous termination may occur, as a proton may split off from the growing ion to yield an uncharged, *unsaturated* polymer incapable of further growth:

$$M_n^+ \to M_n' + H^+$$

This may not be a true termination, as the proton produced may initiate another ionic chain and continue the polymerization; it is then really an example of a transfer reaction. Provided that some other mechanism destroys active centers, the over-all rate is unchanged by transfer, because many such reactions can proceed at the same rate as a single-chain growth and consume the same total number of monomer molecules. The total number of chains formed, however, will be greater than the initial number of active centers.

In a free-radical polymerization, termination reactions other than those occurring between a pair of radicals appear unlikely. The possibility of ring formation between the growing ends of a biradical chain is quite remote.    It is probable that the principal types of free-radical termination reactions are:

1. Coupling of a growing chain and a free radical, the latter being either an initiator fragment or another growing chain.

2. Reaction of two growing chains by disproportionation.

3. Transfer of activation to another molecule, such as polymer, monomer, or impurity, which readily can form a free radical.

It is difficult to determine which is the predominant mechanism except in special cases, but kinetic studies have indicated that most termination reactions are bimolecular and are probably of the first type. Following are examples of the above types of bimolecular terminations.

1. The union of the radicals by a *coupling* or combination mechanism:

$$2R \cdot CH_2 \cdot \overset{*}{C}HX \rightarrow R \cdot CH_2 \cdot CHX \cdot CHX \cdot CH_2 \cdot R$$

2. The transfer of a hydrogen *atom*, yielding both a saturated molecule and a molecule having an unsaturated terminal group, by a *disproportionation* mechanism:

$$2R \cdot CH_2 \cdot \overset{*}{C}HX \rightarrow R \cdot CH_2 \cdot CH_2X + R \cdot CH:CHX$$

These two types of termination reactions can be distinguished experimentally if the polymer molecule can be shown upon analysis to contain either one or two initiator fragments or that half the molecules have unsaturated end groups.    The disproportionation mechanism would also yield a polymer of lower average molecular weight than the combination mechanism; this would be observed in the size distribution curves for the two types of reactions.    The above two processes are believed to be the principal means of termination in nonionic polymerizations.

3. The transfer of activity from a growing polymer to a monomer ($M$) or solvent ($S$) molecule:

$$M_n^* + M \rightarrow M_n + M^*$$
$$M_n^* + S \rightarrow M_n + S^*$$

This process is termed *chain transfer*.[11]    While it does not destroy the growth process, it does decrease the average degree of polymerization. Examples of chain transfer processes are:

a. Chain transfer with monomer:

$$R \cdot CH_2 \cdot \overset{*}{C}HX + CH_2:CHX \rightarrow R \cdot CH_2 \cdot CH_2X + \overset{*}{C}H:CHX$$

[11] Flory, P. J., *J. Am. Chem. Soc.*, **59**, 241 (1937).

b. Chain transfer with solvent:

$$R \cdot CH_2 \cdot \overset{*}{C}HX + S \rightarrow R \cdot CH_2 \cdot CHXY + S*$$

where $Y$ is a fragment from the solvent molecule.

In both processes, the chain is stabilized by the transfer of a monovalent atom from either the monomer or the solvent, and this forms a new radical which may continue the chain. The new chain, if derived from the monomer, would contain no initiator fragment but would contain a fragment of the solvent molecule if solvent transfer is involved. The latter process has been confirmed for polymerization in halogenated solvents; e.g., styrene in carbon tetrachloride:[12]

$$M_n^* + CCl_4 \rightarrow M_nCl + \cdot CCl_3$$

$$\cdot CCl_3 + M \rightarrow \overset{*}{M}CCl_3 \rightarrow \rightarrow \overset{*}{M}_nCCl_3 \xrightarrow{CCl_4} ClM_nCCl_3 + \cdot CCl_3$$

As further evidence, when styrene is polymerized in a solvent, the resulting polymer has a lower molecular weight than the polymer formed in the absence of a solvent; the effect varies with the solvent. The molecular-weight-lowering by solvents can be accounted for by chain transfer reactions between the growing polymer and the solvent.

Note that chain transfer does not greatly affect the over-all rate of polymerization *since the active center is maintained* but, as in the above example, the average molecular weight is appreciably reduced. In the solvent transfer process, if the new radical, $S*$, is not sufficiently active to react with monomer and thus propagate the chain, then the solvent radicals will destroy each other by coupling and the solvent may be regarded as an inhibitor.

Branching may occur (1) when two active chains form an inactive polymer and a molecule with two regions of activation, the latter continuing to grow in two directions, (2) when a growing chain combines with a polymer with continued growth of the combined product, or (3) when a free radical removes a proton from the middle of a chain, thus forming a new region of activation. Cross-linking may occur when a growing branch reacts with another growing branch (or with the main chain of another polymer molecule).

The yields actually obtained from a "catalyzed" addition polymerization in a given time depend on (1) the rate of decomposition of the initiator, (2) the yield of free radicals from the decomposing initiator, (3) the fraction of these free radicals which actually initiate chains, (4) the rate of chain growth, and (5) the rate at which the growing polymer radicals destroy one another.

[12] Breitenbach, J. W. and Maschin, A., Z. *physik. Chem.*, **A187**, 175 (1940).

### Kinetics of Addition Polymerizations [†]

Since the process of addition polymerization is a chain reaction in the kinetic as well as the structural sense, the over-all rate of polymerization and the sizes of the polymer molecules formed are determined by the rates of the separate processes of initiation, propagation, and termination; hence, in formulating the complete mechanism of an addition polymerization the kinetics of each of the processes must be specified.

To illustrate the general kinetic problem, consider a simple case in which the polymerization is determined by the elementary processes of initiation, propagation, and termination, neglecting such complications as chain transfer and branching. The initial activation process may exhibit a first- or second-order dependence upon monomer concentration, or may be determined by collision with an initiator molecule, or by the light absorbed (photochemical activation). It will be sufficient for the present to assume the general initiation process $M \rightarrow M_1^*$ (with rate constant $k_i$) [‡] without specifying its exact nature. The propagation process involves only the addition of monomer to the polymer radical; hence the rate of propagation is $k_p M C^*$, where $C^*$ is the concentration of all polymer radicals. If long chains are formed, the rate of propagation must be much greater than that of termination. Since simple termination involves the destruction of radicals in pairs, either by coupling or disproportionation, the rate of termination is $k_t C^{*2}$. [‡] The complete reaction will therefore be

| | | Rate Constant | Rate |
|---|---|---|---|
| Initiation | $M \rightarrow M_1^*$ | $k_i$ | $v_i$ |
| Propagation | $M_1^* + M \rightarrow MM^*$ | $k_p$ | $v_p$ |
| | $\cdot \quad \cdot \quad \cdot \quad \cdot \quad \cdot \quad \cdot$ | | |
| | $\cdot \quad \cdot \quad \cdot \quad \cdot \quad \cdot \quad \cdot$ | | |
| | $M_{n-1}^* + M \rightarrow M_n^*$ | $k_p$ | $v_p$ |
| Termination | $M_n^* + M_m^* \rightarrow M_{n+m}$ | $k_t$ | $v_t$ |
| (coupling) | | | |

*Assuming that the rate constant of propagation, $k_p$, is the same for all steps* (i.e., that it is independent of radical size), then the over-all rate of monomer consumption is

$$-\frac{dM}{dt} = v_i + v_p = v_i + k_p M C^* \tag{17}$$

[†] The author is indebted to Prof. C. E. H. Bawn and his publisher for permission to adapt much of the material in this section relating to the kinetics of addition polymerizations from Bawn, C. E. H., *The Chemistry of High Polymers*, Butterworths, London (dist. by Interscience Publishers, New York), 1948.

[‡] Since almost all, if not all, initiation and termination reactions are bimolecular, the corresponding rate equations will contain the factor 2. For simplicity, this factor is here included in the respective rate constants.

When very long chains are formed, the propagation reaction is much faster than that of initiation, the first term will be negligible compared with the second, and $v_p$ will approximate the rate of polymerization.

At the very beginning of the reaction, $C*$ is increasing but, since the rate of disappearance of radicals in the termination step is proportional to the square of the radical concentration, the rate of disappearance soon becomes equal to the rate of formation. At this time a steady-state concentration of radicals is operative, and this permits the development of the following relations.

Since, under steady-state conditions,

$$v_i = v_t = k_t C*^2 \tag{18}$$

then

$$C* = \left[\frac{v_i}{k_t}\right]^{1/2} \tag{19}$$

and, substituting in Eq. 17,

$$-\frac{dM}{dt} = v_i + k_p M \left[\frac{v_i}{k_t}\right]^{1/2} \tag{20}$$

Rewriting Eq. 17 as

$$-\frac{dM}{dt} = v_p \left(1 + \frac{v_i}{v_p}\right) = v_p \left(1 + \frac{1}{\gamma}\right) \tag{17}$$

where

$$\gamma = \frac{v_p}{v_i} \tag{21}$$

($\gamma$ is known as the kinetic chain length and is defined as the average number of monomers consumed per unit initiation process), then, from Eqs. 17 and 19, it follows that

$$-\frac{dM}{dt} = k_p M C* \left[1 + \frac{1}{\gamma}\right]$$

$$= k_p M \left[\frac{v_i}{k_t}\right]^{1/2} \left[1 + \frac{1}{\gamma}\right] \tag{22}$$

When the chains are long, $1/\gamma$ becomes negligible and the term in the right brackets approximates unity; i.e.,

$$-\frac{dM}{dt} = k_p M \left[\frac{v_i}{k_t}\right]^{1/2} \tag{23}$$

The over-all rate of polymer formation may now be derived by introducing the appropriate value for the rate of initiation. Following are some examples:

1. Photochemical initiation

$$v_i = f(I)M \tag{24}$$

where $I$ = intensity of absorbed light; by substituting in Eq. 23

$$-\frac{dM}{dt} = \left[\frac{f(I)}{k_t}\right]^{1/2} k_p M^{3/2} \tag{25}$$

2. First-order initiation

$$v_i = k_i M \tag{26}$$

$$-\frac{dM}{dt} = \left[\frac{k_i}{k_t}\right]^{1/2} k_p M^{3/2} \tag{27}$$

3. Uncatalyzed (thermal) second-order initiation

$$v_i = k_i M^2 \tag{28}$$

$$-\frac{dM}{dt} = \left[\frac{k_i}{k_t}\right]^{1/2} k_p M^2 \tag{29}$$

4. Catalyzed initiation, of which the most general case would be a bimolecular reaction between the initiator, $B$, and a monomer molecule

$$v_i = k_i MB \tag{30}$$

$$-\frac{dM}{dt} = \left[\frac{k_i}{k_t}\right]^{1/2} k_p M^{3/2} B^{1/2} \tag{31}$$

In studying rates of polymerizations, the interpretation of data is complicated when high concentrations of monomers are used because of the effects of the changing solvent medium on the kinetics. In dilute solutions, the over-all rates of many vinyl polymerizations have been found to be first order with respect to monomer concentration and one-half order with respect to the initiator; i.e., the rate of initiation is proportional only to the initiator concentration:

$$v_i = k_i B \tag{32}$$

whence

$$-\frac{dM}{dt} = \left[\frac{k_i}{k_t}\right]^{1/2} k_p M B^{1/2} \tag{33}$$

In general, it may be stated that in *homogeneous* systems, the rate of peroxide-initiated vinyl polymerization is proportional to the square root of the initiator concentration.

A number of relationships can be derived for use as checks on the mechanism.

By substituting Eq. 21 into Eq. 17,

$$\gamma = -\frac{\dfrac{dM}{dt}}{v_i} - 1 \tag{34}$$

or, neglecting the second term, which is insignificant for long chains,

$$\gamma = -\frac{\dfrac{dM}{dt}}{v_i} \tag{35}$$

Hence, for a second-order catalyzed initiation reaction (Eq. 30), by substituting Eqs. 30 and 31 in Eq. 35

$$\gamma = \frac{k_p}{(k_i k_t)^{1/2}}\left[\frac{M}{B}\right]^{1/2} \tag{36}$$

and the kinetic chain length is proportional to the square root of the monomer concentration and inversely proportional to the square root of the initiator concentration.

For an uncatalyzed (thermal) second-order initiation (Eq. 28), by substituting Eqs. 28 and 29 into Eq. 35

$$\gamma = \frac{k_p}{(k_i k_t)^{1/2}} \tag{37}$$

and the kinetic chain length is independent of the monomer concentration.

Where termination of growth occurs without stoppage of chain growth, the process is known as a chain transfer reaction (with either monomer or solvent). It is then necessary to introduce transfer reactions:

$$M_n^* + M \rightarrow M_n + M_1^* \quad \text{monomer transfer} \quad k_{tr}$$

$$\left.\begin{array}{l} M_n^* + S \rightarrow M_n + S^* \\ S^* + M \rightarrow S + M_1^* \end{array}\right\} \text{ solvent transfer } \left\{\begin{array}{l} k_{tr'} \\ k_s \end{array}\right.$$

The degree of polymerization is now given by

$$\overline{DP} = \frac{\text{rate of chain growth}}{\text{rate of chain termination by } all \text{ processes}}$$

$$= \frac{k_p M C^*}{k_t C^{*2} + k_{tr} M C^* + k_{tr'} S C^*} \tag{38}$$

where $S$ is the solvent concentration. Since, for a catalyzed reaction,

$$C^* = \left[\frac{v_i}{k_t}\right]^{1/2} = \left[\frac{k_i M B}{k_t}\right]^{1/2} \tag{19 and 30}$$

then, by inverting Eq. 38 and substituting for $C*$,

$$\frac{1}{\overline{DP}} = \frac{(k_i k_t)^{1/2}}{k_p}\left[\frac{B}{M}\right]^{1/2} + \frac{k_{tr}}{k_p} + \frac{k_{tr'}}{k_p} \cdot \frac{S}{M} \tag{39}$$

For an uncatalyzed reaction, Eq. 39 reduces to

$$\frac{1}{\overline{DP}} = \frac{(k_i k_t)^{1/2}}{k_p} + \frac{k_{tr}}{k_p} + \frac{k_{tr'}}{k_p} \cdot \frac{S}{M} \tag{40}$$

In the absence of a solvent, the last term is zero, and the average degree of polymerization is

$$\frac{1}{\overline{DP_o}} = \frac{(k_i k_t)^{1/2}}{k_p} + \frac{k_{tr}}{k_p} \tag{41}$$

By combining Eqs. 40 and 41

$$\frac{1}{\overline{DP}} = \frac{1}{\overline{DP_o}} + \frac{k_{tr'}}{k_p} \cdot \frac{S}{M} \tag{42}$$

By plotting $1/\overline{DP}$ against $S/M$, a straight line with intercept $1/\overline{DP_o}$ and with slope $k_{tr'}/k_p$ should result.

Many hydrocarbons containing a large number of electronegative substituents, such as carbon tetrachloride, carbon tetrabromide, and pentaphenyl ethane, are very reactive with certain chain radicals. Addition of small amounts of such substances causes large depressions in the molecular weight of a polymer. The latter two substances actually exceed styrene in reactivity toward a styrene chain radical. Compounds having a transfer constant $(k_{tr'}/k_p)$ of the order of one or greater are very useful in controlling the molecular weight of a polymer. By their use the molecular weight can be depressed to almost any desired value. When used for this purpose, they are known as *regulators* or *modifiers* (see Chap. 5). The aliphatic mercaptans, for example, are widely used in the manufacture of synthetic elastomers in order to reduce the polymer chain lengths to a range suitable for subsequent processing.

Another expression utilizing the same reaction rate constants, $k_i$, $k_p$, $k_t$, in conjunction with directly measurable quantities is given by the expression for the polymer molecular weight distribution. It is possible, at least theoretically, to derive a distribution curve as a function of time and of the various rate constants for any proposed reaction scheme. Since different types of initiation and termination mechanisms will lead to different forms of molecular-weight-distribution curves, a comparison of the experimentally determined distribution with that calculated for a proposed mechanism can be used to check the kinetic relationships.

Bawn[13] has derived a general equation which covers the case of catalyzed initiation and includes both solvent and monomer transfer reactions, as well as termination by coupling and disproportionation (steady-state conditions are again assumed):

$$-\frac{dM_n}{dM} = \frac{k_d}{k_p + k_{tr}} \cdot \frac{M_1^*}{M} \cdot q^{n-1} + \frac{(k_{tr}M + k_{tr'}S)M_1^*q^{n-1}}{(k_p + k_{tr})MC^*}$$

$$+ \frac{\tfrac{1}{2}k_t M_1^{*2}(n-1)q^{n-2}}{(k_p + k_{tr})MC^*} \quad (43)$$

where

$$q = \frac{M_n^*}{M_{n-1}^*} = \frac{k_pM}{k_pM + k_{tr}M + k_{tr'}S + k_dC^* + k_tC^*}$$

$$C^* = \frac{M_1^*}{1-q} = \left[\frac{k_i \cdot MB}{k_d + k_t}\right]^{1/2}$$

$k_d$ = rate constant for termination by disproportionation

Following are two simple examples of the application of this equation.

1. Uncatalyzed bimolecular initiation reaction (Eq. 28), no transfer reactions occur, and termination is entirely by disproportionation. In this case, $k_{tr} = k_{tr'} = k_s = k_t = 0$ and Eq. 43 reduces to

$$-\frac{dM_n}{dM} = \frac{k_d}{k_p} \cdot \frac{M_1^*}{M} \cdot q^{n-1} \quad (44)$$

and, upon proper substitution and integration,

$$M_n = \frac{\gamma^{n-2}}{(1+\gamma)^n}(M_o - M) \quad (45)$$

where $M_o$ is the initial monomer concentration, $(M_o - M)m_o$ is the total weight of all *polymer* at any monomer concentration, $M$, and

$$\gamma = \frac{k_p}{(k_ik_d)^{1/2}}.$$

2. Uncatalyzed bimolecular initiation with pure monomer and termination only by coupling; i.e., $S = 0$, $k_{tr'} = k_s = k_{tr} = k_d = 0$. Eq. 43 then reduces to

$$-\frac{dM_n}{dM} = \frac{1}{2} \cdot \frac{k_t M_1^{*2}(n-1)q^{n-2}}{k_pMC^*} \quad (46)$$

Upon proper substitution and integration

$$M_n = \frac{n-1}{2} \cdot \frac{\gamma^{n-3}}{(\gamma+1)^n} \cdot (M_o - M) \quad (47)$$

[13] Bawn, C. E. H., *The Chemistry of High Polymers*, Chap. 3, Sect. IV, Butterworths, London (dist. by Interscience Publishers, New York), 1948.

## Copolymerization

Many important polymers are made by using mixtures of monomers, each capable of polymerization by itself (comonomers). The products formed possess properties which are different from physical mixtures of the homopolymers. Two well-known examples are the vinyl chloride-vinyl acetate and the butadiene-styrene polymers. New combinations are constantly being produced, and this technique is doubtless the most convenient way of producing a polymer having certain desired physical properties.

The number of products possible by homopolymerization is limited, but copolymerization allows an almost infinite number of different polymers to be made. For example, the synthetic elastomers produced in the 1925–1935 decade were almost all homopolymers of either butadiene or chloroprene, but during the next ten years these two monomers became the bases of two copolymer groups. From the chloroprene family, some elastomers have been made having improved oil-resistance or low-temperature flexibility. Until very recently, almost all straight poly-butadienes have had many technical disadvantages, particularly suffering from poor abrasion resistance; as a result, copolymers of butadiene with styrene, acrylonitrile, and other monomers have replaced them. When the other comonomer in a butadiene copolymer is present in greater amount and is a vinyl-type molecule, the number of unreacted double bonds in the final molecule is decreased considerably; vulcanization, which requires only a few cross-links, can still be effected, but the products are much less subject to oxidative degradation because of the diminution of unreacted double bonds (e.g., butyl rubber).

In the preparation of a homopolymer, such as polystyrene, all of the polymer chains formed are identical in composition; i.e., they are composed only of styrene mesomers, but the polymer chains will not be homogeneous in that there will be a distribution of chain lengths. In vinyl *copolymerization* processes, the polymers formed differ not only in the length of the individual polymer chains but also in the composition of the different polymer chains. This is because the composition of the unreacted monomer mixture is *changing throughout polymerization*. Only under certain special conditions can the ratio of monomer composition remain constant during reaction; the comonomers are, therefore, consumed at different rates and the unreacted monomer ratio will change with time. Since the composition of a copolymer chain at any instant will depend upon the residual comonomer ratio at that instant, polymer chains formed at the end of a reaction will have a different composition from those created initially, and a continuous variation of composition will exist from the beginning until the end of a copolymerization process.

The number of reactions required to represent the copolymerization of two or more monomers increases geometrically with the number of monomers involved. The number of chain radicals formed is equal to the number of monomers present. In the copolymerization of two monomers, therefore, two chain radicals are present. Addition of the two comonomers to each of these radicals results in four simultaneously occurring propagation reactions. Although chains may be initiated by activating either comonomer, the alternative possibilities for initiation of chain radicals are unimportant in the presence of an initiator which acts efficiently on both.

When the chains are long, the arrangement of units along a chain is determined almost entirely by the relative rates of the different chain propagation reactions, whereas the over-all rate of polymerization depends not only upon the rates of these propagation steps but also on the rates of the termination reactions.

The propagation reactions occurring when two comonomers $M_1$ and $M_2$ react may be written

$$M_1^* + M_1 \xrightarrow{k_{11}} M_1 M_1^* \tag{A}$$

$$M_1^* + M_2 \xrightarrow{k_{12}} M_1 M_2^* \tag{B}$$

$$M_2^* + M_2 \xrightarrow{k_{22}} M_2 M_2^* \tag{C}$$

$$M_2^* + M_1 \xrightarrow{k_{21}} M_2 M_1^* \tag{D}$$

where the mesomer on the right, bearing the asterisk, is the terminal free-radical-bearing unit.

Radicals containing an activated type $M_1$ mesomer are formed by reactions $A$ and $D$ above, as well as by primary initiation. They are destroyed by reaction $B$ and by termination reactions. If the polymer chains are long, initiation and termination occur very infrequently compared with the propagation reactions above, and, under steady-state conditions, their rates are considered to be equal. It is necessary, therefore, to consider only the propagation reactions for the present, as only the relative concentrations of the two types of chain radicals are of concern. By this approximation, the steady-state condition reduces to

$$k_{12} M_2 M_1^* = k_{21} M_1 M_2^* \tag{48}$$

since the rate of formation of $-M_1^*$ equals its rate of consumption. The same equation may also be derived by application of the steady-state condition to radicals of type $M_2^*$.   The rates of consumption of monomers $M_1$ and $M_2$ are

$$-\frac{dM_1}{dt} = k_{11}M_1M_1^* + k_{21}M_1M_2^* \tag{49}$$

$$-\frac{dM_2}{dt} = k_{12}M_2M_1^* + k_{22}M_2M_2^* \tag{50}$$

Using Eq. 48 to eliminate one of the radical concentrations and dividing Eq. 49 by Eq. 50, there is obtained

$$\frac{dM_1}{dM_2} = \frac{M_1}{M_2}\cdot\frac{r_1\dfrac{M_1}{M_2} + 1}{\dfrac{M_1}{M_2} + r_2} = \frac{M_1}{M_2}\cdot\frac{r_1M_1 + M_2}{r_2M_2 + M_1} \tag{51}$$

where $r_1$ and $r_2$ are known as *monomer reactivity ratios* and are defined by

$$r_1 = \frac{k_{11}}{k_{12}} \tag{52}$$

$$r_2 = \frac{k_{22}}{k_{21}} \tag{53}$$

Thus, $r_1$ represents the ratio of the rate constants for the reaction of a radical of type $M_1^*$ with monomer $M_1$ and with monomer $M_2$, respectively.   The monomer reactivity ratio, $r_2$, similarly expresses the relative reactivity of an $M_2^*$ radical toward an $M_2$ monomer as compared with an $M_1$ monomer; i.e., a ratio greater than one shows a tendency for the growing radical to add to a monomer of its own kind, while a ratio less than one indicates a preference for the other monomer.   The quantity $dM_1/dM_2$ given in Eq. 51 represents the ratio of the two monomers in the increment of polymer formed when the ratio of unreacted monomers is $M_1/M_2$.   It is clear that the former ratio differs in general from the latter; hence, the unreacted monomer ratio will change as polymerization progresses, and this will effect a continually changing composition in the polymer being formed.

In the case in which the two radicals display the same preference for one of the monomers,

$$r_1r_2 = 1 \tag{54}$$

and this has been termed an *ideal* copolymerization.   The values of $r_1 = 1/r_2$ are indicated with each curve in Fig. 3-2.   The straight line for $r_1 = 1$ represents the case in which $k_{11} = k_{12}$ and $k_{22} = k_{21}$; i.e., the two monomers are equally reactive with both radicals.   (The reactivities of the two radicals might differ, however.) The polymer composition is equal to the monomer composition throughout the range in this case.

It should be noted that the sequence of monomer units in an ideal copolymer will be random; i.e., the likelihood of an $M_1$ unit immediately following either an $M_1$ or an $M_2$ unit is the same. The probability of either type of unit entering at any place in the chain is always equal to its mole fraction. This statement refers only to the increment of copolymer formed at a particular instant and not to the total product, which consists of increments formed at progressively changing monomer ratios.

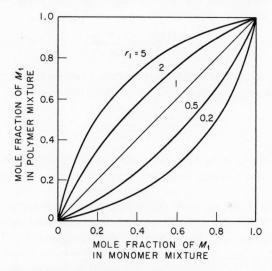

FIG. 3-2. Incremental polymer composition vs. monomer composition for *ideal* copolymerization $(r_1 = 1/r_2)$[14]

If one of the monomers is much more reactive than the other, the monomers will tend to polymerize consecutively (not alternately); i.e., the first portion of polymer formed will contain more of the more reactive monomer, and the other monomer will enter into the reaction only after most of the former has reacted.

There are several procedures available for the determination of the parameters, $r_1$ and $r_2$. All require analysis of the copolymer formed from a series of monomer mixtures. Since the composition changes with conversion, it is necessary either to limit the copolymerization to very small conversions or to treat the integral composition.

The reciprocal of a reactivity ratio expresses the relative reactivity of the two different monomers with a given radical. By a comparison of

[14] Flory, P. J., *Principles of Polymer Chemistry*, p. 181, Cornell University Press, Ithaca, N.Y., 1953.

the reciprocal reactivity ratios, $1/r$, for a series of monomers with the same radical, the monomers can be arranged in the order of their reactivities with the given radical. The fact that $r_2$ rarely is equal to $1/r_1$ (often the difference is very great) indicates that the same order of monomer reactivity does not hold for different radicals. The relative reactivities for a series of monomers depends upon the reacting radical as well as upon the monomers.

Other special cases of copolymerization in terms of the fundamental Eq. 51 can arise. When equimolecular quantities of the starting materials are used, the ratio of the two monomers in the resulting polymer $[M_1]_p/[M_2]_p$ is given by

$$\frac{[M_1]_p}{[M_2]_p} = \frac{1 + r_1}{1 + r_2} \tag{55}$$

Thus, unless $r_1 = r_2$, the initial polymer does not have the same composition as the monomer mixture. This is true only when

$$\frac{r_1 M_1 + M_2}{r_2 M_2 + M_1} = 1 \tag{56}$$

Also, only when $r_1 = r_2 = 1$ does the initial polymer have the same composition as the starting material, *regardless* of the concentration of $M_1$ and $M_2$.

When Eq. 56 is not obeyed, the initial polymer is richer in one of the components. The more reactive monomer is consumed more rapidly, and the initial polymer will be richer in this component. The monomer mixture therefore becomes poorer in this component during polymerization. As a consequence, the polymer formed during the later stages of the reaction is relatively richer in the less reactive component. Thus it is obvious that the polymer mass resulting from complete reaction is a heterogeneous mixture of copolymer molecules of different compositions and chain lengths.

Occasionally pairs of monomers alternate in entering into the copolymer, as shown in the diagram in Fig. 3-3. This type of copolymerization, in which the real and ideal curves cross, has sometimes been termed an azeotropic copolymerization, and the point at which the curves cross, the azeotropic composition, by analogy with two-component distillation.

Commercially, it is usually desirable to prevent variation of composition with extent of polymerization. The initial monomer composition can be calculated to give an initial polymer of the desired composition, but as copolymerization proceeds, the polymer formed will become richer in the less reactive component. If it is desired to produce a polymer of uniform composition, then not only must the reactants be present in the proper ratio, but this ratio must be maintained during the entire polymerization process by continuous and proper addition of the more reactive component.

Strictly speaking, as mentioned earlier in this section, the rate of co-polymerization in a binary system depends not only upon the rates of the four propagation steps but also on the rates of the initiation and termination reactions. A ternary system has even more dependencies. Thus, it may be seen that the subject of copolymerization is extremely complex.

In addition to the types of copolymers discussed above, there are two other types, known as block and graft copolymers, which have recently

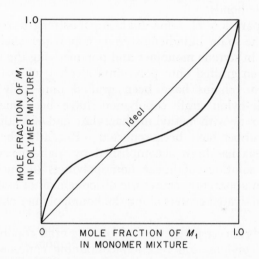

Fig. 3-3. Illustration of an ideal and an azeotropic copolymerization

become the object of renewed interest. Block copolymers are composed of (not necessarily equal) alternations of runs of each of two copolymers:

$$—AA\cdots AAB\cdots BBAA\cdots AABB\cdots BBAA\cdots AABB\cdots BB—$$

Block copolymers of poly(ethylene and propylene oxides) are now being produced for use as surface-active agents. The reaction of certain poly-esters made from two or more glycols and reacted with a diisocyanate to form a polyurethane can form block copolymers. In similar fashion, block copolymers from terephthalic acid with ethylene glycol and other glycols have been reported. Polysulfide resins may be used to link epoxy resins and thus form alternating blocks. Similarly, reaction between epoxy resins and compounds containing reactive methylol groups, such as phenolic-, urea-, and melamine-formaldehyde intermediates, can be made to form block copolymers. As may be noted from the above examples, it is usually easier to form block copolymers by condensation reactions than from addition reactions, although recently success in the latter field has been reported.

Graft copolymers contain one type of linear chain with chains of another polymer branching therefrom:

$$—AAAAA\cdots AAAAAAAAA—$$
$$\begin{array}{cc} B & B \\ B & B \\ \cdot & \cdot \\ \cdot & \cdot \\ \cdot & \cdot \\ B & B \\ B & B \end{array}$$

Branching may occur by chain transfer or by addition of monomer to polymer double bonds.

In the preparation of some high-impact-strength resins, styrene is grafted onto the main butadiene-styrene copolymer chain by dissolving the copolymer in styrene monomer and polymerizing the mixture. Vinyl acetate has been grafted onto poly(vinyl alcohol) chains. Polyethylene and polystyrene chains have been grafted onto poly(vinyl acetate). Ethylene oxide-nylon graft copolymers have been made. Graft copolymers of styrene with methyl methacrylate and of methyl methacrylate with natural rubber have been reported. Recently, the preparation of graft copolymers has been accomplished by high-energy (gamma ray) irradiation of solutions of linear homopolymers in another monomer. The irradiation apparently causes the dislodgement of hydrogen atoms or ions, forming activated centers along the homopolymer chains from which branches grow.

A particularly successful method of forming graft copolymers is to form a chain by a condensation reaction containing components which are sensitive to free-radical-transfer attack and then use a vinyl-type monomer or mixture of such monomers for subsequent "copolymerization."

Since block and graft copolymers have a much "coarser" alternation of mesomers than do the random types, the chemical properties are affected. Whereas random copolymers exhibit properties which are generally *intermediate* between those of the monomers, block and graft copolymers tend to exhibit the properties of *each* of the monomers. For example, if a hydrophobic and a hydrophilic monomer are block or graft copolymerized, the product will show, assuming approximately equal lengths and strengths of groups, solubility in both aqueous and non-aqueous solutions, and will probably make an excellent emulsifying agent.

### REFERENCES AND RECOMMENDED READING

Alfrey, T., Jr., Bohrer, J. H. and Mark, H., *Copolymerization*, Interscience Publishers, New York, 1952.

Bawn, C. E. H., *The Chemistry of High Polymers*, Butterworths, London (dist. by Interscience Publishers, New York), 1948.

Billmeyer, F. W., Jr., *Textbook of Polymer Chemistry*, Interscience Publishers, New York, 1957.

Boundy, R. H. and Boyer, R. F., *Styrene*, Reinhold Publishing Corp., New York, 1952.

Bovey, F. A., Kolthoff, I. M., Medalia, A. I. and Meehan, E. J., *Emulsion Polymerization*, Interscience Publishers, New York, 1955.

Burk, R. E. and Grummitt, O., eds., *The Chemistry of Large Molecules*, Interscience Publishers, New York, 1943.

Burk, R. E. and Grummitt, O., *High Molecular Weight Organic Compounds*, Interscience Publishers, New York, 1949.

Burk, R. E., Thompson, H. E., Weith, A. J. and Williams, I., *Polymerization*, Reinhold Publishing Corp., New York, 1937.

Burnett, G. M., *Mechanism of Polymer Reactions*, Interscience Publishers, New York, 1954.

D'Alelio, G. F., *Fundamental Principles of Polymerization*, John Wiley and Sons, New York, 1952.

Flory, P. J., *Principles of Polymer Chemistry*, Cornell University Press, Ithaca, N.Y., 1953.

Frith, E. M. and Tuckett, R. F., *Linear Polymers*, Longmans, Green and Co., London-New York, 1951.

Groggins, P. H., ed., *Unit Processes in Organic Synthesis*, 4th ed., McGraw-Hill Book Co., New York, 1952.

Hill, R., ed., *Fibres from Synthetic Polymers*, Elsevier Publishing Co., Amsterdam (dist. by D. Van Nostrand Co., Princeton, N.J.), 1953.

Houwink, R., ed., *Elastomers and Plastomers*, Vol. I, Elsevier Publishing Co., Amsterdam (dist. by D. Van Nostrand Co., Princeton, N.J.), 1950.

Langton, H. M., ed., *Synthetic Resins*, 3rd ed., Oxford University Press, London, 1951.

Mark H. and Tobolsky, A. V., *Physical Chemistry of High Polymeric Systems*, 2nd ed., Interscience Publishers, New York, 1950.

Mason, J. P. and Manning, J. F., *The Technology of Plastics and Resins*, D. Van Nostrand Co., Princeton, N.J., 1945.

Plesch, P. H., ed., *Cationic Polymerization and Related Complexes*, Academic Press, New York, 1953.

Powers, P. O., *Synthetic Resins and Rubbers*, John Wiley and Sons, New York, 1943.

Riddle, E. H., *Monomeric Acrylic Esters*, Reinhold Publishing Corp., New York, 1954.

Ritchie, P. D., *A Chemistry of Plastics and High Polymers*, Cleaver-Hume Press, London (dist. by Interscience Publishers, New York), 1949.

Schildknecht, C. E., ed., *Polymer Processes*, Interscience Publishers, New York, 1956.

Schmidt, A. X. and Marlies, C. A., *Principles of High-Polymer Theory and Practice*, McGraw-Hill Book Co., New York, 1948.

Tobolsky, A. V. and Mesrobian, R. B., *Organic Peroxides*, Interscience Publishers, New York, 1954.

Twiss, S. B., ed., *Advancing Fronts in Chemistry*, Vol. I, Reinhold Publishing Corp., New York, 1945.

*Chapter 4*

# CHARACTERIZATION
# OF POLYMERS

In the preceding chapter, polymers were. classified according to their mechanical and chemical behavior. Much of the experimental and theoretical work performed in recent years has been done to elucidate the structures of polymers and the mechanisms of polymerizations. Without this work, purely empirical methods would have to be employed for obtaining useful products, and the burgeoning science of polymer chemistry would never have progressed to its present stage.

In this chapter are presented, in abbreviated form, the principal methods which have been devised to characterize the products obtained from polymerization reactions in the hope that the reader will be impressed with the difficulties that are inherent in obtaining trustworthy results and the technical knowledge and instrumentation that are necessary. Much of the information contained in the preceding chapter has been dependent for its development upon techniques and tests described in this chapter.

## MOLECULAR WEIGHT AVERAGES

The concept of molecular weight presents little difficulty so long as *low-molecular-weight* pure substances are involved. However, a *polymer* mass is nonhomogeneous in that it usually contains individual polymer chains of many different sizes. In other instances, the chains differ not only in length but also in composition. Because polymers are a mixture of such molecules, the molecular weight given to a mixture has a meaning different from that given to homogeneous simple molecules; i.e., the molecular weights assigned to a polymer mixture must refer to an average molecular weight. Each method of determination yields a particular type of average. With a single-molecular-weight species, all of these averages have the same value, but, the greater the nonhomogeneity, the greater is the disparity among them.

It can physically be shown by fractionation that polymers consist of a mixture of molecules differing in molecular weights. As pointed out above, the molecular weights assigned to a polymer mass are an average value, and it has been the custom to designate these average values by a bar over the value considered. Thus, the average values of the number-average molecular weights, weight-average molecular weights, and $z$-average molecular weights are designated, respectively, as $\overline{M}_n$, $\overline{M}_w$, $\overline{M}_z$. In other words, the use of a bar over a value indicates that some kind of average has been taken, although it alone does not designate specifically the kind of average.

Number-average molecular weight is the average molecular weight usually encountered and is defined by

$$\overline{M}_n = \frac{\text{total weight}}{\text{total number of moles}} = \frac{W}{N} = \frac{\sum n_i M_i}{\sum n_i} = \sum N_x M_i = \frac{1}{\sum \left(\frac{W_x}{M_i}\right)} \quad (1)$$

where $W$ = total weight of mixture
$N$ = total number of moles (of all sizes) in mixture
$n_i$ = number of moles of $n$-mer
$M_i$ = molecular weight of $n$-mer
$N_x$ = mole fraction of $n$-mer
$W_x$ = weight fraction of $n$-mer

The number-average molecular weight is obtained by methods which determine end-groups analytically and by osmotic measurements. This value is called a number-average since the molecular weight depends on the *number* of molecules present.

Weight-average molecular weight is obtained by methods which depend upon the *weights* of molecules present, such as by light scattering and sedimentation equilibrium under certain conditions of measurement and also by certain viscosity measurements:

$$\overline{M}_w = \frac{\sum W_i M_i}{\sum W_i} = \sum W_x M_i = \frac{\sum n_i M_i^2}{\sum n_i M_i} \quad (2)$$

where $W_i$ = weight of $n$-mer. In this case the molecular weight of each species is weighted by the weight-fraction of the species. It depends only upon the total weight of polymer in a given volume of solution and has little dependence upon the number of molecules into which the solute is divided. Such common properties as refractive index, specific volume, and heat capacity are of this type.

The $z$-average molecular weight is also obtained by sedimentation equilibrium under other conditions of analysis and is defined by

$$\overline{M}_z = \frac{\sum n_i M_i^3}{\sum n_i M_i^2} = \frac{\sum W_i M_i^2}{\sum W_i M_i} \quad (3)$$

It has been shown[1] that for linear condensation polymers

$$\overline{M}_n : \overline{M}_w : \overline{M}_z = 1 : 1 + p : \frac{1 + 4p + p^2}{1 + p}$$

so that when $p \to 0$, the three molecular weights approach one another in value, whereas, when $p \to 1$

$$\overline{M}_n : \overline{M}_w : \overline{M}_z \to 1:2:3$$

so that the molecular weights of polymers should be referred to specifically. Only when there is one molecular species, all molecules of which have the same molecular weight, will the three averages be equal under all conditions.

Viscosity-average molecular weight is derived from viscosity measurements and is expressed by the following equation when the viscosity-molecular-weight relationship follows Eq. 42:

$$\overline{M}_v = \left[ \frac{m_1 M_1^a + m_2 M_2^a + \cdots}{m_1 + m_2 + \cdots} \right]^{1/a} = [\sum w_i M_i^a]^{1/a} = \left[ \frac{\sum n_i M_i^{a+1}}{\sum n_i M_i} \right]^{1/a} \quad (4)$$

where $a$ is a constant whose value depends upon the polymer-solvent system. When $a$ equals unity, the viscosity-average reduces to the weight-average.

Since various methods of molecular weight determinations yield different types of averages, then, if different molecular weight methods are to be properly compared, it is necessary to know the distribution of molecular sizes in the sample. Since this is frequently not available, as the determination is tedious as well as not very accurate, the methods are usually compared by making measurements on fractionated material. This approach, too, has its difficulties, among which are involved the effects of the use of different solvents and the variable effects of structure, shape, and flexibility of the molecules.

The very high molecular weights and the correspondingly large sizes of polymer molecules make molecular weight determinations more difficult than for ordinary small molecules. Polymer molecular weights are usually derived from one or more of the methods shown at the head of page 65, most of which will be considered in more detail later.

The nonhomogeneity of a polymer mass is determined by separating the mixture into a number of fractions, measuring the molecular weight of each fraction, and then plotting a distribution curve of the fractions.

The separation of a polymer mixture of chemically similar molecules into fractions is based upon a primary property of an individual polymer molecule, namely, its (configurational) size. Such properties as rates of

[1] Flory, P. J., *J. Am. Chem. Soc.*, **58**, 1881 (1936).

|  |  |
|---|---|
| Absolute Methods | Indirect Methods |
| *Physical Methods* | Viscosity measurements |
| Vapor pressure changes | Solubility determinations |
| Cryoscopic measurements | Electron microscope analyses |
| Ebullioscopic measurements | Sound velocity measurements |
| Osmotic measurements | Chromatographic adsorption |
| Sedimentation experiments | measurements |
| Velocity method | |
| Equilibrium method | |
| Light scattering measurements | |
| *Chemical Methods* | |
| End-group analyses | |
| Tracer techniques | |

diffusion and sedimentation, solubility, and volatility are related to molecular weight; hence, the fractionation of macromolecules may be accomplished in several ways. Many of the methods of separating materials into fractions have been tabulated and are given in Table 4-1.

TABLE 4-1. METHODS OF SEPARATION OF MIXTURES INTO FRACTIONS[2]

| *Method* | *Principle on Which Separation Is Based* |
|---|---|
| I. Distribution between two immiscible solvents | Distribution depends on molecular weight |
|   1. Fractional precipitation | |
|     a. By addition of precipitant or removal of a more volatile solvent from a solvent-precipitant mixture | |
|     b. By cooling | |
|   2. Fractional solution | |
|     a. Solvent of varying composition | |
|     b. Varying temperature | |
| II. Rate-of-solution method (diffusion into a single solvent) | Smaller molecules diffuse faster |
| III. Ultracentrifugation | Sedimentation velocity increases with molecular weight |
| IV. Chromatographic adsorption | Smaller molecules are preferentially adsorbed |
| V. Ultrafiltration through graded membranes | Membranes act as graded sieves |
| VI. Molecular distillation | Larger molecules are less volatile |

Fractional precipitation is probably the method in most common use for polymer fractionations. Regardless of the method used, the objective of the separation is to obtain fractions as narrow as possible. To obtain a sharp distribution, it may be necessary to refractionate each of the isolated fractions and then to combine all fractions within the same

[2] Adapted from L. H. Cragg and H. Hammerschlag, "The Fractionation of High Polymeric Substances," *Chem. Revs.*, **39**, 83 (1946).

molecular weight range; even so, there is a practical limit to the sharpness which can be achieved.

The methods for determining the molecular weights of either the unfractionated polymer or of its fractions are considered next. The methods of measurement may be divided into physical methods and chemical methods.

## METHODS OF DETERMINATION OF MOLECULAR WEIGHTS

### Molecular Weights by Physical Methods

Most methods of determining molecular weights require that the substance be in solution. All of the procedures present difficulties. Usually the equations used to calculate the molecular weight are simplified versions of much more complicated and more rigorous forms, which either are not known or cannot be used for lack of complete information. In many cases, the equations are entirely empirical. All, however, have the common property of being more accurate for dilute solutions. In fact, some equations hold only in solutions so dilute that accurate measurement becomes impossible. In such cases, the molecular weight is determined at several low but finite concentrations, and a more correct value is then obtained by extrapolation to infinite dilution.

### Vapor Pressure, Freezing Point, and Boiling Point Changes

Methods which involve a temperature or pressure change in a solvent are of limited value in determining molecular weights of high-molecular-weight substances, since the concentration required to obtain measurable effects may be so high that the relationship of these changes to molecular weight no longer holds. Hence, the methods of freezing-point lowering, boiling-point elevation, and vapor-pressure lowering apply to measurements of molecular weights only up to about 5,000 to 10,000. Even in this low range, the minuteness of the changes in temperatures and pressures precludes their general use because of the limits set by instrumentation.

The osmotic pressure, vapor-pressure lowering, boiling-point elevation, and freezing-point depression of a solution are all different aspects of the same phenomenon. Historically, van't Hoff was the first to prove this interrelationship thermodynamically. Because he gave emphasis to the osmotic-pressure law, these four properties are known, collectively, as *osmotic properties*.

For an ideal solution and a perfect gas phase, Raoult's law holds:

$$p_A = N_A p_A^0 \quad \text{and} \quad p_S = N_S p_S^0 \tag{5}$$

and

$$P = p_A + p_S = N_{x,A} p_A^0 + N_{x,S} p_S^0 \tag{6}$$

where $P$ = vapor pressure of solution
  $p$ = vapor pressure of the component in solution
  $p^0$ = vapor pressure of pure component
  $N_x$ = mole fraction of the component

and subscripts $A$ and $S$ refer to solute and solvent, respectively.

When the solute is nonvolatile, as is the case with high-molecular-weight polymers, the vapor phase consists only of solvent; therefore $P = p_S$. Hence

$$P = N_{x,S}p_S^0 = (1 - N_{x,A})p_S^0 \tag{7}$$

and

$$N_{x,A} = 1 - \frac{P}{p_S^0} = \frac{p_S^0 - P}{p_S^0} = \frac{\Delta \mathbf{P}}{p_S^0} \tag{8}$$

Since

$$N_{x,A} = \frac{N_A}{N_A + N_S} \tag{9}$$

(where $N_A$ and $N_S$ refer to moles of solute and solvent, respectively), for very dilute solutions, $N_A + N_S \doteq N_S$; therefore

$$N_{x,A} \doteq \frac{N_A}{N_S} \tag{10}$$

By substitution into Eq. 8

$$\frac{N_A}{N_S} \doteq \frac{\Delta \mathbf{P}}{p_S^0} \tag{11}$$

Since

$$N_A = \frac{W_A}{M_A} \quad \text{and} \quad N_S = \frac{W_S}{M_S} \tag{12}$$

where $W$ is the total weight and $M$ the molecular weight, then

$$M_A = \frac{W_A M_S p_S^0}{W_S \Delta \mathbf{P}} \tag{13}$$

Because solutions are rarely ideal and because of the assumption made, such equations are not applicable at high concentrations or even for exact calculations at low concentrations. To preserve simplicity, a term, known as the *activity*, is used in place of concentration. Thus

$$p_A = a_A p_A^0 \quad \text{and} \quad p_S = a_S p_S^0 \tag{14}$$

and

$$P = a_A p_A^0 + a_S p_S^0 \tag{15}$$

where $a_A$ and $a_S$ are the activities of solute and solvent, respectively.

These are experimentally determined functions, analogous to concentrations but which include a correction for the deviations from perfect behavior. The activities are calculated from the actual deviations of the system from ideal solution and perfect gas behavior.

The *cryoscopic method* depends upon the amount of lowering of the freezing point of a solvent; the lowering is proportional to the amount and the nature of the substance dissolved in it, provided the substance is completely soluble and does not form a solid solution with the solvent. The equation for the freezing-point curve is

$$\frac{1}{T} - \frac{1}{T_{f,s}} = -\frac{R}{L_f} \ln N_{x,s} \qquad (16)$$

where $T$ is the freezing point of the solution, $T_{f,s}$ the freezing point of pure solvent, $L_f$ the molar heat of fusion of the solvent, $R$ the gas constant, and $N_{x,s}$ the mole fraction of the solvent in the solution. Since $T_{f,s} - T$ is the freezing-point depression $(\Delta t_f)$, this equation then correlates this depression with the composition of the solution and thus enables molecular weights to be determined.

Eq. 16 holds only for ideal solutions. For nonideal solutions, the mole fraction is replaced by the activity, and

$$\frac{1}{T} - \frac{1}{T_{f,s}} = -\frac{R}{L_f} \ln a_S \qquad (17)$$

where $a_S$ is the activity of the solvent. The activity must be determined independently, for example, by vapor-pressure depression, in order to be used in the above equation. This enables the calculation of the freezing-point depression regardless of the character of the solution.

For very dilute solutions, the freezing-point equation reduces to

$$\Delta t_f = K_f C = K_f \cdot \frac{W_A}{W_S} \cdot \frac{1,000}{M_A} \qquad (18)$$

where $K_f$ = molal freezing-point depression constant

$\quad\quad C$ = molality of the solution

$\quad W_A$ = weight of solute dissolved in weight $W_S$ of solvent

$\quad M_A$ = molecular weight of solute

This is a form of van't Hoff's law. The accuracy of this method of determining molecular weights depends upon the accuracy with which $K_f$ is known. $K_f$ can be calculated from

$$K_f = \frac{RT_s^2 M_S}{1,000\, L_f} \qquad (19)$$

or the value may be observed in a compound of known molecular weight by means of van't Hoff's equation. Camphor is often used, as such a substance having a low molar heat of fusion exhibits a large lowering of the melting point with only a small quantity of solute.

It must be remembered that the van't Hoff equation was derived only for the limiting case of infinitely dilute solutions, and thermodynamics does not predict the amount of deviation in the range of finite concentrations. Even in extremely dilute solutions, deviations may occur. Solutes which associate or dissociate give erroneous results. Furthermore, solvents which associate with themselves or form associated compounds or complexes with the solute are to be avoided. These possibilities of error apply to all of the osmotic equations.

The *ebullioscopic method* depends on the raising of the boiling point of a solvent; the raising is proportional to the amount and the nature of the substance dissolved in it.

Thus, the boiling-point elevation relation for nonideal solutions,

$$\frac{1}{T_{b,s}} - \frac{1}{T} = -\frac{R}{L_b} \ln a_S \tag{20}$$

where $L_b$ is the molar heat of vaporization of the solvent, reduces, for very dilute solutions, to

$$\Delta t_b = K_b C = K_b \cdot \frac{W_A}{W_S} \cdot \frac{1,000}{M_A} \tag{21}$$

where $K_b$ is the molal boiling-point elevation constant of the solvent, analogous to the freezing-point elevation constant.

### Osmotic Pressure Determinations

The three previous methods and the osmotic pressure method are used on low-molecular-weight compounds. Some disadvantages of these methods for such compounds are: (1) The vapor-pressure depression is small and such small pressure changes are more difficult to measure than small temperature changes; (2) the cryoscopic method can be used only at the freezing point of the solvent; (3) the ebullioscopic technique is used only at the normal boiling point of the solvent (although pressure changes would cause the boiling point to vary, elaborate equipment would be necessary); decomposition of solute is more likely at elevated temperature; (4) preparation of suitable semipermeable membranes is difficult; the osmotic pressure is quite large.

For high-molecular-weight materials, the first three of the above disadvantages still hold. However, the disadvantages of the fourth method are now advantages; that is, the osmotic pressures lie within the

range of convenient and accurate measurement, and the preparation of
suitable, semipermeable membranes is much easier for large molecules.

When a solution is separated from a solvent by a semipermeable membrane, a pressure differential occurs which is due thermodynamically to
the difference of the fugacity of the solvent in the solution and in the solvent
phase. This pressure differential, known as the osmotic pressure, is
related to the activity of the solvent by

$$\pi = -\frac{RT}{\overline{V}_S} \cdot \ln a_S \tag{22}$$

where $\pi$ is the osmotic pressure, $\overline{V}_S$ the partial molal volume of the solvent, and $a_S$ is the activity of the solvent. The determinations are made in
very dilute solutions, and, in such cases, the partial molal volume of the
solvent is almost equal to the volume of the solution, the activity of the
solvent is almost unity, and Eq. 22 reduces to

$$\pi = CRT = \frac{RT}{M} \cdot c \tag{23}$$

where $C$ is the molar concentration of the solute ($= c/M$). This equation
is another form of the van't Hoff law.

If the van't Hoff equation were generally valid, the value of $\pi/c$ would
be a constant and independent of concentration. This is, unfortunately,
not true of a plot of $\pi/c$ against $c$ for high-molecular-weight polymers.
Only an *infinitely* dilute polymer solution is sufficiently dilute for accurate
application of the above equation.

Thus, for dilute solutions of the same polymer in a series of solvents, a
plot of $\pi/c$ vs. $c$ gives a series of straight lines of different slopes which, on
extrapolation to infinite dilution, give the same limiting value. Only in
the form

$$\lim_{c \to 0} \frac{\pi}{c} = \frac{RT}{M} \tag{24}$$

where $\lim_{c \to 0} \frac{\pi}{c} = \left(\frac{\pi}{c}\right)_o$ may the equation be used for high-molecular-weight
polymers. The value $(\pi/c)_o$ is known as the reduced osmotic pressure and
is obtained by determining the osmotic pressure of a series of dilute polymer solutions of different concentrations and plotting $\pi/c$ vs. $c$ and extrapolating to zero concentration. The reduced osmotic-pressure molecular
weight relation then becomes

$$\overline{M}_n = \frac{RT}{\left(\dfrac{\pi}{c}\right)_o} \tag{25}$$

A semi-empirical relationship between the osmotic pressure and concentration of dilute polymer solutions is

$$\frac{\pi}{c} = \frac{RT}{M} + Bc + Cc^2 + \ldots \tag{26}$$

Neglecting terms in $c^2$ and higher powers gives the relationship

$$\frac{\pi}{c_A} = \frac{RT}{\overline{M}_n} + Bc_A \tag{27}$$

where $B$ (a constant) is equal to $\dfrac{RT}{M_S} \cdot \dfrac{\varrho_S}{\varrho_A}(\frac{1}{2} - \mu)$. In this relationship, $\overline{M}_n$ is the number-average molecular weight of the solute, $M_S$ the molecular weight of the solvent, $\varrho_S$ and $\varrho_A$ the densities of the solvent and solute, respectively, and $\mu$ is a constant which is characteristic of a given solvent-polymer system at a given temperature.

The plot is normally a straight line, although, in the case of some polymer-solvent systems, the $c^2$ term in Eq. 26 becomes operative and the graph then shows a slight curvature. The graph is extrapolated to zero concentration and the molecular weight is calculated from the value of the intercept, $(\pi/c)_o$.

In order to determine the osmotic pressure of a solution, either the static or the dynamic method of measurement may be used. In the static method, the osmotic pressure of the solution is balanced by the liquid column or head that develops by the influx of solvent into the solution; the osmotic pressure is estimated from the increase of pressure with time. The system is relatively simple and easy to construct. Basically, it consists of a semipermeable membrane separating a tube containing the solution and an attached calibrated capillary, and a container for the solvent.

The dynamic method depends upon counterbalancing the osmotic pressure by an externally applied pressure of known value. The external pressure required to prevent the flow of solvent, at zero instrument head, into or out of the solution is equal to the osmotic pressure of the solution. The principal advantage of the symmetrical dynamic type of osmometer is the rapidity with which the measurement can be made, whereas the static method is probably more accurate, except for the limitation of obtaining duplicate capillary tubes in the symmetrical static method.

A more recent technique, known as isothermal distillation, is worth describing. This method is claimed to measure a very wide range of molecular weights with excellent accuracy. In the usual type of osmometer, the chemical potential of the solvent is depressed by the addition of solute molecules; only when this depression is balanced by the greater hydrostatic pressure (the osmotic pressure) of the solution on one side of the membrane is equilibrium reached. In the isothermal still, the chemical potential of the solvent is likewise lowered by the solute molecules, but compensation is obtained by applying a negative hydrostatic pressure to the solvent, rather than by the application of a positive hydrostatic pressure to the solution. At equilibrium, where the chemical potentials balance, distillation between solvent and solution ceases and measurement of the hydrostatic drag gives the osmotic pressure of the solution. With any other hydrostatic drag, finite rates of distillation occur and can be measured; the zero rate of distillation, hence the osmotic pressure, can then be found by interpolation. Unfortunately, this method is extremely sensitive to contamination of the solvent by small molecules, such as water, and extremely precise temperature control is necessary for accurate measurement.

Still another development for more accurate measurement of osmotic pressure is the osmotic balance. In this instrument, the column of solution which provides the osmotic pressure is allowed to develop in a capillary of relatively large diameter, and the weight of this column is measured instead of its height. Since it is possible to measure more accurately a difference in osmotic height by weight than to make a direct height measurement, molecular weights up to one million can be measured fairly accurately.

The quality of any osmotic-pressure measurement depends to a large extent upon the performance of the membrane used. Not only must the membrane be semipermeable, but, practically speaking, it should also have a high rate of solvent transfer. Regenerated cellulose (swollen cellophane, denitrated cellulose nitrate) which has never been dried appears to be the best general-purpose material for the determination of large molecular weights.

The membranes used in osmometry are not truly semipermeable because low-molecular-weight molecules can diffuse back through them; the faster the membrane, the greater is the rate of back diffusion. Because of this, it is difficult to measure accurately the molecular weight of any appreciably heterogeneous polymer of number-average molecular weight less than about 40,000. With suitable precautions, however, it is possible to measure the molecular weight of relatively homogeneous fractions down to about 10,000.

The range of usefulness of the various osmotic techniques depends upon several factors. Most measurements on high-molecular-weight polymers have been made using the freezing-point and the osmotic-pressure methods. In general, the freezing-point method is convenient for the determination of number-average molecular weights of low-molecular-weight polymers, the upper limit being about 10,000. In the molecular weight range of about 40,000 to 500,000 the osmotic-pressure method is probably the most accurate available for number-average determinations. The most valuable use for this method is for the accurate determination of the molecular weights of homogeneous fractions which are necessary for the calibration of simpler and more rapid methods of molecular weight measurement, such as solution viscosity.

All osmotic and viscosity methods are dependent on the complete solubility of the polymer in a suitable liquid and are therefore useless for determinations of materials which are appreciably cross-linked. Hence, most data available on molecular weights are for thermoplastic materials.

### Diffusion and Sedimentation Analyses

The use of the ultracentrifuge is considered the classical method for obtaining molecular weights, because it can give not only the many average molecular weights but also, in principle, the entire molecular-weight-distribution curve. The fact that such instruments are relatively complicated and expensive, the existence of certain theoretical difficulties with long-chain polymers (polydisperse systems), and the development of simpler techniques, such as osmometry, have served to prevent the ultracentrifuge from gaining its rightful position in recent years.

The determination of molecular weights by the ultracentrifuge is due to Svedberg,[3] who used this method originally for the study of protein molecular weights. Its principle of operation is based on the fact that particles suspended in a liquid distribute themselves under a strong centrifugal field so that their concentration diminishes with height according to the size or weight of the particles, and the distribution of the particles bear a mathematical relationship to their weights. Under gravitational influence alone, changes in concentration will occur if the particles are of enormous size; i.e., larger than ordinary molecules. Even with high-molecular-weight polymers in solution, it is not possible, using gravitational sedimentation techniques, to obtain changes in concentration which can be measured with sufficient accuracy to be of value. The concentration difference, however, can be greatly increased by increasing the force up to one million times its ordinary value by the use of an ultracentrifuge, which substitutes centrifugal force for gravitational force.

Ultracentrifuges are used in two ways for the determination of particle sizes: (1) Measurement during the early stages of sedimentation of the rate of fall of the boundary separating the solution from the pure solvent (sedimentation velocity method), and (2) determination of the concentration distribution of the particles when the rates of diffusion and sedimenta-

[3] Svedberg, T. and Pedersen, K. O., eds., *The Ultracentrifuge*, Oxford University Press, London-New York, 1940.

tion are equal (sedimentation equilibrium method). The former method requires very large centrifugal forces (sometimes more than 250,000 times gravity) and several hours for an analysis. The latter method requires smaller centrifugal forces (1,000 to 100,000 times gravity), but days or even weeks of continuous operation are necessary to reach equilibrium. In both methods accurate temperature control and mechanical stability are necessary to prevent mixing by thermal and mechanical convection.

In a *sedimentation velocity* or *sedimentation rate* method, the *rate* of sedimentation of the polymer molecules in solution is measured. Large molecules sediment more rapidly than small ones and, if the boundary between solvent and solution is sufficiently sharp, molecular weights can be calculated from the measured rate at which the boundary moves across the cell. The rate of sedimentation of molecules in a given field varies directly with the centrifugal force causing the movement and inversely with the frictional resistance which the molecules encounter. Although the centrifugal force is proportional to the molecular weight, the frictional resistance depends on both molecular shape and size.

The centrifugal forces are opposed only by frictional resistance, since the centrifugal force is strong and diffusion processes are considered negligible. At a distance $x$ from the center of rotation, the acceleration is $\omega^2 x$, where $\omega$ is the angular velocity, and the centrifugal force on a gram mole of solute is, therefore, $\omega^2 x$ times the effective mass of a gram mole. Since the effective mass of $N$ particles, each of volume $v$ and density $\varrho_A$, in a liquid of density $\varrho_S$ is $Nv(\varrho_A - \varrho_S)$, that of a gram mole is $M_A(1 - \bar{v}_A\varrho)$, where $M_A$ is the solute molecular weight, $\bar{v}_A$ its partial specific volume, and $\varrho$ the solution density. The centrifugal force is balanced by the frictional resistance, $f(dx/dt)$, where $f$ is the frictional constant per gram mole of solute and $dx/dt$ the sedimentation rate at the distance $x$, so that

$$M(1 - \bar{v}_A\varrho)\omega^2x = f\left(\frac{dx}{dt}\right) \tag{28}$$

This equation, the Svedberg equation, can be used only if something is known about the frictional constant, $f$.

For spherical particles, $f$ is given by the Stokes equation

$$f = 6\pi\eta_s N_o r = 6\pi\eta_s N_o\left[\frac{3M\bar{v}_A}{4\pi N_o}\right]^{1/3} \tag{29}$$

where $\eta_s$ is the absolute viscosity of the solvent, $N_o$ is Avogadro's number, $r$ is the radius of a particle, $\bar{v}_A$ is the partial specific volume of the particles, and $M$ is the molecular weight of the solute.

When the polymer molecules are not spherical (this is usually the case), some other means must be used to obtain the value of $f$. If the solute molecules are large in comparison with those of the suspension medium, and if they sediment and diffuse independently of each other, they meet the same resistance during sedimentation as during free diffusion and

$$D_o = \frac{RT}{f} \tag{30}$$

where $D_o$ is the diffusion constant at zero concentration, obtained by plotting $D$ against $c$ and extrapolating to infinite dilution. It is usually assumed that the above requirements hold and $f$, therefore, can be determined by separate diffusion measurements.

Another requirement of this method is the determination of the constant, $s_o$, which is the rate of sedimentation in a unit centrifugal field obtained by extrapolating finite values of $1/s$ vs. $c$ to infinite dilution. It is a characteristic constant of the particular system and is known as the sedimentation constant:

$$s = \frac{\dfrac{dx}{dt}}{\omega^2 x} \tag{31}$$

where $dx/dt$ is the rate of fall of the boundary separating solute from the supernatant liquid, $\omega$ is the angular velocity, and $x$ is the distance of the boundary from the axis of rotation.

If, then, in Eq. 28 $\dfrac{dx/dt}{\omega^2 x}$ is replaced by its abbreviation, $s_o$, and $f$ by its equivalent, $RT/D_o$, there is obtained

$$M = \frac{RT}{1 - \bar{v}_A \varrho} \cdot \frac{s_o}{D_o} \tag{32}$$

where $s_o$ and $D_o$ have to be obtained separately.

This method is not very satisfactory for unfractionated polymers, not only because the experimental data are less accurate, but also because the sedimentation and diffusion constants are measured separately and the extrapolation forms for the two constants may differ, depending upon the shape of the polymer molecules in solution in the two separate determinations. As a result, a hybrid-average molecular weight is usually obtained. It is possible to obtain number-, weight-, and z-average diffusion constants, and number-, weight-, and z-average sedimentation velocities. Singer[4] made an evaluation of the nine different types of averages which are theoretically possible from sedimentation-diffusion work. By making certain assumptions as to the dependence of the frictional factor on molecular weight for the three commonly postulated types of polymer molecules (free draining, matted coil, and unsolvated

4 Singer, S. J., *J. Polymer Sci.*, **1**, 445 (1946).

sphere), and by selecting several types of molecular weight distribution curves, he compared numerically all these different averages. In general, these complex averages fall between $\overline{M}_n$ and $\overline{M}_w$. The more compact the molecule, the higher is its apparent average molecular weight.

The *sedimentation equilibrium* method consists in subjecting the solution of a polymer to a moderate centrifugal field and measuring the change in concentration at definite time intervals and centrifugal fields. The changes in concentration are followed or recorded by measurements of optical changes in refractive index or by light absorption measurements.

In this weaker centrifugal field, the molecular processes of diffusion and sedimentation occur simultaneously. The centrifugal force causes the polymer molecules to sediment, and the originally homogeneous solution separates in two layers. A region of pure solvent is separated from a region of solution by a boundary which is almost always diffuse because of the opposing process of molecular diffusion, which now cannot be neglected. As the polymer molecules sediment, a concentration gradient is formed and the solute molecules tend to diffuse back into the less concentrated layer and thus oppose the effect of centrifuging.

The solution is centrifuged until equilibrium between sedimentation resulting from the centrifugal force and diffusion resulting from thermal agitation is attained. The variation of concentration with distance is determined after the system has achieved equilibrium.

The rate at which the molecules are centrifuged is balanced by the rate at which they diffuse. If $c$ is the concentration of solute at a distance $x$ from the center of rotation, the number of molecules centrifuged in time $dt$ across unit area perpendicular to the $x$-axis at $x$ is $c(\partial x/\partial t)dt$, where $\partial x/\partial t$ is the rate of sedimentation. In the same time, $dt$, the amount of solute diffusing back across the same area is, by the definition of $D$, equal to $D(\partial c/\partial x)dt$. At equilibrium, then,

$$c \cdot \frac{dx}{dt} = D \cdot \frac{dc}{dx} \tag{33}$$

Substituting for $dx/dt$ the value given in Eq. 28, and for $f$ that given by Eq. 30,

$$M(1 - \bar{v}_A\varrho)\omega^2 cx = RT\left(\frac{dc}{dx}\right) \tag{34}$$

Upon integration, there is obtained

$$M = \frac{2RT\ln\left(\dfrac{c_2}{c_1}\right)}{\omega^2(1 - \bar{v}_A\varrho)(x_2^2 - x_1^2)} \tag{35}$$

where $\omega$ = angular velocity

$\qquad \bar{v}_A$ = partial specific volume of the solute

$\qquad \varrho$ = density of the solvent

$\qquad c_1, c_2$ = concentrations at $x_1$ and $x_2$, respectively

$\qquad x_1, x_2$ = positions in the cell (from the center of the rotor)

In the equation for determining molecular weight by this method, activity should properly be used instead of concentration, although in most cases the correction is small. This method is satisfactory for an un-fractionated polymer; however, the molecular weight average obtained depends upon the experimental method of observation. Thus, if the variation of concentration with depth is determined by light absorption measurements, the weight-average molecular weight is obtained; if the variation of concentration *gradient* with depth is determined by refractive index measurements, then the z-average molecular weight is obtained. In this case, $\ln(c_2/c_1)$ is replaced by $\ln(z_2 x_1/z_1 x_2)$, where $z$, the scale displacement, is proportional to $dc/dx$ (the concentration gradient at $x$). However, it is possible to obtain the weight- and z-average molecular weights from each other and, in fact, even to obtain the number-average molecular weight from the weight- or z-average, although in the latter case a constant of integration must be evaluated.

The lower limit of the weight-average molecular weight range which can be measured by an equilibrium ultracentrifuge is about 5,000, while the upper limit is about 500,000, unless extremely dilute solutions are used.

## Light-Scattering Analysis

Although the theory of light scattering by simple liquids and mixtures was worked out by Einstein and von Smoluchowski about 1908, its application to the measurement of polymer molecular weights is relatively recent. This use was put forward by Debye[5] in 1944, and its rapid application to this field was attended with considerable success.

If a beam of light is passed through an absolutely uniform transparent region, such as a vacuum or perfectly crystalline optical quartz, practically no lateral radiation (scattering) takes place. If passed through so-called homogeneous fluids, for example, gases and liquids, thermal motions cause fluctuations in density which in turn produce local variations in the refractive index and result in a scattering of some of the light. In the case of dilute polymer solutions, almost all of the scattering is caused by concentration fluctuations rather than by density fluctuations.

Thus, when a beam of light is scattered through a nonabsorbing polymer solution, the intensity of the scattered light is dependent upon the size and

[5] Debye, P., *J. Applied Phys.*, **15**, 338 (1944).

shape of the polymer molecules.   Except for the equilibrium ultracentrifuge used under certain conditions, the light-scattering method is unique in that it measures the true weight-average molecular weight of a heterogeneous polymer in solution without prior calibration.

If no fluorescence or absorption occurs, all of the light lost is lost by scattering, and the relation of the intensity of the original light to the scattered light is given as

$$I = I_o e^{-\tau l} \qquad (36)$$

where $I_o$ equals the intensity of light entering the cell, $I$ is the intensity of the light leaving the cell, $l$ equals the depth of solution or the length of the cell, and $\tau$ (the scattering) is called the turbidity of the solution.

The turbidity of polymer solutions is related to the molecular weight of the solute.   The basic eqation is

$$\frac{Hc}{\tau} = \frac{1}{RT}\left(\frac{d\pi}{dc}\right) \qquad (37)$$

where $d\pi/dc$ represents the change in osmotic pressure with concentration.

Since the relationship between the osmotic pressure and the concentration of a polymer solution has already been given as

$$\frac{\pi}{c} = \frac{RT}{M} + Bc \qquad (27)$$

Eq. 37 may be rewritten in the form

$$\frac{Hc}{\tau} = \frac{1}{M_w} + \frac{2B}{RT}\cdot c \qquad (38)$$

where $H = \dfrac{32\pi^3}{3\lambda^4 N_o} \cdot n^2 \cdot \left(\dfrac{dn}{dc}\right)^2$

$c$ = the concentration

$n$ = the refractive index of solvent

$N_o$ = Avogadro's number

$\lambda$ = the (vacuum) wave length of light used

$\dfrac{dn}{dc}$ = the change in refractive index of solution with concentration

The molecular weight is obtained by plotting $H(c/\tau)$ against $c$ and extrapolating to zero concentration.   The intercept on the ordinate then gives the reciprocal of the molecular weight.   The only experimental measurements which are necessary for the calculation of the quantity $H(c/\tau)$ are the turbidity at a series of concentrations and the variation of the refractive index of the solution with concentration.

The light-scattering method can be used to measure the molecular weights of polymers down to about 5,000 and even lower; the intensity of the light scattered by a dilute solution of a polymer of lower molecular weight is usually too small to measure accurately. This lower limit for the method represents the upper limit for ordinary cryoscopic measurements.

Some advantages of this method are: (1) An indication of the width of the distribution curve can be obtained; (2) the method is very sensitive to large molecules; i.e., precision of results increases with increase in the molecular weight; and (3) the method is particularly useful at very low concentrations where ideal behavior of polymers in solution is approached.

The accuracy of light-scattering measurements is made difficult by the fact that dust particles or small quantities of coarser particles may easily cause error in the results. The suspensions must therefore be carefully freed from such particles by centrifugation. Low molecular weights and color of the polymer or of the solvent also affect the accuracy of the method.

If any over-all dimension of the individual molecules in solution is greater than about one twentieth of the wave length of the light used, Eq. 38 is no longer accurate. Each molecule can no longer be considered as a point source and scattering from the different parts of the molecule must be taken into account. The light scattered from different parts of a long-chain molecule differs in phase because of the difference in path lengths. This causes an interference effect which results in an asymmetric condition in the angular distribution of the scattered light. This angular asymmetry can be measured and interpreted to give information concerning the shape of the polymer molecule. Further, a knowledge of the angular asymmetry enables corrections to be applied to the above equation so that an accurate value of the molecular weight is obtained.

**Viscosity Measurements**

In most of the methods considered so far, the molecular weight has been obtained from the experimental data by means of equations derived from theoretical considerations. The calculation of molecular weight from viscosity data, however, depends upon the use of an empirically determined relation between molecular weight and viscosity. Because of its relative simplicity, it is useful for obtaining rapidly an estimate of the order of magnitude of the molecular weights of linear polymers.

Slight changes in high-molecular-weight polymer systems have considerable effects upon their viscosities. Since viscosity is relatively easy to measure precisely, many investigations of the relationship between viscosity and molecular weight have been carried out. In the course of these, several methods have been developed that are suitable for the measurement of a very broad range of molecular weights.

The viscosity relations of polymers are appreciably more complicated than those of simpler molecules.  The usual relations do not take into account the forces of attraction between the solvent and dispersed particles. In addition, polymer chains in solution exhibit movement of the molecule as a whole and also movement of the individual segments.  Furthermore, the segments are of molecular dimensions so that the forces of attraction between solute and solvent must be taken into account.  Another complicating factor is that polymers, except for highly branched ones, are characterized by having one dimension great in comparison to the others.

The simplest relationships are obtained from a consideration of a particular solute-solvent combination in which the only factor allowed to vary is the length of the linear polymer chain.  Staudinger,[6] working with linear polymers of relatively low molecular weights, developed the following empirical relationship:

$$\eta_{sp} = K_m \overline{M} c \tag{39}$$

where $\eta_{sp}$ is the specific viscosity ($= \eta_r - 1 = \eta/\eta_S - 1$), $c$ the concentration in base moles[†] per liter of solution, $K_m$ a specific constant for a particular polymer and solvent, $M$ the molecular weight, $\eta_r$ the relative viscosity, and $\eta$ and $\eta_S$ the absolute viscosities of solution and pure solvent, respectively.

Viscosity is a relatively simple measurement to perform and, unlike the situation with osmotic measurements, an increase in the molecular weight does not decrease the precision of measurement.  For these reasons, Eq. 39 was for some time used extensively for determining and reporting molecular weights.  Unfortunately, both theory and experiment indicate that the ratio $\eta_{sp}/c$ is not constant, except for a very narrow range.  The ratio at infinite dilution is preferably used.  This ratio is termed the *intrinsic viscosity* and is designated by the symbol $[\eta]$; that is,

$$\lim_{c \to 0} \frac{\eta_{sp}}{c} = [\eta] \tag{40}$$

Hence, Staudinger's equation is better written

$$[\eta] = K\overline{M} \tag{41}$$

However, even extrapolation to infinite dilution is not always sufficient, since it has been shown that the value of $K$ for a low-molecular-weight polymer, even if so extrapolated, may not hold for the same species of polymer in the high-molecular-weight ranges.  In other words, different

[6] Staudinger, H., *Die Hochmolekularen Organischen Verbindungen*, Julius Springer, Berlin, 1932.

† A base mole is equal to the molecular weight of a monomer unit; i.e., number of moles ÷ $\overline{DP}_n$.

samples of a particular high-molecular-weight polymer, all dissolved in the same solvent, may have different constants.

More recently there have been developed a number of theoretically based equations for homogeneous linear polymers of varying degrees of chain flexibility. These equations reduce to

$$[\eta] = K\overline{M}^a \tag{42}$$

It has been shown that the limits for the constant $a$ lie between 0.5 for perfectly flexible, randomly kinked polymer chains and 2.0 for completely rigid, rod-shaped molecules. This equation has been verified experimentally in a number of carefully fractionated polymers, the molecular weights in most cases having been obtained from osmotic pressure measurements.

Since most polymers are not homogeneous, the nature of the average molecular weight obtained from this equation is not obvious. It has been shown that

$$[\eta] = K\overline{M}_v^a \tag{43}$$

where $\overline{M}_v$ is the viscosity-average molecular weight.

In previous discussions of molecular weight averages, the number-average molecular weight, $\overline{M}_n$, the weight-average molecular weight, $\overline{M}_w$, and the $z$-average molecular weight, $\overline{M}_z$, were mentioned. In Eq. 43, if $a = 1$, the molecular weight is the weight-average molecular weight, $\overline{M}_w$. If, however, $a$ is not 1, i.e., the polymer is not homogeneous, the definition of viscosity-average molecular weight is more complex and is defined by Eq. 4.

The preceding discussion has been concerned with polymers in solution. However, molecular weights may also be calculated by measurement of the viscosity of a molten polymer. At elevated temperatures, some polymers melt sharply without decomposition or degradation; such polymers can be studied by melt viscosity measurements. In general, only those polymers which have a tendency to be crystalline possess melting points sufficiently low and sharp that they can be studied in a molten condition without degradation.

Flory[7] and co-workers have found that the simple empirical relationship

$$\log \eta_m = A + B\overline{M}_w^{1/2} \tag{44}$$

where $\eta_m$ is the melt viscosity, and $A$ and $B$ are constants for a given polymer at a given temperature, holds over a wide range of molecular weights for a number of linear condensation polymers. The values of the

[7] Flory, P. J., *J. Am. Chem. Soc.*, **62**, 1057 (1940); Schaefgen, J. R. and Flory, P. J., *ibid.*, **70**, 2709 (1948).

constants can be determined by measuring the melt viscosities of a series of homogeneous fractions whose molecular weights have been determined by osmotic pressure or light-scattering methods.

Usually the measurement of viscosities is made relative to the known viscosity of a standard substance. The capillary viscometers of Ostwald, Ubbelohde, and Fenske are most frequently used. With these instruments, the time required for a given quantity of liquid at constant temperature to pass from one calibrated mark to another serves as the measure of viscosity.

In the Ostwald viscometer, the viscosity of the standard substance is given by

$$\eta_o = C_s \varrho_o t_o \qquad (45)$$

where $\eta_o$ is the viscosity of the standard substance at a given temperature $T$, $\varrho_o$ is the density of that substance at that temperature, $C_s$ is the viscometer calibration constant, and $t_o$ is the flow time for the meniscus to fall from one line to another. The viscosity, $\eta_x$, of the unknown sample is represented by a similar equation. Dividing one equation by the other gives

$$\eta_x = \frac{\eta_o \varrho_x t_x}{\varrho_o t_o} \qquad (46)$$

This equation requires only a standard material of known viscosity and the densities of both solutions, provided a kinetic energy correction is not required.

One form of the Ubbelohde viscometer does not require density data since the flow occurs under a controlled air pressure. A measured quantity of liquid is used so that the liquid is moved by constant pressure from one sphere to another. The viscosity of the unknown is given as

$$\eta_x = \eta_o (t_x/t_o) \qquad (47)$$

again assuming there is no need for a kinetic energy correction.

**Miscellaneous Physical Methods**

The *electron microscope* has become useful in examinations of polymeric materials. If a polymer can be precipitated from a solution in a curled-up state, its molecular weight should be determinable, provided its density is known, since the resolving power of a magnetic electron microscope is at least 10Å. Furthermore, a "colony count" should give a distribution curve.

The use of *ultramicroscopic photographic techniques* has been useful in clarifying the morphology of various polymers. While quantitative data are not available from this technique, it has been particularly helpful in explaining the physical properties of elastomers, especially by demonstrating that more than one phase exists in the aggregate, each of different average molecular weight.

Another method which has come into recent use has been that of determining the number-average molecular weights of low-molecular-weight liquid polymers based on *sound velocities* through the polymer. The precision of the sound velocity method is estimated to be about three per cent and, within experimental error, these molecular weights are the same as the number-average molecular weights.

The solubilities of linear polymers in suitable solvents or solvent mixtures decrease with increasing molecular weight. The *precipitation titration* method consists of adding a precipitant to a solution of a polymer; the higher the molecular weight of the polymer, the smaller is the amount of precipitant necessary to cause opalescence (incipient precipitation). This method is only of use for relatively homogeneous fractions of an homologous polymeric series. It has been shown that the concentration of precipitant at the critical point is a linear function of the reciprocal of the molecular weight. A calibration curve is prepared from fractions of known molecular weight, plotting critical concentration against molecular weight; it is then possible to obtain the molecular weights corresponding to other critical concentrations.

### MOLECULAR WEIGHTS BY CHEMICAL METHODS

**End-group Analysis**

The *end-group* method of analysis depends upon the presence of one or more detectable terminal functional groups on the polymer molecules, the important point being that the end-mers are left detectably different from the intermediate-mers. End-group determinations are usually chemical, and as a class they are differentiated from the more usual procedures that may be referred to as physical methods. The rapidly growing use of radioactive tracer techniques is an exception.

It is essential that these groups only should react with the test reagent stoichiometrically. This implies that something must be known about the structure of the polymer. Since the method measures the effect of a small group on a large chain, the sensitivity decreases as the molecular weight increases, and accurate results are not usually obtained for molecular weights much above 25,000. Further, the method fails if the polymer contains reactive impurities or cannot be purified; such substances would contribute to the apparent molecular weight. Since the method counts the number of active ends in the given weight of material rather than the actual number of molecules, it will give erroneous results for branched polymers unless the structure is known. The means of identifying the active end-groups may involve drastic chemical treatment; in such cases, it must be known that no degradation occurs under the conditions of the experiment. Each polymer has to be considered on its own merits and individual methods of analysis devised.

The method is particularly applicable to condensation-type polymers and step-addition polymers, for, in most cases, at least one functionally reactive group remains in each polymer molecule. Polyesters have terminal carboxyl groups which can be estimated by direct titration, but again the accuracy of the method depends on a knowledge of the structure. Ethylene oxide, when polymerized in the absence of an alcoholic initiator, contains two terminal hydroxyl groups, which may be determined.

The end-group method was widely used in earlier work when fairly low-molecular-weight polymers were obtained and emphasis was placed on chemical methods of analysis. It has probably been used most extensively in connection with cellulose and its derivatives. Since the end-group method actually counts the number of molecules present, it yields the number-average molecular weight.

It is beyond the scope of this book to discuss in detail the various specific methods of analysis for the various functional groups; however, Table 4-2 should assist in obtaining a picture of the possibilities of this method.

**Tracer Analysis**

*Tracer* analysis depends upon the presence in the polymer molecule of a functional group or groups which have been introduced into the growing molecule either from an initiator or from a reacting solvent. Upon analysis, the percentage of that particular functional group in the molecule serves as an indication of the average molecular weight of the polymer mass. For example, a method for determining the molecular weight of polystyrene, which may be used for other polymers, involves the use of a tracer initiator which reacts with the monomer to form a polymer in which one mole of initiator is absorbed for each chain started. Analysis for bromine, using *p*-bromobenzoyl peroxide as a tracer, has given molecular weights for polystyrene which are in good agreement with those determined by specific viscosity methods.

Of all the methods herein described, determination of molecular weight by viscosity methods is probably the most common, not only because of the relative ease in performing the measurements but also because of the availability and reasonable cost of the equipment. A separate and absolute determination must, however, be made. Osmotic pressure measurements are more accurate, but involve considerable skill and are

TABLE 4-2.   END-GROUP METHODS OF MOLECULAR WEIGHT
DETERMINATIONS[8]

| Polymer | Reacting End Group | Methods |
|---|---|---|
| Hydroxy acid polyesters and amino acid polyamides | —COOH | a. Acid determination<br>b. Salt formation and subsequent determination of metal content |
| Amino acid polyamides | —NH$_2$ | Primary amino group determination |
| Glycol polyethers | —OH | Acid take-up during acetylation |
| Cellulose | Reducing end | a. Copper number<br>b. Oxidation to carboxyl and subsequent acid determination<br>c. Reaction with mercaptan and subsequent sulfur determination |
| Cellulose | 4OH's on one end; 3OH's on other mers | Methylation, hydrolysis, and isolation of tetramethyl glucose |
| End-blocked polymers:<br>Diamine-dicarboxylic acid polyamides blocked with acetic acid<br>Dimethylsiloxanes, ethoxy-end blocked | $\overset{O}{\overset{\|}{—OC \cdot CH_3}}$<br><br>—OC$_2$H$_5$ | Acetate determination<br><br>Ethoxy determination |
| Ethylene | —CH$_3$ | Infrared spectrum |

lengthier.   The other osmotic techniques are limited to the low-molecular-weight ranges.   The ultracentrifuge and the electron microscope are expensive and require specialized training.   Light-scattering equipment is becoming less expensive, is relatively simple to operate, and future developments appear promising.   The chemical methods, particularly the tracer type of analysis, have been used extensively but also are suitable for low-molecular-weight polymers only.   Table 4-3 summarizes the more important methods with a listing of their principal characteristics.

## MOLECULAR WEIGHT DISTRIBUTIONS

It often happens that a particular property of a polymer depends only upon a specific average molecular weight, so that determination of this average alone is sufficient for the interpretation of the property.   This is the case, for example, for colligative properties (number-average), the turbidity (weight-average), and the intrinsic viscosity (viscosity-average).   However, in order to correlate properties which depend upon different

[8] Schmidt, A. X. and Marlies, C. A., *Principles of High-Polymer Theory and Practice*, Table 6-1, p. 236, McGraw-Hill Book Co., New York, 1948.

TABLE 4-3. COMPARISON OF RESULTS OBTAINABLE BY VARIOUS
MOLECULAR WEIGHT METHODS[9]

| Method | Type of Average Molecular Weight | Method Fails or Becomes Insensitive | Effect of High Concentration on Molecular Weight | Additional Data Obtained by the Method |
|---|---|---|---|---|
| **A. Absolute Methods** | | | | |
| 1. Ultracentrifuge<br>a. Sedimentation velocity<br><br>b. Equilibrium | Complex averages; i.e., $\overline{M}_{ww}$, etc. $\overline{M}_n$, $\overline{M}_w$, and $\overline{M}_z$ | For very low mol. wts. | Mol. wt. appears too small | Shape of molecules and distribution of mol. wts.; thermodynamic interaction constant between solvent and polymer $(\mu)$ |
| 2. Osmotic pressure | $\overline{M}_n$ | For very high mol. wts. | Mol. wt. appears too small | Thermodynamic interaction constant between solvent and polymer |
| 3. Light scattering | $\overline{M}_w$ | As refractive index of solute approaches that of solvent | Mol. wt. appears too small | Thermodynamic interaction constant; molecular sizes and shapes; some idea about branching |
| 4. End-group method | $\overline{M}_n$ | For high mol. wts. | | Branching |
| **B. Indirect or Comparative Methods** | | | | |
| 5. Viscosity | $\overline{M}_v$ | For very low mol. wts. | Mol. wt. appears too high | Size, shape, and internal shielding |
| 6. Solubility | $\overline{M}_n$ | For very low mol. wts., also for very high mol. wts. | Solubility decreases with increasing concentration | May gain some idea about branching |

averages, or to compare polymers prepared under conditions which lead to different types of molecular size distributions, a knowledge of the molecular weight *distribution* is necessary.

The experimental method of obtaining the molecular weight distribution involves separating the polymer by fractional precipitation into portions covering comparatively narrow molecular weight ranges, then constructing the distribution curve from the amount and average molecular weight of each fraction. This technique is tedious, sharp separations are seldom obtained, and reliable results require a large number of time-consuming fractionations and refractionations.

[9] Adapted from Boundy, R. H. and Boyer, R. F., *Styrene*, Table 9-37, p. 416, Reinhold Publishing Corp., New York, 1952.

The most significant progress has been achieved through theoretical considerations. The rapid progress in the application of statistical methods, due in large part to a relatively small number of men, has occurred only in the last twenty years. In this short period of time, the theory of polymer distributions has been placed upon a firm mathematical footing.

### Condensation Polymers

The concept of polyfunctionality was summarized by Kienle[10] in 1930 as follows:

1. Polymers are formed only from systems where both reactants have a functionality of at least two.
2. Polymer growth proceeds by chance and random contact of any two mutually functional groups, causing random complexity and heterogeneity.
3. The relative sizes and shapes of reactants and the positions of functional groups determine the physical properties of the polymer.

In 1936 Carothers[11] developed a relationship among functionality, degree of polymerization, extent of reaction, and gel formation. This simple equation correlated much that had previously been disorganized, enabling one to predict the conditions under which gelation would probably occur, the effects of blocking agents, and the extent of reaction required to attain any desired degree of polymerization.

Let $f$ = average degree of functionality; i.e., the *average* number of functional groups per monomer (when two or more reactants are present, they must be present in equivalent amounts)

$N_o$ = total number of monomer molecules initially present

$N_t$ = total number of molecules (of all types) present after reaction has occurred

Then $N_o f$ = total number of functional groups present at start of reaction

$2(N_o - N_t)$ = number of functional groups lost, since two groups react for each bond formed

$\dfrac{2(N_o - N_t)}{N_o f}$ = fraction of functional groups lost = $p$ = extent of reaction

(Note: When $f = 2$, this reduces to $\dfrac{N_o - N_t}{N_o}$; cf. Eq. 1, Chap. 3.)

[10] Kienle, R. H., *Ind. Eng. Chem.*, **22**, 590 (1930).
[11] Carothers, W. H., *Trans. Farad. Soc.*, **32**, 39 (1936).

$$\frac{N_o}{N_t} = \text{number-average degree of polymerization} = \overline{DP}_n = \frac{1}{1 - p \cdot \frac{f}{2}}, \quad (48)$$

Hence,

$$p = \frac{2}{f} - \frac{2}{\overline{DP}_n \cdot f} \quad (49)$$

When $\overline{DP}_n$ becomes very large, the second term becomes insignificant, and

$$\lim_{\overline{DP}_n \to \infty} p = \frac{2}{f} \quad (50)$$

Eq. 50 gives the extent of reaction necessary to reach infinite molecular weight and, as a consequence, the onset of gelation.

If only bifunctional reactants are present, these equations reduce to

$$p = 1 - \frac{1}{\overline{DP}_n} \quad (51)$$

and

$$\lim_{\overline{DP}_n \to \infty} p = 1 \quad (52)$$

Eq. 51 shows that, to reach an average degree of polymerization of only 100, the extent of reaction must be 99 per cent. The necessity for almost complete reaction if high degrees of polymerization are to be attained is obvious. Practically speaking, complete reaction is never achieved, and, no matter how far a strictly bifunctional condensation is carried out, the product is usually fusible and soluble.

The situation is quite different in a typical polyfunctional system. If two moles of glycerol and three moles of phthalic anhydride (or acid) are reacted, the viscosity of the mixture changes slowly at first and then suddenly rises extremely rapidly. The latter stage is accompanied by gelation (intermolecular cross-linking), even though analysis shows that much of the acid is still unreacted. In this system, the two molecules of glycerol contribute $2 \times 3$ functional groups, and the three phthalic anhydride molecules contribute $3 \times 2$ functional groups. Since there are a total of five reactive molecules, $f_{av.} = 12/5 = 2.4$ and, from Eq. 50

$$p = \frac{2}{2.4} = 0.83$$

This means that the reaction cannot be carried beyond the point where 83 per cent of the functional groups have reacted without the formation of a gel, provided, of course, that the reaction is all intermolecular. Since gelation causes immobilization, unreacted and partially polymerized molecules are also present.   If all of the glycerol molecules could be made to react bifunctionally before any react trifunctionally, polyester chains still containing one third of their hydroxyl groups unreacted would be formed, and one third of the phthalic anhydride would also remain unreacted.   At this stage, only two thirds of the functions would be lost ($p = 0.67$).   Since the reaction product would still be a linear polymer, gelation would not occur.   If, however, any further reaction were to occur, it would of necessity involve cross-linking which, in turn, would be accompanied by gelation.   In other words, 67 per cent is the minimum extent of reaction before gelation could occur and 83 per cent is the maximum.   Most experimental values found by various investigators for the extent of reaction at incipient gelation lie between these two values.

The preceding approach is simple and has been useful for qualitative estimations.   However, experimental results have not always agreed too closely with the theoretical predictions of Carothers' equation.   It is really no more than a first approximation to a truly quantitative treatment. One factor not taken into consideration is the distribution of molecular sizes about an average value in any given polymer mass.   The chain length is treated as a unique value at each stage of the polymerization, whereas it actually is the weighted average of a series of different values, as may be shown by the separation of many apparently homogeneous polymer masses into many fractions of different degrees of polymerization. The observed average molecular weight is, furthermore, dependent upon the method of determination, as was brought out in the previous section. Failure to take this last factor into account is probably responsible for most of the discrepancies between experimental figures and those predicted by the Carothers' equation.   A much more satisfactory approach has subsequently been developed in which the statistical probability of the occurrence of each value of chain length is taken into account.   The rest of this section is concerned with this treatment and summarizes the contributions of Flory,[12] Stockmayer,[13] and other workers in this field.

The principle of equal reactivity of all functional groups during condensation polymerizations has been well established.   This means that at every stage of a polymerization process each functional group of a given chemical type has an equal opportunity for reaction, regardless of the size of the molecule to which it is attached.   The chemical reactivity does not, however, necessarily remain constant during the course of the reaction. Then the probability that any given functional group has reacted will be equal to the fraction, $p$, of all functional groups of the same type which have reacted.

[12] Flory, P. J., *J. Am. Chem. Soc.*, **58**, 1877 (1936) *et seq.*
[13] Stockmayer, W. H., *J. Chem. Phys.*, **11**, 45 (1943); *ibid.*, **12**, 125 (1944) *et seq.*

## Bifunctional Condensations

As the simplest case,[†] consider a linear condensation polymer formed from a monomer such as an $\omega$-hydroxy acid. Assume that the terminal hydroxyl group of any molecule has been selected at random and that the probability that this molecule is composed of exactly $n$ units is desired.

$$
\underset{1}{\text{HO·R·}\overset{\overset{\displaystyle O}{\|}}{\text{C}}\text{·O·R·}}\underset{2\quad n-1}{\overset{\overset{\displaystyle O}{\|}}{\text{C}}\text{·····O·R·}}\underset{n}{\overset{\overset{\displaystyle O}{\|}}{\text{C}}\text{·OH}}
$$

The probability that the carboxyl group of the first unit is esterified is equal to $p$. The probability that the carboxyl of the second unit is esterified, this probability being independent of whether or not linkage 1 has been formed, is likewise equal to $p$. The probability that this sequence continues for $n - 1$ linkages is the product of these separate probabilities, or $p^{n-1}$. This is the probability that the molecule contains at least $n - 1$ ester groups, or at least $n$ units. The probability that the $n$th carboxyl group is unreacted, thus limiting the chain to exactly $n$ units, is $1 - p$. Hence, the probability $(P_n)$ that the molecule in question is composed of exactly $n$ units is given by the product of these independent probabilities, or

$$P_n = p^{n-1}(1 - p) \tag{53}$$

If only linear polymer molecules are present, which is assumed, then the probability, $P_n$, that any molecule selected at random is composed of $n$ units must equal the mole fraction of $n$-mers $(N_x)$; hence

$$N_x = p^{n-1}(1 - p) \tag{54}$$

The total number of $n$-mers $(N_n)$ is then given by

$$N_n = N_t p^{n-1}(1 - p) \tag{55}$$

where $N_t$ is the total number of molecules of all sizes. If $N_o$ is the total number of monomer units initially present, then

$$N_t = N_o(1 - p) \tag{56}$$

and

$$N_n = N_o p^{n-1}(1 - p)^2 \tag{57}$$

If the added weight of the terminating groups is neglected, the molecular weight of each species is directly proportional to $n$; hence the weight fraction can be written

$$W_x = \frac{nN_n \cdot m_o}{N_o m_o} = \frac{n \cdot N_n}{N_o} \tag{58}$$

---

[†] This follows the development given by P. J. Flory, *Principles of Polymer Chemistry*, Chap. VIII, Cornell University Press, Ithaca, N.Y. (1953).

The error introduced by this approximation will be significant only at very low molecular weights. Substituting from Eq. 57,

$$W_x = np^{n-1}(1 - p)^2 \qquad (59)$$

The same derivation holds for polymers formed from exactly equivalent proportions of comers. In this case, $n$ represents the combined number of both types of units in the polymer chain.

Solution of Eqs. 11 to 14 in Chapter 3 also yields Eq. 57 above. Both methods of solution have their particular advantages; the statistical method is preferable if the reaction mechanism is simple, but with the more complicated reactions, such as the vinyl polymerizations, the kinetic method has proved more useful.

The maximum concentration for each intermediate is reached at time $t_{\max}$ and may be obtained by substitution of Eq. 16, Chapter 3, in Eq. 57, differentiating, and solving for the maximum

$$t_{\max} = \frac{n - 1}{N_o k} \qquad (60)$$

after which the value decreases and approaches zero as $t \to \infty$.

The maximum concentration of any $n$-mer is given by the relation

$$C_{n(\max)} = \frac{4C_o(n - 1)^{n-1}}{(n + 1)^{n+1}} \qquad (61)$$

If the chains are long; that is, $n \to \infty$, Eq. 61 reduces to

$$C_{n(\max)} \doteq \frac{4C_o}{n^2} \qquad (62)$$

It is often desirable to know the total amount of polymer produced at any time. The weight fraction of condensate *from dimers upward* is, therefore,

$$\sum_{n=2}^{\infty} W_x = \sum_{n=1}^{\infty} W_x - w_1 = 1 - (1 - p)^2 = 2p - p^2 \qquad (63)$$

Therefore, the total amount of polymer is

$$W_p = W(2p - p^2) \qquad (64)$$

where $W$ is the total weight of the system. This may be expressed in terms of $t$ by substituting for $p$ from Eq. 16, Chapter 3.

Graphical representation of the distributions expressed above may readily be made both from the theoretical equations and from actual fractionation experiments. Close agreement of the theoretical plot with the actual graphical representation of an experimental polymeric distribution has indicated the general validity of the statistical theory outlined above.

It can readily be seen, by referral to Fig. 4-1 and Eq. 53, that $P_n$ or $N_x$ decreases steadily as $n$ increases for all values of $p$, and there are, therefore, always more monomer molecules present than there are molecules of any other species.   This, of course, refers to the *number* of molecules; however, on a *weight* basis, these monomer molecules are of negligible importance

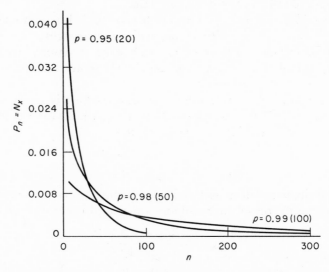

Fɪɢ 4-1.    Mole-fraction distribution (or probability that a molecule is an $n$-mer) plotted for various extents of reaction, $p$, for a linear condensation polymer.   The numbers in parentheses are the number-average degrees of polymerization, $1/(1-p)$[14]

as can be seen by referring to the same information plotted as a weight-fraction distribution for various extents of reaction, $p$ (Fig. 4-2 and Eq. 59), and even more easily in Fig. 4-3, where $p$ is the abscissa and $n$ the para-meter.   This curve indicates that a certain $n$-mer occurs most frequently, that this maximum is progressively displaced toward greater chain length with greater extent of reaction, and that this maximum tends to decrease. Both curves also show that the polymerization products are nonhomo-geneous.

The extent of reaction necessary to give the maximum yield by weight of a particular $n$-mer, i.e., $W_{x(\max)}$, may be calculated from the relation

$$p_n = \frac{n-1}{n+1} \tag{65}$$

which can be derived from Eq. 59 by elementary calculus.   It so happens that, although the size-distribution curves are far from being symmetrical,

[14] Flory, P. J., *J. Am. Chem. Soc.*, **58**, 1877 (1936).

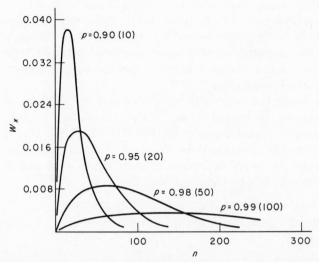

FIG. 4-2. Weight-fraction of $n$-mers $(W_x)$ plotted for various extents of reaction, $p$, for a linear condensation polymer. The numbers in parentheses are the number-average degrees of polymerization, $1/(1-p)$[14]

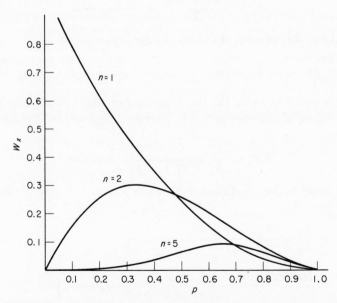

FIG. 4-3. Weight-fraction of $n$-mers $(W_x)$ plotted for various chain lengths for a linear condensation polymer[14]

the $n$-mer present in greatest weight fraction is the one for which $n = \overline{DP_n}$. This relationship is only approximate, coming closer as $p \to 1$.

Another consideration which is of both theoretical and practical importance is the *blocking effect* caused by an excess of one of the reacting monomers or the introduction of a monofunctional reactant. In such a case, even at complete reaction, $n$ is finite, and the degree of polymerization is limited to a lower value.

The depression of the molecular weight caused by addition of monofunctional reactants, or by unbalance in the stoichiometric proportions, has been expressed quantitatively by Flory.[15] Suppose that a small amount of a reactant designated by $B$—$|$—$B$ is added either to a pure $A$——$B$ monomer or to an equimolar mixture of $A$——$A$ and $B$——$B$; $B$—$|$—$B$ may or may not be identical with $B$——$B$.

Let $N_A = $ total number of $A$ groups initially present

$N_B = $ total number of $B$ groups initially present

$r = N_A/N_B$

$p = $ fraction of $A$ groups which have reacted at any given stage of the reaction

The total number of molecules originally present is

$$N_o = \frac{(N_A + N_B)}{2} = \frac{N_A\left(1 + \dfrac{1}{r}\right)}{2} \tag{66}$$

The total number of ends of chains can be expressed as

$$2N = 2N_A(1 - p) + (N_B - N_A) = N_A\left[2(1 - p) + \frac{(1 - r)}{r}\right] \tag{67}$$

and this is equal to twice the total number of molecules. The number-average degree of polymerization is therefore obtained by dividing Eq. 66 by Eq. 67,

$$\overline{DP_n} = \frac{N_o}{N_t} = \frac{1 + r}{2r(1 - p) + (1 - r)} \tag{68}$$

which reduces to Eq. 5, Chapter 3, when $r = 1$. At completion of the reaction ($p = 1$),

$$\overline{DP_n} = \frac{N_B + N_A}{N_B - N_A} = \frac{(1 + r)}{(1 - r)}$$

$$= \frac{\text{(moles bifunctional units exclusive of } B\text{—}|\text{—}B)}{\text{(moles of } B\text{—}|\text{—}B)} + 1 \tag{69}$$

[15] Flory, P. J., *Principles of Polymer Chemistry*, pp. 92–93, Cornell University Press, Ithaca, N.Y., 1953.

The same equations apply to polymers containing small amounts of a monofunctional reactant $B+$, if $r$ is redefined as follows:

$$r = \frac{N_A}{(N_A + 2N_{B+})} \tag{70}$$

Other special cases can be treated similarly, as, for example, when two or more types of added substances are employed simultaneously.

Eq. 69 shows the marked effect of the presence of a small amount of a monofunctional impurity or of even a small excess of one bifunctional reactant on the maximum obtainable molecular weight. One mole per cent of an extraneous unit in the system limits the average degree of polymerization to about 100 units, for example. Thus, the loss of a small portion of one reactant through volatilization or a comparable loss of functional groups through side reactions will have a large effect on the molecular weight attainable.

This principle is of importance for control of polymer molecular weights and of viscosities. Thus, deliberately added functional reactants, known as stabilizers, are used in the manufacture of nylon to eliminate the possibility of slow, progressive after-polymerization which causes a troublesome change in viscosity during spinning and results in non-uniformity of both fiber diameter and strength (see Chap. 8). On the other hand, in the manufacture of poly(ethylene terephthalate) film and fiber, the dimethyl terephthalate is made commercially with a purity of well over 99 per cent in order to obtain the high degree of polymerization necessary for the unusual physical properties desired.

## Polyfunctional Condensations

In a polyfunctional system gelation occurs long before all of the reactants have reacted. Usually, in such systems, there is a sharply defined gel point at which there is a sudden tremendous increase in viscosity and, just as suddenly, an appearance of insoluble product. However, if reaction is continued even after the gel point has been reached, an appreciable weight-fraction of the product is still soluble.

Flory[16] has worked out the statistical analysis of the case of the polymerization of a bifunctional unit $A$——$A$, a trifunctional (branching type)

unit $A$—$\big\langle$, and a bifunctional unit of opposite character $B$——$B$, where

$A$

condensation occurs exclusively between $A$ and $B$ (for example,

[16] Flory, P. J., *Principles of Polymer Chemistry*, pp. 348 ff., Cornell University Press, Ithaca, N.Y., 1953.

$A = - OH, B = - CO_2H)$.   Polymers having structures similar to the following will be formed:

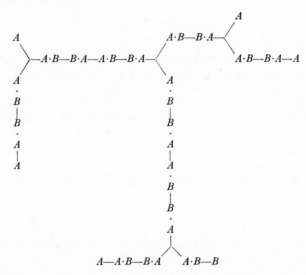

The principle of equal reactivity is again assumed to hold so that the reactivity of a given group is independent of the size or structure of the molecule or network to which it is attached.   It is further assumed that reactions between $A$ and $B$ groups on the same molecule do not occur. This introduces an error which is frequently appreciable.   However, treatment of nonlinear polymerizations without this assumption becomes hopelessly complicated.

Without going into the details of derivation, the following relationships can be obtained:

$$\alpha = \frac{rp_A^2\beta}{1 - rp_A^2(1 - \beta)} \tag{71}$$

or

$$\alpha = \frac{p_B^2\beta}{r - p_B^2(1 - \beta)} \tag{72}$$

where $\alpha$ equals the probability that the chain ends in a branch (poly-functional) unit, $A\!\!-\!\!\diagdown_{\substack{A \\ A}}$, $p_A$ is the probability that any particular $A$ group has reacted, which equals the fraction of all $A$ groups that have reacted, $p_B$ is the probability that the $B$ group on the right of the first $B$——$B$ unit has reacted, which is equal to the fraction of $B$'s reacted, $\beta$ equals the ratio of $A$'s (reacted and unreacted) belonging to branch units to the total number of $A$'s in the mixture, and $r$ equals the ratio of $A$ to $B$ groups initially present ($p_B = rp_A$).

In the application of these equations, $r$ and $\beta$ are determined by the proportions of the initial ingredients employed, and either unreacted $A$ or $B$ is determined analytically at various stages of the reaction. Then $\alpha$ can be calculated employing either of the above equations, depending upon which group is determined directly. Hence, $\alpha$ is readily calculable from experimentally observed quantities.

Where there are no $A$——$A$ units, $\beta$ equals 1 and

$$\alpha = rp_A^2 = \frac{p_B^2}{r} \tag{73}$$

When $A$ and $B$ groups are present in equivalent quantities, $r$ equals 1, $p_A = p_B = p$, and

$$\alpha = \frac{p^2\beta}{1 - p^2(1 - \beta)} \tag{74}$$

When there are no $A$——$A$ units and $A$ and $B$ groups are present in equivalent quantities, $\beta = 1$, $r = 1$, and $p_A = p_B = p$; thus,

$$\alpha = p^2 \tag{75}$$

In a system consisting of bifunctional $A$——$A$ units and $f$-functional units, $R$——$A$, where $A$ may condense with $A$,

$$\alpha = \frac{p\beta}{1 - p(1 - \beta)} \tag{76}$$

If the branch unit is more than trifunctional, the same equations for the calculation of $\alpha$ can be employed. This derivation is not completely general; however, similar ones may be derived for other specific cases.

The critical value of $\alpha$ at which the formation of an infinite network becomes possible may now be obtained. If a branching unit is trifunctional, each chain which terminates in a branch unit is succeeded by more chains. If $\alpha < \frac{1}{2}$, this means that there is less than an even chance that each chain will lead to a branch unit and thus to two more chains or, stated otherwise, there is a greater than even chance that it will end at an unreacted functional group. Under these circumstances, the growth of a network cannot continue indefinitely.

When $\alpha > \frac{1}{2}$, each chain has a better than even chance of forming two new chains. These two chains will, on the average, form $4\alpha$ new chains; thus $n$ chains should lead to the formation of $2n\alpha$ new chains, which will be greater than $n$ as long as $\alpha > \frac{1}{2}$. In this case, branching of successive chains should continue the structure indefinitely and infinite networks are possible. Hence, $\alpha = \frac{1}{2}$ is the critical value for incipient formation of infinite networks in a trifunctional system.

It should be emphasized, however, that, when $\alpha$ is greater than one half, all of the material will not be combined into infinite molecules. Despite the favorable probability of branching, a particular chain may be terminated at both ends by unreacted functional groups, or it may possess a branch at only one end and both of the succeeding two chains may lead to unreacted functional groups. In other words, molecules of finite length will co-exist with infinite networks so long as

$$\tfrac{1}{2} < \alpha < 1$$

A general statement of the critical condition for formation of infinite networks is as follows: The formation of an infinite network becomes possible when the expected number of chains which will succeed $n$ chains, through branching of some of them, is greater than $n$. That is, if $f_b$ is the functionality of the branching unit, gelation will occur when $\alpha(f_b - 1)$ exceeds unity. The critical value of $\alpha$ is, therefore,

$$\alpha_c = \frac{1}{f_b - 1} \tag{77}$$

Note that $f_b$ is not the same as the $f$ of Carothers' function.

Practically speaking, this equation states that the introduction of branch units of successively higher functionality into a polyfunctional system of reactants progressively increases the probability of three-dimensional growth and gelation; i.e., the conversion of a potentially thermosetting system into its thermoset form is thus rendered progressively easier to accomplish.

The size distribution for polyfunctional polymers represented by the self-condensation of a polyfunctional monomer $(f = 3)$, condensation between equivalent amounts of $A{-}\!\!\Big\langle\genfrac{}{}{0pt}{}{A}{A}$ and $B{-}\!\!\Big\langle\genfrac{}{}{0pt}{}{B}{B}$ or of $A{-}\!\!\Big\langle\genfrac{}{}{0pt}{}{A}{A}$ and $B{-\!\!-\!\!-}B$

has also been derived by Flory[17] from probability considerations; Stockmayer[18] has generalized the results to units of any functionality, $f$. The statistical derivations will not be given here, but the general reasoning may be followed by analogy with the size distribution relationships for linear chains.

For trifunctional monomers, an $n$-mer will contain $(n - 1)$ bonds, and so $W_x$, defined as in the case of bifunctional molecules, will contain a

[17] Flory, P. J., *J. Am. Chem. Soc.*, **63**, 3091 (1941); *ibid.*, **74**, 2718 (1952).
[18] Stockmayer, W. H., *J. Chem. Phys.*, **11**, 45 (1943).

factor $p^{n-1}$ and also a factor $(1 - p)^{n+2}$, since there are now $(n + 2)$ end groups. Since structural isomerism occurs when $f = 3$, the simple term $n$ must be replaced by a more complex expression which takes this into account. The actual distribution law for $f = 3$ is

$$W_x = \frac{3(2n)!}{(n - 1)!\,(n + 2)!}p^{n-1}(1 - p)^{n+2} \tag{78}$$

where $W_x$ is the weight fraction of $n$-mers and $p$ is the extent of reaction. The generalized distribution laws for condensation reactions between equivalent quantities of $A{-}\overset{A}{\underset{A}{\big\langle}}$ and $B{-}\overset{B}{\underset{B}{\big\langle}}$ or of $A{-}\overset{A}{\underset{B}{\big\langle}}$ and $B{-\!\!-\!\!-}B$ (again assuming no intramolecular reaction) are as follows:

$$N_x = \frac{(1 - p)^2}{p\left(1 - \dfrac{pf}{2}\right)} \cdot \frac{f(fn - n)!}{n!\,(fn - 2n + 2)!}[p(1 - p)^{f-2}]^n \tag{79}$$

and

$$W_x = \frac{(1 - p)^2}{p} \cdot \frac{f(fn - n)!}{(n - 1)!\,(fn - 2n + 2)!}[p(1 - p)^{f-2}]^n \tag{80}$$

By letting $f = 2$ and $f = 3$, Eq. 80 reduces to those of Eqs. 59 and 78, respectively.

The number-average degree of polymerization for these cases is

$$\overline{DP}_n = \frac{1}{1 - \dfrac{\alpha f}{2}} \tag{81}$$

while the weight-average is

$$\overline{DP}_w = \frac{1 + \alpha}{1 - \alpha(f - 1)} \tag{82}$$

The critical point, beyond which the above equations should not be applied, is reached when

$$\alpha_c = \frac{1}{f_b - 1} \tag{83}$$

since $\overline{DP}_w$ becomes infinite as $1 - \alpha(f - 1) \to 0$ for all values of $p > 0$. This, then, is the gel point where infinite networks begin.

The weight-fraction of $n$-mer for a trifunctional monomer is shown in Fig. 4-4 for three extents of reaction. In contrast to the corresponding diagram for linear polymers (Fig. 4-2), the curves show a continuous decrease with increase in size of $n$; i.e., monomers are always present in greater weight amount than any $n$-mer and, in general, $n$-mers occur more frequently than $(n + 1)$-mers.

The change of composition of the polymer as reaction progresses can be shown more strikingly from Fig. 4-5, which shows weight-fractions of various polymers plotted against extent of reaction for a simple trifunctional reaction.   Here, $\alpha = p$.

It can be seen that the amount of monomer, $W_1$, decreases continuously

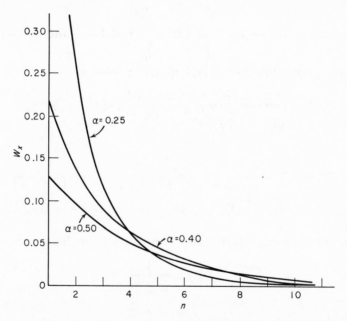

Fig. 4-4.   Weight-fraction distribution for a branched polymer prepared from a simple trifunctional monomer at the $\alpha$'s indicated[19]

as $p \rightarrow 1$; dimer formation, $W_2$, reaches a maximum near $p = 0.2$ and then decreases.   The maximum in the formation of the higher polymers occurs at a progressively later stage of the reaction but never occurs beyond the gel point, $\alpha = 0.5$.

The distribution broadens as condensation progresses, maximum heterogeneity occurring at the gel point, but even here the proportion of highly branched molecules is small.   At the gel point, the generation of infinite networks begins abruptly and the amount of gel, $W_g$, formed increases rapidly as condensation continues.

Infinite networks may also arise by the formation of chemical bonds

[19] Flory, P. J., *Chem. Revs.*, **39**, 137 (1946); *idem*, *J. Am. Chem. Soc.*, **63**, 3091 (1941).

among *linear* polymer molecules. The vulcanization of rubber is a common example of such a process. Through the action of sulfur, accelerators, and other ingredients present, sulfide cross-linkages are created.

### STEP-ADDITION POLYMERS

There also exists a class of compounds which forms polymers by monomer addition only. They are sometimes referred to as "step-addition" compounds. Cyclic monomers, such as ethylene oxide, for

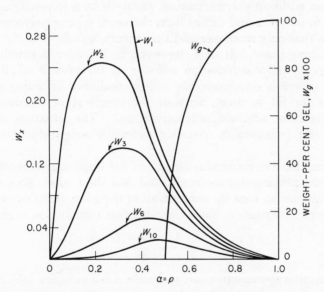

FIG. 4-5. Weight-fractions of various finite species and of gel in a simple trifunctional condensation as a function of $\alpha$, which in this case equals the extent of reaction, $p$[20]

example, may be caused to polymerize by addition of small amounts of substances capable of cleaving the ring with the formation of an hydroxyl group. This product may then add more monomers, as indicated below:

$$ROH \xrightarrow{\overset{O}{\overset{/\backslash}{CH_2—CH_2}}} RO—CH_2—CH_2—OH \xrightarrow{\overset{O}{\overset{/\backslash}{CH_2—CH_2}}} RO—CH_2CH_2—O—CH_2CH_2—OH,$$
$$\text{etc.}$$

Other cyclic compounds, such as lactams and $N$-carboxy anhydrides of $\alpha$-amino acids, may polymerize similarly, regenerating an amino group at each step. The number of polymer molecules formed will equal the number of initiator molecules (e.g., ROH), and the average number of

[20] Flory, P. J., *Chem. Revs.*, **39**, 137 (1946).

monomers per polymer molecule will equal the ratio of monomer consumed to initiator.

Here, the polymer forms according to the following scheme:

$$D + M \rightarrow M_1$$
$$M_1 + M \rightarrow M_2$$
$$M_n + M \rightarrow M_{n+1}$$

where $D$ represents the active functional molecule that starts the reaction. It can be seen that this type of polymerization, although formally resembling an addition polymerization, proceeds by a step-wise addition of monomer to polymer and differs from the usual type of polycondensation reaction in that only monomer addition occurs, no addition of polymer to polymer taking place. It may, however, be considered kinetically as a special type of polycondensation reaction as the growth of all polymer molecules proceeds simultaneously under conditions affording equal opportunities for all to react, without the inactivation termination step obtained in most addition polymerizations. The situation causes the formation of a considerably narrower molecular weight distribution than usual.

Assuming that the molecular weight of the initiating molecule is close to that of the propagating molecule, and that there is an excess of propagating monomer so that its concentration does not significantly change during the polymerization, the weight-fraction distribution is given by[21]

$$W_x = \frac{1}{1 + kt} \cdot \frac{ne^{-kt}(kt)^{n-1}}{(n - 1)!} \tag{84}$$

where $n$ includes the initiator $(D)$ molecule, $k$ is a complex which includes the rate constant, and $kt$ is equivalent to the number of monomers reacted per initiator (or polymer) molecule.

The average degrees of polymerization are given by

$$\overline{DP}_n = 1 + kt \tag{85}$$

and

$$\overline{DP}_w = 1 + kt + \frac{kt}{1 + kt} \tag{86}$$

Since

$$\frac{\overline{DP}_w}{\overline{DP}_n} = 1 + \frac{kt}{(1 + kt)^2} \tag{87}$$

it can be seen that as $t \rightarrow \infty$, the ratio of $\overline{DP}_w$ to $\overline{DP}_n$ approaches unity, indicating a very sharp distribution of molecular weights.

[21] Dostal, H. and Mark, H., Z. physik. Chem., **B29**, 299 (1935); Flory, P. J., J. Am. Chem. Soc., **62**, 1561 (1940).

In an addition polymerization, an individual polymer molecule may be formed in as little time as $10^{-6}$ to $10^{-2}$ second. The total amount of polymer formed is a function of time, but the molecular weight of the polymer is not, since addition polymers of the bifunctional type do not interact with one another. An addition polymerization system, therefore, contains monomers and polymers at all stages of the process.

The expressions for molecular weight distributions for vinyl polymers are considerably more complex than those for condensation products. The various possibilities for initiation and for termination complicate the problem greatly, and each order of initiation and termination will change the shape of the distribution curve. Kinetic, rather than statistical, analyses are almost invariably used, and relationships between molecular weights, degrees of polymerization, and molecular weight distributions are worked out analytically for individual cases, after the necessary simplifying assumptions are made. To illustrate the general technique, the two relatively simple reactions given in Chapter 3 will be used to obtain expressions for the degrees of polymerization and molecular weight distributions.

It may be recalled that the relationship between $n$-mer concentration and monomer concentration for an uncatalyzed bimolecular initiation reaction, in which transfer reactions were assumed not to occur and termination was by disproportionation only, was (Eq. 45, Chap. 3)

$$M_n = \frac{\gamma^{n-2}}{(1 + \gamma)^n}(M_o - M)$$

The weight-fraction, $W_x$, of $n$-mer is then given by

$$W_x = \frac{nM_n m_o}{(M_o - M)m_o} = \frac{n\gamma^{n-2}}{(1 + \gamma)^n} \tag{88}$$

where $M_o$ is the initial monomer concentration, $m_o$ the molecular weight of a mesomer, $(M_o - M)$ the concentration of all polymer at any monomer concentration, $M$, and $\gamma = \frac{k_p}{(k_i k_d)^{1/2}}$. Note that the distribution of molecular weights applies only to the polymer and does not include unreacted monomer, since $(M_o - M)m_o$ is the total weight of all polymers only.

The weight- and number-average chain lengths, $\nu_w$ and $\nu_n$, respectively, have also been derived:[22]

[22] Bawn, C. E. H., "The Chemistry of High Polymers," pp. 79 ff., Butterworths, London (dist. by Interscience Publishers, New York), 1948.

$$\nu_w = 2\gamma = \frac{2k_p}{(k_i k_d)^{1/2}} \tag{89}$$

and

$$\nu_n = \gamma = \frac{k_p}{(k_i k_d)^{1/2}} \tag{90}$$

Note that, in this particular case, the weight-average is twice that of the number-average chain length and that both are independent of the initial monomer concentration and of the extent of reaction.

In the example of an uncatalyzed bimolecular initiation with monomer only present and termination by coupling exclusively (Eq. 47, Chap. 3),

$$M_n = \frac{n-1}{2} \cdot \frac{\gamma^{n-3}}{(1+\gamma)^n}(M_o - M)$$

The expression for the weight-fraction of $n$-mer is, of course,

$$W_x = \frac{n-1}{2} \cdot \frac{n\gamma^{n-3}}{(1+\gamma)^n} \tag{91}$$

However, the average chain lengths are now

$$\nu_w = 3\gamma \tag{92}$$

$$\nu_n = 2\gamma \tag{93}$$

Again, the average chain length is independent of the monomer concentration, but, for this mechanism, the weight-average chain length is only 1.5 times the number-average.

As previously pointed out, the above two cases are relatively simple ones in which the initiation was second order with respect to monomer concentration, and termination was either by disproportionation or coupling of two activated polymers. Initiation may also occur by a zero- or first-order process, and termination other than by mutual destruction of activated polymer chains is also possible. The distribution of molecular weights may be worked out theoretically for these by procedures similar to the preceding ones; they will, however, usually not be simple expressions. In all cases, two simplifying assumptions are invariably made: (1) The rate constant of propagation is independent of molecular size, and (2) the stationary state method is applicable; i.e., $v_i = v_t$. This latter assumption generally holds for reactions in which the average life of activated molecules is very short compared with the average half-life of the total reaction.

### MEASUREMENT OF POLYMER PROPERTIES

In addition to characterizing a polymer by a description of its molecular weight and its molecular weight distribution, the material itself can be subjected to a variety of mechanical, thermal, permanence, optical, electrical, and chemical tests. This phase of the polymer industry is unusually complex because of the many factors which affect the ultimate physical characteristics of the materials. The proper choice of a polymer for a particular application requires a considerable amount of experimentation and study. One of the chief concerns of the polymer industry is to summarize and correlate the physical data. Particularly of interest is the finding of any correlation between physical characteristics and chemical structure. The problem has many ramifications, but a sufficient number of correlations have been obtained to permit their use in prediction of behavior in other applications.

Since the selection of a polymer for a specific use is largely based upon its particular physical and chemical properties, many standards by which polymers, especially plastics, can be compared with one another and with other materials have been established. Among the most important are:

1. Mechanical tests. Weight, tensile strength, compressive strength, elongation, modulus of elasticity, impact resistance, flexural strength, hardness, elastic properties.

2. Thermal tests. Thermal conductivity, specific heat, heat distortion temperature, continuous heat resistance, flammability, thermal expansion.

3. Electrical tests. Dielectric constant, dielectric strength, power factor, volume resistivity, surface resistivity, arc resistance.

4. Optical tests. Colorability, refractive index, light transmission, light scattering, light fastness.

5. Chemical tests. Solubility, chemical resistance, elemental analysis, saponification number, acid number, acetyl number, spot tests, fluorescence analysis, solids determination, water determination.

6. Permanence tests. Corrosion resistance, weather resistance, oil resistance, resistance to chemical agents, heat and light degradation, aging.

7. Physiological tests.

A discussion of the properties of polymers correlated with their uses will be deferred to Chapter 12. Of concern here are the various tests used to characterize polymers, which may be called technical tests, inasmuch as these are used to determine the specifications of a particular polymeric substance for use in various industrial applications.

MECHANICAL PROPERTIES

**Weight**

The weight of a polymeric material is normally expressed by its specific gravity. This, of course, is the ratio of the weight of a given volume of material to that of another substance, usually water, under the same environmental conditions. Polymeric substances, being generally organic, are relatively light materials and thus are of particular interest in the production of airplane parts and for other applications where light weight is an advantage. In general, most polymeric substances are appreciably lighter than other commonly used structural materials.

As expected, the values of unit weight depend upon the chemical type being investigated and upon the relative proportions and individual specific gravities if a mixture is involved. In the latter case, knowledge of the specific gravity and percentage composition of each component makes it possible to calculate the specific gravity of the finished product since the effects are additive.

Of particular importance in the consideration of polymer weights as compared to those of metals are the comparative values of strength per unit weight. The combined characteristics of high strength and low weight have made plastic materials extremely useful in many fields.

**Tensile Strength**

Tensile strength is one of the most commonly measured physical properties. It may be defined as the stress necessary to stretch a strip of the material being tested to its breaking point. The value representing this property is expressed in pounds per square inch of original cross-sectional area. Fig. 4-6 illustrates the comparative tensile strengths of some common plastic materials.

These values indicate the range of strengths which may be produced in the field of polymers. For comparison, the tensile strengths of aluminum and steel are 30,000 to 40,000 and 80,000 to 330,000 psi, respectively. The actual results obtained depend, however, upon many other factors. For example, by compounding, the tensile strength may be enhanced by incorporating relatively large amounts of filler with small amounts of plasticizer. In addition, the nature of both the filler and the plasticizer will influence the properties. The optimum amounts of filler and plasticizer incorporated for any particular use must be determined experimentally.

Tensile strength values may also be altered by proper physical processing of the compounded plastic. The milling of raw rubber produces a tremendous change in the physical properties of the crude material. The method used for molding, or the choice of casting or laminating in preference to molding, will also result in changes in tensile strength. In addition, physical processing after fabrication may cause a variation in tensile strength. For example, the strength of extruded synthetic fibers may be increased substantially by stretching or "cold drawing."

Chemical considerations, as average chain length, degree of branching or cross-linking, and the nature of chemical groups present will also affect

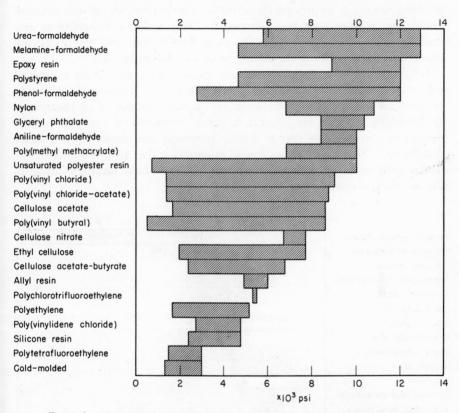

Fig. 4-6. Comparative tensile strength ranges of selected plastics at 73°F

the tensile strength. No general rule may be stated other than that the tensile strength increases with the average molecular weight, finally reaching a maximum, leveling off, then decreasing slightly (see Chap. 10). In the case of linear polymers, the tensile strengths are high because the kinked or curled macromolecular chains can stretch out and straighten. Linear molecules may also slip past each other slightly; thus, during the stretching operation, the groups responsible for secondary valence forces may become aligned and thus increase the tensile strength. If a high degree of cross-linking exists in a polymeric structure, the material cannot be stretched to any great extent, but the tensile strength is generally high. For example, a phenol-formaldehyde resin which has been thermoset has a high tensile strength but low elongation.

### Elongation

The increase in length of a measured plastic strip, when stretched to the breaking point, is expressed in terms of the percentage of the original length and is known as the elongation. The values of elongation and tensile strength are obtained in the same experiment and are of mutual importance in expressing the behavior of a plastic substance.

Tensile strength and elongation are measured by stretching a marked sample at a uniform rate of speed. The elongation is observed by noting the increase in the distance between two parallel marks on the sample at the breaking point. In general, whereas cross-linked types have low elongation values, the simple linear polymers are capable of greater elongation. This property of linear polymers is due to unkinking of the chains with resultant elongation and movement of the chains relative to one another, as mentioned previously.

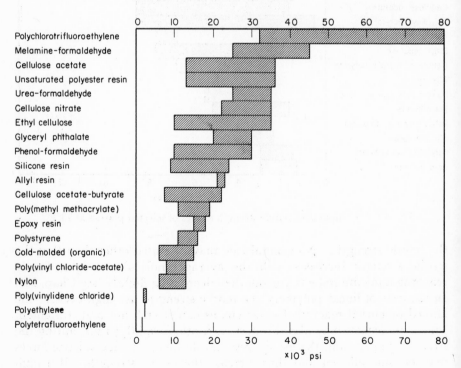

Fig. 4-7.  Comparative compressive strength ranges of selected plastics at 73°F

## Compressive Strength

This property is allied to the tensile strength, but, as the name implies, it is determined by compression rather than by stretching. It is the compression load in pounds at the breaking point divided by the cross-sectional area of resisting surface. The compressive strengths of typical plastics are shown in Fig. 4-7.

## Impact Resistance

Impact resistance is the ability of a material to withstand a rapidly applied load. Resistance of a polymer to sudden shock or impact is a necessary condition for many applications. Measurements are usually made by either the Izod or the Charpy method. These are similar in that they compare the free swing of a pendulum and the swing involved in breaking a notched test specimen of the plastic material. The difference in height to which the pendulum rises when swinging freely and after breaking the test strip is a measure of the energy absorbed in the rupture. The values are expressed in foot-pounds per inch of notch. In the Charpy

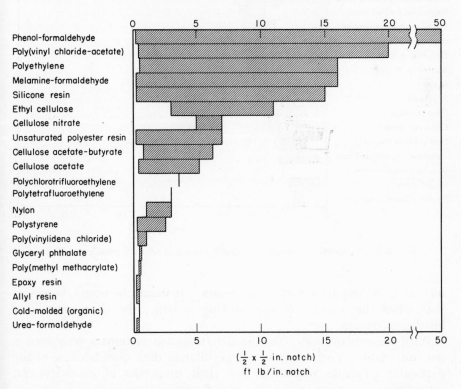

FIG. 4-8. Comparative impact strengths (Izod) of selected plastics at 73°F

method, the notched bar which is to be tested is held horizontally by supports between which the pendulum swings.   In the Izod method, the notched bar is held vertically and is supported at the bottom.   Some approximate ranges of impact resistance for several plastic materials are shown in Fig. 4-8.

The close correlation of physical data with chemical structure is difficult here because of the many other variables which may alter the values.   In general, low-molecular-weight polymers of straight chain or cross-linked type are brittle and have poor impact resistance.   As the molecular size

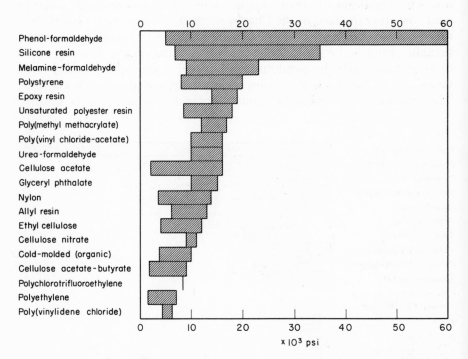

Fig. 4-9.   Comparative flexural strength ranges of selected plastics at 73°F

increases, the impact resistance increases.   It should be noted, however, that when the amount of cross-linking is large, the characteristic of brittleness returns.

With elastomeric materials, the determination of impact resistance is not important.   Their resiliency is peculiar in their class because of the particular structure responsible for their properties of elasticity and extensibility.

## Flexural Strength

Flexural strength, or modulus of rupture, is a measure of the resistance to breaking of a strip as it is bent across its main axis. The property may be measured by determination of the force necessary to cause rupture of a horizontally supported bar. Such variables as rate of deflection, bar measurements, deflections produced, and distance between supports are recorded.

A property often correlated with the flexural strength is fatigue strength resistance, which is determined by measurement of resistance of the plastic to repeated flexing through a known arc.

The values of both flexural strength and fatigue strength resistance are subject to the same types of chemical considerations and physical variations as those which have already been discussed. In general, as the impact resistance increases, the flexural strength also increases. Flexural strength normally will be found to depend upon the macromolecular size and amount of cross-linking of the polymer chains. Long linear chains with accompanying free movement of the macromolecules have a high degree of flexibility. Good fatigue resistance and relatively low flexing moduli result. When rigidity is introduced by excessive branching or cross-linkage, higher moduli and decreased susceptibility to continual flexing are usually obtained.

## Elastic and Plastic Properties

The deformation of a plastic body is composed of two types: elastic and plastic. The former is the principal effect up to a certain stress value which is known as the proportional limit. The proportional limit may be described as the stress above which Hooke's law fails or as the value below which the deformation corresponds to that expected of a perfectly elastic body.

The modulus of elasticity is a measure of the stiffness or rigidity of a material. It can be defined as the load per unit area required to give unit deformation. The modulus of elasticity is measured only within the range of the proportional limit of the substance concerned. For a truly elastic material, Hooke's law states that the stress is proportional to the strain:

$$E = \frac{s \cdot l}{\Delta l} \tag{94}$$

where $E$ is the modulus of elasticity, $s$ the stress applied, $l$ the length of sample, and $\Delta l$ the increase in length; the resultant stress-strain diagram will be a straight line.

Most thermoplastics do not obey this law very closely as they deform permanently under applied loads and continue to deform with time. As has been pointed out in Chapter 3, there is a gradual variation in the value of the modulus of elasticity and other mechanical properties among polymers which causes each polymeric substance to be most useful under specified conditions as an elastomer, plastic, or fiber.

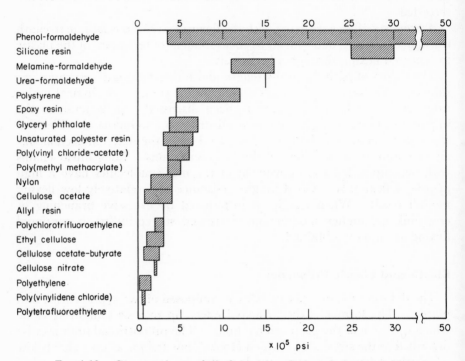

FIG. 4-10.   Comparative moduli of elasticity of selected plastics at 73°F

Certain terms are used to express the types and results of plastic deformation.   The distortion under stress may be classified as either *cold flow* or *creep*.   The former describes a continuous, *constant-rate* deformation at normal temperatures under small stresses.   Creep is also caused by relatively low stresses applied continuously; however, the *rate* of deformation in this case *may change* with time and extensibility of the plastic.   For this test, constant stress is desirable but means for applying a constant load is easier and more common.   Creep is a very slow-speed test compared with tensile strength tests which have a medium velocity and impact tests which have a high velocity.

When small stresses are applied for a long period of time, the plastic deformation becomes greater than when the stress is applied for a short period of time. A temperature increase will lower the value of the elastic limit and will markedly increase the plastic flow.

The result of the distortion involved in plastic deformation is expressed in terms of the amount of distortion (in per cent of original dimensions) which is not recoverable in a specified period of time. This is known as *permanent set*.

## Hardness

Hardness may be divided into two types: resistance to indentation and resistance to abrasion. Both vary according to the ease with which the particles of solid material can be displaced. Scratching, scarring, or wearing by abrasion indicate that fine portions of the composite structure are being displaced. In practice, the effects of abrasion or poor hardness are often expressed in terms of wearing quality, weathering, and permanence of gloss. As might be expected, compounding and service conditions markedly alter the values of these properties.

The general field of amorphous matter may be divided, however, into materials of particularly poor hardness and those of improved hardness. If hardness is considered as merely resistance to penetration, the resinous bodies of relatively low molecular weight and substances of the phenol-formaldehyde or urea-formaldehyde type are particularly satisfactory. If, on the other hand, hardness is thought of as resistance to scratching, the same bodies of low molecular weight are considerably poorer than those of sufficient chain length and resiliency to be classed as elastomers. An increase in the length of the chain and an increase in the amount of cross-linkage cause an increase in this type of hardness.

Four common methods of measuring resistance to indentation are the following:

1. Shore hardness. This is an arbitrary value obtained by a gauge measurement of the resistance offered by the surface to penetration by a needle.

2. Diamond pyramid hardness. This is a value obtained by dividing the load applied to a square-based pyramidal diamond indenter by the surface area of the impression.

3. Brinell hardness. This value is obtained from the value of the force applied in pressing a standard steel ball into the surface of the material being tested, the area of the indentation, and the diameter of the ball.

4. Rockwell hardness. This value depends upon the degree of penetration of steel balls of various sizes when pressed upon the surface of the material undergoing test. Its value is obtained from the increase in depth of impression as the load is increased from a fixed minimum value to a higher value and then returned to the minimum value.

Two methods of measuring resistance to abrasion (mar resistance) are as follows:

1. Abraded spots are made by dropping a specific amount of abrasive (carborundum) through a tube of fixed length onto the sample which is held at an angle of 45° to the path of the abrasive. The gloss of the abraded spot is compared to the original gloss by means of a gloss meter.

2. Taber abrader. The sample is mounted on a turntable revolving at a constant rate. Abrading is done by an abrasive wheel, turning at a different fixed rate. The amount of abrasion is then determined by visual or optical means or by weight-loss measurement after a specified number of revolutions.

Abrasion resistance, brittleness, and the effects of heat play important parts in determining the particular machining operations to be used in the fabrication of polymeric substances.

THERMAL PROPERTIES

Even more than the simpler organic compounds, polymers are changed physically (and often chemically) by heat. Variations in heat conduction and heat absorption are important factors in the commercial utilization of certain plastics.

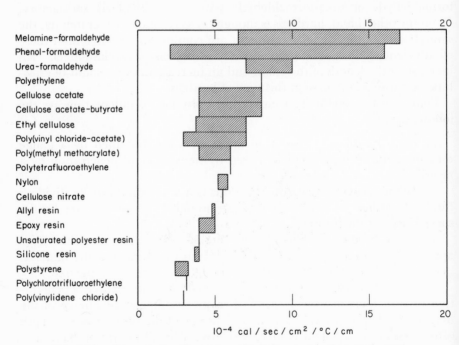

FIG. 4-11. Comparative thermal conductivity ranges of selected plastics

## Thermal Conductivity

This property may be defined as the time rate of transfer of heat through unit thickness and area when exposed to a unit temperature gradient. By reference of the unknown to a standard, the measurements may be determined when the temperature gradients at equilibrium are known.

As a general rule, polymeric substances exhibit low heat conductivities. In some cases, these low values cause the substances to be very desirable for certain applications and, in others, render the materials unfit for use. Low thermal conductivity is particularly unfavorable in the processing of certain plastic materials. Certain chemical and physical changes are brought about in mechanical applications by subjecting the material to heat and pressure. When heat conduction is poor, it is difficult to obtain a uniform product. A knowledge of the thermal characteristics of a polymer is essential for an accurate prediction of the best processing procedure. A relative comparison of the heat conductivities of some common polymers is shown in Fig. 4-11.

## Specific Heat

The specific heat (in calories) of a substance is the amount of heat necessary to raise the temperature of one gram of the substance 1°C. The specific heats of plastic materials are in general appreciably higher than those of metals. It is obvious that the lower the specific heat of a material, the lower the heating costs when it is subjected to a molding process.

TABLE 4-4. SPECIFIC HEATS OF SELECTED PLASTICS

*cal/°C/gm*

| | |
|---|---|
| Silicone resin | 1.3 |
| Ethyl cellulose | 0.3–0.75 |
| Polyethylene | 0.55 |
| Allyl resin | 0.26–0.55 |
| Cellulose acetate | 0.3–0.5 |
| Poly(vinyl chloride-acetate) | 0.2–0.5 |
| Phenol-formaldehyde | 0.28–0.42 |
| Cellulose acetate-butyrate | 0.3–0.4 |
| Cellulose nitrate | 0.3–0.4 |
| Nylon | 0.4 |
| Urea-formaldehyde | 0.4 |
| Poly(methyl methacrylate) | 0.35 |
| Polystyrene | 0.32 |
| Poly(vinylidene chloride) | 0.32 |
| Polytetrafluoroethylene | 0.25 |
| Polychlorotrifluoroethylene | 0.22 |

## Heat Distortion Temperature

The behavior of plastic substances with respect to the characteristic of heat distortion is the basis used for the division of these materials into two

groups: *thermoplastic* and *thermosetting*. As the names imply, the former
exhibits the property of softening with heat, and the latter hardens or
cures permanently when heat is applied. During the hardening process of
a thermosetting resin, the heat causes chemical changes which result in the
formation of a compact, cross-linked system. The lack of free functional
groups in thermoplastic linear polymers prevents further chemical action
when heat is applied and this type remains permanently plastic.

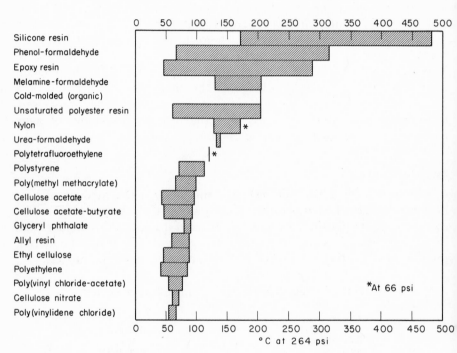

Fig. 4-12. Comparative heat distortion temperature ranges of selected plastics

The effect of heat upon the usefulness of a plastic body depends, therefore, principally on the type of plastic used. In the case of thermoplastics, the softening temperature may be used to represent the highest
practical service temperature, even when no stress is involved. The heat
distortion temperature is specified as the lowest temperature at which a
material being tested (of specific dimensions) yields a specified distance
under a specified loading. Generally, relatively low values are obtained
with thermoplastics, while higher values are found in the case of thermosetting materials. The approximate heat distortion temperatures of some
representative polymers are shown in Fig. 4-12.

## Continuous Heat Resistance

Of great importance in predicting the serviceability of thermosetting types of materials is the value of continuous heat resistance.  This value, also known as the maximum continuous operating temperature, is the maximum temperature at which the sample does not change its form, appearance, or color a specified amount under a specified stress.  This value is the best criterion available of how well the finished plastic will withstand elevated temperatures under actual operating conditions.

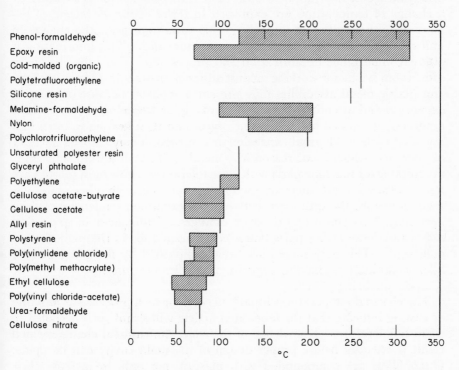

Fig. 4-13.  Comparative continuous heat resistance ranges of selected plastics

Although thermosetting resins do not appreciably soften with heat, excessive or prolonged heat treatment will result in overhardening, contraction, charring, or disintegration.

## Flammability

Certain polymeric substances, for example, cellulose nitrate, show great flammability while others, such as the phenolics, burn with difficulty or not at all.  The compact thermosetting types usually fall in the latter category, while the linear polymers differ from one another according to the nature and arrangement of the atoms present. For example, polymers which contain a high proportion of chlorine in the molecule show reduced flammability. Obviously, a low degree of flammability is usually desirable.

## Thermal Expansion

The high thermal expansion and shrinkage of plastics is often a major disadvantage in their applications. The dimensional changes caused by a change of temperature are expressed in terms of the coefficient of expansion (either linear or cubical). This value represents the change in unit dimensions caused by a unit temperature rise. This information is of great importance in fabrication and processing. Thus, the change in dimensions is a factor working against adhesion of organic surface coatings, and plastic-metal assemblies may present a problem because of unequal expansion and attendant buckling, cracking, or loosening. Plastic parts are frequently tested by chilling the object and then heating it, often in a repeated cycle. Thermal expansion or contraction may throw a part out of tolerance, which is one reason why metals, with their lower coefficients, are suitable for machine parts with close tolerances where most plastics are not. Also, when polymers are used in combination with other materials, such as metals, the difference between the expansion tendencies of each necessitates certain precautions or changes. Differences in expansion may cause loose fitting parts unless compensated for in the manufacture or design. This may sometimes be accomplished by designing plastic-filler combinations having expansion coefficients intermediate to the components being joined.

The elevated temperatures usually needed for such processes as molding or casting indicate that the fabricated article will shrink as it is cooled to room temperature. Knowledge of the exact dimensional changes which result is essential before proper design of the mold cavity can be made. Often fillers are compounded with plastics, not only to increase their strength, but simply because this addition often reduces the coefficient of expansion.

## ELECTRICAL PROPERTIES

Although plastics, in general, have been found to possess excellent insulating characteristics, care must be used in making and compounding them for use as insulators. It is imperative to exclude all moisture from the substances. As a rule, those plastics which have the greatest resistance to moisture also show the highest degree of usefulness as insulators. A careful selection of compounding agents (fillers, plasticizers, lubricants) is necessary, for these added compounds almost always detract from the optimum electrical properties which can be obtained with the polymer alone.

### Dielectric Constant

In an insulator, if a constant electrical force is suddenly applied, there is a restricted displacement of bound charges but no flow.    The amount of displacement increases with increase of potential.    Upon removal of the field, the charges spring back to their original equilibrium positions.    The displacement or charging effect is quantitatively measured by the dielectric constant.    Thus, the dielectric constant is a measure of the ability of a

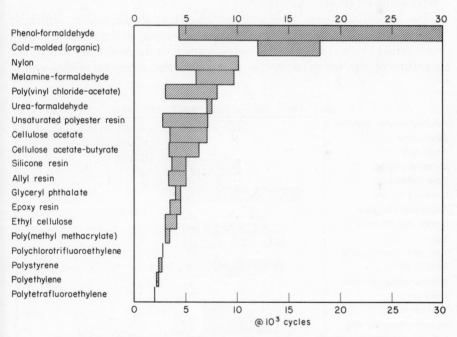

Fig. 4-14.    Comparative dielectric constant ranges of selected plastics

material to store electrostatic field energy in the presence of an electrical field.    It may be defined as the ratio of the electrical capacity of a capacitor using the material under test as a dielectric to the capacity of the same capacitor using a vacuum or air as the dielectric.

The value of the dielectric constant shows a marked variation with change in electrical frequency.    So far as correlation with chemical structure is concerned, it is found that materials of polar nature have much higher dielectric constants than those of nonpolar nature.    In general, the lower the dielectric constant, the better is the material as a dielectric for high-frequency electrical transmission applications.    On the other hand, the higher the dielectric constant, the greater is the electrostatic capacity of a given capacitor using the material as the dielectric.

### Dielectric Strength

The dielectric strength of a material (not to be confused with the dielectric constant) is measured by the electrical field strength which must be applied to cause an arc or spark discharge through the body of the material.    Stated otherwise, values of this property represent the specific resistance of a material to an increasing voltage which may be applied either stepwise or continuously.

The electrical stress produces an electrical displacement which is proportional to the stress and the dielectric constant of the material, up to some critical value; beyond this value, known as the *breakdown voltage*, the structure of the material breaks down and the electrical displacement

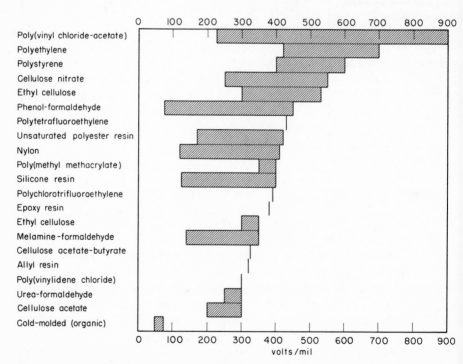

FIG. 4-15.  Comparative dielectric strength ranges of selected plastics.  Step-by-step—⅛in.

increases rapidly.    The dielectric strength is determined from measurements of the thickness of the material and the breakdown voltage and is usually expressed in volts per mil (0.001 inch) of thickness.

The behavior of a material subjected to such a test is somewhat analogous to that of a solid when it is mechanically stressed up to and beyond its yield point.    The breakdown voltage, like the yield stress, is not constant but varies with the conditions of the test.    Thus, the electrical intensity required to cause breakdown varies with such factors as duration and rate of application of voltage, thickness of specimen, frequency of applied voltage, temperature, size and shape of electrodes, and nature of surrounding medium.

## Power Factor

The volt-amperes in an alternating circuit are frequently greater than the watts input, due to inductive or capacitive effects.    The ratio of the power in watts, in a capacitor in which the material under test is the dielectric, to volt-amperes, known as the power factor, is equal to the cos $\theta$, where $\theta$ is the angular phase difference between voltage and current.

Less technically, the power factor represents the amount of power absorbed by an insulating medium from an alternating current field.    For a perfect insulator, there would be no power loss; i.e., no power would be absorbed by the material.    Polystyrene, polyethylene (and quartz) approach the zero value closely, but variations in temperature, moisture content, compounding agents, and electrical frequency cause variations in the power factor.    This property is of great importance in the application of plastics in communications work, since the power factor is a measure of that portion of the energy input which is dissipated as heat and thus is not recoverable.

## Surface Resistivity

Surface resistivity is measured by the resistance between two line electrodes of specified length and distance apart on the surface of a dielectric material.    The resistance is directly proportional to the distance between the electrodes and inversely proportional to their length.

Since electricity is carried along the surface of an insulator as well as through the interior, the effect of humidity on porous insulators is largely the result of the surface conductivity of the pores.    An important factor is whether a *continuous* film of moisture forms readily on the surface of the insulator.    The formation of such a film is determined by the ease with which water wets the surface.    Only hydrocarbon-type (nonpolar) polymers and silicones successfully resist the formation of a continuous film on a clean surface. For this reason, it is customary to coat the surfaces of ceramic insulators with a water-repellent substance, such as a wax, polystyrene, or a silicone. Moisture condenses on such a surface as discrete droplets. Formation of a silicone film *in situ* has been found to be particularly valuable for insulators of the above type.

### Arc Resistance

This test refers to the resistance of the surface of a plastic strip to the passage of an electric arc. In most cases the tendency of organic polymers is to decompose with the formation of carbon tracks. Thus, most polymers have poor arc resistance. In testing arc resistance, point electrodes

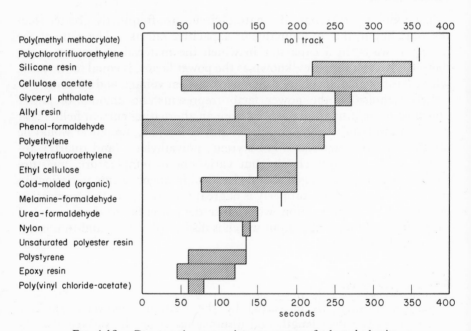

FIG. 4-16. Comparative arc resistance ranges of selected plastics

are placed on two points on the same surface of the insulator. An arc is then passed between the electrodes. The arc first passes through the air, but with time or as the current is increased, the material eventually breaks down and the arc travels along its surface. The length of time is usually measured in seconds and is known as the arc resistance. Polytetrafluoroethylene, urea and melamine resins, and polyacrylates have comparatively good arc resistances.

## Volume Resistivity

In addition to their other electrical characteristics, polymers are valuable because of their general resistance to the passage of an electrical current through them. The volume resistivity is the reciprocal of the current which will pass between electrodes on opposite faces of a unit cube of a material when unit potential gradient exists between the electrodes, or, to put it more simply, is the resistance between opposite faces of a one-centimeter cube. The resistivity of a good insulator should be about $10^{16}$ ohm-cm. Polystyrene has a resistivity of $10^{18}$ to $10^{21}$ ohm-cm, which is excellent. All commercial insulators have imperfections which allow the

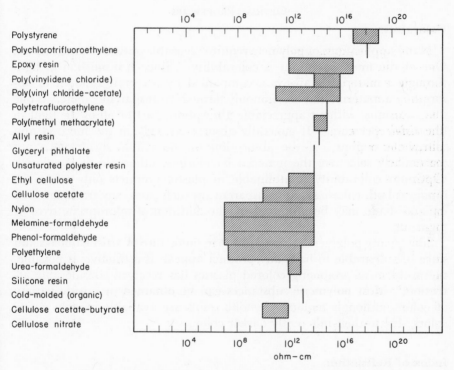

FIG. 4-17. Comparative volume resistivity ranges of selected plastics

material to pass some current when a voltage is applied. These imperfections may be conducting paths, impurities, or crystal-lattice irregularities. Ionic or metallic impurities, particularly in the presence of moisture, appreciably increase the conductivity of an insulator.

Organic polymeric products are less subject to conduction caused by imperfections than are ceramic insulators because their structures are less porous, their plastic nature makes them more resistant to mechanical shock, and their ionic or metallic impurity content is easier to control. Thus, they are superior insulators except at high temperatures and for applications requiring great strength and dimensional stability where ceramic or other materials excel. It is of interest to note that, whereas the resistivity of metals increases linearly with increase in temperature, the resistivity of insulators decreases exponentially.

Volume and surface resistivity measurements are often used to check the uniformity of an insulating material, either to determine the uniformity of processing or to detect trace impurities which affect the quality of the material.

## OPTICAL PROPERTIES

### Colorability

Many applications of polymers require favorable optical characteristics. One of the most important is colorability. Since transmission of light through a material is always accompanied by a certain amount of absorption, a material that is commonly termed "transparent" merely is one that transmits, without appreciable absorption, part or all of the light in the *visible* spectrum. It generally absorbs strongly in the infrared and ultraviolet regions. If the absorption in the visible spectrum is not particularly selective, the material is colorless; otherwise, it is colored. Optimum colorability is attainable in plastic products only when the binder is both colorless and transparent; in such cases, any transparent or opaque shade may be produced by the addition of appropriate dyes or pigments.

Since many polymers are used in the manufacture of artistic objects and since it is desirable to have any product appear as attractive as possible, the problem of producing colored plastics has received considerable attention. Most polymeric substances can be obtained in a wide variety of colors, although molded phenolic resins are available in only a few colors, due to their inherently darker color.

### Index of Refraction

This property is defined as the ratio of the velocity of light in a vacuum (or, often, air) to its velocity in the material being tested. Since direct measurement of the velocity of light in a material is experimentally difficult, the index of refraction is alternatively measured by determining the ratio of the sine of the angle of incidence to the sine of the angle of refraction.

$$n = \frac{\sin i}{\sin r} \qquad (95)$$

The index of refraction is of value for the identification of certain plastics, for the construction of plastic lenses, and for the determination of the reflection of light by plastic materials.

## Light Transmission

The transparency of plastics is measured by determining the fraction of incident light which is transmitted by the plastic. The value is expressed as the percentage of incident light transmitted as measured by a photoelectric cell or by other photometric techniques. Certain polymers, such as poly(methyl methacrylate) and polystyrene, exhibit particularly high values (more than 90 per cent).

## Light Diffusion

Plastics which cause diffusion of the incident light are suitable for a variety of uses in the lighting and decorative industries. Determinations are made by measurements of diffused light by a photoelectric cell held at various angles to the surface of the sample being tested (goniophotometer). Properly compounded urea-formaldehyde plastics make particularly good diffuse reflectors.

TABLE 4-5. OPTICAL PROPERTIES OF SOME TRANSPARENT PLASTICS[23]

| Transparent Plastics | $n_D$ Average | Aging Characteristics (Transparency Before and After Long-time Exposure to "Normal" Light and Atmosphere) | | | |
|---|---|---|---|---|---|
| | | Light Transmission % | | Haze Value† % | |
| | | Origi- nally | After a Year | Origi- nally | After a Year |
| Cellulose acetate-butyrate | 1.47 | 89 | 89 | 8 | 8 |
| Ethyl cellulose | 1.47 | 89 | Very low | 5–12 | Very high |
| Poly(vinyl butyral) | 1.48 | 71 | 10 | 5 | 99 |
| Poly(methyl methacrylate) | 1.49 | 94 | 93 | 2 | 3 |
| Cellulose acetate | 1.49 | 87 | 80 | 5 | 8–28 |
| Allyl resin | 1.50 | 92 | 91 | 2 | |
| Cellulose nitrate | 1.50 | 88 | 38 | 5 | 97 |
| Poly(vinyl chloride-acetate) | 1.52 | 83 | 83 | 7 | 7 |
| Plate glass | 1.52 | Aging effects are slight | | | |
| Polystyrene | 1.60 | 90 | | | |
| Cast phenolic | 1.60 | 85 | | | |
| Diamond | 2.42 | Aging has no effect | | | |

† Haze value is the fraction of light scattered by diffusion. A perfectly transparent material would have a light transmission of 100 per cent and a haze value of zero.

[23] Adapted from Schmidt, A. X. and Marlies, C. A., *Principles of High-Polymer Theory and Practice*, Table 10-5, p. 459, McGraw-Hill Book Co., New York, 1948.

**Light Fastness**

Another desirable property of both colored and colorless plastic articles is a high resistance to color change on aging or exposure to heat and light. This is termed "light fastness" and is often a difficult property to obtain. Poor color retention may be due to instability of the polymer itself or of the dyes and pigments used to impart the color. Many polymers tend to turn yellow or dark upon aging and exposure to heat and light; many dyes and pigments, especially the organic ones, darken, change color, or lose color intensity (saturation) under similar circumstances. A common test is to expose the sample to ultraviolet light or sunlight for a specified length of time and measure the change in color by visual means or by tri-stimulus colorimetry.

CHEMICAL PROPERTIES

**Solubility**

Molecular weights and solubilities of polymeric molecules are so closely related that one cannot be discussed without reference to the other. Three generalizations concerning the solubility of polymers may be summarized as follows:

1. The most general solubility rule in the field of organic chemistry, namely, that a solute is more soluble in a solvent of similar chemical structure, also holds in the case of polymers.

2. Molecules of higher molecular weight are less soluble than analogous polymers of lower molecular weight.

3. The solubility of polymeric chains decreases as the amount of branching increases and drops very rapidly with the introduction of cross-linkages.

The first of these solubility generalizations has been expressed by the simple phrase: like dissolves like. For example, poly(vinyl alcohol) contains a high proportion of hydroxyl groups, hence is soluble in water and low-molecular-weight alcohols; it is insoluble in hydrocarbon solvents. On the other hand, polystyrene is a pure hydrocarbon and is insoluble in such solvents as water and alcohol; it is soluble in hydrocarbon solvents, such as benzene and toluene. This rule is also of importance in selecting the proper type of plasticizer for use with a given polymer, for in this case, also, mutual compatibility is desired.

The relationship of solubility to molecular weight is in accord with the facts observed in the study of simpler organic compounds. As the molecular weight increases, the solubility decreases and the resistance to solvation increases. Furthermore, as the molecular size increases, the interference of each molecule with its neighbors increases, resulting in an increase in viscosity. A series of standard solutions of polymers of differing molecular weights but obtained from the same monomer show a rapid increase in viscosity as the molecular size increases. This relationship between viscosity and molecular weight is the basis of Staudinger's method of determining molecular weights of macromolecules, as was pointed out previously.

The third generalization concerning the solubility of polymers is that solubility decreases with increasing branching and that cross-linked polymers tend to become insoluble. Branching may be so extensive that the branched polymer may closely resemble a cross-linked polymer and have similar properties. When a small amount of polyfunctional reactant is copolymerized with a difunctional reactant, the solubility of the resulting product is invariably less than that from the pure difunctional reactant. Thus, it appears likely that the solubility of a linear polymer is the result of separation of the bundles of chains into single chains by the solvent, which reduces the attractive forces (secondary valences) existing between neighboring chains (see Chap. 10). However, when the binding force between these chains consists of primary valence linkages, separation is impossible, the polymer is insoluble, and the degree of solvation (swelling) is dependent upon the amount of cross-linking present.

### Resistance to Chemicals

The ability to resist the action of various chemicals is of utmost importance in many applications of polymers. Certain generalizations for predicting the behavior may serve as a guide.

First, the presence of any group in the resin or plastic which may be readily attacked will, of course, materially reduce its resistance.

Second, as is well known, the more unsaturation a molecule contains, the more susceptible it is to oxidation. Natural rubber (polyisoprene) has a considerable number of double bonds per macromolecule, hence is easily destroyed by the action of ozone. Polyisobutylene, on the other hand, containing little or no unsaturation, is very resistant.

Third, the effect produced by increasing either the molecular size or the amount of cross-linking in the molecule is comparable to that which would be expected from a discussion of solubility. In both cases the product becomes more resistant to the action of chemicals.

### Qualitative and Quantitative Analyses

Many other chemical tests are often made on polymers. Qualitative analysis may include elemental analysis, spot tests, and fluorescence analysis. Quantitative tests include saponification number, acid number, acetyl number, solids determination, and moisture or water determination.

A discussion of these is beyond the scope of this book; however, students of chemistry and engineering will be familiar with most of these tests.

## Permanence Tests

These tests are designed to show the lasting ability or permanence of the article. The tests may be designed to show the effects of time (aging), light, weather, moisture, and stability under fabricating conditions. They may also reveal the resistance of the material to cracking (dimensional stability) or crazing (chemical stability) under conditions of use or with time.

## Physiological Tests

A consideration in the evaluation of polymeric substances which may not come to mind immediately is the suitability of the material for use in contact with the human body. Eyeglass frames and contact lenses, dentures, and clothing made from modified natural and synthetic fibers must have physiologically harmless properties. Resins and plasticizers used in enamels for food containers and children's toys must be carefully tested before they may be put on the market. These tests are usually conducted by a biological laboratory on animals; it is usually assumed that the results hold true for humans.

### REFERENCES AND RECOMMENDED READING

Barron, H., *Modern Plastics*, John Wiley and Sons, New York, 1945.

Bawn, C. E. H., *The Chemistry of High Polymers*, Butterworths, London (dist. by Interscience Publishers, New York), 1948.

Billmeyer, F. W., Jr., *Textbook of Polymer Chemistry*, Interscience Publishers, New York, 1957.

Boundy, R. H. and Boyer, R. F., *Styrene*, Reinhold Publishing Corp., New York, 1952.

Bovey, F. A., Kolthoff, I. M., Medalia, A. I., and Meehan, E. J., *Emulsion Polymerization*, Interscience Publishers, New York, 1955.

Burk, R. E. and Grummitt, O., eds., *The Chemistry of Large Molecules*, Interscience Publishers, New York, 1943.

Burnett, G. M., *Mechanism of Polymer Reactions*, Interscience Publishers, New York, 1954.

D'Alelio, G. F., *Fundamental Principles of Polymerization*, John Wiley and Sons, New York, 1952.

Delmonte, J., *Plastics in Engineering*, 3rd ed., Penton Publishing Co., Cleveland, 1949.

Encyclopedia Issue, *Modern Plastics*, Plastics Catalogue Corp., Bristol, Conn., 1956.

Fleck, H. R., *Plastics*, 2nd ed., Chemical Publishing Co., Brooklyn, N.Y., 1949.

Flory, P. J., *Principles of Polymer Chemistry*, Cornell University Press, Ithaca, N.Y., 1953.

Frith, E. M. and Tuckett, R. F., *Linear Polymers*, Longmans, Green and Co., London-New York, 1951.

Groggins, P. H., ed., *Unit Processes in Organic Synthesis*, 4th ed., McGraw-Hill Book Co., New York, 1952.

Hill, R., ed., *Fibres from Synthetic Polymers*, Elsevier Publishing Co., Amsterdam (dist. by D. Van Nostrand Co., Princeton, N.J.), 1953.

Houwink, R., ed., *Elastomers and Plastomers*, Vols. I and III, Elsevier Publishing Co., Amsterdam (dist. by D. Van Nostrand Co., Princeton, N.J.), 1948–50.

Kraemer, E. O., ed., *Advances in Colloid Science*, Vol. I, Interscience Publishers, New York, 1942.

Langton, H. M., ed., *Synthetic Resins*, 3rd ed., Oxford University Press, London, 1951.

Mark, H. and Tobolsky, A. V., *Physical Chemistry of High Polymeric Systems*, 2nd ed., Interscience Publishers, New York, 1950.

Mark, H. and Whitby, G. S., eds., *Advances in Colloid Science*, Vol. II, Interscience Publishers, New York, 1946.

Mark, H. and Whitby, G. S., eds., *Collected Papers of Wallace Hume Carothers*, Interscience Publishers, New York, 1940.

Mason, J. P. and Manning, J. F., *The Technology of Plastics and Resins*, D. Van Nostrand Co., Princeton, N.J., 1945.

Meyer, K. H., *Natural and Synthetic High Polymers*, 2nd ed., Interscience Publishers, New York, 1950.

Richardson, H. M. and Wilson, J. W., eds., *Fundamentals of Plastics*, McGraw-Hill Book Co., New York, 1946.

Ritchie, P. D., *A Chemistry of Plastics and High Polymers*, Cleaver-Hume Press, London (dist. by Interscience Publishers, New York), 1949.

Schmidt, A. X. and Marlies, C. S., *Principles of High-Polymer Theory and Practice*, McGraw-Hill Book Co., New York, 1948.

Seymour, R. B. and Steiner, R. H., *Plastics for Corrosion Resistant Applications*, Reinhold Publishing Corp., New York, 1955.

Simonds, H. R., Weith, A. J., and Bigelow, M. H., *Handbook of Plastics*, 2nd ed., D. Van Nostrand Co., Princeton, N.J., 1949.

Society of the Plastics Industry, *Plastics Engineering Handbook*, 2nd ed., Reinhold Publishing Corp., New York, 1954.

Twiss, S. B., ed., *Advancing Fronts in Chemistry*, Vol. I, Reinhold Publishing Corp., New York, 1945.

## Chapter 5

# METHODS OF POLYMERIZATION

Theoretically, monomeric substances are capable of polymerizing in the gaseous, liquid, or solid phase. No high-molecular-weight polymer is known which remains stable under the drastic conditions necessary to maintain it in the gaseous state, although some polymer reactions are called gas-phase reactions, as the reactants and low-molecular-weight polymers initially formed may be present as gases. At the other extreme, while some solid-phase polymerizations are known, the rates of diffusion are so slow that the rate of polymerization is impracticably long. Practically speaking, therefore, almost all, if not all, commercial polymers may be said to be polymerized in the liquid phase.

It will be convenient to classify liquid-phase polymerizations into the following types:

| Homogeneous (initially) | Heterogeneous (initially) |
|---|---|
| Mass | Emulsion |
| Solution | Suspension |

## INITIALLY HOMOGENEOUS SYSTEMS

In all processes classified as homogeneous, there is only one phase present at the start of the reaction. There may or may not be more than one phase present during the polymerization process or at the end of polymerization.

### Mass Polymerization

Mass polymerization is also known as block, bulk, or cast polymerization. Here one phase exists because no solvent or dispersing medium is present. Frequently, the unreacted monomer acts as a solvent for the polymer and the polymer may also act as a solvent for the monomer; i.e., monomer and polymer are compatible. An example of this is the mass polymerization of styrene or methyl methacrylate wherein the viscosity of the liquid gradually increases until the whole mass solidifies into a clear, homogeneous mass. On the other hand, a monomeric substance may polymerize to produce a polymer which is incompatible with the monomer. In this case, two phases are present during the later stages of

130

the process. Polyacrylonitrile and poly(vinylidene chloride), for example, will precipitate as they are formed (above a minimum low molecular weight).

In both cases initiation obviously occurs in the monomer phase, as there is no other phase initially present. In the case of addition polymerizations, an initiating agent, such as an organic peroxide, is usually present. Condensation polymerizations normally do not require a catalyst; if one is used, it is usually a trace of acid. Whenever catalysts or initiators are used, they are soluble in the monomer. In the case in which an addition polymer is insoluble in its monomer, it is likely that propagation of polymerization occurs in the monomer-swollen precipitated polymer particles, because, for example, polyacrylonitrile is not soluble in its monomer, yet very high molecular weights may be obtained by the mass polymerization of acrylonitrile.

There are several desirable features to the mass method of polymerization. It is the simplest system known, as nothing is normally added to the reaction except catalyst or initiator, if used. In addition to the saving in materials needed for other processes, the lack of added materials means that there are no separation, purification, and recovery steps necessary after polymerization is complete. Further, the products obtained are, in general, in an inherently pure state. This, of course, is desirable, as the optical, electrical, and other properties are optimum.

Very infrequently are advantages obtainable from a process without concomitant disadvantages. Many polymerization reactions are highly exothermic. In most vinyl polymerizations, for example, from 20,000 to 30,000 calories per mole of monomer reacted are evolved. This means that the problems of heat removal and of maintaining a uniform temperature in the reaction mass become more difficult.

Further, in a system which is homogeneous throughout the process, the viscosity of the mass increases until solidification occurs. As a result, agitation of the mass to aid in heat removal and to maintain a uniform temperature becomes increasingly difficult and eventually impossible. At any rate, if agitation is used, heavy and powerful stirring equipment and elaborate cooling systems are usually necessary. The center of the mass having the poorest heat control may overheat, causing the reaction to "run away," since, as the temperature rises, the rate generally increases rapidly, causing an even greater evolution of heat. This cycle may continue until reactions of explosive violence occur. At any rate, solid polymers are produced which may not be uniformly polymerized throughout the mass. This, of course, means that the molecular weight distribution will be broader than desired. Then, too, dissolved and entrained gases are likely to produce pockets or bubbles in the solidified mass which may render the article useless if a homogeneous casting is desired. Very slow cooling or slow preferential cooling of the mass from one end or side may help to avoid these bubbles.

For these reasons, mass polymerization of addition compounds is usually confined to small castings, especially where at least one dimension is relatively thin. For larger scale production, mass polymerization is often carried out in two stages, the initial stage being conducted on large masses with good agitation and heat removal while the mass is still low in viscosity, the final stage being one of removal of the partially polymerized material to smaller, more easily controlled molds.

Mass polymerization is more successful with condensation type reactions, as this type of reaction is not, in general, as highly exothermic as most addition reactions. Also, the higher temperatures normally necessary for condensation reactions produce a greater temperature differential between the reactants and their container and the surrounding medium (usually air); hence they contribute to the more rapid dissipation of heat.

If the polymer is soluble in the monomer, as frequently is the case, the course of the reaction can be followed by determining the increase in the viscosity of the liquid. The rate of polymerization can also often be obtained by determining the change in freezing point, refractive index, absorption spectrum, or by determining the amount of unchanged monomer by distillation or extraction methods. When the polymer is insoluble in the monomer, the course of the reaction can often be followed by measuring the amount of precipitate formed in a given length of time. The amount of by-product—for example, water, ammonia, or a salt, formed as a result of a condensation polymerization—is a convenient measure of the extent of reaction.

Continuous mass polymerization has been practiced with some monomers for many years; however, its use has been primarily confined to other countries. It has been pointed out,[1] however, that the only continuous process other than suspension or emulsion by which liquid monomer can be converted to pure polymer would eventually involve heating of the polymer to a rather high temperature where the polymer is sufficiently molten to be pumped. At these high temperatures there is always a tendency to produce lower-molecular-weight material either directly from the residual monomer or by re-equilibration of the higher-molecular-weight products; also, at these temperatures any air leaks in the equipment are naturally deleterious to the color of the product.

## SOLUTION POLYMERIZATION

The other type of initially homogeneous polymerization is known as solution or solvent polymerization. In this process, the monomeric sub-

[1] Boundy, R. H. and Boyer, R. F., *Styrene*, p. 272, Reinhold Publishing Corp., New York, 1952.

stances are dissolved in an inert liquid, such as a saturated hydrocarbon. Again, the polymer may or may not be soluble in its monomer or in the solvent. The catalysts or initiators, if used, are of the same types as those used in mass polymerization.

The only effect of adding a solvent which is completely inert, acting only as a diluent, is to reduce the monomer concentration; the rate of polymerization is decreased in proportion to the decrease in monomer concentration; likewise, the molecular weight is normally lowered correspondingly. It has been observed that on dilution with certain solvents, the rate of an addition polymerization decreases in the way expected, but the molecular weight decreases far more rapidly than can be explained by dilution. An explanation is that the polymer radicals attack the solvent chemically, removing the most weakly bonded hydrogen or other atoms. The polymer radical therefore ceases to grow and the small radical formed initiates further polymerization. Thus, the number of monomer molecules polymerized per radical initially generated is not affected, but a larger number of polymer molecules is produced (see chain transfer, Chap. 3).

There are conditions, however, under which moderate amounts of solvents can actually raise the molecular weight of a finished polymer, for the following reasons: (1) In an addition polymerization, a volatile solvent may maintain a blanket of vapor which excludes air, keeping the oxygen content and the peroxide concentration low, thus producing a higher-molecular-weight polymer; (2) a volatile solvent may evaporate as the temperature tends to increase, thus providing internal cooling; (3) by lowering the viscosity, a solvent may permit the polymerization to be carried out without excessive local temperature rise; thus, the rate and the degree of polymerization are more uniform throughout the mass.

Unfortunately, there are certain disadvantages to this process, too. As mentioned previously, the average molecular weight is usually reduced, due to lower monomer concentration and the possibility that the solvents or certain impurities therein may act as telogens or chain-transfer agents. Many organic solvents show some chemical reactivity with polymerizing systems. Carbon tetrachloride is an example of a solvent which readily combines with a growing addition polymer chain. In so doing, the chains may be terminated to form, as with styrene, $Cl_3C(CH_2CHC_6H_5)_nCl$, and the average molecular weight of the polymer is markedly reduced. It should be pointed out that the effect of solvents in limiting the final degree of polymerization may be either an advantage or disadvantage, depending upon the molecular size desired in the final product.

Agitation may be troublesome because of the high viscosities of concentrated polymer solutions. Thus, heavy equipment similar to that required in a mass polymerization may be necessary. Complete removal of the solvent from the polymer generally requires prolonged vacuum drying, and the solvent and unreacted monomer must be recovered. To accomplish these things while avoiding discoloration and foreign matter in the polymer requires expensive engineering and equipment. Further, if the solvent is to be used only as a heat-transfer medium, it must be non-reactive to polymerization and should, ideally, be nonflammable, of the proper volatility, and a relatively poor solvent so that it is easily released from the polymer.

If both the monomer and polymer are soluble in the solvent, the polymer is recovered by evaporating the solvent and the unreacted monomer, or by precipitating it by the addition of a nonsolvent. In other cases, the polymer is insoluble and precipitates as formed.

However, on the credit side, better heat control through somewhat easier agitation and dilution is obtained, and the product may usually be isolated in a fairly pure state by suitable solvent removal processes. Frequently, the product is one which is normally used in solution. In this case, if the solvent or solvent mixture required in the end use is suitable as a polymerization solvent, the product can be sold as made and no solvent removal, recovery, purification, and recycling are necessary. This, of course, will appreciably reduce the over-all cost of the product.

This method of polymerization lends itself particularly to condensation types of reaction, although some addition polymers are prepared in this manner. For the higher temperatures generally required for condensation reactions, quite accurate temperature control may be maintained if a solvent can be selected which will reflux at the desired reaction temperature. The changes in temperature are thus automatically controlled by the rate of reflux. Many condensation polymers are prepared in this manner, especially alkyd resins used in the coating field.

In summary, solution polymerizations are substantially mass polymerizations in which the monomer is soluble in an added solvent. This added solvent may be a complete solvent, a partial solvent, or a nonsolvent for the polymer. The solvent may be chosen so that all polymers precipitate regardless of molecular weight, or only polymers of definite minimum or higher molecular weights will precipitate. This may be accomplished by selection of solvents or by a mixture of them. Normally, both mass and solution processes are carried out at moderate temperatures, up to 250°C, and at ordinary pressure. For the preparation of certain addition polymers, however, such as polyisobutylene, very low temperatures are customary, often below − 50°C.

## INITIALLY HETEROGENEOUS SYSTEMS

Heterogeneous systems include the emulsion and suspension methods of polymerization. There are distinct differences between them. However, both processes involve two-phase systems, the dispersed phase and the dispersion medium. Other reagents are normally added to both types to obtain particular advantages; these will be discussed later. The important thing to remember is that in heterogeneous systems the monomeric substances are dispersed by various means in an inert liquid which merely acts as a suspension medium for the reactants.

In one sense, both emulsion and suspension processes are extensions of the solvent method of polymerization although their mechanisms are different. When the reactants are so finely divided that individual molecules are separated, the reactants are said to be in solution and only one phase is present. When the average particle size of the dispersed phase becomes larger, a two-phase system is obtained. Depending upon a rather arbitrary classification, these two-phase systems are known as emulsions and suspensions. As an approximation, systems in which the dispersed particles range in size from 1 millimicron to 1 micron ($10^{-4}$ cm) may be termed emulsions, and those which are greater than 1 micron, suspensions. Stable emulsions are usually readily obtained, the ease generally diminishing as the particle size increases. Suspensions, being composed of particles of relatively large mass, are formed with somewhat greater difficulty, and the two phases tend to separate more readily if not agitated sufficiently. In the discussion which follows it is assumed that the monomers are practically insoluble in the dispersion medium and that, in general, the systems are similar to any other dispersion system except for the fact that a chemical reaction (polymerization) occurs in one or the other or both phases.

### EMULSION POLYMERIZATION

In the process known as emulsion polymerization, which is confined almost exclusively to addition processes, two basic components are necessary: the dispersed phase, which includes the polymerizable material, and the dispersion medium. Several other components are usually desirable, the number depending upon the particular system. In general, however, an emulsifying agent and an initiator are almost always used. One possible classification of ingredients is as follows:

1. Dispersion medium
2. Monomer(s)
3. Emulsifying agents
    (a) Surface tension regulators
    (b) Buffers
    (c) Protective colloids
4. Initiators
    (a) Activators (promoters)
    (b) Polymerization regulators (modifiers)

Each of these will be discussed in some detail, as each component has a particular function which helps produce the result desired.

The *dispersion medium* serves as the suspending agent for the dispersed phase. It should be inert with respect to the dispersed phase. Most frequently water serves admirably for this use, although certain oils have been used.

The *dispersed phase* consists principally of the monomeric substances used in the process. This may be a single monomer, comonomers, or even comers. As much as three fourths of the total system may be composed of the dispersed phase.

*Emulsifying agents* are added in order to reduce the interfacial tension between the two phases sufficiently to allow easy and stable emulsification with simple agitation. Useful emulsifying agents include common soaps, salts of long-chain carboxylic and sulfonic acids, alkylated aromatic sulfonic acids, and salts of long-chain amines.

As the system changes from a monomer emulsion to a polymer emulsion, a change in interfacial tension often occurs. *Surface tension regulators* are substances added to the system to help maintain a proper interfacial tension between the two phases as polymerization progresses. Certain aliphatic alcohols in amounts up to 0.5 per cent of monomer weight are effective.

The pH of the polymerizing system often has a great influence upon the rate of polymerization. Since the pH may fluctuate due to the hydrolysis of certain components in the system, it is frequently desirable to stabilize the system at the desired pH. This is accomplished by the addition of suitable *buffers*, among which may be mentioned the usual phosphates and acetates. Up to 3 per cent addition of a buffer is common practice.

*Protective colloids*, such as casein, gums, gelatin, dextrin, globulin, hydrolyzed starch, poly(vinyl alcohol), and carboxymethyl cellulose are frequently added to the system to prevent premature precipitation of either the monomer or polymer emulsion and particularly to prevent adhesion of the sticky, partially polymerized products often obtained in the intermediate stages of polymerization.

It is found that this method of polymerization is most useful for addition, rather than condensation, reactions, especially for vinyl and diene type polymerizations. The addition reactions are, in general, carried out at temperatures below the boiling point of water, indeed often well below its freezing point (an antifreeze must then be used), whereas most condensations require appreciably higher temperatures for effective rates of reaction. Hence, in the following discussion, it will be understood that the mechanisms refer to addition polymerizations.

Emulsion polymerizations are characterized by: (1) A high rate of reaction in comparison with the mass and solution processes, (2) the relatively high molecular weights of the products formed, and (3) the use of *water-soluble* initiators. The effectiveness of water-soluble initiators raises the question, not only of the mechanism upon which this process is based, but also of the phases in which different parts of the process take place.

Emulsion polymerization with water-soluble initiators formerly was believed to occur in the aqueous phase. It is now considered likely that the polymer chains originate in the aqueous phase and then continue their growth in the dispersed monomer-polymer phase. The separation of the growing polymer molecules from the aqueous phase seems to shield them from chain-terminating agents, so that emulsion polymerization can give products of very high molecular weight in a very short time. The procedure differs from the simple suspension polymerization system in that the monomer is either dispersed into droplets which are stabilized by an adsorbed layer of soap molecules or is solubilized in the soap micelle which is present in aqueous soap solutions. The work of McBain, Harkins, Hartley, and others[2] has helped to explain the mechanism of this type of reaction. A somewhat simplified explanation follows.

In emulsified systems of the kind discussed, the presence of lamellar (or possibly spherical) micelles has been established. These consist of a number of double layers of soap molecules which have been oriented with the polar hydrophilic groups on the outside facing the water, while the nonpolar hydrophobic chains are facing each other. Between each double-layer is a layer of water, whose thickness is dependent upon the soap concentration. This can be visualized by referring to Fig. 5-1.

Upon addition of liquid monomer, a small amount of soap is transferred from the micelles to the surface of the emulsion droplets, where it acts as a stabilizing agent. However, the primary function of the soap here is its solubilizing action on the water-insoluble monomer. Some molecules of the monomer are transferred into each double-layer and lie between the rows of paraffin chains, the terminal groups of which face each other. The double-layers of soap molecules are then separated farther from each other. See Fig. 5-2.

The monomer absorbed in this way has been called "solubilized" and explains the ability of soap solutions to dissolve a certain amount of monomer without showing heterogeneity. If excess monomer is added, a heterogeneous emulsion is formed, in which the excess monomer distributes

[2] Harkins, W. D., *J. Chem. Phys.*, **13**, 381 (1945); *ibid.*, **14**, 47 (1946); Harkins, W. D. and Stearns, R. S., *J. Chem. Phys.*, **14**, 214 (1946); Harkins, W. D., Mattoon, R. W., and Corrin, M. L., *J. Colloid Sci.*, **1**, 105 (1946), and *J. Am. Chem. Soc.*, **68**, 220 (1946); McBain, J. W. and Salmon, C. S., *J. Am. Chem. Soc.*, **42**, 426 (1920); Merrill, R. C., Jr. and McBain, J. W., *J. Phys. Chem.*, **46**, 10 (1942); McBain, J. W., *Advances in Colloid Science*, Vol. I, pp. 99–142, Interscience Publishers, New York, 1942; McBain, J. W. and Merrill, R. C., Jr., *Ind. Eng. Chem.*, **34**, 915 (1942); McBain, J. W., *Colloid Science*, D. C. Heath and Co., Boston, 1950; Hartley, G. S., *J. Chem. Soc.*, **1938**, 1968.

itself throughout the aqueous solution in little drops which are more or less stabilized by some of the soap molecules as outlined above.

In addition to the unlikelihood that water-soluble initiators can initiate the polymerization in the monomer phase, it has been shown experimentally that activation begins in some part of the aqueous phase. By demonstrating that monomer and aqueous solution of initiator need be connected only by a vapor phase in order to start polymerization in the

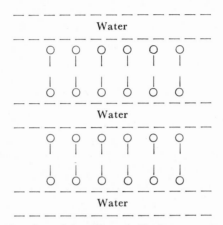

FIG. 5-1.    Cross-section through lamellar micelles in a concentrated soap solution[3]

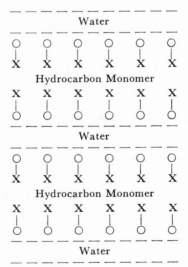

FIG. 5-2.    Cross-section through lamellar micelles in the presence of a hydrocarbon[3]

[3] Houwink, R., ed., *Elastomers and Plastomers*, Vol. I, Fig. 30, p. 59, Elsevier Publishing Co., Amsterdam (dist. by D. Van Nostrand Co., Princeton, N.J.), 1948.

*aqueous solution*, it also appears unlikely that initiation begins on the surface boundary between the two phases.

It thus seems most likely that the locus of initiation is located in the water layers of the micelles. The growth of the activated particle will then first take place in the micelles where, for a time, sufficient monomer is available. Later, monomer, supplied by diffusion from the emulsion droplets and other micelles, is necessary. Several investigators have shown that the rate of diffusion is, in fact, sufficient to support the propagation process, in spite of the rapid rate at which the latter proceeds.

It next appears that, having attained a certain size, the growing polymer particles are expelled from the micelles. However, so long as monomer is present, the micelles can be refilled and the activation continued. The growing particle which has been expelled also takes up monomer, swells, and adsorbs a layer of soap molecules on its surface. Eventually the soap disappears from the micelles and is adsorbed onto the newly formed droplets which consist of growing polymer swollen with monomer. The polymeric chain radical eventually is terminated by combining with another growing chain radical to form a stable polymer particle.

The solubility of monomer in polymer is such that each polymer particle is swollen with approximately an equal amount of monomer. Free radicals are not formed in these particles, but enter them from the surrounding water phase in which the initiator is dissolved. Upon entry of a radical into a particle, polymerization is initiated and continues until it is terminated by entry of another free radical.

If free radicals formed in the aqueous phase must enter the particles to start chain propagation, and if there is no mechanism for their transfer out of the particles, then a radical, once having entered a particle, must continue to propagate until entry of another radical permits mutual termination. Hence, a large number of growing radicals may coexist without mutual self-termination. In comparison to mass or solution polymerization, the lifetime of a growing free radical is increased by a factor of $10^4$ to $10^6$. This, then, is the reason for the ability of a molecule to reach a high molecular weight before being terminated. This growth proceeds simultaneously in many particles, since they are separated from one another by the intervening water phase, with the result that a growing polymer radical in one particle cannot terminate one in another particle. The over-all rate is therefore high.

Most initiators used in addition polymerizations are oxidizing agents, such as peroxides. It has been found that addition of a reducing agent often greatly increases the rate of polymerization. Such additives are known as *activators* or *promoters* and are particularly useful in promoting relatively low-temperature polymerization. As has been previously pointed out, the higher the temperature of polymerization and, usually, the more rapid the rate of polymerization, the lower is the average molecular weight of product. Activators often enable higher-molecular-weight products to form because a lower temperature is necessary to activate the initiator while at the same time they appear to have little detrimental influence upon the molecular weight in spite of the increased rate of reaction. Many improvements in the synthetic elastomer field are due to the use of such materials, enabling improved products, such as the so-called "cold rubbers," to be made. Temperatures well below freezing have been commercially utilized. This, of course, requires refrigeration. This process of activation of initiators by a reducing agent is known as *reduction activation* or *redox*. A number of compounds have been found effective as activators, among them, iron, copper, sulfurous acid, sulfites and bisulfites, hydrosulfites, thiosulfates, and hydroquinone. For a possible mechanism for this reaction, refer to Chapter 3. The principal advantage claimed for the reduction-activation type of initiator is that it is possible to obtain much higher rates of polymerization than those obtainable with a straight peroxide or persulfate initiator due to a more rapid decomposition into free radicals; the quantity of initiator used may also be reduced with beneficial effects upon the ultimate heat stability of the polymer. Ionic catalysts, such as aluminum chloride and boron trifluoride, while useful for many nonaqueous polymerizations, are not effective in aqueous emulsion or suspension polymerizations, as they are hydrolyzed by the dispersion medium.

Persulfates and hydrogen peroxide may also be activated by the cupric ion in systems containing from 0.1 to 1.0 per cent of the sodium salt of sulfonated methyl oleate as an emulsifying agent. Minute quantities of cupric ion are required, in the range of 0.05 to 0.45 ppm, the addition being made as a water-soluble salt, such as copper sulfate. This "copper effect" is further enhanced if polymerization is carried out in the presence of oxygen; in this case, 0.01 to 2.0 ppm of cupric ion is used with a residual pressure of 0.02 to 0.1 atmosphere of oxygen remaining in the autoclave.

In addition to activators, compounds known as polymerization *regulators* or *modifiers* are frequently added to addition-type polymerizing systems. In the development of synthetic elastomers especially, by the emulsion copolymerization of vinyl and diene monomers, it has been found that addition of certain compounds, such as mercaptans, other organic sulfur compounds, or chlorinated hydrocarbons, suppresses the formation of gelatinous and partially insoluble polymers, particularly at high conversions. These substances influence the degree of polymerization by reducing molecular weights by chain-transfer reactions.

Because the bulk of the polymerization occurs within the polymer particles, which are kept more or less saturated with monomer, monomer concentration remains relatively constant so long as any free monomer phase exists (50 to 60 per cent conversion). Hence, unlike the case of mass polymerization, the rate of any cross-linking reaction (as well as that of the polymerization reaction) remains constant up to 50 to 60 per cent conversion. In other words, in emulsion systems, the cross-linking reaction proceeds at a uniform but faster rate than in mass systems during the first half of the polymerization, owing to the higher concentration of polymer at the locus of reaction. Beyond that point, the cross-linking rate increases as the polymer concentration increases.

Under the above conditions, insoluble polymer networks will be formed in emulsion systems if and when the molecular weight of the polymer becomes sufficiently large to contain one cross-linked unit per weight-average chain, the frequency of cross-links remaining more or less constant up to 50 per cent conversion. The suppression of such networks is achieved in the synthetic elastomer industry by means of modifiers or chain regulators which keep the length of the polymer chain below the critical limit for gel formation.

From the fairly long list of additives enumerated above, it can be seen that emulsion polymerizations are considerably more complex than the homogeneous types of polymerization. In addition to the greater number of reagents necessary, the cost of production is increased further by the necessity of using as inert a dispersion medium as possible in order to prevent unwanted telomerization. For this reason, water, which is usually used as the dispersion medium, is often purified by ion-exchange or other methods before use.

Further, the product, which is obtained as a latex, must be precipitated or coagulated by addition of a suitable electrolyte, by extraction with a suitable solvent, or by freezing in order to separate it completely from the dispersion medium. The precipitated latex must then be thoroughly washed free of the additives used and then carefully dried.

However, there are so many advantages to this process that they usually outweigh the disadvantages. Excellent control of temperature is easily obtainable, especially when water is used as the dispersion medium, as the dispersed phase is intimately surrounded by a high-specific-heat cooling liquid. As a result, a more uniformly polymerized product is obtained. In addition, there is little or no viscosity increase, as in the mass or solution methods of polymerization, since the polymer is not in solution. When water is used, the cost of the dispersion medium is nominal, even with purification, as compared with organic solvents; further, the absence of a flammable liquid is a definite advantage.

The product is obtained in a finely divided state which is frequently suitable for direct further processing into manufactured articles without time-consuming and costly size reduction. Then, too, some addition polymers are marketed in latex form and the product of emulsion polymerization can then be used directly, after, if necessary, suitable removal or neutralization of the reagents used in the process.

Aside from these physical advantages, there are several chemical improvements obtained from emulsion polymerization. The rate of polymerization is usually much greater than that of homogeneous polymerizations, reactions often being completed in hours or even minutes, whereas it may take days, weeks, or even months to achieve the same results by the previous methods. Corrective reagents are much more effective by addition to a suspended system and thus the control of the reaction is greater; this control is also improved by the fact that emulsion processes are easily interrupted at any stage of the process, enabling addition of desired reagents or correction of an undesirable condition at any time. It is also interesting to note that many comonomers, which copolymerize slowly or not at all by mass methods, react readily in emulsion form. In fact, it is generally observed that addition reactions, which go slowly by mass methods, go much more rapidly in emulsion form without the expected loss in average molecular weight.

### SUSPENSION POLYMERIZATION

This is the latest method of polymerization, known as the suspension, bead, or pearl type. This method is an outgrowth of the emulsion method and is, in certain respects, similar. One of the disadvantages of emulsion polymerization is the difficulty in coagulating and separating the polymer from the latex. Very fine precipitates are often obtained which filter slowly, making the removal of coagulating salts and initiator residues slow, expensive, and incomplete. Suspension polymerization was designed to overcome some of these difficulties and to produce a granular product directly. As in emulsion polymerization, there are a dispersed phase and a dispersion (suspension) medium. The principal difference is in the average particle size of the dispersed phase. The monomeric particles are much larger, generally between 1 and 10 microns initially; no emulsion exists but instead there is obtained a simple physical suspension of polymerizing drops or beads which will coalesce rapidly upon cessation of agitation.

Thus, again the primary requisites are the suspended phase and the suspending medium. Usually two other classes of agents are used, initiators and a suspension stabilizer, the latter of which is roughly analogous to the emulsion stabilizer or protective colloid used in emulsion polymerization. For reasons enumerated previously under the discussion of emulsion polymerization, the usual and preferred *suspension medium* is water, although inert organic liquids may be used so long as monomer and polymer are insoluble therein.

The *suspended phase*, which is the dispersed phase referred to in emulsion polymerization, contains the substances to be polymerized and the initiator, if used. It has been found that the mechanism of polymerization by the suspension method is analogous to the mass and solution methods of polymerization rather than to the emulsion method. There is no emulsifier to establish intimate contact between the two phases, hence each bead or pearl of monomer acts as a minute, discrete mass polymerization system. For this reason, when copolymerization is employed, only systems which react under the mass polymerization system are found to react by suspension technique. Similarly, mutual inhibition of monomers in mass systems also occurs in a suspension system. Aside from the above outward chemical similarities between the two systems, kinetic studies also indicate the similarity between mass and suspension polymerizations.

The *initiators* or *catalysts*, if used, function as before; i.e., they accelerate the rate of reaction or decrease the length of the inhibition period. In agreement with the previously mentioned similarities between the mass and suspension methods of polymerization, it is found that organo-soluble initiators perform best, although water-soluble initiators have been used on rare occasions. Two types which are currently favored are the organic peroxides and hydroperoxides. Among the peroxides used are benzoyl peroxide, many other acyl and alkyl peroxides, including acetyl benzoyl peroxide, o-chlorobenzoyl peroxide, alkoxy benzoyl peroxides, lauroyl peroxide, and dibutyryl and dicaproyl peroxides. Unsaturated peroxides, such as crotonyl peroxide, have also been used. Naturally, if the dispersion medium is water, ionic catalysts which react with the medium are unsuitable.

A *suspension stabilizer* is usually a desirable addition to a suspension polymerization system. As noted above, the relatively large drops of monomer are kept suspended by continuous agitation. The system is in reality a dynamic, rather than a static one, in that the separate droplets collide, coalesce, and, with proper agitation, are redispersed. At the partially polymerized stage of the reaction, these drops, consisting of monomer dissolved in polymer, become increasingly viscous and tacky. It then becomes necessary to prevent this tackiness from causing these particles to agglomerate. The function of the suspension stabilizer is to coat the drops to prevent sticking or, by a change in interfacial tension, to prevent coalescence of the particles. Of course, once coalescence and redispersion cease, the system becomes a static rather than a dynamic one; hence the average particle size is established by the nature of the stabilizer used and the state of subdivision obtained before polymerization has progressed too far. It is also possible to protect the dispersed monomer globules by adjustments in the density and viscosity of the dispersion medium.

Common stabilizers are inorganic oxides, hydroxides, and salts which are water-insoluble, and organic water-soluble polymers, such as poly-(vinyl alcohols), methyl cellulose, gelatin, and metal salts of carboxymethyl cellulose and poly(acrylic acids). The stabilizer is of such a nature that it is readily removed from the surface of the bead by simple washing, and since no emulsifying or coagulating agents have been added, the product is considerably freer of impurities than that normally recovered from an emulsion polymerization.

It is of interest to point out that if the monomer is at all soluble in the suspension medium, polymerization may take place in both phases, producing two humps in the molecular weight distribution curve, rather than one. This broadening of the distribution is usually undesirable; hence the two phases are selected so as to be as mutually insoluble as possible.

Many condensation reactants are highly polar, oxygenated compounds whose solubility in water is appreciable. This solubility in the dispersion medium is usually undesirable, as pointed out above. For this reason, as well as the temperature limitations when water is used as the suspension medium, suspension polymerization, like emulsion, is best suited for polymerization of addition polymers. Some polyamide condensation polymerizations have been successfully carried out in mineral oils, however.

The advantages in the use of suspension polymerization are, in general, those of the emulsion method plus the advantages gained from a simpler system, better drop size control, no latex precipitation step, and a somewhat purer and more easily handled product. Control of water purity is not as critical as in the emulsion system. However, maintenance of agitation and its rate are more critical in order to obtain and retain the desired particle size, which grows during the course of polymerization.

In summary, it is apparent that all of the previously mentioned methods of polymerization are useful and workable methods for obtaining a polymer, and that the choice of a particular method involves careful consideration of the organic technology and engineering processes involved. The problem has been well stated by Boundy and Boyer:[4] "It is evident that a rigorous cost comparison of the various polymerization schemes becomes a detailed problem in chemical engineering. It can be answered only on the basis of accurate laboratory and semi-plant data, further tempered by the specialized background of the group doing the work, and by the intended use of the product. One of the most important questions is the scale of operation."

[4] Boundy, R. H. and Boyer, R. F., *Styrene*, p. 269, Reinhold Publishing Corp., New York, 1952.

## REFERENCES AND RECOMMENDED READING

Boundy, R. H. and Boyer, R. F., *Styrene*, Reinhold Publishing Corp., New York, 1952.

Bovey, F. A., Kolthoff, I. M., Medalia, A. I., and Meehan, E. J., *Emulsion Polymerization*, Interscience Publishers, New York, 1955.

Burnett, G. M., *Mechanism of Polymer Reactions*, Interscience Publishers, New York, 1954.

D'Alelio, G. F., *Fundamental Principles of Polymerization*, John Wiley and Sons, New York, 1952.

Flory, P. J., *Principles of Polymer Chemistry*, Cornell University Press, Ithaca, N.Y., 1953.

Groggins, P. H., ed., *Unit Processes in Organic Synthesis*, 4th ed., McGraw-Hill Book Co., New York, 1952.

Houwink, R., ed., *Elastomers and Plastomers*, Vol. I, Elsevier Publishing Co., Amsterdam (dist. by D. Van Nostrand Co., Princeton, N.J.), 1950.

Kraemer, E. O., ed., *Advances in Colloid Science*, Vol. I, Interscience Publishers, New York, 1942.

Riddle, E. H., *Monomeric Acrylic Esters*, Reinhold Publishing Corp., New York, 1954.

Schildknecht, C. E., ed., *Polymer Processes*, Interscience Publishers, New York, 1956.

*Chapter 6*

# TECHNOLOGY OF MANUFACTURE: NATURAL PRODUCTS

As has been pointed out in Chapter 3, high-molecular-weight substances have been classified in many ways: according to use, methods of fabrication, chemical similarity, method of manufacture, or origin. Each author has preferred one or another system, according to his intended development of the subject. Here, we shall classify according to origin, subclassifying according to chemical similarity.

In this way, it is possible to divide all organic polymers and high-molecular-weight substances into three principal categories, according to origin: natural, modified natural, and synthetic. Natural products are those which may be used as obtained from nature, except possibly for *physical* treatment in order to isolate and purify the material desired. Modified natural products are all substances of natural origin which require *chemical* treatment (in addition to physical isolation and purification) in order to obtain the product desired. They have sometimes been called artificial products. Synthetic products are those which are not derived from natural sources but are obtained by chemical synthesis in the laboratory and chemical plant.

This chapter will be devoted to the natural products, their sources, purification, general constitution, and properties. Subsequent chapters will cover the technology of manufacture and properties of the modified natural and synthetic polymers.

### "Natural" Resins

Many of the natural resins described in this chapter are not truly high-molecular-weight polymers but are instead substances of resinous character whose average molecular weights are in the hundreds, rather than in the thousands and higher. They are, in general, composed of crystalline, organic compounds of complex structure and relatively high molecular weight, admixed with noncrystalline organic compounds and natural impurities which account for the resinous characteristics of the products. Being natural, rather than synthetic, their compositions are not uniform and vary greatly according to source and treatment. Never-

146

theless, they are considered and used commercially as interchangeable with the synthetic and modified natural polymers, hence merit consideration in any discussion of polymeric and resinous substances.

Products of vegetable origin are obtained from living plants, as are rosin, certain waxes, and natural rubber, or from fossilized plants, as are amber and the copals. Many of these products flow naturally from trees and bushes as a result of cuts, insect bites, or other injuries to the bark. The material is a protective coating for the injured vegetation and, if gathered while on the trees, is known as a "recent resin." If an overabundant secretion occurs, the liquid falls to the ground or collects in crotches, absorbs dirt and dust, and slowly forms a harder or semifossil resin. Still other resins, found in deposits beneath the surface of the earth, have been formed from aging of semifossil resins or from the direct fossilization of vegetable matter which has been buried for a long time. These are the fossil resins and may be centuries old. Most of the above resins are named for some distinguishing characteristic, or for their geographic origin or port from which they are shipped.

Natural resins are often called gums by the trade. This terminology is incorrect, since the true gums are related to the carbohydrates and are more or less soluble in water and insoluble in organic solvents and oils, while the natural resins show the opposite solubility tendencies and are generally characterized by a conchoidal fracture.

In general, the natural resins, except for rosin and lignin, which are from domestic sources, come from the Congo district of Africa and adjoining territory, New Zealand, the Netherlands (East) Indies, and the Philippines. They are obtained from definite species of trees in a systematic manner, usually under governmental supervision. Mantell has classified these so-called natural resins as shown in Table 6-1.

The classification in Table 6-1 is rather arbitrary, since there is practically a continuous gradation in solubility and hardness, from the fresh tappings of living trees, represented by the softest dammars, to the hardest copals of the fossil type. Note that this classification does not include lignin or rosin, both certainly resins of vegetable origin, the latter of which is produced and consumed in quantities far greater than all the rest of the natural resins combined. Perhaps the reason for the usual separate classification of rosin and lignin by other authors is because of their different geographical sources or, more likely, because of their relatively recent commercial importance.

Natural rubber will also be included herein as a polymeric substance of vegetable origin. Although considered an elastomer, rather than a resin, it, too, is obtained from the tapping of living trees and should be included in any discussion of naturally occurring polymers.

*Dammars.* The dammars are recent resinous exudations of certain

TABLE 6-1.   CLASSIFICATION OF NATURAL RESINS[1]

I.  Dammars
    A.  Batavia
    B.  Singapore

II.  East India
    A.  Batu
    B.  Black
    C.  Pale East India Singapore
    D.  Pale East India Macassar

III.  Copals
    A.  Manila
        1.  Melengket
        2.  Loba
        3.  Philippine Manila
        4.  Pontianak
        5.  Boea
    B.  Congo
    C.  Kauri

IV.  Miscellaneous Resins
    A.  Accroides
    B.  Elemi
    C.  Mastic
    D.  Sandarac

trees which are indigenous to the Malay peninsula and nearby islands, although the dammars used in the United States come from Sumatra and Borneo in the Netherlands Indies. The word "damar" originally referred to a torch made by mixing leaves and bark with the powdered resin.

The resin is secreted by the sapwood either upon accidental injury or by systematic tapping. From 10 to as many as 50 pounds per year of dammar per tree may be obtained, collection of the resin usually occurring at intervals of from three to six months. After the resin is dried and delivered unsorted to the port, it is scraped, screened, sorted, graded, and packed for shipment. Grading of dammars is based upon color and impurity content.

Dammar contains one or more resin acids and an $\alpha$- and $\beta$-resene, together with small amounts of an essential oil of a terpenic nature.

The $\beta$-resene, known as "dammar wax," is only slightly soluble in common lacquer solvents. The resin is, therefore, dewaxed to remove the $\beta$-resene before use in lacquers. This is accomplished by dissolving the resin in a suitable solvent, such as an aromatic hydrocarbon, and then precipitating the wax with alcohol. The $\beta$-resene content of dammar varies between 8 and 11 per cent.

The resin varies in color from almost water white to yellow. Since its films do not yellow but instead bleach to form colorless films upon exposure to sunlight, the resin is a very desirable constituent of pale

[1] Mantell, C. L., Kopf, C. W., Curtis, J. L., and Rogers, E. M., *The Technology of Natural Resins*, Table 1, p. 8, John Wiley and Sons, New York, 1942

lacquers. Dammar has a very low acid number for a natural resin, the value generally lying between 25 and 35.

The dammars (and the related East India resins) are soluble in drying oils without requiring thermal processing. They are also compatible with many other resins, waxes, and cellulosic derivatives. They are only partially soluble in alcohols and esters, but easily soluble in hydrocarbons and chlorinated hydrocarbons.

*East Indias.* In comparison to the dammars, the East India resins are of greater age and hardness. They are not obtained by the tapping of living trees but are obtained from collections found on trees and from deposits in or on the ground where they have fallen or have been transported, such as at the seashore, on river banks, in former river beds, or even in the water. They may be considered as semifossilized dammars and are sometimes known as hard dammars.

The East India resins are also low in acid number, having slightly higher values than the dammars, to which they are related. They are divided into three classes: pale East India, black East India, and batu.

The pale East Indias are semifossil resins, generally of a reddish cast. They are sometimes known as hiroe (Macassar) and rasak (Singapore). Like the dammars, they are soluble in oils without the need for thermal treatment. They are obtained from the Moluccas Islands, Borneo, and Malaya.

Black East India is a darker-colored semifossil resin, closely related to the pale East India and batu resins. Its acid-number range is also similar to that of the dammars, but its solubility characteristics and applications are similar to the other East Indias. The principal sources of this resin are Java, Madoera, and Malaya.

Batu is also a semifossil East India resin, related to the dammars and, like them, soluble in oils by simple heating. The resin is opaque and, although dark initially, bleaches with age. The principal sources are the Celebes and Borneo.

*Copals.* The copal resins are made up of the manilas, congo, and kauri, in increasing order of age and hardness.

The manilas, whose name is taken from the port of shipment, originated in the Philippines, where both the tree and the resin are known as almaciga. They are obtained from accidental wounds and by deliberate tapping of the Agathis tree. The method of tapping differs from that of the dammars in that manila resin is obtained from the bark only. Average annual production is around 25 pounds per tree. Borneo, Celebes, the Moluccas, the Philippines, and New Guinea are the principal sources of manila copal.

The softest grade of manila, gathered from one to four weeks after tapping, is known as melengket. Half-hard manila, manila loba, refers to the resin gathered from one to three or more months after tapping. This resin has hardened sufficiently that the pieces do not stick together as does melengket. The fossil or hard grade of manila comes from the Celebes and other parts of the Netherlands Indies and is known as boea. Some boea is found where it has long since exuded in the crotches of trees still standing, while the darker grades are obtained from the ground.

Pontianak, a semifossil copal, is also a member of the manila class but originates from a different species of tree. It comes from Borneo.

The African copals are known as congo and are obtained from the Belgian Congo. Such names as Zanzibar, Accra, Benguela, and Angola are old names for various sources of congo, but are now little used. The congo is collected from deposits in the ground, which are usually found at depths of 3 inches to 3 feet and are located by prodding the ground with metal-tipped poles. Accumulations are also often found in river beds.

Congo copals, considered the hardest of the natural resins, are incompatible with other resins and insoluble in oils and solvents. In order to make congo compatible with the oils and solvents used in varnish making or for other uses, thermal treatment of the resins, known as "running," is necessary. This consists in heating the resin to a temperature of 300° to 325°C in an open kettle and holding at this temperature for a period of time, during which moisture, gases, and cracking products are evolved. The resin loses from 10 to 25 per cent of its original weight, and the product incurs both a reduction in acid number and softening temperature; also, its compatibility greatly improves, since it becomes highly soluble in common solvents and oils. Congo and other copals can also be made soluble by mastication of the resin between hot rollers; the improvement in solubility of the resin is attributed to the partial breakdown of its molecular structure by the mechanical force.

Congo is known as the universal resin of the varnish maker. Varnishes prepared with it are comparable in quality to those containing the well-known modified phenolic resins.

Kauri, a fossil resin of the same general class as congo and boea, was formed from a pine tree believed to have reached an age of nearly 3,600 years and no longer extant. The resin is found underground in hilly clay ranges and peat swamps, principally from the most northern territories of North Island, New Zealand.

Kauri has the lowest acid number of the fossil copals (60 to 80). Although in its original form it is compatible with a wide range of vegetable, mineral, and petroleum waxes, the temperatures of combination are such that thermal processing takes place. After thermal processing similar to that of congo but of a more moderate nature, kauri is compatible with all animal and vegetable oils.

*Miscellaneous.* Gum accroides is also known as gum acaroid, yacca, and Botany Bay resin. It occurs throughout Australia and Tasmania. The resin accumulates at the base of dead leaves along the stems of certain trees.

Accroides differs from the other natural resins in that it contains appreciable quantities of free benzoic and cinnamic acids and thus is related to the balsams. Further, it is the only natural resin which, as marketed, is heat-reactive like the thermosetting phenol-formaldehyde resins. When heated to approximately 250°C, the resin is converted into a hard, insoluble product. The resin is soluble in alcohol but is insoluble in hydrocarbons.

Elemi is known as an oleoresin, since it contains a greater quantity of essential oils than do the other natural resins. It is compatible with vegetable, fish, and animal oils and is completely soluble in aromatic hydrocarbons and esters but not in aliphatic solvents, alcohols, or ketones.

Most of the elemi of commerce is obtained from the island of Luzon in the Philippines. The resin is obtained as an exudate by stripping pieces of bark from the trunks of certain trees. The viscous fluid is removed from the tree at definite intervals and is not allowed to accumulate, since it yellows upon aging.

Mastic is the resinous exudation from a species of tree which is found throughout the Mediterranean coastal region. Most of the resin, however, is obtained from the island of Chios near the coast of Turkey, where the species is cultivated for this purpose. Mastic is formed by spontaneous exudation, but, since the yield obtained this way is small, the tree is tapped for commercial production. The average production is from 10 to 12 pounds per year per tree.

Mastic is a soft resin, having a low softening temperature and acid number. It is soluble in alcohol and aromatic hydrocarbons but is insoluble in aliphatic hydrocarbons.

Commercial sandarac is obtained from a certain species of tree found in Algeria and Morocco in northern Africa and also in Australia. The resin is obtained in a manner similar to that for mastic.

Sandarac is a pale, brittle, and transparent resin. Its acid number is high, comparable to the manilas, the range being 117 to 155. It is soluble in alcohols, but insoluble in both aromatic and aliphatic hydrocarbons. It is usually incompatible with varnish oils.

Perhaps the best known natural resin is the fossil type found in the blue earth of the Baltic coast, commonly called amber or succinite. Amber is superior to all other natural resins in its surface hardness, strength, and heat resistance. For these reasons and because of its scarcity, it is classified as a semiprecious material.

The chemical composition of the above natural resins has been studied by several investigators during the first quarter of this century.   Their results were inconclusive, many differences in their analyses being attributed to impurities in the samples.

Relatively little work has been done on elucidating the structures of all the imported natural resins during the past thirty years.   In view of the fact that modern techniques and equipment should help considerably, it may seem strange that more study has not been undertaken.   It must be borne in mind, however, that these resins are complex mixtures of complex compounds, varying in composition from lot to lot, with many of these compounds being sensitive to oxidation and having, perhaps, many isomeric forms.   Further, with the advent of the myriad modified natural and synthetic resins, the importance of the natural ones has diminished considerably.

The principal uses of the natural resins have been as ingredients of varnishes, paints, lacquers, inks, linoleum, plastics, polishes, and sizes. These applications have decreased steadily because the many modified natural and synthetic resins, with their greater purity, uniformity, availability, and "tailor-made" properties, have gradually supplanted them. They are still preferred, however, for some purposes where their individual properties are yet unmatched by the newer resins.

**Rosin**

Rosin is a component of the resinous exudation of many pine trees throughout the world.   It is obtained in the United States from pine trees in the southeastern states either by tapping the trees or by extraction from pine stumps.   Gum rosin is the residue remaining after steam distillation of the oleoresin obtained from the living tree.   Wood rosin is recovered from the mixture extracted from pine stumps by the use of a solvent. Rosin also occurs in appreciable quantity in tall oil, a by-product of the sulfate paper pulp industry.

For the collection of gum rosin, a cup and gutters are attached to the tree and, just above them, a groove is cut in the tree.   The oleoresin exudes and flows into the gutters and then into the cup.   The gum contains about 68 per cent rosin, 20 per cent turpentine, and 12 per cent water. The residue, after distillation of the turpentine and water, is gum rosin.

A process for the recovery of rosin and terpenes from pine stumps was developed early in this century when it was thought that the rapid depletion of virgin pine forests would soon cause a shortage of naval stores products.   Stumps used are generally from trees which have been cut from seven to ten years previously, because aging leaves principally heartwood, which has a high rosin content.

The stumps are removed from the ground by bulldozers.   The wood is ground and shredded and is then conveyed to extractors in which rosin is extracted by a solvent, sometimes under pressure. A low-boiling solvent, usually benzene or gasoline, is used since it can readily be separated from the turpentine and other products by distillation. The extracted wood is steamed to recover residual solvent.

Turpentine, dipentene, and pine oil are distilled from the solution and fractionated. The rosin remaining behind is dark red in color and is decolorized by either of two methods. In the solvent-extraction method of decolorization, the rosin is dissolved in a petroleum naphtha, in which the colored components are relatively insoluble. A solvent, such as furfural, which has poor solubility in the naphtha at room temperature but has good solvent properties for the color bodies, is then added. By heating the mixture to about 50°C, all components become miscible; upon cooling, the furfural, containing most of the dark-colored material, separates. The whole extraction process may be repeated if a very pale product is desired. The furfural is eventually recovered by steam stripping. By varying the temperature, the time of contact, and the ratio of furfural to naphtha, the amount of decolorization can be varied to produce a variety of color grades.

The other rosin decolorization process utilizes the principle of adsorption. The dark rosin is dissolved in a petroleum naphtha. Washing with water removes some of the dark components. The naphtha solution is then pumped through towers filled with clay or adsorbent (fuller's) earth. All of the rosin is absorbed initially but, as the process continues, the darker constituents are preferentially adsorbed while the lighter-colored, unoxidized rosin is released and passes through. The adsorbent is reactivated periodically by displacing the color bodies with fresh naphtha which is recovered by stripping from the product by steam.

The rosin obtained from tall oil is equivalent to gum and wood rosin. Tall oil contains approximately 45 per cent rosin and an approximately equal quantity of fatty acids. Although several methods of separation are available, a common process is that of fractional distillation under reduced pressure. A good separation of components is obtained.

Most of the acid components of rosin have been isolated and their structures generally established. The composition of rosin varies slightly from grade to grade, depending upon the source and method used in producing it. Both American gum and wood rosins are composed of about 90 per cent rosin acids and about 10 per cent nonacidic materials (resenes or terpenes). The approximate composition of rosin is given in Table 6-2.

The abietic acid found in processed rosin is an isomerization product of the principal constituent of the oleoresin, levopimaric acid. This acid, upon heat treatment, isomerizes and disproportionates to form an equilibrium mixture of various acids. The adducts of maleic anhydride and

TABLE 6-2.   COMPOSITION OF ROSIN

|                                                     | Per Cent |
| --------------------------------------------------- | -------- |
| Abietic and similar type acids        .    .    .    . | 53       |
| Dehydroabietic acid        .    .    .    .    .    .    | 2        |
| Dihydroabietic acids        .    .    .    .    .    .   | 13       |
| Tetrahydroabietic and dextropimaric acids     .    .  | 16       |
| Oxidized acids        .    .    .    .    .    .    .     | 6        |
| Neutral fraction     .    .    .    .    .    .    .     | 10       |

phenolic resins with rosin are believed to involve the isomerization of abietic acid to levopimaric acid before such additions can take place (see Chap. 7).

Following are the generally accepted structural formulas for the principal acids in rosin:

Abietic            Levopimaric            Neoabietic

Dehydroabietic       Dihydroabietic       Tetrahydroabietic

Dextropimaric            Isodextropimaric

The chemistry of the neutral or unsaponifiable portion of rosin is not yet clear.   The constituents of this portion probably play the most important part in the differing physical properties of the individual rosins. These neutral materials are composed of approximately 60 per cent of esters of resin and fatty acids (saturated and unsaturated) with different alcohols of unknown composition, high-molecular-weight hydrocarbons (including terpenes), and some waxes or resenes.

Earlier in this century, rosin was widely used in formulations for varnishes and printing inks, soaps, leather, matches, core oils, electrical insulation, linoleum, solder flux, and adhesives. More recently, most of the rosin produced has been chemically modified in order to obtain more stable and improved products (see Chap. 7). Hence, current uses of unmodified rosin are relatively small. It still does find use, however, as a linoleum ingredient, as an electrical potting and insulating compound, as an ingredient of solder fluxes, and as a binder in foundry core oils and in certain thermoplastic molding compounds.

### Lignin

The most important noncellulosic portion of wood is known as lignin. It is the resinous binder for the cellulose fibers and is removed during the process of paper manufacture. Various woods contain from 35 per cent to almost 90 per cent of lignin, and the paper industry alone produces several million tons of waste lignin annually. In addition, huge amounts of lignin are present in sawmill waste and straw. Although many attempts have been made to utilize this inexpensive, thermosetting polymer, most of it is still unused.

A fibrous material can be made by treating wood chips with steam at high pressure for a short time. The lignins are softened by the hot steam, and, upon sudden release of pressure, are exploded by the high internal pressure into a mass of fiber bundles, which still retain their natural coating of lignin. The resultant fibrous material can be formed into mats under high pressure and temperature.

Lignin is a polymeric mixture as yet only partially characterized but known to contain aromatic rings having methoxy and a few free hydroxyl groups appended. It has been considered a complex polyphenol derivative of propyl guaiacol (o-methoxy phenol) or a complex polyether of various polyhydroxy n-propyl benzenes, with a molecular weight of about 4,000. (This is the source of methanol obtained in the destructive distillation of wood.) One possible configuration for the characteristic portion of the lignin molecule is as follows:

$$H_3CO-\underset{HO}{\underbrace{\bigcirc}}-C-C-CH$$

Since the number of free phenolic hydroxyl groups is small, it is believed that most are involved in the formation of polyether chains. The material known as sulfite lignin is recoverable from the waste liquors obtained from the pulping of wood by the acid sulfite process. The lignin has reacted with the cooking liquor and is present as lignosulfonates rather than as lignin itself. The solubility of lignin in sulfite liquors has been ascribed to the opening of condensed ring systems throughout the polymer network to yield soluble lignin sulfonic acids:

$$\text{(structure)} + HSO_3^- \rightarrow \text{(structure)}$$

Sulfate lignin, on the other hand, is a lignin prepared by acidification of waste liquors from either the kraft or soda process. The latter type of lignin, regardless of wood used or variations in the process, has similar properties, being soluble in alkali and, unlike the sulfonate, insoluble in acid. A third material which has received some attention is the insoluble ligneous residue resulting from the hydrolysis of wood for the manufacture of ethyl alcohol.

Sulfate lignin and partially desulfonated sulfite lignin have been found to be of value as a reinforcing agent for various elastomers. The combination of properties obtainable with this lignin when coprecipitated with natural, GR-S, nitrile, or neoprene elastomers, is surprising. Tensile strengths appear to be as good as, and sometimes superior to, those obtained with the carbon blacks, and, in addition, good abrasion and tear resistance are obtained. Since lignin has a lower specific gravity (1.3) than any of the other pigments commonly used, lightweight articles having the same volume as heavier items made with other reinforcing agents can be made.

Lignin, recovered as basic calcium lignosulfonate from the sulfite pulping process, can be converted to a number of derivatives, each with different properties. Calcium can be replaced by other metals, while other parts of the molecule can be altered by varying the degree of desulfonation, demethylation, or oxidation by proper control of pressure, temperature, and pH.

Vanillin, the first lignin derivative sold and still an important product, is made by treating spent sulfite liquors with lime to precipitate the inorganic materials. More lime is added to precipitate basic calcium lignosulfonate. (Some of this material is isolated directly by spray drying, but the bulk of it is dissolved in sulfuric acid. By adding different metal sulfates, various lignosulfonates are obtained.) For vanillin manufacture, the basic calcium lignosulfonate is treated with caustic soda, oxidized, and partially desulfonated. The vanillin thus formed by splitting some of the lignin molecules is isolated and purified.

A large portion of the calcium lignosulfonate manufactured is used for its dispersant properties. Over 60 million pounds of organic dispersants were required in 1953 for control of viscosity in oil-well drilling muds; of this quantity, an appreciable portion was made from calcium lignosulfonates.

Other commercial uses for some of the lignosulfonate derivatives are as a dispersant for pigment dyes; in insecticide formulations and industrial metal cleaners; as a scale preventive in boiler water treatment compounds; as a tanning agent in the leather industry, replacing a part of the vegetable tans ordinarily used; as a stabilizer in asphalt emulsions; as a deflocculant and binder for ceramics; and as an extender or replacement for phenols in phenoplasts.

*Humic Acids.* Although synthetic humic acids can be made by suitable treatment of polyhydric phenols and carbohydrates, the natural ones are quite abundant and of some interest from the viewpoint of commercial utilization. The naturally occurring humic materials are formed from vegetable matter while it is slowly undergoing conversion to coal. The rate of conversion and the types of final products obtained depend upon the biological and geological conditions. While sugars dissolve and proteins are completely decomposed, the conversion of the cell walls of living matter is slower. It is this cell-wall material, consisting principally of cellulose and lignin, that forms the humic substances, yielding humus and peat, and, eventually, brown coal, bituminous coal, and anthracite. Although cellulose was formerly thought to be the chief raw material from which the humic materials were formed, the belief now is that it is lignin from which these are derived; thus, humic substances can be considered as intermediate products in the conversion of lignin to coal. Under the influence of heat and pressure, accompanied by oxidation, hydrolysis, and microbiological action, some of the methoxy groups are lost and carboxylic acid groups are formed. Carbonyl and phenolic hydroxyl groups are also present.

Humic materials obtained from peat and brown coal have been evaluated for possible use as a rubber reinforcing agent with encouraging results. Of course, this possibility has been engendered by the close chemical and physical similarity of humic acids to lignin.

**Natural Rubber**

Naturally occurring rubbery materials were known as long ago as 1521, as reported by early explorers in Mexico. Joseph Priestley, the discoverer of oxygen in 1774, is credited with introducing the word "rubber," as one of its earliest uses was that of rubbing out pencil marks. Charles Macintosh, an Englishman, produced a rubberized type of fabric about 1820, whence the name *macintosh* for that type of raincoat. The term *vulcanization*, referring to the heat treatment of rubber and sulfur, was introduced by Thomas Hancock.

No large-scale use of rubber was made until 1839, when Charles Goodyear, an American, hardened a mixture of raw rubber and sulfur by heat, thereby widening its useful temperature range and decidedly improving many of its other properties. It was soon found that certain alkaline substances, such as lime, magnesia, and litharge, not only increased the speed of reaction between rubber and the sulfur but also yielded better products. In 1906, Oenslager, in the United States, discovered that addition of aniline to a rubber compound materially accelerated the rate of vulcanization. This was the beginning of the modern rubber industry. Inspired by this discovery, a considerable amount of research was carried on between then and the early 1930's, with the result that many other chemicals were found which produce similar results; these are called "accelerators."

The discovery was made early in other fields that the deterioration of many organic substances is due to oxidation and that certain chemicals inhibit this action. In 1924 the first commercial rubber antioxidant was introduced. Since then, many chemicals designed to improve the aging and fatigue resistance of rubber have been developed.

A huge industry, in large part the result of the growth of the automobile industry, has been established around rubber. Although it began before the synthetic plastics industry and, while often regarded as a plastic substance, rubber has usually been considered an independent field.

Natural rubbers are obtainable from a variety of trees, shrubs, and vines, principally those indigenous to the tropics. The plants yield a milky latex, which is an emulsion of polyhydrocarbon droplets in an aqueous serum, stabilized by naturally occurring proteins, soaps, and lipoids. The bully tree of South America yields balata, the gutta-percha tree of Malaya, Borneo, and Sumatra yields gutta-percha, the guayule shrub of Mexico and California yields guayule, and the Hevea tree of (originally) Brazil yields caoutchouc or Hevea rubber.

Because of its adaptability to plantation production, as well as the high yield and excellent properties of its polyhydrocarbon, the Hevea tree has become the principal source of natural rubber. Before World War II, it supplied almost all of the world's rubber, of which 98 per cent came from plantations in the Far East, 1 per cent was "wild rubber" from Brazil (Pará rubber), and the rest came from Liberian and South American plantations. Work is currently being carried on in the United States for the preparation of high-quality rubber by the deresination of guayule.

The unqualified term "natural rubber" almost invariably refers to Hevea rubber.

The latex obtained from the rubber tree is not from the sap, but is found in capillary vessels severed and exposed by cutting the bark of the tree. A mature tree yields only about 5 grams of rubber per day or about 4 pounds of rubber per year. The approximate composition of latex is given in Table 6-3. Among the inorganic constituents are trace amounts of iron, copper, and manganese salts.

TABLE 6-3. COMPOSITION OF RUBBER LATEX

|  | Per Cent |
|---|---|
| Water | 59–66 |
| Rubber hydrocarbons | 30–36 |
| Proteins | 1–2 |
| Stearin, fats, soaps | 1–2 |
| Quebrachitol | 0.5–1 |
| Inorganic constituents | 0.3–0.7 |

As shown in Table 6-3, the latex contains about 40 per cent of total solids, an average sample after coagulation containing about 86 to 91 per cent rubber hydrocarbons and 1 to 10 per cent moisture. Coagulation of the hydrocarbon is effected by addition of electrolytes, alcohol, acetic or, usually, formic acid, or by evaporation to dryness; the spongy mass, after mastication, is known as *crepe rubber*. *Smoked sheet* is the term applied to the crude coagulum after drying by smoking for export.

In 1826 Faraday deduced the empirical formula $C_{10}H_{16}$ for the rubber hydrocarbon. The controversy over the actual structure of rubber continued until recently, such men as Tilden, Weber, Harries, Pickles, Pummerer, and Meyer and Mark contributing to the elucidation of its structure. It is now known that rubber is a linear, high-molecular-weight polymer of isoprene, $C_5H_8$,

$$\underset{\displaystyle [-CH_2 \cdot C:CH \cdot CH_2-]_n}{\overset{\displaystyle CH_3}{\displaystyle |}}$$

in which $n$ is of the order of 2,000 (corresponding to an average molecular weight of between 100,000 and 500,000) and which possesses the *cis* configuration. Balata and gutta-percha, isomers of rubber, possess the *trans* configuration and, as a result, are much more thermoplastic and less elastomeric.

Crude rubber is converted at the factory into a useful product by the following processes: (1) The rubber is masticated or kneaded between warm rolls, during which process it gradually loses its reversible extensibility and becomes plastic as a result of degradation of the polymer chains; (2) at the same time or immediately subsequent to mastication,

the necessary compounding ingredients are mixed into the rubber; and
(3) the mixture is transferred to molds where it is vulcanized by heat or
is vulcanized in the cold by immersion of the molded object (usually in
sheets) in a solution of sulfur monochloride in carbon disulfide or benzene.

The first operation outlined above involves the physical plasticization
of the solid stock and is known as the *breakdown*.  In practice, the process
consists of subjecting the rubber to a severe mechanical shearing stress
by the use of either a two-roll rubber mill or a Banbury mixer.  The

Fig. 6-1.   Mastication of rubber on a two-roll mill.   At this stage, the rubber is compounded with the necessary additives.   (*Courtesy Goodyear Tire & Rubber Co.*)

milled rubber has greater plasticity and ease of solvation, and a lower
viscosity in solution than the untreated rubber.   One explanation for
these effects is that chemical reaction occurs under the influence of the
mechanical stress, involving oxidation and subsequent cleavage of the
rubber polymer molecules.

The second stage in rubber processing is called *compounding*.   Both the rubber mill and the Banbury mixer can be used for the mixing of the additives with the rubber. The more important compounding agents and their functions will be briefly discussed.

*Reinforcing agents.* Certain inorganic compounds improve the tensile strength, elastic modulus, abrasion resistance, and tear resistance of rubber. Channel carbon blacks, some clays, magnesium carbonate, and barium sulfate are useful for these purposes.

*Inert fillers.* These ingredients have little or no beneficial effect on strength and resistance but improve processing properties or hardness. They may also act merely as diluents to lower the cost of the product. Fillers include soft carbon blacks, barytes, whiting, slate flour, factice, limestone, and talc.

*Softeners.* These materials aid in mastication and subsequent processing of rubber compounds. Lower elastic moduli and higher elongations are obtained by their inclusion in compounding formulations.

The term "softener" is a widely inclusive designation. It was formerly used for miscellaneous oils and pitches, such as palm oil, coal tar, and pine tar, which were used principally to obtain better processing through improved softness and tack. With the advent of the flexible plastics and synthetic elastomers, the number of materials has been greatly increased and the scope of their functions has been enlarged. They are now used as processing aids for uncured stock, softeners for cured stock, freezing-point depressants, organic reinforcing agents, and extenders. Softeners which are used as processing aids for uncured stock have been classified as plasticizers, lubricants, tackifiers, and dispersing aids, depending upon their specific function.

*Vulcanizing agents.* The various materials added to accomplish vulcanization may be classed as follows:

a. Vulcanizing agents. Sulfur has remained the principal vulcanizing agent since its early use by Goodyear and Hancock. Many other materials can be used, among which are sulfur monochloride, selenium, tellurium, thiuram disulfides, polysulfide polymers, and alkyl phenol sulfides.

b. Accelerators. These materials, containing nitrogen or sulfur, or both, are used to increase the rate of vulcanization or allow the use of lower vulcanizing temperatures, or both. By their use, the percentage of sulfur required for vulcanization may be considerably reduced. They may be divided into four general chemical classes, there being also some miscellaneous types: (1) mercaptothiazoles and derivatives, (2) dithiocarbamates and thiuram sulfides, (3) guanidine derivatives, and (4) aldehyde-amine reaction products.

In order of increasing effectiveness, accelerators are grouped as normal or moderate, semi-ultra- or rapid, and ultra-accelerators. The first includes derivatives of guanidine and aldehyde-amines.   A favorite semi-ultra-accelerator is mercaptobenzothiazole:

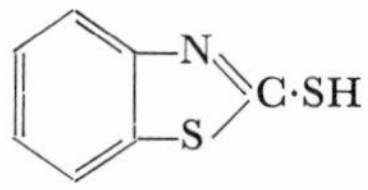

Among the ultra-accelerators are tetramethylthiuram disulfide and zinc salts of dithio acids, such as zinc diethyl dithiocarbamate, $[(Et_2N \cdot CSS)_2Zn]$.

The ultra-accelerators cause curing below 100°C in a few minutes; the semi-ultra or rapid accelerators require temperatures of 100° to 130°C for 20 to 40 minutes; the normal or moderate accelerators are effective at 140° to 150°C and require a longer time for action.

c. Activators.   These compounds, both organic and inorganic, are used to activate or increase the accelerating effect of materials included in the group above.   Most accelerators require both zinc oxide and a fatty acid in order to develop the best quality in the compound.   Hence, it is almost universal practice to add zinc oxide and stearic acid to rubber compounds.   Further activation and improved properties can often be obtained by the use of additional activators, such as litharge, magnesium oxide, amines, or amine soaps.

*Antioxidants.*   Rubber is extremely sensitive to decomposition by the action of oxygen, particularly in the presence of light.   Various organic compounds are used to retard the oxidation of the finished products and thus slow down deterioration due to exposure.   These substances inhibit the reaction of rubber with atmospheric oxygen and are, therefore, known as protectors against aging or antioxidants.   Compounds used are aromatic amines, chiefly those of the naphthalene series, and certain phenol derivatives.   Examples are phenyl-$\beta$-naphthylamine, $p,p'$-diamino-diphenyl methane, and aryl amine-ketone reaction products.

*Colors or pigments.*   Pigments or dyes are sometimes added to impart a desired color to the finished product.   These ingredients may be inorganic pigments, such as iron oxide, titanium oxide, or cadmium sulfide, or they may be organic dyes.

In addition to the above substances generally used, there are a number of materials, such as antiseptics, blowing agents for sponge rubber, odorants, peptizing agents, and retarders, which are used in special cases.

The above compounding agents are incorporated in a rubber mix immediately after the breakdown period.   A typical compounding formula, giving the amounts and the usual order in which the materials are added, is as follows:[2]

---

[2] Mason, J. P. and Manning, J. F., *The Technology of Plastics and Resins*, p. 142, D. Van Nostrand Co., Princeton, N.J., 1945.

|  | | | | | *Parts* |
|---|---|---|---|---|---|
| Rubber | . | . | . | . | 100 |
| Softener | . | . | . | . | 5 |
| Reinforcing agent | | . | . | . | 100–200 |
| Accelerator | | . | . | . | 1 |
| Antioxidant | | . | . | . | 1 |
| Activator | . | . | . | . | 5 |
| Sulfur | . | . | . | . | 2.5 |

Sulfur is usually the last agent to be added in order to prevent partial premature curing (scorching) while the mixing operation is being performed. A retarder is sometimes added for this purpose, organic acids serving effectively.

To the best of our present knowledge, it appears that sulfur vulcanization is a free-radical-initiated chain reaction, which is started by production of a free radical furnished by the accelerator or, in its absence, by sulfur in its chain form. This free radical removes a hydrogen ion from an isoprene mesomer, forming an active center on the mesomer. (See Chap. 3 for details of this mechanism.) Next, a sulfur molecule ($S_8$) combines with the center and releases some free sulfur. The activated sulfur-isoprene addition product then reacts with a mesomer in another chain, removing another hydrogen ion, or reacts at a double bond with the formation of a cross-link (probably —S·S—), which is stabilized by a hydrogen transfer. In both cases, an activated mesomer is regenerated. Other reactions also occur, including intramolecular reactions with the formation of heterocyclic rings.

The action of accelerators appears to be that of decomposition with the release of free radicals, as mentioned above, or possibly that of catalysis of the conversion of the cyclic sulfur ($S_8$) to a more soluble and reactive form. The probable action of zinc oxide is to form zinc mercaptides which later decompose to yield cross-linked mono- and disulfides, which, by their action, suppress the formation of cyclic compounds. Generally speaking, one atom of zinc and two of sulfur produce one cross-link. It also appears probable that the function of the stearic acid added and other fatty acids naturally present is to aid in solubilizing the zinc oxide.

The properties of crude rubber and vulcanized rubber differ considerably. Raw rubber is much inferior to vulcanized rubber both in elasticity and tensile strength. Vulcanized rubber has a breaking strength some twenty to thirty times that of raw rubber, while its elasticity is much less subject to change with changes in temperature.

Thus, during the process of vulcanization, rubber undergoes a great reduction in plasticity while elasticity is maintained. In addition, there is obtained increased resistance to the action of solvents, since with vulcanized rubber, swelling occurs but is not accompanied by solution. This behavior is due, of course, to the cross-linked structure of the vulcanizate.

It has been said that vulcanized rubber is remarkable for its resistance to abrasion; its flexibility, elasticity, extensibility, resilience, absorption of shock; inertness to water, solutions, and gases; high frictional resistance when dry, low frictional resistance when wet; high electrical resistance; low thermal conductivity; resistance to moderately high temperatures; and plasticity under proper conditions. This very unusual combination of properties enables rubber to be used in a multitude of ways, possibly not exceeded by any other substance.

*Reclaimed Rubber.* Many of the thousands of rubber products manufactured today owe at least part of their properties to *reclaimed* rubber, both natural and synthetic. When most sources of natural rubber disappeared at the beginning of World War II, reclaimed rubber to a large extent maintained the flow of transportation until large-scale production of synthetic elastomers took over. By 1951 the reclaiming industry in the United States amounted to about 355,000 long tons per year.

There are many processes for the reclaiming of rubber, the principal one being the digestion of shredded scrap in large autoclaves with a dilute zinc chloride or caustic solution under heat and pressure. This defibers, desulfurizes, and devulcanizes the rubber in one operation and produces a reclaim of very good quality.

Although reclaiming was originated specifically to provide a substitute for new rubber, reclaim has emerged as a raw material in its own right, having unique properties and advantages over new rubber in several applications.

In general, reclaim permits faster and easier mastication and mixing than new rubber. It is also less susceptible to premature vulcanization. Because it is less thermoplastic than new rubber, molded or extruded articles containing reclaim retain their shape better during vulcanization. In some products, it gives better quality than can be obtained with new rubber, and its use often results in equal or better quality at lower cost.

Large quantities of reclaim are used in automotive equipment, such as battery boxes, floor mats, radiator hose, and window channeling; in fact, automobile manufacturers utilize an estimated two thirds of all reclaim produced. A first-quality tire for passenger car use normally contains from 3 to 4 pounds of reclaim; an automobile floor mat may contain 5 pounds, and a battery case an equal amount. Other large uses of reclaim are in the manufacture of adhesives and mechanical and molded goods. Since adhesives made from reclaim have lower viscosities for equivalent concentrations of solids, and the films obtained therefrom possess high moduli, reclaim is particularly valuable in their manufacture.

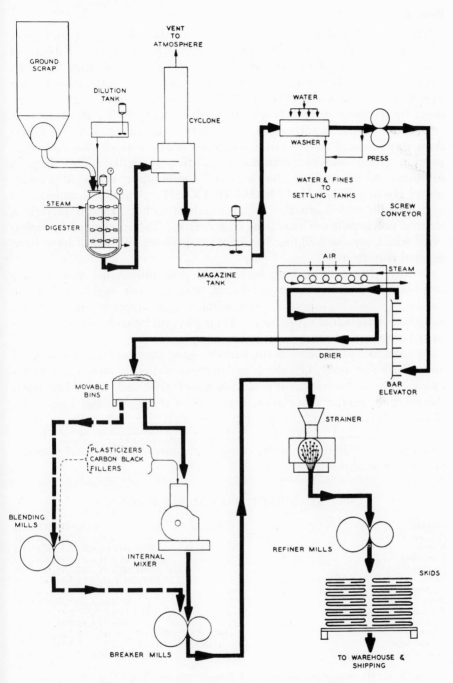

FIG. 6-2.  Rubber reclaiming flow sheet.  (*Courtesy Modern Chemical Processes*)

**Proteins**

The term "protein" covers what is probably the largest and most widely diversified group of complex nitrogenous organic substances known. In spite of this diversity, however, their molecules are constructed principally of relatively few and simple organic substances, known as $\alpha$-amino acids, $R \cdot CH(NH_2) \cdot COOH$. These are combined with each other by means of secondary amide bonds, $R \cdot CO \cdot NH \cdot R'$, also known as peptide bonds, or, in a few cases, by tertiary amide bonds, $R \cdot CO \cdot NR'R''$. Both proteins and nylons (from $\omega$-amino acids) contain this recurrent peptide group and are commonly called polyamides. The simplest substance which utilizes this form of combination is the dipeptide, glycyl glycine, $NH_2 \cdot CH_2 \cdot CO \cdot NH \cdot CH_2 \cdot COOH$. Additional amino acid units may be added at either or both ends of such a structure to yield a series of polypeptides of increasing complexity. Table 6-4 gives the amino acids which are the building blocks of the proteins and which have been isolated therefrom.

Because they contain both basic and acidic side-chains, proteins are amphoteric electrolytes. Nevertheless, due to their highly polymeric nature, colloidal properties predominate and suppress many of the expected crystalloidal properties. Their physical behavior depends upon the pH of the medium in which they are placed.

At a definite pH, known as the *isoelectric point*, the dissociation as an acid and a base are equal; i.e., the concentration of dipolar ions is at a maximum. The isoelectric point is usually about pH 4 to 5, depending upon the relative specific dissociation constants of the acidic and basic side-chains. At this point the protein zwitterion does not migrate upon electrolysis (cataphoresis), and such physical properties as solubility, conductivity, colloidal stability, osmotic pressure, swelling, and viscosity are at a minimum.

TABLE 6-4.   STRUCTURAL UNITS OF PROTEINS[3]

| | |
|---|---|
| Glycine | $CH_2(NH_2)COOH$ |
| Alanine | $CH_3CH(NH_2)COOH$ |
| Valine | $CH_3CH(CH_3)CH(NH_2)COOH$ |
| Norvaline | $CH_3CH_2CH_2CH(NH_2)COOH$ |
| Leucine | $CH_3CH(CH_3)CH_2CH(NH_2)COOH$ |
| Isoleucine | $CH_3CH_2CH(CH_3)CH(NH_2)COOH$ |
| Norleucine | $CH_3CH_2CH_2CH_2CH(NH_2)COOH$ |
| Serine | $HOCH_2CH(NH_2)COOH$ |
| Threonine | $CH_3CH(OH)CH(NH_2)COOH$ |
| Cysteine | $HSCH_2CH(NH_2)COOH$ |
| Cystine | $HOOCCH(NH_2)CH_2SSCH_2CH(NH_2)COOH$ |
| Lanthionine | $HOOCCH(NH_2)CH_2SCH_2CH(NH_2)COOH$ |
| Methionine | $CH_3SCH_2CH_2CH(NH_2)COOH$ |

[3] Meyer, K. H., *Natural and Synthetic High Polymers*, 2nd ed., Table 1, p. 500, Interscience Publishers, New York, 1950.

TABLE 6-4
(Continued)

Phenylalanine . . . . . . . $\langle\text{C}_6\text{H}_5\rangle\text{CH}_2\text{CH(NH}_2)\text{COOH}$

Tyrosine . . . . . . . $\text{HO}\langle\text{C}_6\text{H}_4\rangle\text{CH}_2\text{CH(NH}_2)\text{COOH}$

Dibromotyrosine and diiodotyrosine . . . $\text{HO}\langle\overset{I}{\underset{I}{\text{C}_6\text{H}_2}}\rangle\text{CH}_2\text{CH(NH}_2)\text{COOH}$

Dihydroxyphenylalanine . . . . . $\text{HO}\langle\overset{OH}{\text{C}_6\text{H}_3}\rangle\text{CH}_2\text{CH(NH}_2)\text{COOH}$

Aspartic acid . . . . . . . . $\text{HOOCCH}_2\text{CH(NH}_2)\text{COOH}$
Glutamic acid . . . . . . . . $\text{HOOCCH}_2\text{CH}_2\text{CH(NH}_2)\text{COOH}$
$\beta$-Hydroxyglutamic acid . . . . . . $\text{HOOCCH(OH)CH(NH}_2)\text{COOH}$
Lysine . . . . . . . $\text{NH}_2\text{CH}_2\text{CH}_2\text{CH}_2\text{CH}_2\text{CH(NH}_2)\text{COOH}$
Hydroxylysine . . . . . . $\text{NH}_2\text{CH}_2\text{CH(OH)CH}_2\text{CH}_2\text{CH(NH}_2)\text{COOH}$
Arginine . . . . . . $\text{NH}_2\text{C(:NH)NHCH}_2\text{CH}_2\text{CH}_2\text{CH(NH}_2)\text{COOH}$
Canavanine . . . . . . $\text{NH}_2\text{C(:NH)NHOCH}_2\text{CH}_2\text{CH(NH}_2)\text{COOH}$

Tryptophane . . . . . . $\begin{array}{c}\text{—C—CH}_2\text{CH(NH}_2)\text{COOH}\\ \|\\ \text{CH}\\ \text{N}\\ \text{H}\end{array}$

Histidine . . . . . . . . $\begin{array}{c}\text{N——C—CH}_2\text{CH(NH}_2)\text{COOH}\\ \|\quad\quad\|\\ \text{HC}\quad\text{CH}\\ \text{N}\\ \text{H}\end{array}$

$N$-Methylhistidine . . . . . . $\begin{array}{c}\text{N——C—CH}_2\text{CH(NH}_2)\text{COOH}\\ \|\quad\quad\|\\ \text{HC}\quad\text{CH}\\ \text{N}\\ \text{CH}_3\end{array}$

Proline . . . . . . . . . . . $\begin{array}{c}\text{H}_2\text{C——CH}_2\\ \text{H}_2\text{C}\quad\text{CHCOOH}\\ \text{N}\\ \text{H}\end{array}$

Hydroxyproline . . . . . . . . . $\begin{array}{c}\text{OH}\\ \text{HC——CH}_2\\ \text{H}_2\text{C}\quad\text{CHCOOH}\\ \text{N}\\ \text{H}\end{array}$

168 POLYMERS AND RESINS

The enormous range in sizes of protein molecules has been measured by a number of methods. The earliest estimates were obtained by stoichiometric calculations. The measurement of the osmotic pressure of a solution of proteins has also proved to be extremely useful. However, the best-known method for determining the molecular weight of proteins is the ultracentrifugal method, developed by Svedberg[4] and applied to the study of egg albumin and hemoglobin in 1926, and extensively developed since then (see Chap. 4). Molecular weights for various proteins range from approximately 12,000 to 15,000 for ribonuclease to as high as $4 \times 10^7$ for certain plant viruses.

Proteins are found in all living cells, whether of plant or animal origin. Every living cell must contain many different protein components, for the chemical reactions that are characteristic of the life process are catalyzed by enzymes, and enzymes are proteins.

The proteins comprise so large and diversified a group of substances that there are few properties that are common to all of its members. Their outstanding chemical property is that a mixture of $\alpha$-amino acids is produced when they are completely degraded by treatment with hot acids or alkalies, or, at the proper pH, with proteolytic enzymes. Almost thirty of these acids have been obtained by the hydrolysis of one protein or another. All but two are simple $\alpha$-amino acids, while the exceptions, proline and hydroxyproline, contain nitrogen as part of a simple heterocyclic ring. Most proteins yield about eighteen amino acids; however, they differ widely in the proportions of these acids.

The usual method of classification of the proteins divides them on the basis of composition into two major groups, the *simple proteins* and the *conjugated proteins* (proteides). The simple proteins on complete hydrolysis yield only $\alpha$-amino acids, whereas the conjugated proteins yield, in addition to the amino acids, some other substance.

The classification of the simple proteins upon a logical chemical basis has not yet been possible and, for lack of a better means, they have been divided into groups on the basis of solubility. Table 6-5 lists the simple proteins together with their unusual properties, solubility characteristics, and some of their places of occurrence.

A different subdivision of simple proteins is possible, into fibrous (fibrillar) and nonfibrous (globular) proteins. Fibrous proteins (the scleroproteins) include silk, wool, tendons, hides, horns and hooves, and are not visibly crystalline. Nonfibrous proteins include at least the albumins and globulins, and probably the glutelins. They can form crystals and are more reactive and soluble than the fibrous proteins, although their solutions are easily coagulated. Thus, the glutelins and

[4] Svedberg, T. and Pedersen, K. O., eds., *The Ultracentrifuge*, Oxford University Press, London-New York, 1940.

TABLE 6-5.   SIMPLE PROTEINS

| Protein | Solubility | Typical Occurrence | Remarks |
|---|---|---|---|
| Protamines | Soluble in water | Sperm of fish | Strongly basic Low molecular weight |
| Albumins | Soluble in water Amphoteric | Egg, serum, milk, wheat, muscle | Coagulated by heat |
| Globulins | Soluble in dilute neutral salts Insoluble in water Weakly acidic | Body fluids Grain seeds | Coagulated by heat |
| Glutelins | Soluble in dilute acids or bases Insoluble in neutral solvents | Wheat (glutenin) Rice (oryzein) | |
| Prolamines (Gliadins) | Soluble in 75% alcohol Insoluble in neutral alcohol and water | Wheat (gliadin) Barley (hordein) Corn (zein) Milk | Vegetable proteins |
| Albuminoids (Scleroproteins) | Insoluble in most liquids | Glue, gelatin (collagen) Horn, wool, hair, feathers (keratin) Silk (fibroin) Ligaments (elastin) | Contain much sulfur Resist hydrolysis |
| Histones | Soluble in water Insoluble in dilute $NH_3$ | Animal tissue White blood corpuscles Sperm of animals | Contain sulfur |

the globulins are insoluble in neutral water but dissolve in dilute acid or alkali.    However, strong acids and alkalies transform them from their original state to an insoluble or *denatured* state.    Soluble proteins can be denatured by other methods—by heating (as, for example, by the boiling of an egg), by the addition of electrolytes or organic solvents, by irradiation with ultraviolet light, or even by shaking.    It appears that the change is physical, since little or no chemical difference is observed between the two forms.    At the present time, denaturation appears in many cases to be a transformation from the native condition, in which the protein chains are folded, to a state in which the chains are folded in a different manner or are even unfolded.

Although the proteins are essentially linear in structure, there is considerable evidence that the backbones of adjacent molecules are united by cross-links, both primary and secondary.    A process involving the controlled cross-linking of protein chain molecules is the tanning of leather, which consists essentially of collagen.    Untanned leather is attacked by microorganisms and is very sensitive to moisture and heat.

The collagen fibers are almost nonelastic, but, when wet, the mass is very plastic (due to the plasticizing effect of the imbibed water) and can be molded. Tanning agents improve the resistance to moisture and heat, and their mechanism appears to involve the blocking of hydrophilic groups (such as amino and carboxyl) and the formation of a cross-linked network. Thus, formaldehyde, an irreversible tanning agent, probably acts as follows:

$$-NH_2 + CH_2O + -NH_2 \rightarrow -NH \cdot CH_2 \cdot NH- + H_2O$$

Chrome tanning very likely consists of the formation of cross-linkages by complex formation; for example, by basic chromium ions diffusing into the skin and reacting successively with protein carboxyl groups. Vegetable tannins (multivalent phenols of high molecular weight) probably act similarly, although here it is the amino groups of the protein which are involved. These types of tanning are reversible.

The conjugated proteins (proteides), as mentioned earlier, contain other (prosthetic) groups which are themselves quite complex and vary considerably. The phosphoproteins and lecithoproteins contain complex phosphoric acid derivatives; the nucleoproteins, which occur in all living cell nuclei, contain a high-molecular-weight organic acid composed of cyclic nitrogen bases, a sugar, and phosphoric acid; the chromoproteins contain a complex pigment group; the lipoproteins, a fatty acid; and the glucoproteins, carbohydrate derivatives. The casein of milk is a phosphoprotein, lecithin is a lecithoprotein, hemoglobin is a chromoprotein, and egg whites contain glucoproteins. It is of interest to point out that hemoglobin of blood is composed of hemin, the prosthetic group, and globin, the protein group. Hemin is a red complex composed principally of four linked pyrrole nuclei coordinately bound to an atom of iron. A similar structure is found in chlorophyll, the green coloring matter of plants, where the four linked pyrrole nuclei are here bound to an atom of magnesium.

In addition to the almost universal occurrences of proteins mentioned previously, they also are found in toxins (and antibodies), viruses, enzymes, and hormones. Toxins, secreted by pathogenic organisms and responsible for their lethal effect, include those of diphtheria, tetanus, botulinus, and snake venom. Viruses, substances that can transmit diseases but which are smaller than microorganisms, include the nucleoprotein, tobacco mosaic, a protein of extremely high molecular weight (ca. 40,000,000) and one capable of reproduction. Enzymes are catalysts which control the many living processes, are generated by living organisms, and generally contain a metallic ion. A familiar one is maltase which changes maltose to glucose. Among the hormones, a protein known for more than half a century is insulin, used for control of diabetes. A more recently known and well-publicized pituitary hormone is the adreno-corticotropic hormone, for obvious reasons called ACTH.

An interesting application of chemistry to a natural protein is that of the "permanent" waving of human hair. Ammonium thioglycollate, used in most cold-wave applications, acts by breaking the sulfur cross-links in the keratin of hair. The hair is then mechanically curled, and the cross-links are re-established by an oxidizing agent, called a "neutra-lizer," usually sodium bromate.

Since proteins, like cellulose, are high-molecular-weight polymers, it is not surprising to find that some of them are used as industrial plastics—notably casein (from milk), zein (from maize), arachin (from peanuts), and soya protein (from soya beans). These will be discussed in the next chapter.

*Gelatin.* Gelatin is a soluble protein product obtained by the hydrolysis of collagen, the major intercellular protein constituent of the white connective tissue of animal skins and bones:

$$85°C$$
$$\underset{\text{Collagen}}{C_{102}H_{149}O_{38}N_{31}} + H_2O \longrightarrow \underset{\text{Gelatin}}{C_{102}H_{151}O_{39}N_{31}}$$

Like the molecules of most other proteins, gelatin molecules are very large and complex. Values of the average molecular weight of gelatin have been obtained from 10,000 to 250,000. Upon complete hydrolysis, gelatin yields a number of simple amino acids of known structure; however, their arrangement in the gelatin molecule is not known.

Commercial gelatin is a tasteless, odorless, transparent, brittle solid, colorless when pure. Its uses depend on its gel-forming ability, the ease of its reversible transition from gel to sol, its high viscosity, and its effectiveness as a protective colloid.

Gelatin is widely used in the food, pharmaceutical, photographic, and other industries. Edible gelatin is used in gelatin desserts, candies, jellied meats, consommé, bakery products, ice cream, and other dairy products. In the pharmaceutical field, it is used in capsules, ointments, cosmetics, suppositories, medication carriers, hemostatics, blood-plasma substitutes, tablet coatings, and emulsions. A very large quantity is consumed in making photographic emulsions and miscellaneous products.

*Glues.* Strictly speaking, the term "glue" refers only to the adhesive derived from collagen. The difference between gelatin and glue is the degree of purity, glue being impure gelatin (possibly of lower molecular weight also). Contrary to popular belief, glue cannot be obtained from such noncollagen proteins as hair, hooves, and horns. The word "glue" is frequently used, however, to refer to any adhesive material irrespective

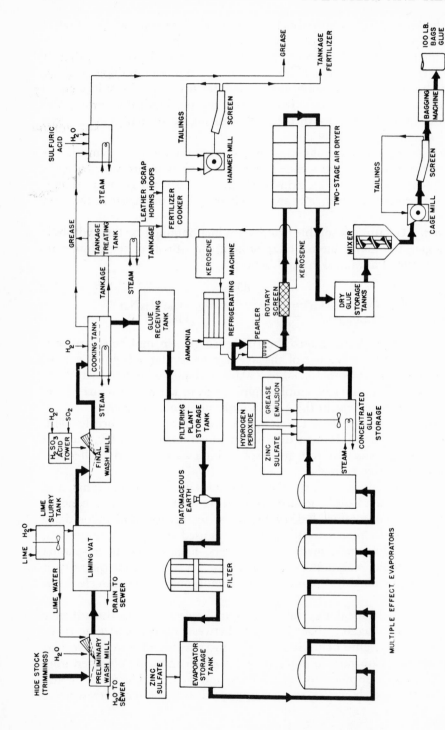

Fig. 6-3.   Animal glue flow sheet.   (Courtesy Modern Chemical Processes)

of source or type.   Although glue has been known and used for thousands of years, the first commercial plant was erected in Holland in 1690; it was first commercially produced in the United States in 1808.

Dry animal glue, whether derived from hides, skins, sinews, or bones, is an amber-colored material.   The two principal types are hide glue and bone glue, the former being the stronger and more versatile type.   Like most proteins, glue absorbs water readily, forming an elastic gel or viscous solution having great adhesive properties.   Glycerol is the only other known solvent for animal glue and even it requires the presence of some moisture to effect solution.   Perhaps the most characteristic property of animal glue is its tendency to form reversible gels in aqueous solution.

Two types of glue are obtained from fish by-products.   Swimming bladders, upon extraction with hot water, yield a high-grade product which, after clarification and filtration, is marketed as fish gelatin or isinglass.   It is too costly for use as a commercial adhesive but finds use as a protective colloid in the clarification of beverages.   The second type is a less expensive product, made from the heads, skins, and skeletal waste of various fish, and is used primarily as a cold, liquid adhesive.

### Cellulose

Cellulose, the major constituent of plants, is the most abundant and widely used organic chemical in the world.   Billions of tons of it are created annually by photosynthesis.   In the form of wood, paper, cotton, rayon, film, plastics, and coatings, as a fuel, and for countless other uses, there is consumed throughout the world almost half a billion tons of cellulose per year.

Cellulose is the fibrous component of vegetable tissues which gives them coherence and form.   It occurs in combination with various noncellulosic carbohydrates, their acidic oxidation products, and with the lignins.

Although cellulose may be obtained from many vegetable sources, the scarcity, problems of collection and isolation, or quality have kept all sources less important than those of wood and cottonseed hairs.

Wood, the principal source, is found everywhere, since the branches and trunks of the higher plants are composed of it.   The composition of wood varies with the species and location of the sample, but, on a dry basis, it contains approximately 40 to 50 per cent cellulose, 20 to 30 per cent lignin, and 10 to 30 per cent hemicelluloses and polysaccharides other than cellulose.   Other constituents are resins, gums, proteins, and minerals.

The other important source of cellulose is cotton, whose fiber contains the lowest percentage of noncellulosic material, 4 to 12 per cent.   However, of some importance is the kapok fiber which is widely used, particularly in life preservers, because of its buoyancy and moisture resistance.

It contains from 55 to 60 per cent cellulose but is not used as a source of industrial cellulose.

Bast fibers are the long fibers of the inner bark of various plants and include flax, hemp, jute, ramie, and many others of lesser importance. They are widely used in textiles and paper, but, like kapok, are not used industrially as a source of $\alpha$-cellulose. The flax plant is the source of linen, which contains 80 to 90 per cent cellulose. Bleached hemp, containing approximately the same amount of cellulose as bleached linen, is widely used for rope, cordage and bagging, although other fibers have replaced it to a large extent. Jute, the cheapest of the textile fibers, is used for making sacks and bags. Jute fibers contain 65 to 75 per cent cellulose. Ramie, used as a textile fiber in the Orient for thousands of years, has a high tensile strength and a high luster and is relatively little affected by moisture. However, the processing of this fiber is difficult, and its brittleness and inelasticity limit its uses. Purified ramie contains about 85 per cent cellulose.

Since cellulose is the major constituent of the cell walls of plants, there is a huge potential source from the many plants which have no industrial utilization, as well as from the residue from utilized plants. The most important of these wastes and residues belong to the grass family, particularly the cereal straws which have long been used for the manufacture of paper and paper board. Another material extensively used for the manufacture of wall and insulation board is bagasse, the crushed stalks of expressed sugar cane. Other agricultural products which have been utilized include corn stalks, esparto grass, reeds, bamboo, papyrus, and palm.

Cellulose is also found in the mineral kingdom and has been reported to occur in the animal kingdom. In the former, it is found in products of vegetable origin—fossil woods, peat, and certain types of lignite. Peat and lignite fibers have limited use in paper board, in insulating sheets, and even in textiles.

The processing of cellulose through various converting operations into its chief end-uses is shown in Fig. 6-4.

Pure cellulose is a linear polymer composed of individual anhydroglucose (glucopyranose) units linked at the one and four positions through $\beta$-glucosidic bonds. Thus, it has the following structure:

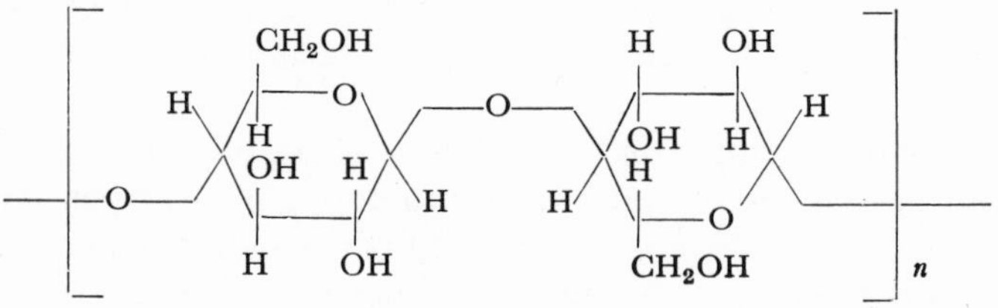

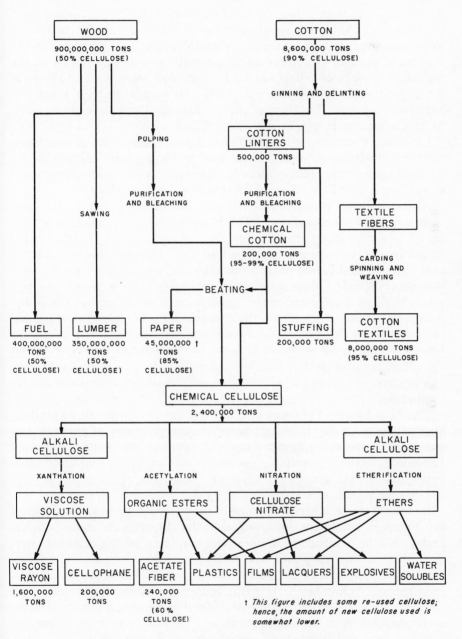

FIG. 6-4.   Cellulose production and distribution[5]

[5] Ott, E., Spurlin, H. M., and Grafflin, M. W., eds., *Cellulose and Cellulose Derivatives*, 2nd ed., Part I, Fig. 1, p. 4, Interscience Publishers, New York, 1954.

where $n$ ranges from a few hundred to about 3,000 in the undegraded polymer. The molecular weight of cellulose is difficult to measure because measurements based on viscosity or osmotic pressure are restricted to the very small number of substances which dissolve cellulose. Further, the molecules are subject to degradation by oxidation, hydrolysis, and thermal decomposition during processing. Molecular weights as high as 800,000 have been reported, but most of the cellulose used commercially appears to have a molecular weight of under 100,000.

Cellulose, therefore, is formed from glucose units, each of which has three free hydroxyl groups. These hydroxyl groups are responsible for its very high softening temperature (which is higher than its decomposition temperature) and its tendency to form crystalline micelles.

Although many properties of cellulose can be explained on the basis of its structure, others cannot. This is partly because cellulose is neither completely crystalline like glucose nor amorphous like a supercooled liquid, but has some properties of both states. The crystallizing tendency of the regular and highly polar anhydroglucose rings is offset by the long, somewhat flexible, mutually entangled chains. As a result, no two cellulose fibers have exactly the same internal structure, and it is the internal structure which affects the strength of the fibers and the rate and extent to which the cellulose in them reacts with reagents. It affects the latter by limiting the access of reagents to the cellulose molecules within the solid; because of this, many reactions which take place easily with glucose do not occur to any appreciable extent with cellulose under similar conditions.

The high hydroxyl content of cellulose might be expected to produce appreciable solubility in water; however, the periphery of primary and secondary hydroxyl groups causes the opposite to occur. Although occasional covalent cross-linking of chains may occur, by ether formation between hydroxyl groups on adjacent chains, the effect of far greater importance is hydrogen bonding among the molecules.

By esterifying or etherifying some of the hydroxyl groups, a number of the hydrogen bonds are destroyed, colloidal dispersion is made possible, and, as will be discussed in the next chapter, the resulting cellulose esters and ethers are thermoplastic and soluble in many solvents. There are, also, a number of reagents which can disperse cellulose by a different mechanism. Schweitzer's reagent (cuprammonium hydroxide) and certain quaternary ammonium hydroxides dissolve cotton linters, yielding a viscous solution in which the cellulose is believed to exist as a complex, copper-containing anion (see Cuprammonium Rayon, Chap. 7). A few other reagents, including calcium thiocyanate, zinc chloride, and trifluoroacetic acid can gelatinize and disperse or dissolve cellulose.

The three major outlets for cellulose—lumber, textiles, and paper—

utilize the strength and toughness of the fibers as they occur in nature; they are cemented with lignin in wood, twisted and woven together in textiles, and matted and adherent to one another in paper.

Since cellulose fibers are not soluble in practical solvents, and since they decompose before melting upon heating, they cannot readily be molded or otherwise converted to other shapes in which their inherent strength could be used to advantage. However, processes based upon the chemical conversion of cellulose to soluble products from which cellulose is regenerated in the desired shape have been developed; e.g., rayon and cellophane manufacture. Another series of processes is based upon the chemical conversion of cellulose to soluble or fusible derivatives which may be shaped to the desired form without regeneration of cellulose. By this means, certain physical properties may also be altered. Acetate fibers, cellulose nitrate coatings, and cellulose ester and ether plastics and films fall in this category. Regenerated cellulose and cellulose derivatives are useful because they also have the properties of strength, toughness, and flexibility.

The chemical reactions of cellulose involve the free hydroxyl groups and the glucosidic linkages. Each glucose residue contains one primary and two secondary hydroxyl groups. In addition, therefore, to esterification and etherification, mentioned above, oxidation reactions may occur. Oxidation of the primary hydroxyl group yields products having carboxyl groups; a number of natural polymers of this type are known and are called polyuronic acids. Thus, alginic acid, obtained from seaweed, is a polyanhydro-$\beta$-mannuronic acid; pectic acid, present in certain fruits, probably is composed of polyanhydro-$\alpha$-galacturonic acid.

The action of caustic soda on cellulose is of interest. To obtain pure cellulose, the lignins are first dissolved out of wood pulp (as in the sulfite process of paper manufacture); treatment of the residue with caustic solution then removes a group of noncellulosic carbohydrate polymers, of lower molecular weight than cellulose, known as *hemicelluloses*. That portion of the residue which is insoluble (arbitrarily) in 17.5 per cent aqueous caustic soda is known as $\alpha$-cellulose. When $\alpha$-cellulose is soaked in cold 17.5 per cent aqueous caustic, it swells and gelatinizes but does not dissolve. The product, known as *alkali* or *soda cellulose*, has an empirical composition varying from $[C_6H_7O_2(OH)_3 \cdot NaOH]_n$ to $[C_6H_7O_2(OH)_3 \cdot \frac{1}{2}NaOH]_n$. Alkali cellulose is unstable and can be washed free of alkali, yielding a regenerated cellulose known as *mercerized* cotton, after Mercer in England who discovered the process in 1844. This cotton has greater affinity for dyestuffs, and the fibers, which have shrunk about 20 per cent in length, acquire a lustrous and silky appearance.

*Pectins.* The pectins are naturally occurring polysaccharides composed principally of colloidal polygalacturonic acids (polyuronides derived from the hexuronic acid, $CHO(CHOH)_4COOH$, related to galactose). These acids are composed of linear chains of anhydrogalacturonic acid residues connected by predominantly $\alpha$-1,4-glycosidic linkages, as shown in the formula:

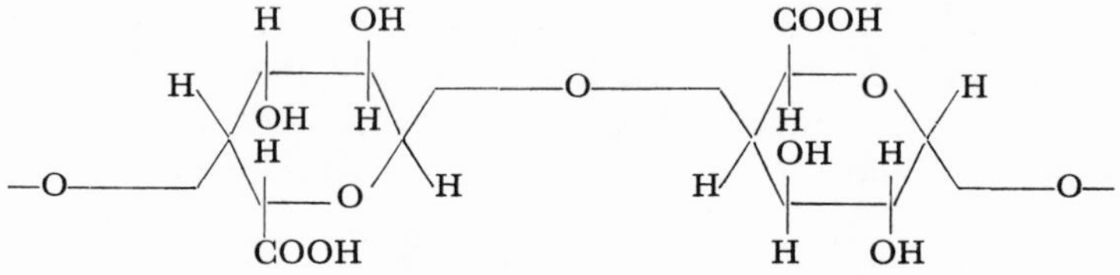

The average molecular weight varies from about 30,000 to 300,000. Dry purified pectin is a white or light-colored solid, slightly soluble in hot water.

Commercial pectin is obtained from apple pomace, citrus peel, and sugar beets. The expressed juices are decolorized and clarified, and the pectin is precipitated with alcohol. Alternatively, pectin can be extracted from citrus fruits with hot, dilute sulfuric acid.

Because of their ability to form gels or jellies with polyhydroxy compounds (especially sugars) or with small amounts of polyvalent ions, commercial pectins are used for the preparation of jams, jellies, preserves, and marmalades. Well over half the world's pectin production is used for this purpose. Pectin is also used for the precipitation of casein from milk, in the production of certain cheese products, in the manufacture of gumdrops, in bakery goods, as a stabilizer in ice cream, as an emulsifying agent in salad dressings, and as a protective coating. It is also used as an ingredient in many infants' preparations, in cosmetics, in the preparation of bacteriological culture media, and as a substitute for agar.

*Agar.* Agar, also known as agar-agar, Chinese moss, and by many other names, is an amorphous seaweed colloid.

Agar consists of D-galactopyranose residues, attached by 1,3-glycosidic linkages. The chain is terminated at the reducing end by a residue of L-galactopyranose. Until quite recently, it was believed that, attached to the rest of the chain through carbon atom 4, the L-galactose residue was esterified at the sixth carbon atom with a sulfuric acid salt. A proposed structure, showing the free acid, is as follows:

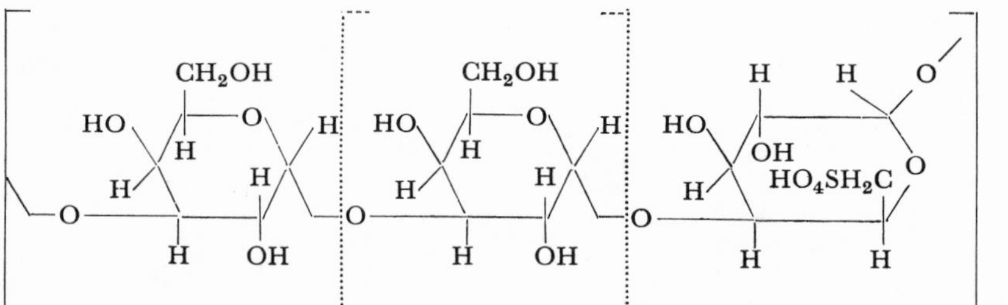

However, growing evidence indicates that little, if any, sulfur is present as an essential constituent, agar instead being simply a calcium galacto-pyranose complex.

Although agar appears in the cell walls of certain seaweeds, probably in the form of its salts, the principal sources of agar are various species of algae. Since agar is soluble in hot water but relatively insoluble in cold water, it is extracted by boiling the algae in water, filtering, and cooling the filtrate to form a gel, which is then cut or chopped up.

In the form of a sweetened and sometimes flavored gel, agar has been used as a dessert by the Orientals for ages. It was introduced from China into Europe and America in the middle of the last century to serve primarily as a gelatin substitute. It is widely used in making jellies and jelly-type desserts and in preparing confections and marshmallows. It serves as a thickener in soups, sauces, and gravies, and as a stabilizer in icings, meringues, fillings, and salad dressings. Agar is useful in canning and preserving meat and poultry, in making sausage casings, in stabilizing icings and sherbets, in making certain cream cheeses, and in preparing malted milk. Agar is commonly used as a roughage, and in certain breakfast foods and special bakery products for laxative purposes, since it is practically indigestible. It is also employed in making pills, capsules, ointments, toothpastes, and other pharmaceutical and cosmetic jellies and creams.

Since Koch in Germany announced agar as a new solid bacteriological culture medium in 1882, agar has become indispensable in microbiological culture media. Agar is extensively used in prosthetic work, where it is the basic material used in most dental impression materials. It is used in clarifying liquors, in sizing paper and textiles, in the manufacture of submarine storage batteries, and in making backings for films and gela-tinous rolls for hectographs.

*Dextran.* The dextrans are a group of high-molecular-weight carbo-hydrates produced from sucrose by a specific group of bacteria or their enzymes. Only the glucose portion of the sucrose is used to make the polymer. The crude dextrans are precipitated from their nutrient sucrose solution with alcohol, are redissolved and reprecipitated from water.

Crude dextran is a water-soluble polymer of glucose having an average molecular weight of more than a million. The empirical formula is $(C_6H_{10}O_5)_n$. The polymer is composed of D-glucopyranose units joined principally by 1, 6-D-glucosidic linkages, but also contains a small number of non-1, 6 linkages. It has been assumed that these bonds have an $\alpha$-configuration.

Since a rather narrow molecular weight range is necessary for clinical use, the crude product is separated by supercentrifugation and, after purification, is chemically degraded to a molecular weight range of about

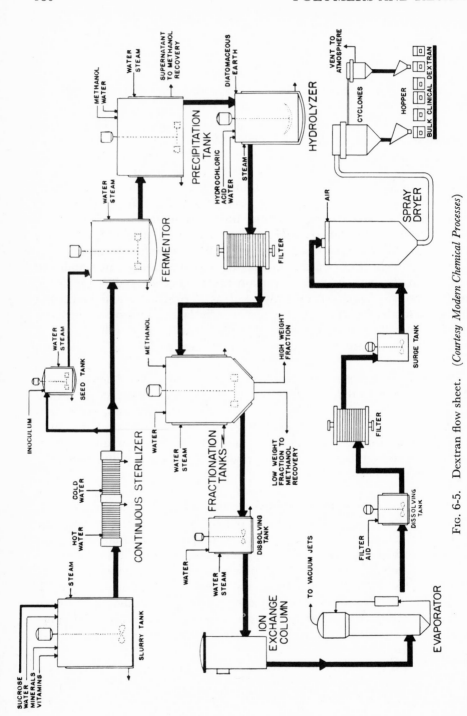

Fig. 6-5.   Dextran flow sheet.   (*Courtesy Modern Chemical Processes*)

75,000 ± 25,000 (light-scattering measurements).   This degraded product is a white, amorphous powder.   It has all the properties of high-molecular-weight polysaccharides, is soluble in water, stable to alkali, and is easily hydrolyzed to glucose by mineral acids.

Its principal use is as a blood plasma expander, temporarily replacing blood in cases of shock or hemorrhage [cf. Poly(vinyl pyrrolidone)]. Other suggested uses are in paper and textile sizes, oil-well drilling muds, and as general thickeners for aqueous solutions.

### Starch

Starch is a naturally occurring, polymeric carbohydrate which serves as the reserve carbohydrate of plants (like glycogen in animals) and thus is found widely distributed in nature.   Starches that are obtained from grains, such as corn (maize); from roots and tubers, such as tapioca, arrowroot, or potato; and from the pith of the stems of certain palms, such as sago, are of principal industrial importance.

Cornstarch is the principal industrial starch of the United States. Tapioca starch (also called cassava starch) is manufactured principally in the East and West Indies and in South America, of which a considerable amount is imported into the United States.   Potato starch is manufactured in Europe and in some sections of America.

Most varieties of starch contain two types of polymers which differ in molecular weight and in chemical structure.   The linear polymer,

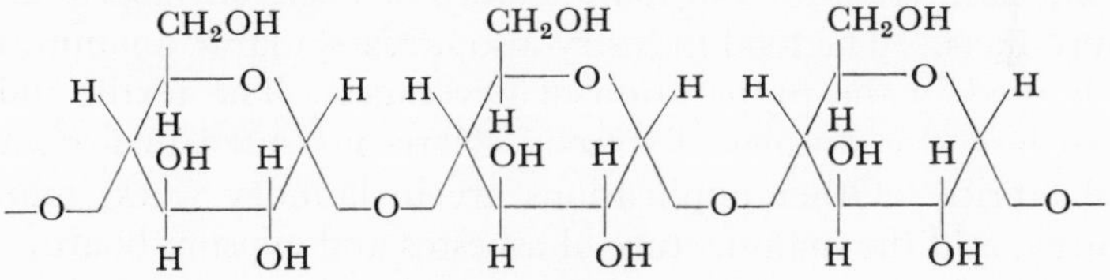

Amylose Chain

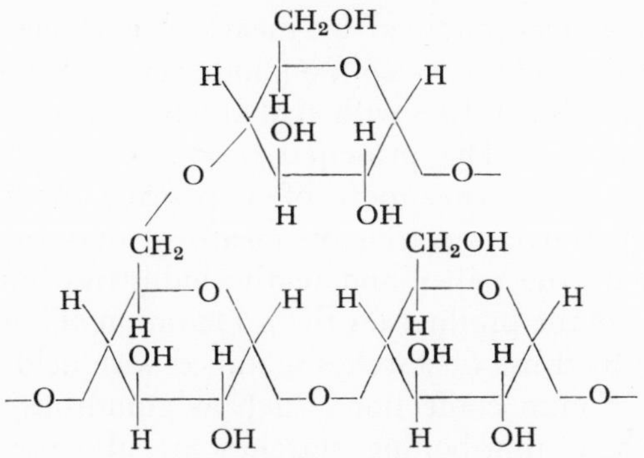

Amylopectin Branch

amylose, consists of glucopyranose units joined through α-1, 4-glucosidic linkages (mol. wt. 10,000 to 400,000) and constitutes about 20 per cent of most starches, whereas the branched or ramified polymer, amylopectin, is made up of glucopyranose units (mol. wt. sometimes greater than 100,000), connected not only by α-1, 4 linkages but also by α-1, 6 linkages.

The amount of amylose obtained varies with the origin of the starch. Starches from the waxy grains, such as waxy corn and sorghum, contain no amylose, whereas the starch from certain varieties of peas contains as much as 75 per cent. The common industrial starches contain about 15 to 30 per cent by weight of amylose.

Dried starch may be modified by heating, with or without the addition of chemical reagents. The product obtained by heating alone is called a British gum, while the product obtained by a combination of partial acid hydrolysis and heating is called a white or canary dextrin.

Before final dewatering, starch slurries may be modified at temperatures below the gelatinization point with chemical reagents. The most important products are the thin-boiling starches, which are made by a partial hydrolysis with sulfuric or other acid, and the oxidized starches, which are made by treating the starch with oxidizing agents, such as hypochlorite (yielding so-called chlorinated starches containing no chlorine) or hydrogen peroxide.

The paper manufacturing and converting industry is the largest user of starch; it is used in the manufacture of laminated and corrugated paper board and adhesives for the manufacture of bags, envelopes, and other paper products. The food industry also utilizes a large amount, much of which is used in the preparation of beverages. The textile industry is the third largest consumer of starch. Here, it is used to size yarns and finished fabrics. Other applications are in laundry work, mining and metallurgy, and the manufacture of asbestos and gypsum board.

Unmodified cornstarch is used primarily in the food industries for the preparation of pies, puddings, salad dressings, and confections. A substantial amount is also modified by means of enzymes. Over half the cornstarch produced by the wet-milling industry is used to make a variety of sugar products by hydrolysis with acid at temperatures above the gelatinization temperature. The principal products are glucose syrup and the refined sugar, D-glucose, more often referred to as dextrose. The brewing industry converts starch by means of diastases (amylase) into fermentable sugar; the paper and textile industries liquefy starch with α-amylases and use the product for the preparation of sizes and adhesives.

The principal food use of starches modified with acid or oxidants is in the production of gum confections, such as gumdrops, fruit slices, and jelly beans. These thin-boiling starches are also used by the textile industry. The lower-fluidity grades are used to size yarn warps before the weaving operation, while the higher-fluidity grades are used in finishing various woven fabrics.

Oxidized starches are used to a large extent by the paper industry in tub-sizing operations or in the preparation of clay coatings which provide a smooth and receptive surface of paper for printing.

Dextrins and gums are used in a great variety of adhesive applications, as well as several of the applications mentioned above.

Since, like cellulose, the glucopyranose units in starch contain an average of one primary and two secondary hydroxyl groups, derivatives can be formed by treating them with acids or their anhydrides to form esters, and with alkyl halides or alkylene oxides to form ethers. Many ethers of a low degree of substitution are water-soluble and are similar to the natural gums in colloidal properties. Highly substituted starch ethers and esters are relatively insoluble in water but are soluble in many organic solvents.

Industrially, the more important starch derivatives have been those of a relatively low degree of substitution, the products being insoluble in cold water. These starch or amylose esters and ethers have been suggested for use in the production of fibers, films, plastics, and coatings. The cost of present manufacturing processes has been a deterrent to their widespread use.

Allyl starch has been made by reacting starch with an allyl halide and an alkaline catalyst. At fairly high degrees of substitution, the product is originally soluble in organic solvents for use in coatings, printing inks, and plastic manufacture. After application and with time, the allyl starch "cures" by an oxidative polymerization to a relatively insoluble state. Its manufacture has been discontinued.

Of the highly substituted inorganic derivatives of starch, the nitrate ester (nitrostarch) is probably the only one to have been made on a commercial scale. It has been used as a demolition agent.

## Shellac

The only resinous substance of animal origin of commercial importance is shellac. Lac is a resinous incrustation found on the branches and twigs of a host tree as a result of the hardening of the secretion of a parasitic insect. The insect absorbs sap from the tree through its stinger. A semipolymerization process occurs and the product is exuded from the insect in the form of a gum or stick-lac. During this period, the female lays her eggs, and the gum, deposited over both the eggs and the insect, hardens into a shell which kills the insect. The hatched young break through the shell and migrate to other trees to repeat the process. The hard crust left on the trees is the crude shellac. The incrusted twigs are broken into sections to become the stick-lac of commerce. Seed-lac is made from stick-lac by crushing and washing, which removes the wood and most of the coloring matter. About 90 per cent of the crude lac comes from India, and small amounts are obtained from surrounding countries.

In producing shellac, the seed-lac is refined by hot expression from a cotton bag, stretching the exudate into sheets and then annealing by slow cooling, after which it is broken into flakes. Shellac is also prepared by mechanical processes which involve a solvent purification process, including filtration.

Bleached shellac is prepared by dissolving shellac or seed-lac in soda ash solution, allowing the impurities to settle, and then bleaching the supernatant liquid with sodium hypochlorite. The resin is precipitated with sulfuric acid, coagulated by heating the suspension, removed as slabs, then drained, ground, and dried. Wax is removed by filtering the soda ash solution of the lac prior to bleaching. Orpiment (arsenic sulfide) is sometimes added in small amounts to produce the light-yellow color often desired.

Shellac is soluble in the lower aliphatic alcohols, but not in hydrocarbons. It is both hard and elastic, and has good film-forming and dielectric properties.

The chemical nature of shellac has been extensively investigated but results reported so far have not been conclusive. In contrast to resins of botanical origin, which contain largely terpenic acids, shellac appears to be composed largely of polyhydroxy aliphatic carboxylic acids and their derivatives.

Shellac is used in many industries. The phonograph record industry formerly consumed a third or more of the shellac produced, but this use is rapidly declining due to the increased use of vinyl and styrene polymers and copolymers for this purpose. The paint and varnish industry is a large consumer of shellac. It is there widely used as a "spirit varnish," as a sealer for wood, and as a constituent of various coatings. In the electrical industry, shellac is used as an insulating varnish and as a binder for laminates. Many molding compositions contain shellac as the thermoplastic resin binder, alone or admixed with phenolic and urea resins, where low cost and gloss and hardness of molded surfaces are desirable.

## REFERENCES AND RECOMMENDED READING

Alexander, J., ed., *Colloid Chemistry Theoretical and Applied*, Vol. VI, Reinhold Publishing Corp., New York, 1946.

Barron, H., *Modern Synthetic Rubbers*, 2nd ed., D. Van Nostrand Co., Princeton, N.J., 1943.

Billmeyer, F. W., Jr., *Textbook of Polymer Chemistry*, Interscience Publishers, New York, 1957.

Brauns, F. E., *The Chemistry of Lignin*, Academic Press, New York, 1952.

Cook, P. G., *Latex: Natural and Synthetic*, Reinhold Publishing Corp., New York, 1956.

Houwink, R., ed., *Elastomers and Plastomers*, Vols. I, II, and III, Elsevier Publishing Co., Amsterdam (dist. by D. Van Nostrand Co., Princeton, N.J.), 1948–50.

Kirk, R. E. and Othmer, D. F., eds., *Encyclopedia of Chemical Technology*, Interscience Publishers, New York, 1947–56.

Kraemer, E. O., ed., *Advances in Colloid Science*, Vol. I, Interscience Publishers, New York, 1942.

Mantell, C. L., Kopf, C. W., Curtis, J. L., and Rogers, E. M., *The Technology of Natural Resins*, John Wiley and Sons, New York, 1942.

Mark, H. and Whitby, G. S., eds., *Advances in Colloid Science*, Vol. II, Interscience Publishers, New York, 1946.

Mason, J. P. and Manning, J. F., *The Technology of Plastics and Resins*, D. Van Nostrand Co., Princeton, N.J., 1945.

Mattiello, J. J., ed., *Protective and Decorative Coatings*, Vol. I, John Wiley and Sons, 1941.

Mauersberger, H. R., ed., *Matthew's Textile Fibers*, 6th ed., John Wiley and Sons, 1954.

Meyer, K. H., *Natural and Synthetic High Polymers*, 2nd ed., Interscience Publishers, New York, 1950.

Ott, E., Spurlin, H. M., and Grafflin, M. W., eds., *Cellulose and Cellulose Derivatives*, 2nd ed., Interscience Publishers, New York, 1954.

Payne, H. F., *Organic Coating Technology*, John Wiley and Sons, New York, 1954.

Ritchie, P. D., *A Chemistry of Plastics and High Polymers*, Cleaver-Hume Press, London (dist. by Interscience Publishers, New York), 1949.

Schildknecht, C. E., ed., *Polymer Processes*, Interscience Publishers, New York, 1956.

Simonds, H. R., Weith, A. J., and Bigelow, M. H., *Handbook of Plastics*, 2nd ed., D. Van Nostrand Co., Princeton, N.J., 1949.

von Fischer, W., ed., *Paint and Varnish Technology*, Reinhold Publishing Corp., New York, 1948.

Wakeman, R. L., *The Chemistry of Commercial Plastics*, Reinhold Publishing Corp., New York, 1947.

Winding, C. C. and Hasche, R. L., *Plastics Theory and Practice*, McGraw-Hill Book Co., New York, 1947.

*Chapter 7*

# TECHNOLOGY OF MANUFACTURE: MODIFIED NATURAL PRODUCTS

Useful as the many natural polymers and resinous materials are, it is often possible to modify them chemically, upgrading one or more properties, in order to increase their usefulness. Increased softening points or flexibilities, better solubilities, new forms, greater stabilities, or certain other properties not available in the natural products are often obtained by chemical treatment, thus greatly expanding the uses of these materials. Hence, in this chapter, there will be discussed the commercially important derivatives of the natural products whose properties and applications may be compared with those of their sources covered in the preceding chapter.

## ROSIN DERIVATIVES

The abietic-type acids contained in rosin oxidize readily, due to their conjugated unsaturation. The pimaric types are relatively inert in this respect. When rosin is exposed to air, the exposed surfaces oxidize rapidly, producing a product of darker color and, in some cases, of lesser value.

One of the ways to stabilize rosin is to decrease the amount of unsaturation by hydrogenation. Either one or both double bonds may be hydrogenated, depending upon the catalyst and solvent used. More vigorous conditions are necessary than is the case with the simpler olefins. The net result in the hydrogenation of rosin is an increase in the dihydro- and tetrahydroabietic acids content. The products are lighter in color and have a slightly lower softening point. Because the hydrogenated products are practically nonoxidizing, they are used to modify alkyd resins and as tackifiers and plasticizers of both natural and synthetic elastomers. They are also, of course, used to replace rosin where their greater stability warrants the increased cost.

Another method of stabilizing rosin against oxidation is by disproportionation. By heating rosin at 270°C for a long time in the presence of iodine, sulfur, certain metals, or mineral acids, part of the molecules give up a mole of hydrogen to form the aromatic and stable dehydroabietic acid by rearrangement, while the hydrogen is absorbed by other molecules to form the dihydro- and tetrahydroabietic acids. Rosin also has been dehydrogenated directly to form the stable aromatic ring compound, dehydroabietic acid. Its use has so far been limited.

Still a third method for stabilization consists in polymerizing rosin by the action of alkyl or metal halides at about room temperature. After a long period of time, a heterogeneous dimeric mixture is formed which contains less abietic-type acids and more tetrahydroabietic acid. Some disproportionation also occurs. By hydrogenating slightly or modifying with maleic anhydride, a product may be obtained which is as stable as a straight hydrogenated rosin. Polymerized rosin has a higher softening point and a higher solution viscosity than rosin, as well as greater resistance to oxidation. It is used as a replacement for rosin where these properties are desirable.

An extremely useful reaction of rosin is that with maleic anhydride or fumaric acid. Although neither abietic nor neoabietic acid reacts with maleic anhydride, the small amount of levopimaric acid present does react to form a Diels-Alder adduct. Upon consumption of the levopimaric acid, the equilibrium among the acids is displaced to form more levopimaric acid, and eventually the mass is converted to the levopimaric-maleic adduct in good yield. The reaction is carried out at above 150°C, and the amount of adduct formed is approximately equivalent to the amount of abietic-type (two-double-bond) acids present. Fumaric acid reacts more slowly than maleic anhydride but yields products having higher softening points.

Rosin acids also undergo typical reactions of the carboxyl group. By reacting the products above simultaneously or subsequently with glycerol, pentaerythritol, or other polyols, esters are formed. Rosin itself is esterified with glycerol to form the neutral ester known as *ester gum*. More recently, the replacement of glycerol with pentaerythritol has produced esters of higher softening points and greater resistance to heat and saponification. Various glycols have also been used. These products are employed extensively in printing inks and protective coatings. Ester gum replaced the more expensive fossil resins in spar varnishes when it was discovered that tung oil and ester gum yielded a good waterproof varnish. Later, modification of ester gum with maleic anhydride and phenol-formaldehyde condensates produced improved and more versatile varnish resins.

Salts of rosin are produced in large volume commercially. Among these are the sodium, calcium (more commonly known as *limed rosin*), zinc, aluminum, and heavy metal derivatives, all known as *resinates*. They are prepared by three methods: the precipitation, solvent, and the fusion processes. The precipitated metal resinates are made by a double decomposition reaction between aqueous sodium resinates and a water-soluble salt of the metal. The solvent-processed resinates are made by refluxing a hydrocarbon solution of rosin with a reactive metal compound. The fused metal resinates are prepared by direct fusion of rosin with the acetate, hydroxide, oxide, or basic carbonate of the metal. Each method has its particular advantages and disadvantages.

Sodium resinate is used extensively in the manufacture of soaps, in the sizing of paper, and in emulsions of the oil-in-water type. Calcium resinate is widely used as a varnish and filler resin in the protective coatings industry. When calcium resinate is dissolved in petroleum solvents with, sometimes, a small amount of oil, the solution, known as *gloss oil*, is used as a component of inexpensive paints and varnishes and as a primer for plaster and cement walls. Zinc resinate is frequently added to enamel and printing ink grinds to improve wetting and dispersion of pigments. Aluminum resinate, actually an aluminum hydroxy resinate, is used as a flatting ingredient in varnishes and lacquers. The resinates of heavy metals, especially those of cobalt, lead, and manganese, are widely used as "driers" for most oleoresinous paints and varnishes where, in minute quantities, they appear to catalyze the absorption of oxygen by the oil and thus accelerate the hardening or "drying" of the film.

Rosin may also be converted by hydrogenolysis of the methyl ester at 300°C and 5,000 psi using a copper chromite catalyst to hydroabietyl alcohol. This colorless, viscous alcohol is used as a resin and as a plasticizer in the protective coatings industry and also as an intermediate in the preparation of ether and ester derivatives. Less important products of rosin are those obtained by ammonolysis and decarboxylation.

One of the most important series of rosin derivatives is that obtained by reacting rosin with phenol-formaldehyde condensates. In spite of the fact that the rosin component is present in excess, the products are known as *rosin-modified* or *let-down* phenolic resins. These products are made to lower the cost of pure phenolic resins and to obtain better color and solubility characteristics than can be obtained from phenolic resins alone.

As will be pointed out in the next chapter, many basic-condensed phenol-formaldehyde condensates are insoluble in drying oils. By adding such a condensate to an excess of liquid rosin, heating until solution is accomplished, and then (usually) esterifying, products are obtained which are superior to rosin or rosin esters for use in coatings and are oil- and solvent-soluble. Acid-condensed phenolic resins are not used, as they do not improve the hardness or viscosity sufficiently. The alkali-condensed phenolic resins do impart hardness and viscosity and do not lose the potential reactivity of their hydroxyl groups.

The mechanism of the reaction, if any, between rosin and a phenolic condensate is still obscure. Some investigators have considered the product to be a solution or colloidal dispersion of phenolic resin in the rosin. However, it is now generally accepted that an addition reaction of some kind does take place between a methylol phenol and a rosin ester. It is possible that products similar to the following may be produced:

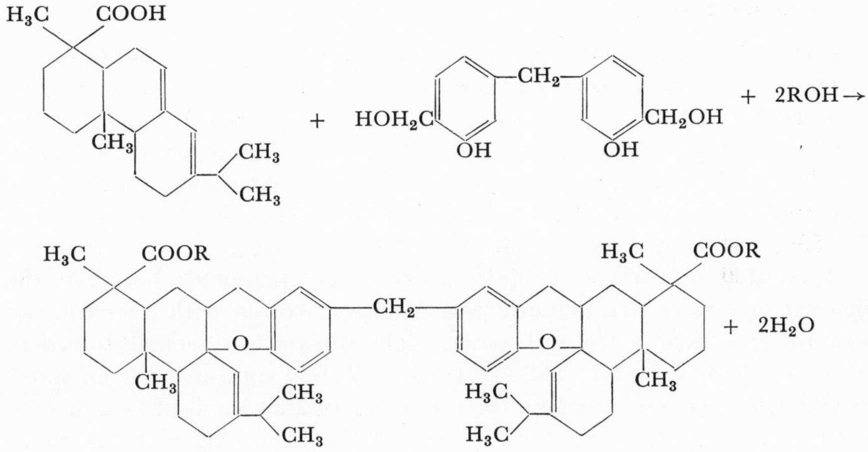

Other natural resins, particularly the copals, have been used to modify the phenolic resins in place of rosin. In most cases, a harder product is obtained. However, due to cost and availability, rosin is now almost exclusively used.

## REGENERATED CELLULOSICS

The regenerated cellulosics are a class of natural products which have been chemically treated in order to solubilize them so that filaments or sheets can be obtained with the usual spinning and casting techniques. In all cases, pure cellulose is regenerated by extrusion of the chemically modified cellulose into a special bath. Due to the chemical treatment, the products after regeneration, while similar to the impure cellulose from which they came, have been changed sufficiently that their properties are different. In most cases, the regenerated cellulosics are purer cellulose and have been degraded somewhat in molecular weight.

In 1924 the term "rayon" was officially adopted in the United States to designate all modified natural and synthetic "silks," including regenerated cellulose and derivatives of cellulose used for fibers. However, due to confusion caused by the use of one term to cover many possible products, in 1951 the meaning of the term was narrowed to include man-made textile fibers and filaments composed of regenerated cellulose only, while the term "acetate" was adopted to indicate man-made textile fibers and filaments composed of cellulose acetate.    Since these two cellulose products are by far the most common modified natural fibers, no generic names have yet been adopted for other cellulose derivatives.

### Chardonnet Silk

Chardonnet "silk," the first modified natural fiber to be produced in appreciable quantity, is now of historical interest only, but was once used extensively.    Although several investigators had previously suggested the use of cellulose nitrate as a textile fiber, Count Chardonnet has been credited with being the first to produce it on a commercial scale.    He patented the process in 1884, exhibited the product at the Paris Exhibition in 1889, and began commercial production in 1891.

A number of variations of the process were patented; however, the general process of manufacture was to nitrate cotton with a mixture of sulfuric and nitric acids and water.    The nitrate was then dissolved in an ether-alcohol mixture and the viscous solution spun into a cold water bath.    Upon passage through the water, the filaments solidified and were then stretched.    A later process involved the dry spinning of the filaments under high pressure.

Because of the hazardous nature of the cellulose nitrate, a later improvement in the process consisted in denitrating the fiber by treatment with ammonium hydrosulfide.    The alkali saponified the nitrate to regenerate cellulose, which was no more flammable than cotton.    Although it enjoyed great popularity for many years, later processes gradually superseded Chardonnet's, primarily because of cost, and manufacture ceased in the United States in 1934 after fourteen years of production.

### Cuprammonium Rayon

In 1857, the German chemist and botanist, Schweitzer, discovered that cotton and paper were soluble in an ammoniacal copper hydroxide solution $[Cu(NH_3)_4(OH)_2]$ (see Cellulose, Chap. 6).    Then, later in the nineteenth century, the American inventor, Weston, produced filaments from such a solution for electric lamp filaments.    In 1890, the French chemist, Despaissis, was granted the first patent for making a cuprammonium artificial silk.    The first commercial development took place in Germany under Pauly's patent but was later abandoned.    Much later, in 1918–19, a German firm, Bemberg A.-G., started production, using a different process, and several plants in Europe produced this type of rayon.    It was not until 1924–25 that an American plant, established by Bemberg, began production in this country.

The principal raw materials used in the cuprammonium process are purified cotton linters or wood pulp, the latter being more generally used today. In one process, aqueous copper carbonate is mixed with the cellulosic material in a shredder to form copper cellulose. After expression of liquid, the residual cake is mixed with aqueous ammonia and caustic soda to form a viscous solution. The solution, containing about 8 per cent cellulose, is stored, filtered, and vacuum deaerated. Glucose is usually added to stabilize the solution and improve spinning properties.

The cellulose now probably exists in the form represented by

where the original ammonia-copper complex is destroyed and two molecules of water are complexed with the copper.

The spinning solution is forced through relatively large holes in nickel spinnerets; subsequent stretching of the filaments reduces their diameter. A thread from a 0.0002 inch orifice may be stretched to as small as one denier in this process. As the filaments emerge from the spinnerets, they pass through coagulating baths, which may be acid or alkaline. Sulfuric acid baths are now less common than alkaline baths. The yarn is then washed, dried, and wound on bobbins. As many as 400 threads are spun simultaneously. After treatment with dilute sulfuric acid to remove residual copper, the yarn is bleached, washed again, and dried.

It is essential that the copper salts and the ammonia used be recovered, else the cost of the process would be prohibitive. In this sense, the production of cuprammonium rayon parallels that of soda ash by the ammonia process, wherein the intermediates are of greater value than the final products, and the process is competitive only because of an efficient recovery process. The ammonia is recovered from the dissolving tank and from alkaline coagulating tanks by passage through an ammonia scrubber. Copper from coagulating baths and from the acid and water purification systems is recovered by precipitation. Approximately 0.57 pound of ammonia, 0.40 pound of caustic, 0.75 pound of copper salt, and 0.92 pound of cotton linters are needed to make one pound of cuprammonium rayon.

Cuprammonium rayon (often referred to as Bemberg rayon because the Bemberg Corporation is probably the sole producer) resembles real silk in fineness of filaments, luster, and softness. However, since it is regenerated cellulose, it also has most of the properties of cotton and viscose rayon.  Probably its chief virtue is its capability of being drawn to very fine filaments, as low as 0.4 denier.  The fineness of filament gives cuprammonium rayon great pliability and good draping qualities; hence it is used in apparel manufacture, especially for women's wear.  It has been widely used as a substitute for silk.

Due to the inherently high cost of manufacture, even with a good recovery process, the production of cuprammonium rayon is very small. In the United States today, probably no more than 3 per cent of the rayon is manufactured by this process, the remainder being made by the viscose process.

**Viscose Rayon**

Although the viscose process for making rayon was the last of the three commercial processes to be developed, it has, since about 1910–11, been by far the most important.  The process is rather lengthy (taking several days to a week) and requires careful control throughout; yet all the raw materials are fairly cheap, with the result that viscose rayon can generally be made to sell below the price of all other rayons.  This is the chief reason for its greater success.

The development of viscose rayon is due mainly to the work of two English chemists, Cross and Bevan,[1] who obtained a patent in 1895 on rayon manufacture.  They discovered that when cellulose is treated with caustic soda and then with carbon disulfide, it is converted into a new compound.  This new compound, when dissolved in caustic soda, produces a viscous solution which Cross and Bevan termed "viscose."

As with cuprammonium rayon, cotton linters or wood pulp are used, the latter being preferred due to its lower cost.  [A viscose plant has been built in the Philippines recently to covert sugar-cane waste (bagasse) into rayon.]  Cellulose pulp from cotton linters, northern spruce, western hemlock, or southern pine is steeped or mercerized in an 18 per cent caustic soda solution to form sodium cellulose.  After expression of liquid in hydraulic presses, the sodium cellulose is shredded into crumbs.  The crumbs are aged for two to three days in steel or iron cans so that partial oxidation and depolymerization occur.  They are then blended with carbon disulfide vapor in large, rotating churns under carefully specified and controlled conditions.  A gelatinous mass of sodium cellulose xanthate is formed [the sodium salt of the cellulose acid ester of xanthogenic (dithiocarbonic) acid, $HO \cdot CSSH$], together with some adsorbed caustic soda:

$$[C_6H_7O_2(OH)_3]_n + NaOH + CS_2 \rightarrow$$
$$[C_6H_7O_2(OH)_2 \cdot O \cdot CSSNa]_n + H_2O$$

[1] Cross, C. F., Bevan, E. T., and Beadle, C., *Ber.*, **26**, 1090, 2520 (1893).

Although almost complete xanthation can be obtained, normally only about one to two hydroxyl groups per cellobiose residue are xanthated, as this is sufficient to allow solution or dispersion of the product in more caustic solution.

A portion of a cellulose xanthate chain may be represented as follows:

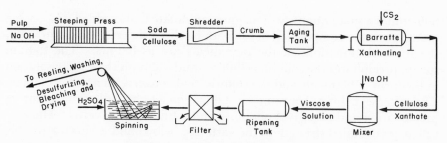

The solubility of this polymer in aqueous media is due to its lack of symmetry, which decreases hydrogen bonding, and to the ionic character

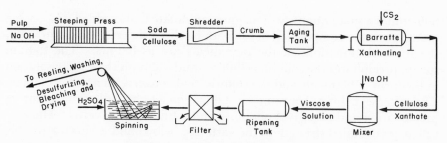

FIG. 7-1.   Viscose process flow sheet

of the xanthate group.   Thus, a dilute caustic solution is added to the xanthate in a mixer, and the mass is stirred until a homogeneous, viscous mass of viscose is obtained.   At this time, the luster of the rayon is controlled.   If nothing is added, a high luster rayon is obtained; to obtain a dull or semidull yarn, a pigment, usually titanium dioxide or a mineral oil, is added which causes the yarn to reflect diffusely.   Since these additives are incorporated into the yarn, they cannot be later washed out.

During the subsequent ripening period, which takes from four to five days and is done in tanks in an insulated room at 15° to 20°C, the molecular structure is retained, but the viscosity slowly decreases, then rises again, partly due to regeneration of some cellulose by slow hydrolysis of xanthate and partly by the salting-out of inorganic by-products.   The regenerated cellulose is maintained in emulsion form by the undecomposed xanthate, which acts as a protective colloid.   During this process, the color of the mass turns from white to an orange-yellow.

After proper ripening, the solution is filtered, vacuum deaerated, refiltered, and spun, as with cuprammonium rayon.   The spinneret may be a platinum alloy containing from 10 to 120 holes for ordinary rayon and more than 3,000 for tire cord and tow. The holes are generally from 0.002 to 0.004 inch in diameter. The final size of the filaments depends more on the rate of supply of the solution to the spinneret and the amount of stretching during coagulation than upon the size of the spinneret holes. All of the monofilaments from a single spinneret are combined into a single thread of rayon yarn.

The spinning bath, made of sheet lead, contains a solution of sulfuric acid and additives maintained at 40° to 55°C. A representative composition is as follows:

|  | | | *Per Cent* |
|---|---|---|---|
| Sulfuric acid | . | . | 9–12 |
| Sodium sulfate | . | . | 17–20 |
| Glucose | . | . | 2– 5 |
| Zinc sulfate | . | . | 1 |
| Water | . | . | 67–71 |

Sometimes a small quantity of magnesium sulfate is also added.

Although the composition of the bath has been determined empirically, the probable functions of the ingredients are as follows. The sodium sulfate precipitates the sodium cellulose xanthate from the viscose solution in the form of filaments and the sulfuric acid converts them into cellulose. The glucose helps to prevent crystallization of the salt formed during precipitation and also gives pliability and softness to the yarn. The zinc sulfate gives added strength to the yarn (see below) and is also responsible for its serrated cross-section, for if it is omitted, the filaments are round or oval and do not accept dyes as well. Sodium sulfate or sodium acid sulfate is always formed in sulfuric acid baths, due to the sodium hydroxide in the viscose. Its concentration is maintained within the limits given above.

The yarn after spinning is impure and relatively weak. Purification consists of washing, desulfurizing (sometimes called sulfiding), bleaching, and washing. The first wash is with water, the second is with sodium sulfide solution, the third with slightly alkaline sodium hypochlorite (followed by neutralization with dilute hydrochloric acid), and the final wash is with water again. Continuous spinning has been achieved by elimination, where possible, of the desulfurizing and bleaching steps.

The regenerated cellulose in the final product is identical to the cellulose from which it came except that the long cellulose molecules have been partly hydrolyzed and degraded into shorter, although still very long, molecules. It should be borne in mind that fibers can be made only from long molecules (see Chap. 12), and that, during and subsequent to the manufacture of a fiber, hydrolytic conditions should be avoided. Some degradation is inevitable, but means to minimize this considerably have been found. In viscose rayon, the cellulose molecules are about one third as long as those in the original cellulose; i.e., the initial degree of polymerization of about 1,100 has been reduced to one of about 350.

The tensile strength of ordinary viscose fiber varies between 25,000 and 50,000 psi; however, the tensile strength drops about 50 per cent upon soaking in water.

High-strength or high-tenacity viscose achieves its greater strength (twice that of ordinary viscose) from orientation of the molecular crystallites by cold stretching during regeneration. Complete regeneration of the coagulated filament is delayed until the filament can be stretched from 50 to 250 per cent, the lower range being used to produce medium-tenacity yarn. The zinc ions added to the bath react with the cellulose xanthate to yield a zinc cellulose xanthate which acts as an outer skin in the form of an elastic gel. This gel decreases the rate of regeneration by the sulfuric acid and facilitates stretching. The presence of zinc ion also appears to improve fatigue resistance of the yarn. For high-tenacity rayon, the concentration of zinc sulfate in the regeneration bath may run as high as 10 per cent, and it is likely that the concentration of sulfuric acid is higher also—from 45 to 75 per cent.

Viscose fibers find more than half their market in tires and other industrial uses; most of the remainder goes into apparel and household fabrics. About nine out of every ten tires made in the United States contain rayon cord; half of this tire cord is used in truck tires. High-strength viscose rayon, such as Cordura, is used in the manufacture of tire cord for heavy-duty purposes. The total amount of yarn presently produced is close to a billion pounds per year. Thus, it is not surprising that the viscose industry is the largest producer of man-made fiber and is the chief consumer of carbon disulfide and a major consumer of sulfuric acid and caustic soda. Viscose is lower in price than all other staple fibers, natural or synthetic.

Staple rayon or "fluff" is made in the same way as filament rayon except that a larger nozzle with from 2,500 to 4,000 openings is used for the spinneret. This produces a ropelike product which is cut into short lengths and then fluffed by blowing air through it. The staple is packed in bales like raw cotton and is used on standard cotton-weaving machines. About one fifth of the viscose rayon made is produced as tow or staple fiber.

In Europe, several regenerated cellulosic fibers are made which are like cuprammonium or viscose fibers but differ in after-treatment or source. Tenasco and Durafil are British products which have higher tenacities than normal rayon. Their manufacture is similar to that of American high-tenacity rayon; i.e., more zinc sulfate or more concentrated sulfuric acid is used in the regenerating bath. Fortisan, both a British and an American fiber, is made by stretching cellulose acetate in steam under pressure and then saponifying the stretched yarn to yield regenerated cellulose. It is the most highly oriented and strongest of any of the modified natural and synthetic fibers yet made, having a tensile strength of almost 140,000 psi.   Since all three fibers have lower extensibilities, moisture regain, and affinity for dyes than normal rayon, they are used only when their greater strength is necessary, as in tire cords, except in the United States, where Fortisan is used in draperies and linings, presumably not only because of its strength but also because of its resistance to sunlight.   In Germany, a wool-like staple fiber, known as Lanusa, is made by a combination of the viscose and cuprammonium processes, which gives it a round cross-section and a wool-like appearance and feel.

### Regenerated Cellulose Film

Regenerated cellulose film, or cellophane, is the most widely used thin, transparent packaging material.   It was first made in France as early as 1908.   Small quantities were imported into the United States until 1924, when American production began.

The method of manufacture of regenerated cellulose film is almost identical to that of viscose rayon.   The principal difference is the method of extrusion.   Instead of forcing viscose through spinnerets, it is extruded from a casting machine into the acid coagulating bath.

The film produced is too brittle for commercial use without the addition of plasticizer.   Suitable plasticizers or softeners improve flexibility and decrease the tendency for the film to rattle.   Water is probably the most efficient plasticizer; to incorporate it into the film, the sheet is passed through a glycerol bath, after removal of sulfur and bleaching.   The glycerol itself has some plasticizing effect but, being hygroscopic, also holds some water in the sheet.   Approximately 7 per cent glycerol is absorbed by the film.   Similar hygroscopic plasticizing agents, including ethylene glycol, glucose, and other polyhydric alcohols, are also used.   The film is finally dried by passage over heated rolls.

Regenerated cellulose film is very sensitive to changes in relative humidity and shows appreciable dimensional variation with such changes. Further, water vapor is readily transmitted by the film, and the plasticizers used are readily leached out.   As a result, when the film was first used for food wrapping, it was found that baked goods, in particular, dried out too quickly.   A moistureproofed sheet was developed in 1927 which opened up thousands of new uses for the product.

The usual method of moistureproofing consists in coating the sheet with a very thin layer of lacquer, which includes cellulose nitrate as the film-forming ingredient, a plasticizer for the nitrate, a resin, and a wax.   The wax, usually paraffin, is responsible for most of the moisture-vapor-transmission resistance of the coating.   Approximately four fifths of regenerated cellulose film is moistureproofed.

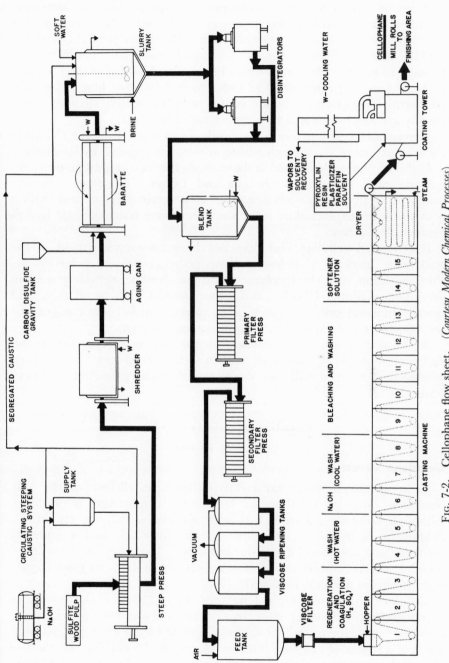

Fig. 7-2.  Cellophane flow sheet.  (*Courtesy Modern Chemical Processes*)

A major reason for using unsupported films is their transparency. Cellulose films are widely used to protect and improve the sales appeal of merchandise. Cellophane transmits most of the ultraviolet light as well as visible light. A newer, similar packaging material (Sylphwrap) is claimed to exclude ultraviolet light; hence, this film should offer greater protection against rancidity. In order to seal cellulose film to itself for packaging uses, a large amount is coated with heat-sealing lacquers which usually are also formulated to be water-vapor resistant.

Regenerated cellulose film is also produced as seamless tubing (Visking) for sausage casing. Although edible, it is not assimilated by the body.

Cellulose film is widely used in the manufacture of transparent, pressure-sensitive tape, such as Scotch tape and Texcel. The tape is usually coated with an adhesive mixture of an elastomeric polymer and various compatible resins, including rosin and coumarone resins or their hydrogenated derivatives.

Regenerated cellulose film does not have an exclusive field in the packaging market. Cellulose acetate, ethyl cellulose, polyethylene, Pliofilm, saran, and vinyl polymers and copolymers are widely used in unsupported films. Glassine and waxed papers, thin metal foils, and many laminated combinations of film, paper, and foil also compete for the very large and rapidly growing packaging business.

So far as is known, *cuprammonium* film has been made only in Europe, and there only on a small scale and in light film gauges. It has been produced there principally for the electrical industry and the millinery trades.

### CELLULOSIC DERIVATIVES

#### CELLULOSE ESTERS

**Cellulose Nitrate**

Cellulose nitrate (often incorrectly called nitrocellulose) is the only inorganic ester of cellulose of large-scale commercial importance. Although cellulosic materials had been nitrated as early as the 1830's, Schönbein, in 1845, nitrated cellulose with mixed acid and is generally credited with the founding of the industry. Twenty years later, Abel found a way to improve its stability sufficiently to allow its manufacture and storage on a commercial scale.

Cellulose nitrate was for a long time made almost exclusively from cotton and cotton linters. The great demands of wartime needs for more cellulose nitrate for propellant uses was responsible for the rapid development of a source of cellulose from wood, and by World War II, most of the cellulose nitrate made in this country (and much elsewhere) came from coniferous wood pulps.

The most important step in the manufacture of cellulose nitrate is the nitration process. The nature of the final product depends upon the degree of nitration and amount of degradation, as shown in Table 7-1.

TABLE 7-1.  CHARACTERISTICS OF CELLULOSE NITRATES

| Nitrogen Content % | Nitrate Groups per Anhydroglucose Residue | Applications |
|---|---|---|
| 10.6–11.3 | 1.8–2.0 | Plastic molding ($\overline{DP}$ ca. 500–600) |
| 11.5–12.2 | 2.1–2.3 | Lacquers and cements ($\overline{DP}$ ca. 150–200) |
| 12.1–13.6 | 2.3–2.9 | Guncotton for smokeless powders ($\overline{DP}$ ca. 2,000–3,500) |

Assuming complete nitration for purposes of illustration, the following summarizes the principal reaction:

$$[C_6H_7O_2(OH)_3]_n + 3nHONO_2 \leftrightarrows [C_6H_7O_2(ONO_2)_3]_n + 3nH_2O$$

This reaction differs from most cellulose reactions in that it is an equilibrium reaction, the extent of nitration at equilibrium being controlled primarily by the composition of the mixed acid. The completely

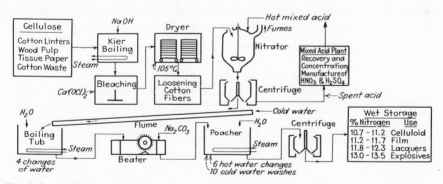

FIG. 7-3.  Cellulose nitrate flow sheet.  (*Reprinted by permission from Chemical Engineering*)

nitrated ester (14.14% nitrogen) is unstable and is not manufactured commercially.  It can be seen from Table 7-1 that commercial cellulose nitrates are made in a wide range of degrees of polymerization, which, in turn, directly controls the viscosity of solutions.

Several methods of nitration have been employed industrially, but for many years the most widely used process has been the so-called mechanical dipper process.  In this method, about 1,600 pounds of mixed acid is charged to a dipper, which is a cylindrical iron or acid-resistant-steel tank fitted with two vertical, slowly rotating, opposed paddles. The mixed acid consists of about 50 to 60 per cent sulfuric acid, 20 to 25 per cent nitric acid, and 10 to 20 per cent water, variations depending upon the intended use of the ester. About 30 to 40 pounds of purified and dried cellulose are added. Larger quantities have been used, but care must be taken to control the exothermic reaction. The large excess of acids is used to minimize concentration changes during the reaction. After about 30 minutes of nitration, the whole mixture is discharged through a valve and pipe in the bottom of the dipper to a centrifuge below, where most of the spent acid is removed. The cellulose nitrate is then carefully washed and stabilized (by boiling in water for several hours), then dehydrated by displacing the water with an alcohol while compressed into blocks in hydraulic presses. The blocks, containing about 30 per cent alcohol by weight, are shredded and the alcohol-wet nitrate is packed in steel drums for shipment.

For use in lacquers (its principal use in peacetime), the cellulose nitrate must be degraded considerably in order to obtain products of low solution viscosity. This is accomplished by digestion of the nitrate in water under heat and pressure. This was originally a batch process but has for many years been done by pumping an aqueous suspension of nitrate through a long pipe, heated at one end and cooled at the other.

Cellulose nitrate is fairly brittle and is not useful as a plastic or film-forming ingredient unless properly plasticized. For fabrication, camphor (the original plasticizer discovered by Hyatt) is still used, along with many others. The moist nitrate is kneaded with plasticizer, stabilizer (urea or amines), and pigments, if desired, and homogenized on heated rollers, which also drives off part of the alcohol. The sheets thus formed may be further dried and broken up to form molding powders or may be welded together by application of heat and pressure to form blocks from which sheets (*celluloid*) are sliced. These must be seasoned under controlled temperature and humidity to insure good dimensional stability.

From the sheets (Pyralin), many useful products are made, including aircraft accessories, buttons, clothes' hamper tops and coverings for toilet seats, decorative and advertising novelties, eyeglass frames, shoelace tips, table-tennis balls, pen and pencil barrels, and women's high-heel coverings.

The specific gravity of the plastic is about 1.35, unpigmented. It is tough, durable, and pliable, and can be readily formed, cemented, and machined. It has excellent dimensional stability and low water absorption. Although resistant to water, hydrocarbons, and dilute acids and alkalies, cellulose nitrate is not resistant to oxygenated solvents or strong alkalies and oxidizing agents. It is also very flammable. It is for this reason, in particular, that other cellulose esters have replaced the nitrate in many otherwise useful applications.

*Pyroxylin* is a term frequently used to designate products containing cellulose nitrate of soluble grade (less than 12.5 per cent nitrogen). *Collodion* is a viscous solution of cellulose nitrate in ether and alcohol, widely used in the past as a temporary bandage or coating for cuts.

### Cellulose Acetate

Cellulose acetate is the organic ester of cellulose made in largest quantity. It was first reported by Schützenberger in 1865. At the end of the century, Cross and Bevan in England discovered milder acetylating conditions, and Miles in 1905 in the United States differentiated between the completely acetylated and the partially hydrolyzed product. Sulfuric acid was employed as a catalyst for the esterification reaction as far back as 1879 and remains the standard agent for commercial use. Cellulose triacetate was first made in the United States in 1914. Since chloroform was the only readily available solvent for the triacetate, the early production was very hazardous.

There is an important difference between the nitration and the acetylation of cellulose. Only cellulose nitrate, of the commercially important cellulose derivatives, reaches equilibrium with the reaction components prior to complete substitution. For this reason, control of mixed acid composition used in nitrating makes it possible to vary the degree of nitration of cellulose. However, for organic esterifications which occur in nonaqueous media, it is not practicable to stop esterification short of complete reaction. This is why the cellulose acetate made commercially always starts with the formation of cellulose triacetate, often called primary cellulose acetate for this reason. Attempts for an intermediate degree of acetylation yield only mixtures of the triacetate and unreacted cellulose.

Commercially, the triacetate is hydrolyzed to a stage part way between the triacetate and the diacetate, yielding a product no longer soluble in chloroform but soluble in acetone, a more convenient, cheaper, and less toxic solvent. This is the method which has made possible the large-scale development of cellulose acetate as a plastic and a fiber, although, quite recently, the triacetate has been used in increasing amounts in molding powders, films, and fibers of high softening points.

The manufacture of cellulose acetate is almost exclusively based upon the acetylation of cellulose with acetic anhydride, using sulfuric acid as a catalyst. Zinc chloride has also, to a limited extent, been used as a catalyst. The reaction is conducted in the presence of glacial acetic acid and is not quite as simple as it may seem. The sulfuric acid reacts rapidly with the cellulose when the acetic anhydride is added at the beginning of esterification, whereas the acetylation reaction is slow. During the process, a trans-esterification reaction takes place while acetyl groups slowly replace sulfate groups. Both reactions have a preference for the primary hydroxyl group of the anhydroglucose unit. The acetic acid is present as a reaction medium for the reactants and the cellulose acetate and also serves to swell the cellulose fibers to insure complete and uniform reaction. In a variation of the process, methylene chloride is also used as a solvent.

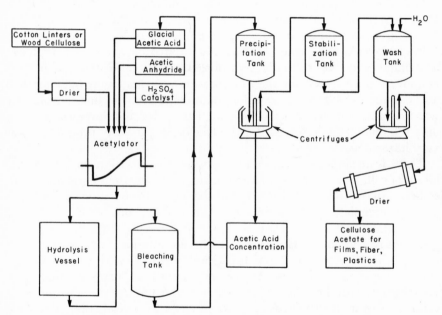

FIG. 7-4.    Cellulose acetate flow sheet.    (By permission from *Plastics Theory and Practice*, by Winding and Hasche, Copyright 1947, McGraw-Hill Book Co.)

Almost all cellulose acetate is made by the solution process. Before acetylation, the cellulose is "activated" by treatment with glacial acetic acid with, often, part or all of the esterification catalyst. This appears to cause intramicellar swelling of the cellulose, so that the hydroxyl groups are made available for reaction. It is then treated with an excess of acetic acid and acetic anhydride. After mixing, the sulfuric acid is added, and the strongly exothermic reaction begins. The containers are usually cooled and the temperature kept below about 30°C in order to obtain a completely homogeneous product. The reaction is stopped by addition of sufficient water or aqueous acetic acid to make a solution of about 95 per cent acetic acid. By hydrolyzing rapidly at an elevated temperature, some chain degradation can be made to occur. If minimum degradation is desired, the hydrolysis is conducted more slowly at a lower temperature. In either case, an acetone-soluble product is obtained. After sufficient hydrolysis has taken place, the secondary acetate is slowly precipitated by addition of excess water or dilute acetic acid.

Two techniques are used to control temperature in the acetylation reaction. The older method is to conduct the acetylation in heavy-duty mixers of the Werner-Pfleiderer type. The mixers and sometimes the blades are water-cooled. The later technique utilizes a low-boiling solvent, usually methylene chloride, to absorb the heat. The boiling solvent is returned by reflux to the vessel. This is the same technique employed in the solvent method for making alkyd resins (Chap. 8), except that a much lower temperature is maintained.

A large volume of dilute acetic acid is obtained as a by-product of the process, and efficient recovery and reconcentration processes are necessary for economic reasons. Solvent extraction and azeotropic distillation methods are currently employed.

The secondary acetate varies in acetyl content, depending upon amount of hydrolysis, which, in turn, is determined by the intended use of the product. Table 7-2 summarizes the common types of acetate made.

Table 7-2. CHARACTERISTICS OF CELLULOSE ACETATES

| Acetyl Content % | Ester Groups per Anhydroglucose Residue | Applications |
|---|---|---|
| 36.5–38.5 | 2.2–2.3 | Plastic molding ($\overline{DP}$ ca. 175–350) |
| 37.5–39.5 | 2.3–2.4 | Fibers and lacquers |
| 39.5–41.5 | 2.4–2.6 | Films and tapes |

The secondary acetate may be dissolved in acetone to form a colorless, viscous solution containing about 25 to 35 per cent acetate. This is known as "dope," and it was in this form that the first large-scale use of cellulose acetate was made—as a coating for the fabric wings of aircraft in World War I so that they tightened up and became impermeable to air. After the war ended, the oversupply of acetate caused a period of intensive research to find new uses for it, and from this developed a method of converting it into an artificial silk, later known as acetate rayon, now known simply as acetate.

The dope, made as above, is passed through spinnerets into (rarely) a precipitating bath or (usually) a stream of air at about 100°C. The solvent evaporates and leaves continuous filaments of acetate which are spun under tension to increase the strength of the fiber by orientation.

Since most of the hydroxyl groups in the cellulose have now been esterified, the fiber is less hygroscopic and more water-repellent than rayon. For the same reason, the product is more susceptible to swelling or dissolution in organic solvents, however.   Acetate has a greater elongation than rayon, both in the dry and wet states.   Acetate yarn is unaffected by dilute solutions of weak acids, but concentrated solutions of strong acids will decompose it.   Concentrated organic acids, such as acetic and formic, will cause swelling or dissolution of the fiber.   Dilute solutions of alkalies have litte effect, but strong alkalies will cause saponification and transform the acetate into a regenerated cellulose form (Fortisan).   It is attacked by strong oxidizing agents.

The tensile strength of acetate varies between 22,000 and 30,000 psi and drops about 40 per cent upon soaking in water.

Cellulose acetate fiber has a soft, warm texture.   It is used in all kinds of women's wear, and in men's wear, including ties, hose, suits, and bathrobes, alone or in blends.   It is also used in draperies and upholstery fabrics.   Like most man-made fibers, it is resistant to bacteria and mildew.

Very recently, a new yarn (Arnel) has been announced which is reported to be cellulose triacetate.   The method by which it is spun has not yet been disclosed.   It is reported to make a light fabric which washes easily and which can be heat-treated to retain creases and pleats easily.

Cellulose acetate molding compositions (e.g., Celanese acetate, Plastacele) are prepared by mixing the precipitated material on heated compounding rolls with plasticizers, dyes, and pigments.   The doughy mass after complete mixing is then rolled into sheets or slabs and blanked out into molding forms or granulated to give molding powder.

In contrast to cellulose nitrate, cellulose acetate is a light-stable, relatively nonflammable material.   It is thermoplastic in nature and is suited for injection molding, whereas cellulose nitrate plastics, unstable in the presence of heat, are not.

Cellulose acetate may be molded without the addition of a plasticizer; however, the unplasticized material possesses an extremely high working temperature.   At very high temperatures, decomposition of the cellulose occurs.   The physical and chemical properties of unplasticized acetates are not very good; they are brittle and their mechanical strengths are low.   Unlike cellulose nitrate, there is no one plasticizer that is suitable for all applications of cellulose acetate.

The useful plastics compositions contain from 60 to 85 per cent of cellulose acetate.   With an increase in the amount of plasticizers used, the tensile strength and hardness decrease, and the elongation, impact resistance, and cold flow increase.   Plasticizers also lower the melting point to a workable temperature and improve such properties as water and chemical resistance.

Cellulose acetate plastics are resistant to dilute acids, gasoline, mineral and vegetable oils, and ethyl alcohol.   Their resistance to water is not as good as that of other cellulose derivatives, a fact which has militated against applications where weathering is encountered.

Cellulose acetate flake is also utilized in the manufacture of surface coatings, sheet, rod, and tube stock, and transparent films and foils.

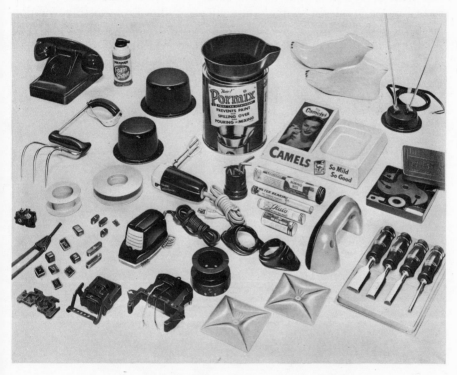

FIG. 7-5.   Molded products made from cellulose acetate.   (*Courtesy Celanese Corp. of America*)

Lacquers made from cellulose acetate are used for insulating purposes, for sealing bottles, for coating colored light bulbs, for coating textiles, papers, and metal foils, for preparing motion picture screens, and for numerous other purposes.

Thin sheets of cellulose acetate are used as transparent wrapping material, and thicker strips are used as safety film, replacing the hazardous cellulose nitrate.   Packaging films are made in many gauges.   The film does not shrink or stretch, is waterproof, germproof, and greaseproof, and is unaffected by humidity or temperature changes.   It presents an excellent surface for printing and can be cemented or laminated easily.

One other large use of acetate is that for tape for magnetic sound recording. In 1955, approximately 6 billion feet of magnetic tape were manufactured, of which about 90 per cent was made from cellulose acetate. The rest was either the cheaper, paper-backed type or the newer, more expensive, but rapidly growing polyester (Mylar) type. These tapes are usually one mil thick, are made in varying widths, and are coated on one side with a very thin layer of iron oxide in a vinyl resin binder. Tape recording is used for home amusement, radio broadcasting, motion pictures, and for diverse scientific applications. Recently, it has even been used for the magnetic recording of television pictures.

Fig. 7-6. Window boxes and overwraps made from cellulose acetate film. (*Courtesy Celanese Corp. of America*)

### Cellulose Propionate

Although cellulose propionate has been known for many years, commercial production was undertaken only recently because of the previous unavailability of propionic acid and anhydride in quantity and at a low price. It is now available under the name Forticel for use in plastic molding powders.

Its manufacture is similar to that of cellulose acetate except for suitable modifications of the process to compensate for the lower activity of propionic anhydride. Like cellulose acetate, mild acid hydrolysis yields a product of improved solubility in such solvents as acetone and dioxan. As expected, the larger fatty acid radical produces a cellulose ester of greater softness.

Cellulose propionate thus requires less plasticizer than the acetate for the same flexural strength and has a higher impact strength. It is dimensionally stable, has good surface hardness without brittleness, and is odorless, even at high temperatures. It is being evaluated and used for such applications as fountain pen barrels, telephone and appliance housings, and football helmets.

### Higher Cellulose Esters

Cellulose butyrate can also be made by a procedure similar to that for the acetate, including the acid hydrolysis step to produce an acetone-soluble product. Due to its increased softness and lower softening point, compared to the acetate and propionate, it has not been offered on a commercial scale.

The higher esters of cellulose cannot be made in good yield by the process used to make the lower esters. Treatment of cellulose with chloroacetic anhydride and magnesium perchlorate or with pyridine or pyridine hydrochloride as catalysts is usually necessary. These higher esters are not, at present, of commercial importance.

### Mixed Esters of Cellulose

Intensive studies have been made of the properties of mixed esters of cellulose in an effort to overcome the deficiencies of each of the straight esters. Cellulose nitrate-acetate was once manufactured but is no longer in production. Of greater interest are the mixed organic esters, especially those of the acetate, propionate, and butyrate. They are prepared by activating cellulose with glacial acetic acid, then reacting the product with mixtures of acids and anhydrides. Each of these products can vary with respect to the total degree of esterification, the ratio of the acyl radicals present, and the molecular weight.

Competitive to cellulose propionate is cellulose acetate-propionate (Tenite III, Hercose AP), developed for the manufacture of tough, dimensionally stable molded parts. The properties and applications are similar to the other cellulose esters. It is used in some surface coatings and in extruded filaments that are interwoven with cotton in the production of special fabrics for fused shirt collars.

The mixed ester made in largest quantity, cellulose acetate-butyrate, is made by esterifying cellulose with a mixture of acetic and butyric anhydrides. The acetate-butyrate most generally used is a material of about 14 per cent acetyl and 36 per cent butyryl content, having a degree of polymerization of 250 to 350. Much less plasticizer is required than with cellulose acetate.

This mixed ester combines the thermal stability of the acetate (Tenite I) with the better moisture resistance and improved dimensional stability of the butyrate. Since the acetate-butyrate retains the desirable features of moldability of the acetate and, in addition, shows great improvement in moldability around inserts, it is widely used in injection molding. It is also extensively employed in the form of extruded strips and tubes for numerous uses.

Fig. 7-7. Telephone housing molded from cellulose acetate-butyrate. (*Courtesy Eastman Chemical Products*)

Cellulose acetate-butyrate shows better weather resistance than the acetate, partly because of lower water absorption, partly because of better compatibility and retention of resistant and nonvolatile plasticizers.

Cellulose acetate-butyrate is used in hot-melt coatings for paper and textiles; by incorporation of waxes and resins, coatings may be made with high impermeability to moisture. Both the acetate-butyrate and the acetate-propionate are used in the manufacture of safety film.

The use of strippable protective coatings has received increased attention in recent years. This type of covering is generally applied by dipping the article to be protected into a molten composition and withdrawing it. The dipped article receives a uniform, heavy coating which quickly sets on cooling to allow immediate storage or packing for shipment. No volatile solvents are used, and so solvent removal and recovery are not required. The previous practice of wax or grease coating, followed by paper covering, is thus superseded by a single-step operation. Not only is the dip covering quickly applied but it is removed with equal ease. A cut is made to start the "peeling," whereupon the whole covering may be removed, generally in a single piece. This type of coating not only excludes water vapor and prevents corrosion but also protects against handling damage. Of the several thermoplastic polymers used in these coatings, ethyl cellulose and cellulose acetate-butyrate are outstanding because of their heat stability, compatibility, and high strength.

One of the most promising applications of acetate-butyrate is for piping, especially in petroleum production. Corrosion problems due to salt water, sour crude, and electrolytic action have been successfully overcome with this plastic. Another advantage in the use of acetate-butyrate pipe is its lower frictional resistance to fluid flow. Flow through extruded acetate-butyrate pipe is approximately 40 per cent more than through clean steel pipe for the same head loss. The country's longest plastic pipeline—nearly ten miles of 3-inch pipe—is now in service transporting crude oil in Montana. Made of cellulose acetate-butyrate, it took only about twelve man-days to lay the entire 52,300-foot line.

### Cellulose Ethers

In many of its reactions, sodium or alkali cellulose behaves as an alcoholate, RONa, e.g., in its ability to form ethers upon treatment with alkyl halides. Methyl, ethyl, and benzyl celluloses have been extensively investigated and, more recently, carboxymethyl cellulose and hydroxyethyl cellulose have been developed. In general, the method of manufacture involves: (1) Preparation of alkali cellulose from linters and 50 to 75 per cent aqueous caustic, (2) concurrent degradation of chain length to the desired degree of polymerization, and (3) treatment at 150° to 200°C in an autoclave with the appropriate etherifying agent.

### Methyl Cellulose

Methyl cellulose is prepared by a process similar to that for ethyl cellulose, substituting methyl chloride or sulfate for the corresponding ethyl analog (see Ethyl Cellulose). Trimethyl cellulose is not readily obtained by this method, but the partly methylated derivative has the most useful properties so that the completely methylated compound is not desired.

Methyl cellulose (Methocel) is produced in several viscosity grades containing from 1.2 to 2.0 methoxy groups per anhydroglucose unit. The commercial product possesses the unusual property among hydrophilic colloids of being soluble in cold water but insoluble in hot. Upon heating, gelation occurs between 40° and 70°C, the precise temperature being a function of molecular weight and concentration.

Six to 7 per cent methyl cellulose dissolved in water produces useful thickening and dispersing agents. In this form, it is used in the formulation of textile printing pastes and in cosmetic preparations and dentifrices. Alone or blended with water-miscible proteins or starches, it is used as an adhesive. Films deposited from methyl cellulose solutions have been used to coat paper. Water-resistant films can be prepared by the addition of water-soluble urea- or melamine-formaldehyde resins. As a thin film, methyl cellulose is highly resistant to greases and oils. Since it is edible, methyl cellulose has been used in salad dressings and other thickened food products.

Recently, a modified methyl cellulose has been produced, which combines many properties of the organo-soluble cellulose derivatives with the properties of the hydrophilic synthetic gums. This compound is prepared by reacting alkali cellulose with both methyl chloride and propylene oxide to form an hydroxypropyl methyl cellulose. The reaction product is purified by successive washings with boiling water.

This product is nonionic, surface active, thermo-gelling in aqueous solution, and can be formed by heat fabrication techniques normally possible only with plastic-type compounds. With this mixed ether of cellulose, it is possible to extrude, mold, or hot cast from nonaqueous solvents a shaped object that is water-soluble.

### Ethyl Cellulose

Ethyl cellulose is manufactured in greater quantity than any of the other cellulosic ethers; hence, its manufacture will be described in greater detail. The first step in the preparation of ethyl cellulose is the formation of alkali cellulose. One method consists of the following steps. After removal of the excess alkali, the wetted material is conveyed to the reactors. Ethyl chloride and excess caustic are added to the reactors. The temperature is raised to 175° to 200°C, and the reaction allowed to continue for a specified length of time. By control of temperature, pressure, reaction time, and ratios of raw materials, it is possible to control the ethoxy content and the viscosity of the product. The over-all reaction for a degree of substitution of one is:

$$[C_6H_7O_2(OH)_3 \cdot NaOH]_n + nC_2H_5Cl \rightarrow$$
$$[C_6H_7O_2(OH)_2(OC_2H_5)]_n + nNaCl + nH_2O$$

When the reaction is completed, the ether and alcohols that are formed as by-products of the action of the caustic on ethyl chloride are flashed off, the vapors scrubbed with sulfuric acid, and the solvent condensed and recovered. As the solvents are removed from the reactors, ethyl cellulose precipitates in a liquor consisting of excess caustic and salt. This slurry is blown to tubs in which the caustic is drained off and the ethyl cellulose is given a preliminary washing. The large granules of ethyl cellulose are then dropped into disintegrators where they are ground to a uniform size. This grinding makes it possible to remove additional salts and caustic by an additional wash and stabilizing treatment. Excess water is then removed in a centrifuge, the product is dried, blended, and stored according to grade. The alcohol and ether formed as by-products are recovered and reconverted to ethyl chloride.

A more recent method of preparation is as follows. The caustic solution is expelled from the alkali cellulose and all traces of free alkali removed by washing with ethyl alcohol, using 95 per cent alcohol for the first washes and absolute alcohol for the last in order to remove all traces of alkali. This method practically eliminates the formation of ethyl ether from the ethylating agent. The alcohol-wet alkali cellulose is suspended in additional alcohol in an autoclave and ethyl chloride gas is added under pressure to the stirred suspension. The temperature is slowly raised to 180° to 200°C under a pressure of 1,000 to 1,500 psi until no further consumption of ethyl chloride occurs, if complete reaction is desired. The final ethyl cellulose flake is obtained by precipitation from an acetone solution, thus assuring complete removal of any occluded salt.

The properties of the resulting ether can be controlled by the degree of substitution, as is shown in Table 7-3.

TABLE 7-3.   CHARACTERISTICS OF ETHYL CELLULOSES[2]

| Ethoxy Content % | Ethoxy Groups per Anhydroglucose Residue | Solubility and Applications |
|---|---|---|
| 14–24 | 0.5–1.0 | Soluble in caustic soda |
| 24–33 | 1.0–1.5 | Soluble in water |
| 33–45 | 1.5–2.3 | Water solubility decreases to zero at 45% ethoxy content |
| 45–47 | 2.3–2.4 | Solubility in nonpolar solvents increases. Softening point decreases |
| 47–48 | 2.4–2.5 | Compatible with waxes and resins; minimum softening temperatures; best commercial grade; tough, stable, and thermoplastic |
| 48–50 | 2.5–2.6 | Soluble in nonpolar but not in polar solvents; softening temperature increases again |

Ethyl cellulose has a specific gravity of 1.14, lower than that of any other cellulose derivative, and is among the lightest plastics. It is produced only in water-insoluble grades. The most common products possess between 44 and 50 per cent ethoxy content. This degree of etherification

[2] Ritchie, P. D., *A Chemistry of Plastics and High Polymers*, p. 172, Cleaver-Hume Press, London (dist. by Interscience Publishers, New York), 1949.

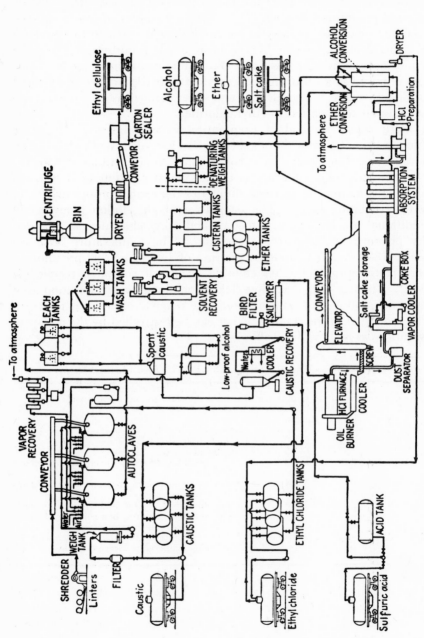

Fig. 7-8. Ethyl cellulose flow sheet. (*Reprinted by permission from Chemical Engineering*)

corresponds to alkylation of about 2.2 to 2.5 hydroxyl groups per anhydro-glucose unit, a range in which optimum solubility in both polar and non-polar solvents is obtained.

Since its introduction in the United States about 1935, ethyl cellulose (Ethocel) has found favor in both coating compositions and molded plastics because of several advantages which it possesses over other cellulosic plastics. It is unusually tough and flexible and, suitably plasticized, retains these characteristics even at temperatures as low as −40°C. For any given flow quality and rigidity, it requires less plasticizer than either cellulose acetate or nitrate. Ethyl cellulose does not embrittle as rapidly as the cellulose esters as temperatures are lowered and its low-temperature flexibility has made it a useful material for nonstructural components in aircraft. An important characteristic of ethyl cellulose is its ability to be compounded with an amazing variety of plasticizers, gums, waxes, natural and synthetic resins, and solvents. By proper selection of these ingredients, almost any desired combination of gloss, weatherability, hardness, flexi-bility, and surface adhesion may be produced. It exhibits good resistance to alkalies and aliphatic hydrocarbons, fair resistance to dilute acids, but is decomposed by concentrated mineral acids and is soluble in most aromatic solvents, esters, and alcohols.

Ethyl cellulose exhibits excellent electrical resistance. In addition, films of ethyl cellulose have excellent flexibility and good water resistance, two factors which are of considerable importance in wire insulation coatings. The good adhesive properties of the material are apparent in its self-sealing properties and its application to low-pressure cloth laminates. Ethyl cellulose is also available for application as a hot-melt strip-coating for the preservation of metal parts.

One of its favorable characteristics is its stability to heat and light. In the case of cellulose nitrate lacquers, breakdown is accompanied by acid decomposition products which promote further decomposition. Since ethyl cellulose is an ether rather than an ester, heat resistance is notably superior to cellulose nitrate. Since it is compatible with cellulose nitrate in all proportions, it is utilized to augment a variety of pyroxylin coatings.

Ethyl cellulose, when compounded, may be used in countless ways. Its applications include packaging papers, wrapping foil, artificial leather, lacquers, adhesives, furniture trim, automotive parts, wire insulation, toilet articles, novelties, fabric coatings, and flexible rubberlike tubing.

Ethyl cellulose film is made by casting from an alcohol-toluene solution onto a moving, continuous surface. The film is characterized by resistance to attack by alkali and dilute acids, resistance to light discoloration, and good flexibility and toughness at low temperatures. It has relatively low water absorption and better toughness than cellulose acetate; however, since ethyl cellulose is not inherently moisture-vapor-proof, this property is added by incorporating in the formulation a moisture-vapor-resistant material, such as paraffin wax.

Ethyl cellulose has never been used on a commercial scale to produce a fiber. Its solubility in a wide variety of solvents, some of them well-known dry-cleaning agents, and its comparatively low softening point have restricted its use in the textile industry.

Benzyl cellulose is manufactured in Europe but not in the United States. Ethyl hydroxyethyl cellulose is made here and is similar in properties and applications to ethyl cellulose, except for better solubility in aliphatic hydrocarbons.

### Carboxymethyl Cellulose

Carboxymethyl cellulose was first developed in Germany toward the end of World War I, but it was not until late in the 1930's, and particularly during and since World War II, that large-scale uses began to emerge and commercial production appeared justified.

Carboxymethyl cellulose is an ether of cellulose and hydroxyacetic (glycolic) acid. The cellulose is treated with alkali, then reacted with sodium chloroacetate to yield sodium carboxymethyl cellulose. An anhydroglucose unit with a degree of substitution of one would be:

$$CH_2OCH_2COO^- \ Na^+$$

Theoretically, complete reaction would mean the introduction of three carboxymethyl groups per anhydroglucose unit. In any actual molecule, the substituent groups are scattered randomly along the chain, some on primary and some on secondary hydroxyl groups (with no units substituted in both secondary positions). The optimum combination of physical properties of the commercially available sodium salt is achieved with a substitution of 0.4 to 1.3 (0.7 being the most common). The free acid formed at a degree of substitution of 1.3 or below is insoluble in water, whereas the sodium salt at degree of substitution of 0.3 or above is soluble. Thus, upon acidification of aqueous solutions of sodium carboxymethyl cellulose, the free-acid form precipitates. The acid form is infusible and cannot be dissolved without being neutralized; therefore, the product is not widely useful. On the other hand, a stable, colloidal dispersion of the free-acid form in water can be prepared by ion exchange between an aqueous solution of sodium carboxymethyl cellulose and a strong, acid-type cation exchange resin. In this form the free acid has unique properties which indicate its possible usefulness as a film former.

The two best-known processes for the manufacture of sodium carboxymethyl cellulose are the German batch process and the continuous process. In the batch process, the principal steps are the reaction between bleached sulfite pulp and caustic soda to form alkali cellulose, and reaction of the latter intermediate with dry sodium chloroacetate to form sodium carboxymethyl cellulose and sodium chloride. Excess caustic is neutralized with sodium bicarbonate, and the product (CMC, cellulose gum) is ground and packaged.

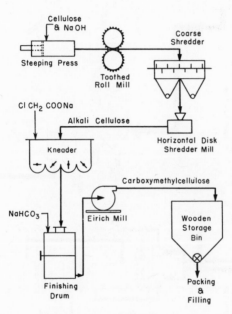

Fig. 7-9. Carboxymethyl cellulose flow sheet (German process). (*Courtesy Modern Chemical Processes*)

The continuous process consists of spraying powdered cellulose first with caustic solution and then with chloroacetic acid as the solid cellulose is tumbled in a rotary drum. For most industrial uses, a dried form, containing 5 to 6 per cent moisture, is produced. The wet sodium carboxymethyl cellulose from the reactor, after aging for eight to ten hours, may be dried by several methods. Flash drying yields the product in its most desirable physical form (Carbose).

Pure sodium carboxymethyl cellulose is a white powder, soluble or dispersible in water or alkaline solutions. Aqueous solutions are highly

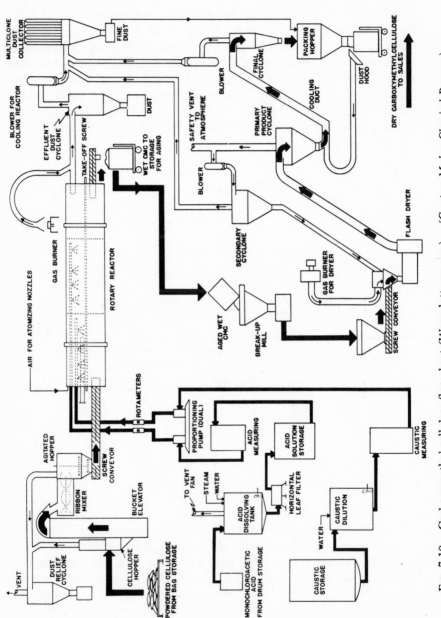

Fig. 7-10. Carboxymethyl cellulose flow sheet (Wyandotte process). (Courtesy Modern Chemical Processes)

viscous, and for this reason are useful for their thickening, suspending, and stabilizing properties.

In pure form, the powdered product is odorless, tasteless, and physiologically inert. Considerable use is expected for purified grades which can be added to food, cosmetic, and pharmaceutical preparations. Carboxymethyl cellulose is an excellent stabilizer for ice cream, since, by inhibiting the formation of ice crystals, it decreases the amount of beating required for the incorporation of minute air bubbles which improve the consistency and decrease the density of packaged ice cream.

It has proved of value in water-soluble adhesive compositions, in stabilization of latices, and in ceramics, where it serves as a dispersing agent to help keep ceramic glazes in suspension. In the paper industry, it has been used to increase the bursting strength of liners, to increase the gloss on coated box boards, and to help suspend ink for subsequent removal in de-inking systems. The European textile industry has employed carboxymethyl cellulose for warp sizing; this application has not yet been very successful in the United States. Less than 1 per cent carboxymethyl cellulose added to oil-well drilling mud improves mud viscosity control and helps to plug porous formations in the bore, preventing loss of water from the mud.

Probably the material's greatest potential lies in the laundry field, where detergent improvement uses larger quantities of carboxymethyl cellulose each year. In addition, the product has been found effective as a laundry sizing. Although evaluation has not been extensive, there are indications that carboxymethyl cellulose may improve the physical characteristics of soil in somewhat the same manner as the acrylic-type soil conditioners do.

### Hydroxyethyl Cellulose

Although hydroxyethyl cellulose has been described in the technical literature for the past thirty years or more, few uses in commerce have developed. Depending upon the degree of substitution, three general types have been made—one of low substitution, dispersible in chilled caustic solutions; a medium degree of substitution, soluble in caustic at room or elevated temperatures; and a water-soluble grade, of a higher degree of substitution.

Hydroxyethyl cellulose (Cellosize) is made by metathesis between ethylene chlorohydrin and alkali cellulose or by direct reaction of ethylene oxide upon cellulose itself. The over-all reaction for a completely substituted product can be written as follows:

$$[C_6H_7O_2(OH)_3]_n + C_2H_4O \xrightarrow{\text{NaOH aq.}} [C_6H_7O_2(OC_2H_4OH)_3]_n$$

The function of the sodium hydroxide is to swell the cellulose fibers uniformly and to catalyze the etherification.

The product varies in appearance and properties from a fibrous, water-insoluble material, superficially similar to cellulose, to a waxy, water-soluble material with increasing ethylene oxide content.

Hydroxyethyl celluloses have been used as filaments, in sheet form, in textile finishes and sizes, in paper coatings, as a thickener for textile printing, as fixing agents for pigments, as leather coatings, as fillers for greases, and as additions to hydraulic cement used in lining deep wells to retard its solidification at high pressures and temperatures.

A combined ether, carboxymethyl hydroxyethyl cellulose, is also made which is similar in properties and applications to carboxymethyl cellulose, but is more compatible with various salt solutions.

**Cyanoethyl Cellulose**

By treating cellulose first with caustic, then with acrylonitrile, a series of cyanoethylated celluloses are obtained. Depending upon the temperature, mole ratios of caustic and acrylonitrile to cellulose, and time of reaction, various degrees of substitution are obtained. As with the products just previously discussed, cyanoethylated cellulose is an ether:

$$[C_6H_7O_2(OH)_3]_n + nCH_2{:}CHCN \rightarrow [C_6H_7O_2(OH)_2(OCH_2CH_2CN)]_n$$

Alkaline hydrolysis of the product yields carboxyethyl cellulose.

Depending upon the reaction conditions, which control the degree of substitution, the products may be alkali-soluble, water-soluble, or organic-solvent-soluble.

A considerable amount of research has been done upon the cyanoethylation reaction, with both wood and cotton, in an effort to upgrade the properties of cellulose. Water-soluble yarns, twistless yarns, and related products have been claimed. Further, by achieving a degree of substitution of from 0.3 to 2.0 cyanoethyl groups per glucose residue (organic-solvent-soluble), it is claimed that the properties, especially the tensile strength, wear resistance, stiffness, and moisture and mildew resistance, of cotton fabrics are improved. Applications under investigation at present include the use of cyanoethylated cotton in tarpaulins, filter fabrics, awnings, fish nets, tobacco shade cloths, and similar items where permanent resistance to rot, mildew, and bacteria and improved abrasion and stretch resistance are desired.

Even paper has been cyanoethylated. The treatment improves the water resistance and dimensional stability. These properties are particularly important in punched cards used in automatic business machines. The chief drawback to the cyanoethylation of cellulose in all forms so far has been its relatively high cost.   It is likely that increased interest in the application of this process to cellulose will occur as the cost of acrylonitrile decreases.

### Zelan

It has been found possible to etherify partially the cellulose of woven cotton fabrics, thus rendering the goods water-repellent.   Products marketed as Zelan (stearoxymethyl pyridinium chloride or acetate) here and Velan in England have found use for this purpose.   When Zelan-treated cotton is warmed, reaction occurs readily and stearoxymethyl groups are introduced into the surface layers of the cellulose molecules:

$$[C_6H_7O_2(OH)_3]_n + nC_{18}H_{35}OCH_2N(Cl)C_5H_5 \rightarrow$$
$$[C_6H_7O_2(OH)_2OCH_2OC_{18}H_{35}]_n + nC_5H_5N\cdot HCl$$

### ALGINIC ACID DERIVATIVES

Alginic acid, one of the main constituents of seaweed, is a polymer of $d$-mannuronic acid.   Its structure is probably

The molecular weight has been estimated at 15,000 or greater.   Alginic acid can thus be seen to be composed of long, linear molecules containing reactive carboxylic groups.   Sodium alginate (Kelcosol) is a hydrophobic colloid and has found use in ice cream, jellies, marshmallows, and puddings.   It has also been used in adhesives and as a lubricant and binder in extrusions, as has the amonium salt (Superloid).   The calcium salt is used for waterproofing concrete and fireproofing wallboard.

Considerable development work has been carried out in England on the use of alginic acid and its salts as textile fibers.   Solutions of sodium alginate are readily soluble in water and, being very viscous, are suitable for spinning.   They can readily be converted to alginic acid by spinning into an acid bath or to calcium alginate by spinning into a coagulating bath containing calcium salts.   The filaments so obtained are fairly satisfactory with respect to strength, but unfortunately dissolve rapidly in a solution containing a fraction of a per cent of soap and soda ash; thus they will not stand laundering.   Because of this difficulty, investigation has been made of the properties of other alginates in the hope of finding one that would satisfactorily withstand the action of alkaline baths.

Attempts to spin solutions of sodium alginate into coagulating baths containing solutions of salts other than calcium, e.g., those of chromium and beryllium, have proved unsatisfactory.  It has proved preferable in the preparation of heavy metal alginates to weave or knit calcium alginate into fabric and then to convert the calcium alginate fabric into a heavy-metal alginate fabric.  The alginates of chromium and beryllium are satisfactorily resistant to the action of dilute alkali, but, since chromium alginate is green and beryllium compounds are toxic, their utility for general purposes is restricted.

Many other alginates have been made.  Probably the best so far is aluminum alginate; it has a much higher wet strength than calcium alginate and can be washed safely in neutral but not in weakly alkaline soap solutions.  It is at present the only fabric suitable for apparel which is both flameproof and washable.  As a matter of fact, all of the metallic alginates have the outstanding virtue that they are flameproof; they are difficult to ignite and the flame is self-extinguishing.

The manufacture of an alginate fiber consists, briefly, of the following steps.  Seaweed is collected, dried, and milled.  The powdered weed is treated with aqueous sodium carbonate and caustic soda which converts the alginate present to the sodium salt; the pigment and the cellulose present in the weed are not dissolved.  The viscous solution of sodium alginate is purified by sedimentation and is then bleached and sterilized by the addition of sodium hypochlorite.  The alginic acid is then precipitated from the sodium alginate solution by acidification.  Alginic acid is washed and reconverted to the pure sodium salt.  A dilute, sterile solution of sodium alginate is made, filtered, then spun on a viscose spinning machine into a coagulating bath containing normal calcium chloride solution, 0.02 normal hydrochloric acid, and a small quantity of a cationic surface-active agent.  The sodium alginate is thus precipitated in filament form as calcium alginate.  The filaments are drawn together, washed, lubricated, dried, and wound.

Calcium alginate, which is the only alginate fiber presently made commercially (and only in England), is unsuited for applications where washability is required, but its very solubility in dilute alkali has turned out to be an advantage in several applications.  Various fabrics may be woven from a combination of alginate yarns and very fine worsted yarns. After the fabric has been woven, it is treated with an alkaline solution until the scaffold of alginate fibers is dissolved, leaving a very fine worsted fabric—one so fine it could never have been woven directly.  For embroidery work, an interlocked pattern in viscose rayon is embroidered on calcium alginate woven fabric.  Upon washing, the embroidery is left in a netlike form which resembles lace.   There are several other textile uses in which calcium alginate may be advantageously employed. Although the use of the alginates in textiles is still in its infancy, it seems possible that this polymeric material may some day become a factor in the industry.

Early attempts to prepare organic derivatives of alginic acid met with little success; the drastic conditions required to accomplish substitution by the usual reagents largely destroyed the colloidal properties of the polymer.   Recently, alginic acid has been found to react under mild conditions with various alkylene and substituted alkylene oxides to give a unique series of algin products.   These water-soluble alkylene glycol alginates give viscous solutions at relatively low concentrations.   In contrast to sodium alginate, these esters are soluble in acid solutions. Propylene glycol alginate is now available commercially (Kelcoloid):

$$
\begin{array}{c}
\overset{H}{\quad}\quad\overset{H}{\quad} \\
-O-\overset{|}{\diagup}\underset{H}{OH}\ \ HO\diagdown\overset{|}{\quad} \\
\diagdown\underset{\phantom{O}}{\quad}-O\diagup\,L-O- \\
\overset{|}{C:O} \\
\overset{|}{O} \\
H_2C\cdot CHOH\cdot CH_3
\end{array}
$$

Its pronounced thickening and emulsifying powers in acidic solutions have resulted in commercial applications in such uses as in French dressing, salad dressing, flavor emulsions, meringues, pharmaceutical jellies, and foam stabilization.

## REGENERATED PROTEINS

Of the myriad sources theoretically available for proteinaceous matter, relatively few have been commercially exploited.   At present, protein from milk, soya beans, peanuts, and corn constitute the principal sources of supply.

### Polyamides from Milk

By far the most important protein, so far as the plastics industry is concerned, is rennet casein.   For applications other than plastics use, the casein is precipitated from skimmed milk either by allowing the latter to become naturally sour (lactic casein) or by the addition of a small quantity of an acid, such as hydrochloric (acid casein).   Much more acid casein is made than rennet casein.   It should be noted that only a relatively small proportion of the world production of casein of all types enters the plastics industry, considerably larger quantities being consumed by the food, adhesives, paper coating, and other industries.

At least seventeen different amino acids have been isolated in the hydrolysis products of casein, which has a molecular weight of about 375,000 (by ultracentrifugation). In addition, the hydrolysis of casein also yields a phosphoric acid derivative known as a nucleic acid. Consequently, casein is classed as a phospho- or nucleoprotein.

The first use of protein material for plastics applications was in 1897 when Krische and Spitteler in Germany demonstrated that casein could be hardened by immersion in a formaldehyde solution. Since celluloid was the only man-made plastic then available for commercial use, interest was shown in the casein product because of its advantage over cellulose nitrate in flame resistance.

Casein plastics were commercially introduced in Germany during the year 1900. They were named Galalith (milkstone), a term which became a general one for casein plastics. In comparison to flammable cellulose nitrate and the soon-to-follow dark-colored phenolic resins, Galalith had the advantages of being both nonflammable and light colored. Its major deficiencies were the long processing time required and high water absorption. When this plastic was introduced in the United States in the early twenties, it was found that climatic conditions here made its general utilization impractical; the development of cellulose acetate, urea-formaldehyde, and vinyl resins soon restricted the use of casein plastics to the production of buttons and similar small objects.

For the preparation of casein for plastics use, fresh skimmed milk, consisting of a suspension of casein in water together with soluble salts, albumens, lactose, etc., but freed from milk fats, is heated to about 40°C. A small quantity of the enzyme, *rennin*, obtained from the inner lining of the fourth stomach of calves, is then added, and the mixture is agitated until curd begins to form. After a period of standing, to allow the formation of a firm curd, stirring is resumed to break up the curd. The casein is then allowed to settle, and the whey (the liquid part) is drawn off. After repeated washings, the moist casein is put into bags in which the product is pressed until the moisture content falls to about 40 per cent. The cake is then roughly ground and the rennet casein finally dried at a temperature below 65°C.

Solid casein plastics are made (the "dry" process) by mixing rennet casein with 30 to 40 per cent of water, together with suitable dyes, pigments, or lakes, then extruding the heated mixture in the form of rods or tubes. If sheets are desired, extruded rods are laid side by side and flattened in an hydraulic press. The products are cured by immersion in 4 to 5 per cent formaldehyde solution.

Experiments on amino acids in equilibrium with formaldehyde have shown that the ε-amino group (of lysine), as well as the unsubstituted α-amino group, can bind one or two moles of formaldehyde, depending on the concentration of the latter. The first mole is more firmly bound than the second. In addition to lysine, other amino acids have side-chain groups which may react with formaldehyde. Several of these amino acids, when treated with formaldehyde under varying conditions, undergo internal cyclization through the α-amino groups, but the results are of restricted application to proteins, which contain relatively few substituted α-amino groups. There is no experimental proof that the peptide group reacts extensively with formaldehyde; if such reaction did occur on a large scale, all formaldehyde-treated proteins would show definitely larger quantities of stable formaldehyde content than have been found. Whatever the reaction, formaldehyde does accomplish a cure of protein polymers.

Since the hardening process may require from one week to a year, depending on the size of the product being processed, it is desirable to machine into the final form before hardening. Also, the plastic material which is machined off before hardening can be reused, whereas the hardened plastic scraps cannot. After proper hardening, the treated articles are removed from the bath, seasoned to allow evaporation of the water, and finally straightened, if necessary, between steam-heated platens under relatively low pressure.

Casein sheets, rods, and tubes may be machined and fabricated into buttons, buckles, and ornamental jewelry. The products may be buffed to a smooth surface, but a more permanent and less expensive gloss can be obtained by immersion in a hypochlorite solution.

In 1929, it was discovered that moistened casein, containing a small quantity of alum, could not only be easily extruded and machined but could also be molded before hardening. As a result of this discovery, most of the casein plastics manufacturers in the United States were con-solidated with the button producers. The process at present employed in the manufacture of buttons and buckles from casein consists of extruding rods from a mixture of casein, water, coloring material, and about 2 per cent of alum. Buttons are made from the rods in automatic screw machines, which turn out the buttons in essentially their final shapes, or from disk-shaped blanks, which are turned into button forms. The forms are hardened in a 4 to 5 per cent formaldehyde solution; since the buttons are thin, the hardening process requires only a few days. Buttons are then drilled and glazed or polished. Buckles are punched from a ribbon extrusion. Although casein buttons are made by several com-panies, the quantity of casein plastics available in the form of sheets, rods, and tubes is limited.

The most serious fault of casein plastics is their lack of water resistance.

Protein plastics are hygroscopic and are therefore affected by atmospheric moisture changes. The absorption of water causes severe warping in large sizes. From the beginning, these inherent weaknesses limited their use to simple products requiring no great strength or weatherability. Although improvements have been introduced in the fabrication methods and the physical properties, these weaknesses have never been entirely eliminated.

More recently, casein has grown in popularity because of its use in the production of wool-like fibers. Because wool has proved to be eminently suitable for clothing, a large number of attempts have been made to produce a modified natural fiber having similar properties. Early attempts to make a commercially acceptable fiber from casein were unsuccessful; it was not until 1935 that an Italian, Ferretti, succeeded in making pliable fibers with certain wool-like characteristics. An Italian rayon producer purchased Ferretti's patents and began large-scale production of a casein fiber, known as Lanital, from milk. In the United States, research was carried out independently, and in 1939 production of a casein fiber, named Aralac, was begun. However, in 1948, the plant which used to manufacture Aralac was sold to another company who used the facilities to make Vicara fiber from corn protein. So far as is known, Aralac is not at present being manufactured.

The method of manufacture of both Lanital and Aralac is similar. Skimmed milk is heated to 40°C and acid is added to coagulate the protein, which separates as a curd. The whey is discarded, the curd is washed to remove acid and salts, most of the water is removed mechanically, and the curd, consisting of casein, is dried. One hundred pounds of whole milk yields 3 pounds of casein, from which about the same weight of fiber can be produced.

After blending, the casein is dispersed in aqueous caustic soda. The solution is clarified and extruded through jets into a coagulating bath and collected as tow. The coagulating bath contains 100 parts of water, 2 parts sulfuric acid, 5 parts formaldehyde, and 20 parts glucose. The function of the sulfuric acid is to precipitate the casein from the sodium caseinate solution; the formaldehyde acts as a partial hardening and insolubilizing agent, while glucose increases the rate of dehydration of the fiber. The casein is coagulated under slight tension in order to yield a stronger fiber.

The tow is then finally hardened by treatment with more formaldehyde; this is necessary in order to obtain a fine fiber which will withstand wetting. Aralac, but, so far as is known, not Lanital, is then given an acetylation treatment in order to improve its stability to boiling water.

Aralac was designed as a blending fiber, and a predetermined amount, together with rayon, wool, or cotton staple, or a combination, were blended, and the mixed fibers drawn into strands, then combed and twisted until a fine strand of blended yarn was obtained. This single strand was a uniform mixture of casein and other fibers and was used for weaving. About the only application in which Aralac was used unblended was in woven interlinings for women's winter coats. In other uses, which included a wide variety of textiles, the Aralac content in the finished cloth ranged from 20 to 50 per cent.

The outstanding properties of casein fiber are its warmth and softness of hand. Casein fiber will not felt, but the admixture of a small proportion of casein fiber with wool increases the feltability of the wool.

The principal defect of casein fiber is that, when wet, its tenacity is very low. The specific gravity is 1.29—close to that of wool. Casein fibers are sensitive to alkali, but they are stable to mild buffered alkalies, such as sodium bicarbonate. The fiber is attacked by clothes' moths and carpet beetles and is subject to mildew; it is in this respect similar to the natural hair fibers. Solvents normally used in dry cleaning have no effect. Water absorption is similar to that for wool—about 14 per cent under standard conditions. The stability of the fibers to light is similar to that of wool.

Merinova is a newer casein fiber made in Italy. It is a soft, creamy fiber supplied only as staple. Its process of manufacture is very similar to that of Lanital. The fiber obtained after spinning is treated in autoclaves with formaldehyde in order to give it wet strength and some resistance to alkali. As it is still somewhat susceptible to alkali but resistant to boiling dilute sulfuric acid, it withstands the usual wool-dyeing process. Because of the formaldehyde treatment, it is mothproof and shrinkproof; its specific gravity and moisture regain are similar to those of wool. Its uses are similar to those of Lanital.

A curled casein fiber has been developed in the United States for use in applications for which horse hair, with its high resiliency, was once found uniquely suitable. The fiber is known as Caslen. Used as a single filament a few thousandths of an inch thick, it is cheaper than the best quality of horse hair, equally resilient, more sanitary, more uniform, and more dependable as to availability. It can be treated so that it is mildew-, moth-, and bacteria-proof.

Acid casein is also made in large quantities for other uses. One modern process uses the following procedure. Skim milk is heated with warm water in a multiple-pass heater. Diluted muriatic (commercial hydrochloric) acid is fed into the acidifying chamber. In the 15 seconds it takes the curd to pass through the chamber, the casein precipitation is completed, and the spongy mass of curd drops out on a coarse screen. The whey that passes through the screen is caught in a tray and is drained off for further processing.

The fresh curd contains about 85 per cent water. It is transferred to a ribbon conveyor which kneads and breaks the curd and allows the whey to drain and to be combined with the whey from the screen drain tray. When the curd reaches the top of the draining conveyor, it contains about 70 per cent water. It then drops through a curd breaker where the curd is forced through a series of small holes. The broken curd is washed with water to dissolve occluded salts. The water is removed by squeeze rolls and the moisture content is reduced to about 50 per cent, at which point the curd is about as dry as can be obtained by mechanical means. The curd is then further dried in a conveyor dryer which is heated in zones from 55°C to as high as 80°C. The casein comes off the conveyor with a moisture content of less than 10 per cent. The casein sheet is then broken up and discharged to a centrifugal blower which cools the granular product while lifting it to a cyclone separator. From the cyclone the casein drops into a roller mill which reduces the casein to 20 to 30 mesh. From a screen which separates the oversize, the casein is fed to a bagging conveyor.

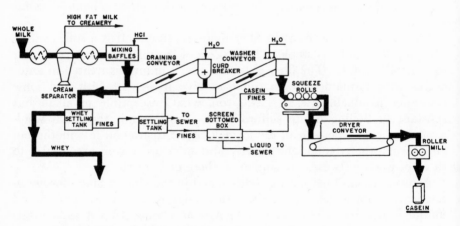

Fig. 7-11. Acid casein flow sheet. (*Courtesy Modern Chemical Processes*)

Acid caseins presently find their widest use in the paper coating field and to a lesser extent in the stabilization of rubber latex emulsions for paints. In the latter field, the stabilizer, although only a minor constituent quantitatively, is of great importance in helping to control stability, brushing and leveling, and to improve pigment dispersion. To be a good stabilizing agent, a substance must not only have protective colloidal properties but must also be compatible with a variety of compounds found in a typical latex formulation. Casein (and soya bean protein) are almost universally used; other substances do not provide their unique combination of dispersing and stabilizing properties.

Casein also is used in the pharmaceutical field in the formulation of special diets for animals. Edible-grade casein is finding increased use in bakery products. Sodium caseinate, made from the whey proteins, is used in various food products where an edible emulsifier and stabilizer is required and in the formulation of some pharmaceuticals and baby foods. Calcium caseinate, also a high-protein product of edible quality and a source of dietary calcium, is important as a fortifying agent in the preparation of foods for special diets. Modified caseins have been proposed for use as wine clarifiers, adhesives for drinking straws, binders in offset and lithographic chemicals, binders for wall-paper colors, for polishes, for leather finishes, and in textile sizings, as a hardener in floor waxes, for use in speciality paper coatings and inks.

## Polyamides from Soya Beans

It was not until 1804 that the soya bean was introduced into the United States, although it had been cultivated in the Orient for centuries. Even then, it remained virtually a curiosity for over a hundred years. Only about the time of World War I was appreciable acreage devoted to its growth, and not until the 1930's was commercial, chemically isolated soya protein produced.

Since that time, the solvent-extracted oil has become an important commodity for the manufacture of margarine and cooking oils, and thousands of acres of land in Europe and the United States are now devoted to the growing of the soya bean. As a result, a large quantity of de-oiled dry meal, containing about 48 per cent protein, has become available. It has been used to some extent in the form of prepared foods for human consumption, but principally for cattle food. Like casein, one of its largest uses is as an adhesive for coated papers (alpha-protein).

Protein plastics derived from this source are mainly used as extenders in phenolic molding powders. Much publicity was given in 1936 to the Ford process of compounding curable phenolic resins with soya protein meal, though it should be noted that about half the meal, being carbohydrate in nature, acted merely as filler. The protein fraction may have exhibited some polyfunctional reactivity, but plastics based *wholly* on soya protein have not so far been successfully developed.

Soya bean fibers have been made by essentially the same method as that used for casein fibers. The beans are flaked and the oil is removed by extraction with hexane. The flakes are then treated with a 0.1 per cent solution of sodium sulfite at room temperature, as this dissolves all the protein. The solution is clarified, and sulfuric acid added with constant stirring until the isoelectric point (pH 4.5) is reached, whereupon the protein precipitates as a curd, which is separated, washed, and dried at a temperature not exceeding 60°C.

The spinning solution is prepared by dissolving the curd in aqueous caustic soda to form a 20 per cent solution and is stabilized by the addition of a small quantity of sodium ethyl xanthate. This solution is aged until it attains the required viscosity and is then spun into a coagulating bath containing a salt and acid. The coagulating bath used is similar to that described for making casein fiber. The soya bean fiber is stretched as it is spun to obtain some degree of orientation, and then, like the other vegetable protein fibers, it is hardened by immersion in formaldehyde.

The fiber is light tan in color but can be bleached. It has a naturally pearly luster and usually does not require the addition of a delustering pigment. As with most regenerated protein fibers, its low wet strength is a disadvantage.

The specific gravity of the fiber is 1.31—practically the same as that of wool. Under standard atmospheric conditions it takes up 11 per cent of moisture and in this respect is about equal to viscose. The fiber is fairly resistant to the action of dilute acids, but is attacked and dissolved by alkalies, although not quite so readily as wool.

Soya bean fiber has been used principally in staple-fiber form for automobile upholstery, and, to a lesser extent, in admixture with wool for felts and upholstery fabrics. In properties and appearance, it is very similar to casein fiber, which in turn is similar to wool. It is not at present manufactured commercially.

## Polyamides from Peanuts

Ardil, developed in Scotland, is a vegetable protein fiber made from the proteins in peanuts. The desired proteins are obtained from solvent-extracted peanut meal by solution in dilute caustic soda. The extract is filtered and treated with acid or sulfur dioxide until the isoelectric point is reached (pH 4.5 to 5.0). The precipitated proteins, free from water-soluble albumins, are centrifuged, washed, and dried.

In the original method of spinning, the protein was dissolved in a concentrated solution of urea, in which it was ripened to increase the viscosity and from which it was spun. Because urea is too expensive a solvent, it was discarded in favor of caustic soda. It was then extruded into a coagulating bath containing 15 per cent sodium sulfate and 2 per cent sulfuric acid at a temperature of 25° to 40°C. The filaments were collected at a rate faster than they were extruded in order to impart a stretch. It was then hardened by immersing it in a bath at 35° to 50°C containing a saturated solution of common salt and about 2 per cent hydrochloric acid. After hardening, the fiber was washed, dried, and cut into staple.

The outstanding properties of Ardil are its warmth and softness. In addition, it will develop a crimp, very similar to that which is characteristic of certain wools, if it is wetted, stretched, and then released. Its strength is not high, as it is not a highly oriented fiber, but it has a high elongation, so that the fiber is resistant to rupture. Its resistance to abrasion is poor, so that pure Ardil fabrics wear badly, but, unexpectedly, when mixed with wool in equal proportions, the resistance to abrasion is sometimes higher than that of an all-wool fabric.

The Ardil which was used in development work had a pale straw color which was probably its greatest defect. It does not felt, but the addition of a little Ardil to wool increases the felting power of the wool. Its moisture content is even higher than that of wool, so that it is suitable for apparel.

An equal mixture of Ardil and wool yields an attractive product, which is warm, soft, and wears satisfactorily. It is mothproof, but does not protect the wool with which it is mixed. Ardil can also be combined with cotton and rayon, adding to their fullness and warmth. Its manufacture was discontinued in 1957.

## Polyamides from Corn

Zein is a by-product of corn processing and becomes concentrated in the gluten fraction during the preparation of cornstarch. The potential yield of zein is about 1 pound per bushel of corn (which contains about 8 per cent protein). The zein may be extracted from the gluten meal in a countercurrent extractor, using 85 per cent isopropyl alcohol at 55° to 60°C. The alcohol extract is cooled and filtered to remove undissolved particles, and the clear extract is mixed with approximately an equal volume of hexane. This mixture separates into two layers, the upper consisting of most of the hexane, a large part of the isopropanol, and almost all of the oil and pigments which it is desired to remove. This layer is removed by centrifuging, leaving a 15 to 20 per cent solution of zein in alcohol, with only a small percentage of hexane and impurities. The remaining hexane may be removed by vacuum distillation.

The zein is then precipitated from the viscous solution by spraying it into a moving body of very cold water, from which it rises to the top in fibrous form and is collected, pressed into cakes, ground, and dried quickly in a stream of hot air.

The zein powder thus obtained has as its outstanding use the coating of paper, to which it gives a pleasing and scuff-resistant surface without high gloss. Paper coated with zein is resistant to the penetration of grease or oils and is useful in the manufacture of food wrappings. Because of its cost, zein is employed as an adhesive only for specialty uses, such as the application of high-grade film veneers.

Zein, like casein, can be used in making plastic materials. Since it reacts slowly with formaldehyde, the formaldehyde necessary for final hardening can be incorporated into the plastic mix, along with plasticizers, pigments, and extenders. The mix is formed into sheets or rods and then partially cured by heating for a short time at 100°C. The material can then be punched, cut, or machined and finally cured by heating at 60° to 100°C for a longer time. Zein plastics can also be made in the same way that casein plastics are made and cured by immersing in formaldehyde solution. The reaction with formaldehyde is catalyzed by acids, strong mineral acids such as hydrochloric being most effective. Small amounts of ammonia or primary amines act as promoters for the reaction but only in the presence of acid.

Like other protein plastics, zein depends upon water as a plasticizer to improve its flow, although smaller proportions are required than for soya bean protein and casein. Zein plastics are used in the manufacture of buttons, buckles, and other novelties. They exhibit better resistance to moisture than the casein plastics.

Corn protein consists of globular proteins (prolamines) having a molecular weight of the order of 40,000 to 50,000. In chemical structure they are similar to the proteins in peanuts and soya beans, and thus similar to wool protein in respect to the amino acids making up the polypeptide chains. It should be noted, however, that these vegetable proteins do not possess the cystine cross-linkages which confer on wool its property of recovery from deformation and resistance to creasing. Nevertheless, a very satisfactory fiber is made from corn protein.

The production of a fiber from zein was developed in the United States. Although a process was patented in 1939 for the production of zein from corn protein, little more was heard of fiber production until 1948. As mentioned under casein fibers, the fiber plant which had formerly been used for the production of Aralac was redesigned and the production of a zein fiber, known as Vicara, was undertaken.

Two methods of manufacture are known. The earlier used the relatively expensive solvent, urea. Just as this material was found uneconomical in the production of Ardil, so, too, it has been discarded in favor of caustic soda for the manufacture of Vicara.

According to the latter method, the zein is obtained from corn meal by dissolving the latter in alkali and precipitating the protein with acid. The protein molecules in natural form are curled or globular, and, to straighten them out, a denaturing treatment with caustic soda is necessary. The fiber is spun from this solution by extrusion through spinnerets into an acid coagulating bath. The fiber is then partially cured, probably by treatment with formaldehyde, and is stretched to complete the uncoiling of the molecules and orient them to increase their strength. It is then further treated in hardening baths to improve the resistance of the fiber to boiling water.

The cure of all azlon (protein) fibers, normally carried out in aqueous systems using formaldehyde, continues, although it has several deficiencies. The most serious one is that the formaldehyde cross-links formed by the reaction are not stable in boiling acid baths, such as are used to dye wool. With zein fibers, rapid curing in aqueous media must be done at elevated temperatures and involves holding the fiber under high tension so that it will not undergo excessive shrinkage. An acetylating treatment of the fiber is often used to modify undesirable effects, such as loss of strength and embrittlement of the fiber. Recently, a new aldehyde cure has been reported which differs from the above method principally in that it is conducted under essentially nonaqueous conditions.

The curing solution is composed of an aldehyde-yielding agent and a relatively strong acid in an inert organic solvent. Paraformaldehyde and hydrogen chloride in toluene is an example. When this cure is applied to raw zein fiber, the acetylation step is claimed to be unnecessary. However, if acetylation is desired, the treatment can be combined with the nonaqueous cure by substituting acetic anhydride for the usual organic solvent. Reduction of shrinkage and the retention of good wet and dry tenacities are advantages claimed by this process.

Zein is an exceptional protein in many ways. It contains a relatively high proportion of amide groups and these improve its stability after curing. Zein fibers are more crystalline, of higher tenacity, and are more easily oriented than fibers from other proteins.

Vicara is light gold in color and has a specific gravity of 1.25. Like wool, it is water-repellent. It is claimed to be more resistant than animal fibers to the action of alkali and to be less flammable than the cellulosic fibers. It is not seriously affected by temperatures up to 175°C. It is not a thermoplastic fiber. The tenacity is high for a regenerated protein.

Since Vicara is insoluble in organic solvents, it can be safely dry-cleaned. It is resistant to mildew and bacteria and is unattacked by moth and beetle larvae; this resistance makes it especially useful for upholstery. Vicara does not felt or shrink. It is odorless and thus lacks the "wet-wool" smell of wool.

Vicara is one of the best of the regenerated protein fibers that has yet been made. It is more likely to be used in blends than alone. Indeed, it has been described as "the fiber that improves the blend." Its moisture absorbency, warmth, and softness, its comparative freedom from static electricity and its consequent freedom from attracting dirt, and its elasticity —all characteristics of a protein fiber—make it suitable for blending with wool without detracting from the valuable natural properties of wool. These properties may also be imparted, to some extent, to the synthetic

fibers which usually lack most of them.    If blended with rayon, it gives
suppleness; with nylon it confers water absorptiveness, and to cotton it
adds resilience.    As with the other protein fibers made in the United
States, production of Vicara has been reported to have been discontinued.

There are several other sources of proteinaceous materials which have
been examined for possible use in the plastics and fiber industries.    Among
them may be mentioned hair (keratin), feathers, nails, horn, whalebone,
blood plasma (fibrinogen), and biological waste products from such
industries as the brewing and other fermentation industries.    Although
some specialized uses for materials prepared from such proteins are known,
the preparation of these materials cannot as yet be called commercial.

### DERIVATIVES OF NATURAL RUBBER

**Hard Rubber**

This product of natural rubber is industrially important and belongs
actually to the plastics family.    Although it has been displaced in many
instances by more recently developed resins, hard rubber is still used for
many articles for its moisture resistance, chemical inertness, strength, and
good dielectric properties.

In modern practice, the amount of sulfur used for making soft rubber
articles seldom exceeds 4 per cent.    When more than this amount is
used, the soft, resilient characteristics of rubber begin to disappear.
Products containing between about 8 and 25 per cent sulfur are somewhat
unstable.    The valuable physical properties of hard rubber are not
attained until the amount of combined sulfur approaches that required
to attain saturation of the double bonds of the rubber hydrocarbon.
This theoretical value is 47 per cent of the weight of the rubber reacted.
The lower limit of usefulness of hard-rubber products is about 25 per cent
sulfur.    As the percentage increases, hardness and heat resistance
improve while impact and tensile strengths decline.

Ordinarily, hard rubber or "ebonite" contains 30 to 45 parts of sulfur
per 100 parts of rubber hydrocarbon.    Compounding ingredients other
than sulfur include accelerators, mineral fillers, and hard-rubber dust.
Reclaimed rubber is often used to improve processing properties before
vulcanization, as are small quantities of waxes, resins, and oils.

Hard rubber becomes flexible at about 100°C, but is unstable above
this temperature, decomposing with evolution of hydrogen sulfide until
it melts with further decomposition at 270°C.    Hard rubber is swollen
but not dissolved by rubber solvents, such as benzene, and is highly
resistant to other solvents and most chemical reagents except strong
oxidizing acids.    Its density is 1.18 and its water absorption is 0.3 per
cent, which is unusually low.

Typical applications of hard rubber include sliding door frames, rails, glazing strips, doors, water-lubricated bearings, storage-battery containers and separators, funnels, jars, sheets, rods, and tubes, valves, gears, telegraph and telephone parts, electrical insulating equipment, and pipe fittings. Hard rubber is widely used in lining metal equipment, such as vats and tanks, tank cars, and conduits.

Hard rubbers may also be made from synthetic elastomers in a manner analogous to those from natural rubber. Depending upon the type of synthetic elastomer used, synthetic hard rubbers may be prepared which are as good as or superior to hard rubbers from natural sources.

### Isomerized Rubber

Since there is one double bond per isoprene unit in a rubber molecule, it is possible by the action of numerous reagents to obtain linkages from one double bond to another, thus forming rings and connective chains. This cyclization forms products of lower unsaturation, most of which exhibit thermoplasticity and strong adhesive properties.

The first cyclorubber was prepared in Germany in 1910. Concentrated sulfuric acid was reacted with rubber at ordinary temperatures, and an amorphous powder, insoluble in the usual rubber solvents, was obtained. Staudinger, in 1926, gave methods for obtaining cyclorubbers of definite degrees of saturation. He prepared these by treating hydrohalides of rubber in boiling toluene with zinc dust, then precipitating the product with alcohol. The reaction left one double bond per two isoprene units, and, if the above reaction were effected in the presence of hydrochloric acid, there was left only one double bond per four isoprene units. The nature of the reactions occurring is not yet known, nor can it be assumed that they proceed with simplicity.

In 1927, Fisher modified the early methods by using a variety of acidic cyclizing agents instead of the usual sulfuric acid. Notable cyclizing agents used were *p*-toluene sulfonyl chloride and various sulfonic acids. Each reagent was mixed with rubber on a rubber mill and the sheeted mixture heated in an oven. These mixtures when subsequently heated were tough and thermoplastic, in some instances resembling shellac and in others resembling balata or gutta-percha.

These rubber isomers are used principally in the formulation of adhesives and paints. They serve as the basis of Vulcalock cement which forms an exceptionally strong bond between rubber and steel or other smooth surfaces. This process of bonding rubber to metal has proved to be of great value in the construction of rubber-lined steel equipment where high temperatures are not encountered.

The cyclized rubbers (also known as thermoprenes) are the basis of a series of rapid-drying acid- and alkali-resistant coatings containing no oils or cellulose nitrate. These coatings form films which have excellent adhesion to properly prepared metals and other surfaces. Films are hard, firm, durable, and exhibit some elasticity. They exhibit good resistance to moisture and most acidic and alkaline chemicals.

A modification of the method of preparation of cyclized rubbers consists in cyclizing in the presence of phenol or naphthol. The products are similar to those already discussed, but they contain free hydroxyl groups and have no adhesive properties. This makes them suitable for use in lacquers and other coatings, impregnants, and molding compositions.

A modification of the Staudinger method of cyclization has been developed in the United States. Instead of using rubber hydrochloride, rubber and salts of amphoteric metals (aluminum, antimony, chromium, iron, manganese, tin, or zinc) are heated to 250°C. Likewise, if dissolved in a suitable solvent, rubber will add many metallic and metalloid halides, such as stannic chloride, titanium tetrachloride, ferric chloride, and antimony pentachloride, which can cause polymerization of certain vinyl compounds. Upon treatment of the resultant addition product with acetone or alcohol, the salt is reformed together with formation of a rubber isomer. Similar results can be obtained with the use of boron trifluoride, fluoroboric acid, or halogenated acids of tin. In the treatment with metal salts, the viscosity at first increases but on continued heating decreases, and still further heating reduces the viscosity greatly. The density increases from 0.93 to 1.06, but this increase in density is not due to halogen, which is absent in the final products. The increase in density has been explained as due to the formation of cyclic compounds. In all instances, the product is more saturated than the original rubber hydrocarbon.

Chemical theories of the preceding reaction have attributed the disappearance of double bonds to cyclizations, in particular to the mutual saturation of double bonds, or their saturation at the expense of broken carbon-hydrogen bonds. The structure of the cyclized rubber has been postulated as both monocyclic and polycyclic. The most widely accepted structure for a monocyclic polymer is:[3]

$$\left[ -CH_2 - \underset{CH_3}{\overset{\displaystyle \bigcirc^{CH_3}}{\bigg|}} - CH_2 - \right]_{n/2}$$

The following[4] has been proposed for a polycyclic structure. In the first step of the reaction, a rubber carbonium ion is probably formed under

[3] Gordon, M., *Ind. Eng. Chem.*, **43**, 386 (1951).
[4] Salomon, G. *et al.*, *Ind. Eng. Chem.*, **43**, 315 (1951).

influence of the strongly proton donor properties of the cyclizing agent—
e.g., sulfuric acid:

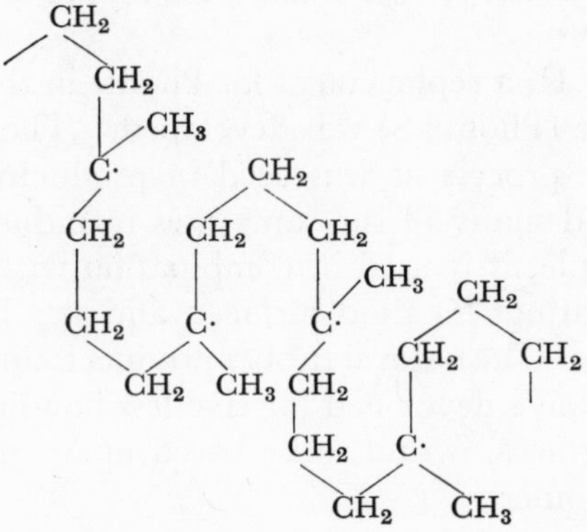

$$
\begin{array}{c}
CH_2 \\
\quad CH_2 \\
\quad\quad | \; CH_3 \\
\quad\quad C\cdot \quad\quad CH_2 \\
CH_2 \quad CH_2 \quad CH_2 \\
CH_2 \quad C\cdot \quad C\cdot \quad\quad CH_3 \quad CH_2 \\
\quad CH_2 \quad CH_3 \; CH_2 \quad CH_2 \quad CH_2 \\
\quad\quad\quad CH_2 \quad C\cdot \\
\quad\quad\quad\quad CH_2 \quad CH_3
\end{array}
$$

In the second step of the reaction, this unstable carbonium ion probably
cyclizes as follows:

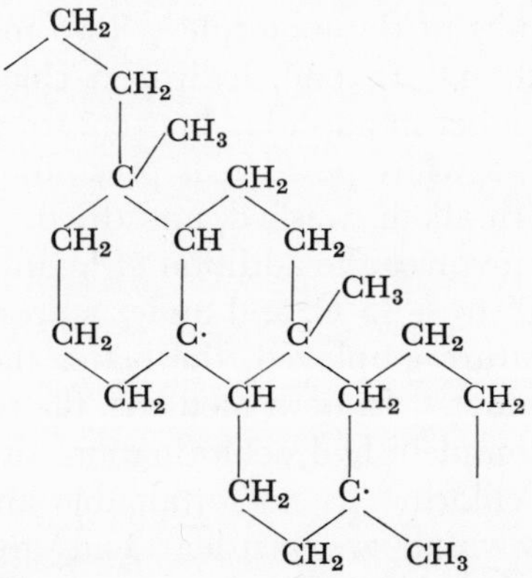

$$
\begin{array}{c}
CH_2 \\
\quad CH_2 \\
\quad\quad | \; CH_3 \\
\quad\quad C \quad\quad CH_2 \\
CH_2 \quad CH \quad CH_2 \\
CH_2 \quad C\cdot \quad C \quad\quad CH_3 \quad CH_2 \\
\quad CH_2 \quad CH \quad CH_2 \quad CH_2 \\
\quad\quad\quad CH_2 \quad C\cdot \\
\quad\quad\quad\quad CH_2 \quad CH_3
\end{array}
$$

This reaction may continue until a chain of ring structures is formed.
It is possible that a cyclized rubber molecule may contain several groups
of rings separated by unchanged isoprene units. The absence of rubber
elasticity and the high softening point of cyclized rubber are probably due
to the loss of chain flexibility by formation of bulky six-membered rings
in the chain.

These products are manufactured commercially under the trade
name Plioform. The resins are thermoplastic, substantially nonelastic,
and resistant to most acids and alkalies. They are much more resistant
than hard rubber to oxidizing acids. They are insoluble in oxygenated
solvents but are soluble in the usual rubber solvents (hydrocarbons).
The materials have given good results in thermoplastic moldings. The

hard types resemble ebonite and serve as good substitutes for it.    Under the name Pliolite, they have been widely used in protective coatings which are resistant to many kinds of chemical attack and as a toughening agent for rubber.

During World War II, a replacement for Pliolite in the form of cyclized synthetic polyisoprene (Pliolite S) was developed.    The cyclized material is made by the same process as was used in producing natural rubber Pliolite.    It has found many of the same uses in industry as the former material.    For example, it is used in combination with wax in hot-melt paper coatings, in coatings for rigid surfaces, and as a base for acid- and alkali-resistant paints.    The natural rubber product is now available again.

Cycleweld, an adhesive developed for rivetless bonding of metal sheets and other smooth surfaces, is said to be based upon rubber compounds, presumably rubber isomers.

### Rubber Hydrochloride

Rubber is capable of adding hydrogen chloride at the double bonds in each of the isoprene units of the molecule.    Two methods are available to carry out this reaction.    In one, hydrogen chloride gas is bubbled through a solution of rubber in naphtha, benzene, or a chlorinated hydrocarbon.    The product, a white powder, is precipitated from solution by alcohol, neutralized with alkali, washed, and dried.

The second method involves the addition of hydrogen chloride at very low temperatures, $-10°$ to $-35°C$, and under a pressure of about 70 psi. The lower the temperature employed, the better the clarity of the film produced from the product.    In both methods, the reaction is stopped at about 88 per cent of complete hydrochlorination, since the fully reacted product (34 per cent chlorine) is not attainable and hydrochlorinated products close to this value are brittle.    Thus the product contains approximately 30 per cent chlorine.

The structure commonly ascribed to rubber hydrochloride is as follows:

$$\begin{array}{ccccccc} & CH_3 & & CH_3 & & CH_3 & \\ & | & & | & & | & \\ -CH_2{\cdot}C{\cdot}CH_2{\cdot}CH_2{\cdot}CH_2{\cdot}C{\cdot}CH_2{\cdot}CH_2{\cdot}CH_2{\cdot}C{\cdot}CH_2{\cdot}CH_2- \\ & | & & | & & | & \\ & Cl & & Cl & & Cl & \end{array}$$

All chlorine atoms of the hydrochloride are attached to the tertiary carbon atoms, in accordance with Markownikoff's rule.    No trace of the presence of a secondary chlorine atom, as suggested in some of the literature, has been found.    Polybutadiene and GR-S, on the other hand, react only at higher temperatures and pressures with hydrochloric acid, with formation of complicated structures with large secondary chlorine fractions.

Rubber hydrochloride is not thermoplastic, since it decomposes before melting. Films of pure rubber hydrochloride become brittle with age, but their useful life can be increased by the addition of stabilizing agents. Plasticizers improve the tear resistance and durability of the films.

Rubber hydrochloride has a density of 1.16; it is colorless, odorless, tasteless, and is unaffected by mold and insects. It burns with difficulty and is resistant to fatty oils, greases, and to dilute aqueous alkalies and acids, except oxidizing acids.

Films of rubber hydrochloride can be cast from solution or calendered on heated rolls. The casting solution is extruded onto a rubber belt, coated with a water-soluble resin. The film is stripped from the belt, passed through a drying compartment, and wound in rolls.

Pliofilm is produced as a nearly colorless, transparent packaging material. It can be bonded with suitable adhesives and lends itself readily to printing. The film possesses a high elongation and has good tear resistance. It may be welded easily by the application of heat and mild pressure. It is very resistant to the passage of water vapor and can withstand considerable deformation, after mild heating, to permit "stretch wrapping" of irregular objects.

Its inertness and ease of fabrication make it important in the field of food packaging and parts protection. Its unique position in the packaging field stems from the fact that its extensibility is over 400 per cent, compared with that of cellophane, which is only 20 per cent. In addition, its tensile strength is approximately four times that of cellophane. These properties make the material suited to accommodate the irregularities of the most diverse packages, from vegetables to complete airplanes. The films are not readily punctured, and the material can be sewn like cloth; hence, it has also been used in making garment bags, raincoats, shower curtains, and umbrellas.


**Chlorinated Rubber**

The reaction of chlorine on rubber was observed as early as the end of the eighteenth century. It was not until 1915, however, that the British chemist, Peachey, patented a commercial process for making chlorinated rubber in solution. Manufacture began in England shortly thereafter under the name Duroprene and, later, Alloprene. In 1930, Tornesit was produced in Germany and was later made here under the same name. The name of the domestic product was subsequently changed to Parlon.

The reaction of natural rubber with halogens is complex. The introduction of bromine and iodine chloride is essentially an *addition* to the double bond; chlorination, however, proceeds differently.   In rubber latex, the first chlorine atom is introduced into the isoprene unit of the molecule by *substitution* in place of an allylic hydrogen atom, leaving the number of double bonds unchanged.   This primary reaction product is unstable.   Theoretical considerations make likely a shift of the double bond:[4]

$$
\begin{array}{c}
CH_3 \\
| \\
-CH_2 \cdot C : CH \cdot CH_2- \; + \; Cl_2
\end{array}
\xrightarrow{\;-HCl\;}
\begin{array}{l}
\nearrow \quad
\begin{array}{c}
CH_2 \\
\parallel \\
-CH_2 \cdot C \cdot CHCl \cdot CH_2-
\end{array} \quad (A) \\[2em]
\searrow \quad
\begin{array}{c}
CH_3 \\
| \\
-CH : C \cdot CHCl \cdot CH_2-
\end{array} \quad (B)
\end{array}
$$

Some cyclization may also occur.   Infrared analysis indicates that (B) is the principal reaction product.   This is gradually transformed on further chlorination into the stable chlorinated rubber:

$$
\begin{array}{c}
CH_3 \\
| \\
-CH : C \cdot CHCl \cdot CH_2-
\end{array}
\xrightarrow{\;Cl_2\;}
\begin{array}{l}
\nearrow \quad
\begin{array}{c}
CH_3 \\
| \\
-CHCl \cdot CCl \cdot CHCl \cdot CH_2-
\end{array} \quad (C) \\[2em]
\searrow \quad
\begin{array}{c}
CH_3 \\
| \\
-CHCl \cdot CCl \cdot CHCl \cdot CHCl-
\end{array} \quad (D)
\end{array}
$$

The commercial product is believed to consist principally of a mixture of (C) and (D).

However, there are some residual double bonds, even at a chlorine content of almost 70 per cent.   This indicates that the process of substitutional addition is repeated, besides addition to the double bond:

$$
\begin{array}{c}
CH_2 \\
\parallel \\
-CH_2 \cdot C \cdot CHCl \cdot CH_2- \; + \; Cl_2
\end{array}
\begin{array}{l}
\nearrow \quad
\begin{array}{c}
CH_2Cl \\
| \\
-CH_2 \cdot CCl \cdot CHCl \cdot CH_2-
\end{array} \quad (E) \\[2em]
\searrow_{-HCl} \quad
\begin{array}{c}
CH_2Cl \\
| \\
-CH : C \cdot CHCl \cdot CH_2-
\end{array} \quad (F)
\end{array}
$$

The latter product is probably the cause of the chemical instability of chlorinated rubber containing 50 to 60 per cent chlorine.

To obtain commercial products yielding solutions of low viscosity suitable for surface-coating applications, the rubber is first given a prolonged cold milling; it is then dissolved in an appropriate solvent, preferably carbon tetrachloride.   Chlorination is carried out in a 4 to 5 per cent solution in glass- or lead-lined equipment.   In the manufacture of Parlon, the hydrogen chloride formed is removed in a tantalum absorber. Upon completion of the chlorination, carried out at 80° to 110°C, the solution is pumped into brick-lined precipitating tanks filled with hot water. The solvent is distilled off and the product is obtained as a granular precipitate, which is washed, centrifuged, and dried. As obtained on the market, chlorinated rubber is a coarse, yellow powder, amorphous and inelastic, with a density of 1.64. Its chlorine content averages about 67 per cent.

Chlorinated rubber possesses one of the highest degrees of water impermeability and one of the lowest degrees of water absorption of the various coating materials. It is odorless, tasteless, nontoxic, and nonflammable. The stability of chlorinated rubber at room temperature in visible light is satisfactory, but ultraviolet light and heat cause appreciable decomposition. The product can be stabilized, however.

Chlorinated rubber is used principally in coatings, which are unaffected by strong caustic and nitric acid, and the strongest bleaches. Even more important, however, is the fact that such common chemically destructive agents as dampness, soaps and other cleaning compounds, vapors and fumes of various kinds, mold and mildew, mineral oils, cement alkali, and plaster lime have little effect. Second only to chemical resistance is rapid drying; paints, synthetic enamels, and printing inks containing chlorinated rubber generally dry in half the normal time.

Chlorinated rubber is considerably more soluble than rubber hydrochloride. Its unique solubility characteristics among highly chlorinated resins and its chemical resistance have made it valuable in the formulation of corrosion-resistant paints. It is used to protect chemical plant equipment; as a basis for concrete, masonry, plaster, stucco, and asbestos-cement board paints; to finish swimming pools; and for numerous other corrosion-resistant applications. Other applications are for use in alkali-resistant printing inks, adhesives, and textile coatings. The resin is also used to a lesser extent for the bonding of rubber and synthetic elastomers to metal.

Other derivatives of natural rubber have been made. None of these, so far as is known, except for the ones already mentioned, has yet achieved commercial exploitation.

## REFERENCES AND RECOMMENDED READING

Alexander, J., ed., *Colloid Chemistry Theoretical and Applied*, Vol. VI, Reinhold Publishing Corp., New York, 1946.

American Viscose Corporation, *Rayon Technology (Including Acetate)*, McGraw-Hill Book Co., New York, 1953.

Barron, H., *Modern Plastics*, John Wiley and Sons, New York, 1945.

Barron, H., *Modern Synthetic Rubbers*, 2nd ed., D. Van Nostrand Co., Princeton, N.J., 1943.

Billmeyer, F. W., Jr., *Textbook of Polymer Chemistry*, Interscience Publishers, New York, 1957.

Delmonte, J., *Plastics in Engineering*, 3rd ed., Penton Publishing Co., Cleveland, 1949.

Dubois, J. H., *Plastics*, 3rd ed., American Technical Society, Chicago, 1945.

Elliott, S. B., *The Alkaline Earth and Heavy-Metal Soaps*, Reinhold Publishing Corp., New York, 1946.

Ellis, C., *The Chemistry of Synthetic Resins*, Reinhold Publishing Corp., New York, 1935.

Fleck, H. R., *Plastics*, 2nd ed., Chemical Publishing Co., New York, 1949.

Gordon, P. L. and Dolgin, G. J., *Surface Coatings and Finishes*, Chemical Publishing Co., New York, 1954.

Hall, A. J., *The Standard Handbook on Textiles*, D. Van Nostrand Co., Princeton, N.J., 1946.

Houwink, R., ed., *Elastomers and Plastomers*, Vol. II, Elsevier Publishing Co., Amsterdam (dist. by D. Van Nostrand Co., Princeton, N.J.), 1949.

Kaye, S. L., *The Production and Properties of Plastics*, International Textbook Company, Scranton, Penn., 1947.

Kirk, R. E. and Othmer, D. F., eds., *Encyclopedia of Chemical Technology*, Interscience Publishers, New York, 1947–56.

Mantell, C. L., Kopf, C. W., Curtis, J. L., and Rogers, E. M., *The Technology of Natural Resins*, John Wiley and Sons, New York, 1942.

Mason, J. P. and Manning, J. F., *The Technology of Plastics and Resins*, D. Van Nostrand Co., Princeton, N.J., 1945.

Mattiello, J. J., ed., *Protective and Decorative Coatings*, John Wiley and Sons, New York, 1941–46.

Mauer, L. and Wechsler, H., *Man-Made Fibers*, Rayon Publishing Corp., New York, 1953.

Mauersberger, H. R., ed., *Matthew's Textile Fibers*, 6th ed., John Wiley and Sons, New York, 1954.

Meyer, K. H., *Natural and Synthetic High Polymers*, 2nd ed., Interscience Publishers, New York, 1950.

Miles, F. D., *Cellulose Nitrate*, Interscience Publishers, New York, 1955.

Moncrieff, R. W., *Artificial Fibres*, 2nd ed., John Wiley and Sons, New York, 1954.

Nauth, R., *The Chemistry and Technology of Plastics*, Reinhold Publishing Corp., New York, 1947.

Ott, E., Spurlin, H. M., and Grafflin, M. W., eds., *Cellulose and Cellulose Derivatives*, 2nd ed., Interscience Publishers, New York, 1954.

Payne, H. F., *Organic Coating Technology*, John Wiley and Sons, New York, 1954.

Powers, P. O., *Synthetic Resins and Rubbers*, John Wiley and Sons, New York, 1943.

Ritchie, P. D., *A Chemistry of Plastics and High Polymers*, Cleaver-Hume Press, London (dist. by Interscience Publishers, New York), 1949.

Schildknecht, C. E., ed., *Polymer Processes*, Interscience Publishers, New York, 1956.

Simonds, H. R., Bigelow, M. H., and Sherman, J. V., *The New Plastics*, D. Van Nostrand Co., Princeton, N.J., 1945.

Simonds, H. R., Weith, A. J., and Bigelow, M. H., *Handbook of Plastics*, 2nd ed., D. Van Nostrand Co., Princeton, N.J., 1949.

Stannett, V., *Cellulose Acetate Plastics*, Chemical Publishing Co., New York, 1951.

von Fischer, W., ed., *Paint and Varnish Technology*, Reinhold Publishing Corp., New York, 1948.

Wakeman, R. L., *The Chemistry of Commercial Plastics*, Reinhold Publishing Corp., New York, 1947.

Winding, C. C. and Hasche, R. L., *Plastics Theory and Practice*, McGraw-Hill Book Co., New York, 1947.

Wormell, R. L., *New Fibers from Proteins*, Academic Press, New York, 1954.

*Chapter 8*

# TECHNOLOGY OF MANUFACTURE: SYNTHETIC CONDENSATION PRODUCTS

This chapter is concerned with all commercial polymers whose sources are synthetic and whose principal method of growth is by a condensation-type reaction. It is, of course, impossible to categorize certain products as made by one kind of process or another when more than one process is involved. It is then necessary to compromise or arbitrarily assign those products to one category.

For example, included in this chapter are the unsaturated polyester laminating resins. The final products are made by the addition reaction of a vinyl-type monomer with an unsaturated polyester made by a condensation reaction. Obviously, this subject could just as well have been deferred until the next chapter. In such cases, the preference of the author has been followed.

There is also a class of polymers which is formed by an addition type of polymerization, according to strict organic terminology; this includes the polyurethanes and the step-addition compounds, during whose growth no by-product molecules are split off. However, in accordance with Flory's distinction between a polymerization process and the type of polymer formed therefrom (see Chap. 1), these polymers are preferentially included in this chapter, since hydrolysis yields monomeric end products that are different in composition from their mesomers.

Further, it is felt that the principal mechanism of growth of these compounds, particularly the ring types, follows more closely that of the true condensation polymers rather than that of the free-radical-initiated or ionic-catalyzed addition polymers. For example, increasing the time of reaction results in an increase in the average molecular weight of the polymer, contrary to the results encountered in vinyl polymerizations. In fact, the growth of polymers from the monomers under discussion resembles that of polymers obtained from unsaturated monomers only in the superficial fact that they add monomer to polymer.

242

## PHENOPLASTS

The reaction between phenols and aldehydes was first described in Germany in 1872 by Baeyer who, basing his conclusion upon many experiments with phenols and aldehydes, stated that the reaction was a general one. By 1900 a number of investigators were studying the products obtained from the reaction of phenol and formaldehyde. Formerly, when it was found that reaction products could not be crystallized and possessed no definite melting point, they were discarded. Now they were studied to see what new properties they might possess. From a commercial standpoint, a shellac substitute was very attractive at this time, and several investigators were engaged in trying to find such a substitute.

As a result, the first truly synthetic resins produced industrially were the phenolics, or phenoplasts, developed in the United States between 1905 and 1914. It was Baekeland,[1] an American chemist of Belgian birth and education (who had already made a name for himself by developing Velox photographic paper), who first produced a commercially exploitable product.

Baekeland studied the phenol-formaldehyde condensation products from 1905 to 1909. He introduced two techniques for overcoming the difficulties previously experienced in molding the phenoplasts. They were the use of a filler, such as wood flour, to reduce the brittleness and the use of heat *and pressure* during molding. The application of pressure greater than the vapor pressure of water prevented the bubbling and porosity which the early investigators had observed, and the temperature could then be raised sufficiently high that a short molding time was possible.

Concurrently with Baekeland's work, other investigators, notably Aylsworth, and Redman and his co-workers, Weith and Brock, also contributed significantly to the development of these products. Three companies were formed to develop the products of these three independent interests and, after considerable patent litigation, they were merged in 1922 to form one corporation. Upon expiration of the basic patents in 1926, many new producers entered the field.

During the early stages of their development, the phenoplasts were used principally in the manufacture of electrical insulating parts. The advantages were that they were nonconductors, were relatively tough, could be machined, and the molding cost was low when large-scale production was undertaken.

Research soon showed that fabrics and paper could be impregnated with phenolic resins and subsequently laminated to form tough sheets which were resistant to moisture and to many chemicals. As a result, the laminating industry has grown concurrently with the molding industry.

[1] Baekeland, L. H., *Ind. Eng. Chem.*, **1**, 149 (1909).

Varnish manufacturers did not at first accept these early resins, so that phenolic coatings were restricted to metal lacquers for a long time. Improved resins of greater oil compatibility were later developed and have since come into widespread use in various types of varnishes. Cast phenolic resins also came into prominence during this latter period.

In general, phenols react with aldehydes to form condensation products if there are free positions on the benzene nucleus ortho or para to the phenolic hydroxyl group. Because of its greater reactivity and low cost, formaldehyde is by far the most widely used aldehyde.

Phenol is obtained commercially from the fractional distillation of coal tar and from synthetic sources. The various synthetic processes which have been commercial are indicated below by unbalanced equations:

1. Sulfonation process:

2. Chlorobenzene (carbonate) process:

3. Chlorobenzene (caustic) process:

4. Raschig process:

5. Oxidation process:

6. Cumene process:

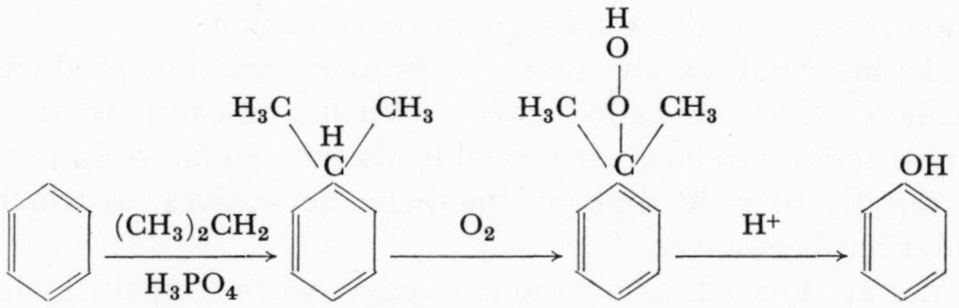

Of the above, the sulfonation, caustic, Raschig, and cumene syntheses are of present large-scale commercial importance.

Formaldehyde is made today by three processes:

$$1.\ CH_3OH + O_2 \xrightarrow[450°-600°C]{Ag} HCHO$$

$$2.\ CH_3OH + O_2 \xrightarrow[350°-450°C]{Fe\text{-}Mo\ Oxide} HCHO$$

$$3.\ CH_4 + O_2 \xrightarrow[400°C]{pressure} HCHO$$

The first method is the oldest and commonest. The third uses natural gas, one version using principally methane, another chiefly propane and butane. All of the above reactions for making phenol and formaldehyde produce by-products, and the economic balances required make an interesting study which, unfortunately, is beyond the scope of the present discussion.

The reaction of phenol itself with formaldehyde in the absence of any other reagent is slow, and catalysts are almost always added to accelerate the reaction. The nature of the reaction products depends considerably upon whether an acidic or basic catalyst is used and upon the ratio of phenol to formaldehyde.

The mechanism of the addition of formaldehyde to a phenol is still not entirely clear. Whatever the exact mechanism may be, the phenolic hydroxyl group activates the benzene ring so that a methylol ($—CH_2OH$) group always enters the nucleus in positions ortho and para to the hydroxyl group. When one or more of the ortho and para positions are already occupied, the reaction becomes much slower; when all of the above positions are unavailable, no reaction occurs. The presence of substituents in the meta position also has a pronounced effect. Alkyl or hydroxyl groups in the meta position tend to accelerate both the initial condensation reaction and the subsequent resinification.

When alkaline catalysts are used, the primary reaction products are phenol alcohols, which are called *resoles*. When acid catalysts are used, the primary reaction products are probably also phenol alcohols, but they rearrange rapidly to yield diphenyl methane derivatives, to which the name *novolacs* has been given.

The resoles are formed, as mentioned above, when formaldehyde acts upon a phenol in alkaline solution. Reference has also been made to the fact that the methylol groups enter the ring ortho or para to the phenolic hydroxyl group. When more than one such position is available, poly-methylol compounds may be formed, the products depending upon the phenol-formaldehyde ratio. Thus, from phenols having three reactive positions, the methylol derivatives shown below may be formed:

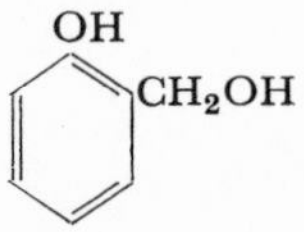

Saligenin 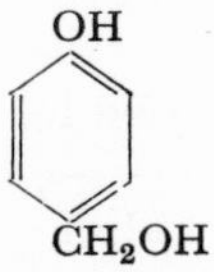          Homosaligenin

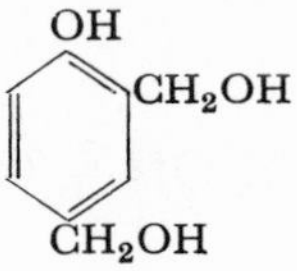

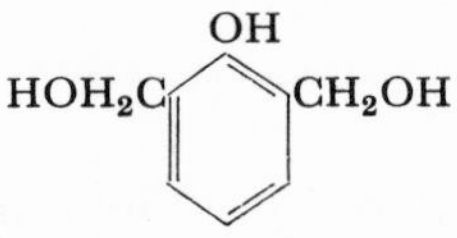

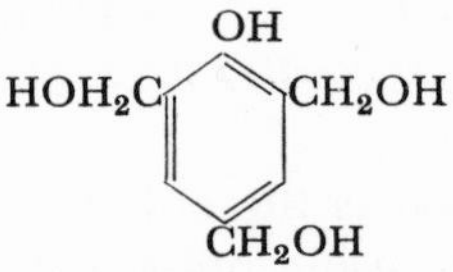

Mathematical analysis of data from chromatographic studies with the methylol phenols has provided kinetic values for the reaction of each phenolic compound and has also yielded reactivity ratios among the compounds. The reactions have been found to be of second order, and significant differences in both position and molecular reactivity have been found. In phenol, an ortho position is slightly less reactive than the para; in saligenin, the reverse is true. Furthermore, introduction of an ortho methylol group enhances the reactivity of the remaining active nuclear positions, while the same group in the para position retards further activity. The effects are multiplied in the dimethylol analogs, and 2,6-dimethylol phenol is by far the most active compound.

The mechanism by which the phenol alcohols condense to form resins is very complex. For convenience, the curing mechanism has been divided into three phases which are not clearly defined but pass gradually from one to the next. This classification was first made by Baekeland and later amplified by Lebach.

*A-stage resin* (resole). This represents the initial condensation product of a phenol and formaldehyde, the product consisting principally of phenol alcohols.

*B-stage resin* (resitol). This represents the second stage of condensation wherein the resin is no longer soluble in alkalies because the molecular weight has increased to such an extent that the alkaline salts are no longer soluble. The product is partially or completely soluble in oxygenated organic solvents. Cross-linking has just begun and the resin is still softened and plastic while hot, although hard and brittle when cold.

*C-stage resin* (resite). This is the final stage of polymerization. A large amount of cross-linking has occurred and the resin is completely insoluble and infusible.

It has been generally accepted that the phenol alcohols condense, with the elimination of water, to yield three-dimensional macromolecules cross-linked by methylene bridges. In the case of phenols with three reactive positions, the curing reactions are so rapid and complex that, until recently, little progress has been made in isolating and identifying compounds formed during the later stages of the reaction.

In order to simplify the problem, recent workers have studied the curing reactions of phenols in which one or two of the reactive ortho or para positions were blocked. Since only mono- or di-alcohols could then be formed, the formation of insoluble, cross-linked products was minimized. In most cases, good yields of crystalline products were obtained; these products could be identified and their further reactions studied.

As a result of such studies, it has been shown that the phenol alcohol, formed from the condensation of a phenol and formaldehyde in *alkaline* solution, undergoes a series of complex reactions. The extent to which the various reactions occur depends upon the structure of the phenol as well as the temperature and length of reaction. Of the many reactions which can and do occur, probably the most important ones are (1) the formation of methylene ($-CH_2-$) bridges between two or more molecules by the following type of reaction:

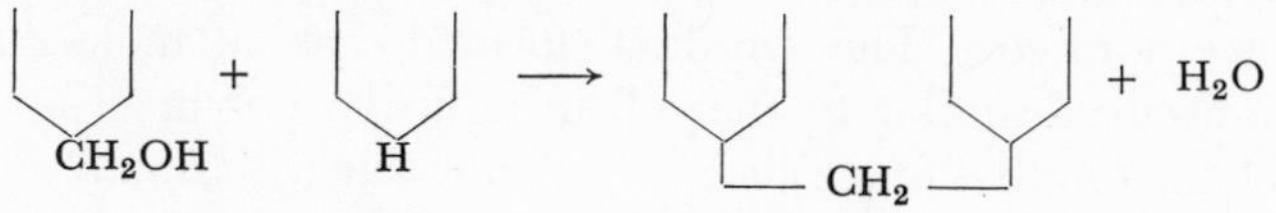

and (2) the formation of ether ($-O-$) bridges:

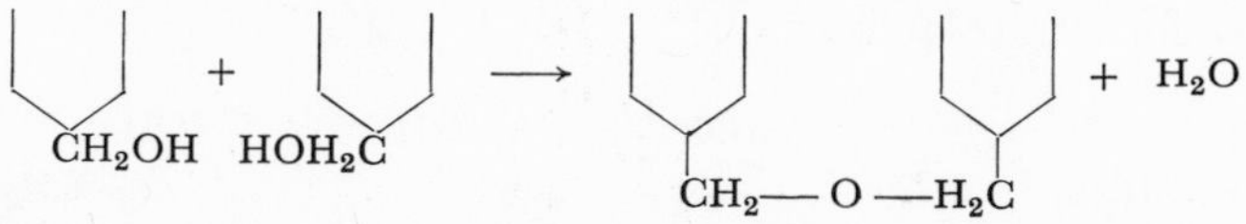

Other intermediates and products which have been identified or postulated include cyclic ethers, phenol aldehydes, and various methylene quinone compounds.   The latter type of intermediate is of interest since it can give rise to polymerization by various *addition* reactions.

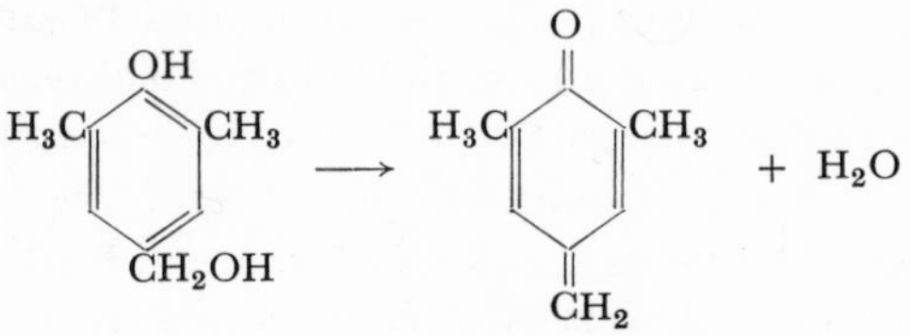

A methylene quinone

When phenol is condensed with formaldehyde under *acid* conditions, the products formed are quite different from those obtained in alkaline solution.   When less than six moles of formaldehyde are used per seven moles of phenol, the products are permanently fusible and soluble (novolacs).   The novolacs are long-chain polymers, in which the phenolic nuclei are connected only by methylene bridges.   It is likely that the initial compound formed is also a phenol alcohol which, however, condenses instantly under the influence of the acid catalyst to yield a diphenyl methane derivative.

The simplest type of novolac is dihydroxy diphenyl methane.   In the case of phenol itself, three isomers are possible, since substitution may occur in either the ortho or para position:

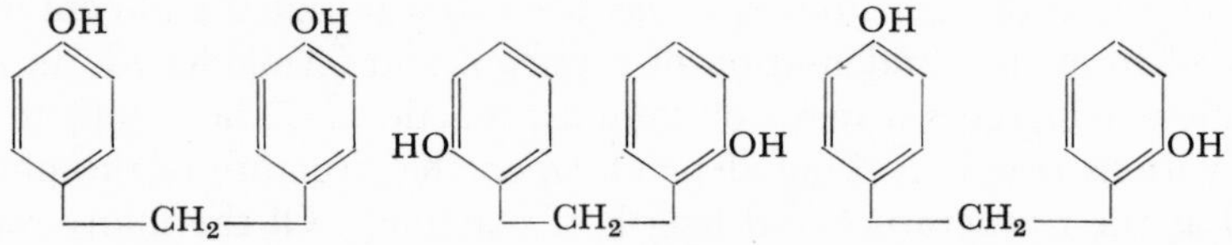

Good yields of dihydroxy diphenyl methane are obtained only when a large excess of phenol is used.   At lower phenol-formaldehyde ratios, as is usual commercially, a series of long-chain compounds with varying chain lengths are formed.   The product formed has a molecular-weight-distribution curve similar to that of an addition polymer; however, the average chain length is much shorter.   A novolac will usually contain only eight to twelve units, whereas a commercial addition polymer, such as polystyrene, may contain more than a thousand units.   A possible structure for a novolac is:

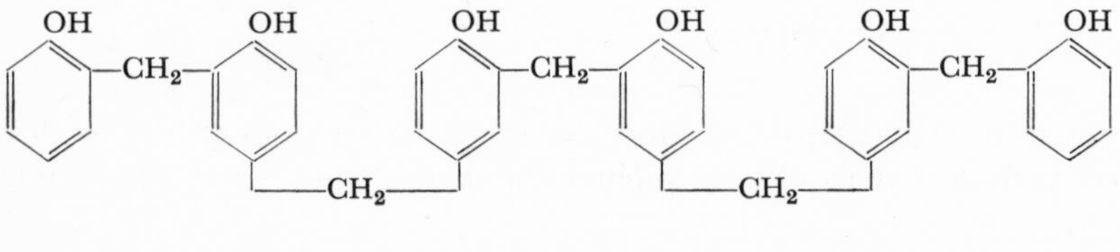

This illustration is only one of many possible structures. The phenolic nuclei are connected by methylene bridges in ortho and para positions in a random manner. Thus, a very large number of isomers is possible, depending upon the number of reactive positions on the phenol nuclei and the lengths of the individual chains. Phenols having only one reactive position available, such as 1,2,4-xylenol, yield only dihydroxy diphenyl methanes; they cannot form resins, as they have no active positions free for further condensation.

The novolacs are permanently fusible and, because the phenolic hydroxyl group is still present, are soluble in caustic solution. For most commercial uses, they are further reacted with formaldehyde. The novolac may be condensed with more formaldehyde in *alkaline* solution or the novolac may be mixed with hexamethylene tetramine. In the former case, one or more methylol groups is added to the novolac chain, yielding a complex phenol alcohol of the type exemplified by the following structure:

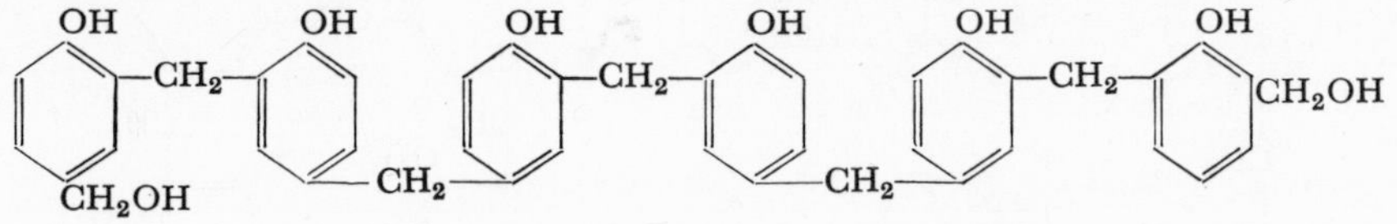

Since these compounds are typical resoles, with free methylol groups, they can undergo any or all of the curing reactions which have already been outlined for the resoles. In the latter case, the hexamethylene tetramine furnishes a source of methylene groups for cross-linking, the ammonia acting as a catalyst in the final curing process.

It is thus apparent that the fundamental difference between a resole and a novolac is the presence of one or more free methylol groups on the former; it is through reaction of these methylol groups that cross-linking occurs.

While phenol and formaldehyde react in slightly less than equimolar amounts to form an acid-condensed thermoplastic polymer, more than one mole of formaldehyde is required per mole of phenol to form a thermosetting resin. In the latter case, the theoretical ratio of formaldehyde to phenol is 2:1. In the production of molding and laminating resins, ratios ranging from 1.1:1 to 1.5:1 are common practice. In the production of cast phenolics, higher ratios of formaldehyde to phenol are used.

Considerable research has been done upon the catalyst systems used for the formation of both resoles and novolacs. Although sodium carbonate and ammonia are among the most commonly used alkaline catalysts, others, such as sodium, potassium, and calcium hydroxides; magnesium phenoxide; quaternary ammonium hydroxides; and urea have been found satisfactory. Acid catalysts which have been used include hydrochloric, sulfuric, formic, acetic, oxalic, tartaric, and aromatic sulfonic acids.   Resins prepared by the use of an acid catalyst are formed approximately three times as rapidly as those made with an alkaline catalyst, provided the same amount of formaldehyde is used in each case. When an acid catalyst is used, the rate of resinification is proportional to the concentration of acid used; whereas the rate, using an alkaline catalyst, is largely independent of the catalyst concentration.   When polyhydroxy phenols are used in place of phenol, little or no catalyst is required.

Insoluble and infusible cross-linked resins (resites) may be obtained when resoles are treated with acids or with metal chlorides.   They are also formed when a phenol with three reactive positions is condensed with a large quantity of formaldehyde in acid solution and further reacted. As mentioned earlier, permanently soluble and fusible novolacs are formed only when less than six moles of formaldehyde are condensed in

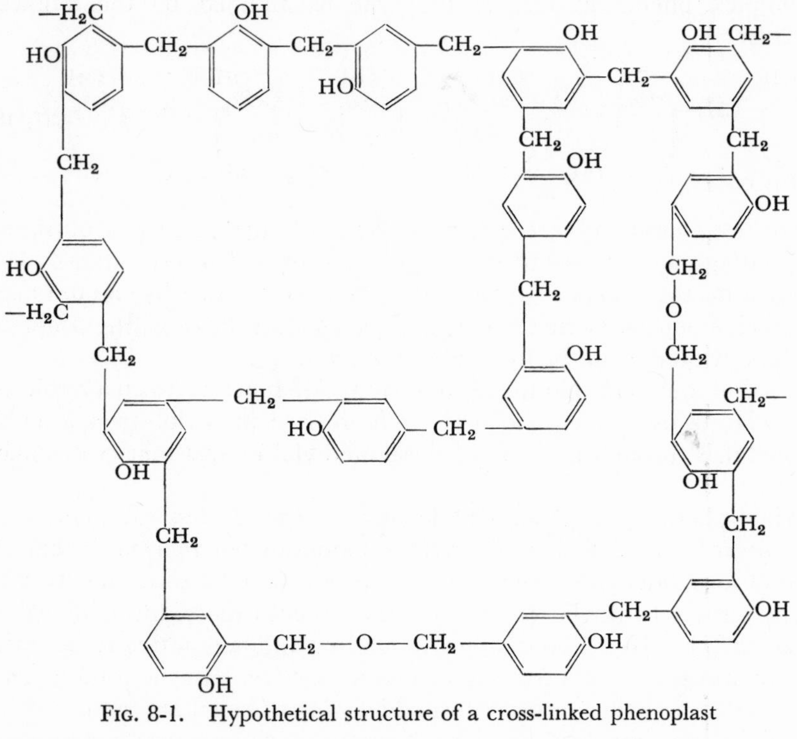

FIG. 8-1.   Hypothetical structure of a cross-linked phenoplast

acid medium with seven moles of phenol.   When a higher ratio of formaldehyde to phenol is used, the resins formed become insoluble.   Under acid conditions, the formation of an insoluble resin is thus dependent upon the quantity of formaldehyde employed, although the reason therefore is not yet known.

To make commercial rapid-curing phenoplasts, the reaction conditions differ from the purely scientific studies.  In order to obtain rapidity of cure and maximum resistance to solvents, the technical products are generally made from phenols having three free reactive nuclear positions, such as phenol or *m*-cresol.  More than one mole of formaldehyde per mole of phenol is employed when the resoles are formed.  The cured product thus has a large amount of branching and cross-linking in three dimensions and is practically insoluble in all solvents.  Fig. 8-1 indicates the type of structure which is probably present.

### Other Aldehydes

Although by far the greatest quantity of phenolic resins is made from formaldehyde, other aldehydes are occasionally used.  There are three reasons for the preference for formaldehyde: (1) The use of formaldehyde generally yields resins having shorter curing times than those of other aldehydes; (2) formaldehyde is subject to few side reactions in the presence of the condensation catalyst; and (3) formaldehyde is the cheapest aldehyde.  The Cannizzaro reaction (disproportionation) is the only side reaction of account under ordinary conditions of phenoplast manufacture.  Most other aldehydes not only undergo the Cannizzaro reaction but take part in more complex reactions, such as aldol condensations and self-resinification when treated with strong acids or bases, since they contain active α-hydrogen atoms.

Among the aldehydes which have been used are acetaldehyde, butyraldehyde, chloral, acrolein, and furfural (furfuraldehyde), of which furfural is the only one of commercial importance (Durite resins).

Furfural contributes special and useful flow properties to the phenolic resins of commerce.  It is primarily used with synthetic phenols to prepare lump resins, which in turn are ground and blended with fast-curing phenol-formaldehyde powdered resins.  Another method is to react mixtures of furfural and formaldehyde with phenol in the reaction kettle itself.

Furfural is obtained by treating pentosan-containing cereals with sulfuric acid.  Among the raw materials containing pentosans are oats and oat hulls, corn cobs, and rice hulls.  Wood waste and bagasse are also potential large sources for the chemical.

Although there is some similarity between the formaldehyde and furfural reaction with phenol, they differ in certain important respects.  Furfural contains not only an aldehyde group, but also two double bonds:

In the reaction with phenol, it behaves as a saturated aldehyde until the final stages of gelation and curing are reached, when cross-linking accompanied by the disappearance of double bonds occurs.  It thus seems likely that the unsaturated aldehyde molecule exhibits a functionality greater than two, and that, in addition to elimination of water by condensation of the aldehyde group with reactive o- and p-hydrogen atoms, there is a vinyl-type polymerization due to the unsaturated furan ring.  A typical unit in a cross-linked cured structure may have a constitution of the following general type:[2]

Furfural reacts in general as do all α-substituted aldehydes, but is slower reacting than formaldehyde.  Strong alkaline catalysts are usually required to obtain high yields in a reasonable time at reflux temperatures. Sodium hydroxide is the preferred catalyst.  Water has a strong inhibiting action in making a lump resin from phenol and furfural.  Except for the specific preparation of alkali-soluble adhesive resins, the best way to react phenol and furfural is probably in the absence of water or with continuous removal of water during the reaction.

When one or more moles of furfural are reacted with one of phenol in the presence of alkali, the condensation is rapid and, without control of the heat of reaction, the product will pass to the completely thermoset, inert stage.  With proper control, the reaction can be stopped at a point where the condensation product is a hard, brittle, fusible mass.  With further heating, this intermediate resin will condense through the methylol groups to give a cross-linked thermoset product.  Resins of this general type are usually compounded or mixed with modifying ingredients and used for molding compounds, impregnating solutions, bonding agents, coating materials, and adhesives.

A series of permanently fusible, potentially reactive resins can be made by lowering the ratio of furfural to phenol to 0.5 or lower.  Under these conditions, the furfural is reacted almost quantitatively; the excess phenol may be recovered by vacuum distillation.

When one mole of phenol is reacted with less than one mole of furfural

[2] Ritchie, P. D., *A Chemistry of Plastics and High Polymers*, p. 114, Cleaver-Hume Press, London (dist. by Interscience Publishers, New York), 1949.

in the presence of an acid catalyst, the initial reaction appears to be the formation of dihydroxy diphenyl furan methane by the condensation of one mole of furfural with two moles of phenol. Continued reaction links more phenol groups together to form a novolac or permanently fusible type of hard, brittle resin. This resin is largely a linear polymer of relatively low molecular weight containing about eight to ten phenol groups per molecule. Since only two of the active positions in the phenol ring have been substituted, this product is capable of further reaction with condensing agents or more furfural to form cross-linked resins.

Phenol-furfural novolacs are unusual in that the lower-molecular-weight members of the series are soluble in drying oils, such as tung and dehydrated castor, and in aromatic solvents. However, the greatest observable difference between formaldehyde and furfural resins is that there is no gradual transition through the A, B, and C stages with furfural. Gelation is apparently hindered by the presence of a ring structure. As a consequence, the phenol-furfural resins undergo a sharp transition from the plastic, softened state to the cured, infusible state.

This property of furfural resins is of industrial value. The unmolded, uncured material has little tendency to gel before the actual curing conditions are reached. Samples of the unhardened product may be maintained for considerable periods just below molding temperatures without appreciable hardening. During early efforts to adapt injection-molding methods to thermosetting plastics, this fact was important, for it permitted their use in injection-molding equipment without jamming the plasticizing chamber or its orifice. Thus, furfural played a significant role in phenolic resin blends which helped make possible the first large moldings. Other phenolics, however, have now been developed for injection molding, and the process, slightly modified, when applied to thermosetting plastics in general, has come to be known as jet molding (see Chap. 11).

Furfural derivatives have exceptional impact and tensile strengths when properly cured. Slight superiority over the common phenolics in electrical characteristics may also be obtained. Finished phenol-furfural articles are resistant to the continuous application of temperatures of 10° to 20°C higher than those recommended for phenol-formaldehyde resins. Other properties, such as chemical inertness, dimensional stability, general adaptability (and poor colorability) are common to both formaldehyde and furfural derivatives.

Furfural has other features which enhance its use as a replacement for formaldehyde. Due to its considerably higher molecular weight, furfural will yield more resin (approximately 35 per cent) when reacted with phenol on an equimolal basis. There is a processing advantage in that formaldehyde is normally furnished as an aqueous solution (37 per cent), and a considerable quantity of water must be removed by vacuum distillation after resinification proceeds to the desired stage. Although reaction with furfural is also a condensation reaction and the water of reaction must be removed, furfural does not require a water solvent at the time of addition to the resin kettle. For these reasons, furfural is sometimes used in place of formaldehyde in spite of its higher cost.

Aside from its use as a resin-forming ingredient, furfural possesses excellent qualities as a plasticizing agent for phenol-formaldehyde resins, exerting considerable influence on the flow qualities of the final compositions. The amount of filler which can be added is generally increased by addition of furfural. Probably one third of all the phenolic molding powder made is modified with phenol-furfural resins. The unusual wetting and penetrating properties of furfural have made possible the successful application of phenol-formaldehyde-furfural resins in the development of resinoid abrasive grinding wheels.

While most of the furfural market is based on its use as a modifier, substantial applications also exist in the phenolic resin industry in which furfural is not a modifying aldehyde but rather the primary aldehyde which contributes the desired properties to the phenolic resin. Appreciable amounts of phenolic molding powders are manufactured from 100 per cent furfural-phenolics. These unblended compounds are used for molding thick castings and parts having heavy sections. There is some sacrifice in the curing speed but the slower cure allows better heat penetration and results in less case hardening from a rapidly cured surface.

Another application is in the manufacture of asphaltic storage battery cases. Most of the automotive storage battery cases manufactured in recent years have been made from a composition containing asphalt, a small amount of synthetic resin, a mineral filler, and an organic fiber. The majority of these cases contain a fluid furfural-phenol reaction product as the synthetic resin. The purpose of the resin is to render the molding composition resistant to attack by the battery acid.

Furfural also plays an important role in the production of a phenol-based laminating varnish. The use of furfural with lesser amounts of formaldehyde in combination with phenol results in a varnish with equivalent electrical and better mechanical qualities than are usually obtained with a cresol-based varnish.

The natural phenol, cashew nut shell liquid (see below), by reaction with furfural, produces dark liquid resins, fusible solids, or infusible solids with properties not obtainable with other aldehydes or phenols. In general, the resins have unusual evenness of frictional characteristics over wide temperature ranges; hence, they find applications as binders or constituents of friction compositions used in automotive brakes and clutches.

**Other Phenols**

Commercially, the monohydric phenols (phenol, cresols, xylenols) are by far the most important, since they are more readily available and less expensive. In most cases, desired properties may be obtained from them alone. It is possible to control the rate of cure of commercial phenol-formaldehyde molding powders within wide limits, and to dictate the nature of the final resite by the choice of phenol or by using a selected blend of different phenols, as well as by varying the catalyst and the phenol-formaldehyde ratio.

Flexibility in a cured phenol-formaldehyde resin can be increased by the presence of very long chain substituents on the aromatic ring. For example, the liquid obtained from cashew nut shells contains some 10 per cent of cardol and 90 per cent of anacardic acid, the latter of which yields anacardol upon heating (decarboxylation).

| Cardol | Anacardic acid | Anacardol |

This mixture can be condensed with formaldehyde to yield flexible resites. Cardol resins excel in their resistance to strong alkali. They are used for electrical insulating purposes and in brake linings, where they show a certain plasticity when hot.

The polyhydric phenols are, in general, much more reactive than the monohydric phenols, since the second hydroxyl group enhances the activity of the benzene ring. Probably the only polyhydric phenol used commercially in phenol-aldehyde resins is resorcinol ($m$-dihydroxy benzene), made by alkali fusion of $m$-benzene disulfonic acid, which, in turn, is obtained from phenol.

Resorcinol is used in place of phenol to produce thermosetting resins which cure at low temperatures. Resorcinol resins are available which will cure from room temperature to slightly above the temperature of boiling water. Presses may thus be heated by hot water, giving a more uniform heat distribution. In the manufacture of laminates, the low temperature of cure is useful with materials which would be affected by higher temperatures.

Resorcinol resins are prepared with an excess of resorcinol over formaldehyde, although the deficiency is made up at the time of application, when paraformaldehyde is added. Of particular interest is the fact that at pH 7, resorcinol-formaldehyde resins are in a highly reactive state. This is, of course, the point of minimum corrosive action of chemical solution, so that no acid or alkaline damage will occur to materials with which such a resin comes in contact.   The discovery was made in 1946 that the gelation time on heating a fusible resorcinol-formaldehyde resin with additional formaldehyde is dependent on the pH of the curing mixture in a way quite different from phenol-formaldehyde resins.   Gelation was found to be slowest at a pH of 3 to 4; at pH values of less than 3, there is a reaction catalyzed by hydrogen ions; at pH's greater than 3, by hydroxyl ions.   It is this latter reaction which enables neutral cold-setting resins to be formed from resorcinol but not from phenol.

The physical properties of these resins are similar to those of the phenolics, but they have not replaced the phenolics in molding powder applications to any great extent because of their much higher cost.   They also are considerably darker in color, which prevents their use in any but the darkest colors.

Resorcinol-formaldehyde resin adhesives are available which, with the proper hardening agents added, will cure at approximately room temperature.   By adjustment of the reaction mixture, almost any desired curing temperature may be selected.   A special latex, based on a dispersion of these resins, has been developed which has proved to be very effective as an adhesive for bonding rubber to cotton and rayon cords in the production of cord fabric for tires.

It may be mentioned that there are other phenolic resins, containing no aldehydes, which are prepared by the catalytic reaction of *p*-alkyl phenols with acetylene in the presence of an inert diluent at elevated temperature and pressure.   In the molecular weight range of 800 to 1,100, they are brittle solids, resembling, in some respects, the oil-soluble alkyl phenol-aldehyde condensation products.   The *p-tert*-butyl phenol-acetylene resin, known as Koresin, developed first in Germany and now made in the United States, is one of the most effective tackifiers for GR-S known.

### Fillers

The addition of a filler to a phenoplast in order to produce a combination which could be molded satisfactorily was one of Baekeland's pioneer contributions.   A filler is any substance, either organic or inorganic, which is blended with a resin to produce a nonhomogeneous mixture which can subsequently be molded.   The primary purpose in adding a filler is to improve the physical properties of the molded article.   The filler, to a great extent, controls the mechanical and strength properties of the finished molded product; to a lesser extent it affects the electrical and heat resistance properties.   The resin itself must give the proper flow and the proper bond and must cure in a reasonable length of time.

Among the many fillers which are used in molding compounds, the following may be mentioned: cellulose derivatives (including ground flours, cellulosic fibers, and comminuted paper), lignin, proteinaceous fillers, and mineral fillers (including carbon, asbestos, mica, diatomaceous earth, metal salts and oxides, and glass fibers).

Wood flour is the most common filler and is used for general-purpose molding compounds. Wood-flour-filled resins flow easily in the mold and yield articles possessing excellent appearance. Poor to fair electrical properties, fair impact strength, good tensile strength, and low heat conductivity characterize the moldings. For more severe impact requirements, cotton linters yield articles which are better in this respect, while chopped fabric, shredded textiles, sisal fiber, and long-fibered wood pulp (kraft) give molded objects of outstanding resistance to shock.

Since the fillers just discussed are organic, none of them yields molded articles possessing high heat resistance. For this purpose, mineral fillers, such as diatomaceous earth or, still better, mica or asbestos, are preferable. Mica is used to improve heat resistance, dimensional stability, and electrical properties. It is superior to untreated asbestos for this type of service and at the same time imparts excellent water resistance. Graphite is often used to improve frictional characteristics of phenolic parts. In the latter case, electrical conductivity is, of course, increased. Asbestos is more commonly used than either of the above fillers.

The fillers for laminated phenoplasts differ from those used in molding powders in that the fillers for the former are usually continuous webs rather than discrete particles. The chemical nature of the fillers is quite similar: paper, cotton or linen fabric, sisal mat, or woven asbestos or glass. The filler greatly increases the strength properties of the laminate over those of the pure resin; the increase is greater than is obtained with molding powders because of the continuous web.

### Oil-Soluble Resins

During the period 1910 to 1916, there were developed in Germany a series of substitutes for the fossil resins. These products were made by dispersing phenol-aldehyde resins in rosin, followed by esterification of the abietic acid with glycerol (Albertols). Introduction of the resins to the American market was begun in the middle twenties. These resins at first received limited acceptance as substitutes for the fossil resins. However, it was discovered in 1926 that, when the resins were combined with tung (Chinawood) oil, the resulting varnishes would dry in about four hours. This rapid drying quality enabled the oleoresinous varnishes to compete with the cellulose nitrate lacquers which were then just coming into widespread use. In addition, these varnishes and the enamels made from them exhibited excellent resistance to outdoor exposure. Two years later, pure oil-soluble phenolic resins, unmodified with natural resins were introduced in the United States.

The growth of the oil-soluble phenolic resins has been rapid. When combined with drying oils, these resins form coatings which have outstanding durability, rapid rate of drying, toughness, alkali and acid resistance, and waterproofness. Tung oil was the principal drying oil used originally, but the shortage and price of tung oil in recent years has caused other oils, such as linseed, oiticica, perilla, and dehydrated castor, to be used, and resins have been developed which work successfully with these, alone and in combinations.

The oil-soluble phenoplasts may be divided into the *pure* or *100 per cent* phenolic resins, which are made by condensation of substituted phenols with formaldehyde and contain no modifying or solubilizing agents; and the *modified* phenolic resins, which are made by disperson of a phenoplast in a natural resin, chiefly rosin (see Chap. 7). Some phenoplasts, in pure form, are insoluble in oils, but the dispersed resins are soluble.

Pure phenolic resins made from trifunctional phenols, such as phenol itself or *m*-cresol, are insoluble in varnish oils. It is thus necessary to use a phenol which is substituted in either an ortho or the para position by an alkyl or aryl group. This substitution yields a bifunctional phenol, which cannot form a highly cross-linked resin, and, further, it improves the resin's solubility in the oil, since alkyl or aryl groups are oleophilic.

Both *o*- and *p*-substituted phenols form oil-soluble products, but the para derivatives are generally used because varnishes made from them discolor less upon exposure to weathering. The ortho derivatives tend to yellow; the reason for this is not known for certain, but the tendency is usually ascribed to the formation of a *p*-quinone structure which cannot form when the para position is occupied.

A large number of substituted phenols may be used to produce oil-soluble phenoplasts. However, many of these either are unavailable commercially or do not yield satisfactory varnishes. The most important substituted phenols used in the manufacture of oil-soluble phenoplasts are: *p*-cresol, *p-tert*-butyl phenol, *p-tert*-amyl phenol, *p*-phenyl phenol, and Bisphenol A [2,2-bis(4-hydroxy phenyl)propane].

### Cast Resins

The manufacture of cast phenolic resins (Catalin, Durez, Haveg, Loven, Pliophen, Resinox) is undertaken when a small quantity of a variety of shapes is required, since casting into simple molds is often more economical than the more elaborate procedure of preparing steel molds for hot pressing. In addition, the resins possess good clarity and brilliance and can be made in a wide variety of colors. To insure light color, pure nickel or nickel-clad apparatus is used, and the raw materials are carefully purified.

The first step in the manufacture of a phenolic casting resin is similar to that for a resole.  A high ratio of formaldehyde to phenol (2:1 to 3:1) is used so that the resin will contain a large number of methylol groups. When the (alkaline) condensation has reached the proper stage, the reaction mixture is neutralized with a weak organic acid, such as lactic or phthalic.  The water is then removed under reduced pressure (30 to 50 mm Hg), and heating is continued until the resin has reached the desired viscosity.  Colors and pigments are then added, together with a compound, such as glycerol, which serves as a common solvent for the resin and the water of reaction; the resin is then poured or cast into thin lead molds.  The molds are held at a temperature of 60° to 100°C in an oven for three to seven days until the resin has formed a hard, infusible mass. The lead molds are then stripped off, and the casting is trimmed to remove the flash.

**Manufacture**

Phenol-formaldehyde resins, other than cast resins, may be manufactured in two different ways.

*One-stage resins* are those in which all of the formaldehyde is added at one time.  An *alkaline* catalyst is used and the phenol-formaldehyde ratio is usually about 1:1.5.  Condensation is interrupted while the resin is still thermoplastic and soluble.  These spirit-soluble resins are used for laminating, although molding materials for special purposes can also be prepared from them by adding fillers and catalysts to the carefully dried resole; subsequent application of heat completes the conversion to resite.

*Two-stage resins* are those in which the formaldehyde necessary for cross-linking is added in two successive steps.  An *acid* catalyst is used, and the phenol-formaldehyde ratio is usually about 1:0.8; this produces a novolac resin which is permanently thermoplastic and soluble, because of the absence of free methylol groups.  Molding powders are then prepared by mixing the powdered resin with fillers and pigments, together with a source of sufficient methylene bridges to yield a resite upon subsequent thermal curing.  As a methylene source, paraformaldehyde or, more commonly, hexamethylene tetramine (hexamine) is added since it liberates no water, a desirable feature when resins of high electrical quality are being prepared.

Since the ultimate form of a finished phenoplast may be a molded product, a laminate, a surface coating, or an adhesive, the operations involved in the manufacture of phenoplasts will differ somewhat as the products approach the finished condition.  Resins for molding powders (Bakelite, Durez, Resinox) are made from pure phenol or from mixtures of tar acids containing chiefly phenol.  Cast resins are made from pure synthetic phenol in order to obtain as good a color as possible.  Before World War II, laminating resins were produced largely from cresols and xylenols; more recently, because of cresol shortages, they have been made in considerable quantity from phenol.

A typical procedure for the manufacture of a phenolic resin will be described. The phenol is charged from a measuring tank into a resin kettle, followed by the formaldehyde and catalyst. If the product is to be a molding powder, a modifier, such as aniline, is often added. Its functions are to obtain better flow of the molding compound and to slow the curing reaction slightly so that the mold will be filled completely before curing takes place.

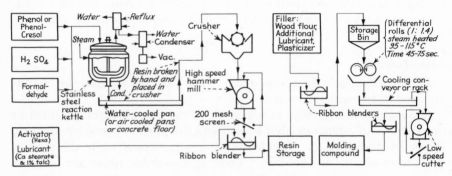

FIG. 8-2. Phenol-formaldehyde molding powder flow sheet. (*Reprinted by permission from Chemical Engineering*)

The resin kettle, usually having a capacity of from 1 thousand to 3 thousand gallons, is supplied with good agitation, preferably a scraper-type agitator, because the resin becomes very viscous during dehydration and it is necessary to scrape the resin film from the sides of the kettle in order to maintain good heat transfer and prevent local overheating. The kettle jacket is principally used for heating the charge to reaction temperature. Once reaction has begun, the heat of reaction is usually so great and the reaction rate so rapid that reflux, rather than jacket cooling, must be used to remove the heat. The kettle and condenser are usually constructed of iron, if color is not important; if light color of the product is essential, as with casting resins, nickel or nickel-clad apparatus is customary. The equipment handling formaldehyde is usually made of aluminum.

By using a high formaldehyde-phenol ratio, under strongly alkaline conditions, a condensate consisting largely of phenol di- and trialcohols is produced, having a high solubility in water; upon neutralization of the catalyst, an aqueous solution is obtained which has little tendency to react further, since the reactivity of the methylol groups is diminished by the diluting effect of the water. Such water-soluble phenolics are used for adhesives or impregnants, subsequent curing being effected by heating in the presence of added catalyst.

If an acid catalyst has been used, the mixture, after initial reaction, will separate into two phases; the heavier phase is the resin, while the lighter phase contains the water of reaction plus the water present in the formaldehyde solution. The water may be separated by decantation or by vacuum distillation. In either case, the resin phase is dehydrated by heating under vacuum.

When a solid, alkaline-catalyzed resin (resole) is desired, the dehydration is also carried out by very careful heating under vacuum. Heating a resole for too long a time or at too high a temperature will cause premature cross-linking, accompanied by violent exothermic reaction, to occur in the kettle. As soon as the resin is dehydrated, it is quickly run out of the kettle onto a cooling floor, which is constructed of sheet iron plates welded together to form a smooth surface. Since the resin is a resole, it is very reactive and will set-up unless cooled quickly. Once the resin has cooled to a brittle solid, it is broken up with sledges into small pieces which are ground to a coarse powder, then pulverized in an impact mill.

In the manufacture of molding powders, the finely ground resin is first mixed with small amounts of lubricants, such as waxes or stearates, which aid in causing flow during molding, in separating the piece from the mold, and in improving the finish of the molded piece. If a novolac-type of resin is used, hexamethylene tetramine is mixed at this stage. The resin compound, filler, and color are next intimately mixed in a ribbon-type mixer. A large proportion of phenoplast molding powders is colored black by the addition of carbon black or black dye. In general, dark shades must be used in order to hide the color of the resin and minimize the darkening which always occurs upon aging or exposure to light.

Since laminates differ from molding powders in that the filler usually consists of a continuous web, the usual type of mixer cannot be used, and the web must therefore be impregnated with a varnish or solution of the resin. Alcohol solutions are usually employed for the heavier cotton fabrics and frequently for papers; some papers, however, are impregnated with a water-soluble resin.

## Applications

The great bulk of the phenoplasts made are consumed in making molded objects. Other applications include the aforementioned laminates, varnish resins, and cast resins. Some of the other applications and newer developments will be briefly mentioned.

Foamed phenolic resins receive attention periodically and, recently, foamed phenolic resins have found an interesting application as a packaging material. Fragile articles can be pressed into the foam and shipped safely. Foams weighing less than 0.4 pound per cubic foot can be made which have only one seventh the density of shredded paper. Phenolic foam has also been used to fill voids between walls in seagoing vessels. This replaces balsa wood, which had to be hand fitted.

A use which absorbed only experimental quantities of synthetic resins a few years ago is the shell foundry molding process. Shell molding was developed by Cröning in Germany and was introduced in this country in 1945; it has since undergone intensive development work by foundry-men and resin manufacturers. The process consists in mixing together measured quantities of sand and powdered resin. The mixture is invested (dumped) onto a heated steel pattern. A thin shell, approximately one quarter of an inch thick, adheres to the hot pattern as the resin flows and fuses the grains of sand together. After excess sand is removed, the shell is cured by baking and the two halves of the mold, in the form of a thin shell, are ready for the casting operation after cores, if any, are inserted. The molds are about one tenth as heavy as conventional molds. They use much less sand, as well as finer sand, which improves the surfaces of the cast pieces. To illustrate the rate of growth of this process, only some 3 million pounds of phenolic (and urea) resins were used in 1955; by 1956, their use had jumped to about 9 million pounds, and by 1957 the foundries probably used as much as 50 million pounds.

Phenol-formaldehyde adhesives are boilproof, can be soaked indefinitely, and in weather exposure will outlast the wood. The boilproof quality permits steaming of phenolic-bonded plywood to soften it for bending and forming operations. Extreme resistance to the action of molds and fungi is another important property. A disadvantage of phenolic adhesives is that they stain thin veneers.

Phenolic adhesives that require temperatures above 100°C to effect their cure in a reasonable length of time are considered to be high-temperature setting. These are usually set by an alkaline hardener. Intermediate-temperature-setting adhesives (between 25° and 100°C) are cured by either alkaline or acidic hardeners. However, the nearly neutral or mildly alkaline adhesives are more common and are usually preferred because of the possibility of wood weakening by strongly acid adhesives. (Urea-formaldehyde adhesives are invariably catalyzed by acids or acid-forming salts. The intermediate-temperature-setting melamine-formal-dehyde adhesives are catalyzed by acids, but the hot-press melamine resins usually are neutral.) The setting of resorcinol-formaldehyde adhesives is obtained by adding formaldehyde or paraformaldehyde. These are really not catalysts but resin-forming ingredients.

In using continuous synthetic filaments for reinforcing molded rubber goods, it is necessary to pretreat the fiber with an adhesive to assure good bonding to rubber. An adhesive commonly used for this purpose is

FIG. 8-3. Phenolic resins are used in this shell-molding process. Blow-holes are eliminated because the shell is porous, allowing the gases to escape during the pouring operation. (*Courtesy Bakelite Co.*)

prepared by partially condensing one mole of resorcinol with three moles of formaldehyde in dilute sodium hydroxide solution, and adding this solution to a mixture of natural rubber and GR-S latices.

Just recently, a new, glass-reinforced phenolic plastic, which has exceptional properties, has been reported. At 260°C, it has a tensile strength of 40,000 to 50,000 psi and a compressive strength of 30,000 to 35,000 psi. A temperature of 260°C is far above the limits—about 150°C —of glass-laminated polyester and epoxy plastics, and is even superior to the tolerances of aluminum and magnesium.

## AMINOPLASTS

The principal aminoplasts of commercial importance are those based on the reaction of formaldehyde with urea and melamine and, to a much lesser extent, thiourea, aniline, and benzene- and toluene-sulfonamides. Although useful resins may be prepared from a number of other amino compounds, few have shown the desirable properties and relatively low cost possessed by the above group. Among other compounds which have been extensively studied as resin-forming materials are dicyandiamide, guanidine, and alkyl-substituted ureas.

There are two conditions which appear to be necessary for an amino compound to form *thermosetting* resins: (1) The compound must have at least two reactive primary amino groups, and (2) except for aromatic diamines, the nitrogen of the amino group must be adjacent to a carbon atom which has a double bond so that tautomerism is possible. Urea, melamine, ammeline, guanidine, dicyandiamide, and thiourea have this characteristic form of tautomerism and all can yield infusible resins with formaldehyde. Compounds having only one amino radical react with formaldehyde but do not form infusible products. Mono-*N*-alkyl substituted ureas, aniline, and aryl sulfonamides, to name a few, are in this class, as are also the aliphatic diamines which cannot tautomerize.

### Urea-Formaldehyde Resins

The first mention of a product obtained by the reaction of urea with formaldehyde was in 1884. It was not until 1920, however, that a Czechoslovakian, John, was granted the first patent in this field. Three years later, other patents issued to the Viennese chemist, Pollak, served as the basis for commercial development of a transparent "organic glass" (Pollopas). Similar products were soon made in France and England. These were cast resins and, while their surface hardness was far less than that of glass and the products lacked good weather resistance, it was at one time predicted that they would be used to replace glass in architectural uses; this hope was never realized.

In 1926, a molding powder using a combination of urea and thiourea was produced in England. Patent rights were acquired in the United States, and molding powders of thiourea plastics were put on the domestic market in 1929 under the trade-mark, Beetle. Molded pure thiourea plastics were, however, short lived for reasons pointed out later.

The actual development of a successful pure urea-formaldehyde molding powder was the result of an investigation at Mellon Institute, beginning in 1928, for a plastic which was light in color and which could be used to replace the heavy enamel cast-iron frames of scales. During the decade which followed the initial commercial development of urea resins, other investigations led to their application as adhesives and surface coatings. The combination of the two properties, thermosetting and complete lack of color, was not present in any resin previous to that time.

The sources of formaldehyde have already been briefly discussed under phenolic resins. Urea (carbamide) is made from ammonia by several processes. (Woehler's famous synthesis of urea by isomerization of ammonium cyanate is now of historical interest only.) All methods now in use depend upon the reaction of ammonia with carbon dioxide under high pressure and temperature to form ammonium carbamate, which, in turn, splits off water to form urea:

$$2NH_3 + CO_2 \xrightarrow[\text{2--6,000 psi}]{160°\text{--}210°C} NH_2 \cdot COO \cdot NH_4$$
$$\downarrow -H_2O$$
$$NH_2 \cdot CO \cdot NH_2$$

The chemistry of the reactions between urea and formaldehyde is very complex, and the constitution of the condensation products is still uncertain. It is known, however, that urea reacts with formaldehyde under *neutral* or *alkaline* conditions to yield monomethylol urea and symmetrical dimethylol urea, depending upon the ratio of the reactants.

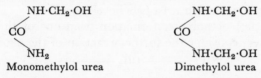

Monomethylol urea      Dimethylol urea

Tri- and tetramethylol ureas are not known, although all of the amino hydrogens can be replaced to form a class of compounds known as urons, which are inner ethers. The mono- and dimethylol ureas may be regarded as the monomers of the urea resins.

These compounds are, in one way, analogous to the hemiformals, formed from an alcohol and urea with formaldehyde under the same conditions:

From an alcohol      From urea

Under *acid* conditions, bisamides are formed, analogous to the formals produced from the reactions of alcohols with formaldehyde:

From an alcohol      From urea

At the present time, four principal mechanisms have been advanced for the first stage of reaction of the methylol ureas under acid conditions. Using monomethylol urea, there are possible:[3]

1. Methylene bisamide formation:
   $NH_2 \cdot CO \cdot NH \cdot CH_2OH + NH_2 \cdot CO \cdot NH_2 \rightarrow NH_2 \cdot CO \cdot NH \cdot CH_2 \cdot NH \cdot CO \cdot NH_2 + H_2O$
2. Methylol methylene bisamide formation:
   $2NH_2 \cdot CO \cdot NH \cdot CH_2OH \rightarrow NH_2 \cdot CO \cdot NH \cdot CH_2 \cdot N(CH_2OH) \cdot CO \cdot NH_2 + H_2O$
3. Ether formation:
   $2NH_2 \cdot CO \cdot NH \cdot CH_2OH \rightarrow NH_2 \cdot CO \cdot NH \cdot CH_2 \cdot O \cdot CH_2 \cdot NH \cdot CO \cdot NH_2 + H_2O$
4. Azomethine formation:
   $3NH_2 \cdot CO \cdot NH \cdot CH_2OH \rightarrow 3NH_2 \cdot CO \cdot N = CH_2 + 3H_2O$

In addition, chemical modification of the methylol ureas before condensation may introduce new factors into the polymerization scheme. The marked effect of the hydrogen-ion concentration must also be considered. This has led to theories which take into account the resonance forms, some ionic, in which urea is believed to exist.

As an example[3] of polymer formation from one of the intermediates postulated above, consider the further reaction of the azomethine trimer

[3] Wohnsiedler, H. P., *Ind. Eng. Chem.*, **44**, 2679 (1952).

with formaldehyde under acid conditions. In the formation of the azomethine amide (Schiff base), one —NH$_2$ group acted as an amino group. In the trimer, the —NH$_2$ groups may now behave as amide (—CO·NH$_2$) groups to form, with more formaldehyde, methylene bis linkages (—CH$_2$—), as indicated in diagram on preceding page.

Under *alkaline* conditions, monomethylol urea forms, upon heating, water-soluble condensation products, which may be considered to correspond roughly to the B-stage phenolic resins, although they are more soluble. Upon acidification and heating, the following reaction probably occurs:

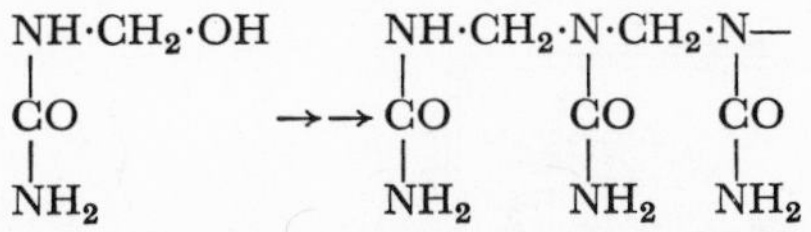

$$
\begin{array}{cccc}
\text{NH·CH}_2\text{·OH} & & \text{NH·CH}_2\text{·N·CH}_2\text{·N—} \\
| & & | \qquad | \qquad | \\
\text{CO} & \rightarrow\rightarrow & \text{CO} \quad \text{CO} \quad \text{CO} \\
| & & | \qquad | \qquad | \\
\text{NH}_2 & & \text{NH}_2 \ \ \text{NH}_2 \ \ \text{NH}_2
\end{array}
$$

With dimethylol urea, cross-linking doubtless occurs, as an insoluble, infusible product is obtained.

Many other theories have been proposed for the reaction of urea with formaldehyde and for the subsequent polymerization, some of which appear to be highly improbable. Which, if any, of the various theories gives the true picture of the mechanism of the urea-formaldehyde resinification process is still in considerable doubt, although there is general agreement on the ultimate occurrence of cross-linking.

The normal methods of manufacturing urea-formaldehyde resins were evolved somewhat empirically. The urea-formaldehyde ratio is usually between 1:1.3 and 1:1.8, the theoretical ideal limit of 1:2 causing heavy evolution of gases during hot molding, probably by elimination of some formaldehyde from the large number of methylol groups. A high proportion of formaldehyde produces harder resins at low pH, probably as a result of an increased number of cross-linkages. However, larger amounts of formaldehyde may cause crazing of molded products on aging.

In the production of urea molding resins, it is common practice to employ the more readily controllable alkaline conditions to accelerate the initial reaction. Aqueous solutions of urea and formaldehyde are mixed in a reaction kettle, together with a weakly alkaline catalyst, such as calcium or dilute sodium hydroxide, ammonia, or an alkanolamine. Because of the potential clarity of the finished resins, extreme cleanliness is observed, and condensation is carried out in nickel-clad, glass-lined, or stainless-steel reactors.

During the initial stages of reaction, conducted at about room temperature, the reaction results in the formation of products which are water-soluble, and which consist mainly of the condensation products, mono- and dimethylol ureas. The solution is then heated to boiling and held until it becomes a viscous, syrupy mass or is partially vacuum dehydrated.

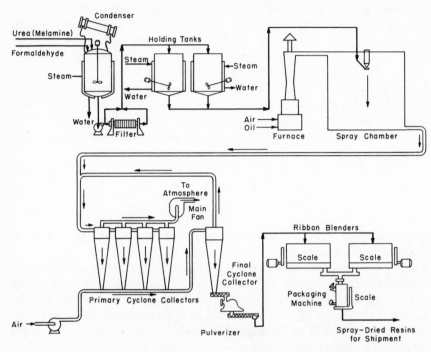

Fig. 8-4. Urea-formaldehyde flow sheet. (*By permission from Chemical Engineering*)

To make a molding powder, the filtered liquid resin is mixed with a filler (which is usually about 30 to 40 per cent of the final composition) and the damp mixture is screened, then dried in thin layers in an oven. The coarse powder is then thoroughly blended with compounding ingredients (pigments and dyes, lubricants, stabilizers, and curing agents) in ball mills to reduce the mixture to a fine, uniform powder.

In an alternative process, the liquid resin is spray-dried by spraying it in the form of fine droplets into a mixture of hot furnace gases. The dried resin dust is separated from the gases in cyclone separators. Fillers and other additives may then be added to the urea resin powder.

A filler is always incorporated in a urea molding powder to impart strength to the polymerized resin and to prevent cracking due to changes in moisture content or as a result of changes in the chemical structure which may occur in the resin after hardening. The fillers most commonly employed with urea resins are bleached paper pulp ($\alpha$-cellulose) and wood flour, because the desirable characteristics of translucency and colorability are maintained. These materials have a fibrous structure which gives rise to moldings of good strength (tensile strengths, for example, of 7,000 to 10,000 psi).

Addition of α-cellulose corresponds to incorporation of fillers in phenolic resins. The effect of adding α-cellulose to urea resins differs from the use of fillers in phenolics, however, in that examination of the molded product does not show individual particles of cellulose physically admixed with resin. It is believed that the cellulose is dispersed in the resin in a molecular state of subdivision, either by solid solution or, more likely, by actual chemical union, possibly by the formation of cellulose semi-acetals.

The α-cellulose is obtained by digesting wood chips for several hours at 100° to 135°C with a reagent which dissolves most of the lignin and other noncellulosic constituents of wood without destroying the fibrous nature of the cellulose. In the sulfite process, a solution containing dissolved bisulfites, with some free sulfur dioxide, is used. In other processes, sodium hydroxide solution, or a mixture of sodium hydroxide and sodium sulfide in solution is used. The pulp is further purified by bleaching, which assists in the removal of residual traces of fats and resins, and is then washed with water.

Cheaper than bleached pulp, wood flour is used in the manufacture of lower grades of urea molding powders. Wood-filled powders yield more opaque molded products than those using α-cellulose. The more suitable grades of wood flour are obtained from the soft woods, such as fir, spruce, poplar, basswood, and cottonwood. The wood is ground to a fineness of about 100 to 200 mesh in such a way as to avoid destruction of the fibrous character of the material. Fillers which have been used in lesser amounts for imparting special properties are cotton, walnut-shell powder, nylon, keratin, and mineral fillers. Other ingredients which may be added are stabilizers, lubricants, plasticizers, and pigments or other colorants.

An acid is used to catalyze the final conversion of the molding powder from the initial stages of resin formation to the infusible, insoluble product. Two types of acid materials are used and are known as *direct* and *latent* catalysts. The former are true acids and are, therefore, effective at all temperatures. Typical are inorganic and organic acids; acid salts, such as sodium acid sulfate; and acid esters, typified by acid alkyl phosphates (with alkyl groups containing more than three carbon atoms).

Latent catalysts form acid products at elevated temperatures, in many cases in conjunction with moisture liberated during the molding operation. In the absence of moisture, they are ineffective at room temperature. Typical latent catalysts include salts and esters which develop acidity upon heating. Dimethyl oxalate, amine hydrochlorides, sodium and barium salts of ethyl sulfuric acid, sodium sulfite, and benzoyl or phthaloyl mercaptobenzothiazole are examples of such catalysts.

Urea, thiourea, or substituted ureas are often added to the molding powders. These act to prevent excessive shrinking and cracking of the molding by combining with unreacted (excess) formaldehyde and free methylol groups which would decrease water resistance. They may also act as plasticizers and help insure uniform flow and curing.

In cases requiring a long flow time in the mold or when delayed action of final polymerization is desirable, lime, soda ash, or other weakly alkaline salts may act as efficient retardants. In making large or intricate moldings, this action is often necessary.

The outstanding property of molded urea plastics is their light color. The resins themselves are transparent. The natural color of α-cellulose-filled ureas is a translucent milky white which can be converted to an opaque white by addition of titanium dioxide, or to numerous pastel shades by addition of other stable pigments. Unlike many other plastics, these resins do not lose luster by handling.

Ureas are considerably less resistant to water than the phenolics and are not used in frequent or prolonged contact with hot water. When well cured, however, they are sufficiently resistant at room temperature to permit their use in bathroom fixtures and "unbreakable" tumblers. Continued exposure of urea-formaldehyde plastics to an atmosphere of varying humidity will often give rise to cracks, as the result of alternate absorption and loss of water. This behavior has recently been greatly improved.

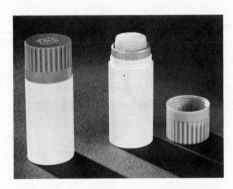

Fig. 8-5. Molded urea-formaldehyde cosmetics container. (*Courtesy American Cyanamid Co.*)

Urea plastics show good resistance to weak alkalies and are unaffected by organic solvents, including greases and oils. They are not resistant to acids or strong alkalies. They possess neither taste nor odor.

Unlike phenolics, heat-resistant ureas cannot be compounded by adding inorganic fillers, because the unique effect of α-cellulose is essential to obtain proper strength and good moldability. Further, the presence of asbestos in a urea-formaldehyde resin destroys its colorability, and it is partly the absence of asbestos filler that reduces the heat resistance of urea-formaldehyde resins as compared with the heat-resistant phenolics.

Upon passage of an electric arc across their surfaces, urea-formaldehyde plastics do not carbonize, as do the phenolics; therefore, the ureas are utilized where arc resistance is of importance (see Chap. 4). Their fair resistance to cracking and good arc resistance, coupled with relatively high dielectric strength, adapts the ureas to fabrication of electrical parts. Among molded plastics, ureas exhibit unusual surface hardness; however, machinability is poor.

The lightness of color and good molding qualities of urea plastics (Beetle, Plaskon) have caused them to be widely used for the manufacture of many articles. Their fair resistance to mild alkalies permits their use in bathroom fixtures and tumblers. Lack of taste and odor, and resistance to greases and oils, have enabled them to be used in the manufacture of shatterproof dishes. Grease, oil, and general chemical resistance properties have also encouraged the widespread use of urea plastics for bottle closures, cosmetic containers, and similar molded articles.

Because of their unique combination of colorlessness, controllable translucency, and high light efficiency, urea-formaldehyde plastics are widely used in the manufacture of electric light shades and reflectors. Many of their applications involve the ability of these resins to act as light-diffusing bodies. In the manufacture of lighting fixtures and decorative paneling, diffusion of light without glare is often desirable. No other resin is as suitable for this effect. As a result, portable lamp diffusers, reflector bowls for commercial lighting, various types of lenses and shades for transparent lighting, and numerous types of decorative lamps are made of urea resins. Light weight, as well as good impact resistance, gives these materials an advantage over glass and ceramics.

The manufacture of urea-formaldehyde products by casting is not widely used because of excessive shrinkage during curing and poor aging characteristics of the product. By careful regulation of the process, however, cast urea resins may be made.

Urea-formaldehyde resins are also widely used as adhesives. For such uses, the resinous material is prepared in a soluble form which may be converted to the permanently infusible form by proper treatment during bonding. These adhesives are usually obtained as highly viscous liquids, of high resin content (70 to 90 per cent), which have a limited period of stability. The resins are also available as dry powders which, when mixed with small quantities of water, form liquid adhesives equivalent to those above. These powders have, of course, a longer shelf life.

The liquid adhesives are generally prepared by condensing urea and formaldehyde under slightly acid conditions to a predetermined degree. The solution is then neutralized and the water removed by vacuum distillation until the required viscosity or solid content is obtained.   The liquid adhesives are converted to the dry powder form either by feeding through hot rolls, and subsequently scraping off the dried resin film, or, more often, by spray drying.   By the latter method, the resin is rapidly dried with little further condensation occurring.

Although urea adhesives can be hardened alone by hot pressing, they are almost always used in conjunction with acid catalysts (hardeners) in order to reduce pressing times.   The hardeners are generally sold separately from the adhesive itself and are mixed with the latter immediately prior to application.   In some cases, however, powdered hardeners may be mixed with the dry adhesives, remaining inactive until moistened.

Fig. 8-6.   Foundry sand cores bonded with a urea resin.   (*Courtesy Catalin Corp. of America*)

For many purposes urea adhesives are modified by the addition of a filler.   Advantages are the use of a relatively cheap material to reduce the cost, an increase in viscosity of the mixture so as to diminish the tendency for the liquid resin to penetrate the wood more than necessary, and an increase in the smoothness and consequent ease of application.

These adhesives have been used on a large scale for the production of plywood and for veneering, which can be machined in the same way as other laminates. Also popular are the light-colored laminates in which the surface sheet is impregnated with a urea resin, while the body of the plastic may be either a urea or phenolic resin. Decorative laminates of this type, often backed with plywood, find wide utility as table and counter tops (Formica). Further, like the phenolics, urea resins are widely used as laminating resins to impregnate either cloth or paper

FIG. 8-7. Decorative wall panels are made by laminating seven sheets of resin-impregnated kraft paper, a patterned sheet, and a covering translucent sheet. (*Courtesy Formica Corp.*)

which can be wrapped into complicated shapes over inexpensive forms. They are cured by application of heat under low pressure.

Waterproof adhesives have been obtained under suitable conditions by reacting a urea resin with starch. This adhesive becomes water-resistant upon drying only and does not depend upon a subsequent reaction with, for example, ammonium salts, as do other cold-setting urea-resin adhesives.

Amino resins, particularly the alkyl ethers, are used in the textile field to increase the crease resistance of cotton and linen and some lower-grade wool and rayon fabrics. These resins have also been applied successfully to woolen fabrics to reduce shrinkage.

Amino resins are capable of conferring good wet strength to paper. Wet-strength paper is paper that has been treated so that it retains a considerable proportion of its dry tensile and bursting strengths when saturated with water. Considerable impetus has been given to the production of wet-strength paper by demands for blueprint paper, map paper, paper towels and napkins, and containers for overseas shipment which do not disintegrate easily when soaked with water. There is also a large market for wet-strength wrappings for moist or iced vegetables, fruits, meats, and other foodstuffs.

The original hydrophilic urea-formaldehyde resins could be used only to a limited extent for surface coating purposes. It was later discovered that, by carrying out the condensation in the presence of an alcohol which had only a limited compatibility with water, resins could be obtained which were not only capable of forming very hard, insoluble films on curing, but which also were compatible with the usual organic coatings solvents and other resins used in surface coatings manufacture. The formation of resins of this type is accomplished by chemical reaction of methylol groups and the alcohol. Ethers of the methylol ureas may be regarded as the primary condensation products from which the relatively water-insensitive urea coating resins are derived.

Three general types of ethers have been prepared; the monoethers of monomethylol urea, the monoethers of dimethylol urea, and the diethers of dimethylol urea:

$$
\begin{array}{ccc}
\text{NH·CH}_2\text{·OR} & \text{NH·CH}_2\text{·OR} & \text{NH·CH}_2\text{·OR} \\
\diagup & \diagup & \diagup \\
\text{CO} & \text{CO} & \text{CO} \\
\diagdown & \diagdown & \diagdown \\
\text{NH}_2 & \text{NH·CH}_2\text{·OH} & \text{NH·CH}_2\text{·OR}
\end{array}
$$

These compounds may be prepared by reacting the appropriate methylol urea with the alcohol in the presence of an acid catalyst or by reacting urea and formaldehyde using the alcohol as the solvent. By varying the temperature and the proportion of reactants, each of the above types of compounds may be isolated. These ethers are white, crystalline solids which are stable at room temperature. The methyl ethers are readily soluble in water but solubility diminishes with increasing chain length, and the butyl ethers are only sparingly soluble. When the ethers are melted and maintained at temperatures above their melting temperatures, resinification occurs with a liberation of a portion of the alcohol. The nature of the chemical changes which occur is not yet clear, although it is believed that, during the resinification process, approximately one molecule of alcohol is split off per molecule of diether. It is likely that reactions of the following type occur:

$$n \, CO \underset{NH \cdot CH_2 \cdot OR}{\overset{NH \cdot CH_2 \cdot OR}{\Big\langle}} \rightarrow CH_2 : N - [-CO \cdot N(CH_2OR) \cdot CH_2 \cdot NH -]_{n-1} - CO \cdot NH \cdot CH_2 \cdot OR + n \, ROH$$

These resin solutions may be converted to a fully hardened state by prolonged heating. During this process, cross-linking probably occurs through the reaction of alkoxy groups with secondary amino hydrogen atoms, resulting in the elimination of further alcohol molecules:

$$
\begin{array}{cccc}
| & & | & | \\
CO & CH_2 & CO & CH_2 \\
| & | & | & | \\
N \cdot CH_2 \cdot OR \; H \cdot N & \rightarrow & N \cdot CH_2 \cdot N & + ROH \\
| & | & | & | \\
CH_2 & CO & CH_2 & CO \\
| & | & | & | \\
NH & & NH & \\
| & & | &
\end{array}
$$

The amount of cross-linking which occurs, however, is small, since analysis of the hardened resins, even after long curing times, still reveals considerable retention of alkoxy groups. In all cases, resinification is accelerated by the presence of acid.

Propylated and butylated urea-formaldehyde resins, which are the ones most commonly used in the coatings field, are viscous, colorless liquids which are thinned to permit spray or brush application. When fully hardened, they yield colorless, transparent films which are extremely hard and resistant to solvent attack. The films formed from these resins alone are brittle and have poor adhesion. In practice, therefore, they are almost invariably plasticized. The most satisfactory plasticizers are oil- or phenolic-modified alkyd resins. The use of this type of plasticizer not only results in a flexible film having good adhesion but also may accelerate the curing of the urea resin, since the alkyd resins normally have an appreciable residual acid content. It is believed by some that the alkyd resin enters chemically into the urea-resin structure, since residual hydroxyl groups from the polyol used in the alkyd manufacture may react with some of the alkoxy groups, liberating the alcohol and forming ether linkages. The properties of the mixtures depend on the proportions of alkyd and urea resins employed; the former contributes durability, flexibility, and adhesion; the latter, hardness and light fastness.

These alkyd-urea combinations are in widespread use for coating metal kitchen and bathroom fixtures, hospital equipment, and refrigerators, as well as other articles which are finished in light shades which must not discolor and which will be relatively immune to soap, oil, solvents, and other chemicals. To provide greater water resistance for washing machines and other laundry equipment, as well as for automotive primer coats, the phenolic-modified alkyds are frequently used in combination with the urea resins.

Urea resins have been the subject of some investigation from the point of view of their use for conversion to fibers. As a class, however, they have not shown much progress in this direction; although higher melting than analogous polyamides and polyurethanes, they exhibit poor thermal stability and appear to be more difficult to prepare in a pure state.

### Melamine-Formaldehyde Resins

Although melamine has been known for more than a century, only recently has this compound been obtained in good yield commercially. It appeared on the American market in 1939.

Calcium carbide is first made from lime and coke in an electric furnace, using a smothered electric arc:

$$3C + CaO \xrightarrow{\Delta} CaC_2 + CO$$

The second step is exothermic, but requires external application of heat to raise a part of the charge to the initiation temperature (over 900°C):

$$CaC_2 + N_2 \rightarrow CaCN_2 + C$$

Fluxes, such as calcium chloride or fluoride, are added to increase the rate of reaction or cause it to proceed at a lower temperature.

By acidifying the calcium cyanamide with aqueous carbon dioxide or dilute sulfuric acid, free cyanamide ($H_2CN_2$) is formed which dimerizes to form dicyandiamide ("dicy"). By further polymerizing dicy at high temperature and moderate pressure, sometimes in the presence of ammonia, melamine is formed. The over-all reaction is

$$3H_2N \cdot C(:NH) \cdot NH \cdot CN \rightarrow 2 \quad \underset{\underset{NH_2}{\overset{\displaystyle |}{\underset{\displaystyle C}{}}}}{\overset{\displaystyle N}{\underset{\displaystyle N \quad N}{\underset{\displaystyle \|}{H_2N \cdot C \qquad C \cdot NH_2}}}}$$

although guanidine appears as an intermediate.

Melamine, like urea, reacts with formaldehyde under neutral or slightly alkaline conditions to give methylol melamines. As is the case with the methylol ureas, the methylol melamines may be regarded as the monomers of melamine-formaldehyde resins. The processes of resinification are also similar to those observed in the case of urea resins. Melamine differs from urea in that all six hydrogen atoms can be replaced by methylol groups upon reaction with formaldehyde; however, only between two and three methylol groups are usually introduced for the production of insoluble, infusible resins.

As with the urea-formaldehyde resins, the reaction is usually carried out in corrosion-resistant equipment. Stainless steel, nickel-clad steel, and nickel alloys have been used. Since conditions for formation of melamine-formaldehyde resins are somewhat different than those for urea-formaldehyde resins, due to the low solubility of melamine in water and aqueous formaldehyde at ordinary temperatures, the condensation with aqueous formaldehyde is usually carried out at temperatures of 90°C or higher. Water may be removed at low temperatures by vacuum evaporation to keep the resin from condensing to an infusible state. The effect of acidity

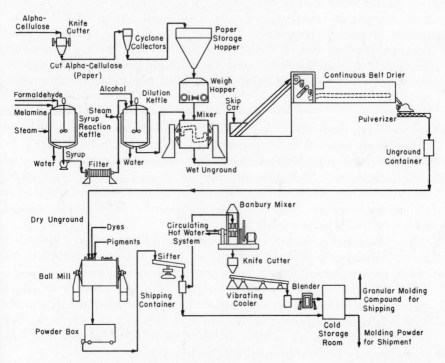

FIG. 8-8. Melamine-formaldehyde flow sheet. (*By permission from Chemical Engineering*)

and alkalinity on the condensation is not so great, nor does the pH need as careful control as with urea resins.

Melamine molding powders (Cymel, Plaskon, Resimene) are manufactured by processes similar to those described for urea. As mentioned previously, the resins used in molding powders usually have a melamine-formaldehyde ratio of between 1:2 and 1:3. These resins harden more rapidly than urea resins at molding temperatures and thus the quantity of acid catalysts and stabilizers added may be less; further, these materials may sometimes be combined with slightly alkaline fillers or with other resins, such as the phenolics, which set-up under alkaline conditions.

The pure resins are colorless; hence molding powders can be produced in light, pastel shades. These plastics are also odorless and tasteless. Melamine is more costly than urea, but the properties of melamine moldings are superior to those from urea for many applications. Melamine resins combined with α-cellulose filler produce translucent moldings which are considerably harder and more heat- and chemical-resistant. However, unlike the urea plastics, they do not require α-cellulose for strength; asbestos filler is therefore advantageously used for maximum heat resistance. Absorption of water by melamine molding resin is one half to one third that of urea resin. For short periods of time, urea-formaldehyde molded parts will stand temperatures as high as 120°C, but cannot be used at temperatures above about 85°C continuously, since discoloration and loss of translucence and strength occur. Melamine-formaldehyde resins are better in this respect and will withstand temperatures well above 100°C continuously. Thus, melamine molding compounds are especially useful in those applications where urea resins fail or reach the limit of their usefulness; e.g., for domestic appliances and for lamp sockets, automobile distributor caps, and similar articles which are continuously exposed to temperatures in the neighborhood of 100°C or which have exceptional requirements with regard to water resistance and surface hardness. Melamine moldings are more suitable for tableware, for in addition to the advantages already mentioned, they are less readily stained by beverages, possess a glossier appearance, and can be washed without damage in automatic dishwashers.

The first use of melamine resins in the United States was in the production of laminated materials, particularly for light-colored surface sheets which are bonded to phenolic bases and for the hot bonding of plywood. They are used as impregnants to impart high wet strength to paper cartons. As little as 3 per cent melamine resin incorporated in a paper pulp results in a paper whose wet strength is nearly as great as its dry strength. There is no accompanying embrittling effect and the fold resistance may be increased several hundred per cent.

Melamine resins suitable for use as adhesives may be obtained by methods similar to those employed in the case of urea adhesives. Melamine and formaldehyde in a 1:2 or 1:3 ratio, for example, may be condensed at 80°C under neutral conditions to the desired water tolerance, then concentrated under reduced pressure to yield a viscous, liquid adhesive of limited stability or spray-dried to give a more stable powder. These adhesives may be hardened by hot pressing alone or, more rapidly, in conjunction with acidic hardeners, to form wood bonds which retain their strength even after long immersion in boiling water. Both organic and inorganic extenders may be used for the same purpose with melamine as with urea adhesives. Melamine adhesives are not suitable for cold-pressing applications, because they harden only slowly, even in the presence of strong acids, at temperatures below about 50°C.

Lower alkyl ethers (especially the methyl) of methylol melamines are widely used for the shrinkproofing of wool. Diammonium acid phosphate is employed as a catalyst to cause polymerization of the resin intermediate after application to the fabric. These resins have also been utilized abroad for several years as textile finishing agents, especially in the manufacture of crease-resistant fabrics. Fabrics treated with urea or melamine resin, together with a reactive, hydrophobic group, become durably water repellent. Melamine resins have also been applied to leather in the monomeric form and subsequently polymerized after penetration into the skin.

Melamine-formaldehyde coating resins may be prepared by methods similar to those described for urea coating resins. In both cases, temperature and pH have to be carefully controlled, due to the tendency for condensation of methylol groups to take place more rapidly than the etherification of these groups. Melamine-formaldehyde ratios of 1:3.5 to as high as 1:6 are used in the preparation of these resins.

Although more expensive than the corresponding urea resins, melamine coating resins are in many ways superior. The colorless, transparent liquids are appreciably less viscous than urea resins of the same solid content. In addition, they have a greater compatibility with hydrocarbon solvents, are more rapidly cured, and yield films having considerably better heat, water, and chemical resistance. The nontracking and excellent insulating properties of their films, coupled with their excellent heat and oil resistance, make them valuable in the formulation of varnishes for electrical equipment.

As with the urea coating resins, melamine coating resins alone form brittle films having poor adhesion and must be plasticized, preferably with an oil-modified alkyd resin. Melamine resins, however, require about twice as much alkyd to give films of hardness, adhesion, and flexibility comparable to those obtained with urea resins.

Although melamine finishes cure much more rapidly than urea finishes at temperatures above about 80°C, they are very slow to harden at room temperature.   Considerably more catalyst is required and, even so, the time required to produce a hard, marproof surface is unduly long.   As a consequence, they are seldom used in air-drying finishes.

### Aniline-Formaldehyde Resins

Strictly speaking, the foregoing aminoplasts are not amines but are amides or amidines.   True amines, such as aniline, do react with formaldehyde, but the process of resinification is fundamentally different.

A number of commercial plastics of limited importance are based on the condensation of aniline and formaldehyde.   This condensation, like that of phenol and formaldehyde, depends both upon the pH of the reaction mixture and the aniline-formaldehyde ratio.   Under neutral or slightly acid conditions, formaldehyde reacts with the amino group only, probably first forming $N$-methylol aniline or azomethine (Schiff base) products, with eventual formation of a cyclic trimer and a linear polymer.

Under strongly acid conditions, on the other hand, both the amino group and the $o$- and $p$-hydrogen atoms are attacked.   If the aniline-formaldehyde ratio is 1:2, the primary chains formed are cross-linked by $p$-methylene bridges, the excess formaldehyde also forming $o$-methylene bridges.   These reactions are summarized by the following chart:[4]

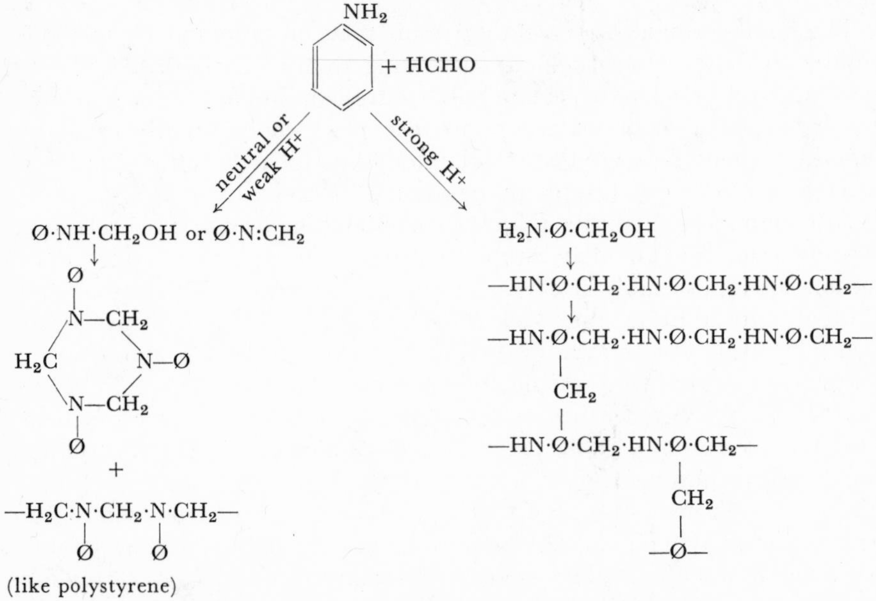

(Ø represents the variously substituted benzene ring)

[4] Adapted from Ritchie, P. D., *A Chemistry of Plastics and High Polymers*, p. 126, Cleaver-Hume Press, London (dist. by Interscience Publishers, New York), 1949.

When only one mole of formaldehyde is condensed with one mole of aniline in acid solution, the resin formed is fusible and soluble. As the proportion of formaldehyde is increased, the resin becomes more insoluble and infusible. Thus, a condensation product can be produced which is practically insoluble and can be molded readily; however, high temperatures are required. Fillers are not ordinarily used.

Since most aniline-formaldehyde resins are made from equimolecular amounts of aniline and formaldehyde, they exhibit typical thermoplastic properties. The pure resin is translucent and of a reddish-brown color. It is unaffected by alkalies and is insoluble in the common organic solvents; however, it is not resistant to strong acids. Moisture or oil absorption is negligible.

Since the resin has good electrical properties, it is useful as an insulating medium in high-frequency electrical fields. Often used to replace mica, ceramics, phenolics, or polystyrene, the aniline-formaldehyde resins (Cibanite) are of value because of their low power factor, high dielectric strength, mechanical strength, inertness to moisture, and ease of machining. Such applications as coil forms, antenna housings, and tube bases are important. Terminal boards, strips, and blocks are other applications for which the material is especially suitable, in these cases because of its low conductivity in the presence of moisture.

## Miscellaneous Aminoplasts

Guanidine (imino urea) reacts with formaldehyde to give resinous products. Guanidine resins have not, so far, been used commercially to any appreciable extent, although references have been made in the literature to their use as modifiers for urea resins in certain processes.

Urea has been reacted with other aldehydes, notably acetaldehyde, acrolein, and furfural. However, so far as is known, these materials are not made commercially.

The use of thiourea with formaldehyde to produce a resin has already been mentioned. However, so far as is known, thiourea resins are not used alone but only in combination with urea or other resins where they impart better curing properties and enhanced water resistance to the products. The early urea-thiourea powders were eventually replaced with the present rapid curing urea powders. The advent of melamine-based molding powders has provided a material with water resistance comparable with that of the original urea-thiourea compositions and without the drawbacks associated with these compositions, particularly the staining of steel molds and lack of heat stability during molding at temperatures higher than about 135°C. Mixed urea-thiourea aqueous syrups are still employed on a limited scale for laminating purposes because of their self-curing properties and stability during the early stages of condensation.

The guanamine-type resins have recently been developed for use as supplements to both melamine and urea resins. The most promising members of the group are the methyl, phenyl, and benzyl guanamines, and the halogenated phenyl guanamines. A large amount of research has been carried out, principally in the United States and Great Britain, on polytriazoles and poly(amino triazoles). Work has also been performed on the synthesis of polypeptides, which form the basis for the natural proteins. It is probable that commercially useful products will eventually be developed from some of these compounds.

### Sulfonamide-Formaldehyde Resins

Saccharin has obtained widespread recognition as a noncaloric substitute for sugar. During the synthesis of this material from toluene via $o$-toluene sulfonamide, $p$-toluene sulfonamide accumulates as a by-product. In order to decrease the cost of production of saccharin, much research has been carried out to find technical uses for the $p$-sulfonamide. One of the most promising fields has been that of the synthetic resins when it was found that, by condensing $p$-toluene sulfonamide with formaldehyde in equimolecular proportions, a semisolid, viscous mass was obtained which set to a hard, colorless resin upon heating to 110°C.

These resins are believed to form by the following general sequence:

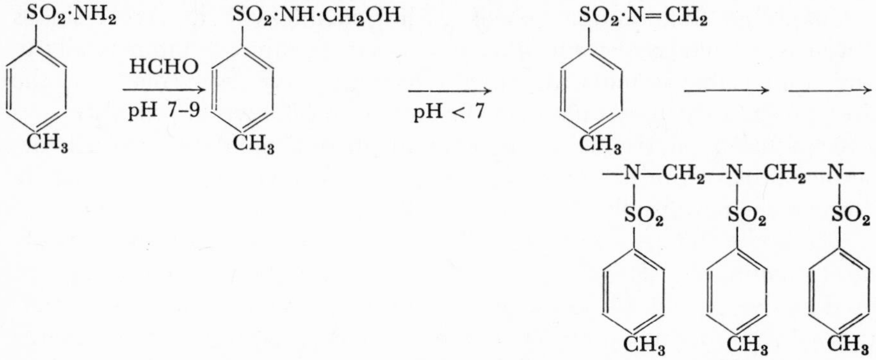

The functionality of the sulfonamide group can be limited by alkylation. Thus, an $N$-alkyl sulfonamide can form only monofunctional $N$-methylol derivatives, which by themselves are incapable of forming resinous products but are useful as plasticizers (Santicizers).

To date, only thermoplastic sulfonamide resins are commercial articles (Santolites). They range in color from light yellow to water white. They are insoluble in water and aqueous acids but dissolve in alkalies accompanied by slow decomposition. They are soluble in most organic solvents, except aliphatic hydrocarbons and fatty oils, and are compatible with poly(vinyl acetate) and shellac as well as with the cellulose derivatives.

Sulfonamide-formaldehyde resins exhibit excellent adhesive properties and have been used in the manufacture of laminated safety glass where their stability to light is also an advantage. Combined with cellulose acetate, they increase the latter's retentivity of plasticizers and reduce exudation of plasticizer from acetate films. They can also be used to improve the hardness and water resistance of cellulose nitrate films as well as the flexibility and toughness of ethyl cellulose. The sulfonamide resins are also used with cellulose nitrate or other resins in the production of heat-sealing lacquers.

The possibility of using polysulfonamides as fiber-forming materials has been considered; however, these compounds are alkali-soluble and are not likely to form linear polymers of good crystallinity. Copolymers have been made, but there is yet no commercial product containing the sulfonamide group on the market.

## POLYESTERS

### Saturated Polyesters

When $\omega$-hydroxy acids are heated or when a dibasic acid reacts with a dihydric alcohol, both being of sufficient chain length, the product is a linear polyester which, in the latter case, may be terminated by either carboxyl or hydroxyl groups, or both, depending upon the ratio of the reactants. Polyfunctional acids and alcohols, on the other hand, react to form eventually cross-linked, three-dimensional esters. There is, therefore, a marked difference between polyesters prepared from bifunctional reactants only and those made from polyfunctional intermediates. The former possess linear structures which are permanently thermoplastic, unless the presence of unsaturated bonds or other reactive groups allows cross-linking to occur by addition polymerization, oxidation, or vulcanization.

Relatively few linear polyesters are produced commercially. A number of balsamlike materials, based on phthalic, succinic, and sebacic acids, are available as plasticizers for cellulose nitrate, various elastomers, and other resins (Paraplex). Some are also used to a limited extent in caulking compounds and adhesives.

It was discovered in 1942 that saturated polyesters having low softening temperatures could be compounded with pigments and, surprisingly, cured with peroxides to form elastomeric masses. For example, a saturated polyester made from sebacic acid and a mixture of propylene and ethylene glycols and with a molecular weight of approximately 20,000 has an elongation of over 500 per cent. However, the tensile strength and elongation after aging at 150°C are too low to be usable. By including small amounts (3 to 5 per cent) of maleic anhydride or fumaric acid in the polyester, more reactive polymers are obtained which can be cured with smaller amounts of peroxide. Such vulcanizable polyesters, originally designated Paracon and later known as Paraplex rubbers, were produced on a pilot-plant scale for several years during World War II.

Outstanding characteristics of the polyester elastomers are their stability on exposure to high temperatures, oxidation, and weathering; their resistance to hydrocarbon solvents; and their excellent low-temperature flexibility without plasticizers. Their range of service temperature is much wider than that of the butadiene copolymers but not so wide as that of the silicones. Their resistance to water is good up to about 60°C, but in steam the cured polyesters disintegrate quickly. Their electrical properties are similar to those of neoprene or of plasticized poly(vinyl chloride). They are no longer commercially available.

It is in the field of synthetic fibers that the use of saturated polyesters has recently grown rapidly. As fiber-forming polycondensates, polyesters were the earliest class to be discovered; the aliphatic polyesters formed the basis of much of the research of Carothers and co-workers during the years 1928 to 1932. When it was realized that, for fiber formation, very high-molecular-weight polymers were required, polyesters of the requisite molecular weights were first obtained by direct condensation and prolonged heating in a molecular still so as to force the reaction to the required extent. It was soon realized that satisfactory products could be produced under less drastic conditions by heating under conditions such that water was removed; e.g., by bubbling a dry, inert gas through the molten reaction mass. Examples of fiber-forming aliphatic polyesters first prepared by Carothers and Hill are poly(trimethylene hexadecamethylene dicarboxylate), poly(ethylene succinate), poly($\omega$-hydroxy decanoate), poly($\omega$-hydroxy pentadecanoate), and poly(ethylene sebacate).

These same investigators showed that condensates having terminal —$CO_2CH_2CH_2OH$ groups (i.e., prepared with an excess of glycol) can continue to polymerize by a process of ester interchange, glycol being evolved:

$$2(-R \cdot COO \cdot CH_2 \cdot CH_2 \cdot OH) \rightarrow$$
$$-R \cdot COO \cdot CH_2 \cdot CH_2 \cdot OOC \cdot R- + HO \cdot CH_2 \cdot CH_2 \cdot OH$$

It thus became evident that, unlike polyamide manufacture, a balanced system was not required; the use of excess glycol has subsequently proved to be of great value in the production of poly(ethylene terephthalate).

The early polyesters made in the United States suffered, as fiber-forming materials, from two defects: (1) They were too readily hydrolyzed and lacked the chemical stability characteristics of nylon, and (2) their softening temperatures were too low to withstand ironing.   Carothers then devoted the major portion of his efforts to polyamides, a course which resulted in the development of nylon.   British research chemists, however, after studying the published works of Carothers, decided to investigate more fully the possibilities of polyesters.

Because of their low softening temperatures and poor resistance to hydrolysis, the *aliphatic* polyesters have achieved no technical importance for making synthetic fibers.   The work of the English investigators led to the discovery of higher melting and more resistant polyesters based upon symmetrical *aromatic* dicarboxylic acids.   Many aromatic polyesters have now been prepared and characterized; the products are high melting, crystalline, and fiber forming if they are based upon $\alpha$, $\omega$-glycols and symmetrical, aromatic dicarboxylic acids.   The work resulted in 1943 in the discovery of a fiber now known in England as Terylene (Melinex for film).

In 1946, the United States patent application on the polymer and fiber produced therefrom was purchased by an American company.   Before the fiber was trade-marked Dacron, it was temporarily called Fiber V. Extruded sheeting is known in this country as Mylar and photographic-film base as Cronar.

Poly(ethylene terephthalate) is, at present, the only fiber- and film-forming saturated polyester of commercial importance.   The manufacturing method used involves: (1) Esterification (methylation) of terephthalic acid, (2) ester interchange between the resultant dimethyl terephthalate and an excess of ethylene glycol, yielding a mixture of bis($\beta$-hydroxyethyl)terephthalate and low-molecular-weight polymers having terminal $\beta$-hydroxyethyl ester groups, and (3) heating of the condensate under vacuum to effect removal of glycol and to form a high-molecular-weight product.

Until required for the manufacture of poly(ethylene terephthalate), terephthalic acid was unavailable commercially, but the development of this polymer has caused considerable attention to be given to its synthesis. During the development work in England, the terephthalic acid was prepared by the two-stage oxidation of $p$-cymene.   Present production is principally based upon the oxidation of $p$-dialkyl benzenes.   Among the many routes to the free acid or its esters, the following either are commercial or are being actively investigated for their commercial possibilities: (1) Oxidation of $p$-xylene in two stages, using nitric acid; (2) oxidation of $p$-xylene in two stages, using air for the first-stage, liquid-phase oxidation, then nitric acid for the more difficult second stage; (3)

$$CO_2H$$

$$CO_2H$$

$$CH_3OH \qquad\qquad\text{Esterification}$$

$$CO_2 \cdot CH_3$$

$$CO_2 \cdot CH_3$$

$$CH_3OH \quad (CH_2OH)_2 \qquad\qquad\text{Ester interchange}$$

$$CO_2 \cdot CH_2 \cdot CH_2OH$$

$$CO_2 \cdot CH_2 \cdot CH_2OH$$

$$(CH_2OH)_2$$

$$-O \cdot (CH_2)_2 \cdot O_2C \cdot \varnothing \cdot CO_2 \cdot (CH_2)_2 \cdot O_2C \cdot \varnothing \cdot CO_2-$$

air oxidation of toluene to form benzoic acid which is converted to its potassium salt, then disproportionation between two moles of the salt to yield benzene and potassium terephthalate; (4) oxidation of $p$-xylene in a one-step process, using a heavy-metal catalyst activated by bromine; (5) one-step oxidation of $p$-diisopropyl benzene in the liquid phase by nitric acid or by a cobalt-catalyzed air oxidation; and (6) liquid-phase air oxidation of $p$-xylene to form toluic acid, then liquid-phase air oxidation of the methyl ester of toluic acid to yield the monomethyl ester of terephthalic acid, which can then be converted either to the free acid or the dimethyl ester. Still other routes have been proposed. The reasons for the many processes are, of course, both legal and economic; i.e., to avoid using a patented process, to utilize available raw materials, to use the cheapest raw material, to use the cheapest process, or a combination of the above.

Purification of the free acid is quite difficult because of its high melting point and general insolubility. One solution to this problem consists in converting the crude acid to its dimethyl ester, which can easily be purified by vacuum distillation or by recrystallization from a solvent or by a combination of both processes.    Esterification is accomplished by heating with methanol in the presence of a mineral acid.

The other intermediate, ethylene glycol, has been produced on a large scale for many years.    One process involves the treatment of ethylene (obtained from the cracking of petroleum) with chlorine water (HOCl) to give aqueous ethylene chlorohydrin which is then heated with a mild alkali to yield the glycol.    An alternative process involves the catalytic oxidation of ethylene to form ethylene oxide, which is subsequently hydrated to the glycol.

Ester interchange occurs upon heating the dimethyl ester with more than two equivalents of the glycol, the reaction being accelerated by a catalyst. The reaction mixture is heated to about 195°C, the methanol formed is removed by distillation as it is formed, and heating is continued until ester interchange is complete.    At this stage, the hot condensate is a colorless liquid and is purified by pressure filtration.    Further condensation is then brought about by raising the temperature of the stirred mass to about 280°C and reducing the pressure to less than one mm Hg, during which time most of the excess glycol is evolved.    Heating is continued for several hours until the desired degree of condensation is obtained.    The reactor used is usually of stainless steel, fitted with a good agitator, and designed so that a good vacuum may be drawn.

The molten polymer, a clear, pale-yellow liquid of high viscosity, is discharged through a heated valve in the bottom of the reactor by applying nitrogen pressure after the vacuum is released.    The cooled melt is formed into a ribbon which, like Nylon 66, is cut into small pieces. Unlike nylon, however, poly(ethylene terephthalate) is amorphous as it comes from the reactor and retains its amorphous form upon rapid cooling.    Crystallization occurs upon reheating, and the polymer then loses its transparent, glassy appearance, turning opaque and white or pale cream in color.    The crystalline polymer is a tough, white, opaque solid which melts at 249°C.    It is insoluble in most organic solvents.

The polymer is converted to filaments by melt spinning, as is nylon, but any trace of absorbed water must be removed prior to fusion, else hydrolysis and consequent decrease in molecular weight will occur.    The fibers are stretched about 400 per cent to yield a highly oriented material. Fine fibers may be advantageously stretched hot; however, coarse fibers, owing to their poor thermal conductivity, have to be stretched cold.

Dacron has excellent resistance to degradation by bleaches and common solvents.    Resistance to weak acids and alkalies is good even at boiling temperatures; to strong acids, it is good in the cold; resistance to strong alkalies is not as good.    Most alcohols, ketones, soaps, detergents, and dry-cleaning agents have no effect on Dacron; however, trifluoroacetic acid and various phenolic substances will dissolve it.

Fig. 8-9.   Dacron tow being fed from 20-odd cans is on its way to the drawing machine.
*(Courtesy E. I. duPont de Nemours and Co.)*

In many respects the yarn bears a close resemblance to nylon.  It is strong; resistant to bacteria, mildew, and moths; and can be made dimensionally stable at high temperatures.  It has a very low moisture absorption and its wet strength is almost as good as its dry strength.  It is superior to nylon in that it is not severely degraded by the action of light.

Blends of cotton with Dacron are widely used in women's blouses, dresses, and men's shirts. Dacron is used in upholstery, in fiber form as a filling for pillows, and in suits in place of wool. Since Dacron is virtually insensitive to moisture, its use in suits for summer wear under conditions of high humidity is very desirable.

Dacron's high resistance to degradation by heat and its good chemical resistance has caused it to be widely adopted for use in such fabrics as sailcloths, curtains, upholstery, tapes, webbings, work clothing, and as filter cloths in chemical industry.

Compared with wool, Dacron suffers from three disadvantages: (1) Whereas wool will absorb up to 30 per cent moisture and still feel dry to the touch, Dacron becomes saturated with perspiration at a moisture content below 1 per cent; (2) unlike wool, Dacron fabrics "wick," so that rain is quickly transferred from the outside to the interior of a garment; and (3) Dacron has a very low heat of wetting. (Wool and other protein fibers give off heat upon wetting and this is believed to help keep the wearer of such a garment warm.)

In addition to ethylene glycol, the higher homologous $\alpha,\omega$-alkylene glycols have been condensed with terephthalic acid or its dimethyl ester, giving a series of polyesters, all crystalline and fiber forming but having lower softening temperatures; none of these polymers is, at present, of commercial importance. As a matter of fact, substitution of other glycols or other dibasic acids results in products which are, in general, lower melting than that from ethylene glycol and terephthalic acid. The same is true of copolyesters.

*Linear Polycarbonates*

A very recent development in the field of condensation polymers has been the synthesis of organic polycarbonates. Research was reported to have begun both in Germany and the United States in 1953, and experimental products were announced in 1957 in both countries.

The most general reaction for the formation of an organic carbonate is that between an alcohol and carbonyl chloride (phosgene):

$$2ROH + COCl_2 \longrightarrow R_2CO_3 + 2HCl$$

To form a polymeric product, the alcohol (or phenol) must, of course, be at least bifunctional. A large number of polycarbonates have been made in the laboratory, using a variety of bifunctional alcohols and phenols. Easily made bisphenols, such as Bisphenol A (see Epoxy Resins), are being favored for development work. By treating such a compound in the presence of caustic soda or an organic base (pyridine, quaternary ammonium compound, etc.) with phosgene or an alkyl or aryl carbonate, a polycarbonate is formed. (Cf. the only other carbonate monomer now produced, diethylene glycol bis(allyl carbonate), under Linear Unsaturated Polyester Resins.)

$$n\,NaO\!\!\begin{array}{c}CH_3\\|\\C\\|\\CH_3\end{array}\!\!ONa + n\,COCl_2 \longrightarrow (-O\!\!\begin{array}{c}CH_3\\|\\C\\|\\CH_3\end{array}\!\!\begin{array}{c}O\\||\\O\cdot C\!-\!)_n\end{array} + 2n\,NaCl$$

Another recently reported method of preparation is by the use of organo-titanium complexes as catalysts with self-condensing biscarbonates by a transesterification process; e.g., *p*-xylyene glycol bis(ethyl carbonate) in the presence of titanium butoxide:

$$n\ \ \begin{array}{c}O\\||\\CH_2\cdot O\cdot C\cdot O\cdot CH_2CH_3\\ \\ \\ \\CH_2\cdot O\cdot C\cdot O\cdot CH_2CH_3\\||\\O\end{array} \xrightarrow{Ti(OBu)_4} \left[\begin{array}{c}CH_2\cdot O-\\ \\ \\ \\CH_2\cdot O\cdot C-\\||\\O\end{array}\right]_n + n(CH_3CH_2)_2CO_3$$

Note that these products are the diesters of carbonic acid and contain the carbonate linkage:

$$\begin{array}{c}O\\||\\-O-C-O-\end{array}$$

The polycarbonates made thus far are colorless, transparent solids, having varying degrees of crystallinity and softening between 150° and 300°C (Lexan). They are reported to have low gas permeabilities and good electrical and mechanical properties. For example, the heat distortion temperature of one product at 264 psi is 140°C—exceeded only by the phenolic resins. Further, the impact strength is reported to be unusually high. Although these polymers are attacked by alkalies, they are resistant to acids and strong oxidizing agents.

Current interest is in producing film, particularly for electrical insulating uses. Other possible applications of the polymer are for electrical coil forms, electronic components, and as a replacement for metal (bronze) die-cast gears and bushings.

### Unsaturated Polyesters

*Polymerized Oils*

Useful vulcanizable materials are derivable from polymerized drying oil acids. If more than one unsaturated fatty acid occurs in a triglyceride, bridges to neighboring molecules may be formed by suitable reactions. When three points of unsaturation are present in the molecules, three-dimensional polymers are formed as insoluble, coherent masses. Such reactions have been known for a long time. They occur in the drying of linseed and other oils and also in the preparation of factice.

The term "factice" (often called "rubber substitute") is used for certain semi-elastic materials which are sometimes mixed with rubber during the manufacture of rubber goods to lower the cost of the product and to confer upon it certain properties. Erasers, for example, are prepared with the addition of factice. White factice, a solid, insoluble substance, is obtained by the action of sulfur monochloride on oils, chiefly castor. The reaction is similar to cold vulcanization of rubber. Brown factice is obtained from half-dried or dried oils by the action of sulfur at 140° to 160°C. This reaction is comparable to the heat vulcanization of rubber.

It is a well-known fact that drying oils through which air is bubbled will absorb oxygen and become more viscous. This is also true of heat-bodied oils. The rise in viscosity indicates an increase in molecular weight. After long exposure to air, linseed and some other oils become insoluble. If oil paints are spread out in thin layers, an insoluble, durable film is formed. Similarly, linoleum is made by the oxidation of linseed oil compounded with sawdust and other fillers.

The reactants in the above examples are highly unsaturated fatty acids (or their esters), which are principally linoleic (9,12-octadecadienoic) acid and linolenic (9,12,15-octadecatrienoic) acid in linseed oil (nonconjugated) and $\alpha$- and $\beta$-eleostearic (9,11,13-octadecatrienoic) acids in tung oil (conjugated). When linseed oil is heated, migration of some of the double bonds occurs to form a conjugated system and, as a result, the oil becomes more reactive.

*Oxidative* polymerization is believed to occur[5] by a complex series of reactions. The exact mechanisms are not yet known, but there is general agreement in the field of oil oxidation that the first product of the reaction, associated with the increase in the size of the molecule, is a peroxide. The most recent views concerning the initial reaction favor the formation of a hydroperoxide. The theory has been advanced that an oil oxidation mechanism is a function of a free radical reaction.

The following hypothesis for the mechanism for hydroperoxide formation has been put forth. The original entrance of oxygen into the unsaturated system occurs at the double bond, resulting in the formation of an unstable complex, which in effect loosens the attachment of one of the hydrogen atoms on an adjacent methylene group. This structure then rearranges to form a hydroperoxide and reform the double bond elsewhere:

$$-CH{:}CH{\cdot}CH_2{\cdot}CH{:}CH- \xrightarrow{O_2} -CH{\cdot}CH{\cdot}CH{\cdot}CH{:}CH- \rightarrow -CH{\cdot}CH{:}CH{\cdot}CH{:}CH- $$
$$\underset{O-O}{} \quad \underset{H}{} \qquad \underset{OOH}{}$$

[5] Hess, P. S. and O'Hare, G. A., *Ind. Eng. Chem.*, **42**, 1424 (1950).

This hydroperoxidic structure under favorable conditions should be capable of a diene-type polymerization because of the conjugation.

According to some investigators, oxidative polymerization occurs by the interaction of these hydroperoxide groups and double bonds. It is believed that this reaction occurs between a hydroperoxide group in one molecule and either a double bond in another molecule or a remote double bond in the same molecule to give mainly dimerides of the ether type [—C(OR)·C(OH)—]. However, because of the presence of the hydroperoxide, it is also conceivable that the near double bond is in a highly activated state and consequently intramolecular addition may occur at this point. Subsequent rearrangement might lead to the following possible intermediate structure:

$$-CH \cdot CH{:}CH \cdot CH{:}CH- \rightarrow -CH \cdot CH{:}C \cdot CH_2 \cdot CH_2-$$

$$\underset{OOH}{|} \qquad\qquad \underset{\substack{O \quad HO \\ (-) \quad (+)}}{\overset{\parallel \quad |}{}}$$

The hydrogen bond of this chelated structure is labile and, therefore, other resonance forms are possible. Accordingly, in an oxidative polymerization, products similar to the following may be formed by hydrogen bonding:

$$\underset{CH_3(CH_2)_nC{:}O...HO \cdot C \cdot (CH_2)_nCOO \cdot CH_2}{\overset{CH_2 \cdot OOC(CH_2)_nCH_2 \cdot C \cdot OH...O{:}C \cdot (CH_2)_nCH_3}{}}$$

In summary, then, the chemistry of oxidative polymerization in the early stages of the reaction may consist of three fundamental steps: hydroperoxide formation; hydroperoxide consumption, followed principally by an intramolecular arrangement to an intermediate; an association of intermediates to form higher-molecular-weight products.

Other research has shown that an hydroxyl group may be formed during the oxidation of an oil. Thus, the polymerization of fatty acids upon oxidation may be due to an esterification of an hydroxyl group of one acid with the carboxyl of another:

$$-CH_2 \cdot CH(CH_2)_nCOOH \xrightarrow{\;-H_2O\;} -CH_2 \cdot CH(CH_2)_nCOOH$$

$$\underset{OH \; H:OOC(CH_2)_nCH_3}{|} \qquad\qquad \underset{OOC(CH_2)_nCH_3}{|}$$

*Thermal* treatment[6] of natural drying oils involves the creation of poly-

[6] See Wheeler, D. H., *Ind. Eng. Chem.*, **41**, 252 (1949); Bradley, T. F. and Tess, R. W., *ibid.*, 310.

basic acid esters by addition polymerization of the unsaturated fatty acid radicals. Disagreement exists, however, with respect to the mechanisms of the double-bond reactions. Presently favored is a 1,2-1,4 addition mechanism (Diels-Alder reaction), even for nonconjugated dienes, since, as indicated earlier, thermal isomerization to the conjugated form is believed to occur. This may be a principal reaction, but it is certain that others occur also.

Based upon various physical and chemical properties of fractions obtained by molecular distillation, thermal polymerization has been tentatively formulated as follows, using methyl linoleate as an example:

$$
\begin{array}{cccc}
\text{CH}_3 & \text{CH}_3 & \text{CH}_3 & \text{CH}_3 \\
| & | & | & | \\
(\text{CH}_2)_5 & (\text{CH}_2)_5 & (\text{CH}_2)_5 & (\text{CH}_2)_5 \\
| & | \quad (\text{CH}_2)_5\text{CH}_3 & | \quad (\text{CH}_2)_5\text{CH}_3 & | \\
\text{CH} & \text{CH} & \text{CH} & \text{CH} \\
\| & \text{CH} \quad \text{CH} & \text{CH} \quad \text{CH} & \text{CH} \quad \text{CH} \\
\text{CH} & \| \quad | & \| & \\
\text{CH} & \rightarrow \text{CH} \quad \text{CH—CH} & \rightarrow \text{CH} \quad \text{CH} & \text{CH} \quad \text{CH} \\
\| & \text{CH} \quad \text{CH} & \text{CH} & \text{CH} \\
\text{CH} & | \quad | & | & \\
(\text{CH}_2)_7 & (\text{CH}_2)_7 \quad (\text{CH}_2)_7 & (\text{CH}_2)_7 & (\text{CH}_2)_7 \quad (\text{CH}_2)_7 \\
| & | \quad | & | & | \quad | \\
\text{C:O} & \text{C:O} \quad \text{C:O} & \text{C:O} & \text{C:O} \quad \text{C:O} \\
| & | \quad | & | & | \quad | \\
\text{O·CH}_3 & \text{O·CH}_3 \quad \text{O·CH}_3 & \text{O·CH}_3 & \text{O·CH}_3 \quad \text{O·CH}_3 \\
\text{Monomer} & \text{Dimer} & \text{Trimer} &
\end{array}
$$

Reactions of this type apply to soya bean, linseed, tung, dehydrated castor, and other drying oils. The acids and esters obtained by polymerizations of vegetable oils may, since they contain more than one carboxyl group, serve for the production of polyesters by condensation with glycols, and, since such polyesters are still unsaturated, they may be vulcanized by heating with sulfur and accelerators, and indeed can be polymerized and cross-linked by heat alone. There can thus be obtained, from vegetable oils, products superior in strength and extensibility to factice and, in fact, possessing rubberlike properties sufficient to render them useful as rubber substitutes.

During the period 1942–43, considerable effort was devoted to the development of such products. When polyesters were prepared by the condensation of the dimeric acids or methyl esters of soya bean oil with ethylene glycol, there were obtained, by further polymerization followed by sulfur vulcanization, elastic materials. The work was centered at the Northern Regional Research Laboratory of the United States Department of Agriculture; hence, the products were termed Norepols. It was demonstrated that various elastomeric articles having a reasonable degree of usefulness could be made from these polymers, but no extensive commercial development followed, because soya bean oil was allocated to food uses.

A limited quantity of the Norepols was actually manufactured and used in the manufacture of jar rings, floor tile, washers, and rubberized cloth. The products showed good retention of elastic properties at subzero temperatures. They were not resistant to petroleum solvents and oils but were unaffected by alcohol and water. Their tensile strength was considerably less than that of rubber and their elongation was not as good. For some mechanical applications, such as packings and glass-jar rings, however, their properties were sufficiently satisfactory. For such uses, they played a minor but significant role during the rubber shortage.

In further experimental work, it was shown that the dimeric fatty acids could be condensed to yield vulcanizable polymers with other glycols, amino alcohols, diisocyanates, and diamines. The first resins prepared from these dibasic acids and diamines were termed Norelacs because they, too, originated at the Northern Regional Research Laboratories. They are now referred to as polyamide resins (Versamids) and were commercially introduced in 1947.

Two basic types are now manufactured. One is a condensation product of thermally polymerized dibasic acids with ethylene diamine. The other is obtained by the condensation of the dibasic acids with diethylene triamine. The sources of these dibasic acids are vegetable oils, such as soya bean, cottonseed, and corn, which contain a relatively large quantity of linoleic acid. Either the acids or the methyl esters may be dimerized by heat to provide the desired dibasic acids.

Most of the uses of these resins involve the formation of thin films. Polyamide resin films are very glossy and are unusually flexible, even without plasticization. Their moisture-vapor-transmission resistance is excellent. In addition, the films are extremely resistant to grease, alkalies, dilute acids, oils, and solvents. One of their outstanding properties is their ability to form strong bonds under the application of heat; thus, the nonblocking resins are used as heat-sealing adhesives for bonding a wide variety of surfaces and as water-vapor-resistant coatings for paper, plastic films, and metal foils. They have also shown promise as adhesive bonding resins for cloth, leather, cork, metal foils, cellophane, wood, and certain plastics; as protective and decorative coatings; as binders for wood flour, sawdust, paper pulp, cork, leather, and textile fibers; as coatings for textiles; and as finishes, fillers, and base coatings for leather. One of their most recent successful uses is as a combined curing agent and plasticizer for epoxy resins.

*Alkyd Resins*

The term "alkyd" was coined by Kienle[7] to designate the resinous reaction products of di- and polyhydric alcohols and acids (al-cid). This implies that the term includes all thermoplastic and potentially thermosetting polyesters, both saturated and unsaturated. At the present time, the term also includes all modifications of such polyesters, in view of the fact that a large proportion of alkyd resins now made are modified in some way.

The first reported preparation of an alkyd was in 1847 when Berzelius in Sweden prepared glyceryl tartrate. It was not until 1901, however, that the Englishman, Smith, esterified glycerol with phthalic anhydride. He carried out a number of reactions between phthalic anhydride and glycerol, and obtained a series of glasslike products.

A few years later, Friedberg, in the United States, was retained by a large company to continue his investigation of this class of resins, in which he had become interested. The products of this research were known as Glyptals. Stimulated by this early work, the sponsoring company undertook a detailed investigation of these resins between 1910 and 1916.

Alkyd resins were first developed as bonding agents for mica flakes and were used for electrical insulating purposes. Early chemists had incorporated saturated fatty acids in alkyds, and in 1921 Kienle conceived the idea of modifying alkyds with drying oils, but it was not until three years later, when the same thought had then occurred to others, that he and Hovey began a series of investigations which, in 1933, resulted in the issuance of a broad patent[8] covering this field. This development was largely responsible for their phenomenal acceptance as surface coatings. When Kienle's patent was declared invalid in 1935, many others entered the alkyd production field and, as a result, there are today a large number of manufacturers.

Another important event of the 1920's was the discovery that both oil- and rosin-modified alkyd resins were compatible with cellulose nitrate, yielding surface coatings which showed improved adhesion and gloss retention. This development led to widespread acceptance of alkyd finishes by the automotive industry, first in combination with cellulose nitrate, then alone, and later in combination with aminoplasts.

By far the largest amount of alkyd resin produced is made from a combination of phthalic anhydride and glycerol. The tremendous popularity of phthalic alkyd resins and phthalic ester plasticizers is based upon the good properties of both the anhydride and its resins, and the relatively low cost of the anhydride. The low cost was made possible by the discovery by Gibbs and Conover during World War I that naphthalene

[7] Kienle, R. H., *Ind. Eng. Chem.*, **21**, 349 (1929).
[8] Kienle, R. H. (to General Electric Co.), U.S. Pat. **1,893,873** (Jan. 10, 1933).

in the vapor phase could be oxidized by air in high yield to give phthalic anhydride. Previous to that time, phthalic anhydride was little more than a specialty chemical. Phthalic anhydride is now also made in large quantities by the oxidation of $o$-xylene obtained from petroleum by hydroforming.

One good feature of phthalic anhydride for the manufacture of resins is that it is relatively stable to heat and light; it sublimes without decomposition and also resists decomposition by ultraviolet radiation, transmitting this quality to the resins made from it.

Glycerol (glycerine) was obtained for many years solely as a by-product of the splitting (saponification or hydrolysis) of fats and oils in the soap-making industry. Its price was dependent, to a large extent, upon the ups and downs of the soap industry. Now, however, glycerol is also obtained synthetically from propylene, and this second source, from an abundant petroleum supply, has helped materially to stabilize the price.

Glycerol and phthalic anhydride will react at a temperature of about 160°C or higher to form a liquid resinous product, which gradually increases in viscosity as heating continues until gelation suddenly occurs. When cooled, the product is hard, clear, and brittle, and is insoluble and infusible. A portion of the resin may be represented as shown in Fig. 8–10, although some secondary reactions also occur:

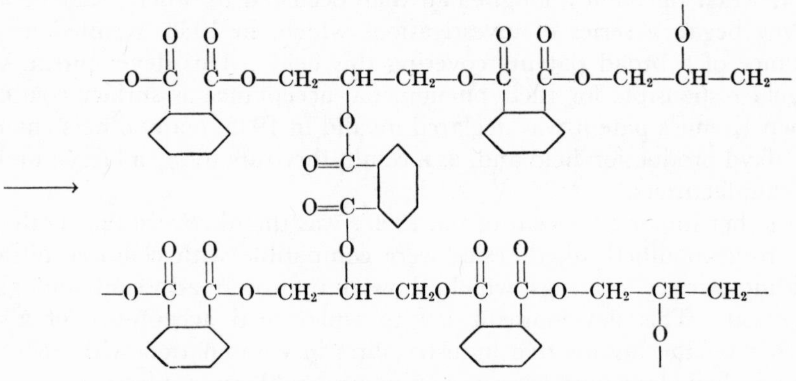

FIG. 8-10. Hypothetical portion of a cross-linked alkyd resin

In the first stage, normal chain growth proceeds predominantly by reaction of the more reactive primary hydroxyl groups of glycerol with the dicarboxylic acid present. When approximately one third of the free acid remains, esterification continues with a slow decrease of the acid content and production of the resin in the gelled or insoluble state. During the latter process, the effects of a slight increase in esterification are noticeable by the rapidity with which the molecular weight increases and with which the solubility and fusibility decrease as the amount of cross-linking increases.

Unmodified glyceryl phthalate resins have not been widely used industrially because of their poor solubility characteristics. Their original use as a bonding agent for mica has been mentioned, and there are certain other specialty uses for this type of alkyd in molding and casting (Catalin) applications. However, the field of use for *modified* alkyd resins is very large indeed—so large, in fact, that before the very recent development and tremendous growth of the vinyl-type polymers, the production of alkyd resins was rivaled only by phenolic resins among the synthetics. Thus, most alkyds are not only composed of di- and polyfunctional acids and alcohols, but they are also modified in diverse ways. Alkyd resins are usually modified with drying or nondrying oils and both natural and synthetic resins. In addition, more than one alcohol or acid may be used in the same alkyd resin to obtain special properties. Thus, the term "alkyd resin" includes a very wide variety of resinous products.

Due to the greater availability of polyhydric alcohols, almost all alkyds commercially manufactured are made from a dibasic acid and either a polyhydric alcohol or a mixture of dihydric and polyhydric alcohols. There may, of course, also be combinations of dibasic acids used; however, few polybasic acids are used commercially.

One fundamental purpose of modification is to alter somewhat the average functionality of the reactants so as to change the time of onset of cross-linking with respect to the extent of reaction. The plasticizing action of long-chain fatty acid modifiers is also of great value. Further, the unsaturation occurring in these modifiers, if fatty acids or oils are used, enables further cross-linking between molecules to occur when films laid down from a resin solution are exposed to the air and/or heat.

The majority of commercial resins, regardless of modification, are capable of being cured to form three-dimensional structures. The use of these modified resins in surface coatings, which is by far their largest use, in general depends upon arresting reaction just prior to gelation, at which point the polyester can still be dissolved in suitable solvents, with or without the addition of drying oils and pigments, to form a varnish or enamel. When laid down as a film, the solvent evaporates and the residual resin cures by thermal or oxidative polymerization to a cross-linked, insoluble form.

The most important group of resins which are generally designated by the term "alkyd resin" is the oil-modified, glyceryl phthalate type. They are the reaction products of glycerol and phthalic acid (phthalic anhydride), modified with drying, semidrying, or nondrying oils. The type of oil selected depends upon the conditions under which the film will be dried and the color-retention properties required. Air-drying alkyds are made with the good drying oils, such as linseed and dehydrated castor, but the semidrying soya bean oil may also be used in medium- and short-oil alkyds.

The utilization of drying oils represented a great advance in alkyd technology because the products not only possess solubility characteristics similar to those of the nondrying-oil modified alkyds, but they also yield hard films upon air drying. As a matter of fact, they air-dry more rapidly than the oils from which they are prepared. The dried films are tough and durable, weather well, and, in addition, possess high gloss, excellent adhesion, and good resistance to light, heat, and chemicals. The films may also be baked, whereupon they show even better characteristics.

Nondrying oils are used in making nondrying alkyds, which are not normally used to form a hard film alone. They are used principally in combination with aminoplasts, silicone resins, or cellulose nitrate lacquers as plasticizers. Because of their low degree of unsaturation, the nondrying alkyds have unusually good color retention.

The most important oils used to modify alkyds are soya bean, linseed, cottonseed, castor and dehydrated castor, tall, tung, and fish. Perilla, oiticica, sunflower, safflower, and walnut oils have been used in lesser amounts. Although alkyds modified with soya bean oil are somewhat slower drying than those prepared with tung, linseed, or dehydrated castor oils, nevertheless, the former oil is very widely used, yielding light-colored, low-cost varnishes. Most of the alkyd resins manufactured today for use in surface coatings are linseed oil- or soya bean oil-modified. Tung oil, in spite of its superior drying qualities by itself, is not very satisfactory as a modifier for alkyds because it is too reactive; low-acid-number resins can be prepared from it only with difficulty.

Oil-modified alkyd resins may be made from fatty acids, rather than from the fatty oils or glycerides. A large variety of fatty acids is commercially available at present for the manufacture of alkyd resins. Their use permits the production of resins having special properties, such as improved drying, better water resistance, or maximum color retention. This improvement of properties is not possible when the oils are used, because, as pointed out earlier, vegetable oils are mixed glycerides. For example, if alkali-refined linseed oil were used, the product would contain the usual percentages of oleic, linoleic, and linolenic acid radicals found in the original oil. However, if the oil were split and the fatty acids separated, they could be used to make three types of alkyd. That made with linolenic acid would dry rapidly, the one containing linoleic would be slow to dry, and the oleic acid alkyd would be nondrying. The degree of yellowing of these three alkyds, however, would be in inverse order.　The first would yellow appreciably with age, since linolenic acid is believed to be the major cause of yellowing of resins containing it.

The recovery of tall oil from the sulfate process for paper making is well known.　The fractionation of distilled tall oil has produced fatty acids having a very low rosin content, which are suitable for use in making alkyd resins; their production and consumption for this purpose are growing rapidly.

Varying amounts of monobasic acid or oil may be used in an alkyd resin.　The ratio of ingredients is expressed by the oil length or phthalic content of the resultant product.　An approximate classification is shown in Table 8-1.

TABLE 8-1.　CLASSIFICATION OF ALKYD RESINS

| Alkyd Resins | Phthalic Anhydride % | Fatty Acid or Oil % |
|---|---|---|
| Short oil length . | 40–50 | 30–40 |
| Medium oil length . | 30–40 | 40–50 |
| Long oil length . . | 20–30 | Over 50 |

Solubility of the oil-modified resins varies with oil length.　Greater compatibility with petroleum thinners and, therefore, reduced cost result from greater proportions of oil or fatty acid.　The long-oil resins are generally used for exterior applications, whereas medium- and short-oil resins are used principally for interior applications.　Since drying-oil-modified alkyd resins are excellent binders for pigments, most interior household enamels now use them for the vehicle portion of the coatings.

Although glycerol and phthalic anhydride are by far the most important fundamental components of commercial alkyds, many others are used. Maleic anhydride is the second most valuable dibasic acid intermediate, even though in the majority of maleic alkyds, maleic anhydride is not used as such but rather as its rosin adduct (see Chap. 7) or as a replacement for part of the phthalic.　Other dibasic acids used to some extent are fumaric, succinic, adipic, azelaic, and sebacic.　Alkyds based upon sebacic acid are particularly well known, as they find special use as plasticizers for finishes based on other resins.　They are also used in special caulking compounds and adhesives.　A recent addition to the list is isophthalic acid, which shows promise of conferring even better heat stability and weatherability to alkyd resins.　Other dibasic acids also used in smaller quantities are adducts of maleic anhydride with such doubly unsaturated compounds as cyclopentadiene and terpenes.　Monobasic acids, especially benzoic and *p-tert*-butyl benzoic, are sometimes used in small quantities to lower the average functionality of alkyd reactants.

Although glycerol is the most widely used polyhydric alcohol, several other alcohols are used, either alone or in combination. Pentaerythritol, a tetrahydric alcohol, is probably the second most popular polyol. Di- and tripentaerythritol are used to a small extent. Ethylene, diethylene, and propylene glycols are often used in conjunction with alcohols of higher functionality in order to lower the average functionality of the reactants. Trimethylol ethane and propane are newer commercially available trihydric alcohols and, in certain properties, show advantages over glycerol. Sorbitol and mannitol are hexahydric alcohols sometimes used. Although a high degree of reactivity and hard, fast-drying resins would be expected, they have four secondary hydroxyl groups, which increase the difficulty of esterification; they also tend to form inner ethers.

Alkyd resins are also frequently modified with other synthetic and modified natural resins. In some cases, this amounts only to a physical combination, as in the use of oil-modified alkyds in conjunction with cellulose nitrate, ethyl cellulose, and chlorinated rubber. In others, a chemical combination occurs, and the modifying resin, such as a silicone intermediate, may be chemically combined with the alkyd. Alkyds may by modified with modified natural resins, such as congo ester or ester gum, or with synthetic resins, such as the phenoplasts or aminoplasts. Resin modification usually produces faster drying times, and the phenolic modification also improves water and alkali resistance. Except for the aminoplasts, these doubly modified alkyds are darker in color than the straight oil-modified alkyds. Generally, the addition of such resins hardens the film obtained from the alkyd, but by the use of oils in conjunction with the resins, numerous degrees of hardness are possible.

Styrenated alkyds became available commercially in 1948. Their development was spurred by the large production capacity for styrene and its relatively low cost after World War II. The styrenated alkyds may be considered to be a type of resin-modified alkyd to which the styrene confers better toughness, durability, and paler color. However, they are not as durable under exterior exposure as the pure oil-modified alkyds and their mar resistance is poor. Their principal advantage is their very rapid drying characteristic.

Quite recently, copolymers of the usual alkyd ingredients and vinyl monomers other than styrene have been introduced commercially. They have some desirable properties, among which are their very rapid rate of drying and light color. Vinyl monomers which have been used include acrylates, methacrylates, and acrylonitrile, alone and in combination with styrene.

Polyisocyanates are just beginning to be used in commercial coatings, and this intermediate has interesting possibilities for future exploitation in alkyd reactions.

The manufacture of alkyd resins requires careful control of the ratio of reactants, temperature, uniformity of mix, and time of reaction. The cooking operation is carried out in stainless steel kettles, since contact with iron produces dark-colored resins. Heating may be done by oil, gas, or electricity, depending upon the local relative costs. Each kettle holds from one to several tons and is equipped with a reflux condenser, agitator, sparger, often a foam breaker, and suitable means for sampling and discharge. In order to maintain a light color, the reactions are usually carried out under an inert atmosphere, usually carbon dioxide or nitrogen. Some plants are equipped to apply a vacuum to the reactors.

In the manufacture of oil-modified alkyds for surface coatings, the reaction is usually carried just short of the point at which gelation will occur—a point determined by experience. Since there is, therefore, the possibility that the retained heat will be sufficient to gel the resin before it cools, it is common practice to thin the resin with an appropriate solvent just before gelation and insolubility occur. By running the hot alkyd into a tank of solvent, the mixture is cooled sufficiently to stop further reaction. Although some alkyds are supplied as pure resin, the majority are sold as solutions.

Alkyd resins are made by two techniques, the fatty acid and the monoglyceride processes. Both may be carried out by direct fusion of the materials (fusion method) or by reacting in the presence of a solvent (solvent reflux method). In the fatty acid process, the ingredients, one of which is a fatty acid, are heated to temperatures ranging from 160° to 260°C. The batch is held at reaction temperature until the desired acid value and viscosity have been reached. It is then pumped, blown by inert gas pressure, or dropped by gravity into the thinning kettle and reduced to the required solid content.

It may appear uneconomical to split an oil into fatty acids and glycerol, and then to recombine the fatty acids with glycerol to make oil again in the fatty acid process. However, if oil is used instead of fatty acid, glyceryl phthalate will precipitate as it is formed because it is insoluble in oil whereas glyceryl phthalate is soluble in fatty acids. Another reason for preferring the use of fatty acids instead of oils, as mentioned before, is that oils contain a mixture of fatty acid residues, whereas the fatty acids made from these oils are refined and, often, fractionated. Thus, it is possible to be more selective in the choice of fatty acids than of oils.

In preparing alkyds from oils, the oils themselves, except for castor oil, are not reacted directly with the acid and polyol, but are first converted to a monoglyceride by heating with the alcohol in the presence of a catalyst, such as calcium or lead oxide, before addition of the acid. This process is a reaction between a glyceride (an ester) and an alcohol, and results in a re-establishment of equilibrium. The reaction is commonly known as *alcoholysis* (cf. ester interchange in the manufacture of Dacron). A typical reaction is as follows:

$$
\begin{array}{ccc}
\text{R·COO·C} & \text{HO·C} & \text{R·COO·C} \\
| & | & | \\
\text{R·COO·C} + 2\ \text{HO·C} \rightarrow 3 & \text{HO·C} \\
| & | & | \\
\text{R·COO·C} & \text{HO·C} & \text{HO·C}
\end{array}
$$

The decision of whether to use the fatty acid or the monoglyceride process is usually based upon the relative costs of the free fatty acids and the oils.

The designation "solvent method" or "solvent reflux method" for alkyd resins simply means that the resin is processed in the presence of a solvent which is immiscible with water. The solvent serves as a temperature regulator and as an efficient means of removal of the water of esterification by azeotropic distillation. The amount and volatility of the solvent determine the reflux temperature, thus enabling close temperature control. By means of a separator, water is removed and the solvent returned to the batch. The solvent also must be a solvent for the phthalic anhydride, if used; otherwise, the reflux condenser will become choked with the unreacted sublimed acid. Xylol (commercial xylene) is commonly used in amounts of from 3 to 10 per cent of the batch.

One of the principal advantages of the solvent method is that it serves to control the reaction temperature closely. This is, in reality, a solvent polymerization rather than a mass polymerization. The reactants are diluted; therefore, the rate of reaction is slower and the polymer size is more uniform. The solvent method is particularly desirable in the preparation of the shorter-oil-length resins, since their rates of reaction are faster and their reactions more difficult to control than those of the longer-oil-length resins.

Another advantage of the solvent method is that determination of the extent of the reaction and consequently of the rate of the reaction can conveniently be made, since the amount of water collected is proportional to the extent of esterification. Further, loss of phthalic anhydride by sublimation does not occur with the solvent method.

Alkyd-type resins are widely used in such varied applications as enamels, lacquers, textile finishes, metal primers, caulking compounds, slushing mixtures, protective films, leather coatings, and water-emulsion paints. The products may be applied by spraying, brushing, dipping, hot-melt, knife-spreading, and roller coating techniques. Automobile, railway, and metal household appliance primers and finishes represent a very important outlet for these materials. They are used in house paints, marine paints, printing inks, and in air-dry wood furniture finishes. Applications outside of the coating industry include the use of alkyds in gaskets, printers' rolls, flexible insulation, and as binders for mica and pigments.

The nondrying alkyds are also referred to as plasticizing polyester resins. They are used principally as plasticizers for cellulose nitrate in lacquers. In this use, they are superior to resins of low molecular weight since they possess film-forming properties of their own and do not have the tendency to exude from the film. They improve the adhesion to metal and the stability of cellulose nitrate. They are also utilized in coatings for linoleum, leather, fabrics, and rubber, often in conjunction with other resins.

*Unsaturated Polyester Resins*

In recent years, a number of unsaturated polyester resins have been produced industrially which possess a number of advantages compared with the usual types of thermosetting resins, such as the alkyds, the phenoplasts, and the aminoplasts. These advantages are all based on the fact that the curing of these unsaturated polyester resins is due to a polymerization reaction which causes cross-linking among the individual linear polymer chains. However, *in contrast to the other thermosetting resins, no by-product is formed during the curing reaction* and the resins can be, therefore, molded, cast, and laminated at low pressures (and temperatures). Not only does this simplify the design of the necessary molds, but, even more important, the low-pressure molding and laminating technique permits large articles to be fabricated which cannot be made by high-pressure processes because of the high cost and physical limitations of such equipment.

The final products have been variously called polyester resins, contact resins (because of the low molding pressure needed), and low-pressure laminating resins. There appears to be no clear-cut and unambiguous terminology for these resins. It is perhaps suitable to call the ester portion a linear, unsaturated polyester and the combination of the unsaturated ester and the unsaturated vinyl-type monomer, i.e., the final product, an unsaturated polyester resin.

We have seen, in the section on saturated polyesters, how long-chain polyesters may be made from dibasic acids and dihydric alcohols. The only present product of great interest from saturated reactants is the fiber- and film-forming poly(ethylene terephthalate). The shorter chain, linear, saturated polyesters are of very limited value, as they are generally of a soft, resinous character, suitable for plasticizers in many cases, but, for this reason, of little use for structural applications.

If either or both of the saturated bifunctional reactants is replaced with reactants containing unsaturation, linear unsaturated polyesters are formed, whose physical properties are not very different from those of the saturated polyesters. The maleates and fumarates of ethylene glycol were prepared by Vorlander in Germany as long ago as 1894.

It may be recalled that Kienle's work with alkyd resins in the middle twenties included the introduction of both drying and nondrying vegetable oils into the alkyd molecule. The basic alkyd patents included not only saturated acids, like phthalic anhydride, but also unsaturated dibasic acids, such as maleic. Small amounts of maleic anhydride were found to be useful in oil-modified alkyds, but complete replacement of phthalic with maleic turned out to be impractical, since insoluble glyceryl maleate formed before the fatty acid could enter into the reaction. This was not the case with phthalic anhydride and glycerol, which form a homogeneous mixture with the fatty acids. Experiments with glycols in place of glycerol, in attempts to overcome this difficulty, led to the discovery that glycol maleates could slowly form insoluble products in the presence of air.

For example, ethylene glycol and phthalic anhydride, both of which are bifunctional, form a linear, thermoplastic polymer:

$$—C·C·O·\overset{\overset{O}{\|}}{C}\quad C·O·C·C·O·\overset{\overset{O}{\|}}{C}\quad C·O·C·C—$$

Another example of this type is poly(ethylene terephthalate), discussed previously. However, when ethylene glycol (bifunctional) and maleic anhydride (potentially tetrafunctional) react under proper conditions, they first form a linear, *unsaturated* polyester:

$$—C·C·O·\overset{\overset{O}{\|}}{C}·C:C·\overset{\overset{O}{\|}}{C}·O·C·C·O·\overset{\overset{O}{\|}}{C}·C:C·\overset{\overset{O}{\|}}{C}·O·C·C—$$

If allowed to stand long enough, the polyester, with the aid of an initiator, is slowly converted from a viscous liquid to an insoluble, rubbery gel. If this gel is heated, it is eventually transformed into a hard, tough, transparent, and easily machined plastic. The prolonged curing time required here, however, is impractical for commercial products.

In 1936, a patent was filed on the use of vinyl monomers as cross-linking agents for glycol maleates. It was found that polymerization could be greatly accelerated and valuable structural materials obtained by reacting the unsaturated polyesters with such monomers as vinyl acetate, styrene, and methyl methacrylate. This discovery may be considered as the beginning of the modern unsaturated polyester (laminating) resin industry.

By first making a linear unsaturated polyester, then adding to it a vinyl monomer, cross-linked, three-dimensional resins are formed. For example, if styrene is added to the glycol maleate illustrated above, one or more styrene units will join the polyester chains by opening of the double bonds:

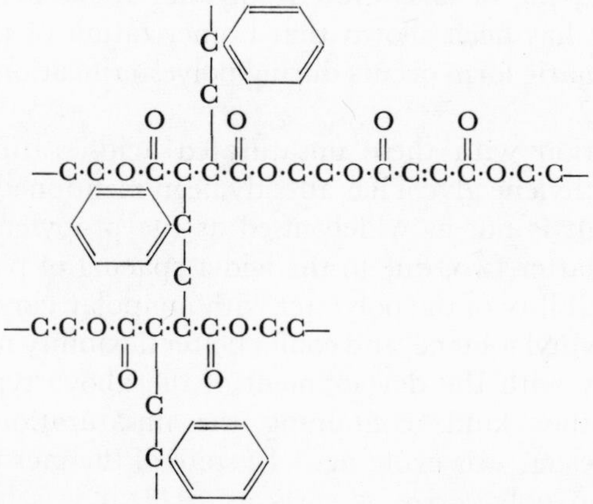

$$-C \cdot C \cdot O \cdot C \cdot C \cdot C \cdot C \cdot O \cdot C \cdot O \cdot C \cdot C \cdot C \cdot C \cdot O \cdot C \cdot C-$$

$$-C \cdot C \cdot O \cdot C \cdot C \cdot C \cdot O \cdot C \cdot C-$$

It is apparent that copolymerization can quickly form highly cross-linked, three-dimensional polymers. The net effect is that a soluble and thermoplastic polyester is converted into a fast-curing, thermosetting, insoluble resin. These copolymers have physical properties which are much superior to those of the unsaturated polyester alone. The products are thermoset and, when filled, make useful articles of outstanding mechanical strength.

In order to form the final product, two kinds of suitable monomers must be employed: (1) Unsaturated dibasic acids must be condensed with saturated glycols or vice versa, and (2) an unsaturated vinyl-type monomer must be added for the copolymerization. Theoretically, many monomers of both types could be employed. So far, although many have been investigated, few have been utilized for industrial practice, although the number is growing daily. Styrene is used, however, most frequently in the second step because of its cost, availability, and desirable physical properties.

A pure glycol maleate-styrene copolymer is rather brittle. Tougher and more flexible resins may be obtained by spacing the double bonds in the polyester molecule farther apart to decrease the amount of unsaturation and subsequent cross-linkage per molecule. This may be accomplished by using glycols of longer chain length, or by replacing part of the maleic anhydride with a saturated acid, such as phthalic, or with a long-chain aliphatic dibasic acid, such as adipic or sebacic. Maleic anhydride and fumaric acid are the commonest unsaturated acids used, and, recently, another unsaturated acid, itaconic, has become available. Although styrene copolymerizes well with maleic anhydride, maleic acid, and maleic half-esters, it does not copolymerize well with maleic diesters. However, styrene does copolymerize well with fumaric diesters.    It thus appears likely that the fumaric double bond is responsible for the satis-factory cross-linking of unsaturated polyester resins derived from maleic anhydride.    It has been shown that isomerization of the maleic double bond to the fumaric form occurs during polyesterification at a temperature of about 200°C.

In combination with these unsaturated acids, saturated glycols are often used.    Ethylene glycol has already been mentioned; it is the simplest of the series but is not as widely used as the propylene and diethylene glycols.    The latter two, due to the wider spacing of polar groups, allow greater compatibility of the polyester with nonpolar vinyl monomers, such as styrene and vinyl toluene, and confer better flexibility upon the products.

Concurrently with the development of the above type of unsaturated polyester, another kind, containing the unsaturation in the alcohol portion of the ester, was evolving.    In spite of the fact that allyl acrylate was reported to polymerize as early as 1873, it was believed for many years that allyl esters were difficult, if not impossible, to polymerize. In 1940, however, in the United States Garvey[9] reported the copolymeri-zation of diallyl succinate with vinyl acetate.    A portion of the resulting copolymer may be represented as follows:

$$
\begin{array}{c}
\text{O:C·C  O:C·C} \qquad\qquad \text{O:C·C  O:C·C} \\
\mid \qquad \mid \qquad\qquad\qquad \mid \qquad \mid \\
\text{O} \qquad \text{O} \qquad\qquad\quad \text{O} \qquad \text{O} \\
\mid \qquad \mid \qquad\qquad\qquad \mid \qquad \mid \\
-\text{C}\cdot\text{C}\cdot\text{C}\cdot\text{C}\cdot\text{C}\cdot\text{C}\cdot\text{C}\cdot\text{C}\cdot\text{C}\cdot\text{C}- \\
\mid \\
\text{C} \\
\mid \\
\text{O} \\
\mid \\
\text{C:O} \\
\mid \\
\text{C} \\
\mid \\
\text{C} \\
\mid \\
\text{C:O} \\
\mid \\
\text{O} \\
\mid \\
\text{C} \\
\mid \\
-\text{C}\cdot\text{C}\cdot\text{C}\cdot\text{C}\cdot\text{C}\cdot\text{C}\cdot\text{C}\cdot\text{C}\cdot\text{C}\cdot\text{C}- \\
\mid \qquad \mid \qquad\qquad\qquad \mid \qquad \mid \\
\text{O} \qquad \text{O} \qquad\qquad\quad \text{O} \qquad \text{O} \\
\mid \qquad \mid \qquad\qquad\qquad \mid \qquad \mid \\
\text{C·C:O  C·C:O} \qquad \text{C·C:O  C·C:O}
\end{array}
$$

[9] Garvey, B. S. and Alexander, C. H. (to B. F. Goodrich Co.), U.S. Pat. **2,202,846** (June 4, 1940).

Shortly after this development, production of resins made by polymerization of diallyl phthalate were announced. Thus, by esterification of one mole of phthalic anhydride with two moles of allyl alcohol, diallyl phthalate is obtained. This compound is tetrafunctional and may be polymerized alone (by mild polymerization, using only one of the allyl groups) to form linear polymers which may be further polymerized to yield thermosetting, highly cross-linked compounds. It is, therefore, not necessary to add any other polymerizing monomer, and pure allyl-ester thermosetting resins are available. Diallyl phthalate monomer is also often used as a cross-linking agent for modified maleate polyester resins, particularly in molding powders where a high-boiling cross-linking agent is desirable. Other unsaturated alcohols are now available.

A number of other allyl esters have proved useful because of the readiness with which they form fluid, soluble, partial polymers. The latter can be converted by themselves into hard, thermoset resins by heating with peroxide initiators or at lower temperatures can form similar products by copolymerization with styrene or other vinyl monomers. Among these compounds are diethylene glycol bis(allyl carbonate), diallyl maleate, diallyl fumarate, and diallyl benzene phosphonate. Resins from such esters as allyl itaconate have been patented, and numerous publications have shown interest in such esters as methallyl methacrylate. Of these, only diallyl phthalate and diethylene glycol bis(allyl carbonate) (CR39) have been produced on a large scale. The method of preparation of the latter may not be obvious; the probable steps, starting with diethylene glycol, are:

$$
\begin{array}{ccc}
\text{O}\!\!\diagup\!\!\begin{array}{l}\text{CH}_2\!\cdot\!\text{CH}_2\text{OH}\\[1mm]\text{CH}_2\!\cdot\!\text{CH}_2\text{OH}\end{array} & \xrightarrow[\ \ \ \ ]{\text{COCl}_2} & \text{O}\!\!\diagup\!\!\begin{array}{l}\text{CH}_2\!\cdot\!\text{CH}_2\!\cdot\!\text{O}\!\cdot\!\overset{\displaystyle\text{O}}{\overset{\|}{\text{C}}}\text{Cl}\\[3mm]\text{CH}_2\!\cdot\!\text{CH}_2\!\cdot\!\text{O}\!\cdot\!\underset{\underset{\text{O}}{\|}}{\text{C}}\text{Cl}\end{array} & \xrightarrow{\ \text{CH}_2\text{:CH}\cdot\text{CH}_2\text{OH}\ }
\end{array}
$$

$$
\text{O}\!\!\diagup\!\!\begin{array}{l}\text{CH}_2\!\cdot\!\text{CH}_2\!\cdot\!\text{O}\overset{\displaystyle\text{O}}{\overset{\|}{\text{C}}}\text{O}\!\cdot\!\text{CH}_2\!\cdot\!\text{CH:CH}_2\\[4mm]\text{CH}_2\!\cdot\!\text{CH}_2\!\cdot\!\text{O}\underset{\underset{\text{O}}{\|}}{\text{C}}\text{O}\!\cdot\!\text{CH}_2\!\cdot\!\text{CH:CH}_2\end{array}
$$

This monomer is noteworthy for its ability to form clear castings having high scratch resistance, a high heat distortion temperature, and good optical properties. As is true of all allyl monomers, cure is relatively slow, and the material is not frequently used as a laminating resin but rather as a cast resin because of its good optical properties.

Quite recently, another allyl compound, triallyl cyanurate, has received considerable attention because of its ability to produce, in combination with unsaturated polyesters, resins having high heat distortion temperatures. Its probable synthesis is:

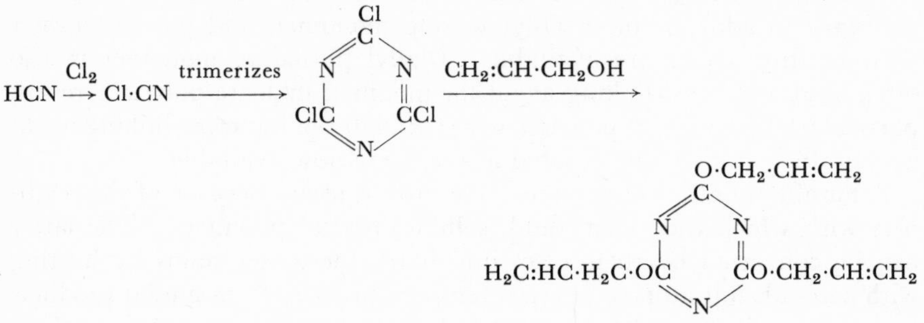

It may thus be seen that, by varying the acids and glycols, both in relative amount and nature, an enormous number of unsaturated polyesters may be prepared. However, the vinyl-type monomers used commercially for copolymerization are limited because they must be relatively low in cost, have a satisfactory volatility range, and not have too low a boiling point. As mentioned previously, styrene is the most commonly used vinyl monomer. Others frequently used, alone or in combination with styrene, are vinyl toluene, acrylic and methacrylic esters, and vinyl acetate. Divinyl benzene has found only limited use with the polyesters.

Most unsaturated polyesters are unstable on storage, particularly at high temperatures and in the presence of air. The tendency to cross-link and gel is, of course, much greater when they are dissolved in a vinyl monomer. Therefore, it is customary to add to the polyester-monomer solution a small amount of an inhibitor, such as *p-tert*-butyl catechol, hydroquinone, *p*-nitroso dimethylaniline, or similar compound, which will increase the lifetime of the product to about half a year at room temperature or lower; this is done by the manufacturer.

The controlled polymerization of polyester-monomer mixtures to yield fully cured solids requires the use of an initiator. Since the final curing is essentially a vinyl-type polymerization, free-radical initiators, such as peroxides and azo compounds, are used. The fact that the action of organic peroxides can be modified by activators and promoters and their ready availability at reasonable cost have led to their extensive use. Some of the available peroxide-type initiators, arranged in groups according to the approximate temperature range in which they initiate polymerization readily, is given in Table 8-2.

TABLE 8-2. PEROXIDE INITIATORS

Low-Temperature Types (30° to 60°C)
Acetyl benzoyl peroxide
Peracetic acid
Methyl ethyl ketone peroxide
Cyclohexanone peroxide
Cyclohexyl hydroperoxide
2, 4-Dichlorobenzoyl peroxide
Cumene hydroperoxide

Intermediate-Temperature Types (60° to 100°C)
tert-Butyl hydroperoxide
Methyl amyl ketone peroxide
Lauroyl peroxide
Benzoyl peroxide
tert-Butyl perbenzoate
Di-tert-butyl diperphthalate

High-Temperature Types (100°C and above)
p-Chlorobenzoyl peroxide
Di-tert-butyl peroxide
Dibenzal diperoxide

The chemical identities of commercial activators and promoters, used in conjunction with initiators, in most cases have not been revealed. Cobalt, in the form of its ethyl hexoate (hexanoate) or naphthenate salt, is a good, general-purpose activator for use with ketone peroxides. It causes rapid curing at room temperature and tends to reduce surface tackiness. Concentrations as low as 30 ppm of cobalt metal will activate a system.

Promoters used with acyl peroxides include tertiary dialkyl aryl amines, such as diethyl aniline, and aliphatic thiols, as, for example, lauryl mercaptan. Concentrations used are most often in the range of 0.05 to 0.5 per cent of active substance. As can be seen, promoters usually are strong reducing agents and initiators are strong oxidizing agents.

The commercial photopolymerization of the vinyl-type monomers has received particular attention since the development of the unsaturated polyester resins. The photopolymerization process has several advantages over thermal polymerization and is especially useful in applications where long pot life is desired, together with rapid gelling at a low temperature. A photosensitizer of polymerization must absorb light and, with the energy so acquired, dissociate into radicals which have sufficient energy to initiate polymerization. Dozens of inorganic and organic compounds have been claimed to be effective. Of the many compounds described in the literature, benzoin appears to have the best general activity and applicability, whereas biacetyl is preferable for the acrylates.

The copolymerization of a polyester-vinyl monomer combination is highly exothermic. The amount of heat generated will depend upon the type of resin and, in particular, upon the amount of unsaturation. The temperature within the polymerizing mass will be governed by the difference between the speed at which heat is evolved—which is dependent upon concentration and type of initiator and promoter, and the temperature at which polymerization was initiated—and the rate at which heat is removed.   Thermal conductivity of the mold itself, if used, dimensions of the article, heat transfer coefficient to the mold or air, and the ambient temperature will govern the latter.   Empirical experimentation must be performed to find the right combination of initiator and promoter for a particular manufacturing operation.

The use of inert mineral fillers with polyester resins has proved to be of considerable interest in potting (electrical) and press mold applications, and for hand lay-ups, particularly in conjunction with glass-fiber reinforcement.   The most commonly given reason for using a filler with these resins is to extend the resin in an attempt to reduce material costs; because of the high density of most fillers, the actual savings are usually less than expected.   There are, however, many other reasons, more important than cost reduction, for adding fillers.   They are used to impart opacity, to increase the hiding power of color pigments, to increase the apparent heat distortion temperature, to increase the hardness of the

Fig. 8-11.   The panels of this truck are made of reinforced unsaturated polyester resin, which considerably lightens the weight of the truck and increases its cargo-carrying capacity.   (*Courtesy Celanese Corp. of America*)

cured resin, and to change the flow characteristics of the resin for hand lay-up work, as in the construction of large tanks.

The largest use of the unsaturated polyester resins is in conjunction with a reinforcing filler, such as glass, paper, or cloth. Glass fiber, woven or as roving, is most frequently used, and provides a laminate of outstanding strength and durability. However, continuous-filament glass fabrics as they come from the loom contain an oily, starch size which prevents fast, complete wetting out by the plastic during impregnation, and prevents good adhesion of the plastic to the glass. In order to obtain good laminates, the size must be removed from the fabric and a glass-to-polyester coupling or finishing agent must be applied. The desizing and finishing processes convert the fabric from a poor to an excellent reinforcing agent for the unsaturated polyester resins. Among the finishing agents which have been used are a number of organosilicon compounds and organochromium complexes.

In many applications, for example, in lay-up work, it is desirable that the resin have a rather high viscosity so that proper tack, film thickness, and minimum flow may be obtained. High-viscosity resins, however, suffer from such disadvantages as slow penetration and impregnation, and it is difficult to disperse and dissolve initiators and fillers and to remove air bubbles. The so-called pre-gel technique is a convenient means of using fast-penetrating resins which are rapidly thickened after impregnation. A promoter is added to the resin which, at room or slightly elevated temperature, reduces the time usually required for gelling the resin. Pre-gelled structures have sufficient rigidity to be handled, and final cure is subsequently obtained in ovens. In some cases, with a very rapidly reacting activator, curing begins immediately following the gelling, and oven cure may not be necessary. In all cases, an initiator is still necessary; promoters and activators only change the relation between and absolute length of the induction period (time until gelled) and cure time (time to become fully cured). For a fuller discussion of the molding techniques, see Chapter 11.

Polyester resins can be colored with light-fast, durable pigments, producing a variety of colors built right into the products. Using glass fibers or other reinforcing materials to add strength and toughness, they yield products that are as strong as, but only one third as heavy as, steel and only two thirds the weight of aluminum. They do not rust, rot, or corrode and need never be painted. They are tremendously resistant to impact and will not dent or shatter. If their elastic limit is exceeded, they will crack, but the damage can easily be repaired using the same unsaturated polyester resin from which the product was originally made.

Since the products are impervious to corrosion, they are useful in fabricating air-conditioner drip pans, fans and impeller blades, swimming

Fig. 8-12.    (*top*) Production line for the manufacture of glass fiber-and-nylon-reinforced unsaturated polyester resin translucent panels; (*bottom*) An installation of these panels in a greenhouse.    (*Courtesy Filon Plastics Corp.*)

pools, and tanks and piping for chemical, plating, and photographic solutions. One of the largest applications of reinforced polyester tanks is for electroplating tanks. They are replacing wood, steel, or concrete tanks lined with lead, rubber, or poly(vinyl chloride). The tanks are light, easy to install, and are ready to use as soon as they are in place. Having high electrical resistance, the resins are used in many electrical applications. Because of their high impact and abrasion resistance, they are useful in the fabrication of luggage, storage bins, helmets, truck

FIG. 8-13. "Geodesic" structure of reinforced unsaturated polyester resin designed for use as a military shelter in the Arctic. (*Courtesy Lunn Laminates, Inc.*)

bodies and cabs, and trays. In several plants, pressure-molded reinforced polyester tote trays are completely replacing enameled steel, steel, stainless steel, monel, and aluminum trays. Having excellent weatherability and resistance to water, these resins are used for boats, fishing rods, and washing machine tubs. Since they are translucent when unpigmented, they are widely used for walls and skylights for factories, offices, schools, and greenhouses.

## LINEAR POLYAMIDES

The word "nylon" is a generic term for any long-chain synthetic polymeric amide which has recurring amide groups as an integral part of the main polymer chain, and which is capable of being formed into a filament in which the structural elements are oriented in the direction of the axis. Of all fiber-forming, synthetic, condensation polymers, these polyamides have received the most attention and have reached a stage of intensive commercial development.

From many glycols and acids Carothers prepared polyesters (polymeric esters) and it was these products which gave the first indication of being a useful synthetic fiber (see Saturated Polyesters). However, the fibers first made from the polyesters were not altogether satisfactory. Then Carothers substituted polyamides (polymeric amides) for polyesters;

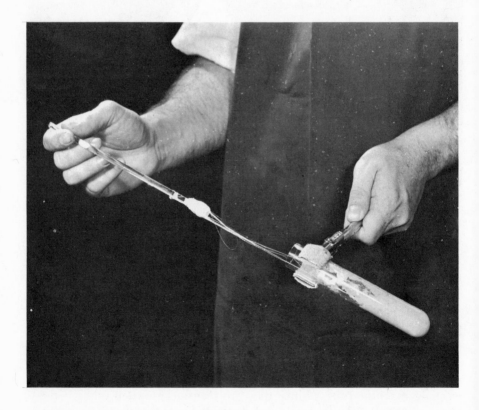

FIG. 8-14. It was an experiment such as this that suggested to Carothers the fiber-forming possibilities of polyamides. (*Courtesy E. I. duPont de Nemours and Co.*)

these showed such a big improvement that research on these products was assiduously followed up and resulted in the very successful fiber, nylon.

These polyamides are made from diamines and diacids in the following manner:

$$H_2N(CH_2)_6NH_2 + HOOC(CH_2)_4COOH \rightarrow$$
$$^+H_3N(CH_2)_6NH_3^+\cdot{}^-OOC(CH_2)_4COO^-\rightarrow$$
"Nylon 66 Salt"

$$H_2N(CH_2)_6NH\cdot OC(CH_2)_4COOH + H_2O$$

and then two molecules of this condensate will react to give

$$H_2N(CH_2)_6NH\cdot OC(CH_2)_4CO\cdot HN(CH_2)_6NH\cdot OC(CH_2)_4COOH + H_2O$$

and this molecule will further react with more similar molecules, eventually forming a long polymer.

Another way in which the polyamides may be made is by starting with a molecule which has an amino group at one end and a carboxylic acid group at the other or with the cyclic lactam derived therefrom. Either can react with a similar molecule in this way:

$$2H_2N(CH_2)_5COOH \rightarrow H_2N(CH_2)_5CO\cdot HN(CH_2)_5COOH + H_2O$$

except that, with the lactam, ring opening first occurs and no water is evolved. Further reaction would occur as above. The former method was first chosen for use in preference to the second simply because it was easier and cheaper to make diamines and dicarboxylic acids than it was to make amino acids.

Normal nylon, made from hexamethylene diamine, $H_2N(CH_2)_6NH_2$, and adipic acid, $HOOC(CH_2)_4COOH$, is referred to as Nylon 66 or the 66 polymer because each of the two reactants contains six carbon atoms. A similar polyamide is made from hexamethylene diamine and sebacic acid, $HOOC(CH_2)_8COOH$, hence is known as the 610 polymer. The 6 polymer, made from ε-caprolactam,

$$HN\cdot CH_2\cdot CH_2\cdot CH_2\cdot CH_2\cdot CH_2\cdot C = O$$

which reacts as if it were ε-amino caproic acid, $H_2N(CH_2)_5COOH$, is also made. Still another variety, the 11 polymer, is obtained from ω-amino undecanoic acid, $H_2N(CH_2)_{10}COOH$.

Of these, the 66 type has been preferred, partly because of the superiority of the fiber—it has, for example, a melting point higher than the other polymers—but also because organic compounds containing six linear carbon atoms are easily and cheaply derived from benzene or its derivatives.   Sebacic and undecylenic acids are made from castor oil, which is not as readily available nor as cheap.

It is possible to synthesize adipic acid and hexamethylene diamine in many ways, but the method first used began with phenol.   The sources of phenol have already been mentioned in connection with phenol-aldehyde resins.

Phenol may be reduced in the vapor or liquid phase with hydrogen to

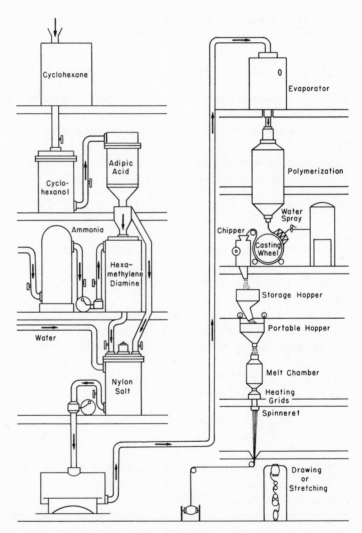

Fig. 8-15.   Nylon flow sheet.   [Houwink, R., ed., *Elastomers and Plastomers*, Vol. II, Elsevier Publishing Co., Amsterdam (dist. by D. Van Nostrand Co., Princeton, N.J.), (1949)]

yield cyclohexanol. The cyclohexanol may be oxidized with, for example, concentrated nitric acid to form adipic acid, the ring being cleaved. This route is no longer used. A more recent process is the reduction of benzene or the cracking of petroleum to yield cyclohexane, the oxidation of cyclohexane to cyclohexanol and cyclohexanone, with further oxidation breaking the ring and yielding adipic acid. A third synthesis, developed during World War II in Germany, is by the reaction of acetylene and formaldehyde in the presence of copper or silver acetylide; the 2-butyne-1,4-diol formed is reduced to 1,4-butanediol which is then dehydrated to give tetrahydrofuran. In the presence of nickel carbonyl, this compound reacts with carbon monoxide to yield adipic acid. In the United States, tetrahydrofuran from furfural has been converted to adipic acid by the same process.

The other reactant, hexamethylene diamine, may be made from adipic acid itself by treating it with ammonia to form the ammonium salt, which may be dehydrated over a suitable catalyst to give the amide, then the corresponding nitrile. The nitrile may be reduced with hydrogen in the presence of a cobalt or nickel catalyst in an autoclave to form the diamine:

$$(CH_2)_4(COOH)_2 \xrightarrow{NH_3} (CH_2)_4(CONH_2)_2 \xrightarrow{-H_2O}$$
$$(CH_2)_4(CN)_2 \xrightarrow{H_2} (CH_2)_4(CH_2NH_2)_2$$

Alternatively, the adiponitrile may be made from furfural, which is converted to furan with lime, reduced to tetrahydrofuran, hydrochlorinated in the presence of sulfuric acid to give 1,4-dichlorobutane, then treated with alcoholic sodium cyanide to yield the nitrile.

A still different source of adiponitrile is butadiene. Butadiene, obtained from petroleum or from alcohol, is chlorinated to form 1,4-dichlorobutene which is reacted with cyanide to give the unsaturated dinitrile which, upon reduction, yields adiponitrile.

It may thus be seen that there are usually several possible routes to the production of an organic intermediate; which process is favored depends upon the prices and availability of the raw materials and processing costs, all of which may vary over a period of time. At the present time, adipic acid is made from cyclohexane, whereas hexamethylene diamine comes from adiponitrile via furfural or butadiene. Figure 8-16 shows graphically the interrelation of intermediates and the many possible methods of synthesis of adipic acid and hexamethylene diamine.

Commercial nylon fibers are linear and have molecular weight averages of the order of 12,000 to 20,000. If the average molecular weight is below 6,000, little or no fiber formation is possible; fibers formed from

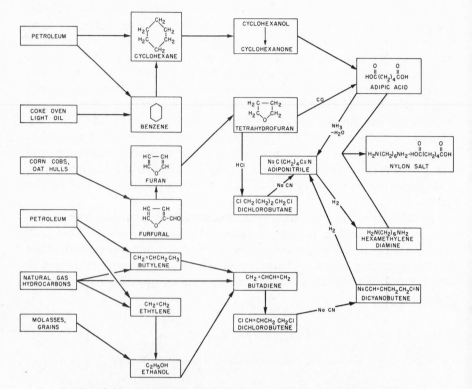

Fig. 8-16.   Synthesis routes to the manufacture of nylon[10]

polymers with an average molecular weight of about 6,000 to 10,000 are
weak and brittle; as the average molecular weight increases above this
range, the fibers become stronger.   However, if the molecular weight
runs much over 20,000, the polymer becomes too difficult to melt or
dissolve.   Therefore, the process of polymerization must be stopped in
the desired average molecular weight range.   This is accomplished by a
process known as *stabilization*.   If, instead of taking exactly equivalent
quantities of reactants, an excess of either the acid or amine is used, *all* of
the long polymeric molecules will eventually have carboxylic or amino
groups at both ends, instead of having a carboxylic group at one end and
an amino group at the other.   When this occurs, condensation cannot
continue, and the polymer is stabilized.

Stabilization can also be effected by using equimolecular quantities of
diamine and diacid and adding a small amount of a monofunctional
reagent; this has the same effect as an excess of bifunctional reactant.
It is thus apparent that the reacting materials must be very pure;

[10] Bunn, H., *Ind. Eng. Chem.*, **44**, 2132 (1952).

the presence in them of a small quantity of impurity may be sufficient to prevent the polymer from attaining even the minimum molecular weight desired.  In practice, a ratio of one mole of diamine to 1.02 moles of diacid will form a polymer having a stabilized average molecular weight of about 12,000—suitable for nylon fiber manufacture.

That a two mole per cent excess of diacid (or, for that matter, diamine) will produce a polymer of ultimate molecular weight of approximately 12,000 may easily be calculated, using the relationship given by Eq. 69, Chapter 4:

$$r = \frac{N_A}{N_B} = \frac{2.04}{2.00} = 1.02$$

$$\overline{DP}_n = \frac{1 + r}{1 - r} = \frac{2.02}{0.02} = 101$$

Since the molecular weight of hexamethylene adipamide is 244, the *average* molecular weight of a comer is (244 − 18)/2 (allowing for water evolved) or 113; hence, the average molecular weight of the polymer is 101 × 113 = 11,413, or, roughly, 12,000.

Note that we have started with the condensation of one mole of diamine

FIG. 8-17.  Nylon salt.  (*Courtesy Chemstrand Corp.*)

with one mole of diacid to form the product known as "Nylon 66 salt." Commercially, the salt can actually be made, then isolated and purified, in order that exactly equivalent amounts of the two will be present. Then a known excess of one of the reagents, or, often, acetic acid, is added and polymerization is continued.

The salt may be made by the reaction of the two components in a solvent, such as methanol, in which it is comparatively insoluble. After formation, it is filtered off, impurities or excesses of the reagents remaining in the mother liquor. After washing with methanol and drying, the salt, a white, water-soluble, crystalline powder is ready for polymerization. Alternatively, the salt may be formed directly by reaction of the two components in water. This method eliminates the solvent recovery problem, but great care must then be taken that both intermediates be of the highest purity, inasmuch as the resulting solution contains all of the products added and, since no crystallization is involved, any adventitious impurities remain. The latter method is now also used in the United States, as high purity intermediates are available. The correct ratio of reactants is maintained by continuous pH control (7.8 ± 0.1). After decolorization and filtration of the aqueous 20 per cent salt solution, it is concentrated to 60 per cent solids in a vacuum evaporator.

The salt solution is run into a stainless steel autoclave and the necessary quantity of stabilizer is added. (When a delustered product is desired, an aqueous suspension of titanium dioxide is added to the reaction mass during the polymerization, about 0.3 per cent being sufficient.) The temperature is raised and the system purged of air by the issuing steam. After sealing the vessel, the temperature is raised to about 220°C, at which time a pressure of about 250 psi develops. After one to two hours, the temperature is gradually raised to 270° to 280°C, during which time steam is bled continuously so that the pressure remains at 250 psi. After reaction is complete, the pressure is slowly reduced to atmospheric. Operating conditions are such that sufficient water is present to maintain the reaction mass in a fluid condition, the ebullition of water providing good agitation. Since the polymer melts at 264°C, by the time all of the water is evolved, the polymer is in a molten state. The melt is heated at atmospheric pressure for about an hour in order to establish equilibrium. The molten polymer is extruded under nitrogen pressure in the form of a thin ribbon onto a casting wheel equipped with a water spray. The cooled ribbon then is cut into small pieces or chips which are screened and then dried.

The chips are fed through a hopper into a spinning vessel in which they are melted. The molten nylon is metered by a pump and extruded through the usual melt-spinning orifices. As soon as the fibers emerge from the orifices, the filaments freeze. The method of melt spinning is advantageous in that it avoids the necessity for solvent recovery and the losses which always occur with such an operation, and it is well adapted to high spinning speeds. The filaments are cold-drawn by stretching some 400 per cent between rollers running at different speeds. The filaments thus become much thinner as well as lustrous and strong, due to orientation of the molecules.

Although Nylon 610 is not used as a textile fiber, it is manufactured in appreciable quantity in this country for spinning into relatively coarse monofilaments. In addition to hexamethylene diamine, the polymer requires sebacic acid for its manufacture. Until fairly recently, this acid was not available commercially, but with the growing use for 610 polymer and the discovery that some of its esters are valuable plasticizers (see Alkyd Resins), the acid is now being made on a sizable scale.

The commercial process involves the treatment of castor oil (containing principally glyceryl ricinoleate) with strong caustic solution at high temperature; saponification and cleavage occur, with the formation of sodium sebacate and 2-octanol. The salt is sprung with acid. An alternative process, although probably not competitive with the castor-oil route, is the Kolbe synthesis based upon the electrolysis of the methyl half-ester of adipic acid. Dimethyl adipate is heated with adipic acid so that re-equilibration occurs with the formation of the half-ester. The sodium salt is subjected to electrolysis in boiling methanol, giving dimethyl sebacate in good yield; the acid is obtained from the ester by saponification and acidification.

Reaction of sebacic acid with an equimolecular quantity of hexamethylene diamine in water or alcohol produces Nylon 610 salt. The salt is polymerized and the polymer obtained as chips by a method similar to that for the 66 polymer.

Because the 610 polymer contains an additional four methylene groups between the polar amide groups, it is lower melting (215°C) and has a lower moisture-absorbing capacity. Because of the latter property, the polymer is used for the manufacture of bristles for brushes and gut substitute for use in tennis racquets and other sports equipment. Under conditions of high humidity, the 610 polymer retains its stiffness to a much greater extent than does the 66 polymer.

Nylon 6 polymer may be made either from $\varepsilon$-amino caproic acid or its lactam ($\varepsilon$-caprolactam), the latter intermediate being preferred since it is easier to make and to purify.

Although several ways of making caprolactam are known, e.g., from sodium azide and cyclohexanone, only one is used for large-scale commercial production. This synthesis involves the production of cyclohexanol from phenol or cyclohexane, the oxidation of the cyclohexanol to cyclohexanone, the treatment of this ketone with aqueous hydroxylamine sulfate to form the oxime, and the rearrangement (Beckmann) in the presence of 80 per cent sulfuric acid or of phosphorus pentachloride in toluene to give the lactam:

$$
\text{OH} \longrightarrow \text{OH} \longrightarrow \underset{\text{S}}{\text{O}} \longrightarrow \underset{\text{S}}{\text{N·OH}} \longrightarrow
\begin{array}{l}
\text{CH}_2\text{·CH}_2\text{·CO} \\
| \qquad\qquad | \\
\text{CH}_2 \qquad\quad | \\
| \qquad\qquad | \\
\text{CH}_2\text{·CH}_2\text{·NH}
\end{array}
$$

The caprolactam is heated under such conditions that the ring opens and forms a linear polymer. Unlike the formation of polyamides from two components, no water is formed as a by-product. Perlon L, a German product, has long been made in this way and nylon has just recently been manufactured by this process in the United States, where at least four companies will be producing it by 1958.

Nylon 11 polymer, developed in France for monofilaments and fibers (Rilsan) and for molding and casting applications, is prepared by the self-condensation of $\omega$-amino undecanoic acid and, like the 610 polymer, is based on castor oil, being in this case derived from undecylenic acid, which is obtained from the oil by pyrolysis of its methyl ester. This acid, by treatment with a hydrohalide in the presence of a peroxide, yields the $\omega$-halo undecanoic acid, which, after separation of the 10 isomer, is treated with ammonia to give 11-amino undecanoic acid:

$$
\text{CH}_2\text{:CH(CH}_2)_8\text{COOH} \xoverset{\text{HX}}{\longrightarrow} \text{X(CH}_2)_{10}\text{COOH} \xoverset{\text{NH}_3}{\longrightarrow} \text{H}_2\text{N(CH}_2)_{10}\text{COOH}
$$

Polymerization is effected by heating the acid alone or in xylenol at about 215°C. Like Nylon 610, the 11 polymer is handled in a manner similar to that of Nylon 66. Nylon 11 melts at about 180° to 185°C; like the other polyamides, it is soluble only in such solvents as phenols and formic acid; it is hydrolyzed by strong acids. Its properties are such that it has found numerous applications in the electrical industry. While most polyamides absorb a certain amount of water (up to 10 per cent), this new material has a very low moisture vapor absorption (of the order of 1 per cent), giving it excellent, constant insulating properties, regardless of ambient conditions. The specific gravity of Nylon 11 is low (1.04) and lies between those of Nylon 66 and polyethylene. A plant to make Nylon 11 from castor oil is now being built in Brazil, and at least one company in the United States is considering its manufacture.

The number of polyamides which can be prepared is very high and many more have been made in the laboratory. However, so far as is known, the ones described are the only ones at present of commercial significance. Of interest, however, is the fact that there has been recently announced research on certain polymers, similar to nylon, known as polyoxamides. For example, 3-methyl hexamethylene diamine will react with diethyl oxalate or a similar ester to form an oxamide. By heating to 240°C under nitrogen, a high-molecular-weight polyoxamide is formed. The strength retention and fatigue endurance limit are reported to be considerably better for this polymer than for Nylon 66. Another reason for interest in this class of polymers is that oxalic acid is cheaper than adipic acid.

Since in the United States, at present, Nylon 66 is the one most widely used, references to nylon, unless indicated otherwise, generally refer to the 66 polymer. Nylon, like all fibers having a high degree of orientation, is very strong. It is stronger than any of the natural fibers but is not so strong as Fortisan, except for special nylons which approach it in strength. Its high wet strength—about 80 to 90 per cent of the dry strength—is a very valuable feature. Nylon has good flexibility and its resistance to abrasion is more than four times that of wool. Nylon is so elastic, for a fiber, that, if it is stretched 8 per cent, it completely recovers its original length upon release of tension.

The specific gravity of nylon (66) is 1.14, which is lower than that of most fibers (viscose is 1.52, cellulose acetate, 1.30); this is desirable for making light-weight fabrics. Although it melts at 264°C, it turns slightly yellow when heated in air at 150°C for five hours; it is slightly better in this respect than silk or wool, but not as good as the cellulosic fibers.

Nylon is unaffected by solvents normally used in dry cleaning. Although not appreciably affected by dilute acids, it is hydrolyzed by long boiling with concentrated hydrochloric acid. This process has been used to recover the original components from nylon waste for subsequent reuse. The stability of nylon to alkali is excellent; treatment with a 10 per cent caustic solution at 85°C for ten hours reduces its strength by only 5 per cent.

Nylon will not support mildew, bacteria, or moth larvae. The equilibrium moisture content is low, only about 3.6 per cent for the 66 polymer. Nylon, like other textile fibers, is degraded by the action of light, more so than cotton but much less than silk. Because it is such a good insulator, it is subject to static charge.

Since the uses of a fiber are determined by its properties, it is obvious that nylon has many applications. Its high tenacity has made it of value for parachute fabric, cords, and harness, and for glider and automotive tow-ropes.

The high tenacity of nylon permits the manufacture of very sheer stockings, as low as 15 denier. Because the filaments can be preset by steaming, ladies' hose are "set" on boards and maintain their shape during wear. Both men's and women's nylon hosiery are now also sold in a stretchable form. These are made by the Helanca process, in which the yarns are set in a coiled form by heat, so that the coils remain permanently but yield to temporary stretching.    Stretch garments simplify store inventories, as only six sizes of hosiery, for example, are needed instead of the twenty or more sizes regularly carried.

The high tenacity of nylon has caused it to be used in the fabric foundation for automobile tires, replacing high-tenacity rayon in premium tires.    In staple form nylon is used extensively for dress fabrics, for upholstery, and, recently, for rugs, either alone or in combination with wool or other synthetic fibers.    Typewriter ribbons made from nylon are thinner, thus giving clearer and sharper impressions and better carbon copies.

Nylon, particularly the 610 type, is extruded into relatively coarse monofilaments (Tynex) for use as brush bristles, fishing lines, surgical sutures, and similar applications.    By progressively varying take-off speeds during extrusion, tapered bristles are produced for use in paint brushes.    Monofilament nylon, spun as a bristle, has been extensively used for tooth brushes, which was, in fact, its first use.    As a matter of fact, most tooth and hair brushes now contain nylon bristles.

FIG. 8-18.    All of the moving parts and bearing surfaces of this textile-spinning apparatus are molded from nylon.    (*Courtesy E. I. duPont de Nemours and Co.*)

Nylon, either melt-extruded or in solution form (Nylon 6 is soluble in aqueous isopropanol), is being used to insulate electric wire for many purposes.

Injection-molded articles from nylon molding powder (Zytel) have appeared more recently; molding powder consumption has, in fact, jumped in 1957 to ten times its consumption (about 2 million pounds) in 1950. Because of its high melting point, unusually high molding temperatures are required—close to 280°C. Extensive use has been made of nylon as a material for the production of bearings and gears. This application may be attributed to the fact that nylon has better mechanical properties and abrasion resistance than other thermoplastics and better chemical resistance and lower dry friction than many common dry metals. In addition, nylon can be easily machined and molded, while its cost compares favorably with many other materials used for bearings and gears. Molded bearings have given excellent service. In many cases they may be operated satisfactorily without any lubrication or by lubrication with water.

Nylon synthetic paper is being made commercially on a Fourdrinier paper machine exactly as paper made from other types of furnishes. The finished paper has high tensile strength and good resistance to heat, wrinkling, bacteria, alcohol, ketones, soaps, detergents, moisture, solvents, and most other chemicals and gases. It also has good electrical properties, high folding endurance, and is reported to surpass many papers in bursting strength. Although all uses have not been tested, the product appears suitable for filters, maps, tracing paper, records, electrical tape, and packaging.

## POLYURETHANES

The fundamental reaction of an isocyanate with an alcohol to form a urethane was discovered by Wurtz in 1848:

$$R \cdot NCO + R'OH \rightarrow R \cdot NH \cdot CO_2R'$$

The linkage is produced by the transfer of the hydrogen atom of the hydroxyl group to the nitrogen atom of the isocyanate group. This is the fundamental reaction in the field of urethane chemistry.

When a monofunctional alcohol is replaced by bi- or polyfunctional alcohols, which may be long-chain compounds or polymers bearing a multiplicity of hydroxyl groups, such as polyesters and polyethers, and the isocyanate is replaced by a di- or polyisocyanate, either linear or cross-linked polyurethanes are formed, depending upon the functionality of the reactants:

$$n \, HO \cdot R \cdot OH + n \, OCN \cdot R' \cdot NCO \rightarrow H-[-O \cdot R \cdot OOC \cdot HN \cdot R'-]_n-NCO$$

The physical properties of the polymer depend upon the nature, functionalities, and ratios of the reactants, all of which can be varied widely. Polyesters which are hydroxy terminated are most often used with the isocyanates; glycols used include ethylene, propylene, butylene, and diethylene; triols used include glycerol, trimethylol ethane and propane, and butane and hexane triols; just recently, pilot-plant production of such unusual polyols as poly(butylene glycol), poly(styrene glycol), and polyepichlorohydrin began; acids frequently used include phthalic, adipic, sebacic, succinic, oxalic, and ricinoleic.

In addition to the preparation of linear polyurethanes by the reaction of a diisocyanate with a glycol, another method is by condensation of a bischloroformic ester of a glycol with a diamine, the intermediate bischloroformate being made by the action of phosgene on the glycol:

$$HO \cdot R \cdot OH + 2COCl_2 \rightarrow ClCOO \cdot R \cdot OOCCl + 2HCl$$

$$ClCOO \cdot R \cdot OOCCl + H_2N \cdot R' \cdot NH_2 \rightarrow \rightarrow$$
$$[-R \cdot OOC \cdot NH \cdot R' \cdot NH \cdot COO-]_n + HCl$$

The polyurethanes are esters of dicarbamic acids, $R(NH \cdot COOH)_2$, and glycols, or intermolecular esters of $\omega$-hydroxy carbamic acids, $HO \cdot R \cdot NH \cdot COOH$. The name "polyurethane" is derived from the use of the word "urethane" used generically to describe esters of (the hypothetical) carbamic acid, $H_2N \cdot COOH$. Specifically, "urethane" refers to the ethyl ester, which has the formula $H_2N \cdot COOC_2H_5$.

The linear polyurethanes are a class of crystalline, fiber-forming polymers, closely allied to the polyamides which contain the amide group,

$$-NH \cdot \overset{O}{\overset{\|}{C}}-$$, capable of hydrogen bonding which permits considerable interchain attraction to occur. However, compared with the polyamide group, the urethane group contains an additional oxygen atom which

forms a part of the main polymer chain: $-NH \cdot \overset{O}{\overset{\|}{C}}-O-$. It is probable that this additional atom makes the chain more flexible; another effect is shown by the fact that polyurethanes have softening temperatures appreciably lower than the polyamides of analogous composition.

A very large number of isocyanates and diisocyanates have been prepared and studied in the United States and abroad. Many have been eliminated from commercial consideration because of price, stability, ease of manufacture, or suitability for the particular application. This has left a relatively small number for development, only a few of which are commercially available at this time. The following list of compounds includes the isocyanates which are found at present to be useful and are either commercially available or potentially so. The first three compounds are probably the most important, the aromatic types being preferred in this country, partly because of their lower toxicity:

CH₃

Toluene (tolylene) diisocyanate (TDI)—(Desmodur T)

$$OCN(CH_2)_6NCO$$

Hexamethylene diisocyanate—(Desmodur H)

Diphenylmethane diisocyanate (MDI)
(and the dimethyl derivative)

1,5-Naphthalene diisocyanate (NDI)—(Desmodur 15)

Triphenylmethane triisocyanate—(Desmodur R)

Xenylene diisocyanate (XDI)
(and the dimethyl derivative) (TODI)

Chlorophenylene-2,4-diisocyanate—(Desmodur C)

The synthesis of diisocyanates may be exemplified by the preparation of toluene diisocyanates from *o*-nitro toluene:

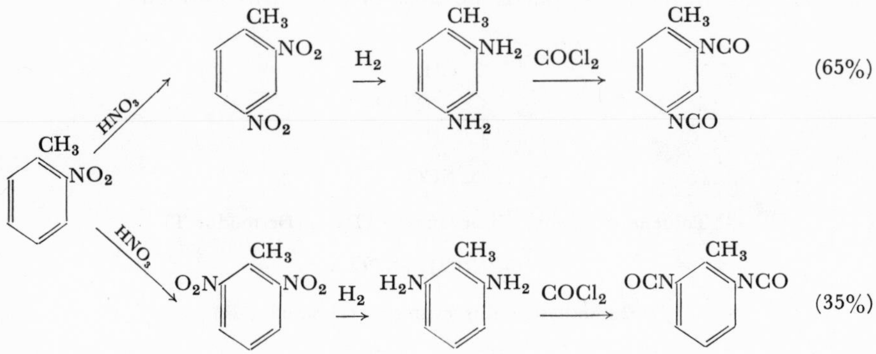

(65%)

(35%)

Another example is the preparation of hexamethylene diisocyanate by the following sequence:

$$H_2N(CH_2)_6NH_2 + CO_2 \rightarrow {}^+H_3N(CH_2)_6NH{\cdot}COO^-$$

$$\downarrow COCl_2$$

$$HCl{\cdot}H_2N(CH_2)_6NH{\cdot}COCl + CO_2$$

$$\downarrow COCl_2$$

$$OCN(CH_2)_6NCO + 4HCl$$

The first two reactions take place in the cold, the latter at 150°C.

Isocyanates are very reactive compounds. Any active hydrogen compound will add to the nitrogen-carbon bond, the labile hydrogen bonding to the nitrogen atom. The relative rates of addition are:

$$R_2NH > RNH_2 > NH_3 > ArNH_2 > ROH > HOH > RCOOH$$

Amines yield substituted ureas, alcohols yield urethanes, water yields a carbamic acid which loses carbon dioxide to give a simple amine, and carboxylic acids react to form anhydrides which lose carbon dioxide to yield amides:

$$R{\cdot}NCO + R'NH_2 \rightarrow R{\cdot}NH{\cdot}CO{\cdot}NH{\cdot}R'$$
$$R{\cdot}NCO + R'{\cdot}OH \rightarrow R{\cdot}NH{\cdot}COOR'$$
$$R{\cdot}NCO + H{\cdot}OH \rightarrow R{\cdot}NH{\cdot}COOH \rightarrow R{\cdot}NH_2 + CO_2$$
$$R{\cdot}NCO + R'COOH \rightarrow R{\cdot}NH{\cdot}COO{\cdot}CO{\cdot}R' \rightarrow R{\cdot}NH{\cdot}CO{\cdot}R' + CO_2$$

Research on polyurethanes was begun principally in Germany prior to 1939. This work led to the development of a product, Perlon U, which was used chiefly for bristle and other monofilament applications; also developed were intermediates, Desmodur-Desmophens, for use as coating compositions, adhesives, and plastics (Igamid U). [The polyisocyanates are

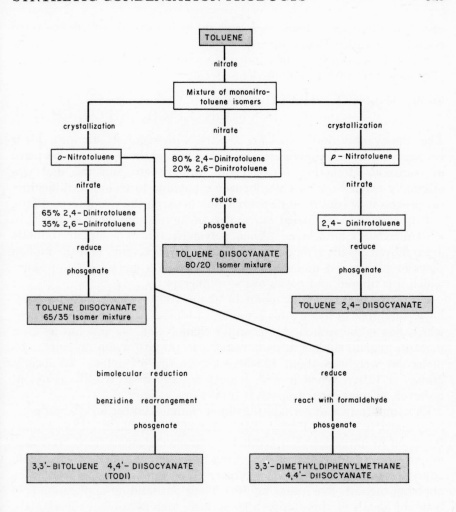

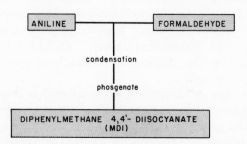

FIG. 8-19. Preparation routes to some commercial isocyanates. (*Courtesy Industrial and Engineering Chemistry*)

called, in Germany, Desmodurs, and the polyesters (polyhydroxy compounds) are called Desmophens.]

Perlon U is formed by the condensation of hexamethylene diisocyanate (Desmodur H) with tetramethylene glycol:

$$OCN(CH_2)_6NCO + HO(CH_2)_4OH \rightarrow \rightarrow$$
$$[—HN \cdot O_2C(CH_2)_6NH \cdot CO_2(CH_2)_4—]_n$$

The diisocyanate and glycol are reacted with vigorous stirring; this is necessary as the two liquids are incompatible, and the reaction takes place in emulsion. Reaction between the diisocyanate and the diol was originally carried out in chlorobenzene, but due to technical difficulties the process now consists of direct reaction between the two intermediates.

Polymerization is carried out under an inert atmosphere at 195°C in a stainless steel autoclave. When polymerization is complete, bubbles are removed by the temporary application of a vacuum, and the molten polymer is then fed under nitrogen pressure to a metering pump, after which it is filtered and passes to the spinnerets.

Perlon U has a melting point of about 180°C which is about 80°C lower than that of nylon; this is too low a temperature for use in apparel which has to be ironed. It is stiffer than Nylon 66 and has a lower moisture regain, similar in these respects to the 610 nylon polymer. Its molecular weight is about 15,000—close to that of nylon. Its specific gravity is 1.21. When heated, it does not brown so readily as nylon; however, in most other respects it is inferior.

One important and perhaps the oldest commercial use for di- and polyisocyanates is in the adhesive field. Formulations based on isocyanates dispersed in natural and/or synthetic elastomer cements have been used to join natural and synthetic elastomers to textiles and metals. Excellent adhesives can be prepared by mixing diisocyanates and glycols, then applying the adhesive immediately. Their outstanding application is in bonding metals to almost any other surface, such as another metal, glass, plastic, or fiber. The bond cures in a few minutes after the application of heat. The isocyanates used are usually toluene diisocyanate, diphenylmethane diisocyanate, and triphenylmethane triisocyanate; almost any polyhydroxy compound will work. Isocyanate cement can be used as a flocking adhesive on papers and fabrics. It will even stick rubber shoesoles to leather uppers, eliminating sewing and providing a waterproof bond of high strength.

In Germany the use of isocyanates for coatings has been developed to a high degree. The coatings are applied in a manner similar to that of the adhesives. The solutions of Desmophens and Desmodurs are mixed and applied to the surface. The coating hardens slowly at room temperature or rapidly if heated. The ability to cure at room temperature is important for coating heat-sensitive objects. The coatings are very flexible and are resistant to water, solvents, and alkalies. They are characterized by high gloss, low gas permeability, and excellent electrical insulating properties. The disadvantages are the need for immediate use of solutions, the difficulty of cleaning equipment, disagreeable vapors, and high cost.

Polyurethane coatings have been successfully used in lining storage tanks of seagoing tankers which haul sour crude oil in one direction and salt-water ballast in the other. On conveyor systems which handle corrosive and abrasive materials, polyurethane paints have given excellent service. Similar coatings are reportedly used on a leading line of American-made rubber toys, providing a tough, glossy, cleanable surface.

A growing use for polyurethanes is in coating magnet wire. Excellent electrical properties, together with high resistance to moisture and heat, have made it the most widely used magnet wire coating material in Europe, and its use is growing rapidly in America. The dominant position in the field of wire coating up to now has been held by Formvar [a poly(vinyl formal) resin combined with an alkyl phenolic resin in a solvent mixture of cresylic acid and/or furfural and naphtha]. The new product, a poly(vinyl formal)-polyurethane wire coating, does not have to be stripped off wires that are to be soldered because the urethane bond breaks at soldering temperatures (360°C), leaving a clean wire surface; the new resin is reported to match the older coating in electrical properties and heat and moisture resistance.

Reaction products of isocyanates and alkyds are reported to give coatings whose films have excellent adhesion to most types of surfaces, good elasticity, low permeability, resistance to weathering, and good electrical properties. Isocyanates are reported also to be of interest for modifying drying oils. Paints and lacquers compounded with these modified oils are said to be superior to those made with the unmodified products, especially in resistance to dilute acids and alkalies. Isocyanates will react with phenol-formaldehyde resins, alkyds, cellulose nitrate, cellulose acetate, modified vinyl resins, and many others. Products of these reactions show improved hardness, reduced thermoplasticity, faster cure, and greater water and solvent resistance. Diisocyanates have been reacted with castor oil, which is basically a trihydroxy alcohol, to form novel polyurethanes. The products are modified during the reactions with glycols, such as hexamethylene glycol. They have good chemical resistance, withstanding caustic and mineral acids, together with fair solvent resistance, and good heat resistance. The materials have also been suggested as potting compounds.

Foams, particularly the elastic types, have shown the greatest amount of success in the isocyanate field. The product is far superior to rubber foams with respect to aging, resilience, and ability to be dry-cleaned. Owing to their low apparent densities and valuable mechanical properties, these foams are used as material for construction and insulation.

For the production of solid foams, a dicarboxylic acid and a triol are partially condensed to form a polyester which contains both free hydroxyl and carboxyl groups. If such an ester is mixed with a diisocyanate, rapid reaction takes place in the syrupy mass with evolution of heat; part of the diisocyanate reacts with the hydroxyl groups to form polyurethane bonds; due to the increase in temperature, the carboxyl groups react in turn with isocyanate groups; cross-links are formed and carbon dioxide is released. The mass thus becomes tough and spongy and finally turns into a very hard foam. This evolution of gas may be supplemented with added thermal blowing agents to give a frothy product which is very light, strong, and rigid.

Toluene diisocyanate is most frequently employed, and a large number of low-molecular-weight polyesters can be used. The product is usually foamed in place by placing the materials in solution and heating with steam. The procedure is simple and a minimum of equipment is needed. The density of the foam may be varied from, say, 3 to 25 pounds per cubic foot and still retain high structural strength. The thermal and insulation properties are excellent.

These foams are used extensively in aircraft construction to give strength with little added weight. Here, they are used in the manufacture of wing tips. An outer skin is formed from aluminum; then isocyanates and polyesters are poured into the hollow of the wing tip and the foaming action fills every crevice. The result is a strong, lightweight wing tip, easily fabricated while saving many man-hours of labor.

Foams of varying degrees of hardness are obtainable. In appearance, soft polyurethane foam resembles finely foamed rubber. In performance, the foam has much more to offer, as it can be sewn by machine or by hand, can be laundered or dry-cleaned, resists the action of sunlight and air, is fire retardant, may be dyed any color, can be combined with other materials, and is tougher than competitive materials. Because they can be made completely porous with no outer skin, polyurethane foams are self-ventilated, offering cooler cushioning material. Since polyurethane foams are only half the weight, by volume, of competitive foams, airlines are installing polyurethane foam seats and backs in passenger planes.

One of the largest volume uses for these foams is expected to be for carpet underlay or rug liners (Unifoam). They require no fabric backing for strength and need not be fastened down, since friction holds them in place. Polyurethane pads have such great resilience that even thin rugs are reported to feel like heavy ones.

Another new field for such foams is in clothing. European dress designers use polyurethane foams to provide lightweight insulation in coats and jackets, and sew shoulder pads of this material into fancy dresses. Since neither detergents nor solvents hurt the foam, linings and pads need not be removed when the garments are cleaned. Recently introduced in the United States is a hooded jacket which weighs less than a summer sport jacket but is as warm as a sheepskin coat; one-eighth inch of polyurethane foam as an interliner makes this possible.

Because of the foam's insulating qualities, perishable-food containers have been made with rigid polyurethane foamed between inner and outer metal shells. A refrigerated trailer-truck with walls made of aluminum-polyurethane-aluminum sandwiches has been developed. It is likely that present weather stripping used on automobiles will be replaced with a

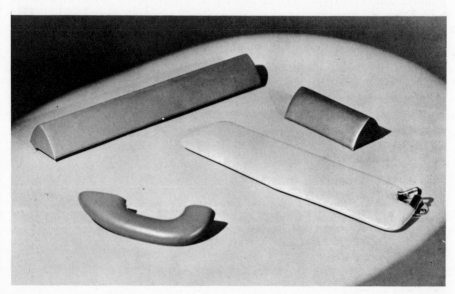

Fig. 8-20. Automobile arm rests, sun visor, and dash padding made from expanded polyurethanes. (*Courtesy Mobay Chemical Co.*)

polyurethane. Its durability is such that it is anticipated that the stripping will retain its original condition for the life of the automobile.

One of the most important uses of the diisocyanates is in the field of elastomers. In Great Britain, research was directed toward the reaction of polyester-amides with organic diisocyanates to produce vulcanizable polymeric plasticizers, designated Vulcaprenes. In Germany, the elastomer known as Vulcollan was developed through studies of the reaction of polyester glycols with organic diisocyanates. The steps for the latter are: (1) Preparation of a linear polyester (adipic acid and ethylene glycol), (2) addition of a diisocyanate which increases the chain length, and (3) treatment of the product with small amounts of water to form a urea and develop a network structure. The diisocyanate must be of a bulky type, like naphthalene diisocyanate. The Vulcollans can be used in solutions for dipped goods, adhesives, and coatings, and can also be worked on a mill. They have the highest resistance to tearing of any synthetic material known. They are highly resistant to aging and to the action of ozone.

In 1953, a new elastomeric polyurethane product, Chemigum SL, was introduced in the United States. The polyester is made from ethylene and propylene glycols, and adipic acid. The useful diisocyanates are the toluene, naphthalene, and diphenylmethane diisocyanates. A storable gum elastomer is prepared by using an excess of polyester and is then cured by adding diisocyanate to the conventional compounding batch. The cure is very rapid. At present, they are difficult to fabricate into tires, and the most successful applications are in cast mechanical goods, coatings, and retreads.

Polyester-isocyanate elastomers (and foams) are cross-linked by entirely different types of chemical reactions than those occurring with most elastomers. These reactions begin as soon as additional isocyanate curatives are added to the raw gum. The principal isocyanate cross-linking reactions are:[11]

$$\begin{array}{cc}
\overset{\text{O}}{\underset{\|}{\phantom{.}}} & \overset{\text{O}}{\underset{\|}{\phantom{.}}} \\
-\text{CO·NH}- \ + \ -\text{NCO} \rightarrow & -\text{CO·N}- \\
& \quad\ \ | \\
& \quad\ \ \text{CO·NH}-
\end{array}$$

Urethane                      Allophanic ester

$$\begin{array}{cc}
-\text{CO·NH}- \ + \ -\text{NCO} \rightarrow & -\text{CO·N}- \\
& \quad\ \ | \\
& \quad\ \ \text{CO·NH}-
\end{array}$$

Amide                         Acyl amide

$$\begin{array}{cc}
-\text{NH·CO·NH}- \ + \ -\text{NCO} \rightarrow & -\text{NH·CO·N}- \\
& \quad\quad\ \ | \\
& \quad\quad\ \ \text{CO·NH}-
\end{array}$$

Urea                          Biuret

Of the three, the latter two predominate.

The physical properties of cured Chemigum SL are very similar to Vulcollan, both exhibiting unusual toughness. Vulcanized Chemigum

[11] Seeger, N. V. et al., Ind. Eng. Chem., 45, 2538 (1953).

SL has a tensile strength of 5,450 psi, an elongation of 750 per cent, and an abrasion resistance twice that of the best cold rubber. Since the polyurethanes are saturated, cut growth resistance is excellent. Even though cuts are initiated by sharp objects, there is no tendency for the cut to grow, even under stress. In this respect, a vast superiority is shown over natural rubber or GR-S. Further, the ozone and oxygen resistance, ultraviolet resistance, oxygen absorption, resilience, and wear properties are excellent.

Resistance of Chemigum SL is poor to high temperatures, hot water, and steam. Another disadvantage is the tendency to harden at low temperatures, since Chemigum SL freezes at $-35°C$, compared with $-65°C$ for cured natural rubber gum. The usual fillers, at best, enhance only slightly and may actually impair the physical properties of these elastomers.

Vulcollan-type elastomers cost today at least ten times as much as present synthetic elastomers, and it is not possible at present to produce a complete tire from them. However, it is indicated that tire life can be increased to a range of 50,000 to 100,000 miles using this type of elastomer.

Potential uses include wear-resistant veneers on pneumatic tires. Soles, heels, belt surfaces, and floorings may be protected by local applications. Since the raw gum stocks are readily soluble in standard solvents, they lend themselves to cement compounding and find use as protective coatings on rubber, plastic, and fabrics. A solution of Chemigum SL, sprayed on the surface of rubber or plastic, gives an adherent, flexible, and scuff-resistant coating that is at the same time resistant to sunlight, ozone, and general weathering.

Adiprene B urethane elastomer is a new polymer announced in 1955. It differs from other diisocyanate elastomers in that it is made from aliphatic polyethers rather than polyesters. An example of such a polyether would be poly(tetramethylene glycol), obtained from tetrahydrofuran. The polyurethane combines in a single product high strength, abrasion resistance, solvent and ozone resistance, and excellent low-temperature properties. Raw Adiprene B is a transparent, amber-colored polymer with a density at room temperature of 1.07. As with other polyurethane elastomers, the transformation of Adiprene B to the elastic state is accomplished by heating with a diisocyanate curing agent. Vulcanization is effected at temperatures of 100° to 150°C; curing times at 15 to 60 minutes at 134°C are the preferred conditions. In contrast to the polyester-based elastomers, Adiprene B can be reinforced with carbon blacks or silicas to improve the hot tensile strength, abrasion resistance, and tear strength. These improvements are accompanied by a sacrifice in resilience, hardness, and compression set.

## SILICONES

Organosilicon compounds were first studied by Friedel, Crafts, and Ladenburg between 1871 and 1874. Although other investigators later studied these compounds, the major theoretical contributions were made by Kipping and his collaborators in England. In 1904, Kipping found that Grignard reagents could be used for the preparation of organosilicon compounds and, during the next forty-odd years, he and his students prepared and studied a large number of them. In attempts to prepare the silicon analogs of the common carbon compounds, they found the differences so many that the foundation for a new field in chemistry was laid. However, the development of modern silicon polymer chemistry during the last twenty years is due principally to Hyde and his associates, Rochow and his associates, and McGregor and Warrick, all in the United States.

Elemental silicon is quite stable at ordinary temperatures; oxidation occurs very slowly below a red heat. Halogens attack it more readily, and chlorine reacts readily at 250°C or higher to form silicon chlorides. In its organic compounds, silicon, like carbon, is usually tetravalent but its electropositive nature and its possible hexacovalency become evident under certain conditions and cause vigorous reactions unknown in the analogous carbon compounds. The rapid hydrolysis of silicon halides and the rupture of silicon-silicon chains by water and hydroxyl ions are examples.

The simplest covalent compounds of silicon are the hydrides, and the simplest hydride is silane, $SiH_4$. The higher hydrides, disilane ($Si_2H_6$), trisilane ($Si_3H_8$), etc., form an homologous series which is structurally similar to the aliphatic series of saturated hydrocarbons. However, chains containing only silicon appear to be limited in length, for the higher silanes are unstable, the highest member of the series so far recorded being hexasilane.

There are four general types of bonds which have been investigated in the formation of silicon polymers:

$$—\overset{|}{\underset{|}{Si}}—\overset{|}{\underset{|}{Si}}—\overset{|}{\underset{|}{Si}}—\overset{|}{\underset{|}{Si}}— \qquad \text{Silanes}$$

$$—\overset{|}{\underset{|}{Si}}—\overset{|}{\underset{|}{C}}—\overset{|}{\underset{|}{Si}}—\overset{|}{\underset{|}{C}}— \qquad \text{Silcarbanes}$$

$$—\overset{|}{\underset{|}{Si}}—N—\overset{|}{\underset{|}{Si}}—N— \qquad \text{Silazanes}$$

$$—\overset{|}{\underset{|}{Si}}—O—\overset{|}{\underset{|}{Si}}—O— \qquad \text{Siloxanes}$$

The silanes represent the first type of bond.    Silane itself is conveniently prepared by the reaction of lithium tetrahydro aluminate with silicon chlorides:

$$SiCl_4 + LiAlH_4 \rightarrow SiH_4 + AlCl_3 + LiCl$$

One method of preparation of compounds containing the Si·C bond is as follows:

$$CH_2Cl_2 + Si \xrightarrow[Cu]{\triangle} —CH_2 \cdot SiCl_2—$$

Neither of the above types of silicon compounds produces satisfactory polymers with the desired properties.    The silazanes do have heat-stable properties, but the polymers hydrolyze easily to form siloxanes and ammonia, from which they are made.    The siloxanes or *silicones* (so named by Kipping because they bear a formal resemblance to the ketones, $R_2CO$) yield the best products.    The basic structure,

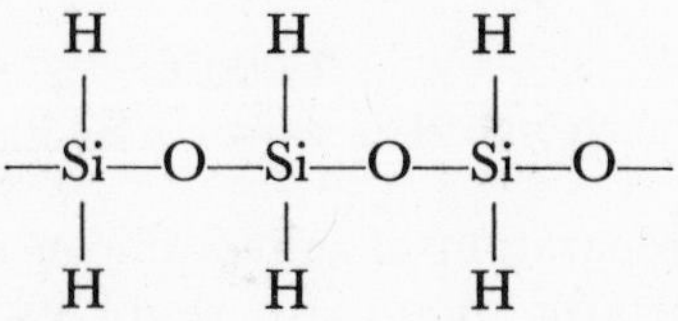

$$
\begin{array}{ccccccc}
& H & & H & & H & \\
& | & & | & & | & \\
—Si & —O— & Si & —O— & Si & —O— \\
& | & & | & & | & \\
& H & & H & & H &
\end{array}
$$

modified by replacement of the hydrogen atoms with hydrocarbon radicals, results in an organosiloxane:

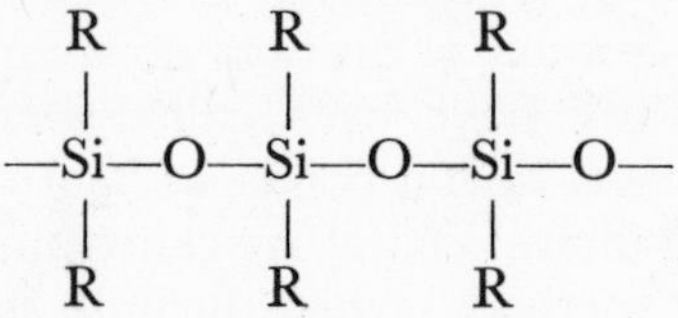

$$
\begin{array}{ccccccc}
& R & & R & & R & \\
& | & & | & & | & \\
—Si & —O— & Si & —O— & Si & —O— \\
& | & & | & & | & \\
& R & & R & & R &
\end{array}
$$

in which two of the bonds of each silicon atom are occupied by organic groups and two are linked to separate oxygen atoms of the polymeric chain.    Since the chain is a stable, oxidized structure, common to silica, quartz, and other silicate minerals, and since certain R·Si linkages are known to be exceedingly inert and resistant to oxidation, the combination provides thermal stability and resistance to some types of reagents to a much greater extent than that found in the purely organic polymers.

The first step in the formation of a silicone is the preparation of elemental silicon.  Sand or quartz rock is heated with coke and charcoal in an electric furnace:

$$SiO_2 + 2C \xrightarrow{\triangle} Si + 2CO$$

(Using an excess of carbon, silicon carbide or Carborundum is formed.) The next step is to convert the element to a halide derivative.  Silicon tetrachloride is useful as the starting compound for making many silicone compounds.  It may be made by the chlorination of silicon at high temperature in a reducing atmosphere:

$$Si + 2Cl_2 \xrightarrow{> 250°C} SiCl_4$$

or

$$Si + 2COCl_2 \xrightarrow{700°C} SiCl_4 + 2CO$$

The chlorinated compound may also be made directly from silica as follows, using coke as a reducing agent:

$$SiO_2 + 2C + 2Cl_2 \xrightarrow{1,000°C} SiCl_4 + 2CO$$

Methods for the preparation of organosilicon compounds (or at least the carbon-silicon parts of them) are restricted to low or moderately elevated temperatures, since carbon-carbon and carbon-hydrogen bonds are not stable at high temperatures.  Rochow[12] has divided the methods on the basis of the reagent involved.  The classical means of synthesis require preparation of one organometallic compound from another, hence first involves the preparation of an organic compound of a metal more active than silicon; these have been called *substitution methods*.  Other methods that form carbon-silicon bonds without the use of other organometallic compounds as intermediates are called *direct methods*.

Of the substitution methods, which include the use of dimethyl and diethyl zinc to prepare the corresponding alkyls of silicon and many of the intermediate substitution products, and the use of sodium or lithium (the Wurtz reaction), the one of greatest interest has been the Grignard reaction, applied by Kipping to the preparation of organic derivatives of silicon tetrachloride.  The latter is a two-stage process.  A suitable alkyl or aryl halide is reacted with magnesium suspended in an aliphatic ether to give the corresponding alkyl or aryl magnesium halide.  This anhydrous mixture is then added to a nonaqueous solution of a silicon

[12] Rochow, E. G., *An Introduction to the Chemistry of the Silicones*, 2nd ed., p. 29, John Wiley and Sons, New York, 1951.

halide or ester. The silicon derivatives remain in solution, from which they may be separated by distillation. Other variations of this process have been developed, some of which involve a one-stage reaction.

In all preparations by the Grignard reaction, a mixture of products is obtained. When the organometallic compound is added to the silicon halide, the primary substitution product formed may react with unreacted reagent just as did the original halide. For example, from silicon tetra-chloride the successive substitution products will be $RSiCl_3$, $R_2SiCl_2$, $R_3SiCl$, and $R_4Si$. The first three of these, still containing active halogen, react with the substitution reagent. It is important to realize that any attempt to prepare an intermediate product always results in a mixture containing the desired compound as well as its less highly and more highly alkylated homologs.

So far as the direct methods of synthesis are concerned, there are several widely different processes which do not require organometallic compounds as reagents or employ stoichiometric quantities of active metals for the preparation of the organometallic reagents. Among these methods may be mentioned the reactions of alkynes (e.g., acetylene) with halosilanes, the rearrangements of certain organochlorosilanes, and the direct synthesis from elemental silicon. Of the direct methods, it is the latter which is of the greatest commercial interest at present.

This method consists of passage of a halogen acid or alkyl or aryl halide in the vapor phase through heated silicon powder, using a mixture of metallic copper and copper oxide as a catalyst. Under such conditions, products of the general type $R_nSiX_{4-n}$ are obtained:

$$Si + 2HCl \xrightarrow[300°C]{Cu} H_2SiCl_2$$

or

$$Si + 2RCl \rightarrow R_2SiCl_2$$

As with the Grignard method, a number of reactions occur simultaneously, forming such products as $RSiX_3$, $R_3SiX$, and others. In other words, a mixture of related organosilicon halides is obtained, from which the components desired must be separated by distillation. Since the production of compounds other than the usually desired type, $R_2SiX_2$, unless in balanced proportions, represents a loss of organic groups or halogen, the direct synthesis is best suited to the preparation of dialkyl or diaryl dihalosilanes. If compounds of the type $R_3SiX$ or $R_4Si$ are required, the corresponding dihalosilane may first be made by the direct method and then alkylated further by one of the substitution methods.

The organosilicon halides are of particular importance because they are the intermediates from which commercial silicone polymers are made. Their reactive halogen atoms enable them to be converted into silanols, alkoxysilanes, or siloxane polymers having the same organosilicon groupings present in the halide.

The alkyl halosilanes react with alcohols to form a series of products variously known as alkyl silicic esters, ethers, or alkyl alkoxysilanes. In these compounds, some organic groups are linked directly to silicon and others are joined through oxygen. They are derived from the halides by replacement of halogen with alkoxy groups:

$$R_3SiCl + R'OH \rightarrow R_3SiOR' + HCl$$
$$R_2SiCl_2 + 2R'OH \rightarrow R_2Si(OR')_2 + 2HCl$$
$$RSiCl_3 + 3R'OH \rightarrow R_3Si(OR')_3 + 3HCl$$

They may also be prepared from the orthosilicates by direct reaction with zinc alkyls or with the Grignard reagent. In general, the alkyl alkoxysilanes are similar to the alkyl chlorosilanes in that they hydrolyze to form various silanols or their dehydration products.

The *monoalkyl trihalosilanes* ($RSiX_3$) are exemplified by methyl trichlorosilane, the simplest member of this series. All of the alkyl trichlorosilanes hydrolyze and are thought to form silanetriols:

$$RSiCl_3 + 3H_2O \rightarrow RSi(OH)_3 + 3HCl$$

No such compound, however, has ever been isolated, since a single organic group apparently exerts insufficient retarding influence on the condensation of an alkyl silanetriol, and it proceeds immediately to split out water, forming polymeric products.

The *dialkyl dihalosilanes* ($R_2SiX_2$) are another series, of which the simplest and probably the most important of all silicone intermediates is dimethyl dichlorosilane. It may be prepared by the Grignard method as follows:

$$CH_3Cl + Mg \rightarrow CH_3MgCl$$
$$2CH_3MgCl + SiCl_4 \rightarrow (CH_3)_2SiCl_2 + 2MgCl_2$$

The direct method may also be used. In this method, methyl chloride and silicon are reacted directly:

$$2CH_3Cl + Si \xrightarrow[\text{Cu}]{\triangle} (CH_3)_2SiCl_2 + \text{many other products}$$

The importance of the dialkyl dihalosilanes has led to the preparation of a large number of such compounds. They react with alcohols to form

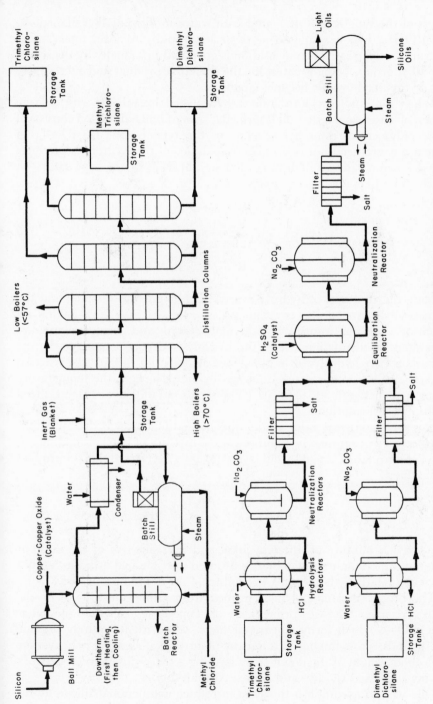

FIG. 8-21. Silicone flow sheet. (By permission from Chemical Engineering)

esters of the type $R_2Si(OR')_2$ and with water to form dialkyl silanediols, $R_2Si(OH)_2$, which condense more or less rapidly to form linear polysiloxanes. The rate of condensation is governed principally by the size of the alkyl group, being greatest for the dimethyl product and successively less as the alkyl groups become larger.

When dimethyl dichlorosilane is hydrolyzed by mixing with a large excess of water, a colorless oil is formed. About one half the oil consists of *cyclic* polymers of dimethyl siloxane of the type $[-Si(CH_3)_2O-]_n$, in which $n$ is greater than two. The remainder of the hydrolysis products consists principally of high-molecular-weight diols of the type $HO[-Si(CH_3)_2O-]_nH$; i.e.,

$$
\begin{array}{ccccc}
& R & & R & & R \\
& | & & | & & | \\
HO-Si- & O-Si & \cdots & O-Si & -OH \\
& | & & | & & | \\
& R & & R & & R
\end{array}
$$

Among the products of hydrolysis are the monomethyl siloxane and the trimethyl siloxane products. Since these may act as a cross-linking reagent or a telogen, respectively, the monochloro- and trichlorosilanes are separated by distillation before the hydrolysis step. Commercially, the halosilanes are hydrolyzed in glass-lined steel kettles. Since the reaction is exothermic, cooling is accomplished by water jackets, the temperature being kept between 30° to 50°C. The separated oily layer is neutralized with soda ash solution.

A reaction of great value to the silicone manufacturer is that of equilibration. For example, by equilibrating a mixture of trialkyl- and monoalkyl chlorosilanes, a good yield of the (usually) preferred dialkyl product is obtained:

$$(CH_3)_3SiCl + CH_3SiCl_3 \underset{}{\overset{AlCl_3}{\rightleftharpoons}} 2(CH_3)_2SiCl_2$$

Similarly, a mixture of different alkyl and aryl silicones of the same or different functionalities may be equilibrated over an acid or basic catalyst to yield a relatively homogeneous product of the desired properties.

The organosiloxane polymers formed from either the dihalo- or the dialkoxysilanes consist principally of repetition of the mesomer, $-R_2SiO-$, which forms linear polymers. As with the purely organic compounds, cross-linking is a means of further increasing the average molecular weight of the polymer by forming a three-dimensional network having increased rigidity and decreased solubility.

One way to accomplish this is to introduce trifunctional silicon atoms at intervals along the siloxane chains and then form oxygen bridges between these monosubstituted trifunctional atoms on different chains:

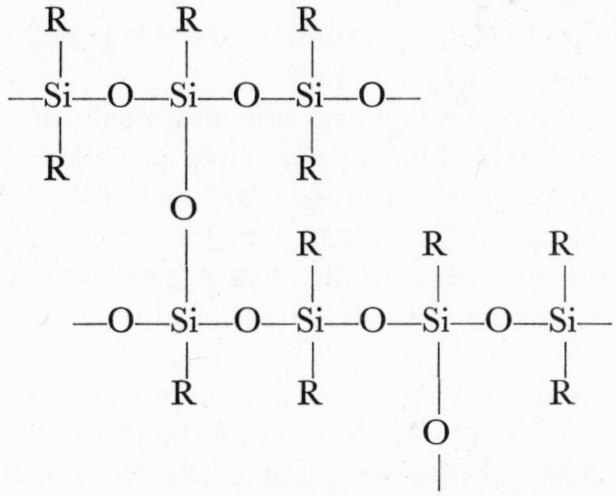

$$
\begin{array}{ccccc}
& R & & R & & R \\
& | & & | & & | \\
-Si & -O- & Si & -O- & Si & -O- \\
& | & & | & & | \\
& R & & | & & R \\
& & & O & & \\
& & & | & & \\
\end{array}
$$

R R R
| | |
—Si—O—Si—O—Si—O—
| | |
R O R
|
R R R
| | |
—O—Si—O—Si—O—Si—O—Si—
| | | |
R R O R
|
O
|

One of the simplest ways to introduce trifunctional groups is to include a small amount of a trihalosilane ($RSiX_3$) with a dihalosilane ($R_2SiX_2$); upon hydrolysis, there is then available a quantity of silanetriol as well as the diol, and cross-linking occurs to an extent determined by the ratio of the reactants.

The *trialkyl halosilanes* ($R_3SiX$), of which trimethyl chlorosilane is the simplest member, being monofunctional, are capable only of hydrolysis and condensation to form such organosiloxanes as the following:

$$2R_3SiOH \rightarrow R_3Si \cdot O \cdot SiR_3 + H_2O$$

This class of silanes is unsuitable for forming polymeric substances; these monofunctional reagents are of value, however, as modifiers (telogens) for the di- and trifunctional compounds.

A special class of alkyl halosilanes is the group containing both Si·H and Si·X linkages. Methyl dichlorosilane, $CH_3SiHCl_2$, for example, is both a hydride and a halide. This type may usually be hydrolyzed without loss of its hydrogen atoms and may also be converted to esters.

Analogous aryl derivatives of the halosilanes may be prepared by similar methods. In addition, many mixed alkyl-aryl chlorosilanes have been prepared commercially. The pure aryl silicones, however, behave quite differently from the alkyl silicones. For example, the hydrolysis of diphenyl dichlorosilane yields pure diphenyl silanediol almost quantitatively:

$$(C_6H_5)_2SiCl_2 + 2H_2O \rightarrow (C_6H_5)_2Si(OH)_2 + 2HCl$$

This diol is quite stable. Acid condensation of the diol yields cyclic trimer, and basic condensation yields the cyclic tetramer almost exclusively.

At high temperatures, linear condensation products are formed. The phenyl silicones formed from both the dichloro- and the trichlorosilanes are weak and brittle, and unsuitable alone for the formation of a useful polymer. The ring-chlorinated products are also brittle and fusible, but will withstand temperatures up to 450°C.

As might be anticipated, alkyl-aryl silicones, made by co-condensing a mixture of alkyl and aryl chlorosilanes, yield products of enhanced usefulness, including high heat resistance and flexibility (from modification of the brittleness of the aryl reactant with the oiliness of the alkyl one). Methyl phenyl silicone, for example, has a good balance of flexibility, infusibility, and strength when the reactants are combined in proper proportion.

At the present time, the most popular area of research is in the field of carbon-functional silicones. These are compounds which contain reactive groups in the organic substituents attached to the silicon atoms. Until recently, most silicone polymer investigations were concentrated on the silicon-oxygen linkages in siloxane and on the intermediates leading up to them. The organic substituents, such as methyl and phenyl, were valued primarily for their inertness. Now, functional groups are being introduced into these organic substituents in an effort to obtain more versatile silicones.

In other words, the modified siloxanes are those in which the basic siloxane structure has been retained and has been substituted with carbon-functional groups. The goals fall into three broad categories. The first objective is to help the parent siloxane perform better in its usual applications and to adapt it to new applications. Particular targets are silicone elastomers and resins having greater strength. Functional groups can also allow investigators to modify compatibilities and cure rates, alter surface properties, and, in general, tailor-make chemical and physical characteristics for individual requirements.

As a second objective, hybrids are sought that retain the good properties of both the silicones and the organic modifiers. One aim is to combine some of the heat resistance of the silicone with the toughness of the organics. Most of this work has been done with the vinyl silicones. Still in the development stages are silicone hybrids of condensation polymers, such as polyesters, polyamides, phenolics, and polyurethanes.

As possible physiological agents, carbon-functional silicones are of interest as a third objective because they afford close analogs to known active compounds. Organisms may find some silicon analogs enough like vital metabolism intermediates for absorption but not similar enough to carry on life processes.

Carbon-functional silicones are still largely in the research stage; nevertheless, a number of products, notably chlorophenyl and vinyl silicones, have already reached the market.    Chlorophenyl silicones are being introduced commercially as high-temperature synthetic lubricants. Methyl chlorophenyl silicone lubricants have a thermal operating range of $-75°$ to $+260°C$; they thus offer a challenge to all known high-temperature lubricants.    Vinyl silicones are being produced commercially as gums for elastomers and as finishes for glass cloth.    What was needed for the latter application was a molecule that could be chemically tied to the glass on one side and the plastic on the other; in this application, vinyl trichlorosilane's double bond performs well.

The great majority of carbon-functional silicones have been made by displacement syntheses involving replacement of carbon-functional groups with other functional groups.    Direct and substitution methods are more attractive industrially but displacement syntheses are simpler for the laboratory.

All commercial silicone products may be divided conveniently into five classes (McGregor[13]): fluids, compounds, lubricants (greases and fluids), resins, and elastomers.

The *fluids* are heat-resistant liquids having low vapor pressures and high flash points.

Fluids in a wide viscosity range are available in which the organic substituents are both methyl and phenyl groups.    The use of phenyl groups improves oxidation stability and lubricating powers, and in some cases lowers the freezing point markedly.    Silicone fluids of the methyl-phenyl type remain liquid at very low temperatures and yet have low volatilities at ordinary temperatures.    Fluids are available with freezing points below $-70°C$ and a flash point of about $290°C$.    Certain of the fluids exhibit smaller changes in viscosity at temperature extremes than any other fluids known; this property makes them indispensable for use as lubricants where wide temperature variations are encountered.

The applications of the dimethyl silicone fluids, which are the commonest, are extremely diverse.    To the layman, probably the best known is that of treated tissue for cleaning spectacles.    Films are also applied to glassware, either by immersion in a dilute solution of dimethyl silicone in a solvent or by treating the glassware with the vapor of a chlorosilane in a chamber containing sufficient water vapor to insure complete hydrolysis.    Polymerization takes place on the surface of the articles to be coated and a water-repellent surface is developed.    Silicones are now being used to reduce bottle breakage; after containers are coated with a silicone emulsion, the breakage rate drops well below that of normal glassware.

Other uses of silicone oils have been as an ingredient of polishes for automobiles, furniture, and floors, and as a mold release agent for elastomers, plastics, and metals.    Another interesting application has

[13] McGregor, R. R., *Silicones and Their Uses*, p. 35, McGraw-Hill Book Co., New York, 1954.

been to glass fibers, creating water repellency by preventing wicking, and developing resiliency. Silicone-treated glass fibers, upon release from pressure, resume their original volume, whereas untreated glass fibers are easily crushed. Both of the above properties have enabled glass-fiber fillers to be used in life jackets.

The fluids are also effective antifoam agents for petroleum oils, hydraulic fluids, tar, thermoplastic adhesives, and also are used in the cooking of resins which have a tendency to foam. The use of premium grade, detergent lubricating oils would be impractical if it were not for the minute trace of silicone added to these oils to prevent foaming.

Another use is as a damping fluid in instruments or to prevent the transmission of vibrations from one part of a machine to another. Torsional vibration dampers using a thin film of a high-viscosity dimethyl silicone are in general use in internal combustion engines. In shock absorbers, silicone fluids offer great permanence and uniformity of action. In overload relays, circuit breakers, thermostatic controls, and similar

Fig. 8-22. Fabrics treated with a silicone emulsion become durably water-repellent and resist soiling. (*Dow-Corning Corp. photograph*)

devices, the silicones are used as a dashpot liquid. Their use gives uniform and reliable damping with minimum maintenance.

The outstanding water-repellent properties of the silicones have encouraged their use in a large number of different fields. Products developed for textile use have the water-repellent properties of the usual fluids but can be cured rapidly at a temperature of about 150°C to a semirubbery material which is unaffected by water and dry-cleaning solvents. While this treatment is applicable to nearly all types of fabrics (including wool and cotton), it is particularly useful with the modified natural and synthetic fibers, such as viscose, cellulose acetate, nylon, Orlon, and the acrylics. It has recently been reported that suede jackets have been "siliconized" to make them as cleanable as fabric and, of course, water-repellent. Shoes are on the market which are treated with a silicone product (Sylflex); this is tanned-in to make shoe upper leather exclude water, stay soft and flexible, and yet breathe. Even ironing board covers, treated with a silicone, are available. The cover is lintless, highly resistant to scorching, and is repellent to water-borne stains.

Paper, properly treated, becomes extremely water-repellent and non-adhesive to partially cured rubber, asphalt, pressure sensitive tapes, and to most other adhesive materials.

The silicone *compounds* are petrolatum-like materials made from the fluids by the addition of small amounts of very finely divided silica. These products vary in consistency from relatively free-flowing liquids to heavy, salvelike materials. They retain the properties of the dimethyl silicones, such as high heat resistance, low freezing point, low volatility, and good electrical properties. The heavier ones do not flow with heat and have excellent water repellency.

Like the fluids, an important application is the use of silicone compounds as an antifoaming agent. The antifoam may be incorporated in adhesives, resins, rubber, chewing-gum bases, cooking oils, surface coatings of all types, detergents, water softeners, dyes, and insecticides.

Another use of silicone compounds is as a lubricant for glass and ceramic stopcocks and joints; they are effective over a temperature range of $-40°$ to 250°C.

The silicone compounds have also found a wide market in the electrical industry. They are particularly valuable as moisture- and water-repellent, high-dielectric-strength sealing compounds for spark plugs, and are used for moisture seals for electrical connectors.

Silicone *lubricants* are made from the fluids, the simplest being the dimethyl siloxane type. Where a greater temperature range is desired, some phenyl groups are substituted for some of the methyl ones. Until recently, lithium soaps and carbon black have been used as thickeners for silicone fluids to make lubricants, but these products can operate only up to about 200°C, since the lithium soaps melt above this temperature. Silicone greases, thickened with aryl urea compounds, function at temperatures from subzero to 260°C.

Silicones are widely used in damping devices, as hydraulic fluids, in porous-bronze bushings, and as lubricants for natural and synthetic elastomers and for many plastics, particularly when the latter are used for fiber gears and bearings, as in synchronous clock motors and meters. Somewhat more viscous compounded silicone fluids are used where a wider operating range is required or where heat stability at higher temperatures is necessary, such as in parking meters, automobile speedometers, ball bearings, oven doors, high-temperature valves, and oven conveyors. Valves controlling the flow of a diverse variety of commercial liquids and gases show much less tendency to seize when this type of lubricant is used. They also make excellent lubricants for rubber when it must move against steel. Certain types of silicone greases have as their outstanding characteristic the ability to lubricate at extremely low temperatures. Another type is used in the ball bearings of motors operating at high speeds and temperatures.

The silicone *resins* are among the new resins that contribute improved properties for certain applications. Notable advances in electrical insulation and protective coatings have been obtained. The distinctive properties of silicone coatings are heat resistance, water repellency, and resistance to corrosive gases and most aqueous chemicals. In applications where the full advantages of these properties are not required, organic film-formers, especially alkyd resins, may be added to the silicone, either by cold blending or by chemical reaction. By such combinations, faster drying and better application properties may often be obtained, although a compromise of properties between the two classes of film-formers will be obtained. Organosilicone coatings containing aluminum flake are available that will withstand temperatures as high as 500°C. However, very high curing temperatures are required. This type of coating is meant for application to metal surfaces exposed to extreme heat, such as hot stacks, furnaces, manifolds, ovens, and high-temperature processing equipment.

Many types of water-repellent solutions and emulsions have been developed for the waterproofing of masonry and concrete. As the solvent is evaporated from a solution of a suitable silicone, a thin film is deposited on the sides of the capillaries in the masonry. Surface weathering does not impair the effectiveness of this treatment which prevents moisture penetration and salt efflorescence.

A very large use of silicones is in resins for application as an insulating medium in electrical uses. Since the passage of an electric current in a conductor is always accompanied by the evolution of heat (as the resistance of the conductor is finite), the current must be limited so that the heat generated is not sufficient to decompose the insulation. Since silicone resins have superior insulating properties and do not decompose as readily at high temperatures as most organic substances, typical applications of the silicone insulation resins are for use in motors and generators.

Silicones are also used as laminating and molding resins. For the latter, they are mixed with appropriate fillers, such as glass fiber, asbestos, or diatomaceous earth, the solvent is removed, and the resin-filler mix held

Fig. 8-23. The silicone-insulated (class H) motor on the right weighs half as much as the class A insulated motor on the left, yet the capacities of the two motors are the same. (*Dow-Corning Corp. photograph*)

at an elevated temperature for a short time. When cool, the mix can be broken up or powdered and is then ready for compression or transfer molding. Typical properties are tensile strengths of 4,000 to 6,000 psi, water absorption of less than 0.2 per cent, continuous heat resistance of better than 250°C, and negligible effect of chemicals.

Certain silicone resins have proved to be very useful as release resins, especially in molding and food baking operations. Baking pans, suitably coated and baked, allow easy release of bread, rolls, cakes, etc. Silicone-coated pans also permit easy release of meats and even frozen foods.

Silicone *elastomers* have some basic properties which are responsible for their unique place in the industrial picture. The usual silicone elastomers are prepared from a mixture of a dimethyl silicone polymer, an inorganic filler, and a vulcanizing agent. The silicone polymer is usually made by polymerization of very pure difunctional silicones in order to obtain a high molecular weight. The usual fillers are employed, except for carbon black, which interferes with the curing action of the peroxide-type of vulcanizing agent commonly used. Further, as heat-resistant silicone elastomers (Silastic) were developed, it became apparent that carbon black could not be used as the reinforcing agent for another reason —because of its limited heat stability. Fortunately, *silica* soot had been developed in Germany as an elastomer reinforcement during World

FIG. 8-24. These bread pans have been treated with a silicone resin. No further greasing is required and the baked loaves will not stick to the pans. (*Dow-Corning Corp. photograph*)

War II. This product is now used in the United States. A mixture of silicon tetrachloride and hydrogen is burned, yielding finely divided "silica smoke" and by-product hydrogen chloride. The collected silica soot has a particle size range of only 4 to 20 millimicrons, its surface area is 300 to 350 square meters per gram, and one gram of this new product contains about $10^{18}$ particles. A silica-reinforced elastomer has a tensile strength of 1,900 psi as compared to 200 to 900 for previous grades of silicone elastomers; this may be compared with 1,500 to 3,000 psi for organic elastomers. In addition, elongations of more than 600 per cent have been achieved, as compared to 50 to 200 per cent for ordinary silicone elastomers.

Elastomers can be made that will withstand temperatures as high as 315°C without serious deterioration; so far as silicone elastomers are concerned, their outstanding characteristic is their stability at elevated temperatures. At 150°C, their life is unlimited for all practical purposes, whereas temperatures above 100°C bring about a rapid softening of most organic elastomers. Further, all of them retain their flexibility down to at least −55°C and some even down to −90°C. Most natural and synthetic organic elastomers have a minimum serviceable temperature of about −35°C. Since the good low-temperature properties are not dependent upon the addition of plasticizers, there is no sacrifice of high-temperature resistance.

The silicone elastomers show the properties of stretch and retraction, bounce, and great flexibility. They do not have as great tensile strength or abrasion resistance as the organic elastomers, but they are useful over a much broader temperature range. They are also resistant to many chemicals that affect the organic elastomers adversely. The arc, corona, weathering, and ozone resistances of all silicone elastomers are, in general, exceptional, when compared with organic ones.

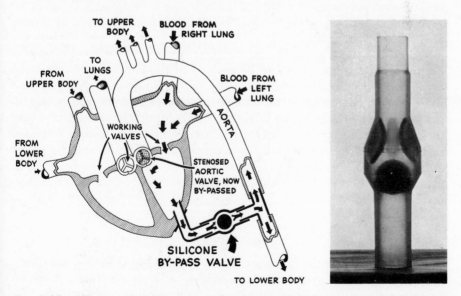

Fig. 8-25. Silicone valve (inset) is used to by-pass defective aortic valve in human heart. (*Dow-Corning Corp. photograph*)

At temperatures above 125°C, gaskets and seals made from most organic elastomers deteriorate rapidly in contact with oil.  Since silicone elastomers resist the action of various oils at temperatures up to 250°C, they are widely used as gasketing material for internal-combustion engines. Their resistance to hydrocarbon solvents is, however, generally poor. Development of fluorosilicone elastomers has improved this property considerably.  For example, a polymer (Silastic LS) made from trifluoropropyl methyl dichlorosilane is reported to be the first silicone elastomer which not only flexes at low temperatures but is also solvent-resistant.

Striking advances have been made in silicone elastomer technology by the development of vinyl curing systems.  Basically, the new system involves reversing the activity of the curing system.  Instead of using a highly reactive peroxide in combination with the highly unreactive methyl groups in the base polymer, the new method is based upon the introduction of reactive, unsaturated, pendant groups into the polymer, and using a relatively unreactive peroxide exhibiting specificity toward the unsaturated groups.  Although this new curing method is applicable to many unsaturated groups, such as allyl and cyclohexenyl, most of the work to date has been done with the vinyl group.  This group can be introduced into the polymer in such forms as ethyl vinyl siloxane, methyl vinyl siloxane, or phenyl vinyl siloxane.  The general class of di-*tert*-alkyl peroxides has been found satisfactory as initiators for the curing of such unsaturated polymers.

A brief word must be said about "bouncing putty," prepared by mixing about 5 per cent boric oxide with a dimethyl silicone and heating the mixture.  This is a putty-like material having a peculiar combination of properties, for, although it can be molded in the hand like putty, it also exhibits good compressive elasticity by rebounding when dropped on a hard surface; although it shows cold flow when left at rest, it can be shattered by a sudden blow; finally, it can be drawn out slowly into long threads.  Some suggested uses for this compound are in damping devices, sealing and filling compounds, as a center in golf balls, and for use in automatic table-leg levelers.  In spite of its unusual combination of properties, however, this material remains relatively unimportant commercially.

## POLYETHERS

Polyethers having the linear structure —O·R·O·R·O·R·O— have been prepared from aldehydes, alkylene oxides, and glycols; and, from the corresponding sulfur analogs, polythioethers have also been obtained.  Up to the present, the latter have not been of commercial importance.

## Polyoxymethylenes

Although formaldehyde is of great value to the synthetic resin industry because of its wide use in the formation of phenoplasts and aminoplasts, its homopolymers are largely of theoretical interest. Paraformaldehyde, or more commonly, paraform, is the most familiar form of formaldehyde polymer, but others may be prepared under specific conditions. Formaldehyde polymerizes in several distinct ways, as follows:[14]

$$
CH_2O
\begin{cases}
\xrightarrow[H_2SO_4]{\Delta} &
\begin{array}{c}
O-CH_2 \\
CH_2 \quad\ O \\
O-CH_2
\end{array}
\ +\
\begin{array}{c}
O-CH_2-O \\
CH_2 \qquad\quad CH_2 \\
O-CH_2-O
\end{array} \\
\xrightarrow{Ca(OH)_2 aq.} & HOH_2C(CHOH)_4CHO + HOH_2C(CHOH)_3CO \cdot CH_2OH \\
\xrightarrow{aq.} & HO(-CH_2O-)_nH \\
\xrightarrow[H_2SO_4]{CH_3OH} & CH_3 \cdot O(-CH_2O-)_nH
\end{cases}
$$

In aqueous media, formaldehyde probably polymerizes from its hydrated form, methylene glycol, $CH_2(OH)_2$, forming polyoxymethylenes or, more correctly, polyoxymethylene glycols. The product, known as paraformaldehyde, is a mixture of linear polyoxymethylene chains of varying lengths, where $n$ has a value of from 10 to 50. A polyaddition mechanism, through the unsaturated carbonyl groups, may be responsible for its polymerization in the pure liquefied state at very low temperatures to give solid polymers of much higher molecular weight, capable of being pressed into films and drawn into short filaments. The end groups may be modified by etherification and esterification, as illustrated by the last equation above.

All polyoxymethylenes are crystalline, yielding well-defined powder diagrams. Some of them have been obtained in the form of fibers, but the polymers, even when of higher molecular weight, have been of little commercial importance as fibers or plastics until very recently. A major defect has been the ease with which depolymerization can occur; in general, most formaldehyde polymers cannot be dissolved in acids or organic solvents nor can they be melted without decomposition occurring.

A new polymer (Delrin acetal resin), now undergoing development, is made from formaldehyde. Although little has yet been revealed concerning its method of manufacture or composition, it is known that it can be made by a continuous process by passing gaseous formaldehyde into an

[14] Ritchie, P. D., *A Chemistry of Plastics and High Polymers*, p. 88, Cleaver-Hume Press, London (dist. by Interscience Publishers, New York), 1949.

inert hydrocarbon reaction medium at or near room temperature and pressure. Stabilization of the polymer chains prevents the depolymerization and chemical sensitivity of the usual formaldehyde polymers. Further, a continuous method of polymerization is believed to be partly responsible for the longer, stronger chains formed which give the product its unique properties.

These properties include a very low equilibrium moisture content (0.2 per cent at 50 per cent relative humidity), a 264 psi heat distortion temperature of 100°C (171°C at 66 psi), a specific gravity of 1.425, a crystalline melting point of 175°C, and a tensile strength of 10,000 psi.

The product is a white powder which can be used in injection and blow-molding operations or can be extruded. Possible uses include gears, tumblers, aerosol bottles, telephone cases, bearings, housewares, automobile parts, and wire coatings. Basically, this polymer is potentially one of the cheapest plastics possible; it may well capture a large share of the thermoplastics market within the next ten years.

### Polyoxyethylenes

Polymers are readily formed from ethylene oxide. These polymers are mixtures which can be separated into fractions which vary widely in molecular weights. Unlike the formaldehyde polymers, they are not depolymerized by heat, but instead yield complicated products including acetaldehyde and acrolein.

The variation in the degradative behavior of the two types of polymers is probably due to the following differences. In polyoxymethylene, rupture can occur only between a carbon-oxygen linkage, whereas in polyoxyethylene rupture can occur at a carbon-carbon linkage as well. Thus, polyoxyethylene is a true ether, whereas polyoxymethylene behaves more as an acetal of formaldehyde and methylene glycol.

It has been previously pointed out (Chap. 4) that polymerization of ethylene oxide involves the preliminary formation of a small amount of ethylene glycol by the addition of water, followed by the addition of more ethylene oxide to the glycol. This intermolecular addition reaction can continue in stepwise fashion until the macromolecule is formed:

$$H_2O + H_2C \overset{O}{\diagup \diagdown} CH_2 \rightarrow HO \cdot CH_2 \cdot CH_2 \cdot OH$$

$$HO \cdot CH_2 \cdot CH_2 \cdot OH + nH_2C \overset{O}{\diagup \diagdown} CH_2 \rightarrow HO(-CH_2 \cdot CH_2 \cdot O-)_{n+1}H$$

It should again be pointed out that the reaction, formally resembling an addition polymerization, is fundamentally different from it, resembling more closely the condensation reactions, since light and peroxides have no effect.

Ethylene glycol is the parent member of the polyglycol series. The monoethyl ethers of ethylene glycol and diethylene glycol are the well-known solvents, Cellosolve and Carbitol, respectively. The remaining terminal hydroxyl group may be esterified to yield an ester-ether product, such as the Cellosolve and Carbitol acetates, widely used as relatively non-volatile solvents.

The poly(ethylene glycols) range from waterlike liquids to waxlike solids (Carbowaxes and Polyglycols). Also known as polyglycols or poly(oxyethylene glycols), these compounds are nonvolatile, unctuous materials, soluble in both water and aromatic hydrocarbons. Because of their unique solubility characteristics, these compounds are used as mutual solubility agents for immiscible liquids. They are employed as water-soluble lubricants for textile fibers and rubber molds and in metal-forming operations. They are used as plasticizers and softeners in glues and composition cork, and as components of printing inks, water-soluble paints, paper coatings, sizes, cosmetic preparations, hairdressings, and pharmaceutical preparations. They are also used as intermediates in the food, agricultural, textile, and petroleum industries.

Commercially, the poly[ethylene (and propylene) glycols] are produced batchwise in steel autoclaves. Using water, ethylene glycol, or diethylene glycol (containing a catalytic amount of caustic) as a reaction medium, ethylene oxide is introduced at such a rate that the temperature is maintained between 120° and 135°C, the pressure on the system at this temperature being about 60 psig. The reaction is exothermic, and it is necessary to cool the batch. After all of the oxide has been added, an additional two to five hours is allowed to permit completion of the reaction, after which the mass is neutralized and filtered.

Aliphatic polyethers have also been made by the reaction of glycols with dihalides to yield products of low to medium molecular weight. Fiber-forming and resinous aromatic polyethers have been made by reacting epichlorohydrin and a dihydric phenol in the presence of alkali (cf. Epoxy Resins).

### Epoxy Resins

The epoxy resins are recently (1947) produced polyethers which were specifically developed, based on theoretical considerations, to have certain desirable properties for use in the coating and electrical fields. The most common types are produced by reaction of epoxy compounds with dihydric phenols to give glycidyl ethers, and are variously called Epi-Rez, Araldite, Epon, and Bakelite ERL and EKRA series resins.

The phenols used must be at least dihydric. Possible ones include catechol, resorcinol, hydroquinone, pyrogallol, and phloroglucinol. However, these phenols are all relatively scarce and expensive. The phenol usually used for the manufacture of epoxy resins is known as Bisphenol A, and is made by condensation of acetone with phenol:

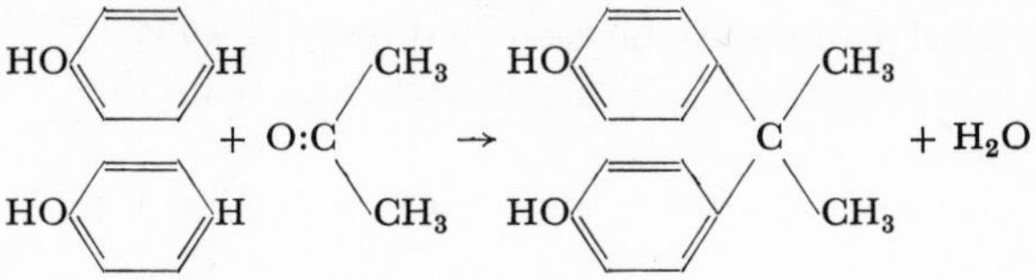

Other related bisphenols are known.

Of the many epoxy compounds possible, the one principally used, because of its availability and cost, is epichlorohydrin, which is made by dehydrochlorination of the isomeric glycerol dichlorohydrins, which in turn are obtained from the chlorination of propylene:

$$CH_2{:}CH{\cdot}CH_3 + Cl_2 \xrightarrow{\ 400°–600°C\ } CH_2{:}CH{\cdot}CH_2Cl$$

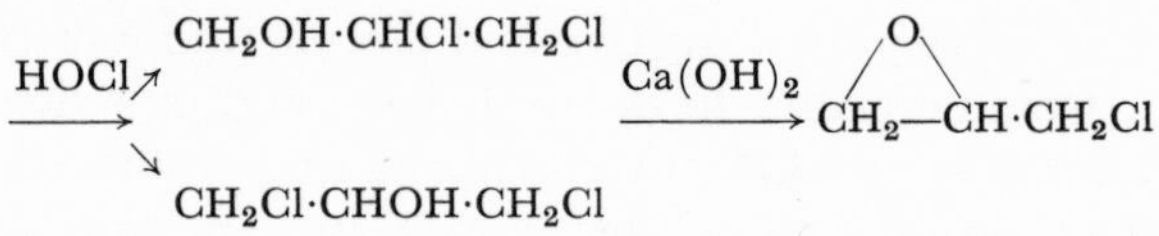

The reaction between Bisphenol A and epichlorohydrin in the presence of alkali yields linear polymers, one possibility of which may be represented as follows:

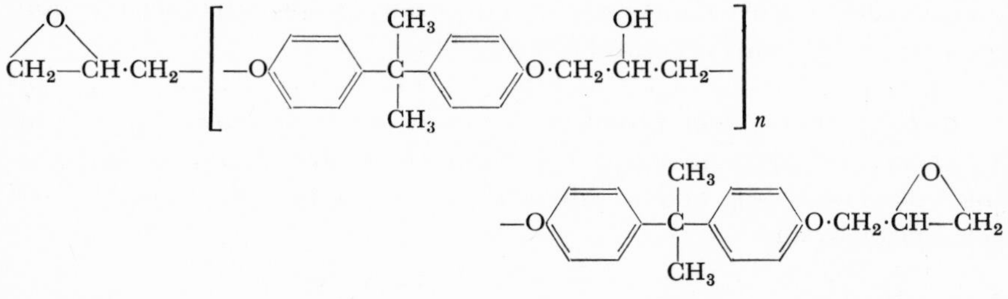

The molecules may be terminated by either of the reactants, depending upon which is used in excess. The commercial resins are usually terminated by epoxide groups. The molecules may also be terminated by a telogen, such as phenol, cresol, etc. This removes end functional groups and increases the inertness of the resin.

Note that, unlike the phenoplasts, the phenolic hydroxyl groups are all converted to ether linkages. Further, since the phenolic hydroxyl group, often a source of color difficulties, has been converted to an ether linkage, resins of improved color and color retention are obtained. The polar nature of the molecule contributes to good adhesion. Because of the chain length and nature of the mesomer, this type of resin forms unusually flexible films which, due to the absence of ester linkages, are quite resistant to hydrolysis and saponification and to a variety of chemicals. The molecular weight of the solid epoxy resins usually lies between about 500 and 1,200.

The unmodified epoxy resins, even when baked, yield films of limited utility. The outstanding properties of adhesion, flexibility, toughness, and chemical resistance are obtained by chemical reaction with curing agents which convert these resins to chemically and mechanically strong, thermosetting polymers.

The reactive epoxide and hydroxyl groups are the points of reaction with curing agents and modifying resins. The chemical activity of the liquid, low-molecular-weight resins is due primarily to the epoxide groups, while the high-molecular-weight resins, having a lower relative amount of epoxide groups, react primarily through the hydroxyl groups. The intermediate resins exhibit both epoxide and hydroxyl group activity.

Numerous organic nitrogen compounds have been investigated for use as epoxy resin curing agents, and the amines, both aliphatic and aromatic, are the most useful. Primary amines are more effective than secondary and tertiary amines. The curing mechanism of tertiary amines is not agreed upon, but, since no active hydrogen is present, the reaction is believed to be catalytic, rather than additive. Polyfunctional aliphatic amines, such as diethylene triamine, are the most effective ones, reacting rapidly at room temperature to form highly cross-linked structures. Elevated temperatures are necessary to obtain optimum cure with aromatic amines, as they cure very slowly at room temperature, resulting in brittle products with low softening temperatures.

Complex or adduct amines have been developed to overcome some of the deficiencies of simple amines. They are prepared by the reaction of two moles of a polyamine with one mole of an epoxy resin. Among the advantages of complex amines are lower toxicity, ease of handling, and improved flow. The Versamid resins, like the amine adducts, were also developed to overcome the volatility and toxicity of the simple polyamines. It may be recalled (see Polymerized Oils) that these are a series of amino-terminated resins. The use of dibasic acid anhydrides is still another recent attempt to find a less toxic series of products for use as difunctional cross-linking (curing) agents for the epoxy resins.

Another useful agent for curing epoxy resins is the mercaptan-terminated, saturated type of elastomer (liquid Thiokols) which can be cured either at room or elevated temperatures. An amine is necessary to catalyze the reaction in order to obtain optimum properties.   These copolymers have excellent oil, water, and solvent resistance and flexibility.

Still another method of curing epoxy resins is by reaction with aminoplasts and phenoplasts.   These types of curing agents usually require curing at high temperatures and a small amount of an acid catalyst.

Epoxy resin esters, prepared by esterification of the resins with fatty or rosin acids under the influence of heat, are the most widely used modification in the coatings field.   If the epoxy resins, which are really polymeric polyols, are reacted with a monofunctional acid, ester linkages are formed with the hydroxyl and epoxide groups.   The fatty acid improves the flexibility and solubility of the molecule, converts the reactive hydroxyl and epoxide groups to ester groups (which are somewhat less reactive) and, if the fatty acid is unsaturated, provides some drying or curing action by means of the unsaturated linkages.

A very large demand exists for epoxy resins in the manufacture of home appliance finishes and drum and can linings.   Highly flexible enamels based on epoxy resins have become highly desirable for use in the metal decorating field where coatings are applied before stamping operations. Excellent abrasion resistance has led to their increasing use for floor varnishes; resistance from chemical attack has made them a premium product for industrial maintenance coatings.   As a protective lining for tank cars, epoxy coatings are ideal for such products as 73 per cent caustic, liquid latex above a pH of 11, and carbon disulfide.   The lining seals off steel contaminants and does not contribute any of its own.

The resins have also found wide applications as industrial adhesives. Epoxy resin adhesives have high bond strengths and require only contact pressure during the curing cycle.   These adhesives can be cured either at room temperature or at elevated temperatures in shorter periods of time. This relatively new type of adhesive produces exceptionally strong bonds with metal parts.   For this reason and because of their good mechanical strength properties, epoxy adhesives are being used to replace soldering, brazing, and riveting in joining metals.   Epoxy adhesives can be used for bonding steel, tungsten carbide, cast iron, aluminum, copper alloys, copper, thermosetting plastics, ceramics, wood, glass, and hard rubber. The adhesives have low shrinkage during cure and good wetting properties.   These factors, together with the inherent strength (cohesion) of the adhesive itself, result in exceptionally strong, permanent bonds.

Plastic dies and jigs can be repaired with this adhesive.   Epoxy resin castings, using metal powder as a filler, are finding use in tool and die work, since they exhibit good dimensional stability as well as high impact resistance over a wide temperature range.   The resins can be used with or without the aid of reinforcing materials to produce castings of high strength.

Epoxy resins cost considerably more than the general-purpose unsaturated polyester resins. By blending as much as 40 per cent of a furfural-ketone resin with an epoxy resin, the cost for laminating uses can be reduced appreciably while maintaining physical properties in resulting laminates exceeding those required by the commonly used specifications. Epoxy-furan laminates also exhibit superior chemical resistance, primarily to acids, in comparison to many conventional epoxy systems. In order to

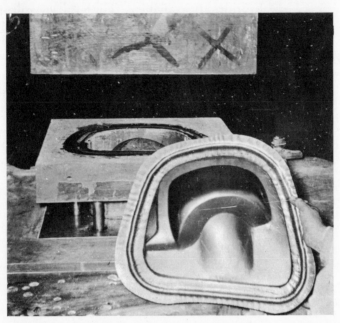

Fig. 8-26. A panel of cold-rolled steel with a complex contour was drawn on the plastic die (background) which has a laminated epoxy resin face. (*Courtesy Marblette Corp.*)

obtain higher impact strength and an increased degree of flexibility, epoxy-furan laminates may be further modified by addition of polysulfide polymers. Impact strength of resulting laminates is comparable to that of conventional epoxy-polysulfide systems.

Epoxy resins have many applications in the electrical field; for example, for potting or impregnating electrical components, such as transformers, capacitors, coils, and windings. For such uses, the end application will determine the desired viscosity of the resin and hardener blend. Potting and encapsulation of electrical parts require the use of a low viscosity resin to impregnate fine structures and fill voids. On the other hand, a sealant requires that the resin stay in place; thus a high-viscosity mixture is desired.    Adhesives require varying viscosities, according to the particular application.

To satisfy the multitude of requirements, the compounded epoxy resins may contain the following ingredients:[15]

| | |
|---|---|
| Epoxy Resins | A wide range of viscosities are available, from low-viscosity liquids to high-melting-point solids. |
| Hardeners | A large number of complex amines and acid anhydrides are available.   The hardener will determine the pot life and have an effect on the viscosity and the properties of the cured resin. |
| Plasticizers | Plasticizers, such as dibutyl phthalate and tricresyl phosphate, have been used to modify the resins. Polymers, such as polysulfides, polyamides, and fatty diamines react with epoxy resins and internally plasticize the cured resin. |
| Reactive Diluents | This class of materials, including such compounds as styrene oxide, epichlorohydrin, and acetonitrile reduce viscosity and react with the resin. |
| Fillers and Reinforcements | These compounds increase impact resistance, reduce the danger of cracks or crazing, increase viscosity, and lower the cost.   Asbestos, mica, silica, aluminum powder, and glass fiber may be mixed with the resin. |
| Pigments | These are used to impart color and opacity.   Pigments may be dispersed as solids or pastes.   They must be able to withstand the high exothermic temperatures developed during curing. |

Primary aromatic sulfonamides, such as $p$-toluene sulfonamide, secondary aromatic sulfonamides, and certain disecondary sulfonamides, will also react with epichlorohydrin to form intermediates, and eventually polymers, containing varying amounts of epoxy groups.   There is a distinct possibility that these products may appear on the commercial market shortly.

## THIOPLASTS

In 1926, Baer observed that polymeric, rubberlike substances were formed by the reaction between alkali sulfides and methylene chloride and other dihalides.   At about the same time, an American chemist,

[15] Sussman, V., *Modern Plastics*, **32**, No. 8, 164 (1955).

Patrick, was endeavoring to find a new antifreeze liquid. During his experiments, he boiled ethylene chloride and sodium polysulfide together in aqueous medium. The resultant product was not a liquid as expected but a yellowish solid with plastic-elastic properties. Patrick followed up his accidental discovery and in 1932 patented the production of the first thioplast, which was named Thiokol A.

A significant difference between the formation of polysulfide elastomers and most other synthetic elastomers is that the essential reaction is a true condensation reaction and not an addition polymerization. Patrick showed that organic dihalides having the terminal grouping $—CH_2Cl$ react readily with inorganic polysulfides, forming linear polymers of high molecular weight. The chain-linking for the thioplasts is through sulfur bridges, $—S_x—$. Although long assumed to have pendent sulfur atoms present, polysulfides are now believed to be purely linear chains. The general reaction is

$$n \ ClCH_2 \cdot CH_2Cl + n \ Na_2S_x \rightarrow (—CH_2 \cdot CH_2 \cdot S_x—)_n + 2n \ NaCl \quad 1 < x < 5$$

Thus, condensation of ethylene chloride with sodium tetrasulfide yields a linear polysulfide having the structure

$$[—CH_2 \cdot CH_2 \cdot S_4 \cdot —]_n$$

which has rubberlike properties and, like natural rubber, gives a sharp X-ray fiber diagram on stretching. Materials of this class form the basis of the Thiokol-type of synthetic, elastomeric materials which have high resistance to oils and solvents. Treatment of the poly(ethylene tetrasulfide) above with aqueous alkali removes two sulfur atoms, forming the disulfide polymer, $(—CH_2 \cdot CH_2 \cdot S \cdot S—)_n$, a hard material which begins to soften at 120°C and also shows an X-ray fiber diagram. The disulfide polymers can also be made directly by the reaction of ethylene chloride with sodium disulfide or by oxidation of ethylene mercaptan. The disulfide can be combined readily with sulfur to form the rubberlike tetrasulfide polymer.

In the commercial production of thioplasts, the dihalide is added slowly, with vigorous agitation, to an aqueous solution of a sodium polysulfide. An agent (magnesium hydroxide) is used to facilitate reaction, and, if latex is desired as the final product, to assist dispersion. Excess sodium polysulfide is used for economy and because a viscous liquid, instead of an elastomer, is obtained if the halide is in excess. The exothermic reaction requires two to six hours and is carried out at about 70°C. At the completion of reaction, the suspension is allowed to settle, and the product is washed free from sodium chloride and excess sodium polysulfide.

The simplest thioplast is represented by Thiokol A, derived, as pointed out above, from ethylene chloride and sodium tetrasulfide. This, the original polysulfide elastomer, is still made in the United States. Due to the unpleasant odor of Thiokol A, other organic dihalides were investigated and successful results were obtained. Thiokol B was produced from bis(2-chloroethyl)ether (Chlorex) and sodium tetrasulfide as follows:

$$n\ O(CH_2 \cdot CH_2 \cdot Cl)_2 + n\ Na_2S_4 \rightarrow [-CH_2 \cdot CH_2 \cdot O \cdot CH_2 \cdot CH_2 \cdot S_4-]_n$$

Thiokol B is no longer made in the United States. The British Novaplas A and the German Perduren G are derived from the same dihalide. Thiokol D, also no longer manufactured, was the polydisulfide made by treating the polytetrasulfide, Thiokol B, with sodium hydroxide. The German Perduren H is made from bis(2-chloroethyl) formal, $[CH_2 (OCH_2 \cdot CH_2Cl)_2]$, and the British Vulcaplas from *sym*-glycerol dichlorohydrin (1,3-dichloro-2-propanol).

It is often advantageous to use a mixture of dihalides in the manufacture of polysulfide elastomers. GR-P (Government Rubber-Polysulfide), made on a limited scale during World War II, was a form of Thiokol N (no longer manufactured) and was based on the use of a mixture of ethylene and propylene chlorides. Thiokol FA, made in the United States, is derived from a mixture of ethylene chloride and bis(2-chloroethyl) formal by reaction with sodium polysulfide of the composition $Na_2S_{1.8}$. As compared with Thiokol A, it has improved resistance to low temperatures and a less objectionable odor. Polymers from the above mixture are serviceable over a range of approximately $-35°$ to $+150°C$.

The usual basic compounding formulation of Thiokol FA has the following ingredients:

| | |
|---|---|
| Thiokol type FA . . . . . . | 100.0 |
| Carbon black . . . . . . | 60.0 |
| Stearic acid . . . . . . . | 0.5 |
| Zinc oxide . . . . . . . | 10.0 |
| Benzothiazyl disulfide . . . . . | 0.3 |
| Diphenyl guanidine . . . . . | 0.1 |

The function of the carbon black is polymer reinforcement. The stearic acid serves as a lubricant. The functions of the last three additives will be discussed later.

In the preparation of several types of Thiokol, a trihalide is included in the reaction mixture to cause a small amount of cross-linking of the polymer chains and thus to reduce markedly the tendency of vulcanizates to undergo cold flow and suffer compression set. Thiokol ST, made from bis(2-chloroethyl) formal by reaction with sodium polysulfide, and Thiokol PR-1, made from a mixture of ethylene chloride and the formal by reaction with a different sodium polysulfide, are thus cross-linked. The cross-linking agent is probably about 2 per cent of 1,2,3-trichloropropane.

In addition to the use of a cross-linking agent in the preparation of the Thiokols just mentioned, treatment causing chain scission is usually involved in their preparation. It has been known for a considerable time that the linear polysulfide elastomers which cannot be broken down to a satisfactory degree of plasticity on a rubber mill can be plasticized by the addition of small proportions of such substances as benzothiazyl disulfide and tetramethyl thiuram disulfide. These may be used alone or in combination with a small amount of diphenyl guanidine which, although not effective by itself, accelerates the action of the disulfide. The disulfide acts as a softening agent, lowering the molecular weight of the polymer by disulfide redistribution:

$$(-SS \cdot R \cdot SS \cdot R \cdot SS-)_n + n\ R'SSR' \rightarrow (-SS \cdot R \cdot SR')_n + n\ R'SS \cdot R \cdot SS-$$

Upon vulcanization, the disulfide linkages are regenerated.

A more recent method of bringing about such scission, to form liquid, low-molecular-weight polymers, is by reductive cleavage of disulfide links by treating polysulfide latex with sodium hydrosulfide and sodium sulfite. The sodium hydrosulfide splits a disulfide link to form a thiol and the sodium salt of a thiol. The extra sulfur atom is taken up by the sodium sulfite:

$$-R \cdot SS \cdot R- + NaSH + Na_2SO_3 \rightarrow -RSNa + HSR- + Na_2S_2O_3$$

The addition of acid to coagulate the liquid polymer in the water dispersion converts the sodium salt to the free thiol.

The liquid polymers are mercaptan-terminated, saturated elastomeric chains, prepared from bis(2-chloroethyl) formal and cross-linked with a small amount of trichloropropane, and are represented by

$$HS(CH_2 \cdot CH_2 \cdot O \cdot CH_2 \cdot O \cdot CH_2 \cdot CH_2 \cdot S \cdot S)_n$$
$$CH_2 \cdot CH_2 \cdot O \cdot CH_2 \cdot O \cdot CH_2 \cdot CH_2 \cdot SH$$

where $n$ may vary from two to twenty-six. They have been used in caulking and casting compounds, in cold-setting adhesives, as a curing agent for epoxy resins, and have been used for impregnation of porous materials, followed by conversion in place to an elastomer of high molecular weight. Air-drying coatings are one of the most recent developments and may be of considerable value.

Types of Thiokol which are terminated in thiol groups can be vulcanized by a wide variety of oxidizing agents. Unlike natural rubber or the usual synthetic elastomers, no added sulfur is used. Zinc peroxide and

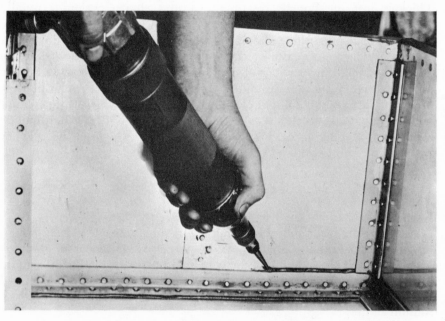

FIG. 8-27.   Filleting an aluminum aircraft fuel tank with a putty compounded from a low-molecular-weight polysulfide elastomer.   (*Courtesy Thiokol Chemical Corp.*)

combinations of zinc oxide and *p*-quinone dioxime, as well as lead peroxide, cumene hydroperoxide, and cobalt driers have been used. However, zinc oxide is the curing agent almost always used. The rate of cure is independent of the amount of zinc oxide; up to 10 per cent, based on the weight of the polysulfide, may be used. The method of action of the zinc oxide is uncertain but may be primarily that of an oxidizing agent, serving to re-form disulfide linkages which, during plasticization, were reduced to thiol groups (see above).

The specific gravity of solid polysulfide elastomers varies from 1.33 to 1.38. They may be obtained in a wide range of hardnesses by proper compounding. Abrasion resistance is one half to three fourths that of a first-grade, natural rubber tire tread. Tensile strengths up to 1,400 psi and elongations of 500 to 600 per cent are obtainable. These values are retained in large measure upon immersion in oil.

From the standpoint of their usefulness, the polysulfides are in some properties excellent, in others quite poor. They have unexcelled solvent and oil resistance and gas impermeability. They possess good aging characteristics and exceptional resistance to ozone. Some types stiffen on aging, although this behavior is less marked in vulcanizates. On the debit side, most of the thioplasts have a disagreeable odor, relatively poor heat resistance, lack of abrasion resistance in tire treads, low tensile strength, and some cold flow. For some applications, of course, some of these characteristics are relatively unimportant or even advantageous; e.g., cold flow in gaskets and cements.

The most important uses depend largely on their excellent resistance to oils, solvents, and water, and their impermeability to gases. They are or have been used in gasoline hose in automobiles and service stations and in oil-loading hose; in printers' rolls and newspaper blankets; as the hydro-carbon-resistant lining of military fuel depots, of boxcars for the transportation of fuel oil, and of bulletproof tanks for airplanes; in protective coatings; for caulking; and as adhesives and binders. They are also used in paint-spray hose, electric-cable covering, and miscellaneous diaphragms and gaskets. The low gas permeability of thioplasts is of advantage in balloon fabrics.

The polysulfides are also available as latices, putties, molding powders, and solutions. The latex has found several applications, including the use as a coating for underground gasoline-storage tanks and concrete tankers. Thiokol putties are employed to seal cracks and seams in aluminum airplane wings and to seal pressurized aircraft cabins. Solid polymers are available in powdered form for flame spraying (Schori process). The most important application of flame-sprayed Thiokol is in coating rudders, struts, and steel shafts for use in military vessels. Other uses of the flame-sprayed material include linings of salt-water pipeline valves, bearings, and low-pressure condenser plates.

Thiokols have also found some application as molding powders. These powders may be molded at a temperature of about 150°C using a pressure of 700 psi. Hard, nonporous, highly polished articles result. The moldings resemble ebonite, but have improved resistance to the absorption of water; electrical properties are moderate but are reasonable compared with those of other synthetic elastomers, although they are not as good as rubber compositions.

Of interest is the fact that a convenient method for the production of crystalline, high-molecular-weight polythioethers by an addition type of reaction, in which dimercaptans are combined with diolefins, has been developed, the reaction being catalyzed by peroxides or ultraviolet light and carried out in solution or in an aqueous emulsion:

$$n \text{ CH}_2\text{:CH·R·CH:CH}_2 + n \text{ HS·R'·SH} \rightarrow$$
$$[\text{—CH}_2\text{·CH}_2\text{·R·CH}_2\text{·CH}_2\text{·S·R'·S—}]_n$$

Many of the products are said to be fiber forming; poly(hexamethylene sulfide) can be melt-spun. However, the melting points of these polysulfides are quite low, ranging from about 60° to 90°C. No commercial fiber is known employing the polysulfide linkage.

### FURAN RESINS

The term "furan resins" is a general one, referring to resinous products obtained from furfural and its derivatives, including furan, tetrahydrofurfuryl alcohol, and especially furfuryl alcohol.

| Furfural | Furan | Tetrahydrofurfuryl alcohol | Furfuryl alcohol |

The reaction of furfural with phenols is of greatest interest and has been discussed under Phenoplasts. Tetrahydrofurfuryl alcohol, the least reactive of the furans, is useful mainly for the preparation of certain esters, used as plasticizers for various cellulosic and vinyl resins. Furan is of limited value, at present, as a resin intermediate.

Of greatest reactivity, from the standpoint of self-resinification, is furfuryl alcohol. It has been commercially manufactured since 1934 by the high pressure (1,000 to 1,500 psi) hydrogenation of furfural in the presence of a copper chromite catalyst at 175°C. The commercial alcohol is an amber-colored liquid, boiling at 170°C. Like furfural, it is subject to auto-oxidation in the presence of air, but may be effectively inhibited by the addition of a small quantity of an amine. In the presence of concentrated mineral or strong organic acids, it polymerizes with explosive violence.

The largest use of furfuryl alcohol is in the manufacture of dark, thermosetting resins, which are outstanding because of their resistance to corrosive chemicals, acids, alkalies, and solvents. Usually the furfuryl alcohol is first partially polymerized to form a soluble and fusible resin, using an acid catalyst, and then is neutralized. The neutralized resin is storage-stable, but is rendered infusible by the addition of acid at the time of use. These liquid prepolymers are used for making tank and digester linings, for making cast equipment, in cementing and reinforcing ceramics, and for the protection of laboratory table-tops.

Control of the exothermic reaction during the resinification of furfuryl alcohol is achieved by regulation of catalyst concentration and temperature. The mechanism of resinification has been inferred, in part at least, from a consideration of the intermediate products formed. The initial and predominant reaction is intermolecular dehydration, involving the hydroxyl group of one molecule and the active α-hydrogen atom of another

FIG. 8-28. Resin-bonded grinding wheels are made from abrasive grains, powdered resin, and a liquid resin by the cold molding process. Furfuryl alcohol is often used as the bonding agent. (*Courtesy Durez Plastics Div., Hooker Electrochemical Co.*)

molecule. Further reaction in the same manner leads to higher-molecular-weight condensation products in which furan rings are linked together by methylene (and probably other) bridges in a manner somewhat analogous to the resoles, since furfuryl alcohol already contains a "built-in" methylol group:

Methylol phenol          Furfuryl alcohol

To a small extent, furfuryl ether and formaldehyde, resulting from thermal decomposition, are found in the reaction mixture.   Experimental evidence has indicated that the formaldehyde recondenses with the intermediate products, and this is thought to be one way in which the chains become cross-linked.   Finally, a network of cross-linkages may be formed by addition polymerization, involving the nuclear double bonds, to complete the resinification, thereby explaining the high degree of chemical resistance of the thermally set resin.   However, little information is available as to the mechanism of such a reaction.   Unlike the vinyl types, furans do not appear to undergo peroxide-catalyzed addition polymerization; it is probable that the peroxide is used up in oxidation of the furan compound. Linkages of the following types may occur in the final resin:

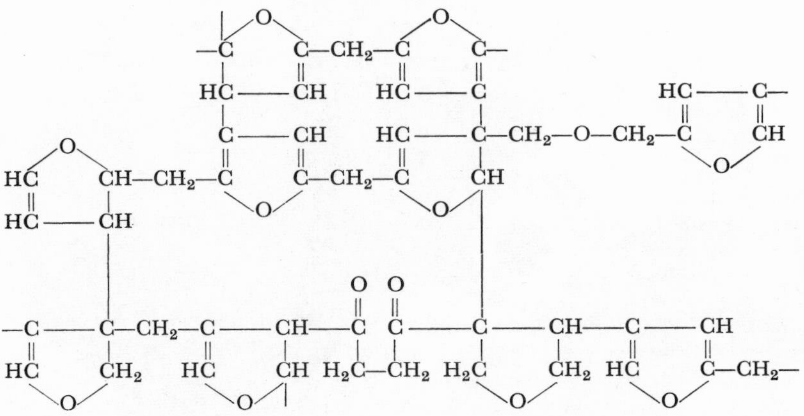

By stopping the reaction at the desired point, viscous resins capable of further polymerizing by themselves or of reacting with other reactive resins are obtained.   These products have found use in making cements, mortaring acidproof brick, and mixing with asbestos and other fillers for the production of chemically resistant equipment.   Thus, acid-catalyzed furfuryl alcohol resin filled with acid-digested asbestos is the basis for cast equipment, vessels, and parts known in the industry as Haveg.   The molded plastic in the form of pipes, ducts, valves, vats, hoods, and tanks is widely used for its corrosion resistance in the chemical, textile, petroleum, and metallurgical industries.   The product is a good heat insulator and is unaffected by thermal shock or sustained temperatures up to 130°C.

The polymerization reaction can also be run *in situ*.   For example, wood or asbestos is impregnated with furfuryl alcohol or with a solution of the partially condensed alcohol and, on acid treatment, forms an inert, thermoset resin. One of the first uses was in the preparation of impervious, chemical-resistant surfaces on wooden, laboratory bench-tops. By the application of alternate coats of furfuryl alcohol and dilute mineral acid, there is produced a jet-black finish, which is inert to the action of common solvents, strong alkalies, and most acids, except for the strong oxidants, such as nitric.

Corrosion-resistant, resinous cements are prepared by mixing an inert filler, such as carbon or silica, with a liquid resin which is catalyzed by acid to the solid and infusible state. The furfuryl alcohol resinous cements have approximately the same handling and physical properties as phenol-based materials, but the chemical resistance is different. They are used extensively because they withstand the attack of alkali of all concentrations —even hot solutions of concentrated sodium or potassium hydroxide. The resistance to acids and organic liquids is similar to that of phenolic cements, except that the latter excel in resistance to mild oxidizing acids. Other points in favor of furfuryl alcohol cements, as compared with phenolics, are the long storage stability of the liquid resin without change in viscosity and the lack of adverse physiological effect on users.

It is interesting to note the use of furfuryl alcohol resin cement in producing a floor covering having a low resistivity. These floors are installed in operating rooms in hospitals in order to reduce the possibility of electrostatic discharges and subsequent ignition of flammable gases used. Conductive floors for explosives manufacture have also been developed.

In the manufacture of resinoid abrasive wheels, furfuryl alcohol serves not only as a solvent for the fusible phenolic resins employed as binders, but also as a reactant with these binders during the curing step. Furfural has long been used as a reactive solvent in this industry, but the alcohol is preferred by some manufacturers because solvent action of the alcohol on the phenolic is slower than that of furfural.

Furfuryl alcohol forms ether linkages readily with other active hydroxyl groups. The best examples of this reaction are the resins formed by reacting furfuryl alcohol with dimethylol urea. Two moles of dimethylol urea mixed with one mole of furfuryl alcohol in aqueous solution and reacted at 100°C, then dehydrated to about 60 per cent solids, gives a viscous solution of a light, amber-colored, heat-hardening resin. This sets rapidly at 150°C. These products give strong paper-base laminates and can be used for high-frequency- or low-temperature-curing adhesives in the woodworking industry. Typical applications of the gap-filling adhesive include lumber-core gluing, edge-bonding of furniture, and other wood-to-wood gluing applications where the joints rarely are uniformly matched. The principal advantages of a furfuryl-alcohol-modified, urea-formaldehyde resin are improved flexibility, increased craze resistance, long stability of the glue line to aging, and increased water resistance over conventional urea-formaldehyde products.

Furfuryl alcohol can be reacted with formaldehyde to yield a viscous mass which can be cured to a thermoset composition by application of heat. An acid catalyst is normally used, such as hydrochloric, phosphoric, or benzoic. The reaction can also be catalyzed by alkaline materials to yield resins which are much more thermoplastic than the acid-catalyzed types.

Although, as stated earlier, the largest quantity of furfural is consumed by the phenolic resin industry, lesser quantities are used in specialty resins, such as acid-catalyzed furfural (similar to acid-catalyzed furfuryl alcohol), furfural-ketone, and furfural-aniline resins.

Carbon and graphite articles are ordinarily porous and permeable to many fluids. In order to utilize the chemical inertness inherent in elemental carbon, synthetic resins are cured in the pores of the material in order to render it impervious. The resulting stock may then be fabricated into tanks, pipes, valves, heat exchangers, and similar equipment for the chemical processing industry. Acid-catalyzed furfural resin was the first synthetic resin employed to render such stock impermeable (Karbate).

Little has been published on the condensation of furfural with ketones, aromatic amines, and similar reactive materials having active hydrogen atoms. However, furfural-ketone reaction products further reacted with formaldehyde produce thermosetting resins. Such resins in general involve the reaction of one mole of furfural with 0.5 to one mole of a ketone in an alkaline medium; the product is then reacted in the presence of an acid catalyst with 0.5 to two moles of formaldehyde. These products are used primarily as resins compatible with synthetic elastomers to increase their resistance to oils and chemicals.

A resinous reaction product of furfural and methyl acetone has been used for many years in a commercial lacquer. The resinous reaction product is a large portion of the solids content of the lacquer, and furfural is also used as a solvent for the resin. The lacquer serves as a final wear-resistant coating on lithographic plates. The coatings when exposed to arc light are insoluble in gasoline, turpentine, and ink oils, and consequently are never removed when the plate is washed.

As mentioned earlier, the high solvent power of furfural, and the fact that the solvent is a reactive one, is taken advantage of in many resin uses, such as the bonding of grinding wheels and cold molding. Here, the furfural is used to soften the resins to permit cold forming and later may be reacted with the resin.

## REFERENCES AND RECOMMENDED READING

Alexander, J., ed., *Colloid Chemistry Theoretical and Applied*, Vol. VI, Reinhold Publishing Corp., New York, 1946.

Barron, H., *Modern Plastics*, John Wiley and Sons, New York, 1945.

Billmeyer, F. W., Jr., *Textbook of Polymer Chemistry*, Interscience Publishers, New York, 1957.

Bjorksten, J., Tovey, H., Harker, B., and Henning, J., *Polyesters and Their Applications*, Reinhold Publishing Corp., New York, 1956.

Blom, A. V., *Organic Coatings*, Elsevier Publishing Co., Amsterdam (dist. by D. Van Nostrand Co., Princeton, N.J.), 1949.

Burk, R. E., Thompson, H. E., Weith, A. J., and Williams, I., *Polymerization*, Reinhold Publishing Corp., New York, 1937.

Carswell, T. S., *Phenoplasts*, Interscience Publishers, New York, 1947.

Curme, G. O. and Johnston, F., eds., *Glycols*, Reinhold Publishing Corp., New York, 1952.

Delmonte, J., *Plastics in Engineering*, 3rd ed., Penton Publishing Co., Cleveland, 1949.

Dubois, J. H., *Plastics*, 3rd ed., American Technical Society, Chicago, 1945.

Dunlop, A. P. and Peters, F. N., *The Furans*, Reinhold Publishing Corp., New York, 1953.

Ellis, C., *The Chemistry of Synthetic Resins*, Reinhold Publishing Corp., New York, 1935.

Encyclopedia Issue, *Modern Plastics*, Plastics Catalogue Corp., Bristol, Conn., 1956.

Fleck, H. R., *Plastics*, 2nd ed., Chemical Publishing Co., Brooklyn, N.Y., 1949.

Gordon, P. L. and Dolgin, G. J., *Surface Coatings and Finishes*, Chemical Publishing Co., New York, 1954.

Groggins, P. H., ed., *Unit Processes in Organic Synthesis*, 4th ed., McGraw-Hill Book Co., New York, 1952.

Hicks, J. S., *Low-Pressure Laminating of Plastics*, Reinhold Publishing Corp., New York, 1947.

Hill, R., ed., *Fibres from Synthetic Polymers*, Elsevier Publishing Co., Amsterdam (dist. by D. Van Nostrand Co., Princeton, N.J.), 1953.

Hopff, H., Muller, A., and Wenger, F., *Die Polyamide*, Springer-Verlag, Berlin, 1954.

Houwink, R., ed., *Elastomers and Plastomers*, Vols. I and II, Elsevier Publishing Co., Amsterdam (dist. by D. Van Nostrand Co., Princeton, N.J.), 1949–50.

Kaye, S. L., *The Production and Properties of Plastics*, International Textbook Company, Scranton, Penn., 1947.

Kirk, R. E. and Othmer, D. F., eds., *Encyclopedia of Chemical Technology*, Interscience Publishers, New York, 1947–56.

Langton, H. M., ed., *Synthetic Resins*, 3rd ed., Oxford University Press, London-New York, 1951.

Mark, H. and Whitby, G. S., eds., *Collected Papers of Wallace Hume Carothers*, Interscience Publishers, New York, 1940.

Martin, R. W., *The Chemistry of Phenolic Resins*, John Wiley and Sons, New York, 1956.

Mason, J. P. and Manning, J. F., *The Technology of Plastics and Resins*, D. Van Nostrand Co., Princeton, N.J., 1945.

Mattiello, J. J., ed., *Protective and Decorative Coatings*, Vols. I and III, John Wiley and Sons, New York, 1941–46.

Mauer, L. and Wechsler, H., *Man-Made Fibers*, Rayon Publishing Corp., New York, 1953.

Mauersberger, H. R., ed., *Matthew's Textile Fibers*, 6th ed., John Wiley and Sons, New York, 1954.

McGregor, R. R., *Silicones and Their Uses*, McGraw-Hill Book Co., New York, 1954.

Meyer, K. H., *Natural and Synthetic High Polymers*, 2nd ed., Interscience Publishers, New York, 1950.

Mills, M. R., *An Introduction to Drying Oil Technology*, Interscience Publishers, New York, 1950.

Miner, C. S. and Dalton, N. N., *Glycerol*, Reinhold Publishing Corp., New York, 1953.

Moncrieff, R. W., *Artificial Fibres*, 2nd ed., John Wiley and Sons, New York, 1954.

Monsanto Chemical Co., *The Chemistry and Processing of Alkyd Resins*, St. Louis, 1952.

Morgan, P., ed., *Glass Reinforced Plastics*, Iliffe and Sons, London—Philosophical Library, New York, 1954.

Nauth, R., *The Chemistry and Technology of Plastics*, Reinhold Publishing Corp., New York, 1947.

Payne, H. F., *Organic Coating Technology*, John Wiley and Sons, New York, 1954.

Post, H. W., *Silicones and Other Organic Silicon Compounds*, Reinhold Publishing Corp., New York, 1949.

Powers, P. O., *Synthetic Resins and Rubbers*, John Wiley and Sons, New York, 1943.

Richardson, H. M. and Wilson, J. W., eds., *Fundamentals of Plastics*, McGraw-Hill Book Co., New York, 1946.

Ritchie, P. D., *A Chemistry of Plastics and High Polymers*, Cleaver-Hume Press, London (dist. by Interscience Publishers, New York), 1949.

Robitschek, P. and Lewin, A., *Phenolic Resins*, Iliffe and Sons (for British Plastics), London, 1950.

Rochow, E. G., *An Introduction to the Chemistry of the Silicones*, 2nd ed., John Wiley and Sons, New York, 1951.

Schildknecht, C. E., ed., *Polymer Processes*, Interscience Publishers, New York, 1956.

Simonds, H. R., Bigelow, M. H., and Sherman, J. V., *The New Plastics*, D. Van Nostrand Co., Princeton, N.J., 1945.

Simonds, H. R., Weith, A. J., and Bigelow, M. H., *Handbook of Plastics*, 2nd ed., D. Van Nostrand Co., Princeton, N.J., 1949.

Sonneborn, R. H., Dietz, A. G. H., and Heyser, A. S., *Fiberglas Reinforced Plastics*, Reinhold Publishing Corp., New York, 1954.

Vale, C. P., *Aminoplastics*, Cleaver-Hume Press, London (dist. by Interscience Publishers, New York), 1950.

von Fischer, W., ed., *Paint and Varnish Technology*, Reinhold Publishing Corp., New York, 1948.

von Fischer, W. and Bobalek, E. G., eds., *Organic Protective Coatings*, Reinhold Publishing Corp., New York, 1953.

Wakeman, R. L., *The Chemistry of Commercial Plastics*, Reinhold Publishing Corp., New York, 1947.

Walker, J. F., *Formaldehyde*, 2nd ed., Reinhold Publishing Corp., New York, 1953.

Whitby, G. S., ed., *Synthetic Rubber*, John Wiley and Sons, New York, 1954.

Winding, C. C. and Hasche, R. L., *Plastics Theory and Practice*, McGraw-Hill Book Co., New York, 1947.

*Chapter 9*

# TECHNOLOGY OF MANUFACTURE:
# SYNTHETIC ADDITION PRODUCTS

Organic compounds containing unsaturated bonds, such as C:C, C:C, C:N, C:N, C:O, exhibit a general tendency to polymerize by an addition reaction. To be of commercial interest, however, an unsaturated compound must be subject to precise control with regard to purity and reaction conditions; otherwise, polymeric products of uniform quality cannot be obtained, since addition reactions, in general, take place much more rapidly than condensation reactions, and it is more difficult to interrupt and modify an addition reaction. For such reasons as raw material costs, ease of purification, control of the reaction, and quality of product, monomers containing only olefinic bonds are the most important for the commercial production of addition polymers.

For convenience, the polymers have been grouped according to chemical similarity of their monomers. This facilitates comparisons of the chemical and physical properties of the polymers with the chemical structures of the monomers.

## ALIPHATIC HYDROCARBONS AND DERIVATIVES
### POLYETHYLENE
**High-Pressure Process**

Prior to 1933, high-molecular-weight polymers from ethylene did not exist, although it had long been known that ethylene could undergo a process of self-addition to form low-molecular-weight polymers. High-molecular-weight polymers from ethylene did not evolve as a gradual improvement over the low-molecular-weight polymers; rather, the development of very high-pressure engineering was required. The first high-molecular-weight polyethylene sample has been variously reported to have resulted from attempts to obtain styrene from a mixture of benzene and ethylene at high pressure without an initiator and from attempts to convert ethylene and benzaldehyde into motor fuels. In either case, the attempts were unsuccessful, but about 1937 this research program in Britain (principally by Fawcett and co-workers) led to the production of a true, high-molecular-weight polymer of ethylene, by polymerization in the presence of carefully controlled amounts of oxygen at temperatures of 100° to 400°C and pressures of about 1,000 to 2,000 atmospheres. The over-all principal reaction is

$$n \; CH_2:CH_2 \rightarrow (-CH_2 \cdot CH_2-)_n$$

By 1939, polyethylene was in production in Britain; in 1943, it was being made in the United States.

The sources of ethylene in the United States may be of interest. One very large source is from the by-product material formed during thermal and catalytic cracking operations employed in crude oil processing. A second method of forming ethylene, and probably the most widely used procedure in this country, is the thermal cracking of such feed stocks as ethane, propane, butane, or naphtha. A third method of forming ethylene is by the passage of hydrocarbon into a chamber through which flows a stream of very hot pellets; the preheated feed is heated further by contact with the refractory pellets and undergoes a cracking reaction, which results in the formation of ethylene, other olefins, and some aromatics. A variation of the latter method is the passage of feed through a regenerative-type checker furnace; ethylene and other products are obtained. Other processes for the formation of ethylene which have not found large use in this country are the partial oxidation of ethane and the hydrogenation of acetylene. The latter is not economical here but has been a standard method in Germany, where acetylene is more readily available than ethylene. There is also a possibility that ethylene could be economically produced through the Fischer-Tropsch reaction if the prices of natural gas and petroleum products continue to rise.

A typical method for the manufacture of high-pressure polyethylene by mass polymerization follows. Ethylene gas of 99.8 per cent purity or better, at 550 psi, is further compressed to more than 20,000 psi and fed to the reactions vessels. At this pressure, in the presence of traces of oxygen and at about 200°C, some ethylene polymerizes to form liquid polyethylene. This is removed from the reactor continuously and, after being separated from any unpolymerized ethylene, is solidified by cooling and cut into cubes. Unconverted ethylene is recompressed and recycled to the reactor. Conversions are about 25 per cent, with overall yields running as high as 95 per cent.

Ethylene may also be polymerized by the "solvent" or slurry process. This reaction occurs at about 200°C and 1,000 atmospheres in the presence of an aromatic hydrocarbon (benzene) and about 20 ppm of oxygen. A stainless steel tubular reactor is employed. Conversions are low—about 17 per cent—but recycling gives a very satisfactory over-all yield.

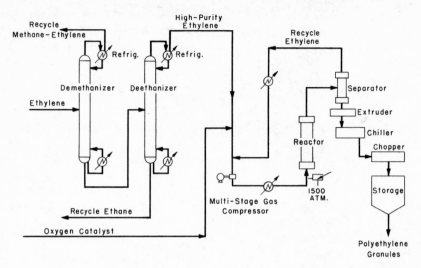

FIG. 9-1. Polyethylene flow sheet—high-pressure process. (*Reprinted from Petroleum Refiner*)

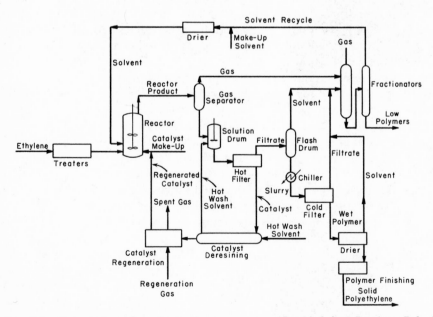

FIG. 9-2. Polyethylene flow sheet—slurry process. (*Reprinted from Petroleum Refiner*)

Oxygen has a great influence upon the character of ethylene polymerization. There is an optimum concentration of oxygen; too much or too little gives slow conversion to polymer. Oxygen in amounts of 0.06 to 0.08 per cent initiates the reaction effectively, although the amount added has to be carefully controlled in order to prevent explosion of the highly compressed gas.

The use of oxygen is of interest in that it is an inhibitor of the polymerization of most other unsaturated monomers. Under the conditions which make it effective as an initiator, it rapidly oxidizes ethylene; therefore, it appears likely that free radicals produced during the oxidation are the actual initiators for the polymerization. Recent research in the field of hydrocarbon oxidations has demonstrated that hydroperoxides appear as one of the first products of reaction. Kinetic studies have shown that subsequent oxidation of the parent hydrocarbon is autocatalyzed by the decomposition of the hydroperoxides, which produces free-radical initiators for the chain reaction. The decomposition of hydroperoxide also leads to the formation of secondary oxidation products, such as ketones, aldehydes, acids, alcohols, water, and carbon dioxide.

Many other compounds have been used as initiators, all of which generate free radicals. Organic peroxides, such as benzoyl peroxide and di-*tert*-butyl peroxide, have been used, in aqueous solution, in solution in organic solvents, or in solution in the compressed ethylene itself. Inorganic peroxy compounds, including hydrogen peroxide and persulfates, normally used in aqueous solutions, are also effective, and their reactivity may be increased by the reduction-activation technique used in other polymerizations. Another class of initiators which is effective is the group of azo compounds.

The exothermic heat of polymerization (22 kcal) is very large and the dissipation of this heat is an important problem in the control of the polymerization. For example, at 100°C and 1,000 atmospheres, the specific heat $(c_v)$ of ethylene is 0.415; hence, the adiabatic, constant volume polymerization of only 1 per cent of a given quantity of ethylene will release almost eight calories per gram and raise the temperature nearly 20°C.

An increase in pressure generally yields products of higher molecular weight, whereas an increase in temperature or concentration of the initiator tends to lower the degree of polymerization. After reaction, if the pressure is released at the high reaction temperature, the polyethylene is obtained on cooling as a compact, solid mass. (If allowed to cool under pressure, the polymer is obtained as a powder of low apparent density.) The usual product is a tough, waxy, colorless, predominantly linear, high-molecular-weight polymer. The molecular weight is normally within the range of 5,000 to 40,000. The structure of the polymer is essentially a sequence of methylene groups; there is also present a small amount of combined oxygen which is believed to act as a bridging atom to form occasional cross-links:

$$—CH_2 \cdot CH_2 \cdot CH \cdot CH_2 \cdot CH_2 \cdot CH_2—$$
$$|$$
$$O$$
$$|$$
$$—CH_2 \cdot CH \cdot CH_2 \cdot CH_2—$$

Branched units also occur in the molecule, although probably not to the extent of more than about one unit in fifty. Both long- and short-chain branching have been detected. The former is caused by intermolecular hydrogen transfer between a propagating chain and a dead polyethylene molecule, with a long side-chain growing from the site of transfer. Short-chain branching occurs during chain propagation, through formation of a transient five- or six-membered ring complex, which results in a $C_4$ or $C_5$ side-branch. In addition, each molecule is believed to contain an average of one vinylidene group.

This branched nature of the polyethylene molecule is reflected in the lower melting point and lower degree of crystallinity than those of high-molecular-weight paraffins made by other means. Superficially, the solid polymer is amorphous, although X-ray diffraction diagrams show appreciable crystallinity. It has been found that, up to about 75°C, about 35 per cent of the material is amorphous. A completely amorphous product can be made by heating the polymer to its softening point, then quenching rapidly. In addition to the imperfect crystallinity due to the partially branched structure, the presence of a tertiary hydrogen atom at each point of branching probably accounts for the oxidation of polyethylene in air at 120°C, although, in general, the polymer is highly resistant to acids, bases, solvents, and oxidizing agents.

[Linear polymers of high molecular weight can be made by other methods. Among these are the catalytic reduction of carbon monoxide by hydrogen (Fischer-Tropsch) and the decomposition of diazomethane. Diazomethane in cold ether solution forms white, solid polymethylene on standing, particularly in the presence of platinum, sodium, copper, or other catalysts:

$$n \, CH_2N_2 \rightarrow n \, N_2 + (—CH_2—)_n$$

Solid polymethylene is also insoluble in organic solvents at room temperature but dissolves in boiling isopropyl benzene and pyridine. This polymer may be as much as 95 per cent crystalline.]

Polyethylene is known in Britain as Alkathene and Polythene, in Germany as Lupolene and Trolen, and, among other names, in the United States as Petrothene and Alathon.

Among the outstanding properties of polyethylene plastics are their good toughness and flexibility over a wide temperature range and their excellent electrical properties. The stiffness of polyethylene is between the rigid plastics, such as polystyrene, and the elastomers, such as highly plasticized poly(vinyl chloride).

Polyethylene softens relatively sharply at temperatures from 105° to 115°C, depending upon the average molecular weight. The specific gravity is 0.92, the tensile strength at 25°C is approximately 1,300 to 2,000 psi, and the water absorption is less than 0.005 per cent.

Although polyethylene is insoluble in any solvent at room temperature, it is swollen by gasoline, benzene, lubricating oils, and carbon tetrachloride. In most solvents, polyethylene becomes readily soluble above a fairly definite temperature which varies somewhat with the solvent but is usually between 60° and 80°C. These solutions, when cooled, form gels. Most oxygenated solvents do not dissolve polyethylene, even when hot, except for ketones and esters containing moderately long alkyl groups.

Except for attack by halogens and concentrated nitric acid, polyethylene is outstanding in chemical inertness. It has good resistance to sulfuric, hydrofluoric, hydrochloric, and acetic acids at room temperature and is unaffected by concentrated caustic.

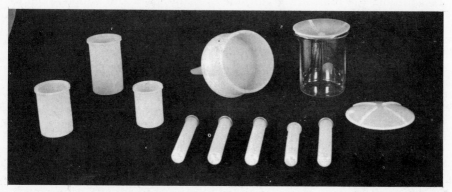

FIG. 9-3. Polyethylene laboratory apparatus. (*Courtesy American Agile Corp.*)

Polyethylene is susceptible to oxidation, however. Stabilizers are desirable when it is exposed for a long time to light in the presence of oxygen. Milling or prolonged heating in contact with air may cause cross-linking; this action can be accelerated by the presence of peroxides or other substances which form free radicals.

Film and sheeting are by far the largest consumer uses (over 50 per cent) of polyethylene and will probably remain so for many years. Packaging probably consumes at least 60 per cent of all polyethylene film made at the present time.  No earlier material possessed all of the desirable properties of polyethylene in such applications; e.g., low density, inherent flexibility, resilience, high tear strength, excellent moisture and chemical resistance, and a low tendency for cuts to run.  Polyethylene has become a strong competitor of cellophane in the packaging field.

The usual methods of calendering and extrusion do not work well for manufacture of polyethylene films, principally because of the narrow temperature range in which the material has optimum plasticity.  Instead, the plastic is extruded through a circular slit and is continuously blown up to form a uniform, thin-walled, seamless tube, much as saran film is made.

Films are used as liners of metal and fiber drums which are used for shipment of liquid, moist, dusty, corrosive, and adhesive products.  They are also widely used in shower curtains, garment bags, and as a laminate with paper to package small portions of food, such as sugar.  Thin films have been used as membranes in brain surgery, and small tubes have replaced sections of blood vessels, while larger tubing has been utilized for intravenous feeding.

Some limitations of polyethylene films are lack of complete transparency and attack by certain hydrocarbons and chlorinated solvents. In addition, the films are permeable to many gases and vapors, such as ethers, gasoline, carbon tetrachloride, and carbon disulfide.  Other limitations of polyethylene include ready flammability, difficulties in obtaining high surface gloss, and limited outdoor stability.

Polyethylene has many other industrial uses, but its outstanding electrical properties make it particularly valuable for insulation in high-frequency equipment.  Air and cellulose combinations have long been used, but cellulose is relatively sensitive to moisture and must therefore be protected from the weather.  Hard and soft rubbers also have been used, but their dielectric properties are poor at high frequencies.  As a result, polyethylene has become the standard insulating material in coaxial cable.  Polyethylene is used as cable insulation in the form of tape, string, or disks, and is also extruded over wire to form a continuously insulated conductor.  The flow of the polymer above its softening temperature permits relatively easy molding and extruding; as a result, many types of polyethylene-insulated coils and sockets, capacitors, and other electrical components are available.

Polyethylene, used as sheathing, also serves as a mechanical protection for wires and cables for power, communication, and control cables.  Its general chemical inertness is an added advantage in this application, since electrolytic or chemical action rapidly attacks metallic sheaths.

Further, the lighter weight of such plastic-sheathed cables reduces installation and transportation costs.

Pipe and industrial equipment account for about 20 per cent of the present volume of polyethylene. Polyethylene tubing, suitably pigmented and stabilized, is used in lightweight irrigation pipes, sewer lines, and industrial piping. Because of its inherent flexibility, a new type of plastic article arose, for example, squeezable bottles and tubes, disposable baby bottles, and flexible ice-cube trays, which are fabricated in tremendous volume.

Certain grades of polyethylene have been developed for injection molding and are widely used for making articles of thin cross-section. Upon cooling after molding, the linear shrinkage is about 3.5 per cent and the cubical shrinkage about 11 per cent; hence, this plastic is confined to applications where dimensional tolerances are relatively wide. Because of its fluidity, less injection pressure is needed than for most other plastics. The blow molding of bottles is an interesting new technique (see Chap. 11).

As a matter of fact, the first plastic container of industrial importance awaited the introduction of polyethylene, shortly after the close of World War II. The forerunner of today's plastic industrial containers was the polyethylene bottle, first introduced to the packaging field in 1946. Blown polyethylene bottles as large as one pint were available by 1949. The development of a five-gallon, blown polyethylene bottle was reached in late 1950, and the bottles have grown larger ever since.

Printing inks do not adhere well to polyethylene; however, several methods have been developed to treat polyethylene so as to provide a suitable surface. Early procedures included physical reorientation of the material by stretching in the cold state, chemical etching to provide relief from surface tension and to provide greater contact area, and chemical treatment with chlorine gas in the presence of ultraviolet radiation to replace some of the hydrogen atoms by chlorine on the surface and increase the affinity for specially formulated inks. The Kreidl heat differential method operates through the release of surface tension by the application of heat. This is accomplished by subjecting the surface to a blast of hot air for a short period of time. Another method which has been used is electron bombardment. Intense energy is caused to impinge upon the surface molecules, releasing some hydrogen atoms and resulting in a substantially unsaturated surface. This provides a surface which will unite readily with inks. Similar results are obtained by a brief flame contact with the surface. All of the above processes have been used, depending upon the specific requirements.

Polyethylene having a molecular weight in the range of 10,000 to 40,000 can be readily melt-spun, and higher-molecular-weight polyethylene can be converted into filaments by solution spinning. The fibers have not, however, been used to any appreciable extent in the textile field because of the low softening temperature of the polymer and the tendency of the cold-drawn filaments to relax at temperatures above about 75°C. Oriented monofilaments have, however, been used in such applications as for the upholstery of automobiles, where higher temperatures are not normally encountered.

Very recently, the hitherto undesirable property of shrinkage has been used to advantage. The use depends upon the "memory" of polyethylene monofilament yarn. The yarn is first prestretched and then is woven with conventional textile fibers on a regular loom. By immersing the completed fabric in boiling water for a few seconds, the polyethylene, which runs lengthwise in the material, shrinks (by as much as 55 per cent) to its original length, pulling the other fibers to form a permanently three-dimensional fabric. The first use of this material (Trilok) will be in automotive and furniture upholstery, where the cushioning effect of the three-dimensional structure is reported to offer unusual comfort and free circulation of air between the person and the seat.

Certain polyethylenes have been used for paper coating, hot-melt adhesives, cable filling, and have been applied as surface coatings by flame-spraying techniques.

Chlorination of polyethylenes has also been investigated. During World War II, chlorinated polyethylene (Halothene) was developed in England and was used for a paper coating and as a dielectric for low-voltage cables. Chlorinated polyethylene containing up to about 30 per cent chlorine is softer, more elastomeric, and more soluble than the unmodified polymer. Although excellent elastomers (containing no plasticizer) can be made from chlorinated polyethylene, their cost is higher than plasticized vinyl chloride polymers with which they would compete.

Polyethylene has been experimentally copolymerized with many compounds, including vinyl chloride, vinylidine chloride, methyl methacrylate, acrylonitrile, butadiene, maleic anhydride, and carbon monoxide. Polyethylene has also been copolymerized with ethyl acetate; small amounts of the acetate appear to produce films having higher tear resistance than those from unmodified polyethylene. Mixtures containing polyisobutylene are of interest, since their electrical properties are almost as good as those of pure polyethylene, yet the polyisobutylene plasticizes the polyethylene, forming softer, more flexible products, particularly at low temperatures.

High-density polyethylenes are now being obtained from the high-pressure process. The modifications are in the manufacturing techniques, rather than in the chemistry involved. The products appear to be similar to those obtained by the low-pressure processes described below.

## Low-Pressure Process

In several respects, the preparation of high-molecular-weight polymers from ethylene was a surprising and remarkable accomplishment. As pointed out in Chapter 3, it had originally been considered necessary for ethylene to be unsymmetrically substituted in order to form polymers of high molecular weight. Then it was discovered in England that suitable polymers could be obtained under unusual conditions. These conditions included higher temperatures and much higher pressures than had ever been used for the commercial preparation of polymeric substances.

During the past few years, research in Germany, Italy, and the United States has demonstrated that high-molecular-weight polymers of ethylene (and, for that matter, of higher alkenes) can be obtained under much milder conditions, using a variety of somewhat unusual catalytic systems.

In Germany, Ziegler[1] announced the formation of high-molecular-weight polyethylenes by a process which involves the passage of ethylene into a suspension of triethyl aluminum and titanium tetrachloride in an aliphatic oil at substantially atmospheric pressure and at a temperature of approximately 60°C. The process is exothermic and cooling is required. Unlike the high-pressure process, high purity ethylene is not essential and an almost quantitative conversion is obtained. Initiation occurs at active catalyst centers bound to the solids present. Organo-metallic compounds which can yield either radicals or ions are found at these centers. Propagation occurs on the solid surfaces, and termination occurs by breakdown of the organo-metallic compounds to form olefins or by combination of radicals.

A proposed growth reaction mechanism for polymerization is one in which the metallic atom is bound to the surface. An ion-radical forms by reaction with adsorbed olefin; olefin molecules are adsorbed on the surface until the resulting polymer is desorbed. More monomer replaces that polymerized and is oriented by the surface. Binding the radical to the surface limits branching by both intramolecular and intermolecular transfer. So long as the surface adsorbs olefin in a regular, oriented fashion, only chain propagation can occur.

The polymer (Hostalen) differs appreciably from conventional high-pressure polyethylene. The product is an almost completely linear polymer, not possessing the branched-chain structure of high-pressure polyethylene. It has a softening temperature some 10° to 15°C higher than conventional polyethylene. It is claimed that the molecular weight can be controlled within the range of 10,000 to approximately 2,000,000,

[1] Ziegler, K. *et al.*, *Angew. Chem.*, **67**, 541 (1955).

whereas the highest molecular weight practically attainable with the high-pressure process is approximately 50,000. Further, the new product has a degree of crystallinity of more than 85 per cent, which is much higher than commercial high-pressure polyethylene.

Several companies in the United States have been licensed to manufacture polyethylene by this process. Among the products made in this country by this type of process are those known as Super Dylan and Hi-fax polyethylene.

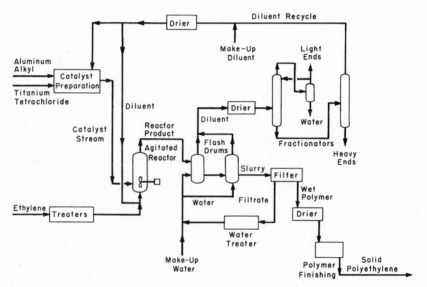

FIG. 9-4.   Polyethylene flow sheet—Ziegler process.   (*Reprinted from Petroleum Refiner*)

At least two other processes have recently been developed here. In one, a catalyst consisting of hexavalent chromium oxide (2 to 3 per cent) supported on a 1:9 alumina-silica carrier is used. The ethylene is polymerized in the liquid phase with a paraffin hydrocarbon diluent (e.g., isopentane) at about 500 psi and 150°C. The polymer (Marlex) is similar to the German material but is not identical. It differs in the types and amount of branching, which is even less than that in Hostalen, and in the prevalence of trans configurations. It is reported to be 93 per cent crystalline. This polymer was first made in 1954 and announced publicly in 1955.

The second American process employs nickel-charcoal and molybdena-alumina catalysts. Both catalysts have little activity in the oxidized state, but heating in the presence of hydrogen activates them by partial reduction. It is believed that the process operates at a pressure of about

1,000 psi and at temperatures of 200° to 260°C. (Another process developed by the same company is reported to use a diperoxy-dicarbonate ester initiator in an emulsion polymerization process.)

The products of the foregoing processes are known in the trade as HT (high temperature, high tensile) materials. It has been suggested that "linear polyethylenes" is a more suitable name for such products than "low-pressure" polyethylenes. All linear polyethylenes of a given weight-average molecular weight, regardless of method of preparation, have similar properties, provided they are free from contamination. More recently, producers of polyethylene, in an effort to find a new name for polyethylene that is more fitting than high- or low-pressure, high- or low-density, linear, etc., are starting to use the term "olefin resins." Such a designation includes both old and new type polyethylenes, as well as other olefin polymers, such as polypropylene, which are being developed at the present time.

The densities of the low-pressure polyethylenes range from 0.93 to 0.96, compared with 0.91 to 0.92 for the conventional high-pressure polyethylenes and 0.935 to 0.940 for the newer high-density, high-pressure types. All of the new polyethylenes can withstand continuous temperatures of 120°C. The older polyethylenes have a softening temperature of 105° to 115°C and are not used continuously above about 75°C. The new polyethylenes would thus become the most heat-resistant thermoplastics in general use except for nylon and the fluorocarbon polymers. In addition, the brittleness temperature of newer polyethylenes, in many cases, is considerably lower than that of standard polyethylene which makes the former particularly attractive for low-temperature use.

The improved properties of linear polyethylene are extremely interesting from the standpoint of structural fabrication. Tensile strength can be as high as 6,000 psi as compared with the maximum of about 2,000 psi for the polyethylene produced by the previous method. Elongation of some of the newer materials is as high as 1,200 per cent. In addition, these materials, in the drawn form, are quite opaque; this is in contrast to the increased transparency found when drawing high-pressure polyethylene. The rigidity of low-pressure polyethylene is much greater than that of the high-pressure material. The stiffness modulus can be as high as 150,000 psi compared with 30,000 psi for high-pressure polyethylene. The vapor and gas transmission rates are about one third the comparable rates in high-pressure polyethylene. This is of considerable interest to packaging and container manufacturers. The bursting strength of pipe is from three to four times as great as that of the same size of pipe of high-pressure polyethylene. Electrical and chemical properties are about equal.

Although high-pressure polyethylene has not been completely suitable for use as a fiber, it appears likely that the higher crystallinity of low-pressure polyethylene will make its development for use as a fiber very promising.

### Irradiated Polyethylene

The discovery that irradiation produces cross-linking in polyethylene was announced in 1953. Polyethylene can be cross-linked in a few seconds by high-energy radiation to such a degree that all its favorable mechanical properties remain essentially unaltered, while its softening range is raised by 15° to 25°C. This increase in softening range is not accompanied by discoloration or other consequences of chemical degradation. This method has led to new commercial types of polyethylene and is now being studied intensively for other polymers.

Polyethylene molecules are essentially saturated straight chains, although there is a certain amount of branching; as mentioned earlier, each molecule is believed to contain one vinylidene group:

$$-CH_2 \cdot CH_2 \cdot C \cdot CH_2 \cdot CH_2-$$
$$\|$$
$$CH_2$$

Neutrons and gamma rays cause the ejection of hydrogen atoms from the chain, leaving an active, free-radical center. According to a recent hypothesis, the free-radical centers move along or across the chains by means of random migration of hydrogen atoms attached to the chain. When these active centers approach a point favorable to reaction with a vinylidene group in a neighboring chain, cross-linking occurs:

$$-CH_2 \cdot C \cdot CH_2- \qquad -CH_2 \cdot \overset{\cdot}{C} \cdot CH_2-$$
$$\| \qquad \qquad |$$
$$CH_2 \; + \; -CH_2 \cdot \overset{\cdot}{C}H \cdot CH_2- \rightarrow \; CH_2$$
$$|$$
$$-CH_2 \cdot CH \cdot CH_2-$$

Irradiation appears to cause very little rupture of the carbon-to-carbon bonds within the main chains; however, the carbon-to-carbon bonds in the side-chains rupture as frequently as do the carbon-hydrogen bonds in the material as a whole.

Cross-linking or vulcanization of polymers by a normal amount of irradiation contributes form stability at 150° to as high as 175°C and also resistance to cracking when the product is stressed or is exposed to the action of solvent or other chemicals.

Irradiated polyethylene does not melt at any temperature if the dose level is sufficient, but changes from a plastic material to an elastic one as it passes above the ordinary crystalline melting range of 105° to 115°C, since the amount of crystallinity is reduced. Above this range, the inherent strength of the material is not sufficient for most applications.

Irradiated polyethylene is offered commercially (Irrathene and Agilene HT). The material has a tensile strength of 1,800 to 2,200 psi, a specific gravity of 0.92, and does not melt at temperatures as high as 175°C; however, for continuous operation at temperatures above 100°C, it must be protected from contact with air.

Although the addition of fillers to polyethylene has been tried, when used alone they have been found actually to degrade polyethylene; unirradiated, filled polyethylene is stiff, brittle, and has no desirable physical properties. Irradiating polyethylene compounded with reinforcing fillers eliminates the stiffness and brittleness caused when fillers are used alone. The tensile strength of the filled, irradiated product is from five to eight times that of the unfilled, irradiated product in the higher temperature ranges. The new material (Vulkene) has better heat and chemical resistance than the conventional high-pressure polyethylene from which it is derived. Another new, irradiated polyethylene (Hyrad) has been announced which will withstand indefinite exposure at 150°C, versus 120°C for Vulkene.

The new low-pressure polyethylenes appear to possess most of the desirable properties produced by high-energy irradiation of high-pressure polyethylene. However, the newer polyethylenes will not necessarily eliminate the need for irradiation but may instead extend the range of base materials applicable for irradiation. Irradiation of low-pressure polyethylene produces still better properties in these materials. Even though these polyethylenes are extremely resistant to stress cracking, they are still not totally free from this phenomenon. Irradiation in proper doses produces a material which is completely free from stress-crack attack.

### Chlorosulfonated Polyethylene

Chlorosulfonated polyethylene (Hypalon), introduced in 1952, is an elastomer whose chemical composition is quite different from natural rubber. All of the other synthetic elastomers, with the exception of Brom Butyl (see Butyl Rubber), involves the polymerization of one or more substances as the principal step in the production of the final product. With Hypalon, on the other hand, the important step is the transformation of a *preformed*, high-molecular-weight, thermoplastic polymer, polyethylene, into a vulcanizable elastomer through chemical reaction with chlorine and sulfur dioxide.

From a theoretical standpoint, absence of chain branching is desirable in a finished elastomer, since the more nearly a strictly linear molecule is obtained, the higher are the qualities of the vulcanizate produced.   On the other hand, chain branching has an appreciable effect in decreasing the crystallinity of the polymer.   Generally speaking, a high degree of crystallinity results in an undesired amount of stiffness in the finished elastomer.   This stiffness causes difficulty in processing of the unvulcanized elastomer.

One of the most practical methods of destroying crystallinity in a high-molecular-weight compound, without destroying other valuable properties, is by the random introduction into the chain of new atoms or groups.   With polyethylene, the introduction of chlorine appears to have the greatest effect upon the degree of crystallinity and at the same time preserves, to a large degree, its desirable properties.   The purpose of also introducing sulfonyl chloride groups is to provide sites of reactivity through which vulcanization can be effected.   These groups are introduced by means of the Reed reaction, involving simultaneous introduction of gaseous chlorine, sulfur dioxide, and a free-radical initiator.

The particular chlorine and sulfur dioxide content chosen was one which was felt to have the most useful balance of properties for general service.   Hypalon is derived from a polyethylene having a number-average molecular weight of about 20,000.   The product contains about 1.5 per cent sulfur and 27.5 per cent chlorine, or approximately one chlorine for each seven carbon atoms and one sulfonyl chloride group for every 90 carbon atoms.   All of the sulfur appears in sulfonyl chloride groups, probably attached predominantly to secondary carbon atoms in the chain.   The chlorine atoms not attached to sulfur presumably are distributed more or less randomly along the polyethylene chain.   Thus, they may occur in primary, secondary, and tertiary positions.   The composition is indicated in the structure:

$$\left[ (-CH_2 \cdot CH_2 \cdot CH_2 \cdot CHCl \cdot CH_2 \cdot CH_2 \cdot CH_2 -)_{12} -\underset{\underset{SO_2Cl}{|}}{CH}- \right]_{17}$$

By varying molecular weight and its distribution, chain branching, and degree of crystallinity, a wide variety of derivatives may be prepared. The one offered commercially is a white, fluffy crumb with a specific gravity of about 1.1 when molded.   Tensile strengths of gum stocks are as high as 3,500 to 4,000 psi and are not dependent on fillers, such as carbon blacks or silica gels.

Chlorosulfonated polyethylene is a completely saturated elastomer, depending primarily upon the reactive sulfonyl chloride groups for cure.   The curing systems which have been studied most intensively are based upon a polybasic metal oxide or polybasic metal salt of a weak acid (litharge or magnesia), an organic acid, and an organic accelerator.   For the organic acid, hydrogenated wood rosin is preferred, since it is less subject to oxidation and discoloration than the unsaturated, naturally occurring acids. Mercaptobenzothiazole is the safest known accelerator for this system.

The principal cross-linking reaction in this metal oxide curing system is believed to be due to the reaction between the metal oxide and sulfonic acid groups on the polymer chain. The first step in the cure is the hydrolysis of sulfonyl chloride groups to form the free acid. The second step is the formation of a sulfonate bridge. The following equations have been postulated to explain the curing reaction taking place:

$$2R \cdot SO_2Cl + 2H_2O \rightarrow 2HCl + 2R \cdot SO_2 \cdot OH$$
$$PbO + 2HCl \rightarrow H_2O + PbCl_2$$
$$PbO + 2R \cdot SO_2 \cdot OH \rightarrow H_2O + (R \cdot SO_2 \cdot O)_2Pb$$

The cross-linking reaction takes place at significant rates only under curing conditions where water is formed, and the rate of hydrolysis of a sulfonyl chloride group to the sulfonic acid group is rapid. The presence of more or less water affects only the rate of the cross-linking reaction and not the extent of the reaction.

From a processing standpoint, Hypalon differs from other elastomers in two important respects; first, the effect of milling on breakdown, and second, the effect of temperature upon the viscosity of the polymer. Natural rubber and many of the important synthetic elastomers must be broken down by milling in order to make them plastic enough to work on rubber equipment. Hypalon, on the other hand, requires no breakdown in order to obtain material which has satisfactory viscosity and smoothness on a rubber mill. Further, its viscosity decreases more rapidly with an increase in temperature than does that of most other elastomers.

Hypalon, unlike GR-S, does not require the addition of carbon black in order to produce vulcanizates of good quality. Vulcanizates having good tensile strengths can be obtained by the addition of vulcanizing ingredients only. In this respect, the polymer resembles both natural rubber and neoprene.

This polymer, properly compounded and cured, has an excellent combination of properties, including complete resistance to ozone; excellent resistance to abrasion, weather, heat, and crack growth; low moisture absorption; good electrical properties; a wide color range (since it does not require carbon black for reinforcement); good chemical resistance; and oil resistance close to that of neoprene. Exceptional mechanical durability and chemical stability of blends of chlorosulfonated polyethylene with GR-S-type copolymers may be obtained.

Hypalon compounds, when properly formulated, have unusually good outdoor durability. Tests have indicated that vulcanizates may be successfully used for tank linings, hose, and similar applications where other elastomers have proved inadequate.

Very satisfactory bonds have been obtained with cements based upon Hypalon. In these cements, the curing agent is *p*-quinone dioxime, which has thus far been found to be superior to other curing agents.

POLYTETRAFLUOROETHYLENE

Polytetrafluoroethylene, commonly called Teflon in the United States and Fluon in Britain, is a completely fluorinated polymer. The commercial production of Freon refrigerants, compounds consisting of fluorine, carbon, and (usually) chlorine began in 1931. Further research on this family of products led to the laboratory discovery of tetrafluoroethylene resin in about 1938. Semiplant production of Teflon began in 1941, and the first commercial plant started operation in 1950.

The discovery by Plunkett in this country that tetrafluoroethylene under pressure polymerizes readily was quite unexpected. Until the advent of polyethylene, it had been thought that one or two substituents (and no more) were necessary to disturb the symmetry of ethylene in order for polymerization to occur. Even then, ethylene formed products of high molecular weight only at relatively high temperatures. Tetrachloroethylene shows no tendency to polymerize, whereas pure, uninhibited tetrafluoroethylene will polymerize with violence, even below room temperature.

The commercial synthesis of tetrafluoroethylene is unusual. The monomer is made by the pyrolysis of monochlorodifluoromethane, which is obtained by a Swarts-type, liquid-phase hydrofluorination of chloroform:

$$CHCl_3 + HF \xrightarrow[65°C]{SbCl_5} CHFCl_2 + CHF_2Cl + CF_2Cl_2 + HCl$$

$$\downarrow AlCl_3$$

$$CHF_2Cl + CHCl_3$$

$$2CHF_2Cl \xrightarrow{650°–800°C} CF_2{:}CF_2 + 2HCl$$

The chloroform produced in the second reaction is recycled. Tetrafluoroethylene is a colorless, odorless gas which liquefies at $-76°C$.

A description of the commercial polymerization of tetrafluoroethylene has not been made in the literature, although several laboratory preparations have been described. It is known that the monomer may be polymerized by both mass and suspension methods, although the former is hazardous because of the highly exothermic reaction. In one process, oxygen is used in conjunction with organic peroxides as the initiator. The conditions of the reaction include the presence of substantial amounts of water, a pressure of about 1,000 psi, and a temperature range from 55° to 240°C. An improved method emphasizes the importance of water as a heat transfer medium, the use of inorganic peroxides, the increasing polymerization rate with increase in pressure, and the advantage of a

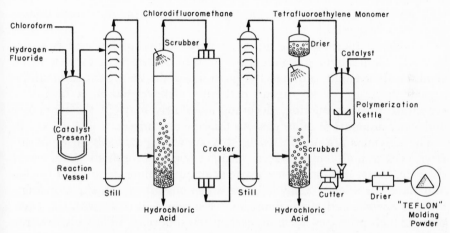

FIG. 9-5. Polytetrafluoroethylene flow sheet. (*Courtesy E. I. duPont de Nemours and Co.*)

buffer to prevent large pH fluctuations. Bisazo compounds have recently been reported to be the preferred type of initiator.

One method for producing an aqueous dispersion involves a temperature of 55° to 70°C, a pressure of 50 to 350 psi, and disuccinic acid peroxide as the initiator in an agitated, aqueous medium. The polymer can also be prepared as an aqueous dispersion, using bis(β-carboxypropionyl) peroxide. These resin dispersions consist of colloidal-sized, negatively charged particles of between 0.05 and 0.5 micron in diameter.

Teflon is produced in three basic forms: as granules, fine powder, and an aqueous dispersion. The granules and powder are used in molding and extrusion processes. The dispersion polymer is used for coating, impregnating, and the production of filled compositions.

The high-molecular-weight polymers of tetrafluoroethylene are the least thermoplastic of the addition polymers. They have outstanding resistance to solvents and corrosive chemicals and display excellent strength and flexibility over an extremely wide temperature range. They are harder and even less elastomeric than chlorotrifluoroethylene polymers. The highly crystalline polymers are white or light gray in color, translucent in appearance, and waxy in feel—similar to polyethylene. Quenched tapes and foils, however, exhibit fair transparency. Since the polymer is insoluble in all solvents, molecular weights cannot be obtained; estimates of 500,000 and higher have been made.

The specific gravity of Teflon is 2.2 to 2.3, the tensile strength 3,500 to 4,500 psi, the heat distortion temperature is 130°C, and the water absorption is negligible. The polymer exhibits considerable cold flow at moderately elevated temperatures; this is responsible for the moderately low heat distortion temperature and is one of the important limitations of the material.

Although a thermoplastic material, polytetrafluoroethylene has a surprisingly high softening temperature of 327°C, and this, as well as its good tensile strength, is due to the small size of the fluorine atoms and the regular structure of the linear molecule. Above 400°C, it begins to evaporate without melting, decomposing slowly to yield the monomer and lesser amounts of other gaseous fluorine derivatives.

The polymers are unaffected by any known organic solvent or plasticizer, even at high temperatures. Aqua regia, chlorosulfonic acid, acetyl chloride, boron trifluoride, hot nitric acid, and boiling solutions of caustic also have no affect. Only molten alkali metals attack the polymers, forming carbon and alkali fluorides. Fluorine will react with the polymers at high pressures, forming carbon tetrafluoride. The polymers are nonflammable. These thermal and chemical stabilities are associated with its very remarkable electrical properties: very low dielectric constant and dielectric loss (power factor). In these respects, it surpasses polyethylene and polystyrene.

Because of general insolubility and the lack of thermoplasticity and ability to be plasticized, conventional fabricating procedures are unsuccessful. Maximum properties can be obtained only when the resin is fabricated at temperatures exceeding the fusion temperature. The fabrication methods resemble powder metallurgy. In one procedure, the finely divided, granular polymer is cold-pressed into a preform under a pressure of 2,000 to 10,000 psi, which then has sufficient cohesiveness after removal from the mold to permit sintering at high temperatures (370° to 390°C). From these masses, gaskets and other simple articles can be machined. Tapes can be shaved from tubes of the polymer mounted in a lathe.

Rods, tubes, and special cross-sections can be produced from molding powder by extrusion. This process involves compacting the cold powder with either a reciprocating ram or a screw, and then forcing the compacted powder through a heated die where it is sintered. Production rates are slow, as compared to conventional melt extrusion, primarily because of the low rate of heat transfer. Ram extrusion provides higher production rates than screw production at lower cost and is the preferred technique.

A copolymer of tetrafluoroethylene with hexafluoropropylene (Teflon 100X) has recently become available. This product is reported to be much easier to fabricate than the homopolymer.

Dispersions of the colloidal polymer, suitably formulated with dispersing agents, spread out on smooth surfaces as deposits which can be converted into tough, thin films. Temperatures above 327°C are required to fuse the polymer particles. These finishes became available in production quantities in 1950. The suspensions produce extremely resistant finishes and can be used for lining reaction vessels of steel, copper, aluminum, glass, or ceramics. Surfaces must be specially prepared and special primer coats are usually necessary in order to obtain adequate adhesion, since the polymer is an anti-adhesive. The surface of the polymer can be dulled by a bath of sodium metal and liquid ammonia; this recent discovery enables the material to be bonded with most commercial adhesives. The finish has such high chemical, heat, and moisture resistance that it is also used to prevent corrosion of equipment and as electrical wire insulation. Since nothing will stick to the finish, its high cost is justified for special applications. In the rubber industry, for example, products are likely to stick to the smoothest metal surfaces and seriously impair equipment operations. As another example, in the packaging industry the long-standing problem of glue sticking to machine parts is solved by the use of this material. In addition to the preparation of thin films, the resin dispersions have been found suitable for impregnating woven fabrics and mat structures to render them chemically resistant.

In spite of its high cost, polytetrafluoroethylene can be used economically as valve seats, diaphragms, packing and gaskets for meters, pumps, agitators, and other continuously operating equipment where replacement of worn parts is frequent or difficult. Tetrafluoroethylene (and chlorotrifluoroethylene) polymers are used as electrical insulators in motors and radio equipment operating at high temperatures.

Sheets as thin as 0.00025 inch are expected to find application as insulation where mica is now used, particularly in the development of more compact radar equipment. Films of polytetrafluoroethylene remain flexible at temperatures as low as −100°C, but are more brittle than chlorotrifluoroethylene polymers at liquid air temperature. Pressure-sensitive tapes made of Teflon film have been announced which are reported to be effective from −65° to 205°C. They can be applied at any temperature within this range without loss of their adhesive properties, and they will stick to glass, aluminum, steel, copper, and brass.

Fiber made from the polymer was introduced in experimental quantities in 1954. Teflon fiber retains the unusual properties of the parent polymer, having excellent chemical resistance, strength, and heat stability. The upper limit of the fiber's useful temperature range is between 200° and 275°C, depending upon the application. The tensile strength of the fiber is 50,000 psi at 23°C, its moisture absorption is zero, its color is brown (it can be bleached), it has poor dyeability, and it is soft and slippery. It is nonflammable and has excellent electrical properties.

Few materials stick to the fiber, and its coefficient of friction is the lowest of any. The flex abrasion resistance of Teflon fiber is above that of rayon and Orlon at room temperature but below that of nylon and Dacron. However, in corrosive chemical atmospheres or at high temperatures, Teflon fiber is superior to the latter two in flex abrasion resistance and freedom from brittleness.

Some of the uses considered for the fiber include filter fabrics; packing for pump and valve shafts; gaskets; laundry textiles for press covers, pads, and roll covers; special conveyors and belting; diaphragms for valves; electrical tapes and wire wraps; and special sewing thread.

### POLYCHLOROTRIFLUOROETHYLENE

The polymerization of chlorotrifluoroethylene was first reported in 1937, but it was not until the atomic energy program during World War II required materials of construction with an extreme degree of chemical and thermal stability, especially for gaskets and valve seats used in highly corrosive fluorine atmospheres, that a high-molecular-weight resin was obtained in good yield. The polymer was first used in the Oak Ridge gaseous diffusion plant in connection with the production of $U^{235}$. Commercial manufacture was undertaken in 1947, and a large expansion of facilities has taken place since that time.

The monomer can be prepared by the dechlorination of 1,1,2-trichloro-1,2,2-trifluoroethane with zinc dust in boiling alcohol:

$$CCl_2F \cdot CClF_2 + Zn \xrightarrow{\text{alcohol}} ZnCl_2 + CClF{:}CF_2$$

Chlorotrifluoroethylene is a colorless gas with a faint, ethereal odor. It has a boiling point of $-28°C$ at a pressure of 1 atmosphere, and its liquid density at 20°C is 1.3.

At room temperature, the liquid monomer reacts rapidly and quantitatively with atmospheric oxygen to form compounds which, upon hydrolysis, yield oxalic acid, hydrogen fluoride, and hydrogen chloride.

A small amount of a water-soluble peroxide is also formed. It has been postulated that the intermediate formed is a cyclic peroxide:

$$
\begin{array}{c}
\text{F} \quad \text{F} \\
| \quad | \\
\text{F·C·C·Cl} \\
| \quad | \\
\text{O–O}
\end{array}
$$

For this reason, the monomer is handled in closed systems or under nitrogen and is stored at dry-ice temperature. The monomer is usually inhibited for temporary room-temperature storage with a small amount of a mixture of terpenes known as Terpene B hydrocarbons. This is removed by fractionation, and the last trace is eliminated by passing the monomer over silica gel.

The monomer polymerizes under the influence of peroxides and in the absence of oxygen; however, relatively slow conversion rates are obtained. Although no information has been released on the commercially employed polymerization techniques, it is known that polymerization can be conducted by aqueous suspension or mass methods and that, although improved commercial methods have been developed, long reaction times and low conversions still are encountered.

Numerous peroxy compounds have been reported as polymerization promoters for this monomer. Polymerization may be controlled so as to yield oils, greases, and waxes in the molecular weight range of 500 to 5,000. This has usually been accomplished by carrying out the polymerization in the presence of a large excess of chloroform (a chain-transfer agent) at a fairly high temperature (150°C). Benzoyl peroxide is used as an initiator. The chemical and thermal stability of the products can be improved by after-treatment with cobalt trifluoride, which removes the hydrogen and more reactive chlorine introduced by the chloroform.

A new initiator for the more rapid polymerization of chlorotrifluoroethylene consists of silver ion for the activation of an aqueous persulfate-bisulfite redox system. Another method for the reasonably fast preparation of high-molecular-weight polymers in high yields is by a suspension polymerization technique, using *tert*-butyl perbenzoate in a sodium bisulfite-ferricitrophosphate system. A new continuous process is now being used for the production of the polymer.

A typical polymer has a specific gravity of 2.12, a tensile strength at 25°C of 5,700 psi, an elongation of 500 per cent, and a negligible water absorption. The high-molecular-weight resins are colorless, high-melting, plastic solids which are insoluble in their monomer. The polymer's chemical inertness, high dielectric strength, and zero water absorption may be attributed to its fluorine constituent. Chlorine contributes to its transparency, is in part responsible for its excellent mechanical properties, and, most important of all, permits this plastic to be molded and fabricated into useful articles by standard production equipment (cf. polytetrafluoroethylene).

Many of the physical properties of chlorotrifluoroethylene resins depend upon the type and extent of their crystallinity. These resins have been described as crystallizable but not necessarily crystalline. The "quick-quenched" resin is primarily amorphous and the "slow-cooled" or "heat-treated" resin is predominantly crystalline. In thin sections, the quenched resin is colorless and transparent. In thicker sections or when heat-treated, the resin varies from an opalescent blue to an opaque white, depending upon the degree of crystallinity.

Chlorotrifluoroethylene polymers (Kel-F and Fluorothene) are hard and rigid rather than elastomeric. Nevertheless, the elastic modulus varies so little with temperature that thin sections will flex without shattering at almost $-200°C$ and yet will retain appreciable strength at temperatures as high as $+200°C$. The plastics are noteworthy for their strength, toughness, abrasion resistance, good aging characteristics, flame resistance, and thermal stability. The polymers are also known for their resistance to oxygen, ozone, sunlight, strong bases and acids (including the fuming oxidizing acids), and a wide variety of organic solvents. Although insoluble in all organic solvents at room temperature, the polymers are swollen by a number of organic liquids, including diethyl ether, trifluoroethylene, carbon tetrachloride, toluene, and ethyl acetate. At high temperatures, many more liquids, including some phthalate esters, swell or even dissolve the polymers. They resist all corrosive agents except molten alkali metals, fluorine, and highly halogenated compounds, and are superior to polytetrafluoroethylene in resistance to the penetration of reagents.

Because polychlorotrifluoroethylene is a true thermoplastic, it can be fabricated by compression, injection, and transfer molding. Rod, tubing, wire insulation, and film are fabricated by continuous extrusion at 250° to 300°C.

The physical properties of the polymers vary widely with degree of polymerization. Softening and molding temperatures range from below 175° to above 300°C. The material is currently being produced in the form of high- and low-density molding powders, ranging in molecular weight from 75,000 to 110,000. The molded material has exceptionally high impact strength, is elastic under stress, and can be machined readily to small tolerances.

Polychlorotrifluoroethylene has many of the same properties and uses as polytetrafluoroethylene. For most properties, however, the trifluoro product does not have as wide a temperature range as the tetrafluoro material. An exception is the resistance to thermal shock. The trifluoro material also has much better resistance to cold flow, a property important for gaskets, **O**-rings, and packings. Its compressive strength is very high for a plastic material, and heat treatment can increase this still further—from 30,000 to 80,000 psi.

Amenability of the polymer to heat treatment makes possible the production of transparent sheet and molded products which have the same properties as the original resin plus the added advantage of light transmission. Use of this transparent material is made in windows and sight glasses for corrosive applications, where a strong yet transparent material is desirable.

Although the polychlorotrifluoroethylene plastics are quite expensive, like the tetrafluoro polymers they give valuable service in many special industrial applications where other materials will not withstand the extremes of chemical attack and temperature involved. Only tetrafluoro-ethylene polymers surpass them in resistance to high temperatures and to chemical attack.

The polymers have been used as gaskets, valve seats, transparent windows, and tubing; as insulators and supports for electrical equipment; and for other applications where properties of extreme chemical inertness, freedom from moisture absorption, and toughness are essential. For many applications, polychlorotrifluoroethylene is preferable to polytetra-fluoroethylene because of easier molding or forming under heat and greater transparency. The lack of complete symmetry in the chain segments opposes the high degree of crystallinity and opacity shown in vinylidine chloride and tetrafluoroethylene polymers.

Recent development of a welding method for polychlorotrifluoroethyl-ene film makes it useful for lining tanks to protect against corrosive attack. The welding procedure is only successful in bonding the film to itself; the lining must be supported inside tanks by an acid-brick structure.

A series of dispersions in water and organic liquids is available. These dispersions permit application of the polymer by spraying, brushing, or dipping, followed by fusion. Hitherto, protective coatings were applied by pressing, extrusion, or compression molding.

The resins are of value to the electrical industry because of their exceptional moisture resistance, chemical and thermal stability, electrical characteristics, and ease of fabrication. The material is used for coatings for magnet wires, insulation for coaxial cable, and supports for radar and FM antennas.

Because practically nothing will stick to polychlorotrifluoroethylene, the polymers are used on conveyor belts that handle sticky materials, on machinery used to heat-seal plastic films, and on the rollers and other components of bread-making machinery. In the food industry, dispersion coatings are used as release agents for bread dough, candy, and meat products. In the medical and pharmaceutical fields, the resins are of great value because items such as tubing and film can be sterilized without distortion.

Liquid and waxlike polymers of molecular weight 500 to 5,000 are useful as plasticizers for the high-molecular-weight polymers and as lubricants where extreme stability is required, particularly to halogens.

A commercially available copolymer resin containing fluorine is the copolymer of chlorotrifluoroethylene and vinyl chloride (Exon 400). It is used as a solution coating and can also be extruded, injection molded, and compression molded.

A recent fluorocarbon elastomer, announced during 1954, is known as Kel-F elastomer. The structure has not been disclosed, but it is a copolymer of chlorotrifluoroethylene with perhaps vinylidene fluoride as the other component. This copolymer contains about 50 per cent fluorine, has rather poor flexibility and elastomeric properties, but is highly resistant to a number of chemicals and possesses good heat stability up to 200°C. It is, however, not very resistant to the ester-based oils. Potential uses include fuel hose, tank linings, gaskets, seals, diaphragms and valve seats, plus coatings for clothes used in corrosive material handling, and for paper, wood, and metal.

### POLYPROPYLENE

As an outgrowth of the intensive research on heterogeneous catalyst systems for the polymerization of ethylene, it has been found that higher alkenes (e.g., propylene, 1-butene) can also be successfully polymerized to form high-molecular-weight, useful polymers. Of great interest at the present time is the pilot-plant production of polypropylene in the United States and in Italy, using the Hostalen- and Marlex-type catalytic systems (see Polyethylene).

Propylene is abundantly available from the high-temperature cracking of petroleum feed stocks and propane.

The over-all polymerization reaction is

$$n \; CH_2{:}CH{\cdot}CH_3 \rightarrow (-CH_2{\cdot}\overset{\displaystyle CH_3}{\underset{\displaystyle |}{CH}}-)_n$$

In the United States, phosphoric acid, copper pyrophosphate, and silica-alumina have been used commercially for many years to produce liquid polymers from propylene and butylene, but the use of a supported chromium oxide (Marlex-type) catalyst to produce high-molecular-weight polymers of ethylene and other olefins is apparently the first use of a solid heterogeneous-type catalyst which has been commercially practical. This type of catalyst promotes the polymerization of a variety of unsaturated hydrocarbons. In general, it is effective in polymerizing all 1-olefins (with no branching closer than the 4-position to the double bond) which contain eight carbon atoms or less. For example, 1-butene, 1-pentene, and 1-hexene form branched, high-molecular-weight polymers by this method. Diolefins, such as butadiene and isoprene, can also be polymerized by this type of catalyst. The observed rule concerning branching closer than the 4-position does not apply to diolefins.

These new alkene or olefin polymers, made by using a heterogeneous and highly specific catalyst, have been termed "stereospecific" polymers. Stereospecific refers to the arrangement of molecules in a predetermined geometric form, rather than in random fashion. The terms "isotactic," "syndiotactic," and "atactic" have been coined to describe the special types of stereoisomerism which occur upon the stereospecific polymerization of vinyl compounds of the type, $CH_2{:}CHR$, which usually do not show stereoisomerism in the monomeric form. By means of stereospecific catalysts, polymerization can be directed to form an ordered arrangement of mesomers, yielding regular sequences (isotactic), alternations of definite steric configurations (syndiotactic), or, with the usual initiators, random sequences (atactic):[2]

```
        R       R       R       R       R

   H    C   H   C   H   C   H   C   H   C

   C    H   C   H   C   H   C   H   C   H

   H        H       H       H       H
                  Isotactic
```

```
        R       H       R       H       R

   H    C   H   C   H   C   H   C   H   C

   C    H   C   R   C   H   C   R   C   H

   H        H       H       H       H
                Syndiotactic
```

[2] Natta, G., *Modern Plastics*, **34**, No. 4, 170 (1956).

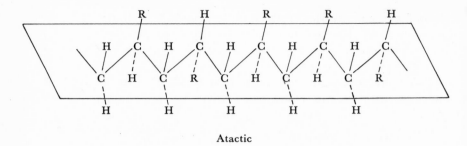

Atactic

(The dotted lines refer to atoms or radicals below the reference plane.) Stereoisomerism is also possible in polymers of conjugated diolefins (e.g., butadiene), and the possible number of forms increases rapidly as complexity of the monomer increases.

These new polymers contain alkyl side groups which are oriented with respect to the tertiary carbon atoms of the chain. These side groups spiral around the main chain, and the spirals fit closely together to yield a regular, crystalline structure. In contrast, the highly amorphous type of polymer, as is that made by high-pressure techniques, has a random arrangement of side groups; this prevents close packing of molecular chains and thus prevents orientation.

The production of such polymers with a regular structure requires that the polymerization take place (1) always in a head-to-tail arrangement, (2) without branching by chain transfer or by copolymerization of monomer with its low-molecular-weight polymers, and (3) in such a way that the mesomers arrange themselves in an ordered steric configuration. The formation of stereospecific polymers from 1-olefins depends upon the presence of solid catalysts bound chemically to the growing polymer chain. It is probable that stereospecific catalysis depends upon chemisorption of monomer molecules on the surface of the solid catalyst so that the adsorbed molecules are always presented to the growing chain in a definite orientation. Investigations so far conducted lead to the belief that the mechanism of this type of polymerization is an anionic one, using catalysts which contain compounds of groups IV to VIII transition elements in an oxidation state lower than the maximum, in combination with metal alkyls. The useful elements appear to be titanium, vanadium, chromium, and zirconium. Titanium trichloride appears to be the preferred salt at present.

Polypropylene has a highly crystalline structure which gives it a high softening temperature (160°C), a high tensile strength (greater than nylon), high resistance to solvents, and none of the waxy feel of polyethylene. Its high softening temperature compares with the range of 105° to 130°C for polyethylene made by various processes. Molded products are reported to be stiffer, harder, and to have better scratch resistance than polyethylene.

Natta and Giustiniani in Italy have succeeded in producing polypropylene in yields as high as 90 to 95 per cent. The product (Moplen), first produced commercially in Italy in 1957, is going principally into molded products, although film will also be made. It is likely that polypropylene fiber will be seriously considered because of the high degree of crystallinity of the polymer. Production of polypropylene (Pro-fax) in the United States began in late 1957.

Because of the low price of propylene (lower than ethylene) and its ready availability in this country, it appears likely that polypropylene will rank with polyethylene as a very large tonnage polymer in the near future.

## POLYBUTENES

Fairly recent polymers on the market are the relatively low-molecular-weight polybutenes, prepared by the polymerization of $n$-butenes, which, in turn, are obtained by the cracking of petroleum fractions or by the dehydrogenation of butane. The feed, from a refinery gas stream containing some $C_3$ and $C_5$ hydrocarbons also, is precooled; a slurry of anhydrous aluminum chloride (containing a small amount of hydrogen chloride gas as an activator) in light polymer is injected into the feed and exothermic polymerization occurs rapidly. By control of the temperature, various low-molecular-weight products are obtained. These saturated, viscous liquids range in molecular weight from about 300 to about 1,500, and have specific gravities of 0.83 to 0.89. They are used as components of sealing compounds, insulation and sound-deadening mastics, caulking compounds, cements, and pressure-sensitive adhesives. They have also been evaluated in the preparation of tracing paper, as a dielectric for capacitors, and as a lubricant in aluminum drawing and rolling.

Most of the early work on the low-temperature polymerization of 1-olefins with Friedel-Crafts catalysts has been done with unpromoted catalysts; i.e., in systems where a co-catalyst was not added. However, it is now known that olefins will not undergo polymerization at low temperatures in the presence of Friedel-Crafts catalysts in the absence of promoters. The so-called unpromoted reaction proceeds because of the presence of traces of moisture or other promoters in reagents that have not been specifically dried or purified (see Chap. 3). Just recently, higher-molecular-weight, solid polymers from 1-olefins have been produced for the first time by use of new heterogeneous catalysts (see Polypropylene).

Of much greater importance at present are the polymers and copolymers of isobutylene (methyl propene), sometimes incorrectly called isobutene. Polyisobutylenes (Vistanex, Isolene, Polyvis) were first developed in Germany (Oppanol B) and were available commercially in Europe about 1936 in a range of molecular weights from about 15,000 to more than 200,000 (Staudinger molecular weight). The homopolymers, ranging from viscous liquids to somewhat rubberlike solids, are produced in relatively small volume in the United States.

To obtain the high quality isobutylene necessary for low-temperature polymerization and copolymerization, the dehydration of pure isobutyl alcohol over alumina at about 400°C was originally used in Germany. In the United States, isobutylene is obtained, along with other alkenes and related hydrocarbons, by the cracking of petroleum fractions. The method in general use of selectively hydrating isobutylene to form *tert*-butyl alcohol, followed by dehydration to the olefin, although a means of preparing isobutylene of high purity, has certain disadvantages, chief among which is the highly corrosive nature of the dilute sulfuric acid used for the hydration. Catalytic depolymerization of $C_8$ homopolymers of isobutylene and its copolymers with *n*-butylene, using attapulgus clay, is very efficient and produces isobutylene of over 99 per cent purity. When necessary, isobutylene can also be obtained industrially by dehydrogenating and isomerizing *n*-butane from natural gas. The isobutylene is then purified by fractional distillation at two to three atmospheres pressure. The monomer boils at −7°C and has a specific gravity at this temperature of 0.63.

Acrylic and vinyl esters, vinyl and vinylidene halides, and other

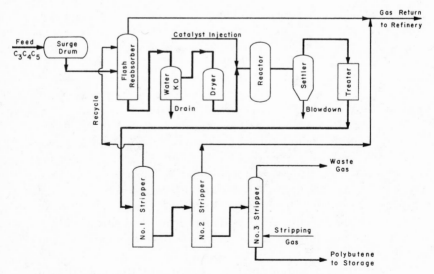

FIG. 9-6. Polybutene flow sheet. (*Reprinted from Petroleum Refiner*)

monomers which have electronegative substituents on the ethylene nucleus respond best to polymerization by heating in the presence of substances which form free radicals. They can also be polymerized by heat or by ultraviolet light alone. They do not usually yield high-molecular-weight polymers under the influence of Friedel-Crafts catalysts, such as boron trifluoride, aluminum chloride, or stannic chloride (cationic polymerization).

On the other hand, monomers which contain relatively nonpolar or electropositive substituents respond best to cationic polymerization. In this category are such monomers as isobutylene, methyl alkenes, α-methyl styrene, and vinyl iso-alkyl ethers. In general, these monomers do not polymerize readily under the influence of alkali metals (anionic polymerization).

In the preparation of commercial isobutylene high-molecular-weight polymers, liquid ethylene is used as a diluent, the polymerization taking place at $-80°$ to $-100°C$. When low-molecular-weight polyisobutylenes are desired for use as tackifying agents, higher temperatures obtained by using diluents other than ethylene are employed; e.g., butane or propane. The polymer is a saturated, linear product:

$$
\begin{array}{cccc}
CH_3 & CH_3 & CH_3 & CH_3 \\
| & | & | & | \\
-CH_2 \cdot C \cdot CH_2 \cdot C \cdot CH_2 \cdot C \cdot CH_2 \cdot C- \\
| & | & | & | \\
CH_3 & CH_3 & CH_3 & CH_3
\end{array}
$$

Polyisobutylene homopolymers cannot be vulcanized in the usual ways because of lack of functionality; however, they can be rendered insoluble by treatment with sulfur chloride and certain other agents. The products resemble factice, are of low tensile strength, and are easily crumbled.

The physical properties of polyisobutylenes change gradually with increasing molecular weight. The lowest-molecular-weight polymers are viscous liquids; then with increasing molecular weight the liquids become more viscous, then change to balsamlike, sticky masses, and finally form elastomeric solids.

The stabilized elastomers are fairly resistant to concentrated acids and alkalies. Unlike natural rubber, the polymers remain flexible at $-50°C$ and are more stable to ozone and oxygen. Like the natural product, they can be degraded in molecular weight by milling.

Elastomeric polyisobutylene homopolymers are not as widely used as was originally anticipated because of their tendency to cold flow, their limited compatibility, and their relatively poor stability. However, they do find applications in adhesives, caulking compounds, as a fortifier of wax in coatings for paper, and related uses where their softness and cold flow may be desirable and where adhesion and waterproofness are required. Because of their tackiness, they have been used in adhesive and pressure-sensitive tapes. The lower viscosity polymers are useful for modifying the viscosity and the viscosity index of lubricating oils. In 1953, a method was developed for greatly increasing the wear and water resistance of leather by impregnating with polyisobutylene. Laboratory tests have shown that the treatment increases wear by about 80 per cent, reduces water absorption by about one half, and effects considerable savings in tanning materials. By far the largest use of isobutylene, however, is as the principal comonomer in making butyl rubber.

## Butyl Rubber

By the middle of 1949, the rubber industry of the United States had consumed more than 650 million pounds of butyl rubber and had fabricated enough butyl rubber inner tubes to equip over 50 million automotive vehicles. Yet Butyl was not invented until 1937 and was not commercially produced until 1943. The war, and the consequent shortage of natural rubber, provided the chief impetus for the great demand for synthetic elastomers. Neoprene and Buna N, in commercial production in 1933 and 1941, respectively, reached high levels of use early in the war, but were subsequently exceeded by Butyl as it found its place in inner-tube manufacture.

The tremendous growth of this elastomer was due to the fact that it had been found in the laboratories of an American company that small amounts of butadiene or isoprene could be copolymerized with isobutylene. Whereas polyisobutylene could not be vulcanized, the copolymers of isobutylene and a diene could be vulcanized because they still contained some unsaturation.

Butyl rubber is made commercially by copolymerizing isobutylene with a small amount of isoprene (1.5 to 4.5 per cent). Both the monomers used in the manufacture of butyl rubber are derived from cracked refinery gases. Isoprene was also prepared on a commercial scale from turpentine during the last war. A process was developed for the production of isoprene from dipentene, which in turn is readily obtainable from turpentine components (see Terpene Polymers).

Isobutylene and isoprene are mixed in the desired proportions with an inert diluent, methyl chloride, which serves to control the violence of the polymerization reaction and also serves as a nonsolvent medium for the polymer. This feed, cooled to about $-95°C$, is supplied continuously to agitated reactors. A chilled solution of catalyst (aluminum chloride in methyl chloride) is mixed rapidly with the cold feed; the polymer forms almost instantaneously. The temperature of the exothermic reaction is maintained at about $-90°C$ or lower by vaporization of liquid ethylene in the reactor jacket. The polymer, a slurry of very fine particles suspended in the reaction medium, passes through an overflow line into a large volume of hot, agitated water. Unreacted feed components are there flashed off and recycled. A small quantity of zinc stearate in suspension is added to prevent agglomeration of the suspension of polymer in the hot water. An anti-oxidant is also introduced to stabilize the polymer; i.e., to prevent deterioration during finishing operations and subsequent storage. The slurry is put through a vacuum stripping section, and then is pumped to a finishing section where the polymer is isolated as crumb by filtration on vibrating screens. The crumb is then dried by passage through a tunnel dryer.

A portion of the structure of Butyl may be represented as follows:

$$
\begin{array}{c}
\text{CH}_3 \quad \text{CH}_3 \quad \text{CH}_3 \quad \text{CH}_3 \qquad\quad \text{CH}_3 \qquad\quad \text{CH}_3 \quad \text{CH}_3 \\
| \qquad\; | \qquad\; | \qquad\; | \qquad\qquad | \qquad\qquad | \qquad\; | \\
-\text{C·CH}_2\text{·C·CH}_2\text{·C·CH}_2\text{·C·CH}_2\text{·CH}_2\text{·C:CH·CH}_2\text{·C·CH}_2\text{·C·CH}_2- \\
| \qquad\; | \qquad\; | \qquad\; | \qquad\qquad\qquad\qquad | \qquad\; | \\
\text{CH}_3 \quad \text{CH}_3 \quad \text{CH}_3 \quad \text{CH}_3 \qquad\qquad\qquad\quad \text{CH}_3 \quad \text{CH}_3
\end{array}
$$

By introducing the slight degree of unsaturation into the chain, an elastomer results which can be vulcanized with sulfur, yet which is very nearly saturated. The reactivity of natural rubber, which is highly unsaturated, is thus eliminated, and the vulcanized product is much more stable to oxygen, ozone, strong acids, and certain metallic salts which cause rapid deterioration of rubber articles.

Various grades of butyl polymers, all copolymers of isobutylene and isoprene, and having different degrees of unsaturation and different average molecular weights, are commercially available. GR-I (now GR-I 50), formerly the standard grade containing 2 per cent isoprene in the feed stock, has been replaced by GR-I 15, having a slightly higher isoprene content and a faster rate of cure.

The density of the vulcanizate at 25°C is 0.93 and the tensile strength is about 2,800 psi. The normal (Staudinger) molecular weight range of butyl rubber is 40,000 to 80,000, although weights as high as 400,000 can be obtained. Butyl rubber is practically odorless, tasteless, and nontoxic. Although the unvulcanized polymer shows less cold flow than polyisobutylene, it still has more tendency to flow under its own weight than has natural crepe rubber.

Butyl is compounded and vulcanized by the same general method as used for natural rubber except for the special precautions required by its low unsaturation. Carbon black is the customary filler, and fabricated articles may be vulcanized by molding or by heating in a steam-pressure autoclave. Reinforcement with carbon black or other fillers does not improve the tensile strength of this elastomer. Resistance to abrasion, cutting, and shock, as well as toughness, are, however, improved.

The properties of butyl rubber, although satisfactory by present standards, are reported to be greatly improved by heat treatment. In the heat-treating process, the raw mixture of butyl rubber and carbon black is either alternately or simultaneously heated and mechanically worked before being prepared for vulcanization. The result is an improvement in tensile strength, tear strength, abrasion resistance, and resilience.

Since the limited unsaturation of Butyl offers fewer locations for potential cross-links, more active accelerators and higher temperatures are required for vulcanization than with other elastomers in order to obtain useful vulcanizates in reasonable periods of time. As in the sulfur vulcanization of other elastomers, a metallic oxide, such as zinc oxide, is necessary for the attainment of good physical properties. Unlike natural rubber and GR-S, the presence of fatty acid is not necessary.

When desirable, Butyl can be vulcanized without the use of sulfur. In the course of studies on methods of vulcanization, it has been found that butyl rubber is rapidly vulcanized, in the presence of oxidizing agents, by nitrogen-containing derivatives of quinone, such as $p$-quinone dioxime and its esters. It appears that oxidation of the dioxime to an intermediate product is the first step in this vulcanization reaction. It has been postulated that the active ingredient involved is $p$-dinitroso benzene, which results from the mild oxidation of the dioxime:

$$
\begin{array}{ccc}
\text{NOH} & & \text{NO} \\
\bigcirc & \xrightarrow{(O)} & \bigcirc \\
\text{NOH} & & \text{NO}
\end{array}
$$

Quinone dioxime is normally used at a concentration of 2 per cent, based on polymer, using lead oxides as the oxidizing agent. In the presence of four parts of lead dioxide, activity is so great that vulcanization occurs at room temperature. This rapid cure is useful in cement work and is carried out by the use of a split-batch technique.

The distinctive chemical and physical characteristics of butyl rubber are caused by the paraffinic nature of the polymer molecules with their low degree of unsaturation and by the sequence of pendent methyl groups attached to the closely packed, linear chains. The vulcanizates are chemically inert and exhibit an unusually high degree of impermeability to gases, the latter property being the result of the dense molecular packing.

The behavior of Butyl in contact with organic chemicals or solvents is like that of other hydrocarbon elastomers. The vulcanizates are swollen by hydrocarbon solvents, particularly of the paraffinic type. Polar solvents have little effect. Unexpectedly, butyl vulcanizates show good resistance to swelling in contact with animal and vegetable oils.

It is important to compare the effect of oxidation in Butyl with that occurring in other elastomers. Whereas the former softens when heated in an oxidative atmosphere, such elastomers as GR-S and Buna N become brittle. Natural rubber softens initially and then gradually also becomes brittle.

In most other respects, the physical properties of butyl vulcanizates are similar to those of natural rubber. Sheets of both Butyl and Hevea are soft, flexible, and elastic. However, upon release from stretching, Hevea recovers more quickly and with greater "snap." The rebound (resilience) at room temperature of unplasticized Butyl is poor; as the temperature is increased, the polymer becomes more resilient and eventually becomes equivalent in resilience to Hevea. As the temperature is decreased, Butyl stiffens rapidly, eventually becoming brittle. Butyl (and Hevea) does not require reinforcing agents for the development of high tensile strength, as does GR-S. The stress developed in an unfilled Butyl vulcanizate may be as high as 4,500 psi, whereas unpigmented GR-S usually fails at stresses under 500 psi.

The tear resistance of Butyl is excellent, and the polymer has the ability to retain its tear strength at elevated temperatures and after extended aging. Although Hevea shows a slight advantage over Butyl in tear strength at room temperature before aging, the latter is distinctly superior after aging due to its resistance to degradation by oxygen.

Because butyl rubber is a nonpolar, essentially saturated hydrocarbon, it possesses excellent electrical properties. Since it also is resistant to water, ozone, weathering, bacteria, and fungi, the polymer is well suited for electrical insulation.

The unique properties of butyl rubber, particularly its air retention (almost ten times better than that of natural rubber) and its resistance to aging and to tearing, led to its early consideration as an inner-tube material. During World War II, butyl tubes were found to perform so satisfactorily that, by early 1944, Butyl had become the only substitute for natural rubber in inner tubes which was acceptable to military authorities. Butyl was channeled by government directive into inner tubes as quickly as it became available by the simple process of prohibiting the use of natural rubber for this product. Satisfactory inner tubes could not be produced from GR-S, the only other readily available elastomer.

Automobile inner tubes are made by extruding a continuous tube of compounded, uncured elastomer, cutting this into proper lengths, applying a prefabricated valve, and then splicing the tube ends together to form a ring. The tube is then inflated to stretch it into a doughnut shape, after which it is vulcanized in a mold.

Since the advent of tubeless tires on a large scale, research has been concentrated on finding new outlets for the large butyl rubber capacity. Recently announced on an experimental basis have been automobile tires made of Butyl. Present tires consist of GR-S elastomer containing a small amount of natural rubber. The new tires were made possible by the perfection of a butyl latex which permitted, for the first time, the bonding of butyl rubber with tire cord using existing plant equipment. Tires made of Butyl are said to offer several advantages over tires of natural and other synthetic elastomers: shorter stopping distances, less noise of operation (butyl tires do not squeal on rounding corners), and better resistance to ozone.

Modern automobiles also use butyl rubber for dozens of other parts because of its extreme resistance to aging or deterioration on exposure to heat, cold, sun, weather, and chemicals. High-voltage electrical cables are made with Butyl because of the superior corona and ozone resistance, combined with excellent heat, cold, and abrasion resistance. Tractor tires are made with Butyl because it gives low tread wear and high resistance to weather, cracking, cutting, and chipping.

In addition to molded items of all types, the natural tackiness of Butyl allows its use in conveyors and hoses for handling strong acid solutions. It can also be calendered into sheets for use as linings in tanks, pipes, and valves.

Butyl rubber cements and coating compositions are made by dissolving the polymer in solvents containing naphtha together with smaller amounts of aromatic hydrocarbons or chlorinated aliphatic solvents. Aqueous dispersions have also been developed for impregnating and adhesive applications.

Butyl rubber, modified by reaction in solution with bromine (about 2.5 per cent), is compatible with natural rubber and GR-S and has a high modulus and good adhesion to other elastomers and metals (Brom Butyl). The bromine probably adds across some of the isoprene double bonds in a random manner. The vulcanization rate is appreciably increased by this modification.

Many other monomers have been copolymerized with isobutylene to yield products of some value. Possibly the group of greatest interest has been the so-called S-polymers, obtained by low-temperature copolymerization of isobutylene and styrene. However, none of these copolymers, other than those of isobutylene with isoprene, has yet become of great commercial importance.

## POLYSULFONES

For many years, it has been known that sulfur dioxide reacts with olefinic compounds to yield thermoplastic resins having physical properties similar to some of the major commercial plastics. The polysulfones are linear polymers in which the reactants usually are combined in equimolar proportions. The structure of the polymer chain made from sulfur dioxide and 1-butene, for example, is presumed to be

$$
\begin{array}{ccc}
CH_3 & & CH_3 \\
| & & | \\
CH_2 & & CH_2 \\
| & & | \\
-CH_2 \cdot CH \cdot SO_2 \cdot CH_2 \cdot CH \cdot SO_2- &
\end{array}
$$

Emulsion polymerization is used to make the polysulfone resins. Sulfur dioxide and an olefinic hydrocarbon, such as 1- or 2-butene, higher aliphatic olefins, cyclo olefins, or butadiene, are mixed with water, emulsifier, such as a sodium alkyl sulfate, and a catalyst. Although a large number of materials will catalyze this system, including oxygen, hydrogen peroxide, and organic peroxides, ammonium nitrate has been found to be quite satisfactory and is much lower priced. The mixture is stirred at 35° to 40°C in a glass-lined autoclave for four to six hours. The reaction pressure drops from about 75 psig initially to about 30 psig as polymerization progresses.

In the case of 1-butene, conversion is 95 to 100 per cent of theoretical. The yield is a fluid latex of about 35 per cent resin content which is coagulated with magnesium sulfate solution, filtered, washed, and dried.

Polysulfones are sensitive to heat, although the products can be stabilized. The polysulfone from 1-butene may be recovered from the latex as a finely divided, white powder. The dry powder has an apparent density of about 0.3 gram per milliliter. The product may be dissolved in solvents and applied as coatings by conventional methods. It can be molded satisfactorily by compression methods at temperatures from 105° to 160°C and can be blended with nylon, other thermoplastic resins, or synthetic elastomers. Copolymers have also been made; i.e., more than one unsaturated monomer may be reacted with sulfur dioxide. These products are now being evaluated for commercial acceptance.

## ALIPHATIC VINYL AND VINYLIDENE COMPOUNDS

### POLY(VINYL CHLORIDE)

Although vinyl chloride was described by Regnault in 1838 and its polymerization reported by Baumann in 1872, the polymer has become of commercial importance only within the last twenty-five years. Much of the development work was carried out in the United States and Germany; the process of monomer manufacture was patented and methods of polymerization by mass and emulsion techniques were developed in Germany about 1930. The discovery of the valuable elastomeric properties of plasticized poly(vinyl chloride) by Semon in the United States in 1932 gave great impetus to the further commercialization of this polymer.

More manufacturers (and more trade names) exist for vinyl chloride products than for any other vinyl-type polymer (Exon, Geon, Koroseal, Marvinol, Pliovic, Tygon, Velon, Vinylite, Vygen). In the plastics field, "vinyl resins" or "the vinyls" almost always refers to vinyl chloride polymers and copolymers. Among the unsaturated monomers, vinyl chloride is equaled only by ethylene, styrene, and butadiene in commercial importance.

In spite of its importance, comparatively little has been published about vinyl chloride polymerization, except in the patent literature. The other vinyl halides have not become important in the polymer field, although vinyl fluoride is now being mentioned in copolymer products.

The three principal methods for the preparation of vinyl chloride are as follows:

$$CH_2Cl \cdot CH_2Cl + NaOH \text{ aq.} \xrightarrow[150 \text{ psig}]{145°C} CH_2{:}CHCl + NaCl + H_2O$$

$$CH_2Cl \cdot CH_2Cl \xrightarrow[(BaCl_2)]{250°-500°C} CH_2{:}CHCl + HCl$$

$$CH{:}CH + HCl \xrightarrow[HgCl_2]{180°C-5 \text{ atm.}} CH_2{:}CHCl$$

The first method was originally the most important commercial process used in the United States. In this method, however, half of the chlorine is converted to salt. The latter two methods are now most widely used for industrial preparation of vinyl chloride.

As shown by the second reaction, vinyl chloride can be obtained by the vapor-phase dehydrohalogenation of ethylene chloride, the latter, in turn, being made by the chlorination of ethylene in the liquid phase at about 45°C and 15 psig. The hydrogen chloride formed can be reacted with acetylene to form more vinyl chloride, as given in the third reaction.

In Germany, the manufacture of vinyl chloride directly from acetylene and hydrogen chloride has always been the principal method. At present, about 55 per cent of the vinyl chloride made in the United States is by this process, the rest by the pyrolysis of ethylene chloride. In the liquid process, acetylene is passed into a hydrochloric acid bath in the presence of catalysts, such as ammonium chloride and cuprous chloride. In the gaseous process, dry hydrogen chloride in slight excess is mixed with dry acetylene gas in a vapor blender; the former is the cheaper of the two reactants and permits the acetylene to react more completely. The gaseous mixture is fed to the top of multitube reactors. The reactors are packed on the tube side with activated carbon pellets, impregnated with

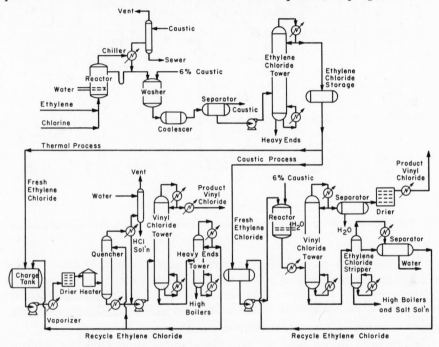

FIG. 9-7. Vinyl chloride flow sheet—from ethylene. (*Reprinted from Petroleum Refiner*)

catalyst, which may be a mixture of mercuric and potassium chlorides. The addition reaction is highly exothermic, requiring cooling of the tubes. The temperature of the reaction varies between 135° and 205°C, depending upon the age of the catalyst. The yield is more than 90 per cent.

As in the case of the preparation of vinyl acetate, the ethylidene derivative (and some aldehydes) is also produced but its formation is decreased by the use of silica gel or highly active carbon as a carrier for the catalyst. The vinyl chloride is condensed and uncombined reactants are distilled off. The monomer, which boils at −14°C, is stable in the absence of oxygen; hence no stabilizer is required for storage.

The pure monomer does not polymerize thermally and only slowly photochemically. Organic, free-radical-forming compounds, such as acyl

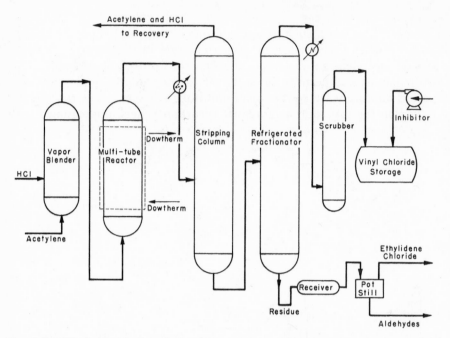

FIG. 9-8.   Vinyl chloride flow sheet—from acetylene.   (*Reprinted from Petroleum Refiner*)

or aryl peroxides and aliphatic azo compounds, initiate polymerization readily at temperatures of 30° to 80°C.   Since the polymer is insoluble in the monomer, it begins to precipitate as soon as polymerization starts. To obtain polymers of high intrinsic viscosity and free from discoloration, rapid reaction at a comparatively low temperature is desirable.

It has been shown that the rate of polymerization increases continuously during the early stages of the reaction.   The rate appears to reach a maximum at about 50 per cent conversion, after which it slowly decreases.   This phenomenon is known as the "gel effect," and no entirely satisfactory explanation has yet been advanced for its occurrence.   It appears, however, that an (apparent) decrease in the reaction rate constant for termination $(k_t)$ is responsible for the increased rate of polymerization.   The phenomenon occurs most frequently in systems yielding polymer which has limited solubility in the reaction medium (which may be solvent or monomer).   It appears likely that the growing radicals become embedded in the precipitated polymer particles and termination reactions become more difficult, due to isolation of a radical in one particle from those in others.

The mass polymerization of poly(vinyl chloride) on a large scale is not practicable, principally because (1) the polymer is formed in large masses which cannot be easily processed, and (2) the heat of polymerization is so great that the reaction is very difficult to control and also causes thermal degradation and discoloration of the polymer. Solvent polymerization of vinyl chloride is sometimes convenient, and the product is relatively free of inorganic contaminants. Although polymerization of vinyl chloride is greatly inhibited by the presence of oxygen, polymerization often proceeds satisfactorily at low temperatures because the monomer vapors escaping during the charging of the autoclave and from leaks help to purge the system of air.

Regardless of whether the mass or solution polymerization technique is used, large-scale reactions cannot be carried further than about 50 per cent before the polymer must be separated; otherwise, local overheating occurs because of poor heat transfer through the polymer-monomer slurry. For this reason, most of the poly(vinyl chloride) produced is made by emulsion and suspension techniques.

The emulsion polymerization of vinyl compounds was an outgrowth of the development of this technique for the manufacture of synthetic elastomers (see Butadiene-Styrene Copolymers). Because of its low water solubility, vinyl chloride is successfully polymerized by this method. Polymerization is carried out in horizontal, rotating autoclaves made of nickel or lined with enamel. The polymerization is carried out at about 45°C, and is 90 per cent complete in 24 hours. The unreacted monomer may be vented and the emulsion pumped directly to a spray drier and atomized with air heated to 160°C.

Further progress in improving emulsion polymerization of vinyl chloride was made by the application of redox techniques (see Chap. 5). Small amounts of reducing agents added to the initiator were found to accelerate the rate of polymerization markedly. Suitable reducing agents are sulfur dioxide, alkali sulfites and bisulfites, sulfoxylates, hyposulfites, and thiosulfates.

Vinyl chloride polymers continue to be manufactured by the emulsion method, although the popularity of the suspension method is growing. In emulsion polymerization, several per cent of emulsifying agents and initiators are used. Since the polymer is produced as a latex, these additives are difficult to remove. In suspension polymerization, the additives amount to less than 1 per cent, and most of them leave with the water when the polymer slurry is centrifuged; the suspension product is, therefore, almost pure polymer. On the other hand, emulsion polymerization readily lends itself to continuous operation, whereas suspension polymerization does not.

For suspension operation, the monomer and water are metered into glass-lined autoclaves, and the mixture is agitated and brought to a temperature of between 45° and 55°C. Initiators and control agents are flushed in.   The polymerization is exothermic and requires close temperature control to maintain uniform high quality.

The density of unplasticized poly(vinyl chloride) is 1.4, tensile strength is 9,000 psi or higher, and elongation is 5 to 25 per cent.   The water absorption ranges from below 0.1 to more than 1 per cent, depending upon contaminants and the type of plasticizers used.

Cyclohexanone is one of the best solvents for vinyl chloride polymers and copolymers.   Among the few other solvents which dissolve the homopolymer of high molecular weight at room temperature are methyl cyclohexanone, dimethyl formamide, nitrobenzene, tetrahydrofuran, isophorone, and mesityl oxide.   Higher alkyl ketones, dioxan, and methylene chloride are solvents for the low-molecular-weight polymers.

The principal drawback of vinyl chloride polymers (and copolymers) is a general lack of stability in the presence of light or heat.   The thermal stability of poly(vinyl chloride) is poor, heat causing evolution of hydrogen chloride and forming a progressively darker product believed to contain conjugated unsaturation in random sequences:

$$-CH_2 \cdot CHCl \cdot CH_2 \cdot CHCl \cdot CH_2 \cdot CHCl \xrightarrow{\triangle}$$
$$-CH:CH \cdot CH:CH \cdot CH_2 \cdot CHCl-$$

Fortunately, the polymer can be stabilized.   Basic stabilizers include alkali or alkaline earth oxides, hydroxides, alcoholates, carbonates, or their fatty acid salts; amines; and other organic nitrogen compounds. Sodium organo-phosphates, barium ricinoleate, and cadmium and calcium stearates have also been used.   Lead stabilizers used include white lead, lead orthosilicate, dibasic lead stearate, and other basic lead salts. Unlike lead chloride, both zinc chloride and ferric chloride catalyze the decomposition of vinyl chloride polymers; hence, zinc oxide and iron oxide pigments are not usually used with these polymers.

The alkylene oxide compounds, especially propylene oxide, are examples of acceptors for hydrogen chloride which are not alkaline.   Low-molecular-weight glycidyl ethers and epoxidated oils, as well as barium and cadmium epoxy compounds, are frequently used.

Another useful group of stabilizers for vinyl chloride polymers are the alkyl and aryl tin compounds.   Such esters as dibutyl tin dilaurate and dibutyl tin dimaleate are particularly effective.

Stabilizers for protection against discoloration and sunlight are also used.   Salicylate and benzoate esters, resorcinol dibenzoate, and alkali metal phosphates have been suggested.

Frequently, a combination of two or more stabilizers is used.   It has been found that certain combinations of stabilizers exert a *synergistic* effect, in that the total stabilization produced by the combination of stabilizers is greater than the effect produced by either one of the stabilizers or by the expected sum of the individual stabilizing effects. Synergistic effects are obtained by many combinations of the above stabilizers, which enables less of each to be used. Careful evaluation of empirical combinations is necessary in order to determine the optimum proportions of ingredients.

The use of unplasticized poly(vinyl chloride) for fabricating sheets, films, and tubes, was developed in Germany during World War II. Completely unplasticized poly(vinyl chloride) has definite chemical and physical superiority over any plasticized or copolymerized vinyl polymer. Rigid poly(vinyl chloride) and unplasticized poly(vinyl chloride) are different materials. By incorporating a relatively small amount of plasticizing agent or copolymer (5 to 10 per cent), fairly rigid sheets, moldings, and other shapes are obtained. These materials are termed "rigid poly(vinyl chlorides)" and are inferior to unplasticized vinyl chloride homopolymers for chemical and anti-corrosive applications, since the plasticizers have a tendency to leach out when in contact with solvents. This causes contamination of the liquid and gradual embrittlement of the polymer.

Unplasticized poly(vinyl chloride) (Agilide) is a hard, horny material that is insoluble in most solvents and is not easily softened. In Europe, rigid vinyl chloride plastics have been used since 1937 in industrial equipment and to replace celluloid, cellulose acetate, and metals. Unplasticized poly(vinyl chloride) was used extensively in Germany during World War II in the form of extruded sheets, rods, and tubes for chemical process equipment and as a substitute for stainless steel. It was also widely used in bristles for brushes and brooms. Until fairly recently, production of rigid poly(vinyl chloride) plastics has been on a relatively small scale in the United States except for special applications. At present, the use of rigid poly(vinyl chloride) is growing rapidly in the United States. Rigid sheeting and articles from vinyl chloride polymers have an outstanding advantage over cellulose derivatives in their non-flammability. One of the present principal and rapidly expanding uses of the rigid polymer is in the manufacture of piping for the transportation of corrosive fluids and other liquids.

Most of the polymer now made is fairly highly plasticized and is used as sheets, other extrusions, or in the form of polymer-plasticizer pastes for making coated fabrics and for molding and dipping. In fact, vinyl chloride polymers in the United States got their start in the field of rubber substitutes. However, the plasticized vinyl chloride resins soon found many uses where rubber was unsuitable. The hardness and elasticity of these resin compositions can be controlled by the plasticizer content and type; in addition, they are nonflammable and are almost transparent and colorless.　Many of the fabricating techniques for plasticized vinyl polymers came from the rubber industry; e.g., milling, calendering, and extruding.

The first important plasticizer for poly(vinyl chloride) was tricresyl phosphate.　Some of the earlier plasticizers which have also proved useful are dibutyl phthalate and sebacate, and tributyl phosphate.　There are now dozens of plasticizers for poly(vinyl chloride) on the market.　Frequently, combinations of plasticizers are used to obtain a better balance of physical properties in the products.　In other words, some plasticizers are general-purpose plasticizers, some confer low-temperature flexibility, some confer flame resistance, some have better nonmigratory characteristics, and some, although not as useful because of their physical characteristics, are lower in cost.

Plasticized vinyl chloride polymers do not possess the "snap" of vulcanized natural rubber, and the permanent set is much greater.　With increasing plasticizer content, the elongation at break increases while the tensile strength decreases.　At low plasticizer concentration, tensile strengths as high as 9,000 psi have been obtained, whereas, with large proportions of plasticizer, elongations of over 500 per cent are attainable. Poly(vinyl chlorides) begin to soften in the range of 70° to 80°C, although the high-molecular-weight polymers do not flow well enough for practical molding much below 150°C.

Communication and low-voltage power cable insulation and sheathing consume large quantitites of plasticized poly(vinyl chloride), which has replaced much of the more flammable and less durable natural rubber. It may seem surprising that a polar polymer is so useful as an electrical insulating material.　However, although the chlorine atoms in the polymer are highly polar, they are relatively rigid and immobile.　The value of vinyl chloride resins as electrical insulation materials is further enhanced by their insensitivity to moisture and relatively good aging performance when properly stabilized.　In contrast to the less polar resins, such as polystyrene, the dielectric constant and power factor of vinyl chloride polymers are quite dependent upon plasticizer content, temperature, and electrical frequency.

Other popular applications of the polymer are for thin, pliable sheeting and film finishes for textiles.　Clear and pigmented sheeting is widely used in shower curtains, rainwear, food covers, and in inflatable toys. Cloth and paper are coated with plasticized vinyl chloride polymers for use in, for example, nonflammable upholstery and raincoats.　Tubing, gaskets, and many other articles are manufactured by extrusion.　In addition to use as an insulator, tubing of this material has proved popular for the transport of chemicals and for garden hose.　A new and very rapidly growing use of poly(vinyl chloride) is in flexible pipe for irrigation.

Shoe soles of plasticized vinyl chloride polymer wear several times as long as leather soles, and vinyl floor tile has proved highly satisfactory.

A recent development is a vinyl-to-metal laminate which produces materials of excellent abrasion, chemical, and weather resistance, in addition to beauty of color and embossed design. A variety of gauges of special vinyl sheeting have been combined with steel, aluminum, magnesium, and copper to manufacture such products as duct work, luggage, instrument cases, panel boards, automotive interior parts, wainscoting, counter tops, television cabinets, business machine housings and parts, wall surfacing, and containers.

The application of elastomeric vinyl coatings from slurries or pastes containing no solvents was originally developed in Germany. Powdered poly(vinyl chloride) is mixed with a liquid with which it is substantially insoluble at ordinary temperatures. The thin or thick liquids or pastes can be spread, molded, or sprayed, or articles can be coated by dipping. A homogeneous film is then obtained by heating to 120° to 150°C until the polymer fuses. Gloves have been made by dipping aluminum forms into poly(vinyl chloride) paste, fusing, then stripping. The pastes or slurries can be applied to paper or fabric and subsequently fused. Plastic coated cloth so formed is used widely for upholstery (one type of artificial leather). The vinyl chloride polymer-plasticizer combinations containing no solvent are called *plastisols*, and those made up with volatile dispersing liquids are called *organosols*. They are used in applying thick protective coatings to such objects as plating racks for plating baths and sink racks for dishes. One of the most promising uses for vinyl plastisols today is for coating nylon for use as tarpaulins which have previously been made of canvas, coated canvas, and neoprene-coated materials, including glass fabric. Tarpaulins of the new type have been made for baseball diamonds, football gridirons, and swimming pool covers. Probably the biggest use will be for cargo covers on trucks, since one man can handle the light-weight, vinyl-coated nylon covering.

A new development in the use of vinyl resins is as a film in photography (Calimar). A deep photographic image, developed by heat all the way through flexible films, is being evaluated for use in such fields as decorating, display, and photo-recording. Calimar consists of an organosol paste containing light-sensitive, dye-forming, and catalytic chemicals. This mixture is drawn down on a supporting substrate to form a photosensitive film which, when cured, is 0.003 inch thick and self-supporting. The material contains no silver compounds and is photosensitive throughout. Its speed of action is comparable to that of lithographic plates. In contact with a standard photographic negative, a film is exposed to ultraviolet light for one minute. This light frees radicals from a chlorinated paraffin present, and the radicals activate metal oxide and dye-formers in the film.   The exposed film is developed by heating it for a few minutes at about 160°C.   The heat causes light-activated compounds in the film to form dyes, and at the same time it passivates any dye-formers not yet catalyzed by the light.

Another valuable vinyl development has been the application of the polymer latex, prepared by the emulsion technique, *directly* for the manufacture of sheets, coatings, and elastomeric articles.   The use of latices avoids the expense of coagulating and separating the polymers from the polymerization system and also eliminates the hazards of using organic solvents.   Techniques of application are similar to those used with natural rubber latex.

Chlorinated poly(vinyl chloride) was developed in Germany and manufactured there during World War II.   Methods of preparing the polymer were (1) chlorination in a tetrachloroethane solution, and (2) chlorination as a suspension in chloroform.   In both cases, the chlorine content of the poly(vinyl chloride) is raised from 57 per cent to 62 to 66 per cent, corresponding to $(—CH_2 \cdot CHCl \cdot CHCl \cdot CHCl—)_n$; the German textile fiber known as Pe-Ce or PC is of this type.

In ultimate average composition, this chlorinated polymer may not be very different from saran.   The purpose of the chlorination was to obtain a product soluble in acetone, which is probably the most convenient of all solvents normally used for spinning.

In one method of preparation, vinyl chloride was polymerized in emulsion in autoclaves at a pressure of 50 atmospheres and a temperature of 65°C.   After spray-drying the polymer at 130°C, it was made into a 25 per cent solution in tetrachloroethane and chlorinated for 30 hours at 80°C in a water-cooled vessel.   After chlorination, the polymer was spray-dried, the solvent being removed by vacuum and recovered.   The after-chlorinated polymer had a softening temperature of 80° to 85°C.

Resistance to chemical attack by acids and alkalies and its nonflammability made fibers spun from this polymer suitable for use as filter cloths, industrial clothing, and rotproof fabrics.   However, these products suffered from low softening temperatures and poor heat stability.   The fiber-producing plant, now in the east zone of Germany, is believed to be inactive at the present time.

Other fibers have been made from straight poly(vinyl chloride), principally in France and Germany.   Filter cloths, protective clothing, nonflammable flying suits, canvas, curtains, and fishing nets are some of the uses for these fibers.   In the United States, fibers from copolymers of vinyl chloride have been preferred.

### Vinyl Chloride Copolymers

The chief vinyl copolymers of commercial importance in which vinyl chloride predominates are those with vinyl acetate and acrylonitrile.   A large number of three-component polymers (terpolymers) have also appeared. In addition, there are important copolymers in which vinyl chloride is a minor constituent. These will be discussed under the comonomer which is the major constituent.

Among the advantages claimed for copolymers of vinyl chloride are a greater range of physical and mechanical properties, lower softening temperatures (enabling them to be processed at lower temperatures), improved heat stabilities, and wider solubilities in organic solvents.

Poly(vinyl chloride), as has been seen, is difficultly thermoplastic, chemically inert, nonflammable, has poor heat and light stability, and is relatively insoluble in all cold solvents. Poly(vinyl acetate), on the other hand, softens at about 40°C, has outstanding light and heat stability, relatively high water absorption, and is soluble in most organic solvents except for aliphatic hydrocarbons. Because of its thermal instability, the high softening temperature of the unstabilized chloride makes milling and molding difficult, whereas the acetate, because of its low softening temperature and sticky nature, also is unsuitable. Thus, poly(vinyl chloride) is used principally in molding and extrusion compositions while poly(vinyl acetate) is used chiefly in solutions or as a latex.

There are many uses in the plastics industry for materials having properties intermediate between those of the chloride and acetate. Mixtures of the two polymers exhibit poor compatibility and have few worthwhile properties. In order to obtain desirable properties, it is necessary to copolymerize mixtures of vinyl chloride and vinyl acetate. In 1928, three companies were performing research on the copolymerization of vinyl chloride with vinyl acetate, and products were introduced on the market in the early 1930's.

The conditions necessary for copolymerization are similar to those used for the polymerization of the pure monomers. Mass polymerization may be used, although solution, suspension, and emulsion techniques are more commonly employed. Aryl and acyl peroxides, tetraethyl lead, and ultraviolet light may be used as initiators.

Most commercial vinyl chloride-acetate copolymers contain from 85 to 95 per cent of vinyl chloride and usually are solvent polymerized. The polymer may be precipitated with the aid of a nonsolvent, such as water. In general, however, the best solvents are those from which the product will separate as a solid phase when the desired degree of polymerization is reached; e.g., butane or toluene. The copolymer is then dried in large, continuous, rotary driers, worked in a masticator, and modifiers added. The resin can then be fabricated either as rigid stock or as an elastomer. In either case, a heat stabilizer is added prior to compounding.

The characteristics of the products are typical of those expected of compounds composed of vinyl chloride and vinyl acetate units; that is, the desirable features of good mechanical strength (characteristic of the chloride) and improved general solubility and compatibility (characteristic of the acetate) are obtained. Thus, the copolymers have excellent strength and good resistance to water, acids, alkalies, alcohols, and oils. However, they exhibit poor resistance to ammonium hydroxide, ketones, esters, aldehydes, aromatic hydrocarbons, and some organic acids. Heat stability below 65°C is fairly good, although elevated temperatures cause an appreciable darkening in color unless stabilizers are used.

The water absorption is low, especially with copolymers containing a high percentage of vinyl chloride units, and is responsible for the good dimensional stability of the copolymers. This latter property is of great value in some of the applications of unplasticized sheets; e.g., watch crystals, drawing, calculating, and navigating instruments, radio and refrigerator dials, and phonograph and transcribing records.

The amount and type of compounding used with this class of polymers depend upon the particular copolymer used and the application for which it is intended. As expected, less external plasticizer is necessary than is used with poly(vinyl chloride) homopolymers because of the internal plasticization afforded by the vinyl acetate present (see Chap. 10). The amount and type of plasticizer may be varied, however, over a wide range, producing stock which can be fabricated into almost any form, ranging from rigid rods and tubes to elastic films or flexible fibers.

The compounded resins are available in granular form and are used for molding and extrusion. Powdered resin may also be obtained by spraying a solution of the resin into another spray of a liquid which is not a solvent for the resin but which is miscible with the active solvent; the resin is thus precipitated in a finely divided state.

The average molecular weights of the copolymers may be varied by altering the manufacturing conditions, including the temperature and type and amount of solvent and initiator. In this way, such properties as tensile strength, elongation, impact resistance, flexibility, and solubility may be altered as desired.

The lowest-molecular-weight resins are used in surface coatings. Their molecular weight range of 8,500 to 9,500 is high enough to form good films, yet, coupled with a chloride content of approximately 86 per cent, it is still low enough to permit adequate solubility. Solvents used are ketones (active solvents which yield solutions of minimum viscosity), extended with aromatic hydrocarbons (diluents). The coatings made from these resins must be baked at relatively high temperatures (125° to 200°C) in order to obtain proper adhesion and flow. They are widely used in the metal decorating field (cans and closures) and in coating aluminum foil, asbestos board, and paper products. For the latter use, air-drying formulations are used.

In order to improve the compatibility and adhesion of vinyl coating resins, a small amount of a third component is sometimes added to the monomer mixture. As an example, a terpolymer containing 86 per cent vinyl chloride, 13 per cent vinyl acetate, and 1 per cent maleic anhydride is used where its better adhesion to metal is an advantage (Vinylite resin VMCH). Another terpolymer (Vinylite resin VAGH) has improved compatibility and adhesion as well as a higher softening temperature and greater chemical reactivity because of its small hydroxyl content (obtained by partial hydrolysis of the acetate present).

The copolymer most suitable for injection molding has an average molecular weight of about 10,000 and a vinyl chloride content of 85 to 90 per cent. This resin flows readily at molding temperature, shrinks only slightly in the mold, and produces articles having optimum strength and toughness. For compression molding, a copolymer having an average molecular weight of slightly over 12,000 and containing 85 to 88 per cent of vinyl chloride is most satisfactory.

The molded products have a wide color range and good dimensional stability. Because the resins shrink only slightly during processing, relatively large moldings can be made and accurate reproduction of such items as scales and phonograph records is possible. Fillers used are usually those which work successfully with the phenoplasts and aminoplasts. The copolymers are similar to the cellulosics in their molding characteristics, mechanical properties, and appearance.

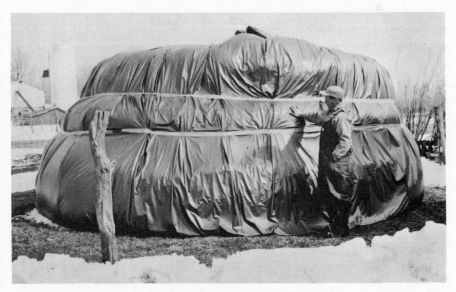

FIG. 9-9. Poly(vinyl chloride) film serves as a convenient silo. (*Courtesy Bakelite Co.*)

For the manufacture of sheet stock, good strength and toughness are required, but the requirement of high plasticity at molding temperatures is not as severe as in injection molding. For these reasons, copolymers of higher average molecular weight (about 15,000) and containing about 90 per cent vinyl chloride are preferred. Because of their strength and water resistance, the sheets are used for dials, instruments, and advertising displays. Plasticizers, pigments, and heat stabilizers are used in compounding these sheets; fillers are ordinarily unnecessary and, as with the molded products, usually decrease the mechanical strength and increase the water absorption of the products.

For the manufacture of elastomeric products suitable for tubing and coating wire, copolymers of still higher molecular weight (above 20,000) and containing about 95 per cent vinyl chloride are compounded with plasticizers on roll mills. Coated wire is made by extruding the plasticized resin around the wire. The electrical properties are fairly good for low-frequency applications, and the aging characteristics are much superior to those of rubber.

It has long been known that homopolymers of vinyl chloride can be drawn out into long filaments. Many chemists have also endeavored to make useful fibers from polymeric vinyl acetate. However, both homopolymers are not very satisfactory for forming fibers for the reasons given earlier. About 1933, the problem was successfully solved by copolymerization, and fibers were obtained to which the name Vinyon was given. This type of fiber, which, like nylon, is a true synthetic fiber, made its commercial appearance at almost the same time (1938–39).

Vinyon is a copolymer of vinyl chloride (88 to 90 per cent) and vinyl acetate, having a molecular weight of approximately 20,000. The polymer is dissolved in a solvent (e.g., acetone), and the solution, which contains about 25 per cent of the copolymer, is used for spinning.

One of the most important properties of Vinyon is that its strength is as great when wet as when dry. Vinyon is unaffected at room temperature by concentrated acids, caustic soda, alcohols, or aliphatic hydrocarbons. It is, however, dissolved by ketones and softened by aromatic and halogenated hydrocarbons. It does not support combustion nor is it attacked by bacteria, molds, or fungi. It has excellent stability to sunlight.

One of its first applications, industrial filter cloths, utilized its excellent chemical resistant properties. Because of its high wet strength, Vinyon is particularly useful for the manufacture of fish lines and nets. It is also used in screen printing. However, its low softening temperature (thermoplastic at 70°C, incipient melting at 150°C) and excessive shrinkage at ironing temperatures preclude its use in textiles that normally are laundered.

Vinyon has been made principally in continuous filament form, although a little staple fiber has been produced. Its unusual properties have enabled it to be used in applications for which most textiles are unsuitable, but, on the other hand, have prevented its use for the more usual applications.

A new family of vinyl fibers, designated as Vinyon N, was announced in 1947. The new fibers possess the excellent combination of properties of the earlier Vinyon fibers and, in addition, have much higher softening temperatures and even better solvent resistance. Vinyon N and dynel, both of which are outgrowths of Vinyon development, have now taken over most of the uses of Vinyon, which probably accounts for the fact that Vinyon manufacture has recently been discontinued.

The copolymer resin used for the manufacture of Vinyon N fibers contains 56 to 60 per cent of vinyl chloride, the other comonomer being acrylonitrile. (For acrylonitrile manufacture, see Polyacrylonitrile.) The monomers are copolymerized by an emulsion process. This reaction proceeds slowly under ordinary conditions but can be accelerated by redox initiator systems. The copolymerization ratio of vinyl chloride and acrylonitrile is rather high in favor of acrylonitrile, and it is necessary to add acrylonitrile continuously during the copolymerization reaction in order to obtain resins of the degree of compositional uniformity desired for the fiber. The resin is produced in the form of a very fine powder resembling flour in appearance. The density of the resin is about 1.3 and its color ranges from light amber to dark brown.

The conversion of the resin to fiber or yarn form is accomplished by either the dry- or the wet-spinning process, depending upon the particular qualities desired in the finished product. The wet process is particularly well suited to the production of staple fiber and heavy denier, continuous-filament yarn. The dry-spinning process is ordinarily employed for the manufacture of continuous-filament yarn in fine and medium sizes. In the latter process, an acetone solution containing approximately 25 per cent of resin and small amounts of stabilizers is used. The unoriented fiber has a tenacity of about 0.7 to 0.9 gram per denier. Vinyon N yarn cannot be cold-drawn at practical rates, but the drawing or stretching operation proceeds smoothly at elevated temperatures. The manufacture of this fiber, which is a continuous-filament yarn, has also recently been discontinued. Its properties are, of course, similar to those of dynel.

Dynel, the staple form of Vinyon N, was introduced in 1951. The word "dynel" is used generically as is "nylon." This copolymer is dissolved in acetone, the solution is filtered and deaerated, and the product is obtained by the usual dry-spinning technique in the form of a tow. The tow is cut into staple lengths and crimped.

Dynel is a light-cream fiber, but can be bleached. Exposure to sunlight causes a mild bleaching of the fiber; at prolonged exposure at high temperatures, dynel darkens somewhat and loses some tenacity. It is sensitive to heat in excess of 115°C, has good covering power, good strength, and dries rapidly. The cross-sectional shape of its filament is irregular and ribbon-shaped, more similar to that of cotton than of wool.

Because of its outstanding chemical resistance and its inability to support combustion, it is widely used for the manufacture of protective clothing for chemical workers and miners, and for chemical filter cloths. Dynel is also used for the covers of paint rollers, providing good absorption and transfer of paint without matting or curling. Blankets made of dynel are easy to launder, impervious to damage by disinfectants, and are shrinkproof and mothproof. Bedspreads and upholstery are other uses for the fiber. Its mothproof and nonallergenic properties make dynel useful for filling cushions and pillows.

Apparel uses include fabrics for coats, undergarments, sleeping garments, knitted blouses, and men's socks, which wash easily, dry quickly, and do not shrink. In addition, dynel is found in blends with both natural and synthetic fibers. With rayon, in women's skirts, dresses, and suits, dynel confers durable pleat, softness and long wear. With wool, in men's suits, dynel contributes crease retention, wet and dry strength, and richness. With cotton, in underwear, dynel gives warmth, loft, washability, and shape retention. One last unusual application of dynel is as hair for dolls; the hair can be washed, waved, brushed, combed, set, and tinted.

Copolymers of vinyl chloride with 5 to 20 per cent vinylidene chloride (Plioflex and the Geon 200 series) are available. These copolymers can be molded at lower temperatures, yet are no more moisture sensitive than poly(vinyl chloride) homopolymers. They are used for molding, extruding, calendering, solution coating, impregnating, and film casting.

The dimethyl and diethyl esters of maleic and fumaric acids copolymerize readily in minor proportions with vinyl chloride, by both suspension and emulsion techniques. These esters alone do not polymerize readily to form polymers. Copolymers containing 10 to 20 per cent diethyl fumarate, or, preferably, maleate have good working properties, good toughness, and relatively high softening temperatures. The vinyl chloride copolymer known as Pliovic A is believed to contain diethyl maleate.

Styrene and butadiene do not readily form copolymers with vinyl chloride, although it is interesting to note that vinylidene chloride does copolymerize with butadiene.

Vinyl chloride has been copolymerized with minor amounts of acrylic esters, particularly methyl acrylate (Igelit MP, Mipolam) in Germany and more recently in the United States. The products have had only limited commercial success to date. Of growing importance in preparing internally plasticized polymers are the vinyl chloride–alkyl vinyl ether copolymers.

New vinyl chloride copolymers include those containing vinyl stearate. The latter may be made by the treatment of stearic acid or inedible animal fats with acetylene in the presence of a zinc stearate catalyst at 165°C and 200 psig. Using suspension or emulsion polymerization techniques, copolymers are easily obtained. The resins containing less than about 20 per cent vinyl stearate are rigid materials while those containing about 35 to 40 per cent resemble vinyl chloride resins that have been externally plasticized with about 25 to 35 per cent plasticizer. The advantage of the copolymer is that plasticizing action on the chloride is obtained internally, without the danger of plasticizer loss by migration, extraction, or evaporation. Both types may be cured with polyfunctional amines (plus sulfur, if desired) at 150°C to yield infusible, insoluble products which may be reinforced with conventional carbon black or silica fillers. The copolymers having high stearate content retain some flexibility after cure and may prove to be useful in certain elastomeric applications.

## Poly(vinyl acetate)

In 1912 Klatte in Germany disclosed the preparation of vinyl acetate from acetylene and acetic acid. Vinyl acetate was then obtained as a by-product of the synthesis of ethylidene acetate, which was of interest as a solvent. Commercial production of poly(vinyl acetate) began in Canada about 1920 and about ten years later in the United States. The reactions for the acetate and diacetate are

$$CH_3COOH + HC\text{:}CH \rightarrow CH_2\text{:}CH \cdot OOC \cdot CH_3$$
$$2CH_3COOH + HC\text{:}CH \rightarrow CH_3 \cdot CH(OOC \cdot CH_3)_2$$

The reaction of acetylene with acetic acid forms both vinyl acetate and ethylidene acetate. By passing acetylene rapidly through a suspension of mercuric sulfate in acetic acid at 70° to 90°C and removing the vinyl acetate rapidly, the yield of ethylidene acetate is reduced; this was the early method of preparation of the vinyl monomer. It was later found that the yield could be improved in the liquid-phase process by the use of lower temperatures and special catalysts. High yields of vinyl acetate may be obtained by the use of either mercuric phosphate or the acidic salt formed from acetyl sulfuric acid ($CH_3 \cdot COO \cdot SO_3H$) and mercuric oxide. The reaction temperature is kept at about 35° to 50°C and acetylene is passed through the suspension at such a rapid rate that most of the vinyl acetate formed is carried out of the suspension with the excess acetylene. With proper control of temperature, catalyst, and circulation rate, yields of 80 to 90 per cent are obtained.

Another method operates in the vapor phase. A mixture of acetic acid vapor and an excess of acetylene at 175° to 200°C is passed over a zinc acetate catalyst deposited on activated charcoal. The vinyl acetate is separated from the unreacted acetic acid by fractionation. The conversion per pass is 30 to 60 per cent, and the yield is almost theoretical. This process is simple and the formation of ethylidene acetate and acetaldehyde is small. A quite recent process, developed in the United States, uses acetic anhydride and acetaldehyde and is based upon the oxidation of butane.

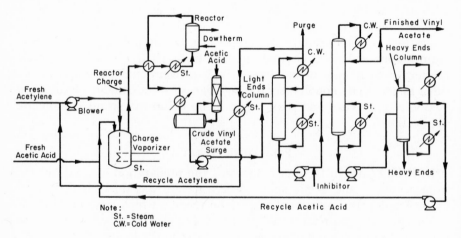

FIG. 9-10. Vinyl acetate flow sheet. (*Reprinted from Petroleum Refiner*)

Vinyl acetate is a colorless liquid boiling at 72°C. In the absence of initiators, the monomer is stable at room temperature; however, it is usually stabilized with about 20 ppm of hydroquinone, although sulfur, amines (diphenyl amine), and copper salts may be used. The monomer is easily hydrolyzed in the presence of acid or base to yield acetic acid and acetaldehyde.

Polymerization usually takes place in an autoclave in the presence of a suitable solvent or diluent (methanol, ethyl acetate, or aromatic hydrocarbon). By varying the conditions, it is possible within fairly wide limits to produce poly(vinyl acetate) of predetermined characteristics. The resin is precipitated, dried, ground, and compounded. Mass and solution polymerizations are now less frequently used than originally; however, they are still employed for the preparation of low-molecular-weight polymers.

Probably the bulk of the poly(vinyl acetate) is produced in the form of aqueous dispersions, commonly (and incorrectly) known as poly(vinyl acetate) emulsions. These dispersions are stabilized by the small amount of poly(vinyl alcohol) formed or by the addition of another water-soluble, high-molecular-weight polymer. By the use of the redox system of activation, vinyl acetate emulsions can be polymerized more rapidly at lower temperatures, thus minimizing hydrolysis. Suspension polymerization, especially in Germany, has also been extensively used.

The commercial resins (Elvacet, Gelva) have relatively low average molecular weights, the values falling between 5,000 and 20,000. The lower-molecular-weight polymers are soft, gumlike resins at room temperature. The higher-molecular-weight polymers are tougher and have higher softening temperatures. When stressed, these polymers deform slowly and do not recover upon removal of the stress. As a result, poly(vinyl acetates) are used primarily as adhesives and coatings, rather than as plastics.

The commercial polymers are colorless, clear, tasteless, and nontoxic, and are supplied in a wide variety of molecular weight (viscosity) ranges. They have a density of approximately 1.2, water absorption varies from 2 to 5 per cent, and the tensile strength ranges from 1,500 to 5,000 psi. The softening temperatures vary widely with the degree of polymerization. Low-molecular-weight polymers can be used for heat-sealing purposes at 70° to 80°C, whereas the highest-molecular-weight polymers require about 125°C. At 250°C, poly(vinyl acetates) discolor and char with evolution of acetic acid; however, they are extremely stable to ordinary ranges of heat and light and do not discolor under long exposure to sunlight or ultraviolet light.

Poly(vinyl acetate) is soluble in ketones, esters, chlorinated hydrocarbons, nitroparaffins, aromatic hydrocarbons, and methanol, but is insoluble in other anhydrous alcohols and in water; however, unexpectedly, the polymer is soluble in 95 per cent ethanol and in other low-boiling alcohols containing about 10 per cent water. The resins are compatible with many natural and synthetic resins.

Poly(vinyl acetates) are not crystalline, giving, instead, X-ray diagrams characteristic of amorphous solids. The polymers are plasticized by most of the common lacquer types of plasticizers, much less plasticizer being required than, for example, with cellulose nitrate.

It is of interest to point out that poly(vinyl acetate) and poly(methyl acrylate) are isomeric. Both are soft, water- and temperature-sensitive polymers whose physical properties have been attributed in part to the lack of chain symmetry and to the polar oxygen atoms exposed on the side-chains. The effect of absorbed water (3 per cent and higher) upon the strength and adhesiveness of poly(vinyl acetates) makes them unsatisfactory for many applications where exposure to high humidity is encountered.

Poly(vinyl acetate) adhesives are widely used to join porous materials, such as cloth, paper, leather, and cork, for applications not requiring high bond strength, rapid drying, or good moisture resistance. Hot-melt adhesives of plasticized poly(vinyl acetate) are used for laminating paper and for book binding, while dispersions have been used for "permanent starching" of clothing. They are used in large quantities in chewing gums as extenders for chicle and other natural gums. Some ten years ago, viscous solutions of poly(vinyl acetate) became popular with children for blowing balloons; these had good plasticity but little elasticity.

When these resins are used as a molding compound, a large amount of filler is incorporated; too much, however, decreases their tensile strength, elongation, and impact resistance. Because of their low softening temperatures (45° to 90°C) and excessive sticking to the mold, the poly(vinyl acetate) resins are not widely utilized alone for molding applications. They are, however, combined with various fillers in the manufacture of plastic floor tile, artificial leather, pressed wood compositions, and surfacing for outdoor signs and panels.

Poly(vinyl acetates) are of value in the formation of films and coatings. The films are tough, have good tensile strength, are fairly resistant to water, dilute acids, salts, and mineral and vegetable oils, and are unaffected by aging. Films and coatings may be deposited from either solutions or suspensions. Since they tend to retain some residual solvent at room temperature, they are usually dried by heating to about 110°C for a short time. The polymer is useful for coating surfaces of wood, cloth, paper, metals, tile, concrete, and ceramics. An important use is as a lining or coating for paper food containers where they impart strength, water, and grease resistance, and transparency to the paper.

They are also useful as an ingredient of other surface coatings; added to cellulose nitrate lacquers, they improve the adhesion, gloss, and toughness. However, the low-molecular-weight polymers tend to block in hot weather and at high relative humidities. The high-molecular-weight polymers, which can be prepared by emulsion polymerization, are preferable, since products can be made having high solid content and low viscosity and can be sprayed without cobwebbing. A very large market for poly(vinyl acetate) is in water-based "emulsion" paints. The inclusion of this resin makes possible the use of such paints for exterior coatings.

A fairly recent development is the use of poly(vinyl acetate) dispersions as admixtures in Portland cement mortars; these show excellent physical properties when cured in air at ordinary temperatures and humidities. This is in contrast to plain cement mortars which require a water or damp curing in order to achieve optimum properties.

Of the copolymers containing a large proportion of vinyl acetate, that with maleic anhydride, used in making Krilium soil conditioner and also used in textile auxiliaries, is of great interest.   Vinyl acetate-crotonic acid copolymer, which dissolves in dilute alkali, finds use as a paper adhesive from which the paper can be readily reclaimed.

In spite of the many applications described above, probably the most important single use of poly(vinyl acetate) is as a raw material or intermediate for the formation of poly(vinyl alcohols and acetals).

## Poly(vinyl alcohol)

Vinyl alcohol has never been isolated.   In all reactions designed to yield vinyl alcohol, the products are ethylene oxide or acetaldehyde, due to rapid tautomeric interchange of a hydrogen atom:

$$\underset{H_2C—CH_2}{\overset{O}{\triangle}} \rightleftharpoons CH_2{:}CHOH \rightleftharpoons CH_3{\cdot}CHO$$

Hence, esters of vinyl alcohol cannot be prepared by the usual method of esterification of an alcohol with an acid.   The polymerized form of vinyl alcohol is, however, quite stable and is prepared from poly(vinyl acetate) by replacement of acetate groups with hydroxyl groups.   Although this reaction has been called both a hydrolysis and a saponification, it is actually an alcoholysis reaction since the reaction proceeds best in anhydrous media.

It was disclosed in 1924 that poly(vinyl alcohols) are readily obtained by the reaction of poly(vinyl acetate) in alcohol with potassium hydroxide. It was also shown that the alcoholysis of poly(vinyl acetates) proceeds most rapidly in practically water-free alcohol, small amounts of alkali or acid being sufficient to catalyze the reaction.   The presence of water greatly retards the reaction rate and also forms slimy products which are difficult to isolate by filtration.

In one general method of preparation, the acetate is first swelled in anhydrous methanol.   The reaction is then catalyzed by the addition of 0.5 per cent or less of caustic or mineral acid.   The alcohol gradually forms at room temperature, more rapidly at higher temperatures.   The product thus made still contains a few per cent of acetate.   By interrupting the alcoholysis, the percentage of acetate left in the molecule may range upward from this minimum.   With polymers of comparable molecular weights, the lower the percentage of acetate left in the polymer, the greater is its solubility in water, the greater its resistance to oils, and the higher is its softening temperature.   A continuous process is now in operation in the United States, making poly(vinyl alcohol) by this method.

Poly(vinyl alcohol) may be re-esterified but does not esterify completely to re-form the poly(vinyl ester) from which it was derived. In other words, not all of the oxygen atoms present in the alcohol are present in alcoholic hydroxyl groups. It is likely that some internal etherification occurs, particularly when an acid catalyst has been used, and that some polymeric structures of the following type are formed:

$$\underset{\substack{| \\ OH}}{-CH\cdot CH_2\cdot}\overset{\overset{\displaystyle O}{\overbrace{\phantom{CH\cdot CH_2\cdot CH\cdot CH_2\cdot CH\cdot CH_2\cdot CH}}}}{CH\cdot CH_2\cdot \underset{\substack{| \\ OH}}{CH}\cdot CH_2\cdot CH\cdot CH_2\cdot \underset{\substack{| \\ OH}}{CH}}\cdot CH_2-$$

Ether formation between chains is also a possibility. Commercial poly-(vinyl alcohol) is also believed to contain a few isolated ketone groups, which may form acetal linkages with the hydroxyl groups of other chains. Branched molecules can then be formed by cross-linkages:

$$
\begin{array}{cccc}
H_2C \diagup & HO\cdot CH \diagup & H_2C \diagup & O\cdot CH \diagup \\
\diagdown & \diagdown & \diagdown \diagup & \diagdown \\
\quad CO\ + & \quad CH_2 \rightarrow & C & \quad CH_2 \\
\diagup & \diagup & \diagup \diagdown & \diagup \\
H_2C \diagdown & HO\cdot CH \diagdown & H_2C \diagdown & O\cdot CH \diagdown
\end{array}
$$

The properties and consequently the uses of poly(vinyl alcohol) depend upon the hydroxyl content of the polymer. Products containing from 70 to 85 per cent of the original acetate groups are insoluble in water but dissolve in aromatic hydrocarbons and aliphatic esters. When the residual acetate radicals are reduced to about 35 per cent, solubility in organic solvents disappears and the product dissolves in cold water but precipitates on heating. At somewhat lower acetate content, the resin is soluble in both hot and cold water. When alcoholysis is as complete as possible (only about 5 per cent or less of the acetate groups remaining), the alcohol only swells in cold water but dissolves upon heating.

Poly(vinyl alcohols) are available under a variety of trade names (Elvanol, Polybond, Resyn, Vinol), having different acetate content and correspondingly different viscosity characteristics. From the large number of possible combinations, the most common commercially prepared products have between 1 and 15 per cent of residual acetate groups. The former are known as the "completely hydrolyzed" types, and the latter are referred to as "partially hydrolyzed" grades.

Poly(vinyl alcohol) is a white-to-cream powder, with a density of 1.3 and a tensile strength as high as 22,000 psi. Dry, unplasticized poly-(vinyl alcohol) powders do not melt, but soften on warming and may then be stretched like rubber, crystallizing in the process. The ester-type, water-immiscible plasticizers commonly used with other plastics are not compatible with poly(vinyl alcohol). The products which have been found to be most effective are some of the high-boiling-point, water-soluble, organic compounds containing hydroxyl, amide, and amino groups. At present, the most widely used plasticizer is glycerol. Ethylene glycol and some of the lower poly(ethylene glycols) are also effective plasticizers. Ethanol acetamide and ethanol formamide have been found to be effective plasticizers, particularly for the partially hydrolyzed grades.

Poly(vinyl alcohols) are quite reactive chemically. This property is useful in the preparation of acetals and other derivatives. Poly(vinyl alcohols) can be reacetylated by heating with acetic anhydride in pyridine. They can also be esterified with other acids, acid chlorides, and anhydrides. By heat treatment or by reaction with dibasic acids, aldehydes, or with copper- and zinc-ammonia complexes, their water solubility can be decreased. Many patents have been issued on processes for the insolubilization of poly(vinyl alcohols) with iron compounds, titanium compounds, diisocyanates, and phenol-formaldehyde and melamine-formaldehyde resins. However, it is generally more practical to make use of a water-soluble formaldehyde derivative, such as dimethylol urea. Also, a number of chromium compounds have proved useful, including sodium dichromate, chromic nitrate, and especially cupric dichromate. Treatment with such dichromates or with diazo compounds, followed by exposure to light, decreases water solubility, a property of commercial utility for printing processes.

However, the reactivity of poly(vinyl alcohols) is disadvantageous in most direct applications. On storage or when heated in the presence of traces of inorganic acids or other impurities, they gradually increase in viscosity and become less soluble in water. The addition of a small amount of alkali will stabilize the polymers against increase in viscosity.

The outstanding property of commercial grades of poly(vinyl alcohol) of low acetate content is water solubility. The alcohols are also soluble in dilute, aqueous, salt solutions. Aqueous solutions of poly(vinyl alcohols) resemble starch solutions in many of their properties, perhaps because internal etherification produces structures somewhat akin to the structure of starch; however, the former are unattacked by bacteria and fungus growth.

In contrast to the water solubility of poly(vinyl alcohols) is their great resistance to organic compounds. Not only are they completely unaffected by oils, fats, or greases, but they are also very resistant to hydrocarbons and to most oxygenated and chlorinated organic solvents.

Poly(vinyl alcohol) films are tough, possess neither taste nor odor, and are highly impermeable to most gases.    Some samples of sheeting molded from unplasticized poly(vinyl alcohol) show tensile strengths of between 9,000 and 17,000 psi—remarkable for a water-soluble material.    Films can be obtained in forms that are soluble in water at room temperature and also in forms that are insoluble in boiling water.    Films are used as tough, protective coatings for highly polished metal surfaces during fabrication and shipment; the film can be removed simply by soaking in water for a short time.

Stretch-oriented films of nonhydrophilic poly(vinyl alcohol), often combined with films of cellulose acetate or acetate-butyrate, have the ability to polarize light and are used in sun glasses and other lenses (Polaroid).

Poly(vinyl alcohol) solutions are used as a warp size for textile yarns during weaving and knitting operations.    In addition to protecting the yarns, the coatings impart reduced resiliency and other physical properties needed during these processes.    The film is later removed by immersing the yarn in warm water.

Paper which is impregnated or coated with poly(vinyl alcohol) shows a marked increase in wet strength with little decrease in the rate of water absorption.    This increase in wet strength lasts a very short time but is sufficiently long for most purposes for which paper towels are used. Poly(vinyl alcohol) is also used to make glassine paper transparent and acts as a softening agent.    Because of its excellent resistance to oils of all types, it is used in the manufacture of greaseproof paper and containers.

Poly(vinyl alcohol) coatings and films are highly impervious to gases. Combined with another coating or film which is more resistant to water, a barrier is formed which is resistant to water, greases, and gases.

Poly(vinyl alcohol) is an excellent adhesive and can be used alone or in combination with other adhesives, such as starch, dextrin, casein, or rubber latex.    The polymers are used as a size in paper manufacture and as binders in the manufacture of milk cartons and fiber boards for boxes.

Poly(vinyl alcohol) is an effective emulsifying agent and possesses the added advantage of functioning in neutral or slightly acidic media.    It is used as an emulsifying or thickening agent in the manufacture of brushless shaving cream and various cosmetic creams and is widely used as a stabilizer in emulsion polymerizations.

Poly(vinyl alcohol) can be compounded with fillers, plasticizers, pigments, and other modifying agents to form molding compounds.    Molding is usually carried out at a temperature of about 130°C and under relatively low pressure.    Rubberlike gaskets, washers, and diaphragms are some typical molded products.

One of the most useful products from poly(vinyl alcohol) is known as Resistoflex.    This elastomeric solid is a plasticized composition, which is extruded in the form of tubes, rods, sheets, and threads.    The products are noted for their high tensile strength, good tear and abrasion resistance, good aging characteristics, excellent flex resistance, and low gas permeability.   Flexible tubing and pipe is used in fuel, brake, and lubrication systems in automobiles, airplanes, and diesel engines, and also for conveying solvents, as well as mineral and vegetable oils.   Sound waves transmitted through Resistoflex tubing suffer little distortion and very little absorption by the tubing.   For this reason, this material is used when sound must be sent through a flexible conduit.

Poly(vinyl alcohol) fibers have been obtained not only by the extrusion of a molding composition, but also by the spinning of an aqueous solution into a precipitating bath containing a salt, such as ammonium sulfate, or an organic precipitant, such as acetone, followed by stretching.   The threads may then be treated with an acid chloride in order to increase their resistance to solvents and moisture.   Poly(vinyl alcohol) fibers have been used as surgical sutures and as supporting threads in lace manufacture (see Alginates).

Poly(vinyl alcohol) staple fibers have been produced in Japan under the name of Kurlon (Vinylon) since 1951.   In this process, vinyl acetate is continuously polymerized in methanol solution, using a peroxide initiator. The methanol solution of poly(vinyl acetate) is continuously transformed into poly(vinyl alcohol) by caustic soda.   The precipitate is filtered, washed with methanol, and dried.   The polymer is then dissolved in warm water to prepare the spinning solution.   This solution, containing about 12 per cent poly(vinyl alcohol), is wet-spun.   The chemical treatment for imparting water resistance to the fiber takes place in the coagulating bath, which contains formaldehyde, sulfuric acid, and Glauber salt (sodium sulfate).

Various treatments can give the fiber the appearance of silk, cotton, hemp, or wool.   It is strong and abrasion resistant, has good dyeing properties, and has good resistance to alkali and acids.   Its hydrophilic nature imparts to Vinylon fiber a property unique among noncellulosics: its water absorbency is high—about 30 per cent.   Vinylon can thus replace cotton in underclothes, sheets, and similar uses where the fiber is in contact with the body.   However, its wet-heat resistance of no more than 115° to 120°C makes ironing a problem.   The fiber may be treated by radiation to increase its resistance somewhat to wet shrinkage.   Irradiated Vinylon has a wet-heat resistance of 150°C.

## POLY(VINYL ACETALS)

The term "poly(vinyl acetals)" is used to designate the products of the reaction of poly(vinyl alcohols) with aldehydes.   This reaction is a condensation but, since the acetals are derivatives of addition polymers,

they are included here.   The term "acetal" is used generically to include
the products obtained by reacting poly(vinyl alcohol) with any aldehyde
and also specifically designates the product obtained by reaction of
poly(vinyl alcohol) with acetaldehyde.   The low-molecular-weight aliphatic aldehydes, formaldehyde, acetaldehyde, and butyraldehyde, are
the only aldehydes which are used to make commercial products.

In Germany, poly(vinyl acetal) products (Mowitals) were made before
1930 and were used for electrical insulation.   Large-scale development of
the acetals has since occurred in America with the development of
poly(vinyl formal) for wire covering and poly(vinyl butyral) for safety-
glass interlayer.

The manufacturing process varies, depending on the aldehyde employed.   Poly(vinyl acetate) can be converted to poly(vinyl acetals) by
first converting to the alcohol, then subsequently reacting with an aldehyde.   If by-products, which probably form to a certain extent, are
overlooked, the resins have the following structure:

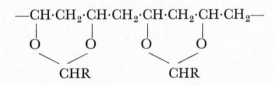

If, instead of aldehydes, ketones are reacted, the corresponding product
is known as a *ketal*.   These have not received wide application in the
United States, but useful poly(vinyl ketals) have been obtained in
Germany from cyclohexanone (Mowital O).

In the manufacture of poly(vinyl formal and acetal), poly(vinyl
alcohol) is not isolated.   The formation of the acetal is carried out in
the same solution in which the alcohol is formed.   Ethanol, containing a
small amount of sulfuric acid, can be used as the solvent; in this preparation, water may be present.   The product is insoluble in the alcohol
solution, so that a separate precipitation step is eliminated.

Like the other acetals, the butyral can be manufactured either by
reaction of butyraldehyde with poly(vinyl alcohol) or by direct reaction
of the aldehyde with poly(vinyl acetate).   However, for the production
of safety-glass-quality poly(vinyl butyral), the polymerization of vinyl
acetate, the alcoholysis of the poly(vinyl acetate), and the condensation
of poly(vinyl alcohol) with butyraldehyde are usually carried out in
separate batch operations, inasmuch as the desired form of this plastic
for use as a safety-glass interlayer contains an appreciable proportion of
free hydroxyl groups.   After the butyral resin has been formed, it is
precipitated by a nonsolvent, such as water, and is then rigorously
purified and stabilized.   Stabilization is necessary in order to prevent

viscosity changes, discoloration, and brittleness on aging and exposure to sunlight. Inorganic alkalies and secondary or tertiary amines are effective neutralizers and stabilizers. The dried material is ground, softened on heated rollers, and compounded with plasticizers and, if not used for safety-glass lamination, with fillers and coloring materials. If used for lamination, it is usually calendered into thin sheets.

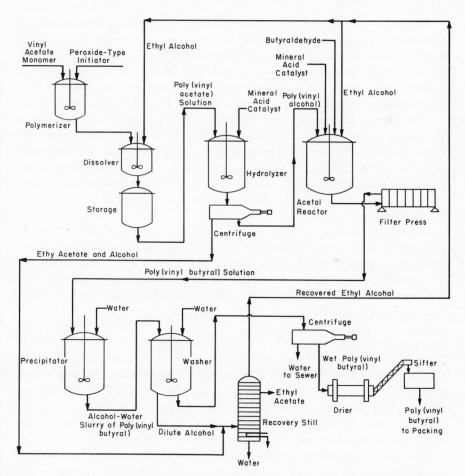

FIG. 9-11. Vinyl butyral flow sheet. (*Reprinted by permission from Chemical Engineering*)

Regardless of the manner by which acetalization is accomplished, the products are only partial acetals because the acetate radicals of poly-(vinyl acetate) are not removed completely by either alcoholysis or acetalization. The degree of alcoholysis and acetalization can be controlled so that acetals having various ratios of acetate, hydroxyl, and acetal groups are obtainable. The properties of the product vary not only with the nature of the aldehyde and the molecular weight of the resin but also with the degree of acetalization. In general, viscosity, insolubility, and strength increase with increasing molecular weight of the poly(vinyl acetate) used and with the degree of acetalization. The partial acetals obtained are tougher and harder than the poly(vinyl acetate) used to make them.

The poly(vinyl acetals) are white powders which are compounded with plasticizers and, frequently, with other resins. In general, about 40 parts of plasticizer are mixed with 60 parts of acetal to make an extremely tough, elastic product. These plasticized resins can be dissolved in suitable solvents or they can be emulsified in aqueous solutions. Poly-(vinyl formals) dissolve in water, whereas the higher homologs do not.

The formals (Formvar), like the alcohols, are particularly resistant to the action of hydrocarbon solvents which tend to soften or dissolve other types of plastic materials. Solutions for adhesives and molding compounds are available. The best solvents for poly(vinyl formal) are chlorinated aliphatic hydrocarbons, aliphatic and cyclo-aliphatic ethers, cyclic acetals, and phenols. Most of these are also good plasticizers for the polymer.

Poly(vinyl formal) is the toughest of the vinyl resins. Its tensile strength is as high as 20,000 psi at 20°C. It has a density of 1.2, a softening temperature of about 190°C, a heat distortion temperature of 65° to 75°C, and a water absorption of about 1 per cent. Because of its inherent toughness, it has until recently been applied only from solution, but new extrusion equipment and techniques have made possible the production of tubes, rods, and sheets. The polymer has excellent warp and abrasion resistance, and a fairly high heat distortion temperature. Since it is completely resistant to oils, gasoline, aliphatic hydrocarbons, fats and waxes, and alkalies, it is useful for automotive and machine parts, and gasoline and oil lines. The resin has also been used in laminating and coating wooden propellers for aircraft and as the inner gasoline-resistant liner of bulletproof (self-sealing) tanks for airplanes. These latter uses were developed in England.

The most important application of poly(vinyl formal) has been in combination with phenolic resins as electrical insulation for magnet wire (Formex). This coating, while as good as the conventional alkyd coating for enameled wire, is much superior in flexibility, extensibility, and resistance to abrasion.

Poly(vinyl acetal) is produced commercially in a variety of grades (Alvar, Polybond). These resins are odorless and tasteless; are soluble in a wide range of alcohols, ketones, esters, and chlorinated hydrocarbons; and are insoluble in aliphatic and aromatic hydrocarbons and in vegetable oils. Their mechanical properties are not as good as the formals; tensile strengths range from 6,000 to 9,000 psi, softening temperatures vary from 135° to 190°C, heat distortion temperatures lie between 75° and 90°C, and water absorption is about 2 per cent.

The acetals are very versatile products, as they are tough, adhesive, and chemically inert. They are used in making coated fabrics, plywood adhesives, and household articles. They have found limited applications in surface coatings for indoor use, especially in combination with cellulose nitrate with which they are compatible, and for some molded products.

Poly(vinyl butyral) resins (Butacite, Butvar, Saflex) were developed specifically for safety-glass application because of their adhesiveness, toughness, clarity, and extensibility when properly plasticized. The product found to be best suited for use in laminated safety glass is a high-molecular-weight, poly(vinyl alcohol) in which approximately 70 to 80 per cent of the hydroxyl groups have been acetalyzed. The resin also contains a very small percentage of acetate groups, unavoidably present, and a relatively large proportion (18 to 19 per cent) of hydroxyl radicals which contribute to the development of adhesion to glass. The resin is supplied in the form of sheets containing about 35 per cent plasticizer. Triethylene glycol di-2-ethyl butyrate and dibutyl sebacate and a few other butyl derivatives are particularly good plasticizers for this product.

This plastic, which first was marketed in the United States in 1936, has outstanding toughness and resistance to shock, even at low temperatures. By 1940, this resin replaced almost all of the other plastics formerly used in safety-glass construction—cellulosics and poly(methyl acrylate). By far the largest user of poly(vinyl butyral) is the automotive industry. However, safety glass is also widely used in railroad cars, television sets, and aircraft.

Poly(vinyl butyral) has a tensile strength of about 8,300 psi, a heat distortion temperature of only about 45° to 60°C, and a water absorption of more than 4 per cent. Although insoluble in water, the butyral resins are hydrophilic because of their hydroxyl content. For this reason, they exhibit good adhesion toward glass which is also hydrophilic and, unlike earlier types of glass laminants, they can be bonded directly to glass without the use of an intermediate adhesive. It is not necessary to seal the edges of the safety glass made from poly(vinyl butyral) because of its water insolubility and excellent adhesion to glass.

Laminates for aircraft consisting of two sheets of poly(methyl methacrylate) joined by a poly(vinyl butyral) interlayer is of great value because it resists breakage from impact with birds. An adhesive to bond the methacrylate to the glass is required.

Poly(vinyl butyral) is unusual among the vinyl elastomers in that, by incorporation of certain ingredients, it can be cured in a manner similar to the vulcanization of rubber. Such curing renders it more resistant to heat and insoluble in most common solvents and also permits the plastic to be compounded and fabricated with rubber processing equipment. Unlike many vinyl resins, the butyral can be calendered at relatively low temperatures to produce films and coatings of good quality. It can be extruded on usual rubber tubing machines; it can be spread-coated from alcohol solution on either rubber- or pyroxylin-type coating equipment and, with certain precautions, can be molded in rubber-type molds. It can also be made into soft or hard sponge of low density by expanding processes common to the rubber industry.

Vinyl butyral elastomer is not a rubber substitute where resilience is required. It is a "dead" material; when distorted, its recovery is slow. It often feels deceptively weak because its initial distortion as a free film or sheet is relatively easy. This low modulus distinguishes the butyral from other vinyl resins and contributes extreme softness of texture without sacrifice of ultimate strength.

During World War II, it was found that this material could be used to coat fabric, forming an excellent substitute for rubberized goods. Raincoats, water bags, life jackets, and pontoon-bridge floats were proofed with poly(vinyl butyral) resins. The value of these coatings was greatly enhanced when ways were found to "vulcanize" the resins by admixture with certain phenolic, alkyd, and urea resins, and with other reactive bi- and polyfunctional compounds, such as diallyl phthalate and organic polyisocyanates, followed by heating. These so-called thermosetting or insolubilized grades of poly(vinyl butyral) are now available commercially and, upon application to cloth and subsequent heat treatment, provide coatings which are tough, resilient, and insoluble in alcohol, acetone, and water.

Because of its partially polar nature, which contributes to good adhesion, poly(vinyl butyral) is also utilized in wood and metal primers and adhesives.

### Poly(vinyl and vinylidene ethers)

The monovinyl ethers, like isobutylene, form homopolymers of high molecular weight only by the action of Friedel-Crafts catalysts. The most common products are the alkyl vinyl ether polymers, which range from viscous, sticky resins to elastomeric solids. These products were available in Germany prior to 1940 and, during the war, their development there was accelerated by a shortage of polyacrylates, which they resemble in physical properties and functions. They were used in large quantities as lacquer constituents, adhesives, and impregnating agents.

Monomers and polymers became available in the United States about 1947–48.

The methods of preparation of these ethers industrially are the reaction of diluted acetylene with alcohols in the presence of sodium or potassium alcoholate under low pressure (1 to 15 atmospheres) and the decomposition of acetals:

$$CH{:}CH + ROH \xrightarrow[130°-180°C]{ROK} CH_2{:}CHOR$$

and

$$CH{:}CH + 2ROH \xrightarrow{Hg^{++}} CH_3CH(OR)_2 \xrightarrow[200°-300°C]{Catalyst}$$

$$CH_2{:}CHOR + ROH$$

Mass or solution polymerization yields viscous, liquid to soft, resinous polymers. Vinyl methyl ether, the lowest member of the series, forms a hard, water-soluble polymer; vinyl isobutyl ether, a rubbery polymer; and vinyl stearyl ether, a waxy polymer. Mass polymerization, using boron trifluoride, is commonly employed in making the polymers. The vinyl methyl ether polymers are notable for their extreme stickiness and for the property of dissolving, at least partially, in water as well as in a wide range of organic solvents, including ethanol, acetone, and benzene.

Poly(vinyl methyl ether) (PVM, Resyn) was made available in the United States in 1948. It precipitates from water solutions in adhesive masses when heated to about 35°C and redissolves below that temperature without loss of original properties. It is suitable as a nonionic, heat-sensitizing agent for natural and synthetic latices. It has been proposed as a tackifying agent for adhesives and cements; as a binding agent in the textile, ceramic, and paint fields; as a plasticizer for cellulose nitrate and chlorinated rubber; as a special sizing agent for paper, textile, and leather applications; and as an auxiliary in the tanning and pigment fields.

An elastomeric, solid poly(vinyl isobutyl ether), called Oppanol C, has been made in Germany. Boron trifluoride, dispersed in liquid propane, is brought into contact with highly purified vinyl isobutyl ether, diluted with liquid propane, in such a way that nearly instantaneous polymerization occurs. The temperature is limited by the vaporization of propane. As the pressure remains near atmospheric, it is believed that the temperature during polymerization is about −40°C. A small amount of an alkyl phenol sulfide is added as a stabilizer to the monomer before polymerization.

This polymer and high-molecular-weight vinyl n-butyl ether polymers have been used, principally in Europe, for the installation of upholstery in motor cars, sealing cellophane and foils, and in cementing materials to glass and metals.   They have also been used, both abroad and in the United States, to replace milled natural rubber, particularly as bases for pressure-sensitive adhesive tapes.   Both the $n$-butyl and the isobutyl ether polymers exhibit qualities of tack, adhesion, and freedom from cold flow which resemble milled natural rubber more closely than polyiso-butylene, butyl rubber, or commercial butadiene-styrene synthetic elasto-mers.   The two ethers also lend themselves to the modification of viscosity and tack by cold milling as in the case of natural rubber.   Among the limitations of stabilized Oppanol C are the high brittle temperature (about $-25°C$) and the limited heat resistance (the polymer is softened at $65°C$).

Many other types of ethers have been made, including the divinyl ethers, allyl vinyl ethers, alicyclic vinyl ethers, aryl alkyl vinyl ethers, aryl vinyl ethers, and copolymers, but they are of even lesser importance at present.

Although ketene (vinylidene oxide), $CH_2:C:O$, and vinylidene ethers (acetals of ketene), $CH_2:C(OR)_2$, contain the unsubstituted methylene group, they do not form linear, high-molecular-weight polymers in good yield, since reaction occurs at the oxygen or OR groups as well as by addition at the carbon-carbon double bond.

### Poly(vinyl ketones and aldehydes)

The polymers of vinyl ketones and aldehydes have not become com-mercially important in the United States, although in England, there has been some small-scale production.   One reason for the slow commercial development of the ketones is that there is yet no economical and efficient method for the synthesis of the pure monomers.

Methyl vinyl ketone can be made by reacting acetone with formal-dehyde to form the methylol compound with the subsequent splitting out of water:

$$(CH_3)_2CO + HCHO \xrightarrow{K_2CO_3} CH_3 \cdot CO \cdot CH_2 \cdot CH_2OH \xrightarrow[360°C]{Cr_2O_3}$$
$$CH_3 \cdot CO \cdot CH:CH_2 + H_2O$$

The yield is very low and the recovery of the monomer in the pure state is very difficult, since more than one $\alpha$-hydrogen atom of acetone may react with formaldehyde, and the monomer polymerizes readily, even in the absence of initiator.   The $\beta$-hydroxy isomer (acetoin), a fermentation product, can also be dehydrated to form methyl vinyl ketone.

The preparation of vinyl acetylene from acetylene (see Polychloroprene) is another method of synthesis of methyl vinyl ketone:

$$2CH{:}CH \xrightarrow{Cu_2Cl_2} CH{:}C{\cdot}CH{:}CH_2$$

Then

$$CH{:}C{\cdot}CH{:}CH_2 + H_2O \xrightarrow[H^+]{Hg^{++}} CH_3{\cdot}CO{\cdot}CH{:}CH_2$$

Methyl vinyl ketone is miscible with water in all proportions and with a wide variety of organic solvents. It is one of the most reactive of monomers in polymerization reactions. This reactivity is probably due to the conjugated arrangement of its double bonds. The completely polymerized, high-molecular-weight polymers are rigid solids, but products containing residual monomer are elastomeric at room temperature.

The usual products are soft resins resembling poly(methyl acrylate). Because of the low softening temperatures, instability, and reactivity o methyl vinyl ketone polymers, attempts have been made to modify and improve the products without much success. Aryl and other alkyl vinyl ketones have been prepared by various means, but interest in them has been even less than that of the lowest member of the series.

The simplest unsaturated aldehyde is acrolein (acrylic aldehyde), $CH_2{:}CH{\cdot}CHO$, whose classical preparation by the dry distillation or by the catalytic dehydration of glycerol is well known. It may also be prepared directly by air oxidation of propylene at 400°C, using a copper oxide catalyst. There are many other methods of preparation.

Addition polymerization of acrolein is complicated by condensation through the aldehyde group, a well-known organic reaction. It is only quite recently that interest in acrolein as a monomer has risen sharply, and it is likely that products will soon be reported. Other unsaturated aldehydes have not yet exhibited any practical value as monomers.

### POLY(VINYLIDENE CHLORIDE)

Vinylidene chloride, like vinyl chloride, has been known since the time of Regnault (1838). Industrial interest in the polymer, however, began about 1930, particularly in the United States. Prior to this time, there had been little progress in the study of vinylidene chloride polymers, since they were insoluble in common solvents and could not be fused or molded without decomposition. As a result of much investigation, successful polymers, particularly in fiber form, were introduced in 1939.

There are several processes by which vinylidene chloride can be made.

Ethylene chloride may be obtained by the chlorination of ethylene at 60°C in the presence of a metal catalyst, such as antimony, iron, copper, or manganese:

$$CH_2{:}CH_2 + Cl_2 \xrightarrow[\text{15 psig}]{45°C} CH_2Cl{\cdot}CH_2Cl$$

Upon further chlorination, *unsym*-trichloroethane is formed:

$$CH_2Cl{\cdot}CH_2Cl + Cl_2 \rightarrow CH_2Cl{\cdot}CHCl_2 + HCl$$

This process is carried out by passing a mixture of 55 to 75 parts of chlorine and 100 parts of ethylene chloride into the bottom of a molten bath of metal chlorides kept at a temperature of 300° to 425°C. Alternatively, the trichloroethane may be prepared by the direct chlorination of vinyl chloride in either the liquid or the gas phase:

$$CH_2{:}CHCl + Cl_2 \xrightarrow[\text{75°C}]{Fe} CH_2Cl{\cdot}CHCl_2$$

The trichloroethane is dehydrochlorinated by treatment with alkali; e.g., a lime slurry or caustic soda at 90°C, the gaseous product being condensed and fractionated:

$$CH_2Cl{\cdot}CHCl_2 \rightarrow CH_2{:}CCl_2 + HCl$$

Alternatively, the trichloroethane may be dehydrochlorinated by pyrolysis at about 400°C. The presence of a small amount of chlorine or oxygen is reported to improve the yield.

Another method of preparation is from chlorine and acetylene. Acetylene reacts so violently with chlorine to form acetylene tetrachloride that a large quantity of inert material must be present, or the reaction is moderated by passing the gases into antimony pentachloride. Acetylene and chlorine, the former being in excess, are then reacted in the presence of the tetrachloride and a catalyst (e.g., ferric chloride). The vapors from the reaction vessel are condensed to recover the acetylene tetrachloride and to yield vinylidene chloride:

$$CH{:}CH + 2Cl_2 \rightarrow CHCl_2{\cdot}CHCl_2$$

$$(CHCl_2{\cdot}CHCl_2) + CH{:}CH + Cl_2 \xrightarrow{135°C} (CHCl_2{\cdot}CHCl_2) + CH_2{:}CCl_2$$

The monomer has a density of 1.2 and a boiling point of 32°C. It may be stored under a layer of aqueous alkali or under nitrogen to prevent oxidation by air. When the liquid monomer is exposed to air at room temperature, oxidation reactions occur in addition to polymerization.

The ease with which the pure monomer polymerizes at room temperature or below has been ascribed in part to the ready reaction with oxygen to form catalytic peroxides while at the same time removing inhibiting molecular oxygen. This reaction with oxygen is typical of many vinylidene compounds:

$$CH_2\!:\!CR_2 + O_2 \rightarrow CH_2O + R_2CO$$

Organic compounds which are satisfactory for inhibition include diaryl amines, diaryl alkylene diamines, tertiary amines, certain aromatic compounds having at least one phenolic hydroxyl group, thiophenols, and other organic sulfur compounds.

Vinylidene chloride polymerizes readily on exposure to light or free radicals, yielding a crystalline, high-softening-temperature polymer which is insoluble in most organic solvents. As with poly(vinyl chloride), the polymer can be prepared by any of the methods of polymerization. Initiators used are similar to those used for vinyl chloride polymerization. These may be phosphorus pentachloride; oxidizing agents, such as ozone; and organic or inorganic peroxides. Copper, metal alkyls (tetraethyl lead), and metal carbonyls have also been used successfully.

The polymerization reaction is

$$n\ CH_2\!:\!CCl_2 \rightarrow \left[ \begin{array}{c} H\ Cl \\ -C\!\cdot\!C- \\ H\ Cl \end{array} \right]_n$$

The mass polymerization of vinylidene chloride is similar to that of vinyl chloride and acrylonitrile in that the polymer separates as formed. When the monomer, with peroxide initiator, is kept below its boiling point, a precipitate of polymer forms slowly; this occurs more rapidly under pressure at 40° to 60°C. Before 25 per cent conversion is reached, the slurry becomes compact, local temperature rise occurs, and polymerization proceeds very rapidly to produce a hard and opaque polymer.

The industrial polymerization is best carried out by the emulsion technique, using redox because of the insolubility of the polymer in the monomer. The softening temperature of the polymer is high, varying from 185° to 200°C, depending upon the degree of polymerization. Unfortunately, the decomposition temperature of the polymer—210° to 225°C—is so close to the softening temperature that, at temperatures suitable for plastic working of the polymer, hydrogen chloride is evolved. Further, the substance is difficult to plasticize, since very few high-boiling liquids remain compatible with poly(vinylidene chloride). Among the most compatible are highly chlorinated aromatic compounds.

High-molecular-weight homopolymers from vinylidene chloride are insoluble in almost all solvents. Tris(dimethyl amido) phosphate has been found to be the only known solvent for poly(vinylidene chloride) which yields solutions which do not revert to gels on cooling to room temperature. Dioxane and tetrahydrofuran are solvents for the lower-molecular-weight polymers and for a number of the copolymers.

Vinylidene chloride polymers when fused and quickly cooled give weak, transparent, and pliable products which, after aging, undergo a transformation to a random crystalline and opaque state. This property is characteristic of vinylidene chloride polymers but is less pronounced in copolymers than in homopolymers and decreases with decreasing vinylidene chloride content. Both the homopolymers and copolymers of high vinylidene chloride content possess unusually narrow softening ranges.

The following properties of poly(vinylidene chloride) homopolymers have been reported: molecular weights of 10,000 to 100,000 and a density at 30°C of 1.8.

Vinylidene chloride polymers and copolymers, like the vinyl chloride polymers, become yellow or greenish in color and change in mechanical properties when heated or aged. Aging appears to be due to the photochemically catalyzed loss of hydrogen chloride with subsequent formation of conjugated double-bond systems, which may then absorb oxygen. The colored reaction products are formed preferentially at the surface, thus protecting the interior of the specimen from further degradation by light. Consequently, as in the case of vinyl chloride polymers, stabilization is usually required, only a mild acid acceptor being necessary.

### Vinylidene Chloride Copolymers

The very high softening temperatures and general insolubility of poly(vinylidene chloride) homopolymers have made them of little interest as commercial polymers; internal plasticization by copolymerization with another monomer avoids many of the difficulties inherent in the handling of the homopolymer.

In 1936, Wiley in the United States disclosed the copolymerization of vinylidene chloride with small amounts of vinyl chloride. Systematic work on the copolymerization of vinylidene chloride was undertaken in the United States, and in 1940 copolymers known as "saran" were offered commercially. Copolymers are also now marketed under the name Velon.

The name "saran" represents a series of vinylidene chloride copolymers with vinyl chloride or acrylonitrile (Saran F). The material is fairly crystalline, the amount of crystallinity varying with the amount and kind of comonomer used. Of these polymers, vinylidene chloride-vinyl chloride copolymers are the best known. Many other copolymers have been claimed, including those containing vinyl acetate, allyl esters, unsaturated ethers, acrylates and methacrylates, and styrene. As with vinyl chloride copolymers, special polymerization techniques are necessary to obtain homogeneous copolymers, due to the fact that the comonomers do not enter the polymer chain at the same rate. The rate at which polymerization of vinylidene chloride proceeds is drastically reduced when copolymerization takes place, even though the comonomer has a rate similar to that of the preponderating monomer. In the vinylidene chloride–vinyl chloride system, vinylidene chloride is the faster reacting component. In order to accelerate the reduced copolymerization rate, it is preferable to increase the temperature rather than to increase the concentration of initiator. As is true of all copolymerizations containing monomers of unequal reactivity, the products contain a wide distribution of copolymer compositions in addition to the distribution of chain lengths.

Among the outstanding properties of saran are general resistance to organic solvents, inertness at room temperature to all common acids and alkalies with the exception of strong ammonium hydroxide, complete resistance to water on prolonged immersion, negligible water vapor transmission, nonflammability, good dimensional stability, excellent mechanical properties, toughness, durability, and resistance to heat warpage and distortion at relatively high temperatures. Saran is attacked by halogens and strong organic amines.

Softening temperatures of copolymers ranging from 70° to over 180°C can be obtained, with consistency varying from soft, flexible products to hard, rigid materials. Saran copolymers contain at least 73 per cent vinylidene chloride; the usual product contains about 85 per cent. Within the range of 85 to 100 per cent vinylidene chloride, insolubility in organic liquids and resistance to chemical attack are practically constant.

The saran resins are supplied in a range of rigid types to meet specific applications; e.g., filaments, tubes, and films. Average values of certain properties of a saran formulation are: average molecular weight, 20,000; specific gravity, 1.7; softening temperature, 120° to 140°C; water absorption, negligible; flammability, self-extinguishing.

Saran plastics have good stability on aging, and sunlight has only slight effect upon the stabilized polymers. The resins are tasteless, odorless, and nontoxic. The yellow-green color of the polymer can be masked by certain dyes and, of course, by suitable pigmentation.

The polymer is usually fabricated by injection molding and extrusion techniques, the products being unusually tough and durable. The surfaces of molds and extrusion machines which come in contact with saran above 130°C are made of magnesium, nickel, or nickel alloys, since thermal decomposition of saran is catalyzed by iron and copper. Unlike other thermoplastics, the molds are maintained at temperatures ranging from 80° to 100°C in order to facilitate crystallization of the plastic article before its removal; once accomplished, the otherwise soft, flexible molding can be ejected from the hot mold in a strain-free, dimensionally stable form. The molds themselves may be made of the usual types of steel because they operate below 130°C; this, of course, applies only to injection and not to compression molds which have to be heated to molding temperatures. Compression molding can be accomplished satisfactorily, although the moldings are less tough than the injected ones, due to lack of orientation.

Satisfactory extrusion is accomplished in a manner similar to injection-molding technique. If heated above its softening range, saran becomes very fluid and can be readily extruded without retention of plastic memory. The extruded product on cooling is still largely amorphous. It slowly undergoes recrystallization, which is accompanied by marked increase in strength and hardness and a slight increase in density. Controlled heat treatment to hasten recrystallization is often carried out on the extruded product. By stretching under controlled conditions at room temperature, orientation as well as recrystallization occurs, and much stronger products are formed.

Saran tubing has many unusual properties which make it suitable for installations where service requirements are too severe for most other plastic materials. It is highly chemical resistant, noncorrosive, and non-scaling. It withstands high pressures and freezing, and is heat-resistant up to 80°C. Its tensile strength at room temperature lies between 4,000 and 12,000 psi. Saran tubing is tough, yet flexible, and possesses excellent fatigue strength. It is used in laboratories to pipe acids and corrosive chemicals. Industrial plants, machinery and mechanized equipment, instrument piping, and home construction are among the practical uses for saran tubing and piping.

Saran rigid pipes and fittings for industrial applications are also available. Pipes have been especially useful for transporting aqueous acids and alkalies which are corrosive to metals. The pipes and couplings are useful at temperatures up to about 65°C and withstand short contact with steam. This pipe is approximately one fourth the weight of comparable sizes of iron pipe. Its rather low heat distortion temperature and brittleness at low temperatures are, however, limitations to the industrial use of saran. Saran-lined steel pipe has grown rapidly in industrial applications and is useful at somewhat higher temperatures. Saran is also used to line electroplating tanks and to coat plating racks.

Vinylidene chloride copolymer latices are available for coating and impregnation uses. Solution coatings are little used because of the low solubility in common solvents. For these purposes, the copolymers with acrylonitrile were developed.

Saran film, with its moistureproofing and vapor barrier properties, plus its high degree of transparency, has received wide acceptance in the packaging field since its introduction in 1953. The polymer is produced in dry, granulated form, and is extruded through a die into a tube. The film is stretched and oriented by injecting compressed air into the tube and forming a bubble averaging about 80 inches in circumference and 0.5 mil in thickness. The bubble is then compressed, wound into a roll, slit, and rewound.

The film may be creased or folded without appreciable effect on its low rate of moisture-vapor transmission. Its bursting strength, in relation to

Fig. 9-12. Stretch-orienting saran film by injection of compressed air into an extruded tube. The flattened tube is then slit and rolled (see upper left background). (*Courtesy Dow Chemical Co.*)

its thickness, is high. Its properties do not change appreciably on aging or exposure to light. It is tough and serviceable at subzero temperatures and is highly resistant to chemicals. The film was developed for metal protection during wartime; however, since the war, odorless and tasteless types have been developed for the packaging of food and other products (Saran Wrap).

A very large part of saran production has been used to make monofilaments. For the manufacture of saran fiber, the copolymer is heated and extruded through an orifice at 180°C. It is cooled in air and the fibers are then stretched. Color is added to the melt before spinning by addition of pigment.

Its strength, aging properties, and resistance to bacterial and insect attack makes saran very suitable for insect screens. Tests have indicated that saran screening will outlast any metal screening available. Its principal use has been for seat covers for automobiles. It has been used for upholstery in buses and restaurants. Its advantages for these purposes are that it is hygienic, can be washed, does not stain, wears well, and does not fade. Filter cloths, cordage, and industrial brushes have also been made from saran. Extruded and oriented filaments and strips have been reported to have tensile strengths as high as 60,000 psi. Their flexibility is excellent and their flexing fatigue life is outstanding.

Undesirable characteristics of saran fiber products are their low softening temperature, which prevents their use in garments that are ironed; their negligible moisture absorption, which renders them unsuitable for underwear; and their slightly yellowish color, which precludes the manufacture of white and bright pastel garments.

A saran elastomer, based upon one of the copolymers, is available in sheet form for tank lining and can be molded and cured much like other elastomers.

## ALIPHATIC ALLYL COMPOUNDS

### POLYACRYLATES AND POLYMETHACRYLATES

Although commercial acrylic products are of relatively recent origin, acrylic acid itself was first prepared a century or more ago. In the 1870's, esters of acrylic acid were made, and a polymer of allyl acrylate was obtained. The earliest preparation of poly(methyl acrylate) was reported by the Swiss chemist, Kahlbaum, in 1880. In 1901, the German chemist, Röhm, completed a study of certain acrylic acid derivatives, and eleven years later he obtained the first patent in this field. In 1927, production of poly(methyl acrylate) began in Germany. Four years later, the American associate of this firm began manufacture of the resin in the United States. It was produced under the trade names Acryloid and Plexigum.

The work of Röhm and co-workers did not reveal any rigid plastics from the *acrylic* ester monomers. However, the investigations were extended from the derivatives of the first member of the series, acrylic acid, to the derivatives of its next higher homologs, methacrylic acid

($a$-methyl acrylic acid) and crotonic acid ($\beta$-methyl acrylic acid). The esters of crotonic acid were found to be difficult to polymerize. Then Hill in England discovered that *methacrylic* ester polymers, especially those from methyl methacrylate, were rigid, optically clear plastics. Röhm had polymerized acrylic esters between glass plates to form clear, elastic interlayers, the laminate comprising a safety glass. However, when methyl methacrylate was polymerized in this manner, instead of forming a laminated structure, the two pieces of glass separated from the polymer after the completion of the polymerization, yielding a transparent, rigid sheet. The sheets so formed were superior to both poly-(methyl acrylate) and polystyrene in toughness, clarity, and stability. Rights under British patents were subsequently granted to an American company. In 1936, rigid sheeting of poly(methyl methacrylate) under the name Plexiglas was introduced in the United States, and production of rods, tube, sheets, and molding powder under the name Pontalite (later changed to Lucite) was announced.

Of the many acrylic and methacrylic esters which have been investigated, methyl methacrylate polymers have become the most important (Lucite, Plexiglas, Perspex). These polymers possess a combination of useful properties which is hard to surpass, including ease of fabrication, outstanding clarity and lack of color, good stability to light and heat, and moderately high softening temperature, all of which makes them the best synthetic, glasslike polymers known.

Although the properties of the acrylic and methacrylic esters are generally similar, their methods of preparation are quite different and their uses somewhat divergent; hence, it is desirable to discuss the evolution of their modern commercial production and their application separately.

*Acrylic Esters*

In 1931, a pilot plant was built in the United States for the production of methyl and ethyl acrylates. Their manufacture was based upon the discovery that acrylic esters are formed in good yield by heating ethylene cyanohydrin with sulfuric acid and an alcohol. The cyanohydrin was prepared by the action of sodium cyanide on ethylene chlorohydrin which, in turn, was obtained from ethylene and hypochlorous acid:

$$CH_2{:}CH_2 \xrightarrow{\ \ HOCl\ \ } CH_2OH{\cdot}CH_2Cl \xrightarrow{\ \ NaCN\ \ } CH_2OH{\cdot}CH_2CN \xrightarrow[H_2SO_4]{\ \ ROH\ \ }$$

$$CH_2{:}CH{\cdot}CO_2R$$

Note that the last step involves simultaneously an hydrolysis, an esterification, and a dehydration.

In order to lower the manufacturing costs, the production of hydrogen cyanide catalytically from natural gas, ammonia, and air was worked out. Then the reaction of ethylene oxide with the hydrogen cyanide to form ethylene cyanohydrin was substituted for the ethylene chlorohydrin–sodium cyanide step in the former process:

$$2CH_4 + 2NH_3 + 3O_2 \rightarrow 2HCN + 6H_2O$$

$$H_2C\overset{\displaystyle O}{\overline{\diagup\diagdown}}CH_2 + HCN \rightarrow CH_2OH\cdot CH_2CN$$

Both processes have two fundamental disadvantages. First, a mole of water is lost in going from the cyanohydrin to the acrylate; this is an economic loss which can be overcome only by having available very cheap cyanohydrin. Second, neither process is as suitable for making acrylates of higher alcohols, such as butyl and octyl, as it is for methyl and ethyl, because the sulfuric acid causes some ether formation from the alcohols. Moreover, the ethers of the higher alcohols have boiling points close to those of the corresponding acrylates so that separation becomes difficult.

The most recent process has been the commercial development of a method based on Reppe's work with acetylene in Germany. By this method, acrylic esters could be obtained from acetylene, carbon monoxide, and an alcohol by either a stoichiometric process or a catalytic process.

In the former process, acetylene, alcohol, nickel carbonyl, and an acid, such as hydrochloric, are reacted at atmospheric pressure and at a temperature of about 40°C to give approximately a 60 per cent yield of an acrylate, based on acetylene. In this reaction, the carbon monoxide entering the reaction comes from the nickel carbonyl. The theoretical equation for the preparation of ethyl acrylate is:

$$4CH\dot:CH + 4C_2H_5OH + Ni(CO)_4 + 2HCl \rightarrow$$
$$4CH_2\dot:CH\cdot CO_2C_2H_5 + NiCl_2 + H_2$$

In practice, however, it was found that undesirable by-products were formed, whose separation, particularly that of ethyl propionate, was difficult because of the closeness of their boiling points. Further, the nickel chloride had to be recovered and reconverted to nickel carbonyl.

Attempts made by Reppe to run this reaction catalytically, while successful, involved a process which was very slow, even at high temperatures and pressures, much recycling was necessary, and part of the nickel carbonyl formed was rapidly decomposed.

A refinement of the latter process was recently developed in the United States. This reaction is run under mild conditions and gives high yields and conversions; the products are readily purified and contain only a very small amount of the propionate. It had been discovered that a stoichiometric mixture of acetylene and carbon monoxide remained unchanged indefinitely when passed through an alcohol containing nickel carbonyl or nickel carbonyl and hydrogen chloride at atmospheric pressure and temperatures of 0° to 75°C. However, if the reactants were first mixed stoichiometrically and the reaction begun, carbon monoxide could then be introduced into the reaction to produce acrylate by combining with acetylene and alcohol under mild conditions. In other words, the catalytic reaction could be superimposed upon the stoichiometric reaction. This process is a continuous one, run at atmospheric pressure. The conversions and yields are high, only excess alcohol need be recycled, and the crude product is readily purified.

Three other acrylate manufacturing processes have been investigated on a pilot-plant scale. One of these, based on β-propiolactone, is being used for the production of glacial acrylic acid, but not for the esters at present. β-Propiolactone is obtained by the addition of ketene to formaldehyde. Ketene, in turn, is made by the pyrolysis of either acetone or acetic acid.

Another process is based upon acrolein; however, the direct conversion of acrolein to acrylic acid has not yet been solved on a practical scale. The main deficiency of this method is the necessity of first adding alcohol to the double bond and then removing it later.

The third process, which has received much attention, is based upon lactic acid. Whereas the other processes depend mainly on coal or petroleum sources, this one can be derived from agricultural raw materials, since lactic acid can be obtained by fermentation of a number of different carbohydrate-containing agricultural wastes. For making methyl acrylate, lactic acid is esterified with methanol, acetylated with acetic anhydride, then pyrolyzed. Again, a considerable portion of the intermediate molecule is lost, so that the economics are unfavorable, even with cheap lactic acid. Unfortunately, at the present time, even the preparation of lactic acid by fermentation is not competitive with the synthetic route. Another disadvantage is that only acrylates which are heat stable can be produced.

*Methacrylic Esters*

The first commercial process for producing ethyl methacrylate used the reaction of sodium cyanide with acetone to form the cyanohydrin. This was then converted to ethyl β-hydroxy isobutyrate by reaction with ethanol and dilute sulfuric acid, and the ester was then dehydrated with phosphorus pentoxide or by pyrolysis:

$$CH_3 \cdot \overset{O}{\overset{\|}{C}} \cdot CH_3 + NaCN \xrightarrow{H^+} CH_3 \cdot \underset{OH}{\overset{CH_3}{\underset{|}{C}}} \cdot CN \xrightarrow[H_2SO_4, \text{ aq.}]{C_2H_5OH}$$

$$CH_3 \cdot \underset{OH}{\overset{CH_3}{\underset{|}{C}}} \cdot CO_2Et \xrightarrow{P_2O_5} CH_2 : \overset{CH_3}{\overset{|}{C}} \cdot CO_2Et$$

A modification of this process for making methyl methacrylate was later developed in Germany and first appeared in the United States about 1930. Although numerous other syntheses have been devised, all of the methyl methacrylate produced in the United States today is made by the modified acetone cyanohydrin process.

In the latter process, a mixture of acetone cyanohydrin and concentrated sulfuric acid is heated to form crude methacrylamide sulfate; the latter (without separation or purification) is reacted with methanol and water, yielding methyl methacrylate:

$$CH_3 \cdot \underset{OH}{\overset{CH_3}{\underset{|}{C}}} \cdot CN \xrightarrow{H_2SO_4} CH_2 : \overset{CH_3}{\overset{|}{C}} \cdot CO \cdot NH_2 \cdot H_2SO_4 \xrightarrow[H_2O]{CH_3OH} CH_2 : \overset{CH_3}{\overset{|}{C}} \cdot CO_2Me$$

It should be pointed out that the production of hydrogen cyanide catalytically from natural gas, ammonia, and air, mentioned earlier, was also an improvement in the process for making the methacrylates.

An experimental process for making methyl methacrylate from methallyl alcohol has been reported. Methallyl alcohol (2-methyl-2-propen-1-ol) is being produced commercially in limited quantities by the high-temperature chlorination of isobutylene, followed by alkaline hydrolysis of the resulting methallyl chloride. The alcohol is catalytically (copper) oxidized at 300° to 350°C by a vapor-phase air oxidation to methacrolein. Liquid-phase oxidation of methacrolein with oxygen gives high yields of methacrylic acid at substantially room temperature under a pressure of 200 pounds of oxygen, using mixed acetates of copper and nickel as the catalyst. The esterification of methacrylic acid to yield methyl methacrylate is easily performed, using excess methanol, with phosphorus pentoxide as the dehydrating agent at reflux temperature. The reactions are:

$$\underset{\text{CH}_2\text{:C·CH}_3}{\overset{\overset{\text{CH}_3}{|}}{}} \xrightarrow{\text{Cl}_2} \underset{\text{CH}_2\text{:C·CH}_2\text{Cl}}{\overset{\overset{\text{CH}_3}{|}}{}} \xrightarrow{\text{H}_2\text{O}} \underset{\text{CH}_2\text{:C·CH}_2\text{OH}}{\overset{\overset{\text{CH}_3}{|}}{}} \xrightarrow{\text{(O)}}$$

$$\underset{\text{CH}_2\text{:C·CHO}}{\overset{\overset{\text{CH}_3}{|}}{}} \xrightarrow{\text{(O)}} \underset{\text{CH}_2\text{:C·CO}_2\text{H}}{\overset{\overset{\text{CH}_3}{|}}{}} \xrightarrow[\text{—H}_2\text{O}]{\text{CH}_3\text{OH}} \underset{\text{CH}_2\text{:C·CO}_2\text{Me}}{\overset{\overset{\text{CH}_3}{|}}{}}$$

*General*

Physical data for methyl acrylate and methyl methacrylate, respectively, the first member of each series, are as follows: boiling point, 80°C and 101°C; specific gravity, 0.95 and 0.94.

An inhibitor is added to acrylic and methacrylic esters to prevent polymerization during shipping and storage. High-boiling inhibitors include *p*-hydroxy diphenylamine, *N*,*N*'-diphenyl phenylenediamine, and 2,5-di-*tert*-butyl hydroquinone. Commoner inhibitors are hydroquinone and its monomethyl ether.

With some bifunctional monomers, spontaneous formation of a porous, granular, insoluble polymer sometimes occurs; the appearance of the polymer has resulted in its being called "popcorn" polymer. Styrene, butadiene, and methyl acrylate have shown a great tendency to form this type of polymer. Unlike the others, however, methyl acrylate is converted to the popcorn polymer in the absence of air, of added initiator, and of chain-transfer agents. In all cases, the popcorn has the ability to act as a "seed," causing the rapidly accelerating growth of popcorn from its surface in the presence of monomer. Available evidence indicates that the insoluble popcorn polymer consists of a series of very long chains connected by a *very* few cross-links. Apparently polymerization conditions under which a very low rate of initiation of free radicals with consequent production of very long chains are necessary; this causes gelation to occur early in the reaction. The first gel particles which are formed act as seeds from which an increasing number of attached radicals grow [cf. the "gel effect"—see Poly(vinyl chloride)], thus yielding a heterogeneous polymerization throughout the monomer. The formation of popcorn polymer does not occur if sufficient initiator or chain-transfer agent is present, both limiting the length of the chains.

Both acrylic and methacrylic esters polymerize readily under the influence of heat, light, or initiators. Industrially, the peroxide-type, free-radical initiators are usually employed. The acrylic esters may also be polymerized by means of anionic but not cationic agents. Oxygen has a pronounced inhibitory effect upon the polymerization of both the acrylates and methacrylates.

Almost all acrylic and methacrylic esters used commercially are liquids, and the polymers are soluble in the monomers. Under similar conditions, using peroxide initiators at moderate temperatures, methyl acrylate polymerizes more readily than methyl methacrylate and ethyl acrylate. Methyl acrylate shows a much greater tendency to form branched or cross-linked polymers than does methyl methacrylate because of its active $\alpha$-hydrogen atom. Poly(methyl methacrylate), when heated above 300°C, depolymerizes in large part, whereas poly(acrylic esters) decompose without yielding the monomer.

*Polyacrylates*

When polymers of the acrylic esters are to be used in a solvent, they are usually prepared by solvent polymerization in that solvent, because of the difficulty of dissolving the polymers when prepared by mass polymerization. This method is preferable for the preparation of polymers of low to medium molecular weight, since the high viscosities of solutions of high-molecular-weight polymers makes the handling of them troublesome.

Emulsion polymerization is the other usual industrial method for the preparation of polyacrylates. In addition to the usual advantages of this technique, there is also the convenience of the application of the polymer as an aqueous dispersion. The acrylic esters may also be prepared by mass and suspension techniques although, because of the tough, adhesive properties of most acrylic ester polymers, these methods are more troublesome.

The properties of acrylic ester polymers depend greatly upon the type of alcohol from which the ester is prepared. Poly(methyl acrylate) is a tough polymer which forms a pliable film that is so extensible that it can be stretched 750 per cent before breaking. The polymer from the ethyl ester is considerably softer, even more rubberlike, and not as tough. In progressing up the list of alcohols, the polymers become softer and tackier at room temperature until the polymer of *n*-hexadecyl acrylate, which is hard and waxlike, is reached.

Polymers from acrylates of primary aliphatic alcohols containing 4 to 12 carbon atoms are soft, pliable, and adhesive. Polymers from acrylic esters of alcohols containing a ring, such as benzyl, cyclohexyl, and phenyl ethyl alcohols, are less pliable and adhesive.

The acrylates give colorless, transparent polymers which have, in addition to their tough, rubberlike extensibility, excellent chemical resistance and especially outstanding aging properties. However, their greatest value is as comonomers, since the acrylates, of all commercial monomers, copolymerize the most readily. Acrylic (and methacrylic) monomers have been extensively copolymerized with other commercially available addition monomers. Benefits which can be obtained by copolymerization with acrylates include improved heat and light stability and improved mechanical stability of copolymer dispersions produced by emulsion polymerization. Probably one of the greatest advantages in the use of the acrylic esters in copolymerizations, however, is that of internal plasticization (see Chap. 10).

The acrylates have been widely used to internally plasticize polymers made from vinyl chloride, vinylidine chloride, vinyl acetate, and acrylonitrile, among others. The acrylic (and methacrylic) esters will copolymerize with practically all types of monomers of widely different polarities. The acrylates are also employed as internal plasticizers for methyl and ethyl methacrylate polymers. These copolymers are used in coatings from organic solvents, in molding powders, and in cast applications.

Because of their low softening temperatures, the acrylates are particularly suited to film-forming applications. One of the major uses for polymers and copolymers has been in coating applications, particularly in the form of aqueous dispersions (Rhoplex) which are prepared by emulsion polymerization. These acrylic dispersions are employed in the paper, rubber, electrical, and textile industries as coatings, adhesives, and impregnants. One of the first applications of acrylic dispersions, and still a large one, was in the finishing of leather. These dispersions are used in leather finishing both as a base coat for cellulose nitrate lacquer finishes and as components of water-finishing systems.

In the search for polymers having better hardness, less cold flow, higher softening temperature, and improved craze resistance over methyl methacrylate polymers, methyl α-chloroacrylate has received considerable attention. Although the best of these polymers are better, they have not become commercially important due to high cost, lachrymatory properties of the monomer, and limited stability of the polymers.

A specialty elastomer, based on esters, such as ethyl or butyl, of acrylic acid, was announced in 1944. Ethyl acrylate is homopolymerized (Lactoprene) or, preferably, is copolymerized with about 5 per cent of a chlorine-containing monomer, such as 2-chloroethyl acrylate or 2-chloroethyl vinyl ether (Lactoprene EV). The copolymer has the advantage in that it may be vulcanized with sulfur and suitable accelerators (polyamines), since the chlorine in the molecule facilitates vulcanization. The homopolymers, although difficult to vulcanize because of their saturation, may be cross-linked with certain alkaline reagents, such as potassium hydroxide, sodium metasilicate, and lead oxide. Cross-linking may occur by elimination of alcohol in a Claisen-type condensation:

$$—CH_2 \cdot CH—$$

$$| $$

$$CO$$

$$|$$

$$O \cdot CH_2 \cdot CH_3$$

$$H$$

$$|$$

$$—CH_2 \cdot C—$$

$$|$$

$$CO$$

$$|$$

$$O \cdot CH_2 \cdot CH_3$$

These acrylic elastomers are of commercial interest (Hycar PA series) because of their ability to withstand sustained high temperatures (up to 200°C) in air and nonaqueous liquids. They are superior in heat resistance to all the commercial elastomers with the exception of the silicones. They also resist flexural breakdown, ultraviolet light, ozone, and gas diffusion. However, they have poor resistance to water and oxygenated solvents. The vulcanized products have found widest use so far in such applications as gaskets for automatic transmissions. Acrylate-acrylonitrile copolymers are also being manufactured for use as vulcanizable elastomers (Acrylon). Although the use of these acrylic elastomers has been limited by their relatively high cost, lower monomer prices, as well as improved processing techniques, are expected to increase their applications in the future.

A fluorocarbon (Poly-FBA) possessing rubberlike characteristics and excellent heat, oxygen, and ozone resistance and good stability in hot, hydraulic ester fluids has been introduced commercially. It is the polymer of 1,1-dihydroperfluorobutyl acrylate [$CH_2 : CH \cdot CO_2 \cdot CH_2 (CF_2)_2 CF_3$].

*Polymethacrylates*

The lower poly(alkyl methacrylates) are stiffer at room temperature than the corresponding acrylates, presumably because of the lesser flexibility and mobility of the methacrylate chain, resulting in part from steric hindrance by the methyl group [see Poly($\alpha$-methyl styrene)]. Thus, poly(methyl acrylate) is a moderately soft polymer, whereas poly-(methyl methacrylate) is the hardest of the common acrylic esters. It can be sawed, carved, or worked on a lathe with ease. As with the acrylic polymers, progressively tackier and softer methacrylic polymers occur as the alcohol portion of the esters becomes larger, in this case until the *n*-dodecyl (lauryl) ester polymer is reached. Polymers from esters higher than lauryl are waxlike solids at room temperature having progressively higher softening temperatures. Solubility in oils and hydrocarbons increases with increase in the size of the alcohol portion of the ester in both the polyacrylates and the polymethacrylates; the butyl ester is the first in both series exhibiting any appreciable oil solubility. The waxy polymers of the higher *n*-alkyl methacrylates are relatively hard, brittle, and opaque, and have fairly sharp melting points. X-ray diffraction studies have indicated that the crystallinity of the tetradecyl and higher ester polymers is due to crystallization of the long alcohol portions of the chains, rather than the usual alignment of the polymer chains themselves. These higher alkyl methacrylates are prepared from methyl methacrylate by alcoholysis.

Some physical data on poly(methyl methacrylate) (Plexiglas) are as follows: light transmission, 91 to 92 per cent; refractive index, 1.49; density, 1.18; tensile strength, 7,000 to 9,000 psi; water absorption, 0.3 per cent.

Unlike tensile, compressive, and flexural strengths, the impact strength of poly(methyl methacrylate) is affected only slightly by temperature variation in the range from $-60°$ to $+80°C$, and water absorption causes little change in any of the strength characteristics. The polymers are stable to sunlight and aging under many conditions of exposure—even at temperatures up to 350°C, at which temperature depolymerization occurs. They are resistant to dilute solutions of acids and alkalies, petroleum oils, aliphatic hydrocarbons, and dilute alcohols. They are not resistant to concentrated alkalies and oxidizing acids, the lower ketones, esters, aromatic and halogenated hydrocarbons, and lacquer thinners.

The commercial mass polymerization of the esters is confined primarily to the manufacture of cast sheets from methyl methacrylate. Careful control of the polymerization is necessary in order to obtain a bubble-free product of good optical clarity. As polymerization proceeds, there is an appreciable decrease in volume (over 20 per cent). The amount of shrinkage decreases as the size of the alcohol portion of the ester increases. Dissolved gases must be removed, adjustment must be made for the change in volume during polymerization, and the highly exothermic polymerization must be controlled. These problems also arise in the use of methyl methacrylate for embedding purposes.

Most of the problems encountered in casting methyl methacrylate can be alleviated by the use of a casting syrup, or prepolymer, which may be prepared either by partially polymerizing the monomer in the presence of an initiator or by dissolving some polymer in monomer. The use of the former technique, which is preferred commercially, shortens the induction period, enables polymerization to be started at a low enough temperature for adequate temperature control, reduces the dissolved gas content and subsequent bubble formation, reduces the shrinkage, and lessens the danger of leakage from the mold.

The sheet-casting mold is constructed of two heat-resistant glass plates separated by a compressible gasket (to allow for shrinkage) and sealed with gummed paper or pressure-sensitive tape. (Usually about four per cent dibutyl phthalate or $n$-butyl acrylate is added to the methyl methacrylate monomer as a plasticizer.) Plasticized poly(vinyl alcohol) tubing or coated rubber tubing may be used as the gasket material.

Heating is carried out either in an air oven or oil bath at atmospheric pressure or in an autoclave at pressures up to 150 psi. The advantage of the latter method is that the boiling point of the monomer is raised; as a consequence, its tendency to bubble is lessened and the use of higher temperatures with resultant faster polymerization rate is possible. A further advantage is that gases trapped or dissolved in the mix are forced into or kept in solution and do not appear as bubbles in the finished casting. In this method, the air is displaced with carbon dioxide or nitrogen, and these gases are then used to develop the desired pressure.

After cooling, the polymer is separated from the glass plates. The finished casting is annealed (to reduce stresses due to shrinkage during polymerization) by reheating for a time. After cooling, the sheet is protected from scratching by covering both sides with a pressure-sensitive adhesive paper or by spraying it with a strippable poly(vinyl butyral) dispersion coating.

Layer or zone polymerization is used in the manufacture of rods. Syrup is poured into a cylindrical aluminum tube which has the bottom closed with a plug of solid polymer. The vertical tube, under nitrogen or prepolymer pressure of about 200 psi, is heated, beginning at the bottom, by hot water. The water level is gradually raised, or the tube is lowered into the water bath. Shrinkage is thus compensated for by the pressure of liquid prepolymer above the polymerizing zone. Tubes may be made in a heated and rapidly rotated horizontal tube containing only enough syrup to cover the walls to the desired thickness.

As with the acrylic esters, solution, emulsion, and suspension polymerization techniques are also used with the methacrylic esters, the method employed depending upon the intended use of the polymer.

Most of the applications of the cast methacrylates are based on their unique optical properties. Their transparency is equaled by no other plastic, except possibly polystyrene. The clarity and lack of color of poly(methyl methacrylate) make it particularly useful in optical and illuminating devices. Rods and sheets of this plastic have the ability to "pipe" light; this is accomplished by multiple internal reflection of light rays. If a polished rod or sheet is curved on a radius large enough so that a beam of light entering it axially makes such an angle (42° or less) with the curved surface that its tangent is equal to or less than the index of refraction of the resin, the light is totally reflected within the material, and light will be carried around the bend. The light cannot be seen from the sides of a rod, if it is completely clear, since the polymer contains no particles to divert the light and cause it to escape by impinging upon the surface at an angle larger than the limiting one. However, by roughening selected areas, so as to produce surfaces at such angles that light impinges upon them at greater than the limiting angle, light can escape; this technique is used to make edge-lighted signs, instrument dials, surgical illuminators, and similar devices.

Cast and formed methacrylic polymers are used in many other applications, one of the best known being transparent airplane windows and cockpit and radar enclosures. Because of its excellent optical properties, low density, resistance to weathering, and retention of impact resistance at low temperatures, these enclosures were used on every combat plane during World War II.

A shortcoming of the methacrylic resins, which has prevented more general application, is their relatively poor scratch and abrasion resistance. This prevents their general use in automobile windshields. It is of interest to point out, however, that certain makes of automobiles have been produced with a transparent section in the roof, which is reported to be composed of this polymer.

Improved properties can be imparted to cast sheeting by mechanical stretching. Multi-axial hot stretching of poly(methyl methacrylate) 100 to 150 per cent converts the amorphous, brittle, cast plastic into an oriented, tough, laminar material. The stretching improves the impact strength, the resistance to both solvent and stress crazing, and has little effect upon the other physical properties of the polymer. Fabricators have developed methods of using this hot-stretched plastic in canopies for jet planes.

Other recent developments in cast as well as molded methacrylates, which have resulted in substantial improvement in surface hardness, include the partial cross-linking by copolymerization with a small amount of a doubly unsaturated monomer, such as methacrylic anhydride. Copolymers of methyl methacrylate and acrylic or methacrylic acid are superior to poly(methyl methacrylate) in hardness and resistance to abrasion and heat but are susceptible to moisture. Polymers of cyclohexyl or cyclohexyl-cyclohexyl methacrylate are clear and capable of being molded and are harder than the polymeric methyl ester. Copolymers of methyl methacrylate with such monomers as allyl methacrylate, allyl esters of dicarboxylic acids, or allyl ethers of dihydric alcohols are also more scratch-resistant than poly(methyl methacrylate), but are not thermoplastic and fabrication is more difficult. Attempts have also been made to coat thermoplastic sheets with a partially polymerized syrup of this type of monomer and to complete the polymerization between hot platens. Other investigators have treated plastic surfaces with silica or polysilicic acid esters. While maleic anhydride reacts with styrene or vinyl acetate only in equimolar ratios, clear copolymers are obtained with methyl methacrylate for all compositions, providing that the molar ratio of methyl methacrylate to maleic anhydride is greater than one (heteropolymers). Clear, solvent, heat- and abrasion-resistant products have been obtained by reacting the surfaces of cast sheets of the 85:15 copolymer of methyl methacrylate and maleic anhydride with alkylene polyamines and metal salts. None of the above treatments can yet be called entirely successful, because of cost, manufacturing or fabricating difficulties, or loss of desired mechanical properties.

Chloro- and fluoroacrylic and cyclohexyl methacrylic ester polymers

Fig. 9-13.    Acrylic pump housing.    (*Courtesy Rohm and Haas Co.*)

have been of interest for optical plastics. Of the monomers investigated, the most interesting are methacrylates from cyclic alcohols. These have comparatively high softening temperatures, form clear castings of high refractive index, and have lower shrinkage during polymerization. Cast cyclohexyl methacrylate polymers have been used for military optical instruments. Although these products are satisfactory for some applications, they still lack desired surface hardness and are brittle. The shrinkage of mass polymerized cyclohexyl methacrylate is almost half that of methyl methacrylate. This permits better precision casting in relatively thick sections for lenses, prisms, and other optical devices. The monomer is prepared by an alcoholysis reaction between methyl methacrylate and cyclohexanol in the presence of an inhibitor.

Poly(methyl methacrylate) is also available in the form of molding powder in both colorless and colored varieties. Molding powder was first made by pulverizing mass-polymerized material. However, this product does not have the narrow molecular weight range and good flow properties required for molding, since it usually has an extremely high-molecular-weight fraction which imparts undesired elastic memory and poor flow. For this and other reasons, the suspension polymerization process is usually used for producing methacrylic molding powders.

Because these resins are thermoplastic, they are usually injection molded. Miscellaneous uses of molded methacrylates include automobile dashboard panels, instrument dials, knobs, and radiator ornaments; highway reflectors, magnifying glasses, watch crystals, shatterproof spectacle lenses, transparent containers and instrument cases, antenna housings, insulation for radio equipment, musical instrument mouthpieces; and novelties, such as combs, pen and pencil barrels, jewelry, handles, bathroom fixtures, and desk sets. Other uses include numerous surgical and medical applications, such as contact optical lenses, jaw and knuckle joints, and parts of many medical instruments.

An important specialty use of molded methacrylates is as dentures, since dimensional and color stability, chemical inertness, and lifelike appearance are necessary properties. A mixture of polymer and monomer is used, the latter serving as a plasticizer to facilitate molding under the relatively low pressures allowable in dental molds. The polymerization has been carried out rapidly at room temperature using benzoyl peroxide with a tertiary amine activator, such as $N,N'$-dimethyl aniline. Allyl methacrylate and ethylene methacrylate are other monomers widely used in the dental plastics field as cross-linking agents; they have also been used in the general plastics industry to improve heat and abrasion resistance, and to minimize crazing of plastics.

The $n$-butyl and isobutyl methacrylate polymers have found some use as special adhesives. The ethyl ester is used as an embedding medium for biological and other specimens, using layer-casting techniques. Butyl methacrylate polymer emulsions have been applied as textile and leather finishes. A copolymer of $n$-butyl and isobutyl methacrylate has found extensive use in aerosol-dispensed "artificial snow" for decorative purposes.

Since plastisols form films which are soft because of their plasticizer content [see Poly(vinyl chloride)], two relatively new products are of interest. Monomer MG-1 and MPL Monomer, which are thought to be

polyethylene glycol dimethacrylate and tetraethylene glycol dimethacrylate, respectively, act as plasticizers for other resins and, upon heating,
copolymerize with them to form a hard resin.

Synthetic polymeric materials whose compositions and molecular
weights can be controlled are particularly valuable for use as viscosity
index improvers in lubricating oils. A few oil-soluble polymeric materials
are now being manufactured for this purpose. Perhaps the best known of
these are polybutenes, alkylated polystyrenes, and polymethacrylates.
The polymers and copolymers from higher methacrylic esters act as
pour-point depressants as well as viscosity index improvers for hydraulic
fluids as well as lubricants.

### Poly(acrylic and methacrylic acids) and Their Salts

Both acrylic and methacrylic acids polymerize under suitable conditions to form hard, polymeric acids which, depending upon the molecular weight, dissolve or swell in water. Unlike the esters, the acids of
high molecular weight are ionizable and, in neutralized aqueous solution,
behave, like the proteins, as heteropolar colloids.

Acrylic acid has been made commercially from ethylene cyanohydrin:

$$CH_2OH \cdot CH_2CN \xrightarrow[175°C]{H_2SO_4, \text{ aq.}} CH_2:CH \cdot COOH$$

It is also made from $\beta$-propiolactone. There are many other methods of
preparation. Methacrylic acid can be obtained from acetone cyanohydrin via methacrylamide; however, it is most conveniently prepared by
saponification of methyl methacrylate and subsequent acidification.
Both acrylic and methacrylic acids are colorless, transparent liquids.
Acrylic acid boils at 142°C and has a density of 1.04 at 25°C; methacrylic
acid boils at 163°C and has a density of 1.01 at 25°C.

The homopolymers of acrylic and methacrylic acids and their alkali
salts are not suitable for use as conventional plastics, fibers, or films
because of their water sensitivity. They are brittle when dry and remain
hard when heated. At high temperatures, they cross-link and finally
char without depolymerization.

Water-soluble salts of poly(acrylic and methacrylic acids) and their
copolymers have been suggested for use as thickeners of printing pastes,
stiffeners in the textile and carpet industries, modifiers of gums and
starch for special aqueous adhesives, protective colloids and emulsifying agents, and leather-treating agents. The water-soluble polymers—
the acids, salts, and amides—are used in sizing warp yarns to protect

them during weaving. The function of a warp size is to hold down the loose fibers and protect the yarn from chafing during weaving.

The alkali salts form viscous solutions in water. Poly(sodium acrylate) is compatible with most anionic and nonionic dispersions and, unlike many natural gums, is not affected by bacterial or hydrolytic action. It is also a basic ingredient in soil conditioners and is used in paint manufacture and in rubber latex compounding.

In many building, civil engineering, agricultural, and military operations, the need arises to alter, temporarily or permanently, certain properties of the soil found on the site. Properties requiring alteration may include mechanical strength, elasticity, permeability, water resistance, chemical inertness, and surface-wearing properties.

The use of (chiefly) calcium acrylate has been very promising. Its soil stabilization effect is the result of a double process. First, the acrylate ionizes in the presence of water to form, among other ions, a positively charged calcium acrylate ion. This becomes attached to a soil particle by replacing, for example, a sodium ion in a typical base-exchange reaction. The displaced sodium ion then reacts with a negatively charged acrylate ion to form sodium acrylate. The second stage is the actual polymerization of the acrylic salts, both those attached to the soil and those remaining dissolved in the water. Long-chain polymers are formed, thus chemically linking the soil particles and the solution. A redox system of initiation is used, ammonium persulfate and sodium thiosulfate being typical examples.

The product is a modified soil which has considerable tensile strength, is water-repellent, impermeable, resilient, and has much less volume change with water-content changes. Army engineers have done considerable work with calcium acrylate for emergency road and airfield surfacing in forward areas where the logistics of cement and asphalt are unfavorable and particularly where muddy conditions are found.

### POLYACRYLONITRILE

The synthesis of acrylonitrile was first reported by Moureu in France in 1893. The product was, however, little more than a laboratory curiosity in the United States until about 1940 when interest in the new German Buna N elastomer (made from acrylonitrile and styrene) caused an American company to initiate production of the monomer.

Moureu's synthesis consisted of the dehydration of ethylene cyanohydrin, prepared from the chlorohydrin and sodium cyanide:

$$CH_2OH \cdot CH_2Cl \xrightarrow{\text{NaCN}} CH_2OH \cdot CH_2 \cdot CN \xrightarrow{P_2O_5} CH_2:CH \cdot CN$$

The early commercial manufacture in the United States was from ethylene oxide and hydrogen cyanide, made by the following processes:

$$CH_2:CH_2 \xrightarrow{\text{(O)}} \overset{O}{\overset{\diagup \diagdown}{CH_2-CH_2}}$$

$$CaC_2 \xrightarrow{N_2} CaCN_2 \xrightarrow[\text{furn.}]{\text{elec.}} Ca(CN)_2 \xrightarrow{H_2SO_4} HCN$$

Then

$$\overset{O}{\overset{\diagup \diagdown}{CH_2-CH_2}} + HCN \rightarrow CH_2OH \cdot CH_2 \cdot CN \xrightarrow{-H_2O} CH_2:CH \cdot CN$$

Alkaline materials, such as calcium hydroxide or sodium formate, are used for the dehydration in the liquid phase. It is also possible to dehydrate the cyanohydrin by vaporizing it at reduced pressure and passing the vapors over activated alumina at 350°C. The above general method of preparation from ethylene cyanohydrin is still in use.

About 1950, new processes for the synthesis of intermediates were announced. Methane is partially oxidized to yield acetylene and is also reacted with ammonia to give hydrogen cyanide:

$$4CH_4 + 3O_2 \rightarrow 2CH:CH + 6H_2O$$

$$2CH_4 + 2NH_3 + 3O_2 \rightarrow 2HCN + 6H_2O$$

Then

$$CH:CH + HCN \rightarrow CH_2:CH \cdot CN$$

This preparation of acrylonitrile from acetylene and hydrogen cyanide was first developed in Germany. The process can be operated in either the gaseous or the liquid phase. The gaseous process uses a catalyst, such as sodium or barium cyanide, on a porous carrier at temperatures of about 500°C.

The liquid-phase process has been more successful. One method is to pass the reactants into an aqueous solution of hydrogen chloride, cuprous chloride, and ammonium chloride at about 80°C, using a large excess of acetylene; the unreacted acetylene is recirculated. The dilute solution of acrylonitrile is concentrated by continuous distillation.

Acrylonitrile boils at 77°C, has a density of 0.80, and is appreciably soluble in water. Molecular oxygen, i.e., air, is an effective inhibitor against polymerization. As permanent inhibitors, ammonia, ammonium carbonate, amines, and hydroquinone are effective.

Acrylonitrile is one of the most rapidly polymerizing vinyl monomers in the absence of inhibitors. Polymerization is readily initiated by the usual free-radical initiators. Acrylonitrile, like the acrylic esters, will not polymerize using the cationic type of catalyst, such as boron trifluoride. Polymerization does occur, however, with anionic catalysts, such as sodium and amides.

The mass polymerization of acrylonitrile is little used commercially, since it is difficult to control on a large scale except perhaps at quite low

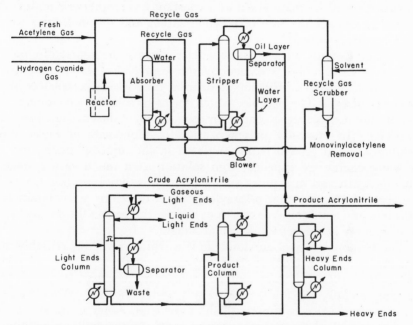

FIG. 9-14. Acrylonitrile flow sheet. (*Reprinted from Petroleum Refiner*)

temperatures. Early in the reaction, the solid polymer, which is insoluble in the monomer, forms with remaining monomer a stiff slurry, and agitation to remove heat becomes difficult. When this occurs, the polymerization becomes violent.

Acrylonitrile can be polymerized in organic solvents, from most of which the polymer separates as it is formed. Only in certain concentrated aqueous salt solutions, in dimethyl formamide, and in a few other solvents will the polymer remain in solution.

Polymerization is best carried out in aqueous media using water-soluble initiators; e.g., persulfates. Acrylonitrile polymerization from aqueous emulsion was studied in Germany about 1930. Polymerization by this method is particularly suited to large-scale manufacture, as the dilution with water results in better control of the polymerization process, and the polymer precipitates as formed in a granular form which is easily recovered by filtration.

The addition of a reducing agent which can be oxidized by persulfate results in a much faster rate of polymerization (redox polymerization). Even the rapid redox system of initiation is greatly accelerated by the addition of certain metallic ions, such as cupric or ferric; a few parts per million of these have a significant effect. These trace metallic-ion impurities must be maintained at a constant level, otherwise undesirable variation in both the rate of polymerization and the molecular weight of the product occurs.

Polyacrylonitrile latex often coagulates during the course of emulsion polymerization. This is caused by the appreciable water solubility of the monomer; part of the polymerization then occurs completely in the aqueous phase. The polymer which forms in solution precipitates, the precipitate then acting as centers for coagulation of the emulsified polymer particles. In emulsion polymerization of monomers of lower water solubility, chain growth is also initiated in the aqueous phase, but the growing chains are expelled from solution at a much earlier stage of chain growth and in a much smaller state of subdivision (see Chap. 5). Emulsion polymerization of acrylonitrile is therefore a combination of solution- and emulsion-type reactions and for this reason the polymer lacks homogeneity in respect to molecular weight.

The homopolymer of acrylonitrile is a white or yellow, crumbly, and opaque material. Unplasticized polyacrylonitrile films free of solvent are quite brittle. The homopolymer is not very thermoplastic, even upon heating, and objects can be molded only with difficulty. When water or an organic plasticizer is present, the polymer is easier to mold. So far as is known, the homopolymers are not used commercially in molding or casting applications.

The high negative polarity, the small size of the nitrile groups, and the hydrogen atoms available for hydrogen bonding are responsible for the strength, general insolubility, and high softening temperature of polyacrylonitrile. It was realized years ago that the physical nature of polyacrylonitrile would lend itself to the formation of good textile fibers; the difficulty was that the polymer could not be melt-spun and, since there was no known suitable solvent for the polymer, it could not be spun from solution either. Research on this problem was in progress in the 1930's in both America and Germany.

Linear polyacrylonitrile somewhat resembles natural silk in that it is composed of long chains containing highly polar and relatively small side groups. As with the polyamides and the cellulosics, the reason for general insolubility is that there are strong secondary valence forces between adjacent chains, in this case formed by hydrogen bonding between the α-hydrogen atoms of one chain and the nitrile nitrogen atoms of an adjacent chain:

$$
\begin{array}{ccc}
\diagdown & & \diagup \\
H-C-CN & \cdots & H-C-CN \\
\diagup & & \diagdown \\
H_2C & & CH_2 \\
\diagdown & & \diagup \\
H-C-CN & \cdots & H-C-CN \\
\diagup & & \diagdown \\
H_2C & & CH_2 \\
\diagdown & & \diagup \\
H-C-CN & \cdots & H-C-CN \\
\diagup & & \diagdown
\end{array}
$$

An effective solvent must thus be one which will break the hydrogen bonds; that is, the solvent must have a greater tendency to bond at those points in the polymer which are hydrogen-bonded, thus breaking the original hydrogen bonds and associating itself with the polymer; such an association becomes, or is the equivalent of, solution. Upon examination of several thousand organic liquids, it was found that quite a number of them, all very strongly polar, would dissolve the polymer. Even so, very slight differences in constitution mean the difference between solvent and nonsolvent properties. The manufacture of fibers from polyacrylonitrile would not have been possible without the discovery of suitable solvents.

Polyacrylonitrile will dissolve in concentrated aqueous solutions of certain salts, such as lithium bromide, sodium thiocyanate, concentrated zinc chloride, and also sulfuric acid. Threads and films may be obtained from the solutions, but these solutions have not proved suitable for commercial use.

The structural requirements of an organic solvent for polyacrylonitrile are quite critical.[3] Not only must an active solvent be able to form hydrogen bonds comparable in strength to those of the polymer chains, but the solvent molecule most possess a suitable nonpolar end for a spacing or separating effect. Thus, dimethyl formamide (I) is a solvent, but not formamide, methyl formamide, or diethyl formamide. Dimethyl sulfone (II) is effective, but diethyl sulfone only swells the polymer. Several other solvents have been discovered recently. Among them are sulfolane (III), N, N-dimethyl acetamide (IV), N, N, N',N'-tetramethyl

[3] Ham, G. E., *Ind. Eng. Chem.*, **46**, 390 (1954).

oxamide (V), ethylene carbonate (VI), dimethyl phosphite (VII), dioxanone (VIII), and tris(dimethyl amido)phosphate (IX).

Several other compounds, found to be active solvents for polyacrylonitrile at room temperature or on heating, include various amides, certain nitriles, lactones, nitro phenols, diamines, and dithiocyanates.

The first commercial polymeric products containing acrylonitrile were the butadiene-acrylonitrile copolymer elastomers developed in Germany (Buna N). These will be discussed under butadiene copolymers.

The principal use of acrylonitrile has been for the manufacture of fibers. Because of its relative infusibility, the fiber is spun by either the wet or dry process, both of which require solution of the polymer. The controlled drawing of the filaments after spinning improves their chemical resistance and strength. This is due to the fact that, when filaments of polyacrylonitrile, especially those containing small amounts of solvent or water, are stretched, a high degree of orientation of the linear molecules can be obtained.

The useful molecular weight range for forming polyacrylonitrile fibers is between 15,000 and 300,000; most commercial polyacrylonitrile fibers probably have a molecular weight between 30,000 and 100,000, depending upon the conditions of the particular spinning process.

Few of the vinyl-type homopolymers have sufficiently high softening temperatures and other properties even approaching those required for general-purpose textile fibers. Realizing the potentialities of poly-acrylonitrile from experimentally made fibers, a program of research on the polymerization, new solvents, and methods of spinning was begun in the United States in 1940. In 1948, Orlon (originally Fiber A) fiber, made from acrylonitrile, became available. Orlon is a synthetic, orientable fiber made from polymers which contain a preponderance of acrylic units, particularly acrylonitrile units, in the chain. The molecular weight of Orlon continuous filament is about 100,000.

Fig. 9-15.   A step in the processing of continuous filament Orlon acrylic fiber.   (*Courtesy E. I. duPont de Nemours and Co.*)

Since the successful introduction of Orlon acrylic fiber, many other manufacturers devoted much research time to an investigation of fibers made from acrylonitrile, alone and with comonomers. In 1951, Fiber X-51, containing acrylonitrile and methyl methacrylate, was introduced, tested, and later sent back for further development. In 1954, Fiber X-54, now named Creslan, was offered as an improvement. Full-scale marketing is planned for 1958. The fiber is reported to be a copolymer of acrylonitrile and other acrylic components (e.g., methacrylamide). Acrilan, offered in 1952, is reported to be a copolymer of acrylonitrile and another minor constituent, possibly vinyl pyridine. Two newcomers, not yet in production, are Verel and Zefran. The former consists of acrylonitrile with one or more comonomers, variously reported to be vinylidene chloride, methallyl alcohol, allyl cyanide, and methallyl cyanide. Zefran has been reported to contain, in addition to acrylonitrile, minor amounts of vinyl pyrrolidone. Dynel has already been discussed under Vinyl Chloride Copolymers.

A principal reason for copolymerizing acrylonitrile with another constituent is that the homopolymer is not receptive to most dyes. The addition of minor quantities of such monomers as vinyl pyridine and vinyl pyrrolidone greatly increases its affinity for dyes, a necessary condition for most commercial fibers. More recently, copolymers of acrylonitrile with about 10 per cent vinyl chloroacetates have shown good affinity toward acid dyes.

Probably the most outstanding property of Orlon is its resistance to outdoor exposure, in which it excels over all common organic fibers. The fiber has good wet and dry strength, fatigue resistance, and flex life. It has very good resistance to mineral acids and excellent resistance to common solvents, oils, greases, and neutral salts; it resists weak alkalies fairly well, but strong alkalies, especially when hot, degrade it rapidly.

Continuous-filament Orlon yarn resembles silk in appearance, stiffness, and hand. The bulking and thermal insulation properties of this fiber are similar to those of wool but the moisture absorption is much lower. The abrasion resistance is not as good as that of nylon, wool, or silk.

Orlon finds its widest use in applications where resistance to sunlight and weather is of paramount importance; for example, curtains, tents, sails, nets, awnings, flags, auto fabrics, and cordage. Because of its chemical resistance, it is used in filter cloths in chemical manufacture. Finer textiles for personal apparel, such as shirts, sweaters, gloves, and socks, became available in 1951. Garments made of Orlon dry quickly without shrinking or stretching.

Acrilan is manufactured by a wet-spinning operation. The fiber is resistant to weak alkalies and is generally very resistant to all other chemicals, including acids (except concentrated sulfuric), common solvents, and dry-cleaning agents. Sunlight causes slight degradation but no aging effect has been discovered as yet. Acrilan softens at 235°C and tends to discolor in dry heat. Due to its warm hand and bulky character, this fiber is widely used alone in apparel, outerwear fabrics, blankets, and inner linings, and in blends with cotton, wool, rayon, and other fibers.

Although Fiber X-51 has been supplanted by Creslan, the properties of both are probably very similar. The properties of Creslan have not yet been made public. The circular cross-section of X-51, similar to that of Dacron, is quite different from the dog-bone cross-section of Orlon, the kidney-shaped cross-section of Acrilan, and the irregular, ribbon-shaped cross-section of dynel; this may indicate that X-51 is the only one of these fibers which is melt-spun.

The color of the fiber is nearly white, and its luster is naturally semidull. The fiber is thermoplastic and is flammable. It becomes tacky at 290°C and shrivels at somewhat lower temperatures; it can, however, be ironed safely at about the same temperature as can nylon.

Fig. 9-16. Acrilan acrylic fiber passing over roller dryers after being spun. The fiber is next cut into staple lengths or shipped as tow. (*Courtesy Chemstrand Corp.*)

This acrylic fiber, like the others, has excellent resistance to outdoor exposure, microorganisms, acids, insects, and most solvents. It has fairly good resistance to caustic. The spun yarns made from staple have been used in filter cloths, blankets, sweaters, knitted jersey, draperies, hosiery, and bathing suits.

Acrylic fibers are also in production or pilot plant in Germany (Dolan-acryl, Dralon, PAN-Faser, Redon, Wolycrylon), France (Crylor), Russia (Nitrilon), Japan (Sinsen), and Holland (No. 53).

A variety of other comonomers with acrylonitrile, including vinyl

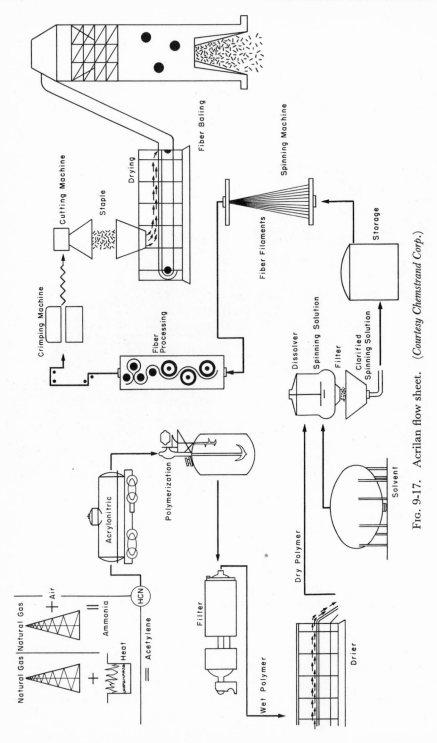

Fig. 9-17.  Acrilan flow sheet.  (*Courtesy Chemstrand Corp.*).

acetate, have been studied. Acrylonitrile-vinyl acetate copolymers containing 60 to 80 per cent acrylonitrile have been studied as fibers.

Higher homologs of acrylonitrile, such as methacrylonitrile, have not yet become of commercial importance, partly because no efficient process for commercial production had been found. However, in 1948, an experimental process for manufacturing both acrylonitrile and methacrylonitrile in yields of 90 per cent was reported. As can be seen from the following reactions, either acrylonitrile or methacrylonitrile can be obtained, depending upon whether propylene or isobutylene, both abundant and cheap, is the starting material:

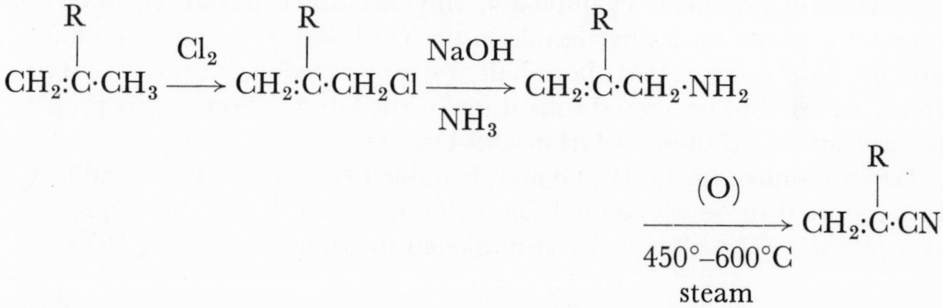

$$\underset{CH_2:C\cdot CH_3}{\overset{R}{|}} \xrightarrow{Cl_2} \underset{CH_2:C\cdot CH_2Cl}{\overset{R}{|}} \xrightarrow[NH_3]{NaOH} \underset{CH_2:C\cdot CH_2\cdot NH_2}{\overset{R}{|}}$$

$$\xrightarrow[\underset{steam}{450°-600°C}]{(O)} \underset{CH_2:C\cdot CN}{\overset{R}{|}}$$

Methacrylonitrile homopolymers have too low a softening temperature and discolor too easily for use as fibers, but the monomer has interesting possibilities as a component of both elastomers and fibers.

### Vinylidene Cyanide

Vinylidene cyanide (methylene malononitrile) is a new monomer of interest in the fiber field. Although the monomer can be made in several different ways, probably the best method is from acetic anhydride and hydrogen cyanide through di(acetyl cyanide):

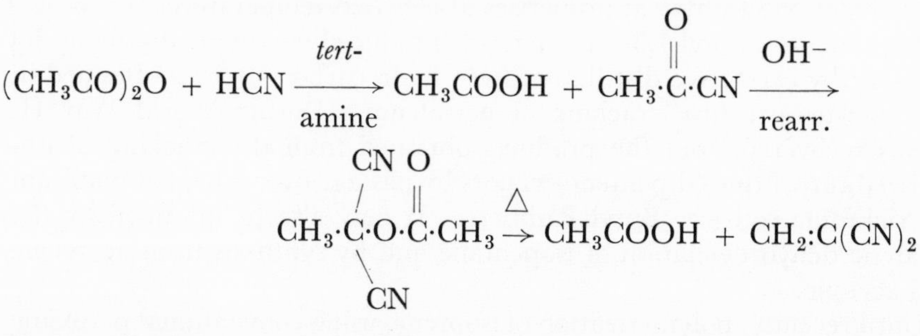

$$(CH_3CO)_2O + HCN \xrightarrow[amine]{tert-} CH_3COOH + CH_3\cdot \overset{O}{\overset{||}{C}}\cdot CN \xrightarrow[rearr.]{OH^-}$$

$$CH_3\cdot \overset{CN}{\overset{/}{\underset{\backslash}{C}}}\cdot O\cdot \overset{O}{\overset{||}{C}}\cdot CH_3 \xrightarrow{\triangle} CH_3COOH + CH_2:C(CN)_2$$

The intermediate, pyruvonitrile, may also be made from hydrogen cyanide and ketene.

The initiation of polymerization of vinylidene cyanide by free radicals is very sluggish. Anionic initiation by such mild agents as pure water, ketones, nitroanilines, alcohols, and amides, on the other hand, is rapid. The polymer is very unstable, undergoing carbon chain-scission in the presence of moisture.

The molded plastic is brittle unless it is oriented.    It has poor electrical properties, as it is very polar.    However, it has outstanding weathering resistance and a high softening temperature.    The polymer is soluble in very few solvents; among the best are dimethyl formamide, dimethyl sulfoxide, ethylene and propylene carbonates, and a mixture of aceto-nitrile and water.

A new fiber first known as Darlan, now called Darvan, reportedly a copolymer of vinylidene cyanide and vinyl acetate, is purported to be the result of a search for a fiber usable in tire cord, but it has not been found suitable for this use.    It is about half as strong as nylon, is similar to wool, and is reported to be a good substitute for the latter.    Some of its proper-ties are similar to those of Orlon and Dacron.

Darvan, unlike the homopolymer, is stable to moisture, bases, and heat. It is reported to be well suited for textile use, and it also shows promise as a plastic.    The fiber was test-marketed in women's coats in 1956.

### ALIPHATIC DIENES

#### POLYISOPRENE

For more than one hundred years, scientists have been endeavoring to produce a synthetic elastomer having the structure and physical properties of Hevea rubber.    The present synthetic rubber industry is based pri-marily on a copolymer of butadiene and styrene (GR-S).    GR-S elasto-mers are satisfactory for use in passenger tires and many other products. However, these polymers, when compared to natural rubber, have certain shortcomings, including high hysteresis, low gum tensile strength, and poor retention of physical properties at elevated temperatures.

Isoprene (2-methyl-1,3-butadiene) is produced commercially today by recovery by extractive distillation from hydrocarbon streams obtained in the high-temperature cracking of petroleum.    During World War II, it was recovered from the products obtained from the cracking of iso-merized turpentine (dipentene) vapors by passage over a heated platinum or Nichrome coil (see Butyl Rubber).    It may also be obtained by the catalytic dehydrogenation of isopentane and by synthesis from acetylene and acetone.

Until recently, polymerization of isoprene, using conventional peroxidic initiators, has resulted in a random addition reaction.    Now, using some of the newly investigated heterogeneous and metal catalytic systems, synthetic polyisoprene has been made which is practically identical in structure to Hevea rubber [poly(*cis*-1,4-isoprene)].

Two synthetic polyisoprenes presently being offered are known as Coral rubber and Ameripol SN. Coral rubber can be made by polymerizing isoprene in the presence of lithium metal at a temperature of 30° to 40°C; it has been polymerized in the pilot plant to an average molecular weight equivalent to or higher than that of the best grade of natural rubber. The molecular weight distribution is also similar to that found in natural rubber. In Coral rubber, there is practically no *trans*-1,4-addition structure; the 1,2-addition structures are also absent. Coral rubber differs from Hevea in that it has slightly less *cis*-1,4 structure and slightly more 3,4 structure. Both Hevea and balata have small amounts of 3,4 structure in the polymer chain, rather than exclusively 1,4 structure, as heretofore generally accepted.

Ameripol SN is similar to Coral rubber in that it contains only minor amounts of 1,2- and 3,4-addition products. The catalyst used has not been specifically revealed but is known to be based on information supplied by Ziegler in Germany; hence, it is presumed to be a heterogeneous type (see Low-Pressure Polyethylene). It is reported that an essentially all *trans*-1,4 polymer can also be obtained.

Coral rubber does not absorb oxygen as readily as natural rubber, has higher thermal stability, and is more resistant to cracking in tire treads. The wear in tire treads is almost equivalent to that of pure natural rubber. Cut-growth of Ameripol is somewhat better than that of Hevea but independent (natural) cracking is inferior. However, practically speaking, the properties of both synthetic polyisoprenes are so close to those of the natural polymer that complete replacement would be possible. It is likely that further research will improve, although perhaps only slightly, the properties of these elastomers. Large-scale production of synthetic polyisoprene could make the United States independent of supplies of natural rubber, which is still required in small amounts in passenger automobile tires and in much larger proportions in truck and airplane tires.

POLYCHLOROPRENE

In 1925 in the United States, Nieuwland reported that a soft, elastic solid was formed when divinyl acetylene was treated with sulfur chloride. This observation aroused the interest of chemists in an American company which had previously become interested in the field of synthetic elastomers—an unknown field in the United States at that time. Under a joint research program, a satisfactory synthesis was worked out for monovinyl acetylene, an intermediate which was found to be of greater promise. There was then developed the production of a new monomer, chloroprene (2-chloro-1,3-butadiene), made by the addition of hydrogen chloride to monovinyl acetylene. Chloroprene differs from isoprene in having a chlorine atom substituted for the methyl group. When polymerized, it forms an elastomer with unique properties. In 1931, the new synthetic elastomer, called Duprene, the name given to polychloroprene, was announced. The name was later changed to Neoprene. The term "neoprene" is now a generic one which denotes a synthetic, rubberlike polymer made by the polymerization of chloroprene or a mixture of monomers containing principally chloroprene.

The most familiar of the neoprenes is the general-purpose type GN (identical with GR-M; i.e., Government Rubber—Monovinyl acetylene); following is a brief description of its method of manufacture.

The first step consists of the partial dimerization of acetylene by absorbing it in an aqueous solution of cuprous and ammonium chlorides:

$$2CH{:}CH \xrightarrow[\text{15 atm.}]{10°C} CH{:}C{\cdot}CH{:}CH_2$$

A small amount of divinyl acetylene is also formed; it is immediately separated from the absorber as an immiscible oil and is burned, since it can be violently reactive. Unchanged acetylene (b.p. $-88°C$) is separated from vinyl acetylene (b.p. $+5°C$) by condensing the latter. The vinyl acetylene is then passed into an aqueous hydrochloric acid solution containing cuprous and ammonium chlorides to form chloroprene:

$$CH{:}C{\cdot}CH{:}CH_2 + HCl \xrightarrow[\text{15 psi}]{30°C} CH_2{:}C(Cl){\cdot}CH{:}CH_2$$

This addition must be carefully controlled in order to minimize the addition of a second molecule of hydrogen chloride to form 1,3-dichloro-2-butene; in spite of careful control, an appreciable quantity of the latter is formed. The formation of chloroprene from vinyl acetylene and hydrogen chloride involves 1,4 addition, followed by rearrangement in the presence of the cuprous chloride.

Chloroprene is a colorless liquid boiling at $59°C$ and having a density of 0.96. When kept in the dark at room temperature, chloroprene slowly and completely polymerizes to form a transparent, resilient, elastic mass resembling soft, vulcanized rubber. Like vulcanized rubber, it cannot be worked on a mill to form a smooth sheet, being nonplastic; it swells but does not dissolve in rubber-swelling agents. This completely polymerized chloroprene is known as $\mu$-polychloroprene. If polymerization is carried only part of the way (about 30 per cent), a plastic material is obtained which is analogous to milled, unvulcanized rubber, and which is designated $\alpha$-polychloroprene. The $\alpha$-polymer can be milled much like raw rubber, various materials being incorporated with it, if desired. It can then be transformed into the $\mu$-polymer by heating or otherwise completing the polymerization process. At ordinary temperatures, the process is slow, but at 130°C the change occurs within a few minutes. The change is accelerated by a number of materials, among them magnesium and zinc oxides. This further polymerization of the $\alpha$-polymer to the fully polymerized product, the $\mu$-polymer, is analogous to the transformation of milled, raw rubber (plastic and soluble) to vulcanized rubber (elastic and insoluble).

Since it is desirable that $\alpha$-polychloroprene be milled and compounded before being cured, methods of controlling the polymerization and substances to be added to the $\alpha$-polymer to prevent it from changing to the $\mu$-polymer, either during milling or when stored for a reasonable period of time, were developed. Many chemicals, among which are amines, phenols, and organic sulfur compounds, are suitable for controlling the polymerization of chloroprene to give a good yield (up to 90 per cent) of the $\alpha$-polymer.

After purification by fractionation, chloroprene is polymerized. The first general-purpose type of chloroprene polymer (Duprene) was manufactured in 1931 by mass polymerization. The development of emulsion polymerization techniques made possible the introduction in 1935 of a second type of chloroprene polymer (Neoprene E); in 1938, a third change in fundamental polymerization methods resulted in a faster curing elastomer (Neoprene G). Since that time, several modifications of the latter type of polymer have been produced commercially, notably Neoprene types GN and RT, none of which is fundamentally different from type G.

In the general polymerization process, the chloroprene is emulsified in water and polymerized at 40°C, using potassium persulfate as an initiator and elemental sulfur as a modifier. A basic polymerization recipe is given in Table 9-1.

TABLE 9-1. BASIC POLYMERIZATION RECIPE FOR CHLOROPRENE

| | |
|---|---|
| Chloroprene | 100.0 |
| Wood rosin | 4.0 |
| Sufur | 0.6 |
| Sodium hydroxide | 0.8 |
| Sodium salt of naphthalene sulfonic acid-formaldehyde condensate | 0.7 |
| Potassium persulfate | 0.2–1.0 |
| Water | 150.0 |

After completion of polymerization, an emulsion of tetraethyl thiuram disulfide is added, and the alkaline latex is aged to increase the plasticity of the polymer to the desired level by the action of the disulfide which cleaves sulfur linkages. The disulfide also stabilizes the final polymer.

The de-emulsification step in the production of neoprene is unusual. The alkaline latex is acidified with acetic acid to a point just short of coagulation; the actual coagulation is accomplished by freezing on the surface of a large, rotating, brine-cooled drum partially immersed in the latex. The film formed on the freeze roll is then stripped from it, washed with water, passed through squeeze rolls, and finally dried in air at 120°C. The dried product is gathered into rope form and cut into short lengths. The elastomer is odorless, is light amber in color, and has a specific gravity of 1.23.

More recently, a new type of polychloroprene has been made available, known as Neoprene type W. This improved polymer has a more uniform molecular weight distribution than any of the other neoprenes, and in addition contains no sulfur, thiuram disulfide, or other compounds capable of decomposing to yield either free sulfur or a vulcanization accelerator. It is a general-purpose neoprene having markedly improved stability, improved processing characteristics, and greater adaptability to variations in vulcanizing systems than the earlier general-purpose types.

It has been postulated that the structure of Neoprene type GN before treatment with tetraethyl thiuram disulfide, is, in part, the following, where $x$ may vary from two to six and $n$ is, on the average, 80 to 110 times $x$:

$$-(CH_2 \cdot C(Cl):CH \cdot CH_2)_n - S_x - (CH_2 \cdot C(Cl):CH \cdot CH_2)_n - S_x -$$

Nonlinear linkages of unknown nature are also present in minor amounts. The sulfur linkage is believed to be cleaved by reaction with the disulfide or its alkaline degradation products by a mechanism which is not yet clear. This cleavage yields a plastic polymer by reducing the average molecular weight below the critical value for gelation. Thus, sulfur, unlike mercaptan modifiers, does not directly control molecular weight, but yields a product whose molecular weight can subsequently be reduced by the amount necessary to render the gel soluble and plastic.

A study of the infrared spectra of polychloroprenes has shown that 1,4 polymerization of chloroprene accounts for the greatest part of the structure of all neoprenes—ranging from about 84 per cent to 99 per cent, depending upon the temperature of polymerization. Of this 1,4 polymer, only 5 to 13 per cent has the *cis* configuration. Small amounts of branched structures are also present. The homopolymer has the following general structure:

$$(-CH_2 \cdot C(Cl):CH \cdot CH_2 -)_n$$

Most neoprenes are homopolymers of chloroprene; however, some are copolymers and these include type RT, made by copolymerizing a small amount of styrene with chloroprene; type FR, a copolymer of chloroprene and isoprene (developed primarily for low-temperature service); and type Q, a copolymer of chloroprene and acrylonitrile, which processes well and has good oil resistance. Many types of neoprene latices are also manufactured for use in latex form directly.

The mechanism of vulcanization of neoprene differs from that of other elastomers. This is demonstrated by the fact that neoprene may be vulcanized by heat alone. However, combinations of zinc and magnesium oxides (5:4) as vulcanizing agents are generally used. Among the organic compounds that are recommended for use with the oxides are ethylene thiourea, $p,p'$-diaminodiphenyl methane, and, more commonly, the di-$o$-tolyl guanidine salt of dicatechol borate. More recently, it has been found that antimony trisulfide is even more effective than the latter agent. In the absence of sulfur, these agents, in combination with zinc oxide, do not vulcanize natural rubber. Although the major structural difference is the chlorine atom in neoprene in place of the methyl group in natural rubber, the small amount of *tert*-allylic chlorine formed by 1,2 polymerization is the important functional difference. In neoprene latex particularly, this active chlorine is gradually liberated, and the polymer becomes cross-linked.

The vulcanization of neoprene with sulfur is of relatively small importance; this reaction is slow, even in the presence of accelerators. It is commonly used only with metallic oxides for the production of special properties in vulcanizates.

Neoprene, unlike most of the synthetic elastomers based upon butadiene, forms vulcanizates of high tensile strength without the addition of reinforcing fillers. The vulcanizates, suitably stabilized by an antioxidant, are extremely resistant to deterioration. Unlike natural rubber, which becomes soft and sticky, neoprene stocks after long aging tend to increase in modulus, decrease in ultimate elongation, and become dry and hard. They are also reported to be superior to nitrile rubber in resistance to deterioration upon exposure.

In general, neoprene vulcanizates are much more resistant to swelling in oil than vulcanizates of natural rubber or of the butadiene-styrene (GR-S) polymers but are less resistant than those of butadiene-acrylonitrile polymers (nitrile rubbers). Neoprenes are, however, more resistant to chemicals than are the latter.

Neoprene, except for certain special-purpose types, does not retain its flexibility to such low temperatures as rubber, becoming leathery at about $-30°C$ and brittle at about $-40°C$. Nevertheless, by the addition of suitable plasticizers in larger quantities than are normally used, the low temperature range may be extended as far as $-60°C$, while oil resistance is retained.

Neoprene was the first synthetic elastomer developed in America and it is still one of the best types.  It can replace natural rubber in most cases and can be used in a greater variety of applications than any other type of synthetic elastomer.  Although tires of fairly good quality can be made from neoprenes, they cannot compete with GR-S tires in cost. Neoprene has become almost a standard engineering material, being specified wherever oil, heat, and abrasion resistance are required, such as at oil-refining plants, for hose and accessories in garages and filling stations, and for gaskets for gasoline engines.  It damps out vibration to a much greater extent than rubber; for this and the above reasons, it is widely used in aircraft production, its value being further enhanced by its virtual nonflammability.

The electrical and moisture-absorbent properties of neoprene are inferior to those of rubber, yet its other properties are so advantageous that it is used to sheathe cables which must be nonflammable and abrasion, oil, solvent, and ozone resistant.

Neoprene is utilized in many forms of clothing, such as aprons, hoods, gloves, and boots, for protection against corrosive materials.  It is widely used in making conveyor belts and in other handling materials where oil and abrasion resistance is necessary.  It is employed in the printing field for a variety of purposes, including such uses as rollers and plates.

Neoprenes are important in the field of rubber-type cements.  Of particular interest is the addition of heat-reactive phenolic resins to cement formulations, giving marked improvement in cohesive strength and good adhesion to cotton, nylon, and Dacron fabrics; steel; glass; Lucite; and Formica.

Neoprene-treated paper is reported to be an economical substitute for cotton duck as a filter fabric.  The cost of the paper is about one fifteenth as much as the cotton duck.  The neoprene confers wet strength to the paper and allows the paper to resist the action of dilute acids and alkalies. Neoprene is used as sponge where oil resistance is required.  A gas-evolving agent, such as sodium bicarbonate, is incorporated as a blowing agent.

Not all of the work on chloroprene elastomers has been carried out in the United States.  The other synthetic elastomer-producing countries were interested at a very early stage.  In Russia, for example, Sovprene, a chloroprene elastomer, has long been available.  Numerous patents have been taken out in Germany relating to chloroprene elastomers.

### Polybutadiene

Because natural rubber is principally a polymer of isoprene, it was natural that the early research work on a synthetic approach to rubber was based upon isoprene.  Only after some time was 1,3-butadiene, the lower homolog of isoprene, examined for its possibilities.

Butadiene was identified in 1863, and, even then, it was made in the laboratory in connection with early attempts to make a synthetic elastomer, since it appeared that isoprene had no obvious advantage over butadiene in the quality of the product obtained. For this reason and because butadiene can be synthesized more cheaply and by a greater variety of reactions than isoprene, butadiene has become the basic monomer in most of the present synthetic elastomer production.

In Germany, a synthetic elastomer (Methyl Rubber) was made in limited amounts during World War I. This elastomer was made by the polymerization of methyl isoprene (2,3-dimethyl-1,3-butadiene), in the presence of aniline hydrobromide. The methyl isoprene was obtained from pinacol, in turn obtained from acetone. Because of the high cost and, at that time, the inferior quality of the product, manufacture was discontinued at the close of the war. With the discovery of improved types of synthetic elastomers, however, manufacture of these was begun in Germany at a later date and has been conducted on a substantial scale.

The aldol process was the preferred method for producing butadiene in Germany before and during World War II. Acetylene was hydrated in the presence of a mercury catalyst to form acetaldehyde, the aldehyde treated with dilute potassium hydroxide to convert it to acetaldol, the latter hydrogenated to form 1,3-butylene glycol, and the glycol dehydrated to make butadiene:

$$2CH\!:\!CH + 2H_2O \rightarrow 2CH_3 \cdot CHO \rightarrow CH_3 \cdot CHOH \cdot CH_2 \cdot CHO \xrightarrow{H_2}$$
$$CH_3 \cdot CHOH \cdot CH_2 \cdot CH_2OH \rightarrow CH_2\!:\!CH \cdot CH\!:\!CH_2 + 2H_2O$$

During World War I, the method selected in England was that from $n$-butanol (obtained by fermentation), which involved simultaneous dehydration and isomerization to form 2-butene, addition of chlorine to the latter, and dehydrochlorination of the 2,3-dichlorobutane to form butadiene:

$$CH_3 \cdot CH_2 \cdot CH_2 \cdot CH_2OH \rightarrow CH_3 \cdot CH\!:\!CH \cdot CH_3 \xrightarrow{Cl_2}$$
$$CH_3 \cdot CHCl \cdot CHCl \cdot CH_3 \rightarrow CH_2\!:\!CH \cdot CH\!:\!CH_2 + 2HCl$$

This process was discontinued after the war, but in 1938 an American company began pilot-scale production of butadiene by the same general method, starting with butenes which were available from the cracking of petroleum. The process consisted roughly of a vapor-phase chlorination, separation and pyrolysis at 580°C of the dichlorides produced, and separation and purification of the butadiene fraction formed.

Other methods which reached only the pilot-plant stage in this country just prior to World War II included the production of butadiene by pyrolysis of cyclohexane, butadiene from fermentation of corn to form

2,3-butylene glycol, and butadiene from acetylene (Reppe process). A full-scale plant for the production of butadiene by the latter process was built in Germany during World War II and operated successfully. The process consisted of reaction of formaldehyde with acetylene at 4.5 atmospheres and 100°C in the presence of copper acetylide to form 2-butyne-1,4-diol, hydrogenation of the latter at 300 atmospheres and 120°C in the presence of a copper-nickel catalyst to form 1,4-butanediol, and dehydration of the diol at atmospheric pressure and 280°C over a sodium phosphate catalyst:

$$CH{:}CH \ + \ 2HCHO \rightarrow CH_2OH{\cdot}C{:}C{\cdot}CH_2OH \overset{H_2}{\longrightarrow}$$
$$CH_2OH{\cdot}CH_2{\cdot}CH_2{\cdot}CH_2OH \rightarrow CH_2{:}CH{\cdot}CH{:}CH_2 \ + \ 2H_2O$$

In 1932, an American company began the operation of an experimental plant to produce butadiene from acetylene, the latter made by the electric arc process. When this operation proved to be uneconomical, butene was used as a raw material, and ultimately the dehydrogenation process was developed by which most of the butadiene is produced today.

In Russia, the manufacture of a synthetic elastomer was begun in 1933. This was obtained by the polymerization of butadiene by metallic sodium. Before World War II, all butadiene used as starting material for the manufacture of synthetic elastomers in Russia was made from alcohol obtained by the fermentation of potatoes or grain; some alcohol for butadiene production is now probably being made from petroleum. The Russian one-step process

$$2C_2H_5OH \rightarrow CH_2{:}CH{\cdot}CH{:}CH_2 \ + \ 2H_2O \ + \ H_2$$

has been operated in Russia for at least twenty-five years. It is believed that the butadiene produced in Russia by the one-step process is less than 80 per cent pure as compared with the 98 per cent or better purity of the American product.

Because of the urgent need in the United States for large supplies of butadiene for synthetic elastomer production, extensive research and development work was undertaken by the petroleum industry. Many processes based on existing or potential petroleum raw materials were considered for commercial exploitation during the years of 1940–43, among which were the following: (1) Thermal cracking of hydrocarbons containing four or more carbon atoms, (2) aldol condensation, based upon acetaldehyde derived from petroleum, (3) chlorination-dehydrochlorination of n-butenes, (4) catalytic treatment of alcohol (ethanol) or alcohol-acetaldehyde mixtures, (5) catalytic dehydrogenation of n-butenes, and (6) catalytic dehydrogenation of n-butane.

Of the many processes considered and developed for making butadiene during World War II, the most economical were those utilizing butenes from petroleum which were, however, badly needed for aviation gasoline. As a result, until petroleum sources could be sufficiently expanded, ethyl alcohol became the major source of butadiene, even though the cost of production was at least four times as much as from petroleum. During the war, 60 per cent of the butadiene in the United States was produced by this process. During 1944 alone, more than 700 million pounds of butadiene were derived from alcohol. By 1945, however, petroleum sources were so far developed that more butadiene was made from petroleum than from alcohol, and the production of butadiene from alcohol subsequently declined to zero. It was not until the outbreak of the Korean conflict that the government reactivated alcohol facilities to meet the great demand for styrene-butadiene elastomers.

In the alcohol process, ethyl alcohol is first dehydrogenated to form acetaldehyde

$$CH_3 \cdot CH_2OH \rightarrow CH_3 \cdot CHO + H_2$$

and alcohol and acetaldehyde are converted to butadiene. The latter process, the production of butadiene from alcohol and acetaldehyde, proceeds by a two-step mechanism—condensation and dehydration of acetaldehyde to crotonaldehyde, followed by reduction of crotonaldehyde by the alcohol:

$$2CH_3 \cdot CHO \rightarrow CH_3 \cdot CH:CH \cdot CHO + H_2O$$
$$CH_3 \cdot CH:CH \cdot CHO + C_2H_5OH \rightarrow CH_2:CH \cdot CH:CH_2 +$$
$$CH_3 \cdot CHO + H_2O$$

The dehydrogenation of ethanol is a well-established process. The catalyst is copper on an inert support, promoted with a few per cent of chromium oxide. Single-pass yields of 30 to 40 per cent of acetaldehyde can be obtained at 250° to 300°C, with a final yield, based on consumed alcohol, of 92 per cent or higher. The chief by-products are butyraldehyde, ethyl acetate, and acetic acid, which are recovered and utilized. The production of butadiene from alcohol and acetaldehyde involves the processing of a mixture of approximately 69 per cent alcohol, 24 per cent acetaldehyde, and 7 per cent water (all by weight) over a 2:98 tantala-silica catalyst at 325° to 350°C and at essentially atmospheric pressure. The ultimate yield of butadiene was 60 to 64 per cent of the theoretical.

Alcohol is at present more expensive than petroleum gases as a raw material for butadiene manufacture. Alcohol produced by the fermentation of vegetables will probably remain a relatively expensive raw material for the manufacture of butadiene, although at times of a surplus of molasses, fermentation alcohol may be in a more favorable position than at present. The production of alcohol made synthetically from ethylene derived from petroleum is a growing practice in this country, and this alcohol will probably be more economical than alcohol by fermentation.

Butene dehydrogenation is now the standard method used in the United States. The butene dehydrogenation process was dependent upon the introduction of the fluid catalytic cracking of oil. This process produces large quantities of $C_4$ olefins, including the *n*-butenes needed for one-step dehydrogenation to butadiene.

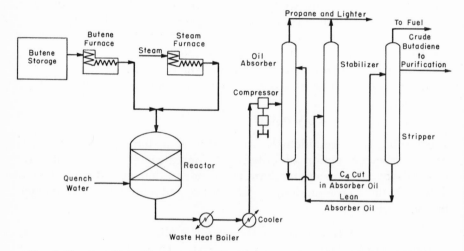

Fig. 9-18.   Butadiene (from butenes) flow sheet.   (*Reprinted from Petroleum Refiner*)

The dehydrogenation step consists of the passage of *n*-butenes and steam through a fixed catalyst bed. The butene is preheated to about 600°C and is mixed at the top of a reactor with steam preheated to 700°C or higher. The use of steam as a diluent, to obtain low *n*-butene partial pressures, has several advantages. At the high temperatures involved, butadiene has a strong tendency to polymerize and to cover catalyst surfaces with carbonaceous deposits. These reactions are minimized by the use of low residence times (a few tenths of a second) and low hydrocarbon partial pressures. Further, necessary reactor temperatures are obtained and the endothermic heat of reaction (22,500 calories per gram mole) is supplied by the superheated steam. The steam is removed from the product gases by simple cooling and condensation. Also, by means of the water-gas reaction, steam either tends to keep the catalyst free of carbonaceous deposits or may be used to remove them from the catalyst. (Cf. the use of steam in this reaction with its use in the dehydrogenation of ethyl benzene to produce styrene.)

A special catalyst mixture had to be discovered which would perform satisfactorily in the presence of large amounts of steam.    Probably the most satisfactory is the one composed of magnesium, cupric, ferric, and potassium oxides.    (The principal portion of the catalyst is magnesium oxide with small amounts of the others.)    A more recent catalyst of greatly improved selectivity has been developed which has been reported to be a chromium oxide-stabilized, calcium-nickel phosphate.

There is at least one plant in the United States now operating by the

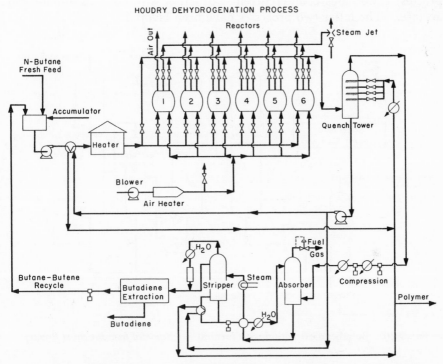

FIG. 9-19.   Butadiene (from butane) flow sheet.   (*Reprinted from Petroleum Refiner*)

single-step dehydrogenation of *n*-butane.   In this process, *n*-butane is preheated to about 625°C and passed through fixed-bed reactors.   Reaction takes place over a chromia-alumina catalyst at about 610°C and at a pressure of 6 inches of Hg absolute.

In all of the major processes for producing butadiene from petroleum, the desired product, butadiene, is contaminated with other hydrocarbons.   Fractionation alone is incapable of separating butadiene of the desired purity from these compounds.   Some of the more important methods that have been used or considered for purifying butadiene are: (1) Azeotropic distillation of crude $C_4$ hydrocarbon fractions with certain compounds, such as ammonia, (2) reversible reaction of butadiene with sulfur dioxide to form a cyclic sulfone

$$CH_2 \cdot CH:CH \cdot CH_2$$
$$\underline{\quad SO_2 \quad}$$

(3) extractive distillation with selective solvents (e.g., furfural), and (4) selective absorption with cuprous salt solutions, including (a recent process) continuous countercurrent extraction with cuprous ammonium acetate. The latter two processes have been favored.

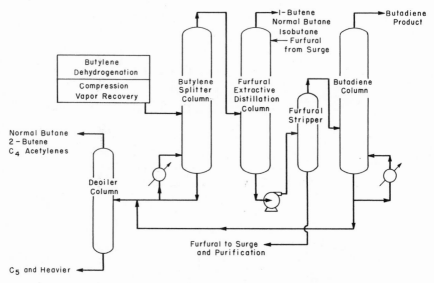

FIG. 9-20.   Butadiene extraction with furfural.   (*Reprinted from Petroleum Refiner*)

Production of butadiene for synthetic elastomer manufacture is an outstanding example of rapid commercial development of a bulk chemical. In the United States in 1940, butadiene was a laboratory reagent handled in small cylinders, whereas one year later it was shipped in railway tankcars.  No other high-purity, synthetic organic chemical had ever before been manufactured in such magnitude.

Butadiene, a colorless liquid which boils at $-5°C$, can be polymerized alone.  Homopolymers of butadiene have not until recently appeared on the American market, but they have been manufactured for many years in Russia and Germany.

Since 1950, liquid (low-molecular-weight) polybutadiene (Butarez) has been manufactured on a small scale.  The process uses a finely dispersed sodium catalyst in a hydrocarbon diluent to control the heat of reaction. It has a molecular weight of approximately 1,300. This liquid polymer, being highly unsaturated and containing cyclo-olefinic rings, thermosets to a hard, transparent coating and has possible uses in protective coatings, as a casting and laminating resin, and as a vulcanizable rubber softener.

Very recently, a new liquid polymer (C-Oil), based on butadiene, has been announced. No information has been released regarding its composition or the polymerization method used in its preparation.

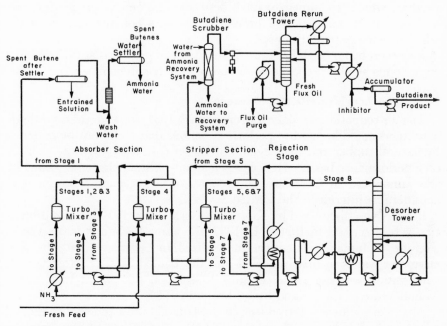

Fig. 9-21. Butadiene extraction with copper salts. (*Reprinted from Petroleum Refiner*)

Early high-molecular-weight butadiene homopolymers were of little commercial value because the elastomer obtained was difficult to process and had poor physical properties. In a new process, reported in 1950, high-abrasion furnace carbon black is mixed with the latex before conversion. Butadiene is mixed with soap and run into a jacketed reactor cooled with methanol. In the refrigerated reactor, butadiene is polymerized at 30°C, using an activated recipe similar to the cold-rubber recipe (see Butadiene-Styrene Copolymers). The reaction takes about ten to twelve hours. The latex is blended with antioxidant, creamed in brine, coagulated with dilute sulfuric acid, dewatered, reslurried, and filtered.

One of the best features of the product is its outstanding processing characteristics.   It can be mixed and extruded at lower temperatures and with lower power requirements than GR-S, cold rubber, or natural rubber.   It is believed that the new product will have its greatest utility in tire treads, probably in blends with cold rubber.   This represents the first successful effort to produce a polybutadiene homopolymer suitable for commercial use in tire treads.

Even more recently, one petroleum company has announced the production of *cis*-1,4-polybutadiene in high yield, using a stereospecific catalyst, which is claimed to have desirable elastomeric properties.   By a slight modification of the process, a *trans*-1,4-polymer can be made which has many potential uses.

However, by far the largest use of butadiene at present is as the principal comonomer in the preparation of elastomeric copolymers.

### Butadiene-Acrylonitrile Copolymers

The introduction of polychloroprene in 1931 showed that synthetic elastomers could be used to perform functions that could not be matched by natural rubber and that, even if of higher cost, they might be cheaper on a performance basis.   Hence, when an oil-resistant elastomer, Buna N, was announced in Germany, the reports of its use were followed with considerable interest in the United States.

Buna N was discovered by Konrad in Germany in 1930, and its properties were described in 1936.   In 1937, the name Perbunan was given to a grade of Buna N being commercialized in Germany, and the new elastomer was then first imported into the United States.   However, its composition was not revealed until 1938 when the patent had issued. Manufacture in the United States began in 1939.

After Perbunan was introduced in the United States and several related polymers had appeared, the class name *nitrile rubber* was given to rubber-like copolymers of unsaturated nitriles with dienes.   Some commercial products are Ameripol, Butaprene, Chemigum, Hycar OR, Paracril, and Polysar N.

For the preparation of nitrile rubbers, many raw materials may be used.   Butadiene and acrylonitrile are by far the most common.   However, in place of butadiene, other dienes, such as isoprene, piperylene, or 2,3-dimethyl butadiene, can be used.   Further, partial replacement of acrylonitrile by the methyl and ethyl homologs has been made experimentally.   Small amounts of other monomers can be added to the two principal components, for example, styrene, methyl methacrylate, ethyl acrylate, or vinylidene chloride.   Specific improvements obtained by the addition of these components are, however, usually obtained at the expense of some other property.

In the emulsion polymerization method for preparing nitrile rubber, which is by far the commonest method, water is used as the dispersing medium. From 180 to 200 parts of water are used per 100 parts of monomer. Distilled, de-ionized, or zeolite-softened water is used, since impurities often have a profound effect upon the polymerization. The water is also often vacuum deaerated in order to remove dissolved oxygen which acts as an inhibitor.

Soaps of fatty acids (oleic, myristic, palmitic) are used to solubilize (by emulsification) the reactants so that the reaction starts in monomer oriented in the micelles (see Chap. 5). Since nonconjugated poly-unsaturation in the emulsifying agent retards the rate of polymerization, many fats are hydrogenated or isomerized before being used for making the soaps. Rosin itself can be used if the nonconjugated unsaturation is removed by hydrogenation or disproportionation. A large number of anionic and cationic emulsifying agents, other than those mentioned above, can also be used by themselves or in addition to soap to modify the course of the polymerization.

The addition of modifiers or regulators (chain-transfer agents) is necessary to regulate the average molecular weight so that the copolymer will be plastic and soluble. If xanthogen disulfides are used at a relatively low temperature, the polymerization can be carried practically to completion and still yield a plastic, easily processed elastomer. When higher mercaptans are used, the polymerization is stopped when it is from 60 to 80 per cent complete; otherwise, the elastomer tends to have a high gel content. A suitable mercaptan modifier is n-dodecyl (lauryl) mercaptan.

Free-radical initiation is generally employed. Peroxides, such as benzoyl peroxide, hydrogen peroxide, potassium persulfate, or cumene hydroperoxide, are used. They are especially effective if there is present a reducing agent which serves to maintain the proper concentration of free radicals (redox system). Mercaptans used as modifiers may also serve this purpose. Others used are aldehydes, sulfites, polyamines, or sugars. This action is promoted by the presence of traces of multivalent ions, such as iron, copper, and cobalt. Salts and organic compounds which form complexes with metal ions are used to buffer the concentration of the ion; sodium pyrophosphate, sodium cyanide, and amino acids are typical examples. A polymerization recipe having a nominal 25 per cent acrylonitrile content is given in Table 9-2.

The polymerization is carried out at as low a temperature as practicable. In general, the lower the polymerization temperature, the more regular is the structure of the polymer, which results in better over-all quality of the product. Temperatures range from a high of 50°C to as low as 5°C. The rate of polymerization is limited, on one hand, by the rate of heat absorption by the cooling medium, and, on the other hand, by the freezing point of the charge. The usual rate of polymerization does not exceed 12 per cent per hour, the complete polymerization usually taking from twelve to forty-eight hours.

TABLE 9-2. NITRILE RUBBER POLYMERIZATION RECIPE

| | |
|---|---:|
| Butadiene . . . . | 75.00 |
| Acrylonitrile . . . . | 25.00 |
| Soap . . . . | 4.50–5.00 |
| Stearic acid . . . . | 0.60 |
| Lauryl mercaptan . . . | 0.50 |
| Potassium chloride . . . | 0.30 |
| Sodium pyrophosphate . . | 0.10–0.20 |
| Ferric sulfate . . . . | 0.02 |
| Hydrogen peroxide . . . | 0.35–0.40 |
| Water . . . . . | 180.00 |

Since nitrile rubber deteriorates rapidly in the presence of metallic impurities and peroxides, a "shortstop," such as hydroquinone, is added to the polymerized latex to destroy radicals and traces of peroxides, and an antioxidant, such as phenyl $\beta$-naphthylamine, is incorporated. Alkyl diphenylamines and hindered alkyl phenols are also used as antioxidants.

The latex is coagulated by flocculating the particles with brine, a sulfonate, and acid. The particles are filtered off on a rotary filter if they are large enough, reslurried in water, and again filtered to remove the soap. Alternatively, the crumbs can be made alkaline to resaponify the soap and are then sheeted on a Fourdrinier, washed, and pressed to form a sheet.

Since there is some cross-linking, the products, in some respects, exhibit the characteristics of slightly scorched natural rubber, with the result that softeners have to be used to impart sufficient plasticity, tack, and processing properties to the mix. Sulfur and accelerators are used for vulcanization, less sulfur being required than for natural rubber, however. The tensile strength of a vulcanized, unpigmented nitrile stock is only a fraction of that of a corresponding natural-rubber compound, but it can be made to closely approach high-grade, natural products by the incorporation of special grades of carbon black. As is true for GR-S, carbon black has a remarkable effect in increasing the tensile strength of compounds made from this copolymer.

By the addition of monomers containing carboxylic acid groups to butadiene and acrylonitrile, active carboxyl groups can be added to the polymer to provide additional active sites for cross-linking reactions which standard products do not have. Vulcanization through the active hydrogen of the carboxyl groups (with zinc oxide) produces an elastomer capable of developing high gum tensile strength. Whereas normal nitrile polymers have a gum tensile strength in the range of 400 to 600 psi and an ultimate elongation of approximately 350 per cent, these recently developed gums can be cured to form products having tensile strengths in excess of 5,000 psi and elongations of more than 500 per cent. Exceptionally good abrasion resistance and excellent low-temperature flexibility are among the unusual qualities of the new polymers.

Nitrile elastomers can be compounded to compare favorably with natural rubber in tensile strength, elongation, and abrasion resistance, but are inferior in adhesion and tear resistance. Their great superiority to both natural rubber and GR-S lies in their excellent resistance to oils, solvents, or chemical reagents, although in some cases chemical resistance is exceeded by that of some of the other synthetic elastomers. They are inherently less resilient than natural rubber by as much as 33 to 60 per cent. Nitrile rubber also has a lower specific resistance than hydrocarbon elastomers because of its molecular polarity.

The property of high oil resistance is the principal factor responsible for the use of nitrile rubbers. This means that the elastomers have low solubility, low swelling, and good resistance to abrasion after immersion in gasoline or oils. The amount of swelling depends upon its compounding, the type of pigmentation, softeners used, and type of cure, although the acrylonitrile content is by far the most important factor. This is shown in Table 9-3, in which nitrile rubbers have been classified broadly on the basis of nitrile content.

TABLE 9-3. CLASSIFICATION OF NITRILE RUBBERS BASED ON NITRILE CONTENT[4]

| Per Cent of Acrylonitrile in Copolymer | Oil Resistance of Vulcanizate |
|---|---|
| 50–60 | Leathery plastic with high resistance to aromatics |
| 35–40 | High oil resistance |
| 25 | Medium oil resistance |
| 15 | Fair oil resistance |
| 2–5 | High swelling in oil |

In general, the nitrile content varies from 15 to 40 per cent. A nitrile content of about 25 per cent is used for general mechanical goods where rubberlike properties are desired over a fairly wide temperature range. Although all products within the range of 15 to 40 per cent nitrile content are resistant to aliphatic hydrocarbons, mineral oils, vegetable oils and fats, only the high nitrile rubber shows good resistance to aromatic solvents. A special polymer containing 15 per cent nitrile is used for fuel tanks. Acrylonitrile elastomers are laminated with another type (natural or GR-S) which swells readily in fuel for self-sealing gasoline tanks for military aircraft.

[4] Whitby, G. S., ed., *Synthetic Rubber*, Table I, p. 799, John Wiley and Sons, New York, 1954.

Although nitrile rubbers swell more in polar solvents than in nonpolar ones, their swelling in water and in antifreeze solutions is low enough to allow their use for automobile radiator hose and similar applications. Their oil resistance is an asset, since oil is sometimes added to antifreeze solutions to reduce corrosion.

The good properties of this elastomer make it extremely useful in the manufacture of carburetor and fuel-pump diaphragms, aircraft hose, and gaskets. Similar applications are gasoline hose for service-station pumps, larger hose for handling oil, and for cables that must be oil- and abrasion-resistant. In these and other applications, the nitrile rubbers compete with Thiokol and neoprene elastomers. Other uses are in molded articles, such as mountings for machinery, shoe soles for service in the presence of oils, and printing rolls, blankets, and plates.

The use of nitrile rubber as a blending agent with other synthetic elastomers and plastics makes it possible to obtain products with particular and useful properties. Nitrile rubber has been blended with natural rubber (with which it is essentially incompatible), with high-styrene copolymers, with polysulfide elastomers, with plasticized poly(vinyl chloride), and with phenol-aldehyde resins.

Butadiene-acrylonitrile copolymers of 25 to 40 per cent nitrile content are particularly valuable as nonvolatile, nonmigrating plasticizers for vinyl chloride copolymers. Nitrile rubber and poly(vinyl chloride) blends form films which are especially useful for food packaging because of their oil resistance and toughness. Microcrystalline wax may be added to decrease still further the water vapor transmission.

Blends of nitrile elastomers and phenolic resins are being used in increasing quantities. The ratio of phenolic resin to nitrile rubber can be varied from low amounts (10 to 25 per cent, based on the nitrile), which have a reinforcing effect, to equal amounts of nitrile and resin. Equal amounts produce hardnesses in the ebonite range but do not have the brittleness of ebonites. By making an ebonite from nitrile rubber, using one sulfur atom per double bond, an excellent bonding agent for grinding wheels is obtained. The addition of nitrile rubber to phenolic resins combines the toughness and flexibility of the elastomer with the high tensile strength and good surface hardness of phenolic resins. The abrasion resistance in certain formulations is remarkable, in some applications even outwearing steel. An adhesive combination of the above, used as a cement or impregnated in tape, is used for the rivetless bonding of brake linings to brake shoes in automobiles (Cyclebond).

Nitrile rubber, particularly as a latex, finds wide application as an adhesive, as a modifier for other water-dispersed resins, as finishing agents for leather, and as impregnants for paper and textiles, particularly non-woven fabrics.

### Butadiene-Styrene Copolymers

Rubber is one of the most important basic raw materials of American industry. Of the world's supply of natural rubber, approximately 97 per cent came from the Far East, principally from British Malaya and the Dutch East Indies. During World War II, not only was the supply of natural rubber largely cut off but also the quantity needed increased. In 1941, the consumptions of natural and synthetic elastomers in the United States were 770,000 and 8,000 long tons, respectively, whereas in 1945, the comparative consumptions were 100,000 and 700,000 tons.

The development and production of butadiene-styrene elastomers in the United States after the beginning of World War II were on a much larger scale than has ever been undertaken for any other synthetic polymer. Hence, it is believed worthwhile to discuss the development of this product in somewhat greater detail than usual.

In 1941, a program for the construction of plants to produce 40,000 tons of butadiene-styrene elastomer annually was made. Later that year, the synthetic rubber program was increased to a capacity of 400,000 annual tons. As the war continued, the program was repeatedly enlarged, and fifteen plants with a capacity of over 700,000 tons annually were eventually constructed.

Prior to the war, neoprene, nitrile, Thiokol, and other specialty elastomers had been manufactured in the United States. Either because of availability of raw materials or cost, these types were not suitable for tires and tubes, which accounted for almost three fourths of the rubber consumption. Fortunately, a number of American laboratories were aware of the development of Buna S in Germany and had performed some research on the emulsion copolymerization of butadiene and styrene. The establishment of a vast industry for the manufacture of synthetic elastomers was undertaken in the United States, the major type produced being GR-S (Government Rubber—Styrene). (It is now made under many names, including Buna S, Butaprene-S, Chemigum IV, Hycar TT, and Buton-S.)

A government agency (the Rubber Reserve) was created to take over-all management of the program, to arrange for information to be exchanged among companies engaged in the program, and to approve of expenditures of government money. The plants were built by the Defense Plant Corporation; then, after the plants were built, Rubber Reserve assumed control and later took over all phases of governmental responsibility, including additional construction.

It was decided to make a product having approximately the same composition as the German Buna-S elastomer. Because of the urgency, the process (the Mutual recipe) and equipment, and the grade of polymer were standardized. To accomplish this standardization, the majority of production facilities were built as identical "standard plants." The "standard plant" design, although representing some compromise among the ideas of the chemists and engineers of different companies, proved to be quite satisfactory.

The conversion (i.e., the polymerization) was conducted by the emulsion process. The study of this technique of polymerization and its rapid improvement in practice have been of great importance in the development of synthetic elastomer (and other polymer) manufacture. In 1917, it took the Germans four months to make Methyl Rubber at room temperature. If copolymerization of butadiene and styrene in the GR-S ratio is carried out by the mass technique without an initiator, almost five months at 55°C is required to accomplish complete polymerization. By using the emulsion process, with suitable initiators, much faster polymerization is obtained. In Germany, where this technique was first used commercially, reaction time was twenty-five to thirty hours at 45° to 50°C. The Mutual recipe adopted in the United States required only twelve to fourteen hours at 50°C. It is now possible to produce a better product at 5°C in only three hours (cold rubber).

Standard GR-S is manufactured by reacting an aqueous emulsion of butadiene and styrene in the presence of soap, polymerization initiators, and regulators at a temperature of 50°C and a pressure of about 45 to 60 psig. The reaction is carried to about 72 per cent of completion, at which point it is terminated by the addition of a "shortstop" (hydroquinone), an antioxidant (phenyl $\beta$-naphthylamine) is added, and the latex is stripped of monomers by vacuum steaming. The recipe, which remained essentially unchanged during the war, is given in Table 9-4.

TABLE 9-4.   POLYMERIZATION RECIPE FOR STANDARD GR-S

| | |
|---|---|
| Butadiene . . . . | 71.00–75.00 |
| Styrene . . . . | 29.00–25.00 |
| Dodecyl mercaptan . . | 0.50 |
| Potassium persulfate . . | 0.20–0.30 |
| Soap (anhydrous) . . . | 4.30–5.00 |
| Hydroquinone . . . | 0.10 |
| Phenyl $\beta$-naphthylamine . | 1.25 |
| Water . . . . . | 180.00 |

Potassium persulfate is used as the initiator in the GR-S formula. When butadiene and styrene are copolymerized in an aqueous emulsion containing only the monomers, emulsifying agents, and a peroxy initiator, the product contains an appreciable quantity of cross-linked polymer which is difficult to process and has little value as an elastomer. By adding to the polymerization system a substance known as a "modifier" or "regulator," which also increases the rate of polymerization and renders the copolymer benzene-soluble, a much easier processing product is obtained. In the preparation of standard GR-S, dodecyl (lauryl) mercaptan is used as the modifier. It functions by a chain-transfer mechanism which decreases the average molecular weight of the polymer (see Chap. 5).

One of the principal advantages of GR-S over unvulcanized German Buna S was the greater softness and plasticity of the former; this was due

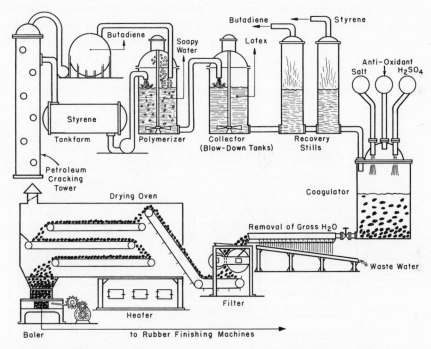

FIG. 9-22. GR-S flow sheet. (Houwink, R., ed., *Elastomers and Plastomers*, Vol. II, Elsevier Publishing Co., Amsterdam (dist. by D. Van Nostrand Co., Princeton, N.J., 1949)

to the relatively high concentration of modifier used in the United States. The modifier used in Germany [bis(isopropyl xanthogen)] retarded the rate of polymerization, hence could be used only in small amounts. The choice of dodecyl mercaptan in the United States was fortunate, not only because of its effectiveness as a modifier, but also because it acted as a reduction activator of the redox type.

The stripped latex is blended and stored in concrete tanks under mild agitation. It is coagulated by the addition of sulfuric acid and salt or by alum. The coagulum is thoroughly washed to remove residual amounts of these agents and soluble polymerization chemicals and is then dried.

Since, at the time the U.S. entered the war, not enough was known about butadiene-styrene polymerization processes to make a continuous polymerization process practical, the plants were designed for batch polymerization. It soon became apparent that a continuous process would have much greater capacity than a batch-operated unit, as well as other advantages, and, as a result, pilot-plant studies on continuous polymerization were carried out. Conversion of some of the reactors was then made and continuous operation was begun early in 1944. Some of the advantages obtained were: (1) The inhibition periods were reduced or eliminated by the maintenance of a closed, oxygen-free system, (2) monomer recovery was smoother because of the constant load on the system, as compared to the surges in batch operation, (3) cooling water

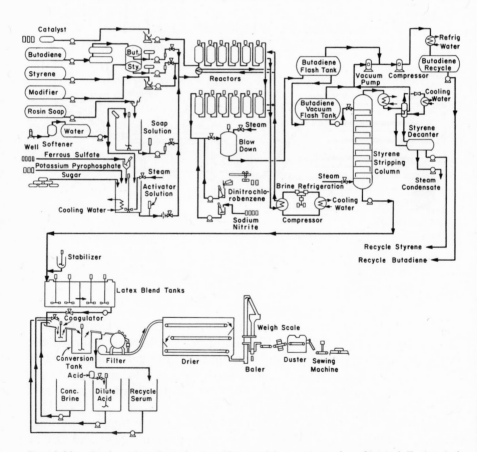

FIG. 9-23.   Cold rubber flow sheet.   (*Reprinted by permission from Chemical Engineering*)

demand leveled off, (4) downtime for charging and discharging batch-wise was eliminated, yielding an appreciable increase in effective capacity, and (5) the polymer produced was equal in quality and better in uniformity to that given by batch operation.

Most of the changes in GR-S manufacture made during the war did not involve radical alterations in the fundamental polymerization recipe. Although it was felt that improvement in polymer quality could be obtained by reducing the temperature of polymerization, the reaction rate dropped off rapidly as the temperature was lowered. During the war, several large-scale polymerizations were carried out at 30°C (instead of at 50°C, the standard GR-S process temperature), but the runs took much longer and little improvement in quality of the polymer was found.

No practical method was known in the United States for carrying out polymerization in a significantly shorter period of time at lower temperatures until immediately after the war, when German redox formulas and their application to polymerization at 5°C (41°F) became available. These formulas were examined and greatly improved and several new low-temperature polymerization systems were discovered. Experimental polymerizations were made in 1946 and 1947 at 5°C; the products were made into tires, and road tests showed marked superiority over tires made from standard GR-S. New furnace blacks developed at about the same time were compounded with the low-temperature polymers and further improved their properties. These products were not only substantially superior to regular GR-S but were better than natural rubber for tread stocks in passenger tires.

The new elastomer was so well received that in 1948 the Rubber Reserve decided to convert a large part of its capacity to the manufacture of cold rubber. Both batch- and continuous-polymerization plants were converted to the new material, and large-scale production was underway in 1949.

A comparison between cold GR-S and regular GR-S illustrates the improvement that has been attained:[5]

|  | Regular GR-S | Cold GR-S |
|---|---|---|
| Ultimate tensile strength, psi | 3,300 | 4,250 |
| Ultimate elongation, % | 630 | 710 |
| Rebound, % | 33 | 38 |
| Flex resistance (flexes to failure) | 100,000 | 320,000 |

The composition of a cold rubber polymerization recipe is given in Table 9-5.

The production of cold GR-S involves the decomposition of a hydroperoxide, forming free radicals, which initiate polymerization by reaction with iron, the latter being introduced as a complex with a pyrophosphate.

[5] Pryor, B. C., Harrington, E. W., and Druesdow, D., *Ind. Eng. Chem.*, **45**, 1311 (1953).

TABLE 9-5.   COLD RUBBER POLYMERIZATION RECIPE

| | |
|---|---:|
| Butadiene | 72.00 |
| Styrene | 28.00 |
| tert-Dodecyl mercaptan | 0.17 |
| Potassium salt of disproportionated rosin | 4.50 |
| Sodium hydroxide | 0.10 |
| Trisodium phosphate | 0.50 |
| Sodium alkyl naphthalene sulfonate-formaldehyde condensation product | 0.10 |
| Potassium pyrophosphate | 0.18 |
| Dextrose | 1.00 |
| Ferrous sulfate heptahydrate | 0.14 |
| Cumene hydroperoxide | 0.01 |
| Water | 200.00 |

Since ferrous iron takes part in the reaction as a reducing agent, it has to be present or polymerization will not occur.   However, the ferrous iron has to be tied up in a nonionized form and released gradually or it will be oxidized too rapidly, with resulting depletion of peroxide initiator. Sodium or potassium pyrophosphate was originally used as the chelating agent to convert the ferrous iron to a sequestered form.   This is a typical redox system of initiation and is used in the preceding recipe.

Recently, all cold GR-S production has been converted to what is known as the "sugar-free" formula.   With only a slight increase in ferrous sulfate and potassium pyrophosphate, dextrose can be eliminated entirely from the recipe.   The activator is slightly lower in cost and is simpler to prepare.   The sugar-free recipe is more sensitive to oxygen inhibition, however.

In 1951, it was found that very small amounts of other metal sequestering or complexing agents, added with the water, reduced the reaction time by as much as four hours.   A typical complexing agent is Versene. Versene Fe-3 is a blend of the tetrasodium salt of ethylene diamine tetraacetic acid and the sodium salt of diethanol glycine.   This material has the ability to hold a large reservoir of ferrous ion in chelated form, releasing it gradually during polymerization as required.

Many other variations of the original recipe, all dependent upon the decomposition of the hydroperoxides by iron, have been devised.   Even the peroxamine recipe, in which no iron is added, although appearing not to depend upon iron, fails to produce polymerization if the reagents used are entirely free from iron (see Table 9-6).   The amount of iron needed in this recipe is very low; e.g., one part in 50 million of the total system; and this quantity is normally contained in the reagents as an impurity.

Most cold GR-S recipes include at least 0.5 part of electrolyte per 100 parts of monomers, in order to maintain the particle size and fluidity of the latex.   Without electrolyte, the latex will gel as it approaches 60 per cent conversion, and agitation and heat transfer would be severely reduced.  Potassium chloride eventually replaced the trisodium phosphate originally used for this purpose.

In place of the benzoyl peroxide widely used in German recipes, cumene (isopropyl benzene) hydroperoxide was employed in the manufacture of the original cold GR-S.   Since then, many new hydroperoxides have been made and investigated.   Cumene hydroperoxide has now been replaced by the more active hydroperoxides of isopropyl cumene and p-menthane, which has made possible the polymerization of cold rubber to 60 per cent conversion in three to ten hours, compared to a former average time of fourteen hours.

A research and development program to reduce the polymerization cycle to thirty minutes or less at 5°C was instituted by one company early in 1951.   Only by achieving this goal could the economic feasibility of making cold GR-S in a tubular reactor of practical length be studied. Production in potentially inexpensive pipe reactors, rather than in present large pressure kettles, is now considered possible.

The term "superfast" was adopted to describe the polymerization recipes developed for use in the pipeline reactor, because reaction rates are fifty times as rapid as those for conventional, commercial, cold-rubber recipes, which are already known as "fast" recipes.   The superfast recipes have been made possible by the availability of very active organic hydroperoxides, increased activator and initiator concentrations, and further refinements of the redox polymerization discoveries.   The rubber produced by this new process promises to be equal in quality to standard cold rubber.

The successful approach to the problem of attaining 60 per cent conversion to polymer in thirty minutes or less at 5°C consisted basically in increasing the concentrations of both the peroxide initiator and iron-pyrophosphate activator of conventional "sugar-free" cold-rubber recipes. Of the six different organic hydroperoxides considered, those initiated with phenyl cyclohexane hydroperoxide exhibited the fastest polymerization rates.   Charges initiated with tert-butyl cumene hydroperoxide were almost as fast.   Replacing potassium pyrophosphate with sodium pyrophosphate unexpectedly doubled the rate of conversion.   It now appears possible that by using a combination of the above reagents, the desired 60 per cent conversion for 5°C GR-S recipes can be reached in under thirty minutes.

The quality of the soaps used as emulsifiers has a large influence upon the initiation and rate of polymerization.   In the standard GR-S recipe, the rate of polymerization is roughly proportional to the concentration of fatty acid soap.   A variety of fatty acids are used to make these soaps, although the standard GR-S formula requires the use of tallow soaps.   The standards now set up for sodium soaps used in standard

GR-S manufacture are quite rigid, and the soaps are tested many times before use. In 1944, another type of emulsifier, a disproportionated rosin soap, came into use for other than standard GR-S recipes. Its behavior closely approximates that of tallow soap.

Although disproportionated rosin soap is still used as the emulsifier in many cold GR-S recipes, others have gained acceptance. For certain products in which rosin must be avoided, potassium fatty acid soap is often used as the sole emulsifying agent. In this case, the peroxamine activation system is usually employed instead of the iron-pyrophosphate system. A typical peroxamine recipe is given in Table 9-6.

TABLE 9-6. TYPICAL PEROXAMINE RECIPE

| | |
|---|---:|
| Butadiene | 72.000 |
| Styrene | 28.000 |
| Potassium fatty acid soap | 4.700 |
| Trisodium phosphate dodecahydrate | 0.800 |
| Tamol N | 0.150 |
| Diethylenetriamine | 0.150 |
| p-Menthane hydroperoxide | 0.120 |
| Ferrous sulfate heptahydrate | 0.002 |
| Versene Fe-3 | 0.020 |
| tert-Dodecyl mercaptan | 0.200 |
| Water | 200.000 |

A more recent formulation used in the production of cold rubber is the sulfoxylate recipe, in which the activator consists of sodium formaldehyde sulfoxylate, ferrous sulfate, and a chelating agent. A typical sulfoxylate recipe is given in Table 9-7.

TABLE 9-7. TYPICAL SULFOXYLATE RECIPE

| | |
|---|---:|
| Butadiene | 70.00 |
| Styrene | 30.00 |
| Potassium soap of disproportionated rosin | 4.50 |
| Trisodium phosphate dodecahydrate | 0.80 |
| Tamol N | 0.15 |
| Sodium formaldehyde sulfoxylate dihydrate | 0.15 |
| Ferrous sulfate heptahydrate | 0.05 |
| Versene Fe-3 | 0.07 |
| p-Menthane hydroperoxide | 0.10 |
| tert-Dodecyl mercaptan | 0.20 |
| Water | 200.00 |

Butadiene may also be polymerized in the presence of sodium, a discovery made by Matthews and Strange in England in 1910; the name Buna is, in fact, derived from Bu (= butadiene) and Na (= sodium). When the polymerization of dienes is initiated by ionic agents, in contrast to those initiated by free radicals, the structure of the polymer chain is greatly influenced by the nature of the additive. Natural rubber and balata are substantially 1,4 addition polymers, whereas GR-S contains about 20 per cent of 1,2 addition. However, sodium produces from butadiene a polymer containing more than half 1,2 structures; potassium, a polymer with a lower; and the alfin-type of catalyst, a polymer with a much lower proportion of 1,2 structures. Because of the marked influence of ionic agents upon the structure of the polymer, and because of the promising results achieved by the new catalyst complexes known as alfin catalysts, and, further, because of the recent remarkable results obtained with ionic catalysts on alkenes, it seems more than likely that the study of ionic catalysts for the polymerization of dienes will be greatly intensified.

Alfin catalysts, very recently developed in the United States by Morton, are derived from the salts of a secondary *al*cohol, combined with those from an ole*fin*. For example, amyl chloride and sodium are reacted to give amyl sodium. Isopropanol is added to destroy at least half of the amyl sodium in such a way as to yield sodium isopropoxide in an extremely fine state of subdivision. Propylene is then passed into the mixture. The reactions are:

$$C_5H_{11}Cl + 2Na \rightarrow C_5H_{11}Na + NaCl$$
$$C_5H_{11}Na + (CH_3)_2CHOH \rightarrow (CH_3)_2CHONa + C_5H_{12}$$
$$C_5H_{11}Na + CH_2{:}CH{\cdot}CH_3 \rightarrow CH_2{:}CH{\cdot}CH_2Na + C_5H_{12}$$

The final catalyst is an insoluble aggregate of ions which is associated with sodium chloride; in fact, half of each aggregate is composed of salt. Coordinate bonds probably hold the aggregate together.

The catalyst, to be effective, must be made from secondary alcohols, at least one branch of which is a methyl group. The olefin must contain the system, $-CH{:}CH{\cdot}CH_2-$, which may even be part of a ring system, as in toluene. Oddly enough, replacement of sodium by potassium destroys the activity of the catalyst, although certain other alkali metals may be used in place of sodium. This catalyst is a three-component system, variation in any component affecting both the rate of polymerization and the molecular weight of the polymer formed.

At a given temperature, alfin-catalyzed polymerizations are completed in a matter of minutes, as compared with hours required by sodium. Alfin-catalyzed polymerizations have been found to produce polymers of high intrinsic viscosity, which are unaffected by the amount of catalyst used; i.e., the reaction appears to be truly catalytic. This is contrary to results of polymerization with an alkali metal, in which the molecular weight of the polymer is decreased with an increased concentration of catalyst. Molecular-weight-distribution determinations have shown that the lowest fraction of an alfin polymer is about $1.5 \times 10^6$, whereas the highest fraction of GR-S is about 750,000 by the same method of measurement. Furthermore, the percentage of 1,2 addition in sodium-catalyzed butadiene polymerizations at 30° to 50°C is approximately 59 to 67 per cent, whereas that in alfin-catalyzed polymerization in the same temperature range is approximately 27 per cent.

The processing difficulties encountered in the practical use of alfin-catalyzed polymers stem from their very high molecular weights and toughness. In order to break down the alfin polymers for suitable viscosity ranges, the use of air appears to be necessary. The aging properties of alfin polymers broken down with air alone seem to be outstanding, especially their flex life, when compared to the effects of aging on milled, low-temperature emulsion polymers and standard GR-S. Polymerization by alfin catalysts, conducted in the presence of oils, has recently shown that polymers possessing reasonably good processing characteristics may be obtained (see oil master-batching below).

The use of sodium hydride has also been investigated for some time. Early work in the United States showed that sodium and lithium hydrides were excellent catalysts for the mass polymerization of butadiene. Physical test data for sodium hydride-catalyzed butadiene and butadiene-styrene copolymers have shown that they are similar to emulsion polymers in stress-strain properties and superior with respect to hysteresis. It appears that sodium hydride-catalyzed butadiene polymers are more similar to emulsion or alfin polymers than to sodium-catalyzed polybutadiene in the amount of 1,2 addition present.

The increased demand by 1950 for both natural and synthetic elastomers was responsible for a study of methods of extension of these products. The principal development is what is known as oil-masterbatched or oil-extended rubber. Oil-extended rubber had gained over 18 per cent of the synthetic elastomer market in the United States by 1953, since it first became commercially available early in 1951. Nearly all of this product goes to tire manufacturers; a small amount is used in footwear. The driving force behind this growth has been economic, since, from a given amount of base polymer, more rubber hydrocarbon can be made at a lower cost.

For many years oil has been used in small amounts as a softener in both synthetic and natural elastomers. Since there was a strong tendency, however, to think of the synthetic elastomers as novel forms of natural rubber, use of oil, known to be harmful in large amounts to natural rubber, met with resistance.

Styrene-butadiene polymers in the vulcanized state may be thought of as long, zigzag polymer chains having relatively few cross-linkages. Soft, lower-molecular-weight polymers between the chains act as an internal lubricant. Without the presence of these softer polymers, the rubber would be too hard for successful processing. Addition of a large amount of oil to regular GR-S makes it too soft, but, if polymerization is carried to a much higher average molecular weight, the product is much harder and contains relatively smaller amounts of lower-molecular-weight polymers. Oil can then be added to reduce the viscosity to a workable range. In effect, oil, in molecular dispersion, replaces lower-molecular-weight polymers as an internal lubricant. Although regular GR-S can be oil-extended, the process is now used only with cold rubber. Oils used are special cuts of standard petroleum refinery feed stocks containing principally naphthenic and aromatic hydrocarbons. In practice, the oil is emulsified with a soap and added to the latex. The two are then co-coagulated. A cold rubber containing 25 per cent of oil has from 10 to 20 per cent more resistance to tread wear in tires than standard cold rubber and is cheaper.

In 1952, another technical development was the successful extension of GR-S with rosin acid derivatives. This work paralleled the 1951 development of oil extension. This is the first successful application of *in situ* polymerization where the extender is an actual part of the emulsion polymerization system.

The amount of vulcanizable unsaturation in butadiene elastomers is less than in natural rubber; hence, the amount of sulfur required for complete vulcanization is less, but more accelerator is necessary. In spite of the use of powerful accelerators, GR-S requires a longer cure than natural rubber and is less susceptible to overcure. It has recently been reported that gamma radiation is effective in curing both natural and synthetic elastomers.

The highly regular, theoretical structure of GR-S is represented by the following skeleton diagram:

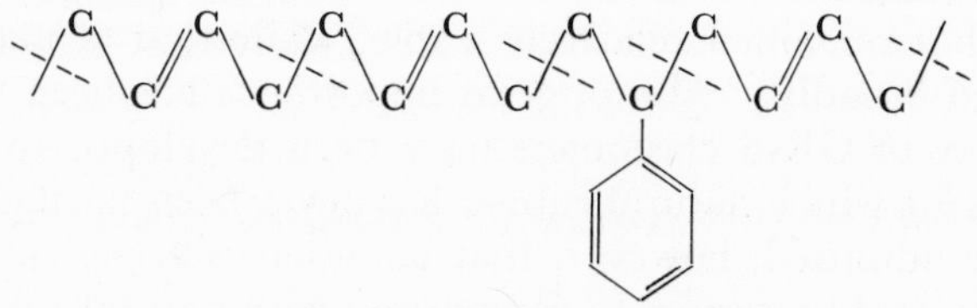

This elastomer shows little tendency to crystallize on stretching (as does natural rubber); this is due to several types of isomerism which, in addition to the presence of the large phenyl groups, decrease the regularity of the molecules, preventing close packing. For example, some styrene radicals probably occur as clusters rather than being evenly distributed along the chains; as mentioned earlier, about 20 per cent of the butadiene adds in 1,2 fashion, instead of 1,4, yielding pendent vinyl groups; polymerization may extend from the pendent vinyl groups or, by chain-transfer reactions, from carbon atoms having allylic-hydrogen atoms on the main chain; and GR-S elastomers contain many more *trans* structures than natural rubber, which is predominantly a *cis*-1,4 polymer of isoprene.

The preceding types of irregularities may be represented by the following sketch:

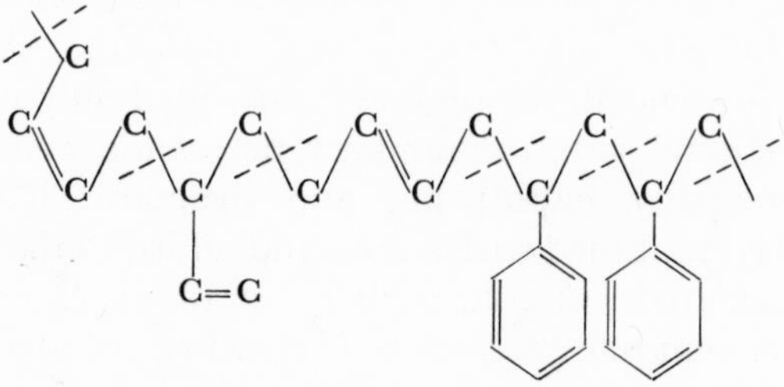

Butadiene-styrene copolymers, like the nitrile rubbers, have comparatively low tensile strengths without the addition of carbon black as reinforcement. In contrast, natural rubber, polychloroprene, and butyl rubber improve little in tensile strength by the addition of carbon black. It is possible that crystalline regions in the latter elastomers have a reinforcing action which can be replaced to some extent in the less crystalline GR-S and nitrile elastomers by fillers. Lignin, a by-product of kraft paper manufacture, has also proved to be an excellent reinforcing agent for GR-S when it is coprecipitated with the latex. It imparts low modulus and high elongation in combination with high tensile strength and hardness to vulcanizates. It is only about three fourths as heavy as carbon black and it has low tinting strength, thus permitting the manufacture of colored products.

GR-S elastomers excel over natural rubber in some properties, such as stability on aging, but particularly in availability and relatively low cost. Their price has remained relatively stable, while that of natural rubber has fluctuated broadly. Also of great importance has been the fact that a wide variety of GR-S elastomers have been developed to meet many special needs for which natural rubber has never been satisfactory.

It must be admitted, however, that butadiene-styrene copolymers are deficient in several properties in comparison with natural rubber. GR-S vulcanizates lack the quick reversible extensibility, liveliness, and resilience of the best Hevea vulcanizates. They also show excessive heat build-up upon flexing (hysteresis); this is one of the reasons that they have not been very satisfactory, when used alone, for the carcass portions of truck and airplane tires. GR-S is poorer in tear resistance, but superior in aging properties and abrasion resistance. Neither GR-S nor natural-rubber vulcanizates exhibit good flexibility at very low winter temperatures or particularly good chemical stability at elevated temperatures for long periods of time.

Since GR-S is a pure hydrocarbon, it has excellent electrical characteristics and is extensively used both for insulation and protective sheathing of cables. While resembling natural rubber in electrical characteristics, it has much better moisture resistance and retains its electrical properties at high operating temperatures for much longer periods of time. It also has good resistance toward ozone. GR-S allows the passage of less air than does rubber.

GR-S is a general-purpose elastomer, and its applications include almost the entire range of elastic products. It is not, however, used where extreme temperature conditions are encountered or in the presence of oils, solvents, or chemicals in general. It is dissolved or swelled by aromatic and chlorinated hydrocarbons.

It is of interest to indicate the approximate distribution of uses for the principal elastomers in the United States:

1. The tires for passenger car and small trucks contain at least 80 per cent GR-S, the rest being natural rubber, whereas in large truck tires the ratio is reversed.

2. Until recently, about 95 per cent of the butyl rubber made was consumed in transportation products. Almost all inner tubes, except those for the largest truck tires, are made of butyl rubber. With the recent change to tubeless tires, Butyl is being exploited for many other uses.

3. Neoprene shows an opposite distribution; almost all is used in non-transportation products, the largest consumption being for wire and cable insulation and the next largest for hose. Of all elastomers used for wire and cable insulation and sheathing, almost 90 per cent is either neoprene or GR-S, the rest being natural rubber.

4. Almost 80 per cent of hard rubber is made from GR-S, most of the remainder being natural rubber.

5. Although more than 70 per cent of boots, galoshes, and allied foot-wear is made from natural rubber, heels and soles use principally GR-S (over 80 per cent).

6. GR-S is used almost exclusively for rubber flooring.

7. Latex foam sponge rubber uses approximately 70 per cent natural rubber, the rest being GR-S. This does not include plasticized poly-(vinyl chloride) or urethane foams, the use of which has recently grown rapidly.

Since the end of World War II, large quantities of high styrene-butadiene copolymers have been made. These are discussed under Polystyrene.

The development of high-strength, rubber-to-steel adhesives long has been an important goal of the rubber industry. A number of products are available, made largely from chlorinated or cyclized rubbers. Although some of these have been highly successful, they have not been able to supersede the older brass-plating processes entirely, where maximum

strength and permanence of bonding are desired.    Copolymers of butadiene and acrylic or methacrylic esters have been studied.    Because of the
polar nature of the carboxyl group and its ability to promote metal
adhesion, such products are considered to be particularly promising as
rubber-to-steel adhesives.

In closing, it is pertinent to point out that the continuation of a huge
synthetic elastomer industry in peacetime is peculiarly an American
achievement, partly, of course, due to our geographical location with
respect to rubber-producing areas.    Only after years of experimentation
has Great Britain's chemical industry decided (in 1956) to establish a
similar industry, but, even so, it intends only to enter the field of special-
purpose products.

## AROMATIC VINYL COMPOUNDS

### POLYSTYRENE

Styrene is the simplest aromatic compound having an unsaturated
side-chain.    Prior to 1930, styrene monomer and polymer were more or
less laboratory curiosities, even though Simon in 1839 published an
article identifying styrene.    A commercial development program was
successfully prosecuted in Germany about 1930, and, in the United States,
one company undertook the production of styrene on a commercial scale
as early as 1925; this venture was, however, short lived.    About 1930 a
research program was begun in the United States for a better process of
manufacture which led to the ultimate development of a cheap and
plentiful supply of styrene.    Large-scale commercial production of
styrene monomer was undertaken in 1937.

Styrene is of particular value in industry in view of its widespread use
in synthetic elastomer manufacture (see Butadiene-Styrene Copolymers)
and because of the remarkably good properties of its polymers made by
injection-molding techniques.    Of the approximately 1 billion pounds of
styrene consumed in 1955, 50 per cent went into polystyrene, 40 per cent
into GR-S elastomers, about 5 per cent into other styrene-butadiene
copolymers, and 5 per cent into miscellaneous uses.

The early method in the United States for the preparation of styrene
involved the dehydrochlorination of monochloroethyl benzene, made by
the chlorination of ethyl benzene, in turn obtained by the Friedel-Crafts
alkylation of benzene with ethyl chloride.    However, the product contained some ring-bound chlorine, which discolored the styrene, and the
process was too costly.

The present commercial process (Dow process) may be outlined by two simple reactions. Ethyl benzene is formed by the alkylation of benzene with ethylene:

$$\bigcirc + CH_2{:}CH_2 \xrightarrow[95°C]{AlCl_3} \bigcirc CH_2{\cdot}CH_3$$

Purified ethyl benzene is then dehydrogenated catalytically in the presence of steam to yield styrene:

$$\bigcirc CH_2{\cdot}CH_3 \xrightarrow{630°C} \bigcirc CH{:}CH_2 + H_2$$

In the first step, ethylene and benzene are reacted in the presence of aluminum chloride and hydrogen chloride under anhydrous conditions,

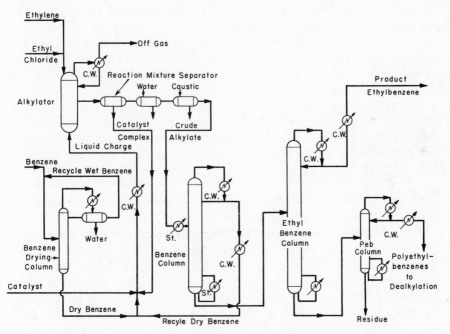

FIG. 9–24. Ethyl benzene flow sheet. (*Reprinted from Petroleum Refiner*)

forming ethyl benzene and more highly alkylated benzenes. High-purity ethylene is not necessary so long as the impurities are hydrogen, light hydrocarbons, or other inert materials. Acetylene is avoided, since it increases catalyst consumption. The ethylene used averages 95 per cent purity, although the process can operate satisfactorily at much lower purities. The benzene used is known as "styrene grade," which corresponds to a purity slightly above 99 per cent. Aluminum chloride, having a minimum purity of 97.5 per cent, is used as the alkylation catalyst. A small amount of ethyl chloride is added to provide hydrogen chloride (as well as ethyl groups), which is necessary to promote high catalyst efficiency.

The alkylation reaction is a reversible one which, at the temperature used commercially, results in an equilibrium mixture of 18 per cent benzene, 51 per cent ethyl benzene, and 31 per cent higher alkylated benzenes. To obtain satisfactory yields, the ratio of ethyl groups to benzene rings in the mixture is reduced and the higher alkylated compounds formed are recycled.

The second step, the dehydrogenation of ethyl benzene, is an endothermic reaction. Since a volume increase occurs with dehydrogenation, decreased pressure aids the reaction. Rather than operate this high-temperature reaction under reduced pressure, steam is added to reduce the partial pressure of the reactants. By the addition of 2.6 pounds of steam per pound of ethyl benzene the partial pressure of the reaction products is reduced to about 0.1 atmosphere. While the theoretical equilibrium at 630°C without steam would give less than 30 per cent styrene in the liquid product, the addition of steam shifts the equilibrium so that a theoretical styrene yield of more than 80 per cent is possible. However, at this temperature, the reaction rate is too slow for practical use. At higher temperatures, at which the reaction rate and the equilibrium would be more favorable, cracking reactions are also increased. Fortunately, certain metallic oxides (zinc, magnesium, iron, aluminum), bauxite, and particularly activated charcoal specifically catalyze the dehydrogenation reaction and permit a high reaction rate at temperatures low enough to minimize cracking reactions.

The addition of steam is advantageous for several other reasons. The superheated steam provides the heat necessary for the dehydrogenation reaction. By mixing the steam with the ethyl benzene just before reaching the catalyst, side reactions are minimized. The use of superheated steam eliminates the necessity for direct heating of the ethyl benzene, so that decoking of furnace tubes is unnecessary. The steam continuously removes carbon deposits on the catalyst by the water-gas reaction, thus eliminating the need for periodic regeneration of the catalyst, which is good for a year or more of active life. The dehydrogenation step is thus a continuous operation, giving ultimate yields of 90 to 92 per cent at conversions of 35 to 40 per cent per pass.

The mixture fed to the dehydrogenation step must have a very low diethyl benzene content, since this material will be converted to divinyl benzene which would polymerize rapidly to form insoluble products

during the purification steps.   If ethyl benzene is overdehydrogenated,
phenyl acetylene is formed.   The use of activated charcoal as a dehydrogenation catalyst enables a lower cracking temperature to be maintained
and minimizes the formation of this impurity.   This material, which is
a polymerization inhibitor and is kept below about a 0.02 per cent concentration in the final product, can be removed by a flash-type hydrogenation of the products from the dehydrogenation step, using the
hydrogen formed and a Raney nickel catalyst.   Since it boils at only
2°C below styrene, separation by physical means is not feasible.

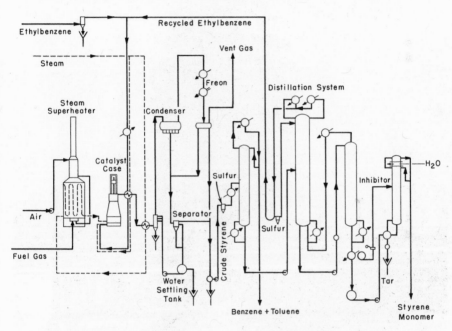

FIG. 9-25.   Styrene flow sheet.   (*Reprinted from Petroleum Refiner*)

The final step is the purification of the crude, dehydrogenated material.
This is the most difficult phase of styrene manufacture.   The boiling
points of ethyl benzene and styrene differ by only 9°C at atmospheric
pressure.   Further, since the rate of polymerization of styrene increases
rapidly with increase in temperature, distillation of styrene at its normal
boiling point (145°C) is not feasible.   In addition, the presence of very
small quantities of certain impurities catalyze the polymerization reaction;
inhibition is accomplished by the addition of elemental sulfur.   Only by
the use of vacuum distillation, inhibition, and special column design can
styrene be purified successfully by distillation.

Since the presence of sulfur is not desirable in the final product, a different inhibitor, usually *p-tert*-butyl catechol, is added for protection during storage and shipment. A more recent variation of this process uses iron oxide as the dehydrogenation catalyst and hydroquinone instead of sulfur as the inhibitor during distillation.

FIG. 9-26.　This elaborate styrene monomer distillation column is a good example of chemical engineering design at work.　(*Courtesy Monsanto Chemical Co.*)

During the latter part of World War II, another method (Carbide and Carbon process) was used commercially to make styrene. The first step (alkylation) was similar to that of the Dow process, except that it was carried out under pressure. However, because of the difficulty of the ethyl benzene–styrene distillation step, a chemical separation method rather than a physical one was employed. The process involved oxidation, hydrogenation, and dehydration to convert the ethyl benzene to styrene.

$$\text{C}_6\text{H}_5\text{--CH}_2\text{·CH}_3 \xrightarrow[125°\text{C}]{(O)} \text{C}_6\text{H}_5\text{--CHOH·CH}_3 + \text{C}_6\text{H}_5\text{--CO·CH}_3 + \text{C}_6\text{H}_5\text{--COOH}$$

Ethyl benzene was oxidized in the liquid phase with air, using manganese acetate as the catalyst. The products included $\alpha$-phenyl ethyl alcohol, acetophenone, and benzoic acid. The latter was removed by a caustic wash, unreacted ethyl benzene was removed by vacuum distillation, and a subsequent vacuum distillation isolated the acetophenone and phenyl ethyl alcohol. Hydrogenation of the latter mixture in the liquid phase at 150°C and 150 psi, using a copper-chrome-iron catalyst, converted the acetophenone to phenyl ethyl alcohol. This alcohol was then passed in the vapor phase over an aluminum or titanium oxide catalyst, which dehydrated the alcohol to form styrene:

$$\text{C}_6\text{H}_5\text{--CHOH·CH}_3 \xrightarrow{200°-250°\text{C}} \text{C}_6\text{H}_5\text{--CH:CH}_2 + \text{H}_2\text{O}$$

The advantage of this process was that the distillation steps were much simpler than those in the Dow process, but, since the economics of this process depended upon utilization of the intermediates and by-products and the over-all yield of styrene (80 per cent), which was lower than that by the hydrogenation method (90 per cent), the process was discontinued for a few years, then was resumed in 1954 because of the increased demand for the by-products.

One other process (Koppers) is in use. This is a vapor-phase alkylation, using a silica-alumina or supported phosphoric acid catalyst at greater than 300°C and 600 psi. Since no provision is made for dealkylation of polyethyl benzenes, the ethylene-benzene feed ratio is kept very low—about 0.2. This, of course, results in higher yields of ethyl benzene, based on ethylene.

A new means of obtaining ethyl benzene went into commercial production in 1957. The ethyl benzene is obtained directly from a mixed xylene stream, containing 15 to 18 per cent ethyl benzene, from gasoline refinery operations. The principal deterrent to the recovery of ethyl benzene in refinery products previously has been the need for critical separation of components boiling only 4 degrees apart. This is now accomplished by the use of very tall and efficient fractionating towers. After separation, the ethyl benzene is converted into styrene by the usual dehydrogenation process.

Pure styrene boils at 145°C, has a density of 0.90, and a freezing point of $-30°C$. It has a sweet, pleasant odor when pure, but usually has a sharp, penetrating odor caused by the presence of aldehydes formed when exposed to air.

The polymerization of styrene proceeds readily, using all methods of polymerization, under the influence of heat alone and/or an initiator. Styrene not only will homopolymerize in the presence of inert materials, such as solvents, fillers, dyes, pigments, plasticizers, rubbers, and resins, but, in addition, forms a huge variety of copolymers. The polymer has the following regular structure:

$$—CH—CH_2—CH—CH_2—CH—CH_2—$$

The rate of the thermal mass polymerization increases exponentially with temperature, requiring months at room temperature but only a few hours at 150°C. The higher the polymerization temperature, however, the lower is the average molecular weight of the polymer formed. As with most polymers, the low-molecular-weight products are weak and brittle, while those of high molecular weight, although much tougher, are more difficult to fabricate. Table 9-8 shows the relationship between temperature of polymerization and the average molecular weight of the polymer produced in an uncatalyzed (thermal) polymerization.

TABLE 9-8.   THERMAL POLYMERIZATION OF STYRENE[6]

| Polymerization Temperature °C | Initial Rate of Polymerization % per Hour | Weight-Average Molecular Weight |
|---|---|---|
| 60 | 0.089 | 2,250,000 |
| 80 | 0.462 | 880,000 |
| 100 | 2.15 | 420,000 |
| 120 | 8.5 | 230,000 |
| 140 | 28.4 | 130,000 |

It is interesting to compare the rate of polymerization of styrene in Table 9-8 with the rate of polymerization when catalyzed. Table 9-9 shows the relation between the initial rate of polymerization and the molecular weight of the product (from viscosity measurements) of a solvent-polymerized styrene monomer initiated with benzoyl peroxide at 50°C.

The rate of polymerization may be greatly increased by the use of reduction activation. For example, a redox initiator in an aqueous

[6] Adapted from Boundy, R. H. and Boyer, R. F., *Styrene*, p. 216, Reinhold Publishing Corp., New York, 1952.

TABLE 9-9.   CATALYZED POLYMERIZATION OF STYRENE[7]

| Benzoyl Peroxide % | Initial Rate % per Hour | Molecular Weight |
|---|---|---|
| 0.0 | 0.045 | 5,500,000 |
| 0.4 | 0.560 | 1,500,000 |
| 1.0 | 0.900 | 1,000,000 |
| 2.0 | 1.250 | 700,000 |
| 4.0 | 2.000 | 540,000 |
| 6.0 | 2.300 | 400,000 |

system gave a 60 per cent conversion in four hours at 40°C and 100 per cent in nine hours.   At 70°C, 60 per cent conversion was obtained in thirty to forty minutes and 100 per cent in ninety minutes.   This clearly illustrates the tremendous acceleration in the rate of polymerization obtainable under certain conditions with some monomers.

As has been seen, it is possible to obtain polymers of widely varying molecular weights by adjustment of the conditions of polymerization. Although polymers having molecular weights in the millions can be made, the most useful products for molding have molecular weights of about 125,000, while polymers of still lower molecular weights (about 35,000) are used in the surface-coating industry.

Although styrene has been polymerized commercially by all known methods of polymerization, it is largely economic forces which determine which method is used.   For large-scale plants, the emulsion process requires less capital investment, the suspension process gives the lowest conversion cost, and the mass process gives the lowest total cost.   The final choice of which plant to install is a matter of specific circumstances and a balance between product quality, capital available, and versatility of equipment.   A discussion of the methods of polymerization and relationship of the various methods to the average molecular weight and purity of the products obtained may be found in Chapter 5.

Commercial polystyrene is a clear, transparent, thermoplastic material, capable of transmitting slightly more than 90 per cent of white light. In these properties, polystyrene closely resembles the methacrylic polymers.

Polystyrene softens slightly above 100°C and becomes a viscous fluid at temperatures around 185°C.   It has a heat distortion temperature of 75° to 85°C, a twenty-four-hour water absorption of about 0.04 per cent, and a tensile strength of 6,000 to 8,500 psi.   Its density of 1.05 makes it one of the lightest plastics.

Polystyrene is resistant to acids, alkalies, alcohols, and to vegetable

[7] Adapted from Boundy, R. H. and Boyer, R. F., *Styrene*, p. 249, Reinhold Publishing Corp., New York, 1952.

oils, fats, or waxes. It is readily soluble in aromatic and chlorinated hydrocarbons and many esters and ketones, whereas it is swelled but not dissolved by aliphatic hydrocarbons and acetone.

Although thermoplastic, polystyrene has very good dimensional stability at room temperature, since it exhibits little cold flow. It is an excellent electrical insulator, having dielectric properties equivalent to those of fused quartz. Its water resistance is outstanding, although, oddly enough, it is permeable to water vapor.

Polystyrene is available commercially for many uses, among which molding compounds rank first in volume (Dylene, Lustrex, Styron). These are available in colorless and colored grades, both transparent and opaque. Of particular interest is the steadily increasing use of this plastic in injection molding, partially replacing cellulose esters. Compression molding is rarely used with polystyrene because the costs are greater and the processing is more difficult, except for the acrylonitrile-modified polymers (see below) which process more easily.

For most applications, polystyrene plastics are used unmodified except in some cases by the addition of pigments, dyes, and lubricants. Since a wide range of softening temperatures and flow characteristics can be obtained by modification of the polymerization process to produce polymers of varying molecular weights, plasticizers are seldom used. Further, the excellent electrical resistance and low moisture absorption are unfavorably affected by their inclusion. Because of the desirable transparency of the polymer, fillers are also rarely used. An exception to this was a product (Styramic) which consisted of polystyrene filled and plasticized with a high-melting, chlorinated biphenyl. This was originally developed primarily as a superior high-frequency insulating material having greater heat resistance than the early polystyrene polymers, which have subsequently been improved.

Polystyrene has also been fabricated into a wide variety of extruded shapes, including monofilaments and oriented sheets (Polyflex, Styroflex). There are on the market expanded forms of polystyrene (Styrofoam) which recently have even been used in an experimental house for the load-bearing walls. It has been claimed that over-all cost for the average home can be reduced almost 10 per cent by its use. Further, because of the excellent insulating qualities of the material, lower first cost of heating and air-conditioning units and lower fuel and electric costs are obtained.

Many important and novel uses of polystyrene depend upon its optical properties. The light transmission of this plastic is not quite as high as that of poly(methyl methacrylate), but it is slightly better than that of the best plate glass. Thus, like poly(methyl methacrylate), the exceptional clarity and transparency of polystyrene lead to such uses as "unbreakable glass" for gauges, windows, and lenses, as well as in countless specialties and novelties. It has a high refractive index (1.60) which, combined with its clarity, allows polystyrene to "bend" light around corners, so that it is used for the edge-lighting of indicators and dials, introduction of "cold" light where heat is objectionable, and manufacture of reflectors.

Polystyrene has fair light stability for all uses except those involving exposure to sunshine or ultraviolet light for a long period of time. The aging of the polymer is due to the photochemically catalyzed addition of oxygen to residual unsaturated groups. Polystyrene is stabilized by strong organic amines [cf. poly(vinylidene chloride) which requires only an extremely mild acid acceptor].

As mentioned under Polymethacrylates, extensive research was undertaken in 1940 to investigate the feasibility of using plastic lenses in military optical instruments. Of the many compounds studied, polystyrene and poly(cyclohexyl methacrylate) were found to possess characteristics sufficiently desirable to warrant production.

Because of its excellent electrical characteristics, extremely low moisture absorption, and good dimensional stability, polystyrene has the distinction of having better electrical properties than most other plastics known at the present time and was one of the major reasons for commercial interest in the resin in the early stages of its development. The volume and surface conductivity and the power factor of polystyrene are almost zero. Furthermore, these properties vary only slightly with changes in temperature and humidity, and are unaffected by alcohol, acids, and caustic. For these reasons, the polymer is widely used in the manufacture of capacitors, insulators, coils, cables, radomes, and many other components for the electrical industry.

The major drawback of polystyrene for electrical applications is its relatively low heat distortion temperature. This has also been a deterrent to its use in other applications. As a result, many attempts have been made to improve polystyrene, so far as its poor heat and solvent resistance and low impact strength are concerned.

Among the early commercial attempts to produce improved polystyrene resins was the chemical modification of the styrene molecule. The only product of this type produced commercially was polydichlorostyrene. Heat distortion temperatures of 110° to 120°C were obtained, which permitted hot-water sterilization of molded objects. Most of the other excellent properties of polystyrene were retained, and, in addition, the high chlorine content conferred nonflammability. However, the impact resistance was not improved and the specific gravity was increased. Copolymers of dichlorostyrene with butadiene produce an elastomer which is superior to regular GR-S in heat resistance and in other properties.  A polydichlorostyrene has been marketed under the trade name of Styramic H. T.  Because of the high cost of the monomer, dichlorostyrene polymers have not achieved large commercial acceptance and have been used only for specialized applications.

One of the first products exploited was a series of styrene-fumarodinitrile copolymers.  These products had heat distortion temperatures of 105° to 120°C.  Unfortunately, the high cost of these products also has limited their commercial acceptance.

Another early attempt involved the addition of small amounts of $p$-divinyl benzene.  As little as 1 per cent produces cross-linked resins with heat distortion temperatures up to 115°C.  These products are, of course, no longer thermoplastic and cannot be molded.  They are available only as cast rods and sheets for machining into small electrical components.  Because of this limitation, they have attained only restricted commercial use.

A much more fruitful modification of styrene has been by copolymerization with minor amounts of other monovinyl monomers.  Although almost every conceivable type of copolymer has been investigated, relatively few have shown sufficient promise to warrant commercial consideration.

With the return of natural rubber after World War II, some of the temporarily surplus styrene and butadiene found use in high-styrene copolymers.  These products, containing 50 to 85 per cent styrene and made by emulsion polymerization, have found use in reinforcing natural and synthetic elastomers.  The properties of natural-rubber vulcanizates containing high-styrene resins differ in some respects from those obtained with GR-S or nitrile elastomers.  The stiffness, hardness, and abrasion resistance are increased, but the tensile strength, per cent elongation, tear resistance, and flex life tend to decrease.

The above products have found particular application in the manufacture of shoe heels, rubber flooring, hard-board stocks, gaskets, caster wheels, electrical insulation, hard-rubber stocks, and many other mechanical goods.  A large percentage of "leather" shoe soles now made probably consist of combinations of a synthetic elastomer and special butadiene-styrene resins.  In the impact-resistant plastics field, where a relatively small amount of rubber is used to plasticize the resin, the products have been used to make golf ball covers, cutting blocks, football helmets, bowling balls, luggage, printing plates, and golf club heads.

High-styrene resin latices have also found considerable use in protective coatings, especially in industrial masonry paints and concrete floor finishes, and in stucco paints, traffic paints, and plaster sealers.  Their most distinctive virtues are that they are resistant to the alkali present in fresh masonry surfaces; they are resistant to water, yet may be formulated to permit a slow rate of moisture vapor transmission necessary in porous masonry coatings; they are resistant to acids and alkalies, sunlight, detergents, and to animal, vegetable, and mineral oils; and they form tough films on masonry that rarely check or peel, flake, or crack. In addition, they are of value as metal primers; as brewery, laundry, and dairy paints; as wallpaper coatings; and in sand finishes and screen inks. Another application of considerable interest is in the formulation of heat-sealing, greaseproof, moisture-vapor-proof solvent coatings for paper. These resins alone are not rigid enough for structural purposes.

Styrene-isoprene copolymers have also been produced for essentially the same end uses as the butadiene copolymers. Styrene-maleic anhydride heteropolymers and derivatives have long been known and have enjoyed application in the textile field. More recently, they have been used as thickening and stabilizing agents, adhesive ingredients, protective colloids, coating resins, and emulsifying agents.

Acrylonitrile has been copolymerized with styrene to produce moldable products having somewhat increased heat distortion temperatures (90° to 100°C) and greater strength and improved weathering characteristics than standard polystyrene. Copolymers of styrene with 5 to 50 per cent acrylonitrile or related monomers are resistant to gasoline and are insoluble or only slightly attacked by carbon tetrachloride; they may be swollen but are not dissolved by aromatic compounds but are soluble in ketones. They are not as thermally stable as polystyrene and are more difficult to fabricate; they have a slightly higher water absorption than polystyrene and are incompatible with the homopolymer.

The most important class of modified styrene plastics for structural applications consists of blends of polystyrene or styrene copolymers with compatible elastomeric materials. There are two basic types of blends available commercially. One type consists of polystyrene combined with a minor amount (probably 10 to 25 per cent) of a styrene-butadiene elastomer. These products, characterized as medium impact materials, have lower tensile strength, higher impact resistance, and heat distortion temperatures approximately equal to unmodified polystyrene.

The most interesting styrene-based plastics for structural uses, however, are the styrene-acrylonitrile copolymers blended with elastomeric butadiene-acrylonitrile copolymers. Most commercial products contain 10 to 25 per cent of elastomer. These products, referred to as acrylonitrile copolymer blends, have been used commercially for several years. They are characterized by high impact strength, fair heat distortion temperatures (80° to 90°C), and excellent molding and extrusion properties. Acrylonitrile copolymer blends have found their greatest acceptance in the form of extruded pipe, which is being used in rapidly increasing quantities in the chemical process, petroleum, and gas industries.

Since protective coatings consume a significant portion of resin production, considerable effort has been expended on the development of
oil-compatible resins from styrene.   Although styrene alone has been used
to a limited extent in the coatings field; that is, in low-molecular-weight
styrene resins and styrene resins modified by plasticization or with phenol
or phenol-aldehyde copolymers; its widest acceptance has been in combination with drying oils which are used as a component of alkyd resins.
Since polystyrene is not compatible with drying oils, a chemical means
was sought for combining styrene monomer with drying oils in order to
obtain homogeneous products with desirable properties.   It was found
that styrene monomer would react or polymerize to some extent with the
unsaturation present in the fatty acid residues of vegetable oils.   In
general, the conjugated oils form homogeneous resins with styrene but
have a tendency toward gelation, whereas the unconjugated oils do not
always form clear resins because of insufficient oil-styrene interaction.
Useful products can, however, be made, and many are commercially
available.   These styrenated oils are used alone or can be used as a
component of alkyd resins.   In either case, they are characterized by
rapidity of "dry" (see Alkyd Resins, Chap. 8).

### POLY($\alpha$-METHYL STYRENE)

The major portion of the $\alpha$-methyl styrene manufactured is made by
the dehydrogenation of isopropyl benzene (cumene).   The first step
involves the alkylation of benzene with propylene to form cumene:

$$\bigcirc + CH_2:CH\cdot CH_3 \xrightarrow[95°C]{AlCl_3} \overset{H_3C\cdot C\cdot CH_3}{\bigcirc}$$

The purified cumene is dehydrogenated catalytically in the presence
of steam:

$$\overset{H_3C\cdot C\cdot CH_3}{\bigcirc} \xrightarrow[600°C]{} \overset{H_3C\cdot C:CH_2}{\bigcirc} + H_2$$

The crude product from the dehydrogenation step is then refined to a
purity of 97 per cent or higher by continuous distillation.   It can be seen
that the whole process is very similar to the Dow process for the manufacture of styrene.

Pure $\alpha$-methyl styrene is a colorless liquid having a boiling point of
165°C, a freezing point of $-23$°C, and a density of 0.90.   The pure
monomer exhibits little tendency to polymerize by thermal or free-radical

initiation. Under normal peroxide initiator systems and also with concentrated sulfuric acid, only dimers and low-molecular-weight polymers are formed. However, the monomer readily polymerizes under the influence of Friedel-Crafts catalysts (cationic polymerization) at low temperatures, yielding homopolymers of high molecular weight. Sodium, aluminum chloride, titanium tetrachloride, and boron trifluoride have been used. It is interesting to note that copolymerization of α-methyl styrene with other unsaturated monomers does occur, using peroxide initiators. Also of interest is the fact that α-methyl styrene will copolymerize with maleic anhydride; this reaction is unique in that neither monomer polymerizes by itself under the influence of peroxide initiators.

Just as the α-methyl group increases the stiffness of methacrylates as compared to acrylates, so it increases the stiffness of poly(α-methyl styrene) as compared to polystyrene. Poly(α-methyl styrene) has a higher melt viscosity, greater solvent resistance, lower elongation, and is harder than polystyrene.

Although α-methyl styrene has been used as a plastic in its own right, as a component of synthetic elastomers, and as a plasticizer, its principal use has been as a modifier of styrene in the reaction of styrene with drying oils. The mass copolymerization of a mixture of styrene and α-methyl styrene with drying oils leads to soluble, homogeneous resins which form clear and useful films. The advantage in the use of α-methyl styrene with styrene is that it exerts a moderating influence on the reaction and thus provides better control when using the more reactive oils; that is, it tends to regulate the growth of polymer chains such that lower-molecular-weight copolymers are formed which are more compatible with the oil portion of the resin.

### Poly(vinyl toluenes)

The principal shortcomings of polystyrene, as have been seen, have been brittleness, lack of heat resistance, and crazing. Impact-resistant styrene resins have been obtained by modification with an elastomeric constituent. While some improvement in heat resistance has been obtained by copolymerization or by reducing the residual content of unreacted monomer in the polymer, the improvement has not been sufficiently great to be of much value. An alternate approach to improved heat resistance is through the use of substituted styrenes, such as the vinyl toluenes.

The name "vinyl toluene," while not the accepted nomenclature, was chosen by industry to avoid any mistake in identity with α-methyl styrene. The proper names for the vinyl toluenes are o-, m-, and p-methyl styrene.

The production of vinyl toluene by the Dow process is similar to the Dow styrene process previously described. Ethylene and toluene are mixed in the presence of aluminum and hydrogen chlorides under anhydrous conditions, and the toluene is alkylated to produce the isomeric ethyl toluenes and more highly alkylated toluenes:

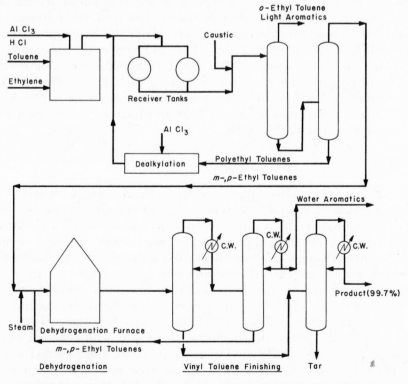

The processing of the products is more difficult than those obtained in the manufacture of ethyl benzene, since three isomeric ethyl toluenes are formed, the *o*-ethyl toluene must be removed, and some toluene is disproportionated to form benzene, ethyl benzene, and xylenes. The crude alkylated benzene is passed through a continuous distillation system, and the various aromatic hydrocarbons are recovered. The recovered higher-alkylated toluenes are equilibrated with toluene in the presence of aluminum chloride.

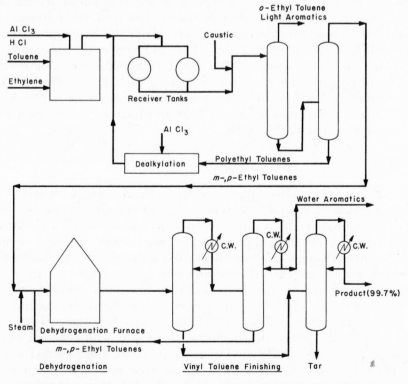

FIG. 9-27.  Vinyl toluene flow sheet.  (*Reprinted from Petroleum Refiner*)

Indene is formed when *o*-ethyl toluene is catalytically dehydrogenated:

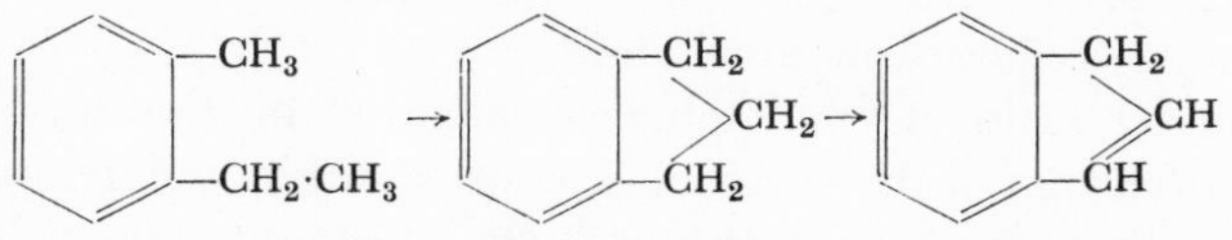

Hence, it is removed from the ethyl toluene isomeric mixture. The separation of the ortho from the meta and para isomers requires an extremely precise fractionation, since the boiling points of the isomers all lie within 4°C of one another.

There is obtained after the final purification step a mixture of *m*- and *p*-vinyl toluenes having a ratio of approximately 65:35 meta to para isomer. This product has a boiling point of 171°C and a density at room temperature of approximately 0.89.

The polymer obtained from this monomer mixture is a transparent, hard, colorless solid, similar to that of polystyrene. The tensile strength and elongation are greater, while the heat distortion temperature and impact strength are less than those of polystyrene. Peculiarly, the polymers and copolymers of vinyl toluene are incompatible with polystyrene.

In 1945, another process was developed for preparing substituted styrenes, especially the vinyl toluenes, by the catalytic cracking of diaryl ethanes. In the Cyanamid process, vinyl toluenes are prepared by a three-step synthesis. Toluene is reacted with acetylene to form a mixture of unsymmetrical ditolyl ethanes. These are cracked in the vapor phase by a process similar to petroleum refinery catalytic cracking. Kaolinite is utilized at temperatures of 400° to 600°C. Purification is accomplished by distillation in the same manner as purification of styrene from ethyl benzene. One mole of vinyl toluene and one mole of toluene are obtained for each mole of diaryl ethane cracked. The reactions for the formation of the para isomer are as follows:

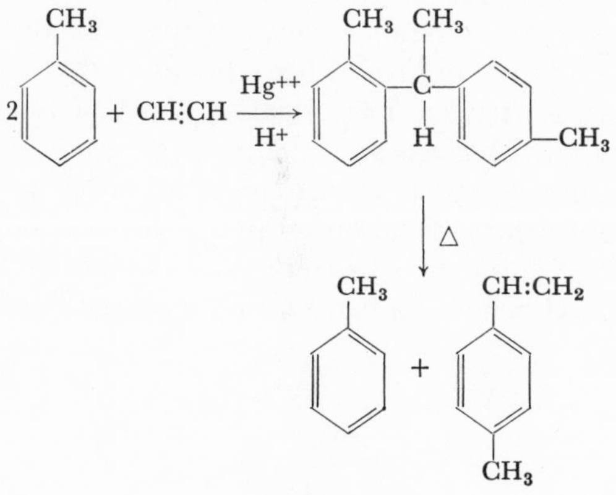

The usual product consists of a mixture of isomers, 65 per cent para, 33 per cent ortho, and 2 per cent meta. Ethyl toluene and other trace impurities are removed by distillation.

The isomer ratio of vinyl toluenes prepared by this process is quite different from that of the vinyl toluenes prepared by the dehydrogenation process. The ortho isomer is the preferred isomer, since it produces a polymer with a higher softening temperature (the meta isomer has the lowest). Hence, this method produces a mixture of vinyl toluenes whose polymers have higher heat distortion temperatures, and the products are therefore of promise as a replacement for styrene in thermoplastic moldings.

Vinyl toluene is of value in the surface-coating industry as a replacement for styrene in the preparation of styrenated oils and alkyds. The higher boiling point of the monomer mixture is an advantage, since higher reaction temperatures may be employed (with equivalent condensing surface). Further, the products are somewhat more soluble in aliphatic solvents—a desirable property for coatings.

### POLY(DIVINYL BENZENES)

Divinyl benzene is a monomer which has associated with it an interest which arises from its unique historical significance. It was used by Staudinger over twenty years ago to show that as little as 0.01 per cent would copolymerize with styrene to form an insoluble product which resembled polystyrene in all respects except that it was insoluble. From this, he postulated that styrene polymerizes to form exceedingly long, linear molecules which needed to be linked together only at a few widely spaced points with the polyfunctional divinyl benzene molecules in order to produce insolubility. This view is now, of course, widely upheld.

Although there are many laboratory methods for preparing divinyl benzene, it is made commercially by starting with an isomeric mixture of diethyl benzenes, obtained as a side stream from the Dow process for making styrene (see Polystyrene). This mixture is catalytically dehydrogenated to give a mixture of divinyl benzenes and ethyl vinyl benzenes in unreacted diethyl benzenes. Fractionation yields a mixture of divinyl benzenes in ethyl vinyl benzenes.

Elaborate inhibitory processes are used in order to prevent polymerization and subsequent gelation of divinyl benzenes during the purification process. No o-divinyl benzene is recovered from the dehydrogenation of a diethyl benzene mixture, since it is converted quantitatively into naphthalene:

The presence of naphthalene is undesirable in the product, since it acts as a plasticizer when present in copolymers, and imparts its characteristic odor to copolymers if present in appreciable amounts.

The monomeric mixture of ethyl vinyl benzene and divinyl benzene isomers is extremely reactive, polymerizing slowly even at 0°C. As a consequence, it is usually inhibited with a phenolic-type inhibitor, *p-tert*-butyl catechol, and kept cool.

Divinyl benzene is not normally polymerized alone, since this results in a cross-linked polymer long before most of the monomer has reacted; the product then contains a large proportion of unreacted monomer which is difficult to remove. Furthermore, the polymerization leads to an amorphous powder which is insoluble in all solvents. As a consequence, divinyl benzene is used as a comonomer, in small amounts, with styrene and synthetic elastomers.

Styrene copolymerizes readily with *p*-divinyl benzene. It serves to cross-link the long polystyrene chains, yielding a three-dimensional polymer which may swell but does not dissolve in the usual solvents. It has been reported that, about 1944, limited production of a series of cast styrene-divinyl benzene copolymers was begun. These materials were primarily designed for insulation in radar equipment used by the armed forces, where excellent dielectric properties and a high heat distortion temperature were needed. Copolymers of styrene and divinyl benzene machine easily because of their resistance to flow, even when heated to 250°C. It is much easier to machine these copolymers than to machine thermoplastic materials.

The development of a better-processing, GR-S-type synthetic elastomer has been accomplished by the addition of a small amount of divinyl benzene to the butadiene-styrene monomer mixture before polymerization. Among the reported advantages of this slightly cross-linked elastomer are low shrinkage, improved surface appearance, reduced swelling, and improved aging characteristics.

## HETEROCYCLIC VINYL COMPOUNDS
### POLY(*N*-VINYL CARBAZOLE)

A large number of vinyl compounds can be prepared from acetylene by reaction with alcohols, amines, mercaptans, carboxylic acids, and other compounds. An example is the addition of carbazole (obtained from coal tar and, recently, synthetically from diphenylene imine) to acetylene to form *N*-vinyl carbazole:

In this reaction, alkali metal hydroxides or alcoholates, potassium carbazole, and other strongly alkaline substances serve as catalysts. Secondary catalysts, such as metallic zinc and certain zinc compounds, are also used. The presence of zinc dust or zinc oxide promotes the reaction and prevents the formation of cuprene-like explosive compounds.

The reaction is carried out in the absence of air under a pressure of 20 to 25 atmospheres and at a temperature of 120° to 160°C. The acetylene is diluted with an inert gas, such as nitrogen or ammonia, the latter of which may serve both as a diluent and as a secondary catalyst. Other liquid diluents or suspension agents used successfully include cyclohexane and hexahydro xylene. (Vinyl carbazole may also be prepared by dehydration of $N$-ethylol carbazole obtained by the reaction of potassium carbazole with ethylene oxide, and by the reaction of potassium carbazole with vinyl chloride.)

$N$-vinyl carbazole, a white solid melting at about 65°C, polymerizes under a variety of conditions, but not in the presence of metallic sodium or strong alkali, to form a linear, thermoplastic polymer:

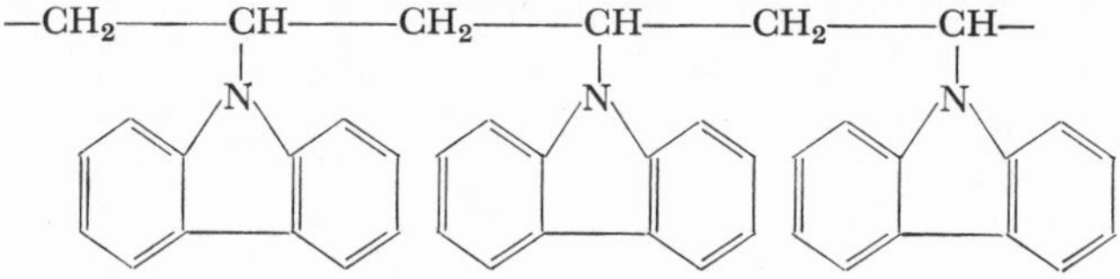

Mass polymerization of $N$-vinyl carbazole yields nearly colorless, clear and glasslike castings. Emulsion or suspension polymerization at 100° to 165°C, using peroxide initiators, forms an opaque polymer which can be injection or compression molded or can be extruded to give oriented, asbestoslike fibers.

Molded poly(vinyl carbazole) at room temperature is a hard, somewhat brittle solid. Its mechanical properties are similar to those of polystyrene at extremely low temperatures. The polymer resembles polystyrene in electrical properties but has much better heat resistance, having a softening temperature of about 200°C, which is abnormally high for a vinyl-type, thermoplastic polymer. It has a very low power factor, a high dielectric strength, and high volume and surface resistivities. Unlike polystyrene and polyethylene, poly(vinyl carbazole) is a fairly polar polymer. However, the dielectric losses are low because of the relative immobility of the bulky carbazole side groups. The specific gravity of pure poly(vinyl carbazole) is 1.2, the water absorption is very low (0.1 per cent), and the heat distortion temperature is over 150°C, which is very high.

The polymer is resistant to dilute acids, alkalies, and even to hydrogen fluoride, but not to concentrated nitric and sulfuric acids. It is insoluble in aliphatic and alicyclic hydrocarbons, as well as in alcohols, ethers, and fatty oils, but is readily soluble in aromatic hydrocarbons and chlorinated solvents.

The unplasticized polymer has the unusual characteristic of developing a macro-fibrous structure upon extrusion or injection molding; that is, it emerges from an orifice as a bundle of strong, fine, rigid, oriented fibers. These fibers can be chopped into short lengths and used as a filler in poly(vinyl carbazole) compression molding powders; this technique provides a unique means for improving the mechanical properties of many articles without addition of large amounts of plasticizer and without incorporation of extraneous fibrous materials of poorer electrical properties. Although it has relatively poor mechanical properties, properly molded poly(vinyl carbazole) can be machined.

The high cost, lack of uniformity, poor color, and poor mechanical properties of poly(vinyl carbazole) have limited many otherwise promising commercial applications. The monomer has been used to some extent by impregnation and polymerization *in situ* in special electrical capacitors. The polymer is manufactured in limited amounts in the United States (Polectron). It is useful in the field of electronics where exacting mechanical requirements are not often necessary but where high operating temperatures may be encountered. The polymer has also been manufactured in Germany for several years (Luvican). As in the United States, the principal applications of Luvican have been in the fields of electrical insulation and electronics.

Copolymers of vinyl carbazole with styrene have been experimentally prepared. These copolymers have promising toughness, a heat distortion temperature of 127°C, and improved molding properties. Since it is somewhat brittle, vinyl carbazole has also been copolymerized with isobutylene in order to minimize this effect.

## POLY(N-VINYL PYRROLIDONE)

Vinyl pyrrolidone was discovered in Germany in the 1930's by Reppe, who was primarily interested in the high-pressure synthesis of new chemicals from acetylene. The following series of reactions, similar to the formation of N-vinyl carbazole, were developed for the production of N-vinyl pyrrolidone (N-vinyl butyrolactam).

Formaldehyde is reacted with acetylene over a copper acetylide catalyst at 300 to 350 psi to produce butynediol. This is hydrogenated at about 5,000 psi over a catalyst containing nickel, copper, and manganese to produce butanediol. Dehydrogenation in the vapor phase over a copper catalyst closes the ring, and treatment with ammonia produces pyrrolidone (butyrolactam). Vinylation is accomplished by treatment with acetylene at more than 200 pounds pressure in the presence of potassium hydroxide:

$$CH{:}CH + 2HCHO \rightarrow CH_2OH{\cdot}CH{:}CH{\cdot}CH_2OH \xrightarrow{H_2} CH_2OH{\cdot}CH_2{\cdot}CH_2{\cdot}CH_2OH \xrightarrow[200°C]{Cu}$$

The butyrolactone intermediate may also be obtained by oxidation of tetrahydrofuran. Another process, recently developed in the United States, is that of reacting butyrolactone with ethanolamine; this avoids the hazards of handling acetylene under pressure.

Poly(vinyl pyrrolidone) was first prepared by mass polymerization, using hydrogen peroxide as the initiator at 100°C. It has subsequently been made by solvent polymerization in water, since the monomer is water-soluble.

The polymer is a yellowish, clear mass of high viscosity. After proper fractionation, the product is a nearly white powder. It is stable to strong acids but not to alkali. Poly(vinyl pyrrolidone) is soluble in both water and organic solvents, resembles albumin in physical properties, and was utilized in Europe during and after World War II in aqueous solution as a blood plasma expander.

Beginning in 1945, research was conducted in the United States by the company which is the sole domestic producer at present. The first significant use for the polymer in the United States, as in Germany and France, was as a blood plasma extender. To sustain the demand, the research was intensified to discover other uses. As an outgrowth of this work, the product is now finding important applications in the drug, cosmetic, food, textile dyeing, paper finishing, and other fields.

Poly(vinyl pyrrolidone) has attracted considerable attention in the pharmaceutical and cosmetic industries because of its unusual combination of properties. Among the characteristics responsible for this interest are its physiological compatibility, its solubilizing action, its ability to prolong the activity of drugs, its detoxifying action, and its ability to protect and stabilize suspensions, dispersions, and emulsions.

Poly(vinyl pyrrolidone) forms water-soluble or water-dispersible complexes with a number of substances which are ordinarily insoluble in water, and, by forming these complexes, detoxifies some of them. As an example, iodine, in the presence of poly(vinyl pyrrolidone), becomes water-soluble. It acts as a detoxifier without destroying the high efficiency of iodine as a virucide or germicide. Although iodine possesses most of the qualities needed to combat a variety of germs and especially viruses, its high toxicity when taken into the system has prevented its use for this purpose. The new combination, known as PVP-iodine, is more effective than iodine alone in treating bacterial infections because it has a longer duration effect, is virtually nonirritating, has been greatly diminished in toxicity, and is harmless to iodine-sensitive people. Despite the detoxification, the iodine reacts chemically as the free form and the therapeutic efficiency is not diminished.

In the cosmetic field, several different applications of poly(vinyl pyrrolidone) have been developed. The best known of these is the use of the polymer as a hair fixative in the very popular "hair nets" or "hair sprays." The flexibility and adhesive properties of the film are utilized in these products to keep the hair in place without flaking off. The fact that poly(vinyl pyrrolidone) is substantive to the hair is probably very important here. The water solubility of the polymer enables the hair to be reset several times with a wet comb and allows easy removal upon washing. For quick drying upon application, alcohol solubility is necessary, and poly(vinyl pyrrolidone) is unusual in that it is a polymer which is soluble in alcohol as well as water. Ethyl cellulose and shellac (also alcohol soluble) are also used in hair sprays. Poly(vinyl pyrrolidone) is being used in other cosmetic applications, such as skin creams and lotions, shaving lathers, and deodorants.

The polymer is of considerable interest as a "chillproofing agent" in brewing of beer, as a clarifying agent in the manufacture of wines and other beverages, and in dentrifices as a means of reducing or preventing staining of teeth by coffee and tobacco. These uses all seem to be associated with its complexing action.

Preliminary work indicates that poly(vinyl pyrrolidone) is an excellent size for several fibers. A solution of poly(vinyl pyrrolidone) (Peregal ST) is used as a dye stripping aid to decolorize or drastically reduce the color of cellulosic fibers which have been dyed with vat, sulfur, or direct dyestuffs. The effectiveness is apparently due to its powerful affinity for dyestuffs. The complex formed is very stable, stability being of sufficient magnitude to prevent redeposition of the dyestuff on the cellulosic fiber from which it has been stripped.

### POLY(VINYL PYRIDINES)

The vinyl pyridines are examples of nitrogen-containing vinyl compounds in which the vinyl group is attached to a nuclear carbon atom instead of to a nitrogen atom (cf. N-vinyl carbazole and N-vinyl pyrrolidone).

2-Vinyl pyridine (α-vinyl pyridine) is prepared from 2-methyl pyridine (α-picoline) obtained from coal tar:

$$\text{(pyridine-CH}_3\text{)} + \text{HCHO} \rightarrow \text{(pyridine-CH}_2\text{CH}_2\text{OH)} \xrightarrow[\text{distil}]{\text{KOH}} \text{(pyridine-CH:CH}_2\text{)} + \text{H}_2\text{O}$$

The monomer is a colorless or yellowish mobile liquid of pungent, unpleasant odor, boiling at 159°C. It dissolves in most common organic solvents and is slightly soluble in water at room temperature.

Solid, high-molecular-weight polymers from 2-vinyl pyridine superficially resemble polystyrene, but are usually yellow or reddish and swell in water. Polymers prepared by mass or emulsion processes, using persulfate initiators, have been proposed as textile auxiliaries and peptizing agents for silver halide dispersions.

The polymers of 4-vinyl pyridine, which is now in commercial production and is made from γ-picoline, are higher melting and less soluble in organic solvents than those of 2-vinyl pyridine.

Poly(vinyl pyridines) resemble polystyrene in their physical properties, as might be expected from the similarity in structures:

$$-\text{CH}_2-\text{CH}-\text{CH}_2-\text{CH}- \qquad -\text{CH}_2-\text{CH}-\text{CH}_2-\text{CH}-$$

Polystyrene                              Poly(2-vinyl pyridine)

The vinyl pyridine polymers, however, require a considerably higher temperature for molding. Chemically, of course, the differences are marked, due to the presence of the basic nitrogen atom in the ring. For example, poly(vinyl pyridines) are soluble in dilute aqueous acids. The tert-nitrogen atom also makes the compounds a convenient starting point for the preparation of polyelectrolytes containing chain polycations. Insoluble ion exchange resins can be made by cross-linking with dihalides, such as ethylene bromide.

In recent years, considerable attention has been directed toward the development of new synthetic elastomers in an effort to improve the present general-purpose synthetic, GR-S. Among the many vinyl derivatives studied, 2-vinyl pyridine has appeared particularly promising as a substitute for styrene. The isomeric vinyl pyridines copolymerize with butadiene in GR-S-type emulsions even more rapidly than does styrene. Early investigators had found that 2-vinyl pyridine, copolymerized with butadiene and with butadiene and styrene, formed polymers which displayed exceptional elastomeric properties. When properly compounded, such polymers were found superior to GR-S in tensile properties, rebound, hysteresis, flex, age resistance, and raw tack. Some have been manufactured in limited quantities.

The copolymer latices have good wetting properties for tire cords. They provide adhesion of rubber to rayon of up to 50 per cent greater than has been obtained without their use. Adhesion of rubber to nylon has been found to be about 300 per cent better than adhesion obtained by ordinary treating methods. The use of nylon in tires is rapidly expanding, and the use of an adhesive of this type is almost mandatory. The major portion is being used by the tire industry; however, there is an increasing demand for fabricators of belts, hose, and other types of coated fabrics.

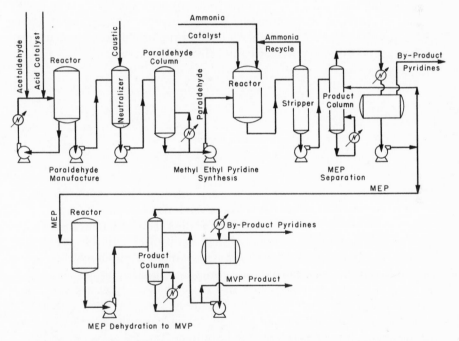

Fig. 9-28. Methyl vinyl pyridine flow sheet. *(Reprinted from Petroleum Refiner)*

Excellent oil-resistant elastomers have become available as a result of the commercial production of 2-methyl-5-vinyl pyridine and the subsequent introduction of butadiene–2-methyl-5-vinyl pyridine copolymers (Philprene VP). To make 2-methyl-5-vinyl pyridine, acetaldehyde is first converted into paraldehyde by trimerization in the presence of a small amount of sulfuric acid. The paraldehyde is then reacted with excess ammonia in the liquid phase to form 2-methyl-5-ethyl pyridine (picolines and other by-products are also formed). This intermediate is a clear liquid which boils over a range of 175° to 180°C. Methyl ethyl pyridine is then catalytically dehydrogenated to yield methyl vinyl pyridine.

The quaternized copolymers of butadiene and methyl vinyl pyridine and terpolymers of butadiene, acrylonitrile, and methyl vinyl pyridine meet many of the basic requirements for an elastomer needed for use in high-temperature-producing aircraft. They give vulcanizates which have excellent resistance to diesters and various other fluids used in modern aircraft, and also have improved low-temperature flexibility. The copolymers and terpolymers are rendered highly oil-resistant by reaction with organic halogen compounds during vulcanization. The halide reacts during cure with the pyridine nitrogen atoms in the polymer, producing polymeric salts (quaternized VP rubber). Quaternizing agents such as *p*-xylene hexachloride, benzotrichloride, or chloranil (tetrachloro-quinone) react to give polymeric salts of the type shown:

$$R^+ \qquad X^-$$

$$-CH_2 \cdot CH{:}CH \cdot CH_2 \cdot CH \cdot CH_2 \cdot CH_2 \cdot CH{:}CH \cdot CH_2-$$

The polymers respond normally to reinforcement by carbon black and are highly reinforced by mineral fillers, such as clay.

Acrylonitrile-vinyl pyridine copolymer fibers are of great interest because they can be dyed with conventional acid dyestuffs. Suitable copolymers for preparation of textile fibers may be obtained from aqueous solutions of the monomers, using persulfates or aliphatic bisazo initiators.

The quality of vinyl polymers made by the emulsion technique has been improved as the result of the discovery that polymers and copolymers derived from vinyl pyridines are valuable emulsifiers for the polymerization of styrene, acrylonitrile, butadiene, methyl acrylate, and other monomers. Latices or dispersions prepared in acidic media, emulsified with a poly(vinyl pyridine), are characterized by high fluidity. Coagulation of the latex with dilute base yields a product which is an intimate mixture of polymers substantially free of emulsifiers or other nonpolymeric contaminants. Systems of this type have been found to offer good process control, high reaction rates, and other advantages inherent in emulsion polymerization, in addition to purity of products usually associated with mass or suspension polymerization.

## CYCLIC UNSATURATED COMPOUNDS

### COUMARONE-INDENE RESINS

It was about the year 1890 that the varnish industry first investigated synthetic resins for improving the properties of drying oils. The earliest research with resins from coumarone and indene appear to have been carried out by the German chemists, Kraemer and Spilker, in that year. During World War I, shortages of natural resins led to the development of these synthetic resins in Europe, where they were frequently used as a substitute, or as a diluent, for linseed oil in the preparation of coating materials. Industrial growth of these resins in the United States began soon afterward (1919). They were one of the first purely synthetic resins to become useful in the varnish industry, but they lost ground rapidly in this field when the phenol-formaldehyde resins were developed.

Coumarone (benzofuran) and indene occur in the solvent naphtha cuts of coal-tar distillates and in smaller amounts in coal and water gases.

Coumarone      Indene

The average content of these chemicals in dry coal tar is about 0.6 per cent, with indene present in greater quantity. A naphtha boiling between 160° and 190°C contains about 30 per cent of coumarone and indene. They are colorless liquids which boil at about 172° and 182°C, respectively. Because of the closeness of their boiling points, they are usually not separated. In fact, they are often polymerized together, using the saturated compounds of the cut in which they occur as a solvent medium; the latter are subsequently separated by distillation and sold as solvents.

The polymerization can be carried out using dilute sulfuric acid as a catalyst, although aluminum, ferric, and stannic chlorides and phosphoric acid are also effective. Mild oxidizing agents accelerate the reaction, but strong oxidizing agents react with coumarone.

Resins of the palest color and highest molecular weight can be obtained by treating purified solvent naphtha fractions with concentrated sulfuric acid at 20°C or lower. The use of alkyl sulfuric acids results in forming resins of pale color but having narrower molecular weight distributions. Polymers of palest color may be made by controlled heat polymerization of cuts containing coumarone, indene, and dicyclopentadiene at 200° to 260°C.

In practice, coal-tar light oil is polymerized under conditions where temperature, monomer content, and catalyst content are carefully controlled. Using sulfuric acid, the reaction is almost instantaneous and highly exothermic. After reaction is complete, the acid tars and sludges are allowed to settle and the catalyst is neutralized with aqueous alkali or by contact with adsorbents, such as Fuller's earth. The polymer solution is then distilled to remove the volatile constituents. Steam distillation may be employed to remove dimers and trimers and is continued until a resin of the desired softening temperature is obtained. Continuous polymerization of coumarone-indene in solvent naphtha has also been carried out, using boron trifluoride etherate. The molecular weight of even the highest-melting commercial coumarone-indene resins is low—of the order of 1,000 to 3,000.

The structure commonly assigned to these copolymers is as follows:

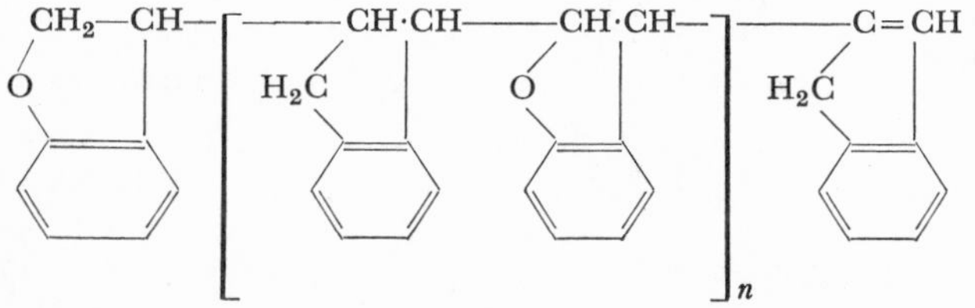

$$CH_2—CH—[———CH·CH———CH·CH—]———C=CH$$

The structure given is a purely formal one, since there is probably an entirely random arrangement of coumarone and indene mesomers in the polymer molecule.

Because of the presence of a double bond in the end group of the relatively low-molecular-weight structure, these resins exhibit appreciable unsaturation. As a result of the cyclopentadiene structure also present in the end group, they are capable of undergoing "fulvenation"; i.e., reaction with an aldehyde at the reactive methylene group, to give a cross-conjugated, chromophoric structure characteristic of fulvenes:

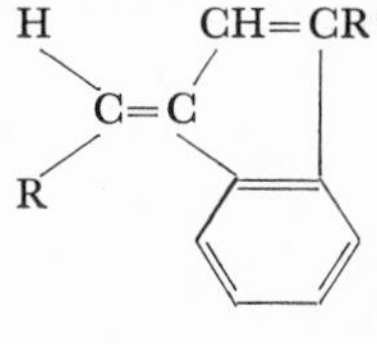

Prolonged exposure to the atmosphere of films made from these resins results in discoloration. It is probable that this is caused by fulvenation as a result of preliminary aldehyde formation obtained by oxidative fission of some of the double bonds of the cyclopentadiene structures present.

Hydrogenation eliminates the double bond and improves color and color stability (Nevillite). The highest priced grades of the hydrogenated resins are water white and retain their clarity upon prolonged atmospheric exposure of thin films. They have found a specialized, but important, outlet in combination with raw rubber in the manufacture of adhesives used in transparent, pressure-sensitive tapes.

Coumarone-indene resins (Cumar, Nevindene, Paradene, Piccou-maron), sometimes called paracoumarone-indene, are available in a wide range of softening temperatures, varying from viscous liquids at room temperature to friable solids softening at over 150°C. Their specific gravities lie between 1.08 and 1.15. Their electrical properties are good and are little affected by moisture. Being substantially hydrocarbon in nature, the resins are practically neutral and are nonreactive with most chemicals, including alkalies and dilute acids. The resins are soluble in almost all hydrocarbons, chlorinated hydrocarbons, and oxygenated solvents except alcohols. They are also compatible with most animal and vegetable oils, with the exception of castor. This wide compatibility allows these resins to be used in varnishes as partial replacements for higher priced resins and, to some extent, ester gum. Since their properties are inferior, however, they are usually considered to be merely diluents. This type of application is somewhat limited by their poor durability and lack of elasticity. However, they are neutral, nonoxidizing, and non-saponifiable, and they impart to varnishes inertness and adhesion, high dielectric strength, and shorter drying time than many natural resins. They are used in paper coatings, artificial leather, oil cloth, shoe polish, printing inks, and linoleum. In fact, a very large portion of the total domestic coumarone-indene resin production is consumed in the manu-facture of floor covering and rubber goods. In the manufacture of mastic floor tile, in which a thermoplastic binder is employed, the resin is plasticized with various selected pitches or specially processed oils.

The use of coumarone-indene resins in molded articles is limited because of their brittleness and low tensile strength, but they find application as a modifier in various molding compositions. The resins are used as a flux to improve the milling and flowing qualities and dimensional stability of vinyl resins to be used for transcription records.

The application of these resins to GR-S compounding is very extensive, especially in formulations containing noncarbon-black fillers. Pure gum GR-S compounds have tensile strengths of only 200 to 300 psi, and the addition of inorganic fillers in large amounts increases the tensile strength only slightly. Fortunately, certain organic materials produce a re-inforcement phenomenon, known as the "organic reinforcement effect," in GR-S which is absent in natural rubber. Coumarone or coumarone-indene polymers exhibit this property. In a pure gum GR-S compound, they do not improve the tensile strength, but when added to a GR-S compound containing mineral fillers, they increase the tensile strength markedly. Although the reason therefor is unknown, the combined effect of coumarone resin and mineral fillers in GR-S is to give appreciably greater tensile strength than can be obtained by the use of either alone. The combination increases the tensile strength from two to seven times. For this reason and because of its moderate cost, coumarone resins are universally used in GR-S insulating compounds containing mineral fillers. The proportion varies from 10 to 20 per cent, based on GR-S. This property has enabled the wire and cable industry to produce satisfactory insulation from GR-S containing no carbon black.

A few modified coumarone-indene resins have appeared commercially. The alkylation of phenols at 90° to 110°C with coumarone and indene yields resinous materials of altered physical properties (Nevillac). The catalyst used for the alkylation may be activated clay or of the Friedel-Crafts type.

These modified coumarone-indene resins, having an average molecular weight of from 400 to 440, are soluble in the same solvents which dissolve coumarone-indene resins, and are, moreover, completely soluble in alcohol. It is probable that the end-group unsaturation of the coumarone-indene polymer is saturated by the addition of a phenolic compound across the double bond to form a mixture of coumarone-indene substituted cresol and cresyl ether polymers, as indicated below, where R may be coumarone or indene:

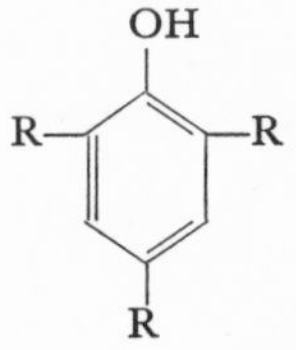

These resins are used in plastics, protective coatings, adhesives, and lacquers, and as solubilizing agents for cellulose esters and vinyl resins.

Resins quite similar in properties to the coumarone-indene type are now being produced on a large scale from petroleum cracking operations. The similarity of the resins from the two sources is due to the close chemical relationship of the constituents of the fractions used, which in both cases contain cyclopentadiene and styrene derivatives, as well as indene.

### POLYCYCLOPENTADIENE

A five-membered ring structure appears to increase the rate of polymerization of unsaturated compounds. The ready polymerization of compounds containing the cyclopentadiene structure has long been known. Polymers are formed by the addition of one molecule by means of a single double bond to a second molecule in the 1,4 position. Inasmuch as the adduct still contains a double bond, the process can continue. The presence of a fused ring does not noticeably diminish the capacity to polymerize, as is shown in the case of indene or coumarone. Although high-molecular-weight polymers seem to be present in the polymerization tar obtained from cyclopentadiene by the action of strong acids, thermal polymerization is practically complete with the formation of heptacyclo-pentadiene.

Cyclopentadiene, like coumarone and indene, is one of the compounds present in coal tar and petroleum, occurring, however, in the lower boiling fractions. It is a volatile liquid, boiling at 41°C. Upon standing, it spontaneously dimerizes to form a solid, melting at 32°C, which has the following structure (Diels-Alder reaction):

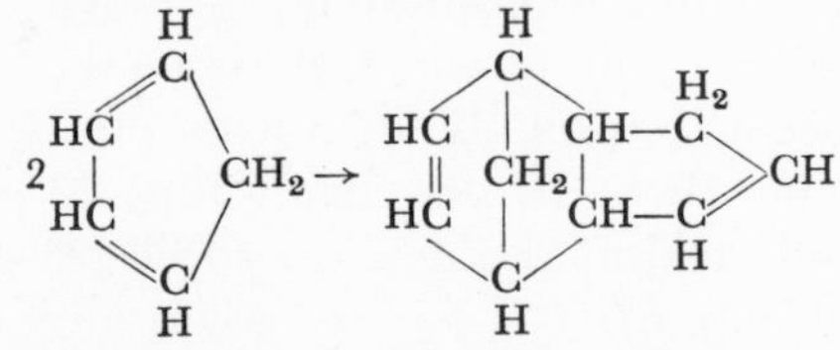

Cyclopentadiene     Bicyclopentadiene

The addition of succeeding molecules may then form a polymer:

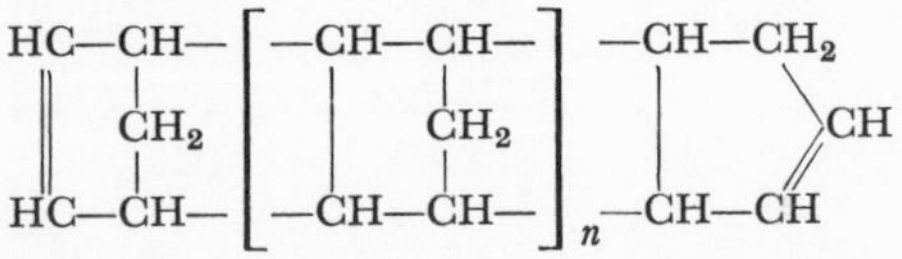

Thermal polymerization is conducted at temperatures above 200°C, the molecular weight of the product being quite low (500 to 600). A commercially produced resin, known as Neville G Resin, has been reported to be made by copolymerization of a natural mixture of bicyclo-pentadiene, indene, and coumarone. The resin is a brittle, dark-red solid, melting at 110° to 125°C. Its uses are similar to those of the coumarone-indene resins.

An unusual dibasic acid, known as Carbic anhydride, is produced by a Diels-Alder addition of maleic anhydride to cyclopentadiene:

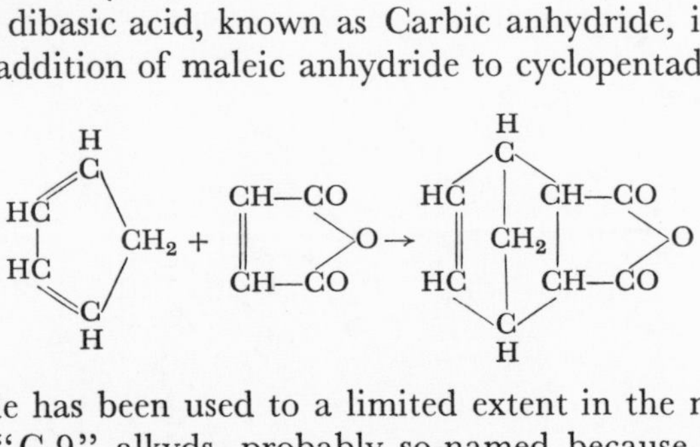

This anhydride has been used to a limited extent in the manufacture of the so-called "C-9" alkyds, probably so-named because the anhydride contains nine carbon atoms.

## POLYTERPENES

Terpenes have been used to produce thermoplastic resins resembling the coumarone-indene resins in physical appearance, properties, and uses. Differences are found, however, in their color stability and in some of their compatibility characteristics.

All terpenes may be considered as low-molecular-weight polymers of isoprene ($C_5H_8$). The monoterpenes, whether linear or cyclic, are based on the dimer, the sesquiterpenes on the trimer, the diterpenes on the tetramer, and the triterpenes on the hexamer of isoprene. From these linear oligomers, mono-, di-, and tricyclic terpenes can be obtained by coiling or folding the chains appropriately.

Of the more complex cyclic terpenes, perhaps the best known are the rosin acids, which occur in rosin obtained from pine trees. The exudate from this tree contains about 12 per cent water, 20 per cent turpentine (a mixture of terpenes, mainly α-pinene), and 68 per cent of rosin (colophony) (see Rosin, Chap. 6).

Polyterpenes are formed by the catalytic polymerization of α- and β-pinenes which occur in turpentine.

α-Pinene                                                        β-Pinene

Anhydrous aluminum chloride and inorganic acids (ionic catalysts) effectively initiate polymerization. By varying the conditions of the reaction, polymers can be obtained which range from viscous liquids to friable resins. The polymerization of α-pinene may be represented as follows:

α-Pinene                Dipentene

$\beta$-Pinene, which already contains a methylene group, polymerizes quite readily with Friedel-Crafts catalysts at low temperatures, forming moderately high-molecular-weight polymers melting above 100°C. Dipentene (limonene) and $\alpha$-pinene (which thermally isomerizes to dipentene) polymerize less readily under similar conditions, forming products of lower molecular weight. The highest molecular weights of these polymers range from 1,600 to 2,000, indicating that there are from 12 to 15 mesomers in the product. Dipentene and other terpene hydrocarbons have been copolymerized with butadiene at low temperatures, using aluminum chloride as a catalyst.

These unsaturated resins (Piccolyte, Nypene) are produced having softening temperatures ranging from 10° to 150°C and densities close to unity. Although light yellow in color they do not discolor appreciably upon aging or heating. They are resistant to dilute acids and alkalies and are insoluble in the lower oxygenated solvents but are soluble in most others. They are compatible with waxes and oils, and with many resins and elastomers. The Piccolyte resins are reported to be thermoplastic polymers of $\beta$-pinene.

Polyterpenes are relatively new in the plastics field and have extremely diversified applications, which include their use as components of laminating compounds, paper coatings, moisture-vapor-proof films, chewing gums, pressure-sensitive and other adhesives, tackifiers for both natural and synthetic elastomers, and oil cloth and linoleum. They are frequently used interchangeably with coumarone-indene resins as modifying agents for other plastics. When mixed with natural or synthetic waxes, they confer both hardness and gloss, and are useful, for the same reasons, as a component of varnishes and paints.

Terpenes, like coumarone and indene, react with phenol under suitable conditions. Thus, phenols having nuclear substitutions are formed which are able to polymerize, as they are still partially unsaturated. Because of their large hydrocarbon content, these resins are very soluble in oils (Super Beckacite 2000). They have not yet found wide application in

Limonene

the paint industry, for which they have been recommended, but have proved useful as adhesives.

Many of the monocyclic terpenes react with maleic anhydride, particularly above 100°C, even though they are not conjugated dienes, to form an adduct, as shown at foot of page 537. In such cases, the hydrocarbon probably rearranges to the conjugated form before reacting. As in the case of Carbic anhydride, these adducts have been used to a limited extent in the manufacture of alkyd resins.

## REFERENCES AND RECOMMENDED READING

Alexander, J., ed., *Colloid Chemistry Theoretical and Applied*, Vol. VI, Reinhold Publishing Corp., New York, 1946.

American Cyanamid Co., *The Chemistry of Acrylonitrile*, Beacon Press, New York, 1951.

Barron, H., *Modern Plastics*, John Wiley and Sons, New York, 1945.

Barron, H., *Modern Synthetic Rubbers*, 2nd ed., D. Van Nostrand Co., Princeton, N.J., 1943.

Billmeyer, F. W., Jr., *Textbook of Polymer Chemistry*, Interscience Publishers, New York, 1957.

Blom, A. V., *Organic Coatings*, Elsevier Publishing Co., Amsterdam (dist. by D. Van Nostrand Co., Princeton, N.J.), 1949.

Blout, E. R., Mark, H., and Hohenstein, W. P., eds., *Monomers*, Interscience Publishers, New York, 1949.

Boundy, R. H. and Boyer, R. F., *Styrene*, Reinhold Publishing Corp., New York, 1952.

Bovey, F. A., Kolthoff, I. M., Medalia, A. I., and Meehan, E. J., *Emulsion Polymerization*, Interscience Publishers, New York, 1955.

Burk, R. E., Thompson, H. E., Weith, A. J., and Williams I., *Polymerization*, Reinhold Publishing Corp., New York, 1937.

Cook, P. G., *Latex: Natural and Synthetic*, Reinhold Publishing Corp., New York, 1956.

Ellis, C., *The Chemistry of Synthetic Resins,* Reinhold Publishing Corp., New York, 1935.

Fleck, H. R., *Plastics*, 2nd ed., Chemical Publishing Co., Brooklyn, New York, 1953.

Gordon, P. L. and Dolgin, G. J., *Surface Coatings and Finishes*, Chemical Publishing Co., Brooklyn, N.Y., 1954.

Groggins, P. H., ed., *Unit Processes in Organic Synthesis*, 4th ed., McGraw-Hill Book Co., New York, 1952.

Hill, R., ed., *Fibres from Synthetic Polymers*, Elsevier Publishing Co., Amsterdam (dist. by D. Van Nostrand Co., Princeton, N.J.), 1953.

Houwink, R., ed., *Elastomers and Plastomers*, Vol. II, Elsevier Publishing Co., Amsterdam (dist. by D. Van Nostrand Co., Princeton, N.J.), 1949.

Kaye, S. L., *The Production and Properties of Plastics*, International Textbook Company, Scranton, Penn., 1947.

Kirk, R. E. and Othmer, D. F., eds., *Encyclopedia of Chemical Technology*, Interscience Publishers, New York, 1947–56.

Marchionna, F., *Butalastic Polymers*, Reinhold Publishing Corp., New York, 1946.

Mark, H. and Whitby, G. S., eds., *Collected Papers of Wallace Hume Carothers*, Interscience Publishers, New York, 1940.

Mason, J. P. and Manning, J. F., *The Technology of Plastics and Resins*, D. Van Nostrand Co., Princeton, N.J., 1945.

Mattiello, J. J., ed., *Protective and Decorative Coatings*, John Wiley and Sons, New York, 1941–46.

Mauer, L. and Wechsler, H., *Man-Made Fibers*, Rayon Publishing Corp., New York, 1953.

Mauersberger, H. R., ed., *Matthew's Textile Fibers*, 6th ed., John Wiley and Sons, New York, 1954.

Meyer, K. H., *Natural and Synthetic High Polymers*, 2nd ed., Interscience Publishers, New York, 1950.

Moncrieff, R. W., *Artificial Fibres*, 2nd ed., John Wiley and Sons, New York, 1954.

Morgan, P., ed., *Glass Reinforced Plastics*, Philosophical Library, New York, 1954.

Nauth, R., *The Chemistry and Technology of Plastics*, Reinhold Publishing Corp., New York, 1947.

Powers, P. O., *Synthetic Resins and Rubbers*, John Wiley and Sons, New York, 1943.

Raff, R. A. V. and Allison, J. B., *Polyethylene*, Interscience Publishers, New York, 1956.

Richardson, H. M. and Wilson, J. W., eds., *Fundamentals of Plastics*, McGraw-Hill Book Co., New York, 1946.

Riddle, E. H., *Monomeric Acrylic Esters*, Reinhold Publishing Corp., New York, 1954.

Ritchie, P. D., *A Chemistry of Plastics and High Polymers*, Cleaver-Hume Press, London (dist. by Interscience Publishers, New York), 1949.

Schildknecht, C. E., ed., *Polymer Processes*, Interscience Publishers, New York, 1956.

Schildknecht, C. E., *Vinyl and Related Polymers*, John Wiley and Sons, New York, 1952.

Sherman, J. V. and Sherman, S. L., *The New Fibers*, D. Van Nostrand Co., Princeton, N.J., 1946.

Simonds, H. R., Bigelow, M. H., and Sherman, J. V., *The New Plastics*, D. Van Nostrand Co., Princeton, N.J., 1945.

Simonds, H. R., Weith, A. J., and Bigelow, H. M., *Handbook of Plastics*, 2nd ed., D. Van Nostrand Co., Princeton, N.J., 1949.

Wakeman, R. L., *The Chemistry of Commercial Plastics*, Reinhold Publishing Corp., New York, 1947.

Whitby, G. S., ed., *Synthetic Rubber*, John Wiley and Sons, New York, 1954.

Winding, C. C. and Hasche, R. L., *Plastics Theory and Practice*, McGraw-Hill Book Co., New York, 1947.

## Chapter 10

# EFFECT OF MOLECULAR STRUCTURE UPON MECHANICAL BEHAVIOR

## GENERAL

This chapter is concerned with the relationship between the molecular structure or configuration of polymers and their mechanical behavior. Since most linear, high-molecular-weight polymers have a similar gross morphology, it is apparent that a closer look at the finer structure and arrangement of molecules is necessary in order to explain why, at a given temperature and at approximately the same average molecular weight, some polymers behave as typical plastic solids, others as elastomers, and still others are peculiarly adapted to the formation of fibers. The treatment of this intensively studied subject will be essentially qualitative in nature, the quantitative treatment being more suitably reserved for advanced works. The subject will furthermore be confined principally to linear polymers, since the knowledge of three-dimensional polymers is in a much more incomplete state. This is so chiefly because the generally infusible and insoluble characteristics of the latter class make experimental verification with theory extremely difficult, if not impossible.

Linear polymers may simply be classified as crystalline or amorphous. However, very few, if any, are completely one or the other; almost all polymeric substances lie between these two extremes of order and disorder. The ratio of crystalline to amorphous content has a great influence on the properties of the polymers.

Let us (after Alfrey[1]) define a crystallite as a region or volume of matter in which the structural units, whether atoms, ions, mesomers, or molecules, are arranged in a regular geometric pattern. Such a region will be called a crystallite even if it contains imperfections, so long as they are local and do not destroy the long-range order of the system. It is not necessary that the crystallites be large enough to be visible, even under magnification, or that their boundaries be of any particular shape. Thus, a polymer will be termed crystalline if there are enough unit cells in each individual

[1] Alfrey, T., Jr., *Mechanical Behavior of High Polymers*, p. 342, Interscience Publishers, New York, 1948.

ordered region to cause definite X-ray interference spots and if the polymer possesses the thermodynamic properties associated with a distinct phase.

On the basis of the above definition, crystallization occurs frequently in high-molecular-weight polymers, although polymers are never completely crystalline. Highly ordered regions (crystallites or micelles) are interspersed with more or less amorphous regions. A single polymer molecule may extend through several phases; i.e., a portion of the molecule may lie in a crystalline region, another part in an amorphous region, and so on.

It may also be seen that there will be portions of a polymer mass in which the degree of order is not sufficient or the size of the ordered region is too small to be called crystalline and yet there may be sufficient orientation of structural units to preclude the use of the term amorphous. Thus, there are present in almost all polymers, regions possessing all degrees of order, from complete crystallinity to complete randomness. Completely crystalline and completely amorphous regions simply represent the extremes of ordered and disordered structural arrangements.

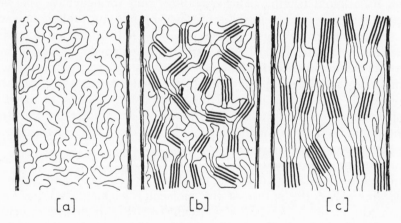

[a]                    [b]                    [c]

FIG. 10-1. Representation of (a) amorphous, (b) crystalline, and (c) oriented crystalline polymers[2]

As might be expected from the foregoing discussion, amorphous polymers may be defined as those which do not yield sharp X-ray diffraction diagrams. These polymers contain few, if any, regions in which the structural units are arranged in three-dimensional regular (crystalline) order. Their structure may be visualized as a tangle of long molecules in which there may be groups of roughly parallel but insufficiently ordered sections of chains.

[2] Alfrey, T., Jr., *Mechanical Behavior of High Polymers*, p. 344, Interscience Publishers, New York, 1948.

Solid, amorphous polymers may occur in the glassy (vitreous), elastic, or plastic state. All noncrystalline polymers become vitreous at low temperatures. This is true not only of polymers which do not crystallize at all but also of crystallizable polymers which have been so rapidly cooled from the melt that they have failed to crystallize. For example, elastomers like rubber, which are capable of crystallization, may form an amorphous, vitreous mass if cooled rapidly enough in the unstressed state.

In addition to the fraction of crystalline material in a polymer mass, the size of the crystallites, their relative positions, and their orientation greatly influence the mechanical properties of the polymer. In a fiber, the crystallites are oriented roughly parallel with the fiber axis; in a crystallized melt, the orientation of the crystallites may be completely random.

It is of great importance to note that a stress greatly facilitates crystallization in a polymer. Thus, rubber, which is amorphous when unstressed, can be crystallized at room temperature if it is stretched to several times its original length. The crystallites thus formed have the same internal structure as the crystallites formed by freezing rubber; however, those formed by stretching are oriented parallel to the direction of tension, whereas those formed by cooling are randomly arranged. Partial orientation can also be induced by compressive stresses under certain conditions. Articles fabricated by injection molding or calendering are stiffer than those made of the same material by compression molding at the same temperature. In the former processes, however, greater partial alignment of the molecular chains during the process of fabrication occurs and the intermolecular cohesion is thus increased.

It thus becomes possible to explain the wide range of properties exhibited by linear polymers on the basis of the kind and extent of molecular order, the nature of the molecular packing, and the forces among the chains. When the molecular order is high, the structural units are geometrically arranged in a three-dimensional lattice, and the solid approaches the degree of perfection of a crystal. At the other extreme, when little or no order exists, the structure becomes that of an amorphous solid. The extent of crystallinity and the properties of the polymer—whether it behaves as a fiber, plastic, or elastomer—are determined by the configuration and chemical structure of the individual chains.

### Plastics

If polyethylene is taken as an example, X-ray examination shows that the molecules have the shape and structure of the long-chain paraffin hydrocarbons, and the properties of the polymer are in many ways similar to those of a crystalline hydrocarbon wax. The forces holding the molecular chains together are the van der Waals forces between the methylene groups of adjoining molecules. These forces are relatively weak and decrease rapidly with distance.

It may be well to digress here briefly to point out that the forces, other than primary valence bonds, responsible for attraction between molecules are of two general types: hydrogen bonds and van der Waals forces. According to the Pauli principle, a hydrogen atom can be associated with no more than two electrons; hence, in the formation of a hydrogen bond, it is not possible for both atoms linked by a hydrogen atom to be attached to it by ordinary covalent bonds. Because of the experimental observation that the linked atoms must be strongly electronegative, it is probable that a hydrogen bond is largely electrostatic or ionic in nature.

The strength of the bond increases, in general, with increasing electronegativity of the atoms bridged with a hydrogen atom; these atoms may be the same or different, but they are restricted almost exclusively to fluorine, oxygen, and nitrogen. In certain instances, hydrogen bonds are formed between carbon and oxygen and between carbon and nitrogen; in such cases, however, the carbon atom always has a strongly electronegative group attached.

The other attractive forces between molecules are due to a combination of several forces, known as the orientation effect (attraction between dipoles), the induction effect (attraction between a dipole and an induced dipole), and the dispersion or London effect (attraction between nonpolar molecules because of electron-induced fluctuating dipole moments). The presence of polar groups on molecules (which are absent in polyethylene) greatly increases their net attraction. This combination of forces is usually known, collectively, as van der Waals or secondary forces. These forces are not as strong as those of hydrogen bonding.

Returning now to the discussion of polyethylene, its soft, waxy nature and relatively low softening temperature are the result of these weak secondary forces and absence of hydrogen bonding, in spite of its high degree of crystallinity. If the hydrogen atoms of the methylene groups are replaced by hydrocarbon groups in a regular manner, as in polyisobutylene or polystyrene, the ease with which the chains can pack together is greatly diminished. Thus, polyisobutylene is like rubber at room temperature and shows extensibility up to many times its original length. Unlike polyethylene, it has no waxlike properties. When stretched, however, it becomes highly crystalline, since the relatively small methyl groups can pack closely together.

In polystyrene, on the other hand, the close-packing paraffinic structure is almost completely lost because of the presence of the large phenyl groups along the chains. The phenyl groups are irregularly spaced along the chains and prevent the molecules from forming regularly packed, crystalline arrangements. For this reason, polystyrene, like glass, is difficult to crystallize, even when stressed.

Replacement of a hydrogen atom on alternate methylene groups of the main paraffin chain in polyethylene by a polar group [as in poly(vinyl chloride) or polyacrylonitrile] or by double substitution [poly(vinylidene chloride), poly(methyl methacrylate)] has a different type of effect. The polar substituent greatly increases the attraction among the chains, since the dipole forces are stronger than other van der Waals forces and thus operate over greater distances. Further, the ease of molecular packing is determined by the chain composition. For small, highly polar substituents, such as chloride or nitrile groups, the dipole-dipole interaction has the greatest influence on chain packing. Polyethylene, on one hand, represents the extreme of nonpolar interaction, while poly(vinyl chloride), poly(vinylidene chloride), and polyacrylonitrile, on the other, represent the extremes of polar interaction. As a result, the latter polymers are much tougher and harder than polyethylene. In the case of polyacrylonitrile, intermolecular attraction is so great that the polymer is soluble only in the most highly polar solvents (see Polyacrylonitrile, Chap. 9). Polymethacrylonitrile, in which the polarity of the nitrile group is reduced by replacement of the hydrogen atom of the :CHCN group by a nonpolar methyl group (thus partially shielding the dipoles from interaction) is a much softer, more soluble polymer. Reduction of intermolecular attraction may also be obtained by copolymerization; for example, acrylonitrile and butadiene copolymers are very flexible and exhibit elastomeric properties.

The polyesters are also harder and tougher than polyethylene, due to the stronger interaction forces of the dipoles. In these polymers, in which carbonyl groups are regularly spaced along the paraffin chains, the spacing is determined by the particular dibasic acid and glycol used, and so the dipole attractions may be spaced by an odd or even number of methylene groups. In even esters, the dipoles all lie on one side of the chain, whereas in the odd esters, the dipoles alternate from side to side. X-ray studies have shown that the dipoles of polyesters coordinate in sheets, the exact way in which this occurs depending upon whether the ester is an odd or even one. The introduction of amine, amide, or hydroxyl groups into a hydrocarbon chain still further increases the intermolecular forces because of the formation of relatively stronger hydrogen bonds.

Summarizing, as the frequency of dipole occurrence increases in a paraffin chain, the intermolecular attraction also increases, resulting in the formation of polymers which become progressively higher melting, harder, more insoluble, and more brittle. Modification of these properties is possible by change of polar spacing, by substitution, or by copolymerization. In the condensation polymers, the choice of reactants is used to control the spacing of polar groups along the chains. With the addition polymers, substitution of hydrogen by alkyl or aryl groups is frequently done. The third method, copolymerization, is used to insert groups which reduce the regularity of the chains and increase the difficulty of packing together to form crystallites. Concomitant effects of the decreased crystallinity in copolymers are lower softening temperatures and increased solubilities in organic solvents.

**Elastomers**

Elastomeric materials differ from all other substances by a combination of two remarkable properties. They are capable of undergoing large deformations upon the application of stress without rupture and the deformed elastomers can recover spontaneously and almost completely upon removal of the stress. In these two properties, they resemble liquids and solids, respectively. This combination of properties, known as *long-range elasticity*, may be exhibited by almost any long-chain polymer under proper conditions of temperature and/or plasticization.

It so happens that all linear polymers above their softening temperatures are characterized by a reversible, long-range extensibility and a low modulus of elasticity. Ordinary glasses are linked together in three dimensions, either by primary valence bonds, as in glass itself, or by secondary valence forces, as in supercooled alcohol. Melting of these substances involves a loosening of all cross-links and the melt behaves like an ordinary liquid. In frozen elastomers, each repeating group (mesomer) is connected by primary valence (covalent) bonds to two adjoining mesomers and by much weaker secondary valence (van der Waals) forces with those in other chains. "Melting" of elastomers affects only the latter bonds, creating a state of matter which lies between the solid and the liquid states. Having been first observed in rubber, this state has been termed the *rubberlike* or *rubbery state*. In addition to the synthetic, high-molecular-weight, linear polymers, within certain temperature ranges, rubbery properties are also exhibited by such biological systems as muscle fibers and membranes of animal cells.

There are several specific conditions which must be met in order for a substance to exhibit rubberlike elasticity. The first requirement is the presence of very long chains, which are necessary in order to obtain high extensibility. These chains are usually connected by some cross-links (see below), but these links must occur infrequently enough that the structure consists predominantly of long polymer chains. Since the long-chain molecules occur in randomly coiled arrangements when the polymer is unstressed, they are able to assume other configurations, particularly more highly extended ones, upon application of a tensile stress. In other words, a large deformation is possible merely by rearrangement of the molecular configurations. During elongation, the molecules partially uncoil and become aligned more or less parallel to the axis of elongation. No other type of structure is known which can undergo such large deformations without suffering permanent internal rearrangement (i.e., flow).

The property which characterizes an elastomer, namely, the ability to recover to its original dimensions, is caused by the development of a restoring force in an elastomer during deformation. This restoring force is due to a tendency for the polymer chains, distorted during deformation, to return to their original, or similar, coiled configurations. Since an elongated chain represents a less probable state (i.e., a state of lower entropy) than a random configuration, the source of the retractive force is the tendency of the molecule to form a more probable (disoriented) state. The calculation of the entropy and its change involves statistical thermodynamics and requires the determination of the number of possible configurations as a function of deformation.

In addition to the requirement of possessing long, linear chains, the system must also have sufficient internal mobility to permit the required rearrangement of chain configurations during both deformation and recovery. Thus, the polymer cannot be either appreciably crystalline or in the glassy state, since both impede or suppress internal motions. The glassy state is avoided by maintaining the temperature sufficiently high, and the crystalline state by proper plasticization.

A third requirement is permanence of structure; else permanent plastic flow, rather than elastic recovery, will occur. This property usually is obtained by introducing occasional cross-linkages, which prevent dissipation of molecular orientation caused by deformation, since even slightly cross-linked chains cannot be completely relieved of such stress except by reversion to their original configurations. In other words, the presence of a permanent network structure is also necessary. (Very high-molecular-weight, noncross-linked polymers sometimes can also exhibit elastic behavior with good recovery, due to the slow rate of relaxation of very long chains.)

The small amount of cross-linking needed for retention of structure does not destroy rubberlike elasticity. An elastomer becomes inelastic only when sufficient cross-linking has occurred to cause the internal structure to become so stiff that slippage of links past their neighbors becomes impossible. This occurs, for example, when rubber is vulcanized with large quantities of sulfur (ebonite or hard rubber).

As will be explained in more detail in the section on Rheology, the ordinary or instantaneous elastic deformation of polymers obeys the same laws as do crystalline substances and metals; at constant temperature, the change in the elastic strain with time is proportional to the applied force, and the recovery upon removal of the deforming stress is instantaneous.

The highly elastic or retarded deformation, on the other hand, lags behind variations in the external force by an amount which depends upon the mobility of the chain segments. At any given temperature, there is a certain finite probability of rearrangement of the molecules and their segments, which depends upon their kinetic motion. The time required for this rearrangement, called the *orientation time* (also sometimes called relaxation time; but cf. Rheology) is greater the lower the temperature; i.e., it is temperature dependent.

If the duration of an applied stress is shorter than the orientation time, the polymer will assume the characteristics of a rigid solid, since there will be insufficient time for the retarded component of elastic deformation to be established. Thus, periodic stresses of high frequency at low temperatures will conceal highly elastic behavior.

As discussed above, the curled, linear molecules are stretched and aligned more or less in parallel when an elastic body is stretched; after the deformation, each segment will have different neighbors (except for the two adjacent ones in its own chain) than it had previously. The segments must therefore exhibit a measure of mobility, as do the molecules of a liquid during flow. In both cases, the rate of flow (deformation) will be impeded by internal friction and heat will be evolved. This internal friction (measured by the viscosity) is about $10^6$ poises for rubber at room temperature, which is one hundred million times larger than that of water.

When the internal friction becomes greater than about $10^{12}$ to $10^{13}$ poises, internal mobility is lost and the substance no longer has the property of highly elastic deformation but becomes instead an amorphous solid. Polystyrene, for example, has an internal viscosity which at room temperature is above the value at which the rubberlike state appears (see Second-Order Transition Temperature), and is thus an amorphous solid. There are, on the other hand, polymers, such as poly(vinyl chloride) and gutta-percha, which are highly crystalline at room temperature and only become reversibly extensible at their softening temperature, when the crystallites are destroyed.

It has already been pointed out that a deforming force partially aligns the linear molecules in an elastomer. If the internal friction is very high, however, this orientation may not disappear after the applied stress has been removed. As a result, the polymer will exhibit a certain degree of anisotropy. For example, during a calendering operation the chains become partially aligned, and the elastic modulus and refractive index become higher in the direction of rolling than in other directions. Similarly, polymers which exhibit elasticity only at high temperatures will have their orientation frozen in upon cooling to room temperature. For this reason, fibers spun under high tension or stretched after spinning exhibit anisotropy and have a higher tensile strength than otherwise.

Another way to accomplish the same result is to vulcanize (cross-link) an elastomer which has been oriented by milling; the anisotropy is permanently retained as a result of the cross-linking, and the modulus of elasticity remains permanently higher in one direction than in any other.

When the molecular segments of an elastomer become completely aligned by a tensile stress, further stress causes rupture of the specimen. However, much greater elongation is possible if crystallization does not occur, as with amorphous polymers (e.g., polystyrene), or is suppressed by heating or by the addition of a plasticizer. In the latter cases, the elongation is not completely reversible, because plastic deformation (flow) has also occurred.

### Fibers

As pointed out previously, many polymers can be stretched to their breaking points without showing any appreciable tendency to return to their original length; this type of stretching is known as "cold drawing." Plastic substances having this property have molecular structures similar to that of an unstretched elastomer (both amorphous), and in both cases oriented crystallites often appear during the stretching operation.

Most fiber-forming polymers are highly (but never entirely) crystalline. In the melted state, the long, linear molecules are curled in irregular configurations, due to the thermal motions of the segments of the chains. When the temperature falls below the melting point, irregular crystal nucleus formation occurs by the aggregation of chain segments which happen to be properly oriented and which are close together. The crystals grow by consolidation of portions of adjacent chains; this tends to cause some progressive straightening out of the chains, but the normally tangled state of the molecules and their natural tendency to assume a somewhat curled configuration impede the process of crystallization, thus leaving amorphous regions scattered throughout the crystalline areas.

In mechanically worked polymers (drawn films, calendered sheets, and fibers), this mixture of crystalline and amorphous regions still occurs, but the stresses incurred cause the crystallites at least to become preferentially oriented. It must be remembered, however, that the crystalline regions are not perfect and that there are no sharp dividing lines between crystalline and amorphous areas; regions of intermediate degrees of order will coexist with highly crystalline and completely amorphous ones.

The ease with which crystallization occurs varies greatly among the types of polymers. Polyethylene always partially crystallizes, no matter how rapidly it is cooled from the molten state. Poly(ethylene terephthalate), on the other hand, can be obtained in an entirely amorphous state by quenching and will remain amorphous for a long time at room temperature. Poly(vinylidene chloride), which can also be obtained in the amorphous state by rapid cooling to room temperature, is then in a metastable condition and slowly crystallizes on aging. As might be expected, the degree of crystallinity of these polymers is inversely dependent upon the rate of cooling from the molten state.

High-molecular-weight polymers having no over-all orientation of the molecules are not usually suitable for textile fiber use; permanent orientation of the molecules parallel to the fiber axis is necessary for the attainment of sufficient strength. By cold drawing the fiber, the requisite orientation is obtained. In other words, for the production of textile fibers, two steps are necessary: the initial formation of unoriented or only slightly oriented filaments, and subsequent cold drawing. It should be borne in mind, however, that drawing cannot be performed successfully below the second-order transition temperature (see next section), since breaking of the fibers then usually occurs.

The drawing of *noncrystallizing* polymers results in a certain amount of molecular orientation which somewhat improves fiber properties. The properties of the drawn fibers will be determined, to a large extent, by the degree of molecular orientation attained, as well as by the length of the molecules. The drawing process results in the expected gradual thinning of the fiber.

The drawing of *crystallizing* fibers differs from those above in that if an unoriented or slightly oriented crystallizing fiber is stretched rapidly, it suddenly becomes thinner at one point, forming a shoulder, and the shoulder moves as more material passes from the undrawn to the drawn portion. The thickness of the drawn fiber remains constant, and further attempts to stretch the drawn fiber result in breakage. The ratio of drawn to undrawn length varies slightly, depending upon several factors, but for most fibers of small diameter, this natural draw ratio varies remarkably little (400 to 500 per cent) at room temperature. In the production of synthetic fibers, the drawing is a continuous operation and the draw ratio is established by the relative speeds of the reels before and after the draw point.

The above phenomena are exhibited by most crystalline polymers, including polyethylene, polyamides, and the aliphatic polyesters. The drawing operation converts such a polymer from one containing randomly oriented crystalline regions into one in which the crystalline regions are oriented, the molecular chain axes being aligned roughly parallel to the fiber axis. It is not always necessary that the undrawn polymer be crystalline, provided that it becomes crystalline during drawing. This can be accomplished as a result of the formation of heat at the shoulder, caused by the work done in drawing, which temporarily increases the amorphous content in a partially crystalline polymer and increases molecular mobility; further, the heat of crystallization on drawing also increases molecular mobility at the shoulder. As a result, the shoulder acts as a focal point at which changes in orientation can occur. The formation of a shoulder and the phenomenon of the natural draw ratio are thus apparently related to the formation of crystallinity in the drawn fibers, for polymers which are noncrystalline both before and after drawing do not exhibit these features.

Now, in the case of solvent or wet spinning, when the extruded solution comes into contact with a stream of hot gas or coagulating liquid, the polymer first precipitates on the surface of the filament, forming a skin; precipitation proceeds inward more slowly, since the solvent must diffuse outward through the skin. At the same time, the filament is stretched and thinned. Further stretching occurs after precipitation of the polymer is complete. It has been suggested that the precipitation stage may correspond to the solidification of melt-spun fibers, while the further stretching occurring after complete precipitation corresponds to cold drawing. However, there is probably little similarity between the processes, other than that of the use of stretching to cause molecular orientation. Neither the shoulder effect nor the natural draw ratio is apparent in solvent spinning, although the fibers produced are crystalline. The orientation process may be quite different from that which occurs in the drawing of melt-spun fibers, partly because the polymer first formed is swollen with solvent. The study of solvent-swollen fibers is a much more difficult task than that of melt-spun fibers, and not enough information has yet been accumulated to permit generalizations to be made concerning the mechanism of orientation in wet-spinning methods.

## TRANSITION AND BRITTLE TEMPERATURES

The commercial uses of polymers are, to a large extent, based upon their individual mechanical properties. Some polymers are plastic, some are elastic, while others are hard or brittle. As has been pointed out in the previous section, temperature influences greatly the physical state of a polymer. When a brittle, high-molecular-weight polymer is heated above a certain temperature, it gradually becomes elastic and, at still higher temperatures, becomes plastic. An elastomer can also attain viscous-plastic properties upon heating and will lose its elasticity to become brittle upon sufficient cooling. In the latter case, the transition from the elastic-plastic state to the brittle state is not usually accompanied by crystallization, but instead results in a glasslike (vitreous) hardening, which is similar to that occurring upon rapid cooling of many low-molecular-weight organic compounds.

The reasons for these phenomena and the conditions governing them must be well understood, because they are necessary for the intelligent application of the many and varied high-molecular-weight polymers. For instance, the stiffening temperature of elastomers must be below their use temperatures, and the temperature range over which these materials exhibit their desirable elasticity should preferably be as wide as possible. The softening temperatures of plastics, on the other hand, must be higher than their use temperatures. It may thus be seen that the stiffening temperature of a polymer determines to a great extent whether it will be classed as a plastic or an elastomer.

Now, a pure, low-molecular-weight, crystalline compound, when heated to its melting point, suddenly changes from a rigid, crystalline condition, showing an elastic response to shear stress, to that of an amorphous material, showing viscous flow instead. At the same time, the values of the primary thermodynamic variables, such as volume, energy, and entropy, and their first derivatives with respect to temperature, also change abruptly. For example, a vertical step in the enthalpy–temperature curve occurs (caused by evolution of the latent heat of fusion), and an equally sudden discontinuity occurs in the heat capacity–temperature curve (since heat capacity is the first derivative of enthalpy with respect to temperature). Such a solid-liquid phase transition occurs at a thermodynamically singular *first-order transition temperature*, known, of course, as the melting temperature or melting point.

Some high-molecular-weight polymers, because of their geometrical regularity, crystallize sufficiently to exhibit a fairly sharp solid-liquid transition (e.g., polyethylene, nylon, polytetrafluoroethylene); in most cases, however, the polymers are amorphous or only slightly crystalline and there is a considerable range for the transition, due to the extreme lengths of the molecules and their resultant hampered mobilities. Because of this lack of a sharp transition in polymers having little or no crystallinity, the term "softening temperature" or "softening range" is preferable to "melting point."

All high-molecular-weight polymers which exhibit first-order transitions differ, however, from compounds of low molecular weight in that, after the transition, while both classes become transparent, the high-molecular-weight polymers become softer but do not become mobile liquids.

This lack of mobility has been explained as follows. Most monomers are mobile liquids at about room temperature. Each monomer molecule vibrates about a mean center, but this center is not fixed, and the particles undergo translational Brownian movement; i.e., they change places with respect to one another frequently. This movement is responsible for flow and for the inability of the liquid to maintain a definite shape under stress. In the case of high-molecular-weight polymers above their softening temperatures, each segment of each chain also vibrates about a mean center; however, since each segment is part of a long molecule, it cannot diffuse far from its original position unless it can take the entire chain along with it. Since movement of chains is hindered by intermolecular attractions as well as chain entanglements, such diffusion is consequently very infrequent unless an external stress is applied. As a result, self-diffusion and flow occur infrequently despite the local high mobilities. In other words, two Brownian movements rather than one occur—that of the individual molecular segments and that of the chains as a whole. These have been termed the internal or micro-Brownian and the external or macro-Brownian movements, respectively.

The value of the first-order transition is influenced by the polarity, symmetry, and orientation of the molecules. Polyethylene, for example, exhibits good strength and toughness at a fraction of the average molecular weight required of polystyrene, in spite of the greater molar cohesion of the latter, because of its greater ease of molecular packing (crystallization). Many polymers, including polystyrene, have such poor molecular symmetry that no first-order transition can be observed, and little or no orientation effects can be obtained, even upon stretching.

In summary then, when a crystalline material melts, a sudden change in mechanical properties occurs within a very narrow temperature range; i.e., the material changes from essentially elastic to essentially viscous mechanical behavior, at the same time changing from a crystalline to an amorphous structure. A noncrystalline polymer does not, of course, undergo the latter change and does not exhibit a sharp melting point.

Now, if a polymer, instead of being heated, is cooled rapidly from above its softening temperature, its viscosity gradually increases and it retains its previous amorphous structure. The same phenomena occur if a polymer is cooled from below its softening temperature, if it is already in the amorphous state. In either case, as cooling continues, the material becomes hard and rigid below a certain temperature, and in this condition is generally known as a "glass." For example, as the temperature of an elastomer is lowered, its rubberlike properties gradually disappear, the material hardens, and finally a narrow temperature range is reached at which the sample becomes brittle and shatters easily. The approximate temperature at which this occurs is known as the *brittle temperature* and is the lower limit of the useful temperature range of the material as an elastomer. At this temperature, there is no sudden change in structure nor does a discontinuity in the primary thermodynamic variables appear. However, at a temperature near the brittle temperature, the first derivatives with respect to temperature of the primary thermodynamic variables, such as the coefficient of expansion and the heat capacity, undergo rather sudden changes. That is, the curves of volume-temperature, energy-temperature, and entropy-temperature change slope sharply. This phenomenon is referred to as a "second-order transition"and the temperature at which it occurs as the *second-order transition temperature* or *glassy temperature*.

In other words, a first-order phase transition, such as a crystallization or vaporization, is characterized by a *discontinuity* in the primary thermodynamic variables, while a second-order transition is characterized by a sudden change in *slope* of these variables; i.e., by a discontinuity in the first derivative with respect to temperature of these variables. This is not a true thermodynamic singularity, hence should not properly be called a phase transition. In order to avoid this terminology, this change has also been called an "apparent second-order transition" or "glassy transition."

With most polymers, the value of the second-order transition temperature is a function of the rate of temperature change. As a result, this temperature has been defined as the lowest temperature at which an observable amount of viscous flow can occur under the influence of the forces acting on the molecules and *within the time limit of the experimental technique*. In other words, when the rate of viscous flow becomes too small to detect under the particular conditions of measurement, a second-order transition is found. Generally, the viscosity of a material at the transition temperature is about $10^{12}$ to $10^{13}$ poises.

For polymers of high molecular weight, the brittle temperature and the second-order transition temperature are close together. However, there are certain fundamental differences in the techniques of measurement of the two temperatures. The methods employed for the brittle temperature determination are more empirical than those for the second-order transition temperature. In the former tests, the values change with such variations as the method of testing, the rate of loading, and the sample dimensions. That is, the brittle temperature is that temperature at which the time interval required for the sample to undergo rupture in the test method used is just equal to the time interval over which the load is applied. At higher temperatures, the viscosity is lower and the sample will deform without breaking; whereas at lower temperatures, the reverse is true and the specimen breaks. It can be seen that the lower the molecular weight, the less the effect of intermolecular forces and chain entanglements, and the higher the brittle temperature becomes.

The second-order transition temperature is usually determined by relatively low-rate tests, such as thermal-expansion or heat-capacity measurements, so that physical deformation of the sample is not normally involved. As will be discussed in more detail later, the second-order transition temperature is that temperature at which sufficient energy is available to the molecular segments to cause them to begin to rotate. As the temperature is raised, increasing segmental rotation occurs, causing brittleness to decrease, so that fairly close occurrence of brittle and second-order transition temperatures is to be expected. However, while the second-order transition temperature depends upon the rate of relaxation of the molecular segments, the brittle temperature depends upon both these relaxation times and those of the sample as a whole. Thus, the different methods of test produce differences in numerical values.

Table 10-1 shows the approximate second-order transition temperatures for various polymers. Samples of the same polymer which have undergone different pretreatment may, however, give somewhat different results. In a given polymeric series, the second-order transition temperature $(T_m)$ gradually rises with increasing degree of polymerization, becoming constant at a molecular weight of about 20,000.

Upon inspection of Table 10-1, it will be noted that the typical elastomers have a $T_m$ of about $-40°C$ or lower, while the typical moldable plastics have a $T_m$ greater than about $+40°C$. Polymers having a $T_m$ between these two approximate temperatures have somewhat mixed properties. This is why either low or high but not intermediate amounts of sulfur are satisfactory for rubber vulcanization, since the $T_m$ of unvulcanized rubber (ca. $-73°C$) rises with increasing sulfur content to about 80°C for ebonite containing about 32 per cent of sulfur; intermediate products are of little commercial value.

The occurrence of a second-order transition has been explained as follows. When a liquid polymer at a temperature sufficiently high to provide extensive rotational, vibrational, and limited translational movements of its molecular segments is cooled, the average kinetic energy in each degree of freedom decreases. Because of the decreasing translational energy, mobility also decreases. As soon as vibrational energy has decreased to the value of the molar cohesion, crystallization begins, provided that recurrence-symmetry (the regularity with which similar structures occur along a polymer chain) requirements are met. Since these requirements are met by relatively few high-molecular-weight polymers and, further, since appreciable copolymerization or plasticization will prevent crystallization, this does not often occur. In such noncrystalline polymers, translation and vibration, and, consequently, mobility continue to decrease with fall in temperature and the polymer becomes increasingly harder and more rigid. If crystallization does, however, occur, translational movement, of course, ceases.

In either case, the rotational energy also decreases, and eventually the temperature is reached at which rotation ceases. This temperature is the second-order transition temperature. Since rotation occurs with molecular segments, molecular symmetry is of no importance, and all high-molecular-weight polymers will undergo a second-order transition, whether or not they exhibit a first-order transition.

TABLE 10-1.   APPROXIMATE SECOND-ORDER TRANSITION
TEMPERATURES, °C

| | |
|---|---|
| Silicone elastomers   .   .   .   . | −123 |
| Polybutadiene   .   .   .   .   . | −85 to −88 |
| Polyisobutylene .   .   .   .   . | −74 |
| Hevea rubber   .   .   .   .   . | −73 |
| Butyl rubber   .   .   .   .   . | −69 |
| GR-S   .   .   .   .   .   . | −61 |
| Thiokol A .   .   .   .   .   . | −50 |
| Neoprene GN   .   .   .   .   . | −40 |
| Nitrile rubber (40% nitrile) .   .   . | −23 |
| Poly(vinyl isobutyl ether)   .   .   . | −20 |
| Poly(vinylidene chloride)   .   .   . | −17 |
| Poly(methyl acrylate) .   .   .   . | 0 to 3 |
| Poly(vinyl acetate)   .   .   .   . | 28 |
| Cellulose acetate-propionate   .   . | 39 |
| Ethyl cellulose   .   .   .   .   . | 43 |
| Nylon 66 .   .   .   .   .   . | 47 |
| Poly(vinyl butyral)   .   .   .   . | 50 |
| Cellulose acetate-butyrate   .   .   . | 50 |
| Poly(N-vinyl pyrrolidone)   .   .   . | 54 |
| Cellulose nitrate   .   .   .   . | 66 |
| Poly(methyl methacrylate)   .   .   . | 60 to 70 |
| Cellulose acetate   .   .   .   . | 70 |
| Poly(vinyl chloride)   .   .   .   . | 75 |
| Ebonite   .   .   .   .   .   . | 80 |
| Poly(N-vinyl carbazole)   .   .   . | 85 |
| Polyindene.   .   .   .   .   . | 85 |
| Poly(vinyl alcohol)   .   .   .   . | 85 |
| Poly(acrylic acid)   .   .   .   . | 80 to 95 |
| Polystyrene   .   .   .   .   . | 81 to 100 |
| Polyacrylonitrile   .   .   .   . | ≫100 |

The ease of segmental rotation in a chain depends upon two factors —steric and polar effects in the individual chain and the effect of neighboring chains.   A chain becomes stiffer and the transition temperature rises as a substituent becomes more polar.   For example, the transition temperature of poly(vinyl acetate) is lower than that of poly(vinyl chloride) because the strong C-Cl dipole attractions in the latter decrease the ease of free rotation.   On the other hand, as the size of the substituent increases, interaction among the molecules decreases and causes a lowering of the transition temperature.   For example, in the methacrylic ester series, the higher esters are much more rubberlike than the lower esters, since the longer side-chain groups separate the chains more and thus act as internal plasticizers; the addition of plasticizers accomplishes the same result.

The introduction of side groups may sometimes increase the second-order transition and brittle temperatures.   For example, poly(methyl methacrylate) contains one more methyl group in each mesomer than does poly(methyl acrylate); the former has a second-order transition temperature considerably above that of the latter.   Here, however, steric hindrance of the methyl group by the bulky ester group may be the responsible factor, since both groups are bound to the same carbon atom and probably cause a decreased internal flexibility of the molecule.

In polystyrene, the bulky benzene groups apparently limit the flexibility of the molecule, thus causing higher brittle and second-order transition temperatures than might otherwise be expected. Polarization of the benzene groups must be appreciable in this polymer and consequent attraction among the molecules must be great, since there are very few external plasticizers compatible with this polymer.

As has been mentioned, the second-order transition temperature is affected by molecular weight (chain length), by stress, by copolymerization, by extent of cross-linking, and by plasticization. Cross-linking or vulcanization raises the second-order transition temperature, since it, in effect, stiffens the individual chains. Plasticization has a very pronounced effect on the value of the second-order transition and brittle temperatures. For example, the second-order transition temperature of poly(vinyl chloride) is about 75°C, but the addition of plasticizer can lower it sufficiently that it becomes an elastomer at room temperature [cf. unplasticized vs. plasticized poly(vinyl chloride), Chap. 9]. Fillers, on the other hand, have little or no effect on the transition temperature.

It should be apparent by this time that probably the most important factor that determines the value of the second-order transition and the brittle temperature is the strength of the intermolecular forces. As can be seen from an inspection of Table 10-1, examples of compounds which have strong secondary valence forces, hence high second-order transition (and brittle) temperatures, are polyacrylonitrile, poly(vinyl alcohol), poly(acrylic acid), and poly(vinyl chloride). Only in compounds having weak secondary valence forces are the molecules sufficiently mobile to form an elastic material at room temperature. As a result, only polymers having a relatively limited number of polar groups exhibit elastomeric properties. The butadiene-acrylonitrile copolymers which exhibit such properties contain only one nitrile group for every ten to fourteen carbon atoms in the chain, while polyacrylonitrile homopolymer contains a nitrile group on every other carbon atom and is hard and inflexible. It can thus be seen that the relation between composition and brittle or second-order transition temperature must be known, at least qualitatively, in order to predict the mechanical properties of polymers.

The appearance of a second-order transition occurs in a large number of tests or measurements, including those of thermal expansion, heat capacity, thermal conductivity, dielectric loss factor, and the modulus of elasticity. Only X-ray diffraction and melt viscosity measurements fail to exhibit a change at the transition temperature. Those measurements which exhibit a transition, although involving rotation of molecular segments, probably differ in the lengths and rates of rotation of the segments. Table 10-2 summarizes some of the measurements commonly made and the characteristic features involved.

TABLE 10-2. COMPARISON OF SOME COMMON TESTS FOR SECOND-ORDER TRANSITIONS IN POLYMERS[3]

| Test | Linear Deformation Required | Speed of Test (cycles per second) | Phenomenon Responsible for Transition |
|---|---|---|---|
| Heat capacity | Negligible | Slow (0.01) | Rotation of segments |
| Thermal expansion | Negligible | Slow (0.01) | Viscous flow |
| Young's modulus | Medium | Slow (0.1–1.0) | Effect of short range forces |
| Brittle point | Large | Rapid ($10^2$) | Uncoiling of polymer chains in highly elastic deformation |
| Dielectric loss | None | Very rapid ($10^2$–$10^6$) | Rotation of dipoles |
| Refractive index (molecular refraction) | None | Very rapid ($10^{14}$) | Change in mobility of electons with intermolecular force fields |

The authors of Table 10-2 have also plotted both second-order transition temperature ($T_m$) and brittle temperature ($T_b$) measurements as functions of the molecular weight of a typical polymeric substance (see Fig. 10-2). In the area below $T_m$, the polymer is a brittle solid in which the molecular segments only oscillate about their equilibrium positions; between $T_m$ and $T_b$, the polymer behaves internally as a liquid in which there occurs sluggish segmental rotation; above $T_b$, the polymer acts as an internally tough liquid, capable of developing rubberlike behavior at high molecular weights because of relatively easy segmental rotation. Fig. 10-2, although an approximation only, indicates how the factors of molecular weight and temperature affect the mechanical properties of polymeric substances. The foregoing discussion should help to explain the differences between the plastic and the elastic states. As has been pointed out earlier, rubberlike properties are obtained only in amorphous polymers of high molecular weight.

It should now be more clearly understood what was meant in the earlier section on Elastomers when it was stated that one of the requirements for a substance to exhibit elastomeric properties was that it must neither be highly crystalline nor must it exist in the glassy state (i.e., it must be above its second-order transition temperature). Thus, while polystyrene is an amorphous, high-molecular-weight polymer which can be given some permanence of structure by copolymerization with a very small amount of, say, divinyl benzene, its second-order transition occurs above normal use temperature and so it is known as a plastic. There are other factors

[3] Boyer, R. F. and Spencer, R. S., in Mark, H. and Whitby, G. S., eds., *Advances in Colloid Science*, Vol. II, Table IX, p. 49, Interscience Publishers, New York, 1946.

involved, of course, but the point made above is an important one. In other words, the value of the second-order transition temperature is of great importance in determining the physical state of an amorphous, high-molecular-weight polymer.

The vitreous, low-molecular-weight resins are also an important class of useful materials. Rosin, many other natural resins, and certain pitches are typical examples. These substances are supercooled, amorphous

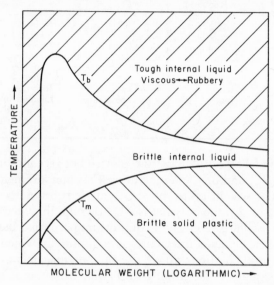

FIG. 10-2.    Proposed second-order phase diagram for polymers[4]

materials. At temperatures below their second-order transition, amorphous, high-molecular-weight polymers resemble them in physical behavior, except that the polymers are less brittle. This difference is, of course, attributable to the higher molecular weight of the polymers; their much longer molecules are inherently more flexible and are thus able to absorb a greater amount of an applied external stress.

## PLASTICIZATION

A plastic solid is one which will retain its shape at use temperature until acted upon by a stress which exceeds its yield value; upon application of an increasing stress, it deforms continuously and permanently. The latter property distinguishes a plastic from an elastomer. A plastic is a solid because there are sufficient attractive forces among the molecules to cause

[4] Boyer, R. F. and Spencer, R. S., in Mark, H. and Whitby, G. S., eds., *Advances in Colloid Science*, Vol. II, Fig. 23, p. 50, Interscience Publishers, New York, 1946.

resistance to flow, until the yield value is exceeded. The strength and character of the attractive forces among the molecules and their segments determine the degree of plasticity, since these internal forces must eventually be capable of being overcome by the application of the external stress in order to cause plastic (viscous) flow.

The *plasticity* of a material may be defined as the extent to which it will exhibit plastic flow. In broad terms, a *plasticizing agent* is any agent that increases the plasticity, although Blom[5] feels that the *reduction of brittleness* is a more accurate description. A *plasticizer* is any *added* substance that increases the plasticity of a mass. On the basis of this definition, heat is not a plasticizer, but can produce the same (or similar) effect as a plasticizer.

Plasticization of a substance increases its flexibility and extensibility, and decreases its yield point, elastic modulus, and tensile strength. Since flow is caused by the movement of molecules with respect to one other, the ease with which this relative motion occurs depends upon the strength of the attractive forces among the molecules. Hence, a plasticizing agent is one which operates by decreasing the intermolecular forces of attraction, thus increasing molecular mobility and, in effect, bringing the substance closer to the true liquid state at room temperature.

Methods of plasticization are commonly divided into two categories: *external* and *internal*. The former method involves the addition of modifying ingredients to a polymer or its solution and is nearly unlimited in its application, although suffering from several disadvantages. The latter involves modification of the polymer molecules themselves and represents the theoretically ideal way of adapting a resin for practical use, but it is, unfortunately, applicable only to a relatively limited extent.

### External Plasticization

Although polymers soften upon heating and are then easily molded, they, like almost all organic compounds, decompose at high temperatures. Historically, plasticizers were first used so that polymers could be molded at proper molding temperatures without damage; their function was, then, to make the composition more plastic (less viscous) at molding temperatures. Another important function, not fully appreciated until later, was to develop resilient characteristics in otherwise inelastic polymers. In addition to these two basic purposes, there are many specific reasons for the addition of particular plasticizers. For example, phosphates and chlorinated compounds decrease the flammability, while hydrocarbon plasticizers may improve the dielectric strength of many resins.

[5] Blom, A. V., *Organic Coatings in Theory and Practice*, p. 15, Elsevier Publishing Co.' Amsterdam (dist. by D. Van Nostrand Co., Princeton, N.J.), 1949.

Thermosetting compositions utilize plasticizers only to provide adequate flow just prior to the molding operation. Upon the application of heat, the plasticizer and resin no longer remain completely compatible, and an excessive amount of plasticizer may then "bleed out" by diffusion to the surface of the molded article.

The functions of plasticizers used in surface coatings are similar to those for the thermoplastic, hot-processed articles mentioned above. The addition of plasticizer increases the distensibility and flexibility and reduces brittleness, thus decreasing the tendency of the coating to check or chip. Although flexibility in coatings applied to rigid surfaces is not a major factor, the impact resistance is improved. Unsupported film and coatings used on cloth and paper, on the other hand, require the development of pliability, and plasticization accomplishes this.

The characteristic that differentiates true plasticizers from solvents and dispersing agents is volatility. True plasticizers are used as permanent components of plastic compositions; hence, they must be relatively nonvolatile compounds. Solvents and dispersion media, on the other hand, while acting as *temporary* plasticizing agents, are not expected to remain in the plastic composition. Certain nonvolatile additives, usually included with the plasticizers, consist of the class of relatively poor solvent liquids and are generally known as softeners. A true plasticizer may be distinguished from a softener in that the former increases the flexibility, workability, or shock resistance of a resinous material, whereas the latter can be substituted for a portion of a true plasticizer without appreciably affecting the mechanical properties of the substance being plasticized; i.e., it acts as an inert diluent.

True solution implies the complete release of molecules from interaction among themselves. This can be accomplished with low-molecular-weight compounds because the number of sites for intermolecular attraction between any two solute molecules is relatively small. Because of the great lengths of the chains and the many sites thereon available for intermolecular attractions, high-molecular-weight substances can rarely be truly dissolved. It is best, therefore, to think of the latter as being *dispersed* to a greater or lesser extent, rather than dissolved, when treated with a so-called solvent or plasticizer. On the basis of the above concept, "solvents" may be considered to be good, plasticizers to be fair, and softeners to be poor dispersing agents for high-molecular-weight substances. Then, plasticizers differ from softeners only in their effectiveness as molecular dispersing agents, while solvents may be distinguished from plasticizers and softeners not only upon the above basis, but also on their differences in volatility. Primary or true plasticizers are often called chemical plasticizers, while softeners are often known as secondary plasticizers or extenders.

Since true plasticizers are fair dispersing agents, forces of attraction exist which tend to bind the plasticizer and resin molecules together. Some high-molecular-weight compounds may not, however, be quite effective enough to disperse a resin at room temperature. By dispersing such plasticizers in the resin by hot milling or by adding it in combination with a volatile solvent which is subsequently removed, a permanently homogeneous dispersion can often be obtained. The molecular size of the plasticizer will determine, to a great extent, whether or not it will dissolve a plastic on contact. If the plasticizer molecules are small enough to penetrate the resin molecules, dispersion will usually be accomplished; dispersion will not occur if the plasticizer molecules are too large, regardless of the activity of the plasticizer. This is due to the fact that the strength of intermolecular forces decreases rapidly with distance, and the plasticizer molecules must penetrate those of the resin in order for the mutually attractive forces to become appreciable.

The dividing line between a plasticizer and a softener is not sharp. Plasticizers usually contain active (polar) groups, such as carbonyl, ether, nitrile, halide, or ester, that are present in low-molecular-weight solvents for the resin. Most of the primary plasticizers are esters. This is not fortuitous. Esters have such polarity and symmetry that their intermolecular forces of attraction are intermediate; they will therefore exhibit good compatibility with a wide variety of substances. However, the effectiveness of a plasticizer containing solvating groups in maintaining a homogeneous dispersion depends also upon the kinds and numbers of other atoms present in the plasticizer molecule.

Practically speaking, plasticizers which do not exude from a plasticized composition after long aging or upon frequent flexing are considered to be primary. Secondary plasticizers, which are nondispersants or, at best, poor dispersants, must always be blended with some primary plasticizer in order to be compatible and nonexuding. Many of the softeners are hydrocarbon-type (nonpolar) compounds. At use temperature, they are not sufficiently miscible with the resinous component to form a true homogeneous phase. Instead, there is present a mixture of a dispersion of the lower-molecular-weight fractions of the resin in the plasticizer enmeshed in a plasticizer-poor network formed by the larger, less soluble resin molecules. At elevated molding temperatures, however, the resin and plasticizer become and remain compatible.

The theory which best explains the mechanism of plasticization is known as the gel theory. Rigidity in an unplasticized resinous mass, as pointed out earlier in this chapter, is caused by a three-dimensional structure formed by individually weak, but collectively strong secondary valence bonds among the polymer molecules at intervals along their long molecular chains. An effective plasticizer penetrates between the molecules and decreases the number of polymer intermolecular attachments, thereby reducing the rigidity of the three-dimensional structure at a given temperature and permitting deformation without rupture. Although some displacement of neighboring molecules must occur when thick sections of material are deformed, the principal resistance to deformation is not considered to be internal friction among the molecules but rather to be due to the elastic resistance offered by the three-dimensional structure present.

With most plasticizers, the distensibility of a plasticized film decreases as the temperature is lowered; with some there is no change; yet with certain plasticizers the distensibility actually increases as the temperature is lowered. The above theory explains the latter unusual phenomenon on the basis that the particular plasticizer used becomes a more effective dispersant for the resin as the temperature is lowered, i.e., it exhibits an inverted dispersion-temperature relationship.

If increased flexibility in a mass is caused by the breaking of bonds between active centers in the three-dimensional network, the same result should be obtainable by introducing any substance into the polymer which will separate the molecules more. This is the explanation for plasticization by softeners. However, they are not satisfactory for such use alone because the active centers on the resin molecules are not neutralized by other active centers, such as are present in true plasticizers, but are instead merely separated by the mass of the neutral substance. Upon cooling, aging, or flexing, the attractive forces among the resin molecules will tend gradually to squeeze out the neutral softener and re-form the rigid structure originally present. This, of course, causes plasticizer exudation and resulting plastic embrittlement. The addition of some primary plasticizer with the softener results in partial neutralization of the active centers along the polymer molecules, thus decreasing the tendency for the resin molecules to reunite and squeeze out the neutral component. This is the reason that some true plasticizer is almost always used in conjunction with the less expensive softeners.

Contrary, perhaps, to expectation, better tear strength is observed in externally plasticized compositions than those which are internally plasticized, even if of equivalent composition. Since a portion of an external plasticizer present can be displaced under the action of concentrated pressure, it appears likely that some of the external plasticizer is squeezed out at the apex of a tear, causing local desolvation, resulting in greater concentration of the resin molecules at that point. This exudation of plasticizer cannot occur in an internally plasticized composition.

External plasticizers have been classified chemically as monomeric (a misnomer) or, preferably, simple, and polymeric, the latter class also being known as resinous. The simple plasticizers are typified by such compounds as the esters of phthalic, phosphoric, adipic, and sebacic acids. These esters are high-boiling liquids of relatively low viscosity, and are widely used in cellulose nitrate and vinyl resin lacquers. It is interesting to note that chemically closely related plasticizers often behave differently; thus, while aromatic phosphates exhibit low oil extraction but poor cold flexibility in vinyl resins, the aliphatic phosphates have a high rate of oil extraction combined with good cold flexibility. This means that, practically speaking, each plasticizer must be evaluated individually in every resinous composition, even though some generalizations are possible.

Polymeric plasticizers include those derived from both linear and polyfunctional condensation polymers, as well as the linear polymers obtained by vinyl polymerizations. Alkyds formed from tri- and tetrahydroxy alcohols as well as from certain glycols often make excellent plasticizers, especially those esterified with such long-chain dibasic acids as adipic and sebacic. Polymeric addition-type plasticizers generally produce flexible compositions of good toughness, even at very low temperatures. Poly(vinyl ethers) and certain polyacrylates are examples. Resinous plasticizers are particularly of value when migration and extraction of the plasticizer must be avoided. Since they seldom are sufficiently fluid to be used alone, blends of resinous and simple plasticizers are frequently used, particularly in formulating plastisol compositions. Vinyl resins can be plasticized with acrylonitrile-butadiene copolymers in the form of a colloidal blend. The nitrile copolymer acts as a polymeric plasticizer which is not easily extracted, does not migrate, and imparts high flexibility even at low temperatures.

It should be kept in mind that, although the lower-molecular-weight fractions of many addition polymers have good plasticizing action, the monomer is detrimental to the development of good physical properties in any polymer.

Plasticizers are used principally in the hot-processing, coatings and adhesives, and safety-glass industries. Hot-processing operations include the molding, calendering, and extruding of thermoplastic resins. By the addition of plasticizers, the working temperature for milling, mixing, and forming is lowered, while greater pliability and impact resistance are conferred on the finished article. Over half of the plasticizer production is consumed in this field. Of this amount, a large portion is accounted for in vinyl resin compositions, particularly those containing poly(vinyl chloride) and its copolymers. The vinyl acetate and vinyl butyral resins, when used in hot-processing applications, generally do not require plasticizers. Polystyrene and the acrylic resins are also not usually plasticized as this process degrades their mechanical properties appreciably because they lack the crystallinity and the high intermolecular forces which help to prevent cold flow. Cross-linking of polystyrene would prevent cold flow but would, however, make the molding process more difficult, unless it were done subsequent to molding, as in the vulcanization of rubber. Poly(vinylidene chloride) and polyacrylonitrile can be externally plasticized by very few substances because of their strong intermolecular attractions and resulting general incompatibilities.

Almost all of the cellulosics, because of their very polar nature, must be plasticized. The acetate and the mixed esters are used principally in hot-processing applications; the nitrate is used principally in coatings (lacquers); and the ethers are used in both fields.

Thermoplastic polymers used as adhesives usually require plasticizers to improve tack and reduce brittleness. The manufacture of safety glass requires the use of a few plasticizers that are specific for this application. As will be recalled, the interlayer in safety glass is composed of plasticized poly(vinyl butyral). The only plasticizers so far found suitable for this application are triethylene glycol di(2-ethyl butyrate), di(butyl Cellosolve)adipate, and dibutyl sebacate.

Thermosetting resins are sometimes plasticized. Since plasticizers are added to a thermosetting mix specifically to increase plasticity just prior to the actual molding operation, rather than to effect modification in the properties of the finished product, the plasticizers used for this purpose are not the conventional types used with thermoplastic resins, and the mechanism of plasticization is not the same, as has been mentioned earlier. The so-called plasticizer probably acts to prevent premature cross-linking at many points which would normally react sooner in the absence of the plasticizer.

Most elastomers are plasticized for reasons similar to those for the thermosetting resins; i.e., to aid principally during processing. The intensive shearing action of a rubber mill or Banbury in the presence of air accomplishes some depolymerization of the polymer, and rubber softeners appear to assist in this depolymerization. Many raw synthetic elastomers require so much softener that so-called vulcanizable plasticizers have been developed. These compounds are capable of attachment to the polymer by primary valence bonds during the vulcanization process. They thus can act as plasticizers during the milling operation, yet cannot bleed from the vulcanizate. Such plasticizers include unsaturated hydrocarbon and vegetable oils which will react with sulfur, and certain phenol-aldehyde resins which are semiliquid at milling temperatures and become cross-linked during the vulcanization process.

There are many properties which must be carefully evaluated to determine the suitability of a specific plasticizer for a specific application. Factors which affect the ease of processing are of great importance. Even the specific gravity is considered because, although plasticizers function by volume, they are purchased by weight. Thus, all aspects of performance, including cost, must be taken into consideration when selecting the most suitable plasticizer for a specific use. The technical requirements desirable in a plasticizer are listed.

*Desirable Characteristics of a Plasticizer*

Wide compatibility
Low vapor pressure
Resistance to migration
High plasticizing efficiency
Resistance to chemical change
Retention of flexibility at low temperatures
Resistance to degradation by heat and light
    (including ultraviolet)
Good electrical characteristics
Ability to impart nonflammability
Freedom from odor, taste, and toxicity
Low viscosity change with temperature change
Resistance to extraction by water and organic solvents

Not all of the above properties will be found in any one plasticizer. It is necessary to select a plasticizer having the most important property or group of properties desired for the particular application. In many cases, a combination of plasticizers is used in order to secure the best compromise in properties.

The minimum quantity of plasticizer is used which will give the desired properties. This is so because, in general, the less the amount used, the better will be the combination of properties in the product. Generally speaking, a plasticizer is used to compensate for the deficiencies in a polymer; the ideal plastic would require no external plasticizer.

### Internal Plasticization

As was stated earlier in this section, the theoretically ideal way to modify a resin so that its physical properties are optimum would be by internal plasticization; i.e., by modification of the polymer structure by introducing appropriately spaced groups of proper polarity and dimensions along the main polymer chain. Because such groups would be bound by primary valence bonds to the polymer molecule, exudation, extractability, and loss by volatilization—the principal deficiencies of external plasticization—could not occur.

Unfortunately, in spite of the many attempts to produce the ideal plastic by this means, resins which have been internally plasticized do not exhibit adequate strength at one temperature when they have been designed for satisfactory flexibility at some lower temperature. This property severely limits the useful temperature range of internally plasticized polymers.

Such polymers are inferior to their externally plasticized counterparts in this respect because, in the latter case, the plasticizer molecules are in dynamic equilibrium (solvating and desolvating) with the polymer molecules at any given temperature and concentration. Since the most useful external plasticizers incur an increase in solvating (dispersing) power as the temperature is lowered, this automatically compensates for the normally increasing rigidity in polymers under the same conditions. Obviously, plasticizing groups held by covalent bonds to the polymer molecules cannot enter into such an equilibrium reaction; thus a polymer, properly plasticized for low temperature use, would be too highly plasticized at room temperature or higher.

An example of this method of chemically modifying an already existing homopolymer is that of partially or totally replacing the acetyl groups in poly(vinyl acetate) with acetal groups; the properties of the resulting polymer; e.g., poly(vinyl butyral); are quite different from those of the unmodified polymer. The technique of graft "copolymerization" is similar in principle.

Nevertheless, many resins are internally plasticized and perform quite adequately. However, the method of internal plasticization utilized commercially consists in the formation of copolymers. A monomer yielding a polymer of high strength or hardness is copolymerized with another monomer which produces a polymer having better flexibility. The plasticizing structure thus becomes a permanent part of the polymer structure. A common example of this type of plasticization is that of vinyl chloride with vinyl acetate (see Vinyl Chloride Copolymers, Chap. 9). Polymers having relatively high softening temperatures, such as poly(vinyl chloride), methacrylic resins, and polystyrene, are thus plasticized internally by copolymerization of their monomers with such monomers as butadiene, isobutylene, isoprene, acrylic esters, and vinyl acetate.

## RHEOLOGY

Rheology is the science treating of the deformation and flow of matter. This is a very complex subject, and only a brief excursion into the field will be made. It must be borne in mind that the behavior of most polymeric substances under stress is determined by a multiplicity of interdependent factors; hence, only "ideal" relationships are amenable to simple mathematical expression and solution. An approach to the problem of mechanical deformation of polymers can best be made by a brief discussion of the principal types of deformation which occur.

The simplest mechanical behavior under stress of an amorphous, high-molecular-weight polymer is represented by three components: an instantaneous elastic response, a retarded elastic response, and, when extended beyond its elastic limit, a flow. The instantaneous elastic response also occurs in low-molecular-weight amorphous materials and is due to the stretching or compression of primary valence bonds and distortion of interbond angles; the retarded or highly elastic response is due to the straightening out of the curled molecules; flow is caused by the motions of the centers of gravity of the chains relative to each other and is always a permanent deformation. Obviously, the nature of the over-all response depends upon the relative magnitudes of these three components.

*Instantaneous elastic deformation* is said to occur when a solid, subjected to a stress, develops a strain (or deformation) which is directly proportional to the applied stress, provided that the latter is not too large (Hooke's law). This is expressed as follows:

$$\frac{\text{unit stress}}{\text{unit strain}} = E \ (\text{Young's } \textit{tensile} \text{ or } \textit{compressive} \text{ modulus of elasticity}) \quad (1)$$

or, in terms of shear stress and shear strain:

$$\frac{S}{\gamma} = G \ (\textit{shear} \text{ modulus of elasticity}) \quad (2)$$

where $S$ is the shear stress and $\gamma$ is the shear strain.

As a visual analogy, it is observed that an unloaded helical spring develops a deformation instantaneously upon the application of a stress and that the loaded spring recovers its original shape completely and instantaneously when the stress is released. This relationship is the only one which is *independent of time*. It is important to remember that Hooke's law holds only for very small deformations; once the so-called proportional limit of the substance is passed, the modulus no longer remains constant, the deformation is usually no longer completely recoverable, and time effects become evident.

A *retarded elastic response* contains a damping resistance to the establishment of elastic equilibrium. This may be expressed mathematically in terms of shear as:

$$S = \eta \frac{d\gamma}{dt} + G\gamma \quad (3)$$

The constant, $\eta$, is the coefficient of viscosity (usually simply called the viscosity) or the internal friction of the substance, expressed in poises. Upon integration,

$$\gamma = \frac{S}{G}(1 - e^{-\left(\frac{G}{\eta}\right)t}) = \frac{S}{G}(1 - e^{-t/\tau}) \quad (4)$$

where $\tau(=\eta/G)$ is known as the *retardation time*. Thus, at constant stress, a substance exhibiting such a response relaxes exponentially at a rate determined by its retardation time.

Thus, when a solid substance is stressed, a deformation occurs. When the stress is removed, the deforming movement will cease, due to the internal friction (viscosity) of the material. The deformation will be permanent or may disappear partly or entirely. The portion of the deformation which recovers is called elastic deformation and is composed of an instantaneous elastic response and a retarded elastic response. That portion of the deformation which is permanent is called flow. This nonrecoverable or plastic deformation (flow) occurs when the stress exceeds the yield value (see below), and is caused by mutual slippage of structural units, either at the molecular level or higher.

*Flow* may be classified as Newtonian and non-Newtonian in behavior. An incompressible Newtonian fluid responds to stress in a simple fashion: shear stresses result in *viscous* flow. If the fluid is incompressible, a uniform compressive stress causes no strain. The term "Newtonian" indicates a direct proportionality between shear stress and rate of flow; i.e.,

$$S = \eta \frac{d\gamma}{dt} \tag{5}$$

or

$$\frac{\text{unit stress}}{\text{unit strain}} = \frac{\eta}{t} \tag{6}$$

[These equations hold only for viscous (streamline) flow.] Thus, in a Newtonian liquid, a force on any section is perpendicular to the plane of that section and no shearing stress exists; i.e., no stress tending to produce a deformation. Such a shearing stress can exist in a solid, even when at rest. Intermediate characteristics are displayed by very viscous liquids (semisolids), since they will not support a shearing stress when at rest, yet can do so when in motion.

With few exceptions pure liquids closely approximate Newtonian behavior; i.e., their viscosities are approximately constant up to very high stress values. Strictly speaking, however, since every liquid is slightly compressible, some deviation from the linear relation between stress and flow does occur, particularly with liquids of high viscosity. As a matter of fact, all real liquids exhibit an elastic as well as a viscous response under shear, despite the usual definition of a liquid as a material which will not support a shear stress except by undergoing flow.

Many solutions of polymers do not possess the simple linear characteristic of a Newtonian fluid (curve 2, Fig. 10-3); their behavior cannot be expressed by a single parameter. The coefficient of viscosity, as previously defined (Eq. 5), now becomes dependent upon the shear stress and thus has no precise meaning. It is often called the "apparent coefficient of viscosity." Non-Newtonian flow can be expressed mathematically by the following general relation:

$$S = f\left(\frac{d\gamma}{dt}\right) \tag{7}$$

Most plastic solids and many solutions of polymers exhibit only elastic deformation when subjected to very small stresses; above a certain value of shearing stress, which is known as the *yield value*, they begin to flow. The appearance of a yield value in solutions of high-molecular-weight polymers can be explained on the basis that the long polymer molecules are held together by intermolecular forces and cannot be torn apart until a certain stress has been reached, at which time flow begins. In cases where the yield value is very large, a solution flowing through a tube flows only along the wall of the tube and is pushed through the center as an undeformed solid, the process being known as "plug flow."

When a polymer exhibits first elastic and then plastic deformation, Bingham's[6] relationship between stress and flow is often of value:

$$S - S_o = \eta \cdot \frac{d\gamma}{dt} \tag{8}$$

where $S_o$ is the yield value of stress. This equation defines purely plastic flow (curve 4, Fig. 10-3). Usually, however, the stress-flow curves of most polymeric substances are more complex, and at low values of flow a nonlinear region often appears, thus making it difficult to determine whether there is, in fact, a yield value or whether the curve actually returns to the origin. In such cases, it is usual practice to extend the linear portion of the curve so as to intercept the $S$ axis; the value of the intercept is then called the yield value (curve 5, Fig. 10-3).

A material which obeys Bingham's relation is called an ideal plastic material. When the stress is less than the yield value, $S_o$, no flow occurs. At stresses greater than $S_o$, steady flow occurs which is no longer proportional to the total stress, $S$, but to the amount by which the stress exceeds the yield value, $(S - S_o)$. Few plastic materials, however, exhibit ideal plastic flow, their stress-flow relationship showing appreciable curvature above the yield value.

Figure 10-3 illustrates the principal types of flow which are found to occur in a diverse array of substances. Curve 2 illustrates true Newtonian flow. Deformation occurs at any shearing stress above zero and is directly proportional to the magnitude of the stress. Permanent deformation of most semisolid or solid substances occurs only after the yield value is exceeded, as shown by curve 4. Moreover, as pointed out previously, with such substances the stress-flow relation is more or less curved, as in

[6] Bingham, E. C., *Fluidity and Plasticity*, McGraw-Hill Book Co., New York, 1922.

curve 5.  Note that while only one viscosity measurement is needed to describe Newtonian flow, two measurements at different rates of shear are required for ideal plastic flow; many more than two are necessary to describe properly the type of flow when the stress-flow relationship is not inear.

Two less common types of flow are known as dilatant and pseudoplastic flow.  In both types, there is no yield point.  Dilatant flow, exemplified by highly pigmented dispersions and suspensions of raw cornstarch in

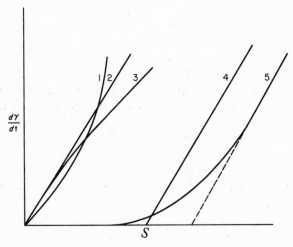

FIG. 10-3.  Types of flow

water (or by wet sand), occurs when the viscosity increases more rapidly than the stress as the latter is increased (curve 3).  In pseudoplastic flow, the reverse occurs (curve 1).  Casein suspensions and many latices exhibit the latter type of flow.  It is obvious that the rate of shear must be given when reporting viscosities by either method.  An equation which will approximate all of the above types of flow is that due to Herschel and Bulkley:[7]

$$(S - S_o)^n = \phi \cdot \frac{d\gamma}{dt} \tag{9}$$

where $\phi$ is some function of $\eta$.  When $S_o = 0$ and $n = 1$, this reduces to Newton's equation; when $n = 1$, this becomes Bingham's equation.

In all of the above cases, the rheological properties were independent of the past history of the material.  On the other hand, there do exist

[7] Herschel, W. and Bulkley, R., "Konsistenzmessungen von Gummi-Benzollosungen," *Kolloid-Z.*, **39**, 291 (1926).

other materials, such as certain clay suspensions, highly pigmented pastes, and certain paints, which gel or solidify upon standing and liquefy upon agitation, the change of state being, at least to some extent, reversible. This phenomenon is known as thixotropy. With such substances, the stress-flow curve will consist of two lines, one representing the properties of the material upon application of increasing shear and the other, those properties upon decreasing shear. Thus, to plot the complete rheological properties of a thixotropic material, twice as many experimental observations are necessary as those required for the other types of non-Newtonian flow and nonideal plastic flow.

The purely elastic relationships between shear stress and shear strain have been outlined above (Eqs. 2 and 4). It has been pointed out that many substances show both an elastic and a plastic (flow) response to stress. This combination of responses may also be related mathematically. Thus, as a relatively simple example, assume that a material under consideration undergoes both an instantaneous elastic response and a flow. The total deformation is, of course, the sum of its elastic deformation and its flow. This may be expressed by the following Maxwellian relation:

$$\frac{d\gamma}{dt} = \frac{1}{G} \cdot \frac{dS}{dt} + \frac{S}{\eta} \tag{10}$$

For a fixed deformation process, $d\gamma/dt = 0$, and

$$\frac{1}{G} \cdot \frac{dS}{dt} = -\frac{S}{\eta} \tag{11}$$

Upon integration (assuming that $G$ and $\eta$ remain constant),

$$S = S_o e^{-\left(\frac{G}{\eta}\right)t} = S_o e^{-t/\tau} \tag{12}$$

where $\tau(=\eta/G)$ is here known as the *relaxation time* and is the time required for the original stress, $S_o$, to decrease to $1/e$ of its original value; i.e., to decrease to the value $S_o/e$. The relaxation *rate* is, of course, the reciprocal of the relaxation time (cf. retardation time).

Unfortunately from the mathematical point of view, in all real substances both the modulus and the viscosity do not remain constant, the latter changing especially rapidly with temperature. The treatment above is merely a special case of the more general relationship in which all of the functions are variable; they may, in fact, vary in quite complicated ways.

For most simple liquids, the relaxation rates are much greater than the flow rates in viscometry measurements. The effects of elasticity can, therefore, be generally disregarded. However, high-molecular-weight polymers and their solutions, because of their high viscosities and low elastic moduli, frequently have much slower relaxation rates; in such cases, the elastic deformation may no longer be disregarded.

In closing, the behavior of vulcanized rubber, as an example of a slightly cross-linked polymer, may be qualitatively described. If rubber were an ideal, viscous liquid, the stress created by a fixed deformation would vanish instantaneously. Since vulcanized rubber is slightly cross-linked, relaxation of chains is somewhat restricted, so that the stress decreases to some limiting value above zero. Unvulcanized rubber and many other elastomeric polymers will have a lower limiting value, but the rate of relaxation will still be much less than that of an ideal liquid. Under the condition of constant stress, on the other hand, the deformation will continue and, upon removal of stress, a permanent deformation will appear; i.e., the specimen will exhibit plastic flow.

### TENSILE STRENGTH DEPENDENCIES

Since mechanical strength properties of all structural materials are of vital interest to the engineer, it is necessary that the dependence of these properties upon molecular constitution and environmental conditions be understood. Most of the information contained in this section has been stated elsewhere in this book, but is scattered and has not been directed specifically to the relationships emphasized herein.

In any linear polymer, the tensile strength is dependent upon two principal factors: the strength of the primary covalent bonds between molecular segments and the strength of the secondary valence forces (and hydrogen bonding), the latter of which, by intermolecular attraction, resist mutual chain slippage. The shorter the average chain length, the fewer will be the points of intermolecular attraction; since the intermolecular bonds are much weaker individually than the intramolecular bonds, a stress is more likely to cause structural failure by the relative movements of chains past one another rather than by the breaking of primary bonds, unless the collective strength of the secondary bonds becomes sufficiently great. Therefore, in order to increase the tensile strength sufficiently, so that failure can occur only by rupture of the strong primary bonds, the chain must be longer than some minimum length; i.e., the length at which the total strength of the intermolecular forces is equal to the minimum primary bond strength.

It is found experimentally that the tensile strength of polymers in general does not become appreciable until the number-average degree of polymerization reaches about 40 to 80 for plastics and about 150 for fibers. Above these values, the tensile strength increases rapidly with increasing chain length, up to a degree of polymerization of about 200 to 250; above this range, the rate of increase becomes less and usually levels off at about 600 to 700.   The leveling off comes at a lower degree of polymerization for polymers whose molecules display strong intermolecular forces.   The above general relationships apply also to impact and flexural strengths.

It seems reasonable to suppose that a low-molecular-weight polymer fails under tension principally by the pulling apart of chain ends caused by the mutual slippage of chains, since the relatively short, adjacent chains can slip past one another.   In a very high-molecular-weight polymer, failure of this type would require the mutual slippage of long, tangled chains.   As pointed out previously, even though the intermolecular forces are individually much weaker than the intramolecular forces, as molecular length increases and the number of points of intermolecular attraction also increases, it eventually becomes easier to break the primary bonds than to force the molecules to slip past each other.

It is more difficult to predict the effect of various molecular weight distributions, or the effect of the presence of very high- or very low-molecular-weight material, upon the tensile strength and related mechanical properties.   So far as is now known, the most important characteristic of a molecular weight distribution appears to be the number-average molecular weight of a sample.   It has been pointed out earlier in this chapter, however, that very short molecules have a greater deleterious effect than their weight-fraction in the polymer would indicate.

Orientation of linear polymers is usually, although not necessarily, accompanied by crystallization, and the determination of the relative importance of the two phenomena on the tensile strength of a polymer is difficult.   Research upon natural rubber has indicated that axial orientation of the molecules has the greater influence.   Lateral orientation of the chains, however, which is equivalent to crystallization, further increases the tensile strength.   Any type of oriented polymer, of course, has appreciably greater tensile strength than amorphous material.   Although not enough information has yet been accumulated to establish a numerical relationship between the degree of orientation and tensile strength, the fact that decrease in amount of disordered areas increases the strength of a polymer is well established.

The strength of a polymer depends not only upon its molecular configuration but also upon the influence of its environment.   For example, water serves as a plasticizer for many polymers, and its effect is to increase toughness and ductility at the expense of tensile strength.   The effect is roughly proportional to the amount of water absorbed; thus, plastics containing an appreciable number of hydrophilic groups (carboxyl, hydroxyl, amino) are more affected than those which are composed of only hydrocarbons or their halogenated derivatives.

The effect of temperature varies, depending upon the type of polymer.

Thermoplastic polymers generally soften and lose their mechanical strength at temperatures well below those which cause appreciable thermal decomposition. Loss of external plasticizer, when used, by exposure to elevated temperatures, even though below decomposition temperature, can cause a decrease in ductility and toughness, even though strength and stiffness are increased. Thermosetting polymers, on the other hand, usually maintain their good mechanical properties up to fairly high temperatures, provided, of course, their decomposition temperature is not reached.

Exposure to very low temperatures affects only slightly the strength characteristics of most plastics unless cracking or checking (caused by insufficient relaxation) occurs or unless a slow crystallization, induced in highly oriented masses by the low temperature, takes place.

## REFERENCES AND RECOMMENDED READING

Alexander, J., ed., *Colloid Chemistry Theoretical and Applied*, Vol. VI, Reinhold Publishing Corp., New York, 1946.

Alfrey, T., Jr., *Mechanical Behavior of High Polymers*, Interscience Publishers, New York, 1948.

Bawn, C. E. H., *The Chemistry of High Polymers*, Butterworths, London (dist. by Interscience Publishers, New York), 1948.

Billmeyer, F. W., Jr., *Textbook of Polymer Chemistry*, Interscience Publishers, New York, 1957.

Blom, A. V., *Organic Coatings*, Elsevier Publishing Co., Amsterdam (dist. by D. Van Nostrand Co., Princeton, N.J.), 1949.

Boundy, R. H. and Boyer, R. F., *Styrene*, Reinhold Publishing Corp., New York, 1952.

Burk, R. E. and Grummitt, O., eds., *The Chemistry of Large Molecules*, Interscience Publishers, New York, 1943.

Buttrey, D. N., *Plasticizers*, Cleaver-Hume Press, London (dist. by Interscience Publishers, New York), 1950.

D'Alelio, G. F., *Fundamental Principles of Polymerization*, John Wiley and Sons, New York, 1952.

Doolittle, A. K., *The Technology of Solvents and Plasticizers*, John Wiley and Sons, New York, 1954.

Fleck, H. R., *Plastics*, 2nd ed., Chemical Publishing Co., Brooklyn, N.Y., 1949.

Flory, P. J., *Principles of Polymer Chemistry*, Cornell University Press, Ithaca, N.Y., 1953.

Frith, E. M. and Tuckett, R. F., *Linear Polymers*, Longmans, Green and Co., London–New York, 1951.

Glasstone, S., *Textbook of Physical Chemistry*, 2nd ed., D. Van Nostrand Co., Princeton, N.J., 1946.

Hill, R., ed., *Fibres from Synthetic Polymers*, Elsevier Publishing Co., Amsterdam (dist. by D. Van Nostrand Co., Princeton, N.J.), 1950.

Houwink, R., ed., *Elastomers and Plastomers*, Vol. I, Elsevier Publishing Co., Amsterdam (dist. by D. Van Nostrand Co., Princeton, N.J.), 1950.

Mark, H. and Tobolsky, A. V., *Physical Chemistry of High Polymeric Systems*, 2nd ed., Interscience Publishers, New York, 1950.

Mark, H. and Whitby, G. S., eds., *Advances in Colloid Science*, Vol. II, Interscience Publishers, New York, 1946.

Mason, J. P. and Manning, J. F., *The Technology of Plastics and Resins*, D. Van Nostrand Co., Princeton, N.J., 1945.

Meyer, K. H., *Natural and Synthetic High Polymers*, 2nd ed., Interscience Publishers, New York, 1950.

Moncrieff, R. W., *Artificial Fibres*, 2nd ed., John Wiley and Sons, New York, 1954.

Payne, H. F., *Organic Coating Technology*, John Wiley and Sons, New York, 1954.

Ritchie, P. D., *A Chemistry of Plastics and High Polymers*, Cleaver-Hume Press, London (dist. by Interscience Publishers, New York), 1949.

Schmidt, A. X. and Marlies, C. A., *Principles of High-Polymer Theory and Practice*, McGraw-Hill Book Co., New York, 1948.

Twiss, S. B., ed., *Advancing Fronts in Chemistry*, Vol. I., Reinhold Publishing Corp., New York, 1945.

Whitby, G. S., *Synthetic Rubber*, John Wiley and Sons, New York, 1954.

## Chapter 11

# FABRICATING AND PROCESSING

In this chapter there will be discussed and illustrated many of the ingenious techniques which engineers have developed to transform powders, granules, sheets, and liquids into the myriad shapes and forms useful for countless applications.

Monomers and polymers (and, for that matter, all other structural materials) are of little or no practical use until the raw product from the manufacturing process has been transformed by more or less standardized fabrication and processing techniques into useful forms. Hence, the task is to convert liquids (in the case of monomers) or solids (in the case of polymers) into physical states and shapes which will be useful for the applications for which they are intended. Note here the distinction between fabrication and application. The former involves a manufacturing technique to put the raw material in the *physical shape* or *state* suitable for use. The latter term involves the *use* of the product for the purpose for which it was fabricated or processed.

Most attempts at classifying the diverse methods of fabrication and processing have met with small success, in large part due to the fact that many final shapes may be obtained by more than one method. A further difficulty in discussing these methods arises from the inexact and often ambiguous nomenclature which has evolved in industry. The following system of classification of fabrication and processing techniques is possibly the most satisfactory method and is based upon the physical state of the raw product, since this will, to a large extent, determine the method of processing.

TABLE 11-1. PROCESSING OF POLYMERS

| *Solids* | *Liquids and Melts* |
|---|---|
| Molding | Coating |
| Extrusion | Expanding or Foaming |
| Calendering | Casting |
| Sheet forming | Spinning |

*Solids and Liquids*
Laminating and impregnating

## MOLDING

Molding is usually defined as "the process of forming in or into a particular shape." This definition is a very broad one, and the term may justly be extended to include extrusion, forming, impregnating, expanding, casting, and spinning, all of which involve a shaping operation of some kind. In order to differentiate between the types of shaping mentioned above and those involving the use of a closed mold, molding, as used in this section, will be defined as the shaping of an article from a plastic material by the application of pressure (and, usually, heat) in a *closed chamber*.

### Cold Compression Molding

Cold molding is one of the oldest methods of shaping plastic materials. The process possesses an economic advantage over most other molding techniques and for this reason has continued to be used. On a percentage basis, its use is decreasing because of the strong competition from the faster, and, in many cases, higher quality molding processes which have subsequently appeared.

This type of molded product first came into use in the United States about 1908–09, at approximately the same time as the advent of the phenolic hot-molded compounds. Both were the result of a search for a heat-resistant, molded, insulating material for use in the electrical and automotive industries. Its predecessor, porcelain, although widely used because of its fireproof, heatproof, and waterproof properties, was so brittle that it frequently could not be used in spite of its excellent insulating qualities. Other products investigated were vulcanized fiber, hard-rubber compounds, and shellac, but, due to individual limitations, all were eventually superseded by compositions made by the cold-molding process.

Cold-molding compounds may be divided into two types, depending upon their compositions and temperature limitations: nonrefractory (organic) and refractory (inorganic). In general, the binders suitable for nonrefractory cold-molding compounds are of two classes, bituminous and resinous. The bituminous class includes asphalt, gilsonite, and pitches, which are blended with drying oils. Resinous binders usually consist of phenolic resins dissolved or dispersed in solvents. This type generally has better electrical and mechanical properties than the bituminous type. Fillers used consist principally of asbestos fibers, silica, and magnesia.

(Refractory cold-molding compounds usually contain Portland cement, clay, lime, silica, or phosphoric acid as the binder, all filled with asbestos; all but the last-named binder are moistened with water before molding.)

Cold-molding compositions differ from all others in that they are

manufactured at the place of molding.   This is so because their preparation requires only simple mixing of readily available components and the
mixed batches have a tendency to dry out or cure if not molded soon after
mixing.

The molding operation is similar to hot compression molding except
that the molds require neither heating nor cooling.   Whenever possible,
the cold-molding powder is preshaped to the approximate shape of the
finished article.   The charge placed in the mold must be accurately
measured, since neither flow nor flash of the material occurs during the
molding operation.   Since cold molding is merely a compression of the
molding mixture, the change in the mold is purely physical.   The pressing

FIG. 11-1.   Electrical components fabricated by the cold molding process; left, an
aluminum silicate-lime refractory item; center, a mineral filled-melamine item; right,
a filled phenolic molding.   (*Courtesy Rostone Corp.*)

operation operates under pressures of from 2,000 to as high as 30,000 psi
and is continued only long enough to mold the material into the desired
shape.   After removal from the mold, the article is transferred to an oven
and is baked at temperatures of 80° to 260°C, depending upon the binder
used.

The molding operation itself is very rapid, since there is no heating or
cooling cycle.   The low cost of the molding material and the high production rate, which usually eliminates the need for expensive multiple-
cavity molds, have served to keep the cold-molding process in use.

Cold-molded parts usually lack the surface smoothness and gloss
associated with hot-molded or cast plastics; even the high pressures
required to compensate for the lack of plastic flow of these materials are
not sufficient to reproduce accurately fine mold design, and, therefore,
cold-molded articles are usually limited to simple shapes.   Since the
articles are primarily of value for their good electrical characteristics,
appearance is not usually of great importance.   Common electrical
products include such items as connector plugs, switch bases, outlet covers,

attachment plugs and caps, and sockets. Other items, such as buttons, checkers, and storage battery cases, are often cold molded.

## Hot Compression Molding

Hot compression molding, because it is much more commonly employed than cold compression molding, is usually called simply compression molding. Its distinguishing feature is the application of pressure to a molding powder in a heated and closed mold. This fundamental idea of shaping a plastic body by heat and pressure was first applied by Baekeland to phenol-formaldehyde resins about 1907. Since that time, the art of compression molding has been continually improved and refined. Although the principle of heating and shaping by pressure in the same cavity is still actively followed, newer developments, such as transfer and injection molding, have demonstrated that the principle of heating and shaping in separate chambers is also of great value.

Thermoplastics can be molded by this technique, but then the molds must be cooled before removal of the shaped article and must be reheated before receiving the next charge. This expense, the time lost, and the development of faster and more satisfactory methods for molding thermoplastics have restricted the process mainly to the molding of thermosetting compounds. Compression molding is used, however, with some rigid and unplasticized thermoplastics which are so viscous or unstable at their maximum molding temperatures that unsatisfactory results by other techniques occur.

In the general process of compression molding, the charge is placed in a heated mold, and the mold is closed, generally under low pressure, until pressure is exerted on the material. The material becomes plastic and, as the mold continues to close, the softened material is forced to fill all the cavities of the mold. High pressure is applied to the mold just before it is completely closed in order to insure complete filling of the mold. The molded article is kept under pressure until it is cured, after which the mold is opened and the molded part is removed. Often the mold is allowed to breathe (i.e., is opened momentarily after first closing it) in order to allow gases present (air, moisture, etc.) to escape before the final closing is performed. From this brief description, it may appear that the process is a very simple one. It is true that the principle is simple, but the actual techniques used, materials of mold construction, and mold design have evolved after many years of engineering evolution. Some of these techniques and considerations will now be briefly discussed.

The mold charge may be used as supplied (i.e., loose granules, beads, chips, scraps of resin-impregnated cord or fabric), or it may be *tableted* or *preformed*. Tableting involves the pressing of the compounded resin into a cylindrical, rectangular, annular, or other simple shape having some common use, singly or in multiple, in various molds in the molding plant. In preforming, the material is roughly pressed into the shape of the molding to be produced.  In rarer cases, where flow is poor (e.g., polytetrafluoroethylene), complete shaping of the preforms to the mold cavity is advantageous.  Tablets and preforms are usually much less dense than is the final molding, but are appreciably more compacted than the original material.

Although it requires a separate operation, tableting or preforming offers several advantages.  The charge may be handled with greater facility, both in loading of the mold and in preheating of the charge.  A big advantage is that automatic premeasurement of the charge is accomplished.  Tablets and preforms are pressed to the desired shape without heat at pressures ranging from 5,000 to 20,000 psi (cf. cold molding).

*Preheating* of the molding material before it is placed in the mold is a common operation.  By its use, less pressure is required for molding, and the cure time is decreased (especially for thick sections); in fact, preheating is a prerequisite for plunger molding (see Transfer Molding). Further, because of the greater fluidity of the charge, preheating makes possible the molding of pieces containing intricate or delicate inserts. The heat also insures using a dry material, resulting in optimum electrical properties and reduced shrinkage.

There are three general types of preheating: high frequency, steam, and air.  The first type is also known as heatronic molding and electronic heating.  This process consists in preheating a plastic by placing it in a high frequency (2 to 70 megacycles per second) electric field prior to the molding operation.  In such a rapidly reversing field, a tremendous amount of internal molecular friction occurs, with the resulting formation of heat.  This method of heating differs from all other types in that the heat is generated within the material being heated, requiring no conduction into the material.  Consequently, the inside of the plastic is hotter than the outer surface because of conduction from the surface to air, whereas the reverse is true using other methods of heating.

High-frequency preheating is in wide use because it enables a molding compound to be heated very rapidly and uniformly.  As a result, more uniform plasticization and faster cures are possible than with other methods. However, the initial cost of the electronic equipment is higher.

This technique, with suitable modification, is applicable not only to compression molding but also to transfer and injection molding, to the curing of laminates and plywood, and to thermoplastic welding operations. It is employed principally for the preheating of preforms used in compression molding, thereby enabling the rate of this process to approach that of injection molding of thermoplastic materials.  The lower frequencies are usually employed for the slow curing of laminates, while the higher frequencies are used for molding, where more rapid heating rates are desirable.

Steam or moist air preheating is not popular at present because it is much slower than high-frequency preheating. However, its cost of installation is less and it can be used to control material moisture content, which, to some extent, influences the shrinkage and dimensional stability of molded pieces. This is of value in molding instrument parts where great accuracy is required.

Dry-air preheating is useful when electrical properties of the product are particularly important because it dries the molding compound more effectively than all other methods. It is the slowest method of preheating and, like moist-air preheating, may cause some precuring because of nonuniform heating caused by conduction from the surface.

Molding is performed under varying conditions of temperature, pressure, and cycle, depending upon the characteristics of the molding compound used. The temperature of the charge may vary from room temperature (no preheating) to about 150°C. At higher temperatures, the rate of cure becomes too great for practical handling of the charge. Mold temperatures vary from 145° to 200°C but are generally in the range of 160° to 185°C, except for the fluorinated plastics for which the temperature may be as high as 380°C. The mold is heated by a variety of methods, which include steam, gas, electrical, and induction heating, and superheating of water. The optimum temperature of molding differs for the various molding compounds and is fairly critical.

The control of pressure is equally important. The pressure exerted during molding is based upon a knowledge of the cross-sectional area of the molded pieces and, in molds where "flash" occurs, from the total area of molding material upon which pressure is exerted. Usually, a combined low-pressure and high-pressure system is used in order to supply a low pressure of 300 to 500 psi during closing of the press and average pressures of 1,500 to 8,000 psi during molding. These pressures are adequate for most materials and, at the same time, prevent fatigue of the steel members of the mold, which can break down the case-hardened metal and cause dimensional inaccuracies in the molded product. Pressures for preforming, on the other hand, may run as high as 40,000 psi, since this operation is performed at room temperature and the molding material has no plasticity.

Molding cycle times depend upon the shape and thickness of the molded article, the type of molding material, and the technique used; they usually vary from a few seconds to several minutes.

Molding may be performed in hand-operated, semi-automatic, or fully automatic presses, depending upon the rate desired and the nature and number of articles to be made. Hand molds are used only for intricate pieces and for very short runs. The assembly, charging, disassembly, and discharging are done by hand. In semi-automatic molding, the mold is permanently mounted in the press and the molded pieces are ejected automatically. This type of molding is most popular, particularly for large pieces. In fully automatic molding, the operator merely supplies

FIG. 11-2. A fully automatic compression molding press. (*Courtesy Hull-Standard Corp.*)

material for each machine and periodically removes accumulated pieces; the loading, molding, and ejection steps are automatic. This method is used for extremely long runs of small pieces, such as closures and tube bases, and, in such cases, is economical in spite of the initial high cost of the equipment.

Compression molds are generally of four different types of design. A *fully positive* mold is one which fully confines the material, the travel of the force being limited only by the material in the mold, since the mold has no land or cutoff. A very small amount of material may escape between the force and the die. The mold charge must be very accurately measured, since the amount determines the thickness of the piece. This type of mold is used when maximum density in a product, such as the high-impact plastics, is desired, since the total molding pressure is applied only to the projected area of the molded piece. This type of mold is used very rarely with thermoplastic materials. It is also not used for multiple-cavity moldings, because the dimensions of the molded articles vary with the charge. Since it usually is impractical to measure mold charges exactly or to confine them closely, there is always some necessary expulsion of surplus or even undesired loss of charge from the mold cavity.

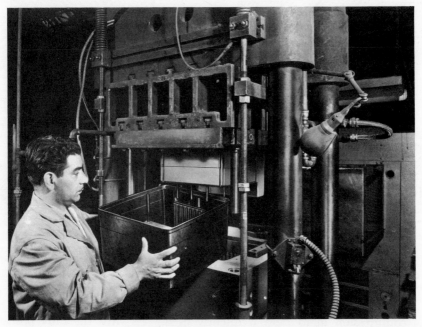

Fig. 11-3. A semi-automatic compression molding press. (*Courtesy Durez Plastics Div., Hooker Electrochemical Co.*)

This excess is called *flash*. The quantity of charge must be sufficient to produce a molding of proper density under proper pressure, yet allow for flash.

Thus, a *flash-type* mold is one in which the material is not confined within the mold cavity until the instant of final closing. A relief must be provided around the cavity on either the upper or lower part of the mold or sometimes on both; thus, only a comparatively small area, called the cutoff, is in contact when the mold is completely closed. Once the mold is completely closed, however, the cutoff prevents positive pressure from being exerted on the contents. As a result, the density of the piece is less. The overcharge, usually about 3 per cent, escapes through the narrowing space between the lands as the mold closes. This type of mold is less expensive and forms pieces of constant dimensions. It is generally used to produce thin, flat pieces.

Combination of the positive and flash-type molds are used, the commonest being usually referred to as a *semipositive* mold. This is the type

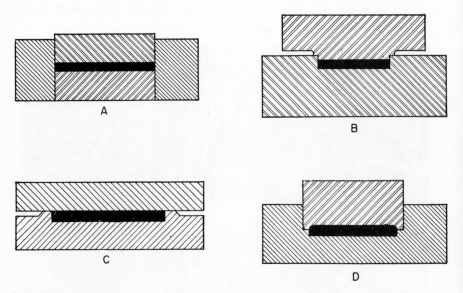

Fig. 11-4. Types of compression molds: (a) fully-positive; (b) semi-positive; (c) flash; (d) landed-positive. (Simonds, H. R., Weith, A. J., and Bigelow, M. H., *Handbook of Plastics*, 2nd ed., D. Van Nostrand Co., Princeton, N.J., 1949)

of compression mold most frequently used. As with the fully positive mold, the upper and lower parts telescope; like the flash type, however, the material is partially confined and has some provision for overflow of the slight excess of charge. The mold produces a piece of maximum density, inasmuch as the material is under positive pressure during the last portion of mold travel and just before the mold has seated on the cutoff edge. Further, positive pressure is maintained without the necessity for such accurate weighing as is desirable or necessary in the positive type of mold.

A *landed positive* mold, which may be either externally or internally landed, is generally used where it is necessary to form a radius, bevel, bead, or some other projection. This type of mold, like the semipositive mold, is a combination of the fully positive and flash types, and differs from the semipositive in that only a small horizontal flash is obtained, full pressure being maintained on this flash and the charge.   As with the other types of positive molds, the halves of the mold telescope to some degree, thus providing better transmission of pressure to the material than in the flash type.   A variation of the landed mold is the *subcavity* mold, which is one having more than one subcavity within the main cavity but having only one force.

Molds are generally made from steel, the quality of the steel ranging from soft mild through carbon steel to the special hard, stainless, alloyed types.   Nonferrous casting alloys, such as beryllium-copper, are often employed for molding thermoplastics where intricate cavities are required and rapid wear is not encountered.   Often tool steel is used for molds. It is machined, then case hardened, after which it is ground and polished. Stainless steels are used when staining of molds must be avoided, as for pastel shades of urea resins.   Molds are often chromium plated, since chromium is very resistant to abrasion and corrosion and increases greatly the working life of a mold.   The surface of chromium plated molds improves release of molded items, resists staining, and imparts a very smooth surface to the products.

For the production of large quantities of identical moldings, multiple molds may be used.   It is usually much simpler and cheaper to use a single mold with multiple cavities, however.   Electroforming over a master mold, made of metal, wood, plaster, etc., is used for both processes and reproduces the original mold form faithfully.   One of the best methods of making multiple cavities, of identical shape and size, is by hobbing.   This process was conceived about 1876, shortly after the Hyatts developed celluloid.   Large-scale production of such items as toothbrush handles and harness buckles could be produced only in steel multiple-cavity molds.   However, production of such molds by machining was not only very expensive because of the handwork involved, but it was also practically impossible to make multiple cavities of uniform size and contour by hand methods.

The hobbing method forces a highly polished and hardened steel master (called a hob) into a piece of cold, soft steel by means of a hydraulic press; the cavity formed has a surface which is as highly polished as the hob.   In addition, the soft steel is so compressed that a finer grain size in the surface of the hobbed cavity results.   All of the cavities produced from a master hob are of the same size and have uniformly polished surfaces.

Very high stresses are developed in both the soft steel of the blank and the tool steel of the hob, since the pressures required for hobbing ordinarily range from 50 to 200 tons per square inch of die impression.   From one to six annealings of the mold are required to relieve these stresses.

It must be remembered that the dimensions of a molded piece will not necessarily be the same as the dimensions of the mold in which it was made, particularly in the case of thermosetting compounds which cure during the molding cycle. Consequently, the mold design must allow for shrinkage of the plastic during the curing operation. Further, molds should be designed so that parts can be readily and rapidly produced; i.e., the molds should be easy to load, easy to clean, and, particularly, the moldings should be easy to remove. The latter step is facilitated by providing sufficient draft or taper on the sides of the mold cavities and the plunger.

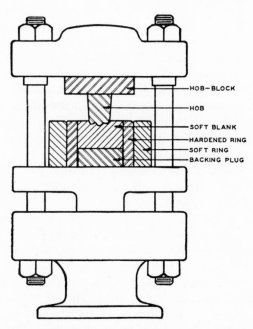

Fig. 11-5. Schematic illustrating a hobbing operation. (Simonds, H. R., Weith, A. J., and Bigelow, M. H., *Handbook of Plastics*, 2nd ed., D. Van Nostrand Co., Princeton, N. J., 1949)

Compression molding is particularly useful for the production of parts of large area and deep draw, having relatively simple shapes. Furniture drawers, radio and television cabinets, instrument and business machine housings, and similar large objects are typical examples. This method of molding is also commonly used for the large-scale production of smaller, simple pieces, such as closures and buttons. Resins most adaptable to compression molding are the thermosetting types, such as phenoplasts, aminoplasts, and reinforced polyester resins.

### Transfer Molding

One big disadvantage of compression molding is the difficulty in completely curing thick webs due to the poor heat transmission of plastics. This difficulty was overcome by the development of transfer molding, a technique developed in 1926 for molding thermosetting compounds in which use is made of a preheating chamber (transfer pot) from which the preheated molding compound is forced into the mold proper when the desired plasticity is attained.

Transfer methods may be subdivided into *pot-type* transfer and *plunger* or auxiliary ram transfer. The latter method has largely, but not entirely, displaced its predecessor, pot-transfer molding. The plunger method uses a small diameter transfer pot in which one or more transfer plungers force the plastic into the mold. It differs from the pot-type system in that the molding material is forced through a very small runner and gate. As a result of friction generated by passage through the restricted openings, the material receives additional heating, and moldings are cured much more rapidly.

In conjunction with high-frequency preheating, plunger molding effects considerable savings by the large reduction in the length of the molding cycle. This method is the best that has been developed for molding thermosetting materials in times approaching those of the injection molding of thermoplastics; in fact, it has sometimes been called the injection molding of thermosetting materials. However, it differs from injection molding (*q.v.*) in that the mold is maintained at the molding temperature, since the parts, being thermoset, can be ejected from the mold without cooling. Another difference is due to the nature of the plastic—throughout a transfer process, the plastic is slowly hardening and only one shot or cycle can be completed at a time. There is some similarity between the

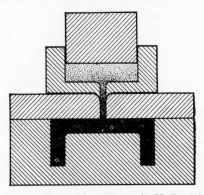

FIG. 11-6. Schematic of a transfer mold. (Simonds, H. R., Weith, A. J., and Bigelow, M. H., *Handbook of Plastics*, 2nd ed., D. Van Nostrand Co., Princeton, N.J., 1949)

two processes, however, since in both the plastic powder is hot and semi-plastic, and flows under pressure evenly into the mold cavity without unbalanced pressures being present to distort any inserts present.   This is another advantage over compression molding.

The molding process consists in placing the molding compound, usually in pellet form, in the preheating cavity, allowing it to become semi-fluid, then forcing it through an orifice by means of a ram into the mold cavity.   The shape of the orifice, which is tapered slightly, is critical, since the material in the orifice (the stalk) is the only flash occurring in transfer molding and it is desirable that it be reduced to a minimum. Since the stalk is very thin, it will harden first, and it thus forms a bung to the mold, so that, as soon as the stalk is hard, the ram may be withdrawn and the heating continued until the piece is fully cured.   After ejection of the cured molding, the small flash stalk is broken off.   Thus, an added advantage of the transfer-molding technique is the small amount of flash produced, which reduces greatly the expensive finishing operation neces-sary in compression molding.

Although a transfer pot provides a more effective and positive means of applying pressure to the charge, additional pressure is required to over-come resistance in the sprues, runners, and gates (the small passageways or openings through which the charge passes into the actual cavity—see Injection Molding).   Therefore, compression pressures are appreciably greater than those used for compression molding—up to three times as great.

Transfer molds must be vented to allow escape of air trapped in the mold during injection of the material.   The vents are small openings usually located on the same half of the mold as the runners and are located at the points which fill last, in order to facilitate the expulsion of air and other gases.

The proper amount of heat and pressure used in molding is extremely important, since the resins used are thermosetting.   Although insufficient heat and pressure will cause insufficient flow, too much may cause the material to harden too soon and may possibly jam the machine.   The material requirements for transfer molding differ to some extent from those for ordinary compression molding.   For this reason and because a longer flow path is involved than in compression molding, materials used must cure somewhat more slowly in transfer molding.   Nevertheless, when used with high-frequency preheating, transfer molding is quite rapid and a good production rate is possible.

The plastics most widely used in transfer molding are phenol-formalde-hyde and melamine-formaldehyde molding compounds.   Urea-formalde-hyde resins can be transfer molded but, because of their greater reactivity and critical behavior in high-frequency preheating, they are not as widely molded by this process as the phenolic and melamine resins. The more recent polyester molding materials are satisfactory for small articles, but their very rapid curing rate has prevented their use in larger molds and for articles where considerable plastic flow is required.   Highly viscous thermoplastics, such as rigid poly(vinyl chloride), may also be transfer molded.

The principal advantage of transfer molding, as has been mentioned,

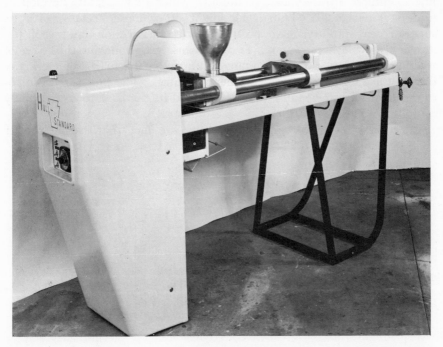

Fig. 11-7.   A fully automatic transfer molding press.   (*Courtesy Hull-Standard Corp.*)

is that complicated shapes, using split molds and complex inserts, can be made.   Other advantages of transfer molding are the extreme accuracy in location of inserts, closer tolerances possible, ease of molding fabric-filled compositions, reduction of molding cycle times, elimination or substantial reduction of rejects for certain types of pieces, lower mold costs, and substantially lower finishing costs, although the loss of the cured sprue and residue in the transfer chamber may result in greater material costs than in compression operations.   Also, shrinkage may be only one fourth as great as in compression molding, probably because of the higher pressures and the fact that the material has been partly cured by the time it fills the mold.

## Injection Molding

Thermoplastics require considerably longer cycle times than heat-hardening materials when compression or transfer molding is used, due to the necessity for alternately heating and cooling the mold. Injection molding was developed in order to allow thermoplastics to be molded as successfully as the thermosetting compounds.

The development of injection molding can be traced back to 1872, when the Hyatt brothers used their newly invented stuffing machine to inject cellulose nitrate plastic (celluloid), which they had also developed, into a closed mold. The development of cellulose acetate, with its superior heat stability, made possible the use of injection molding in the absence of volatile solvents. Further work was done on this type of molding by many people in many countries, particularly in Germany during the early part of the twentieth century. The process was introduced in the United States about 1931, and its use has grown especially rapidly since about 1935.

Injection molding is characterized by the fact that, as in transfer

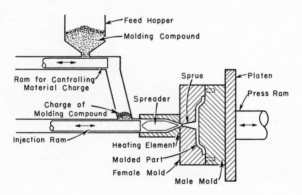

Fig. 11-8. Schematic of an injection molding machine. (Sonneborn, R. H., Dietz, A. G. H., and Heyser, A. S., *Fiberglas Reinforced Plastics*, Reinhold Publishing Corp., New York, 1954)

molding, the mix is (electrically) preheated in a plasticizing cylinder and then is forced by a plunger through a nozzle into a closed mold which, unlike transfer molding, is cold enough to harden the plastic sufficiently for rapid ejection. In some cases, two cylinders are used, one for preheating the material and the second for holding the material at molding temperature until it is injected into the mold. In this case, the first cylinder is known as the preplasticizing chamber. The plasticizing chamber is made large enough to hold a number of charges, usually from four to eight, and is kept filled by addition of feed as softened material enters the mold. This allows sufficient time for the poorly conducting plastic material to become evenly heated and softened. To aid further in rapid and even heating by intimate contact of the molding material with the heated walls of the chamber, a spreader is inserted in the chamber. This torpedo- or pineapple-shaped core, in addition, streamlines the flow of plastic, preventing its partial entrapment.

An injection molding machine consists, in essence, of a split mold which is opened and closed by a clamp. The clamp must be strong enough to hold the mold closed during the filling operation. The exit end of the cylinder contains a small orifice which butts against a corresponding opening (sprue) in one half of the mold. The softened plastic is forced by a plunger from the cylinder, through the sprue, through a constriction (gate), and along channels (runners) into the molding cavities. Since great resistance to flow is incurred by passage of the plastic through the cylinder, sprue, runners, and gates before the material enters the cavities, the pressures used in injection molding are much higher than those required for compression molding, generally running from 5,000 to 30,000 psi.

Fig. 11-9. Large injection molding machine. (*Courtesy Reed-Prentice Corp.*)

The temperature to which the molding compound is heated in the plasticizing cylinder varies, of course, with the particular resin used, the amount of plasticization, the size and complexity of the molding, and the number of cavities. It may range from 140° to 300°C, but is usually between 175° and 275°C.

The temperature of the mold itself is much lower—low enough that the injected plastic is rapidly cooled and solidified so that it may be just as rapidly ejected. In order to prevent undue stressing of the molded article, the mold is usually kept slightly warm, temperatures as high as 120°C being not uncommon.

Like transfer molding and for the same reasons, injection molding produces articles requiring few finishing operations. Because the plastic is injected into an already closed mold, the parting line seldom requires removal; only removal of the gate (degating) is usually necessary.

An advantage in molding thermoplastics is that the gates, sprues, runners, and rejects may be ground up and reused, provided, of course, that they are clean and of the same color. Consequently, loss is kept at a minimum. Another advantage is that unit cost is low, because of short molding cycles, and the number of mold cavities can be reduced. However, a relatively large and expensive machine is used to produce a fairly small article, and the overhead tends to be high. Most injection machines operate automatically, from the initial loading to the final ejection, and automatic controls for the regulation of feed, temperature, pressure, and molding cycle are a necessary adjunct.

Among the many thermoplastic materials formed by injection molding are the acrylics, cellulosics (cellulose acetate, cellulose acetate-butyrate, and ethyl cellulose), which often utilize preplasticizing chambers, polychlorotrifluoroethylene, nylon, polyethylene, polystyrene, and the common vinyl resins.

### Jet Molding

The rapidity of molding and other advantages of the injection molding process served to stimulate research in developing similar techniques for thermosetting compounds. As a result, about 1940, several modifications of the injection molding process were made available for the rapid molding of thermosetting materials, particularly for small articles. The best known are termed jet, flow, and offset injection molding.

The biggest problem that had to be overcome was to prevent premature hardening of thermosetting mixtures when they were preheated in a plasticizing chamber, while heating them sufficiently so that they would flow readily and fill the mold properly. The *jet process* solves this problem nicely by heating the molding mix in the plasticizing cylinder just enough that it will flow under high pressure without appreciable polymerization occurring, then heating the relatively cool mix to a high temperature very rapidly just as it is injected into the mold. Like high-frequency preheating, jet molding is really the application of a new heating technique rather than a new method of molding.

As in injection molding, the molding compound falls from a hopper into a feed cylinder, in which it is forced forward toward the nozzle by the pressure of the injection plunger. Very high pressures are required, from 15,000 to over 75,000 psi, depending upon the composition of the molding powder. The nozzle end of the cylinder is mildly heated, temperatures of 65° to 95°C being the usual range. In spite of the low state of plasticization, the plunger forces the material to flow. In order to allow passage of filled plastics at such low temperatures, the spreader used in injection molding is omitted. As the semiplastic material passes through the nozzle, it is heated almost instantaneously to a temperature of from 140° to as high as 650°C, depending upon the composition of the mix and the size of the mold. This is accomplished by induction heating

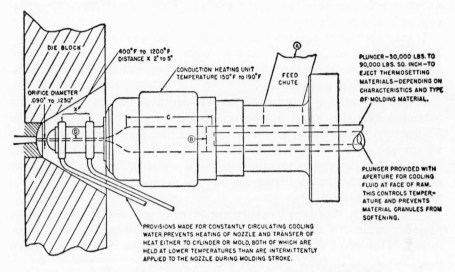

FIG. 11-10. Schematic of a jet nozzle. (*Courtesy Bakelite Co.*)

from two or more electrodes placed around the nozzle. Although the temperature generated in the molding compound is very high, the fluidized mass is forced into the mold so rapidly that it fills the mold before it thermosets.

After injection, pressure in the cylinder is released, heating of the nozzle electrodes is discontinued, and the nozzle is rapidly cooled by water, which circulates through the electrodes. This prevents the plastic remaining in the nozzle from decomposing or thermosetting, prevents undue heating of the mold and cylinder, and also serves to control the break-off point of the sprue. For obvious reasons, jet molding is sometimes known as the hot-cold nozzle process.

The molding cycle for thermosetting materials takes from thirty seconds to two minutes by the use of this process. This is generally a more rapid process than compression or transfer molding, primarily because the molding material requires less handling. Another advantage of this process is that both thick and thin sections of articles can be cured at the same rate, because the entire plastic mass is heated uniformly to the same high temperature before injection.

Although this technique of molding can be used for thermoplastics and even for elastomeric compounds, there is generally no advantage over injection molding. In some cases, particularly for thermoplastics that are heat sensitive, however, the jet molding process may be preferred. In such cases, the plunger pressure is less and the cylinder temperature is lower than normally used in injection molding, the heat required for injection being supplied only at the nozzle. This prevents undue degradation of heat-sensitive materials.

It may appear strange that the jet process enables the molding of many heat-sensitive materials. However, many polymers can withstand intense heat for a short time better than they can endure lower temperatures for longer periods of time.

In the *flow molding* process, no heaters are used on the nozzle. The frictional heat developed during injection serves to plasticize the resin adequately. Sometimes, too, the heating of the cylinder is accomplished by the use of hot oil, steam, or hot water, instead of the usual electric band heaters, in order to minimize local overheating and premature hardening of the thermosetting mixes. In other respects, the process is similar to jet molding.

*Offset injection molding* is another variation of jet molding. A heated preform, which in some cases is heated by a built-in, high-frequency heater, is forced by the plunger sideways into passages in the mold which are offset along its path. By this means, unusually large pieces may be molded inexpensively and rapidly using relatively light molding equipment.

### EXTRUDING

Extrusion is one of the earliest methods of forming plastic materials into relatively simple shapes. It is a process of shaping adopted from the rubber industry which, so far as the plastics industry is concerned, began with the production of casein rods and tubes. It provides a rapid and efficient means of producing long, continuous shapes, such as tubing, rods, sheets, and films, from thermoplastic and, less often, from thermosetting resins.

The general process of extrusion consists in forcing a plastic mix through a die which forms the mix into a strip of material shaped like the die opening. The extrusion machine consists of a hopper, a screw-feed mechanism or a hydraulic ram, a heating chamber, a nozzle, and a die. The hydraulic type of machine is known as a "stuffer" and the screw type as a "screw machine." The feed drops by gravity from a hopper into the cylinder, where it is forced forward through a heating zone, a nozzle, and a die, from which it emerges with a cross-section similar to that of the die. The extrusion may be carried by a conveyor belt under cooling blasts of air, may be allowed to cool naturally, or may be cooled more rapidly by immersion in water or other fluid. It may be seen that extrusion is essentially the same as injection molding, except that

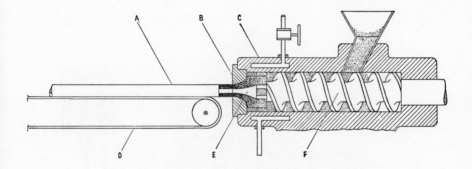

A. Extruded tubing being carried along by conveyer belt.
B. Die.
C. Heating zone.
D. Endless conveyer belt.
E. Mandrel located concentric with the die to produce the inner opening.
F. Screw type conveyer.

FIG. 11-11. Sketch of a typical screw extruder. (Simonds, H. R., Weith, A. J., and Bigelow, M. H., *Handbook of Plastics*, 2nd ed., D. Van Nostrand Co., Princeton, N.J., 1949)

(1) shaping in the former method is accomplished at the exit of the plasticizing chamber, using a die after the nozzle, and (2) no closed mold is used.

The hydraulic types of feed are employed for extrusion of thick sections, since they are capable of exerting a high pressure upon a large amount of material at one time. Articles made from the cellulosics are often fabricated by such units. The screw machines use granulated plastics and can be used with almost all types of raw materials. They usually contain a screw feed which has a decreasing pitch toward the feed end, causing the pressure to increase on the plastic mix at the extrusion end. Sometimes, too, double screws are used. The clearance between the screw and the cylinder wall determines, to a great extent, the amount of pressure developed on the plastic mix. Since pressures are rather high, the materials of construction of the screw and cylinder are carefully chosen.

The machined or forged cylinder is usually made of hardened, corrosion-resistant steel alloys.    The screw, made of tough and rigid steel, is usually chromium plated, except for the land areas, which may touch the cylinder if deflection should occur.    The threads of the screw come close to the cylinder walls in order to maintain pressure, to keep the feed moving, and to prevent local overheating of feed.    Variable-speed drive of the screw is usually employed, to allow for variation in type of feed and size and

Fig. 11-12.    Multiple-screw extruder.    (*Courtesy F. J. Stokes Corp.*)

shape of the die.    Speeds generally vary from 10 to 50 rpm.    The temperature in the cylinder ranges from 100° to 400°C, depending upon the nature of the mix, except for such materials as polytetrafluoroethylene, in which cases much higher temperatures are used.    The die is often maintained at a higher temperature than the plasticizing chamber to assist in the final shaping operation. Bronze wire screens or breakers are sometimes placed either behind or in the die to reduce turbulence and to aid in homogenizing the plastic before extrusion.

The molding powders used for extrusion are similar to those used in molding, except that the particle size is usually larger. Continuous extrusion began with cellulose acetate, but now almost all of the thermoplastics are used, including nylon, cellulose acetate-butyrate, ethyl cellulose, poly(vinyl chloride), vinyl chloride-acetate copolymers, vinylidene chloride copolymers, poly(vinyl acetate), polystyrene and styrene-

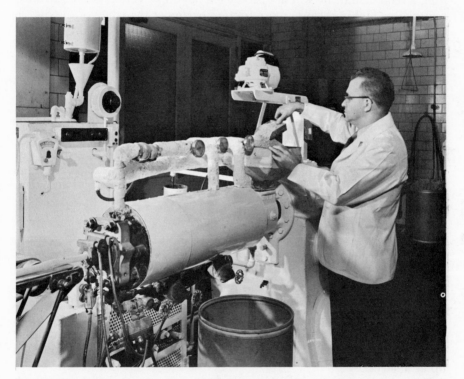

FIG. 11-13.  Laboratory extrusion of a vinyl resin.  (*Courtesy Chemical Div., Goodyear Tire & Rubber Co.*)

acrylonitrile copolymers, poly(methyl methacrylate), polyethylene, poly-(vinyl butyral), poly(vinyl alcohol), the fluorinated vinyl polymers, and even many elastomers.

There are two general methods of extrusion used commercially: the wet extrusion process and the hot or continuous dry extrusion process. Wet extrusion is used principally for the shaping of cellulose nitrate compositions.  Alcohol-wet cellulose nitrate is mixed with solvents and plasticizers, and with colors and pigments, if desired.  After straining, vacuum drying, and blending, the plastic is milled to a jellylike consistency for hydraulic extrusion or into a harder form for screw-type extrusion. Dry extrusion is similar to wet extrusion, except that dry flakes, granules, or powders are used for the feed.  This is the more common technique in use today.

The production of film and sheeting may be performed in several ways. A common method is by extrusion through a slit die, sometimes equipped with a sizing bar for the adjustment of thickness.  Contrary to expectation, a rectangular die will not produce a flat cross-section in the extruded material.  This is because more friction occurs at the edges of the die, so that the cross-section of the film will taper at the edges.  In order to compensate for this effect, the die is made concave toward the center if a rectangular section is desired.  It is also true that a die used for the production of tubing is not necessarily circular.  For tubing, a die forms the outside of the tube, while a core or mandrel, supported by a spider, forms the inside.  Gentle air pressure (1 to 3 psi) is sometimes fed through the spider to the inside of extruded tubing in order to prevent collapse of the tubing before it is hardened after leaving the die.

Certain plastics, such as polyethylene and poly(vinylidene chloride), are especially adaptable to the formation of tubing or sheets by the expanded tube (blown film) method of extrusion. Poly(vinylidene chloride) resins, in particular, are unsuitable for use in casting procedures, because of general insolubility, and in calendering operations, because of the narrow softening range and relative instability at high temperatures. Polyethylene and vinyl chloride resins may be extruded successfully either by the flat film extrusion method or by the expanded tube process.  In the latter method, tubing of small diameter and heavy wall is extruded. Air is introduced inside tubing to blow it up to many times its original diameter, the air being held inside the tube by a set of nip rolls.  In the process of expansion, the wall thickness is greatly reduced.  The tubular film thus formed is rolled up on a mandrel as flat tubing or is slit and rolled up as a sheet.

For extrusion *coating*, a plastic is extruded as a flat film at a high temperature and, while still molten, is drawn through a set of nip rolls where it comes in contact with the substrate, which is also passed between the rolls.  The pressure applied by the rolls laminates the film to the substrate, which is usually paper or cloth.

For wire covering, wire is paid off from a constant tension device. The wire is often preheated to improve adhesion of the coating and to remove residual oil or drawing-die lubricant, after which it passes through a die.  The resin is forced over a guider and out of the circular die, enveloping the wire as it passes through the die.  Nylon, plasticized

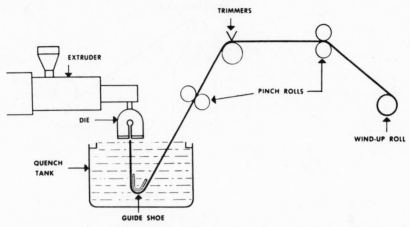

FIG. 11-14. Sketch of a flat-film extrusion process. (*Courtesy Modern Plastics Encyclopedia*)

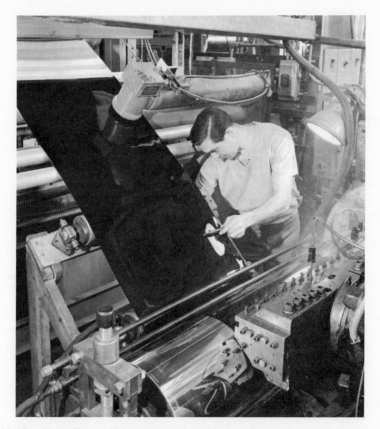

FIG. 11-15. Extruding cellulose acetate sheeting. Note the use of beta-ray film-thickness gauge. (*Courtesy Celanese Corp. of America*)

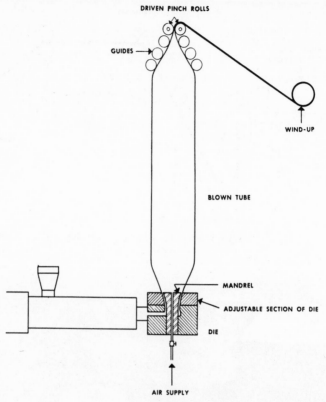

FIG. 11-16. Sketch of a blown-film extrusion process. (*Courtesy Modern Plastics Encyclopedia*)

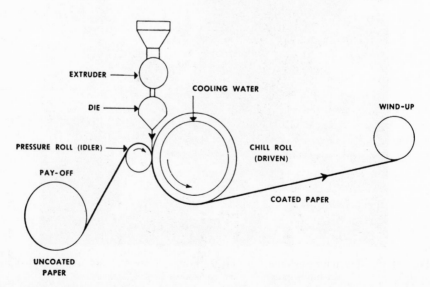

FIG. 11-17. Sketch of extrusion coating. (*Courtesy Modern Plastics Encyclopedia*)

poly(vinyl chloride), and polyethylene compositions, applied by this method, have proved valuable as rubber replacements in electrical wire insulation applications, showing imperviousness to oil, better electrical insulating properties, and little or no tendency to harden or crack with aging. Also made in large quantity is extruded tubing ("spaghetti") of vinyl resins in various colors, which have rapidly replaced varnished cambric tubing as electrical insulation. The tubing is not only more flexible, but is more dependable for electrical insulation.

Many other applications for extruded products have been developed, ranging from thermosetting phenolic tubes to fine bristles of all types. Extruded conduit for electrical purposes and piping for the transport

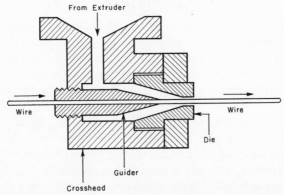

FIG. 11-18. Extrusion wire coating apparatus. (*Courtesy Modern Plastics Encyclopedia*)

of chemicals are in wide use. Extruded cellulosic rods and tubes are used in such items as fountain pen barrels, covers for golf club handles, and tool handles. The original extruded plastic, casein, is widely used in the button manufacturing field. Thin sheets of regenerated cellulose (cellophane) and cellulose acetate (Celanese, Kodapak I, Lumarith, Vuepak) are made by extrusion, as well as by casting or calendering methods. Such sheets are clear and uniform in quality, and are widely used in the packaging field.

A process for the extrusion of thermosetting materials originated in Germany in 1932 and was commercially developed in England about 1935. A pulsating ram works in a barrel or die, in which the zone nearest to the ram is cold and subsequent zones are progressively hotter as the other end of the barrel is approached. As the ram moves back and forth, fresh material is fed into and is forced through the barrel to the far end, where there is a profile of the cross-section required in the extruded material; i.e., the barrel turns into a thick die. The resin, by passing through the progressively hotter zones, becomes thermoset before leaving the die. A braking device retards the rate of extrusion so that the material remains in the die until it is properly cured.

The properties of extruded, thermosetting plastics are similar to those made by compression molding, except that the impact strength of the former is about 50 per cent higher, an improvement ascribed to the orientation necessarily incurred in an extrusion process. Phenolic and urea molding compounds are generally used in extrusion molding of thermosetting compounds. Usually, only wood-flour fillers are used, since asbestos, mineral, and fabric fillers do not produce a surface of good quality.

## CALENDERING

Calendering is probably the most rapid method of making film and sheeting. The process consists of fusing a blended plastic mix in (usually) a Banbury mixer, then squeezing the hot, doughy mix between pairs of internally heated rollers, from which it emerges as a flat film or sheet of uniform and predetermined thickness. The film is then cooled on a chill roll.

Calendering equipment is also used to apply a plastic film to such backing materials as paper and fabric (skim coating). The film and backing are squeezed together between the heated rollers. The process, like extrusion coating, is really a laminating operation.

Among the resins suitable for calendering operations are vinyl chloride polymers and copolymers, vinylidene chloride copolymers, and polyethylene. The vinyl chloride polymers are often calendered in the form of plastigels (plastisols thickened with various gelling agents).

The films and sheets are used for the same purposes as are similar products made by the film casting (see Coating) and extrusion processes. This is another example of a product which can be made by more than one process, the choice of process being dependent upon the type of equipment already available, the relative cost of new equipment, the size of the installation and capacity desired, and the particular characteristics desired in the final product.

## SKIVING

Another method of forming sheets, used principally for cellulose nitrate and, to a lesser extent, for cellulose acetate, is known as *blocking and sheeting* or *block skiving*. The technique is used when sheets are required of greater thickness (e.g., > 0.01 inch) than is practical to obtain by film casting from solutions or where the heat of calendering may be detrimental to the resin. In this process, a block of solvent-softened plastic

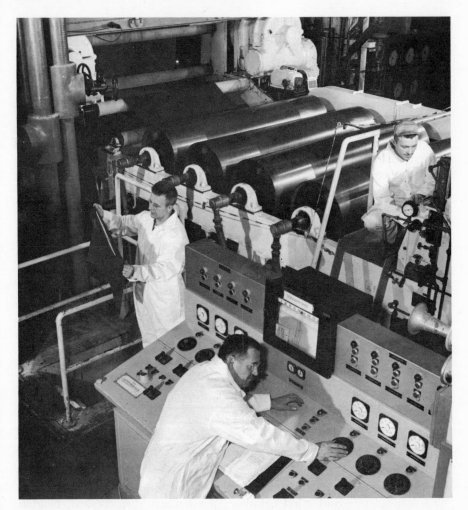

Fig. 11-19. This huge calender is producing vinyl plastic film and sheeting for a variety of end uses. (*Courtesy Monsanto Chemical Co.*)

is first made by compressing a stack of rough sheets, with or without the application of heat. Uniform sheets are sliced or skived from the block by passing it beneath a planing knife. The sheets are then seasoned to remove the residual solvent.

## SHEET FORMING

Forming operations involve the shaping of plastic substances which are already in the form of sheets. The sheets are usually made by the processes previously described. Many of the forming processes are similar and have, in fact, evolved by the refinement of a particular process, as by the application of a new "twist" to an already existing method.

ATMOSPHERIC PRESSURE FORMING

**Cold Bending**

The bending of stiff thermoplastic sheets into slightly curved and cylindrical shapes without the application of heat is one of the simplest and fastest methods of forming. The plastic is held in shape by means of adhesives or metal or plastic fasteners. Thin, rigid vinyl and acrylic sheets are commonly used in this method of forming. Care must be taken in bending, however, as small radii of curvature and sharp bends may cause crazing or embrittlement of the plastic upon aging.

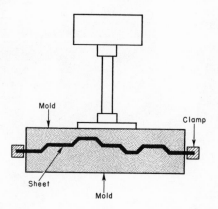

Fig. 11-20. Mechanical pressure forming. (*Courtesy Modern Plastics Encyclopedia*)

Much more common is the cold bending of films, such as cellophane. Cellulose acetate and ethyl cellulose, particularly, are creased, beaded, and formed into various shapes and used for packaging applications. Containers made in this way provide visual access to their contents while offering protection from handling and soiling. Combinations of plastic films with cardboard and other materials are also widely used for the same purpose.

**Hot Bending**

Forming by hot bending consists in draping a hot, pliable sheet of plastic over a form of the desired shape, then allowing the sheet to cool. The edges of the sheet are held in place, if necessary, to prevent curling while cooling.

The molds, which are often made of wood, are usually covered with cloth, felt, flock, or rubber. If better detail is required or if the production run is long, more elaborate molds may be used. Plastic sheets commonly formed by this process include those made from the vinyls, the acrylics, the cellulosics, and butadiene-acrylonitrile-styrene copolymer blends.

Desirable features of this method of forming are that little or no finishing is required, and the investment in tools and the cost of molds are quite low. Only articles of relatively simple curvature can be formed by this method, however, and the optical qualities are only fair.

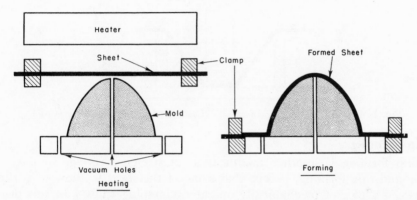

Fig. 11-21. Hot bending (drape forming). (*Courtesy Modern Plastics Encyclopedia*)

### Stretch Forming

Stretch forming is similar to the preceding technique, except that the hot sheet is stretched while being applied to the mold. In some cases, the sheet is clamped along one side and is stretched by pulling from the opposite side. In other cases, the sheet is not clamped but is pulled simultaneously along its edges by several operators. After stretching to the desired shape, the sheet is held in place by a metal ring clamped around its edge until the sheet has cooled sufficiently.

Closer tolerances can be obtained by this method than by the previous procedures. Again, relatively simple and inexpensive molds can be used. Although compound curves are possible, reverse curves cannot be formed.

### Plug-and-Ring Forming

Plug-and-ring forming is a modification of stretch forming. The heated plastic sheet is draped over a male mold (the plug) whose contour corresponds to the inside of the finished article, after which a ring is pressed down over the outside of the sheet. The shape of the ring conforms to the contour of the plug, allowance being made for the thickness of the sheet. The sheet is actually drawn to some extent by passage of the ring over it and, by selecting the proper diameter of the plug with respect to the ring, the sheet may be made to wrinkle or not, as desired.

As with previous methods of forming, tool and equipment costs are relatively low. This method of forming is applicable to all types of thermoplastic sheeting.

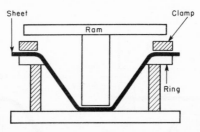

Fig. 11-22. Plug-and-ring forming. (*Courtesy Modern Plastics Encyclopedia*)

### Slip Forming

Slip forming is another modification of stretch forming, similar to plug-and-ring forming, except that some of the sheet is allowed to slip between a pair of mechanically operated clamping rings. In this procedure, the male mold over which the hot sheet is placed is mechanically forced through a draw ring. The sheet is held between the surfaces of a hold-down ring and the draw ring by compressed springs and, as the plug is forced through the draw ring, the sheet slips between the surfaces of the two rings.

As with previous methods, all types of thermoplastic sheeting can be formed by this method. Articles that are slip formed tend to have a more uniform thickness than those fabricated by simple stretch forming. This results in lower optical distortion in clear plastics and less pattern distortion in articles having a grained or textured surface. A disadvantage of this process is that the sheet will slip only a certain amount between the hold-down and draw rings because the springs forcing the two rings together are compressed more and more as the plug enters the draw ring, and eventually a pressure is reached which will not allow further slippage of the sheet between the rings. Once this point is reached, mark-off occurs and the sheet begins to thin.

### Drawing

To draw a thermoplastic sheet, the sheet is placed on a die plate, whose opening corresponds to the projected outside dimensions of the article being made, and a plunger (former) having the exact shape of the finished product is forced into the die, thus drawing the sheet into the die and shaping it around the plunger.   A hold-down plate is used to hold the sheet on the die and to prevent wrinkling of the sheet as it is drawn into the die.   The sheet is softened by the die and hold-down plate, which are heated.   The formed article is hardened by the plunger, which is kept cool.

Thermoplastic sheeting commonly drawn includes the cellulosics, the acrylics, vinyl chloride-acetate copolymers, and the butadiene-acrylo-nitrile-styrene copolymer blends.   This method affords a means of shaping relatively small articles rapidly and in relatively large quantities.

## Die Pressing

Die pressing is one of the earliest methods of forming thermoplastic articles.   It is essentially a compression molding process in which the charge is a blank of thermoplastic sheeting precut to the approximate size and shape of the article desired.   The blank is softened in an oven or on a hot plate and is then transferred to a split mold.   The mold, which may be either hot or cold, is then closed under a pressure of up to 2,000 psi.

This method of forming can be used with any of the thermoplastic materials, so long as they are available in a shape (sheets, rods, tubes) which will approximate the shape of the finished article upon blanking. This is necessary in order that only a minimum amount of plastic flow is required in the mold.   This is a particularly useful technique for shaping cellulose nitrate plastics, since this material cannot be molded in powdered form by hot compression or injection techniques.   The only advantage in its use for other thermoplastics which can be injection molded is that massive articles of simple shape can easily be formed.

## Rotoforming

The Rotoforming process (patented) is unusual in that centrifugal force is used to draw the heated thermoplastic sheet, no contact being made with the mold except at the points of attachment.   The shape of the article formed can be altered widely by varying the direction and magnitude of the centrifugal force.   The operation consists in clamping the heated sheet to a jig, which is then rotated.   The shape of the article is determined by varying the position of the jig with respect to its axis of rotation, and the depth of draw is established by the speed of rotation of the jig and the temperature of the sheet.

This process has been confined principally to the acrylics but can also be used for the other thermoplastics.   The optical properties of articles formed in this manner are very good—comparable to those obtained by free blowing.   An advantage is that many more shapes can be produced than can be obtained by the latter method.

### Veneering

Veneering is the process of applying a sheet of plastic permanently over a form.   The forms are usually made of wood, particularly birch or maple.   Because veneering is usually done by hand, this process is also known as *hand forming*.

The plastic sheet is first conditioned or softened by immersion in an aqueous solution of acetone or by exposing it to acetone vapors.   A cement, usually amyl acetate, is then applied to keep the blank soft and

FIG. 11-23.   A postforming operation.   (*Courtesy Formica Corp.*)

sticky as it is stretched over the wooden form. The sheet is held in place until dry.

Both cellulose nitrate and cellulose acetate are popular for use in veneering operations. Items commonly made by this process are heels for women's shoes, hamper tops, and toilet seats.

## Postforming

Postforming is an operation applied to thermoset plastics. Contrary to earlier belief, fully cured, thermosetting materials, such as compression-molded phenoplasts, can be formed under proper conditions. If such a fully cured material is rapidly heated to a higher temperature than that of the original curing, it will relax sufficiently rapidly to permit forming.

Postforming (or *thermoelastic forming*) differs from low-pressure molding (see Laminating and Impregnating) in two respects: (1) The resin is in the fully cured stage, instead of an intermediate stage, and (2) the surface finish is that of the precured sheet, the surface of the postforming mold having no influence upon the already cured sheet. Although thermoplastic resins may also be formed in this way, postforming is one of the few forming operations which can be used with thermosetting compounds, of which the phenoplasts are the most important class. Thermoset polyester sheets have also been successfully formed by this method.

Postforming is carried out using inexpensive molds, generally of plastic, wood, plaster of Paris, etc., in relatively short cycles, since the piece is held under low pressure in the mold only long enough to allow it to cool sufficiently to retain its shape upon release of pressure. Successful forming of properly heated material depends principally on speed of operation; the material must be placed in the die and formed in less than one-half minute after removal from the source of heat. Sufficient pressure to shape the piece is all that is necessary thereafter.

### FLUID-PRESSURE FORMING

The use of differentials of air pressure has grown rapidly in recent years for the forming of thermoplastic sheeting. Although some work was done in Europe before 1935, most of the development work has been performed since that time in the United States. The technique was used to form poly(methyl methacrylate) sheeting during World War II, but has become a major fabrication method only since 1951.

Either vacuum or air at greater than atmospheric pressure may be used to obtain the desired pressure. The choice depends, among other things, upon the shape of article, the optical quality required, and the maximum pressure required, the latter of which controls the degree of conformity of the sheet to the shape of the mold.    Obviously no more than 14.7 psi differential pressure can be obtained with a vacuum; when this is insufficient, positive air pressure must be used.

## Vacuum-Forming Methods

Vacuum-forming methods utilize the atmospheric pressure of air to force a heated sheet into an evacuated space.    Vacuum forming is more adaptable to the mass-production of thin-walled objects of large area than is any other fabrication process.    The investment in equipment is relatively small and tooling costs are proportionately low.

*Vacuum Forming in Free Space.*    This is the simplest method of vacuum forming.    A sheet of proper size is heated in an oven until it has attained the proper degree of plasticity.    The sheet is then clamped around its periphery over a vacuum chamber.    The sheet may either be stretched across the vacuum-chamber opening or may be allowed to drape into the chamber, depending upon the final shape desired and the amount of stretching involved.    By evacuation of the chamber, the sheet is forced down into the chamber by atmospheric pressure.

The shape of the formed object is determined by the shape of the

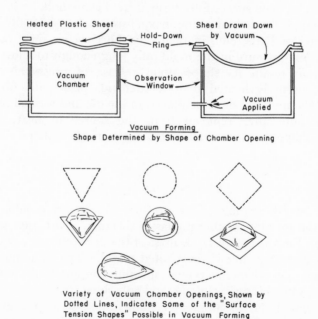

Fig. 11-24.   Vacuum forming in free space.   (Simonds, H. R., Weith, A. J., and Bigelow, M. H., *Handbook of Plastics*, 2nd ed., D. Van Nostrand Co., Princeton, N.J., 1949)

vacuum-chamber opening, the amount of drape permitted before forming, and the amount of drawing performed. The sheet must be drawn rapidly enough to form properly before it hardens, yet not so rapidly that the sheet is torn. In general, acrylic, cellulose acetate, and rigid vinyl sheets are easily formed by this method, which is especially well suited to the forming of sheets when clarity and freedom from scratches, embedded dirt, and surface defects are desired.

*Vacuum Snap-Back Forming.* Snap-back forming requires the use of a plastic possessing elastic memory. The principle involved is that of allowing a vacuum-drawn hot sheet to contract over a male form of the desired shape when the vacuum is released.

As with vacuum forming in free space, a heated plastic sheet is clamped

FIG. 11-25. Reflector fabricated by the vacuum snap-back technique. Note vacuum chamber beneath and male form at left. (*Courtesy Rohm and Haas Co.*)

and drawn into a chamber by vacuum. A male form is lowered into the cavity above the sheet in a position which is close to its surface. By decreasing the vacuum in the chamber beneath the sheet, the sheet contracts, due to elastic memory, encasing the mold in the process. After cooling sufficiently, the mold is removed.

This technique is operable only with those substances which tend to return to their original dimensions after heating and stretching. The acrylics and the butadiene-acrylonitrile-styrene copolymer blends are suitable for such forming. Closer tolerances can be maintained than by the previous methods and reverse curvatures and fairly complex

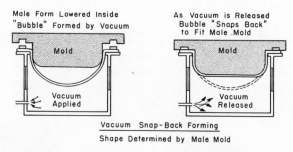

FIG. 11-26.   Vacuum snap-back forming. (Simonds, H. R., Weith, A. J., and Bigelow, M. H., *Handbook of Plastics*, 2nd ed., D. Van Nostrand Co., Princeton, N.J., 1949)

contours may be successfully reproduced by applying air pressure to the other side of the piece after the snap-back has occurred.

*Ridge Forming.*   Ridge forming is a variation of snap-back forming, and will produce articles having compound curves. The process is the same as the foregoing one, except that the male mold, which is recessed, after lowering into the cavity formed by the drawn sheet, is actually pushed into the sheet so as to stretch portions of the sheet into the desired contours. Once this is done, the release of vacuum beneath the sheet allows the sheet to snap back around the recessed mold.

It is possible to vary the tooling and the technique to form articles of unusual design. If the vacuum chamber is divided into sections, so that vacuum can be applied independently to the several sections, fairly complicated shapes can be formed, including flat and rounded sections. Combinations of vacuum below and air pressure above the sheet may also be used. Although developed primarily for the acrylics, ridge forming can also be used with cellulose acetate and vinyl sheets.

*Vacuum Drawing or Blowing.*   Vacuum drawing is essentially the same process as vacuum forming in free space, except that sufficient vacuum is applied to draw the plastic sheet against the contours of the vacuum chamber. The vacuum chamber is perforated to permit the passage of air and serves as the mold. Alternatively, compressed air may be used above the sheet to force it into the chamber instead of using a vacuum beneath the sheet; the process is then known as blowing. Almost all thermoplastic sheet materials can be formed into complex shapes by this method.

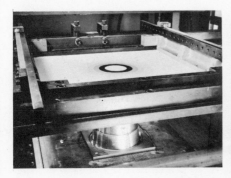

FIG. 11-27. Vacuum forming from rigid vinyl sheeting: *Top Left:* the decorated sheet is clamped and heated over the die; *Top Right:* clamping jig is lowered and the sheet is stretched; *Bottom:* vacuum is applied and the sheet assumes the contours of the mold.
(*Courtesy Bakelite Co.*)

### Pressure-Forming Methods

When vacuum-forming techniques are limited in effectiveness by the heavy gauge of the plastic sheet or by intricate design, conventional pressure-forming methods or custom-designed combination vacuum and pressure techniques can be used. Both employ superatmospheric air pressure or steam to form the plastic.

*Pressure Blowing in Free Space.* Pressure blowing in free space is analogous to vacuum forming in free space, the essential difference being that compressed air, rather than a vacuum, is utilized to shape a heated plastic sheet. Again, variations in the contour of the clamping ring permit objects of different shapes to be formed. By altering the height and shape of the clamping ring, variously shaped flanges may be formed.

The usual thermoplastic sheets can be formed by this method, which produces objects of good optical quality. Since fairly heavy equipment is required, other methods of forming are often preferred, unless the article can be made in no other way.

*Blow-Die Forming.* This operation, which has many modifications and is also known as *blow molding* and *pressure blowing*, is used to make articles, such as balls and bottles, whose circumference is greater than the opening

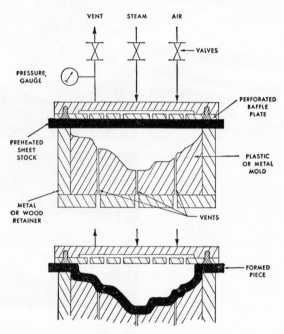

Fig. 11-28. Vacuum drawing or pressure blowing. (Simonds, H. R., Weith, A. J., and Bigelow, M. H., *Handbook of Plastics*, 2nd ed., D. Van Nostrand Co., Princeton, N.J., 1949)

of the mold. The principle is similar to that of vacuum drawing in that the inside surface of the mold or die determines the shape of the finished article. The die is split to permit removal of the article and is dovetailed, so as to be airtight when closed.

A cut or blanked sheet of the desired shape is fastened between a clamp and the die, and the entire assembly is immersed in boiling water. When the sheet is properly softened, a plunger, perforated on the lower half, is introduced into the mold, partially forming the plastic sheet. Steam, admitted through the perforations in the plunger, forces the sheet

FIG. 11-29.  Relief map vacuum-formed from rigid vinyl sheeting.  (*Courtesy Bakelite Co.*)

into complete contact with the surface of the die.  The formed article is hardened by immersion of the assembly in cold water, steam pressure being continued to maintain the shape of the article until the chilling of the die hardens the plastic sufficiently, whereupon the steam is cut off.

Most of the thermoplastic sheet materials can be shaped by blow-die operations, the technique being most applicable to thin sheets and articles of moderate size.  Shapes, such as a hollow sphere or a container having a shoulder, which are difficult or impossible to form otherwise, can be obtained by this process.

Variations involve the use of hot air or steam alone instead of steam and hot water.  A hollow ball may be blow molded by the use of a split-cavity mold having a small opening at the parting line for the introduction of a tube or hollow needle.  Two softened sheets of plastic, with the tube between them, are placed between the two halves of the mold, which are then locked together.  Since the pressure exerted within the mold is not very great and the temperatures to which the mold is exposed are not high, the mold may be made of wood, plaster, aluminum, or tin.

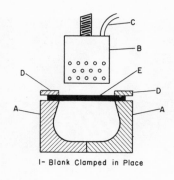

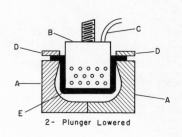

1- Blank Clamped in Place

2- Plunger Lowered

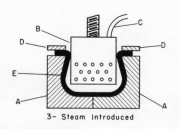

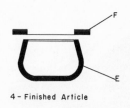

3- Steam Introduced

4- Finished Article

A,A- Split Mold
B-   Perforated Plunger Operated
     by Screw
C-   Steam Connection
D,D- Clamp
E-   Blank and Blown Article
F-   Scrap Removed

FIG. 11-30.  Blow-die forming.  (Society of the Plastics Industry, *Plastics Engineering Handbook*, 2nd ed., Reinhold Publishing Corp., New York, 1954)

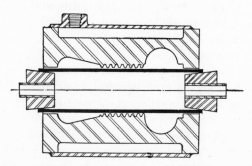

FIG. 11-31.  Blow-die forming.  (Simonds, H. R., Weith, A. J., and Bigelow, M. H., *Handbook of Plastics*, 2nd ed., D. Van Nostrand Co., Princeton, N.J., 1949)

By introducing a jet of hot air or steam through the tube, the two sheets of plastic are forced outward to fit the contours of the mold. After the article has been shaped, the tube is withdrawn, and the two halves of the mold are again pressed tightly together, causing the hole left by the tube to be sealed off. The mold need not be chilled before removal of the product, since the plastic is never hot enough actually to flow.

The material used must be carefully selected. If a plastic, it is usually well plasticized so as to give a rubbery effect when heated; once it is formed, however, the material becomes rigid. The sheets must be of the proper thickness so that they will fill the mold completely without tearing. Hot-water bottles, football bladders, and similar hollow, collapsible items are often made from rubber by this technique. By using steam as the pressure gas, the rubber is vulcanized during the forming process.

A great advancement in the blow-molding process was the introduction of extruded tubing in place of flat sheet stock. This made possible the manufacture of threaded bottles by blow molding. The underlying principle is the same as for sheet stock, but a supporting insert is used to mold the thread. Alternatively, a threaded insert may actually be used as a part of the molded item and the object made in a two-step process (Vlchek process).

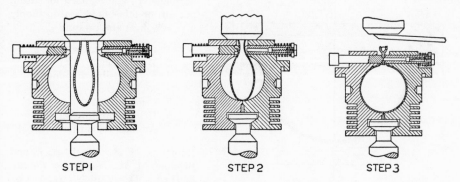

STEP 1    STEP 2    STEP 3

Fig. 11-32. Injection blow-die forming. (Simonds, H. R., Weith, A. J., and Bigelow M. H., *Handbook of Plastics*, 2nd ed., D. Van Nostrand Co., Princeton, N.J., 1949)

Another refinement in the art of blow molding is the recent combination of an extrusion process and a blow-molding process. In this method, the blow mold is placed beneath the nozzle of the extrusion machine, so that, as the material is extruded, an air jet starts to expand the hot, extruded mass. As the mass starts to drop away from the extruder, a mold closes around the tubing and the air jet forces the extruded mass to conform to the mold. As soon as the article is fully blown, the material is nipped off.

For larger production, a battery of inexpensive molds may be set up to
run with one extruder. The same principle has been applied using an
injection machine. Both processes have been used to form such items as
Christmas-tree balls, floating toys, and toilet-ball floats.

Blown articles have been successfully produced from cellulose nitrate,
cellulose acetate, cellulose acetate-butyrate, ethyl cellulose, polyethylene,
polystyrene, and most other thermoplastics. The process has not been
applied satisfactorily to thermosetting plastics.

*Compressible-Diaphragm Forming.* The compressible-diaphragm method
of forming has the advantage of producing formed articles of fairly uniform
wall thickness. A plastic disk is placed on a female mold, a porous wire
ring is laid on top of the plastic, above which is laid a compressible
diaphragm. The mold is closed by pressing a cover against the diaphragm
and clamping. The assembly is heated evenly by introducing steam
through openings above and below the plastic sheet. The plastic disk is
first pressed tightly against the diaphragm, and any entrapped air is
forced out through the porous ring into an annular space. The plastic
softens rapidly and uniformly, permitting the diaphragm to force the
softened plastic downward against the mold when a pressure differential

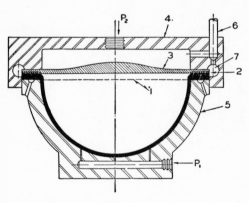

FIG. 11-33. Compressible diaphragm
forming. $P_1$ and $P_2$ inlets for steam,
hot air, or other fluid heat to supply
heat and pressure

1. Plastic disk unformed
2. Wire screen
3. Compressible diaphragm
4. Mold cover
5. Female mold
6. Release pressure inlet
7. Annular relief ring

(Simonds, H. R., Weith, A. J., and
Bigelow, M. H., *Handbook of Plastics*,
2nd ed., D. Van Nostrand Co.,
Princeton, N.J., 1949)

is created by reducing the pressure underneath the plastic. During this
change of pressure, the stretching of the plastic through frictional contact
follows the movement of the diaphragm. In this manner, a uniform
thickness of plastic is obtained through the inversely proportional stretch
of the compressible diaphragm, which is thicker in the center than at the
edges. When the assembly is cooled, the pressure is equalized between
the diaphragm and the blown plastic. The diaphragm returns to its

original position, leaving the plastic against the mold, from which it is easily removed upon disassembly of the mold.

Although this method produces parts of uniform wall thickness, the pieces generally have a low luster and somewhat rough surface. Further, the diaphragm has a comparatively short life at the temperatures used.

## LAMINATING AND IMPREGNATING

The term "laminate" is widely used (and misused) in the plastics industry. It is usually employed to designate impregnated products as well as true laminates. A *laminated* article is that formed by the laying-up of two or more sheets (which need not necessarily be flat). The sheets are usually held together by an adhesive of some kind, applied to their surfaces. An *impregnated* article, on the other hand, is one of porous or fibrous nature whose pores, capillaries, or interstices are filled with a resin or adhesive. By itself, it is not a laminate, but two or more impregnated sheets may be used to form a laminate. Both laminated and impregnated articles are, however, characterized by the fact that their structures are nonhomogeneous; that is, solid matter in the form of sheets, whether fibrous or not, is used in conjunction with a liquid (usually viscous) which eventually hardens by any of various means to yield a completely solid object of great strength and rigidity. Since the term "laminate" is so widely used in the plastics industry for both types of materials, this term is retained herein for the same uses. However, it is to be hoped that more accurate and descriptive nomenclature will eventually evolve.

The strongest products of the plastics and rubber industries are laminates, and it is principally because of them that polymers have invaded the structural field, one formerly served almost exclusively by metals.

*Plywood* is a product made by gluing together under pressure thin, alternately cross-laid wood veneers. By means of this alternate con-

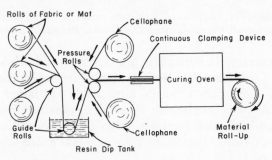

FIG. 11-34. Continuous laminating. (Sonneborn, R. H., Dietz, A. G. H., and Heyser, A. S., *Fiberglas Reinforced Plastics*, Reinhold Publishing Corp., New York, 1954)

struction, the strength and stiffness of the wood fibers in the direction parallel to the grain is distributed in two directions, so that a strong sheet of large area is formed which has many good qualities not possessed by a single layer of wood.    For example, the grain arrangement of the alternating layers minimizes the tendency of wood to shrink and swell anisotropically with changes in moisture content.

*Laminated*† *wood* is a similar multilayered product, having, however, parallel grain direction in all layers.    It is not usually made of thin veneers, but is instead assembled from boards or layers of lumber into timbers, arches, trusses, and similar heavy, load-bearing members.    Such con-

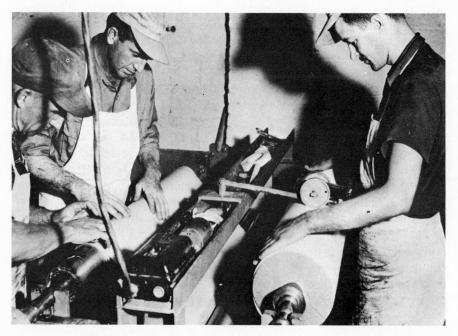

FIG.11-35.    Machine-impregnation of cloth with resin.    Product is subsequently used for the fabrication of laminated articles.    (*Courtesy Brunswick-Balke-Collender Co.*)

struction concentrates the strength in one direction and, while the laminate exhibits most of the characteristics of a single piece of lumber, defects can be eliminated, wider curves can be fabricated, and larger items can be made from smaller pieces of lumber than can be obtained from a single log.

High-pressure-laminated products, other than plywood and laminated wood, consist of fibrous fillers in the form of sheets which are impregnated

† Here the term is used specifically, not generically, in the trade to distinguish the product from plywood, thus adding to the confusion.

or coated with a thermosetting resin (binder) and are compressed under high temperature and pressure to form hard, solid products having great mechanical strength. Stock forms of industrial laminates are known as sheet, tube, rod, molded macerated, and molded laminated.

The first step to make any type of laminate is the impregnation of the filler, which may be paper, asbestos paper, glass mat, or asbestos, glass, nylon, or Orlon fabric. The resins used include melamine, silicone, unsaturated polyester, epoxy, and, most frequently, phenolic types.

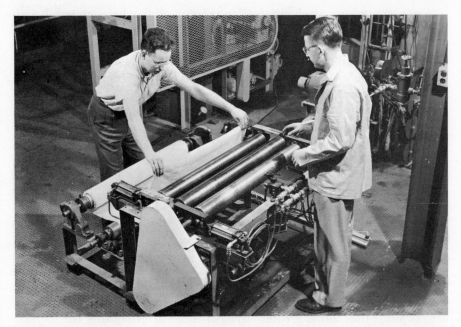

Fig. 11-36. Manufacture of a laminated tube. The resin-impregnated cloth is laminated by passing around the heated center roll. (*Dow-Corning Corp. photograph*)

The resin is dissolved in a suitable solvent to form a spirit varnish with which the filler is impregnated or coated. There are several impregnation processes. One technique, graphically described as the dip-and-scrape method, controls the final resin content of the filler by the resin concentration in the impregnating bath. Another method utilizes a pair of adjustable squeeze rolls or a doctor blade to control the amount of resin left on the coated web. A third method employs a series of roll coaters which meter the resin onto the web as it passes between the rolls.

After impregnation, the wet web passes through a drying oven which drives off the solvent and partially cures the resinous binder, so that the web is no longer tacky but the resin is still subject to further cure. This product is the base material from which the various laminated stock items are made.

*Sheet* stock is made by cutting the base material into pieces of the desired length and stacking them to a height which will result in the required thickness of the finished laminate. The lay-up is then compressed between polished stainless steel plates and cured under heat at temperatures of 130° to 175°C and pressures of approximately 1,000 to 2,500 psi. After cure, the press is cooled and the laminate is then removed.

Some sheets are produced by lamination of the base material with other substances, such as vulcanized fiber, cork, rubber, or copper. An example of the latter is the manufacture of printed circuits which are now widely used in radios, television sets, and other electronic devices.

Laminated *tubes* are made by wrapping the base material upon mandrels which press against heated pressure rolls. The tubes are then either oven baked or pressed in a heated mold until the resin is fully cured. *Rods* are made in a similar manner in cylindrical molds under high temperature and pressure, without, however, the use of a mandrel.

When the production of an article from the above standard forms is impractical, it is often made from a *molded-macerated* material. The base material is cut into small squares, and is compressed and cured in a suitable mold. This type of product is often preferable to that machined from laminated sheet, tube, or rod because its strength characteristics are more uniform.

*Molded-laminated* parts are made by cutting strips of base material into special shapes, depending upon the shape of the desired product. These strips are placed in layers in a mold and are formed and cured under heat and pressure like molded-macerated articles. The advantage in using this technique is that much greater strength is obtained because the laminations conform to the actual shape of the product. These last two methods of making laminates are used when the quantities made warrant mold costs, when a molded finish is desired, or when the shape of the article is such that intricate machining would be required if made from one of the simpler standard stock shapes.

Laminates having simple curvatures may also be obtained by post-forming the laminated sheet (see Forming). A cured sheet of laminate is heated in an oven until it becomes somewhat pliable. It is then quickly placed in a mold or forming die, in which it is held in its final shape until cool.

Phenolic laminates, which, depending upon the filler, may weigh half as much as aluminum, are among the strongest structural materials known, on the basis of their strength-weight ratio. Because of their excellent mechanical properties, thousands of industrial applications utilize gears made from this material. Having excellent electrical properties also, phenolic laminates are widely used in the electrical industry. Their extreme resistance to corrosion, solvents, and acids enables them to be used in many applications in the chemical process industries.

Two of the most popular fillers are asbestos fibers and woven glass fabrics. Both have excellent heat resistance, and glass fibers in particular confer very high tensile strength upon the laminate. The latter filler,

FIG. 11-37. The laminated article in the foreground is made from resin-impregnated paper or fabric sheets by the application of heat and pressure. (*Courtesy Durez Plastics Div., Hooker Electrochemical Co.*)

when combined with phenolic resins, is used for motor insulation and similar applications, where strength and electrical resistance are needed at high temperatures. Melamine resins are combined with glass fiber to produce laminates having, in addition to high mechanical strength, excellent arc and flame resistance. The use of silicone resins results in the formation of laminates whose initial strength is somewhat lower than the above but which exhibit very low dielectric losses and extreme high-temperature resistance. Also of value are the laminates made with diallyl phthalate and epoxy resins; these also have excellent mechanical and electrical qualities. The epoxy resins, although requiring the addition of polyamide, polyamine, or dibasic acid anhydrides as hardeners, produce no undesirable by-products upon curing. They have remarkable adhesion to both glass and metal, as evidenced by the fact that their edgewise compressive strength is higher than that of any other resin. The furan resins, because of their extreme chemical resistance and because they can easily be cured at room temperature, are widely used in the construction of chemical tanks and other process equipment. Unsaturated polyester resins, in conjunction with glass mat fillers, are at present an extremely popular material of construction. These resins also cure without the formation of by-products and, since selection of the proper catalytic system enables them to cure with little or no heat, low pressures may be utilized, breathing of molds is unnecessary, and the molds themselves may often be made inexpensively.

It is often desirable to use certain inert fillers, in addition to the principal filler, in conjunction with the resinous impregnant to lower the cost, raise the viscosity of the liquid resin, or improve the mechanical properties of the product. Among those used are asbestos, silica, clay, mica, talc, and calcium carbonate.

For the production of odd shapes which cannot be made economically or at all from stock shapes, many special molding processes have been developed. These techniques are used with special phenolic, epoxy, and unsaturated polyester resins, particularly in conjunction with the use of glass fibers as the reinforcing medium. These products are known as *reinforced plastics*. This term is now generally employed to include high-strength products made from both laminar reinforcements, such as fabrics or paper, and chopped fiber reinforcements, particularly glass fiber. The common methods of fabrication are known as contact, bag, matched die, and vacuum impregnation molding. The term "molding" is not used here as defined at the beginning of the chapter, since neither a closed mold nor pressure need necessarily be employed.

*Contact Lay-Up Molding.* The term "contact molding" implies that reinforced plastic articles are fabricated without the use of pressure; heat may or may not be used. The reinforcing material is laid by hand in a female mold. The reinforcement is generally of cloth, chopped fibers, or glass mat, and may be either pre-impregnated with resin or untreated. If untreated, it is wetted with a liquid resin applied with a brush, spatula, or spray gun. The filler is rolled or otherwise worked by hand to remove entrapped air and to ensure intimate wetted contact between the plies of filler. The wet mass is then allowed to cure at room temperature or by the application of mild heat.

Although this is one of the simplest means of preparation of reinforced plastics, so far as equipment needed is concerned, dimensional accuracy

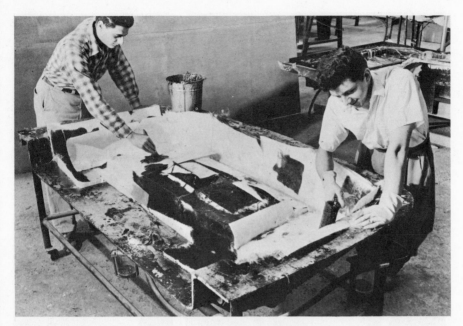

Fig. 11-38. Illustration of roller and brush application of pigmented resin over fiber glass mat by the hand lay-up technique. (*Courtesy Lunn Laminates, Inc.*)

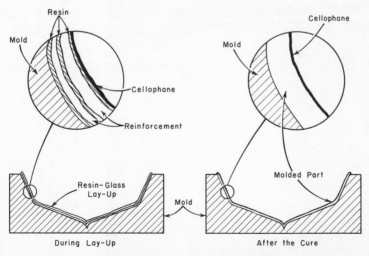

Fig. 11-39. Sketch of contact molding. (Sonneborn, R. H., Dietz, A. G. H., and Heyser, A. S., *Fiberglas Reinforced Plastics*, Reinhold Publishing Corp., New York, 1954)

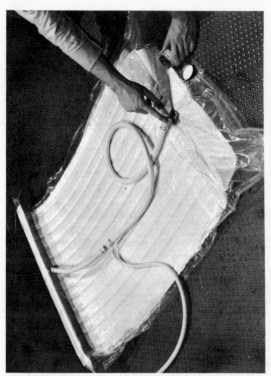

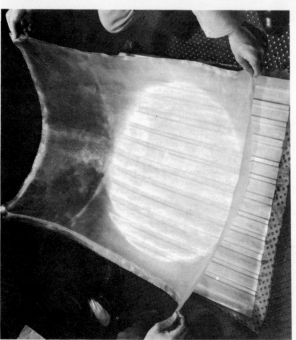

Fig. 11-40.  Vacuum-bag method of forming:  *Top Left:* Layers of glass cloth, previously soaked in liquid resin, are laid over metal form; *Top Right:* after a blanket is laid over the wet lay-up and a dry, coarse-weave glass cloth is laid over blanket to help distribute pressure, entire assembly is enclosed in a poly(vinyl alcohol) bag. Vacuum is applied to inside of bag, causing it to collapse and press lay-up against mold; *Bottom:* wrinkles and air bubbles are removed by hand smoothing.  After curing, formed laminate is removed from mold.  (*Dow-Corning Corp. photograph*)

of molded parts is necessarily low. Further, maximum strength is not developed in this process because the ratio of resin to filler is relatively high. Boat hulls, automobile bodies, chemical tanks, prototype moldings, and other items made in relatively small quantity are often fabricated by this method.

*Bag Molding.* Bag molding follows the general procedure given above, except that pressure is exerted upon the wet lay-up by means of a flexible bag. The use of pressure ensures more intimate contact between the layers of the molding.

The bag, often made of rubber, poly(vinyl alcohol), or other flexible material, is placed over the wet lay-up, after a separating sheet, such as cellophane, is laid down, and the bag is sealed along its edge to the mold. Pressure is then exerted upon the molding by inflation of the bag with air or steam (expanded-bag molding), by evacuation of air from the inside, thus allowing atmospheric pressure to be exerted over the bag and molding (vacuum-bag molding), by applying pressure to the outside of the bag in an autoclave, or by a combination of the above. The particular technique selected is determined by the amount of pressure desired.

The use of pressure permits the fabrication of items having complex contours. Greater uniformity and a higher rate of production than are obtained by contact methods are other advantages of this process. The cost of tooling, while less than that of methods yet to be described, is, of course, greater than that of contact molding. Vacuum-bag molding has been used to make automobile body and aircraft components and prototype molds. The expanded-bag technique has been used to make radomes, small cases, and helmets.

*Matched-Metal Molding.* Matched-metal molding is used when the manufacture of articles of close tolerances at a high rate of production is required. Machined or cast mating molds of steel, aluminum, or cast iron are frequently employed. Because pressures of up to about 200 psi can be exerted upon the material to be molded, a higher ratio of glass to resin may be used, resulting in a stronger product. The cure cycle is extremely short (two to three minutes) so that a high production rate is possible. There are four general ways in which fabrication by matched-die molding can be classified: wet lay-up, preform, pre-impregnated sheet, and premix compounding.

For *wet lay-up* work, the reinforcement is impregnated with the liquid resin outside the mold and, while wet, is laid-up or arranged inside the mold by hand. The two parts of the mold are then brought together, and the article is cured by the application of heat and pressure.

*Preform* molding utilizes chopped glass fibers, which are collected in a chamber on a preform screen rotated on a turntable through which air is drawn. By wetting the fibers on the screen with an emulsified resin and

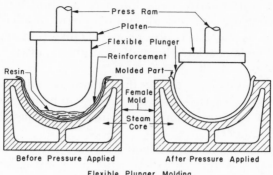

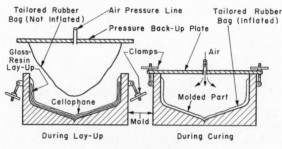

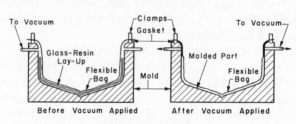

Fig. 11-41. Sketches of bag-molding processes. (Sonneborn, R. H., Dietz, A. G. H., and Heyser, A. S., *Fiberglas Reinforced Plastics*, Reinhold Publishing Corp., New York, 1954)

hardening the mixture by the application of heat, a preform is obtained whose contour is similar to that of the final product. The preform is stripped from the screen, placed in a mold, catalyzed resin is added, and the mold is closed. Chairs, safety hats, instrument housings, and planter boxes are made by this method.

Advantages of this process, other than those already mentioned, are that the product is finished on both sides and, with proper tooling design, holes, cut-outs, etc., may be produced in the molded article. As a result, finishing operations are considerably reduced.

*Pre-impregnated* sheet molding is similar to wet lay-up molding, except that the fabric or mat laid in the mold has already been treated with the resinous binder. This simplified the final molding procedure, since the sheet need only be laid in the mold before the mold is closed and the product cured.

Fig. 11-42. Equipment used for the preparation of preforms. (*Courtesy Owens-Corning Fiberglas Corp.*)

*Premix* molding, also known as "gunk," "goop," or slurry molding, consists in placing a weighed amount of a mixture of chopped fibers, fillers, and liquid resin into a mold. The subsequent molding operation and cure are similar to those of the preceding techniques.

*Vacuum-Injection Process.* Matched molds are used in this process in the same way as previously described for matched-metal molding. They are designed, however, so that the space between the two parts of the mold is the thickness of the wall of the finished article. Rather than compressing the laminate as in the previous method, the space between the two parts of the mold is filled with reinforcing material and liquid

FIG. 11-43.   Matched-metal or -die molding process: *Top:* impregnating glass fiber preform with resin emulsion; *Bottom Left:* placing preform in mold; *Bottom Right:* trimming molded article.   (*Courtesy Structurlite Plastics Corp.*)

resin is drawn in by vacuum to impregnate the filler from a trough surrounding the mold.   There must be, of course, openings at the top of the mold through which a vacuum may be pulled.   Alternatively, the trough may be sealed and a positive air pressure applied to its surface, forcing the resin up into the mold.   Since the resin is usually catalyzed for room temperature curing, the mold is maintained under a vacuum or pressure until cure is effected.

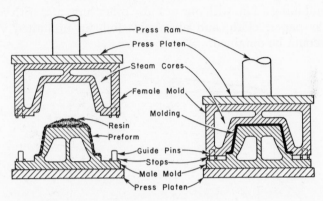

FIG. 11-44.   Sketch of matched-metal or -die forming.   (Sonneborn, R. H., Dietz, A. G. H., and Heyser, A. S., *Fiberglas Reinforced Plastics*, Reinhold Publishing Corp., New York, 1954)

As with matched-metal molding, articles made by this process are finished on both sides.   The amount of waste, handling, and subsequent mess are less than in all other methods.   Since compression is not used, the resin-filler ratio is high, resulting in products of less than maximum strength.   Large items, such as boats and tanks, are easily fabricated.

All of the foregoing laminated products are known as industrial laminates.   Many laminated articles are also made for decorative as well as functional purposes.   The use of decorative laminates is rapidly increasing in homes, schools, offices, stores, theaters, hotels, automobiles, airplanes, and ships.   Particularly because of color considerations, resins most frequently employed are either melamine or unsaturated polyester resins. Melamine laminates require the conventional high-compression techniques and the polyester laminates are made by the low-pressure or continuous methods.   Table tops, wall panels and room dividers, doors, furniture, ornamental signs, skylights, trays, and a host of other items are now made of plastic laminates.   They are outstanding for their attractive colors and patterns and for their resistance to wear.

In addition to the types of laminated articles covered in the foregoing discussion, a large class of laminated products, not used for structural purposes, is that of laminated films. As will be recalled, regenerated cellulose (cellophane) was the first flexible film of commercial importance. Its growth was so rapid and successful that, to satisfy the demand and extend the market even further for flexible film for packaging purposes, new plastic films, such as Pliofilm, cellulose acetate, saran, the vinyls, polyethylene, and Mylar, were developed. Although each type of film had its own distinctive and desirable properties, it soon became evident that for many applications no single film was satisfactory. It was found that, by combining a film with one or more other films and with such other materials as paper, cloth, and aluminum foil, an unlimited variety of properties could be obtained.

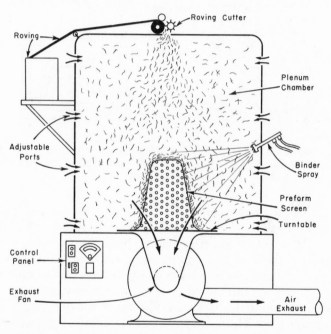

FIG. 11-45. Sketch of preform molding. (Sonneborn, R. H., Dietz, A. G. H., and Heyser, A. S., *Fiberglas Reinforced Plastics*, Reinhold Publishing Corp., New York, 1954)

Most foil or film laminations are made by one or more of the following methods: (1) Wet laminating, using an adhesive in water or organic solvent solution; (2) thermoplastic or hot-melt laminating, using a heated thermoplastic for bonding; (3) contact laminating, using a pressure-sensitive adhesive without the use of heat; and (4) calendering and extruding, whereby one film is calendered or extruded onto a flexible substrate. The latter technique is not, strictly speaking, a laminating process, but a laminated product is formed.

In addition to packaging uses, other important applications of laminated films and foils are in the production of metallic yarns, insulating wraps for pipes and electrical uses, and wallboard and table and counter tops.

## Cellular Laminates

A cellular laminate or sandwich construction consists of a relatively thick core of low density bonded between two thin, high-strength faces or skins. The function of the core is to stabilize the skins of the sandwich so that they can develop a substantial portion of their ultimate compressive strength without buckling. This construction provides a very stiff structural panel of low weight which may be used for decorative as well as purely functional purposes. Such a panel may be fifty times as rigid in bending as a sheet of skin material of the same weight.

Core materials used include "honeycomb"; balsa wood; expanded cellulose acetate, polystyrene, polyurethane, silicone, and phenolic resins;

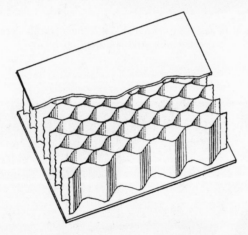

Fig. 11-46.   Cellular laminate.   (Simonds, R. H., Weith, A. J., and Bigelow, M. H., *Handbook of Plastics*, 2nd ed., D. Van Nostrand Co., Princeton, N.J., 1949)

sawdust board; and cellular rubber hardboard. Honeycomb is made from reinforced plastics, metal foil, and paper. The skins are usually of glass-reinforced plastics, metal, or plywood. Almost any combination of core and skin material may be combined, depending upon the product desired. High-strength adhesives which adhere well to both skin and core are used for bonding.

Two general methods are employed in sandwich construction. The more usual method is to prefabricate skins and cores separately, then bond them together. This requires that the cores be machined or expanded to the correct shape in the initial core manufacturing operation.

(a) Installation of resin-impregnated paper honeycomb core in panel
assembly and bonding jig.

(b) Metal-faced honeycomb panels as removed from bonding press.

FIG. 11-47.  Examples of sandwich construction using a honeycomb core with metal
and plastic skins.  (*Courtesy Aircomb Section, Douglas Aircraft Co., Inc.*)

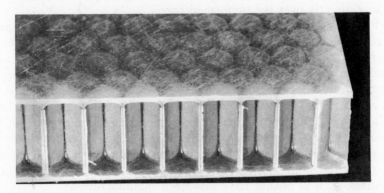

(c)  Plastic-faced honeycomb panel.

(d)  Plastic-skinned honeycomb structure for naval vessel.

Plastic skins are molded by one of the techniques discussed earlier or by molding directly over the preformed core.

A less common method of fabrication consists in foaming or expanding the core in place inside prefabricated and positioned skins. Since preshaping of the core is eliminated, this process is often employed in the manufacture of aircraft radomes or wing tips where accurate preshaping of core material is very expensive or where the location is difficultly accessible.

A very useful type of panel can be made by bonding a flexible, honeycombed, resin-impregnated glass cloth or paper core between thin laminations of glass cloth, metal, or hardboard. Panels of extremely high strength and very low weight for use as structural members in automobiles and particularly in aircraft are thus made. Much thicker, built-up structures, such as beams, have also been manufactured.

By proper selection of components, specific nonstructural advantages can be obtained from cellular laminates. Facings and core can be selected for their electrical properties (as in radomes); an impermeable facing can be used as a moisture barrier; and core materials can be selected to provide high thermal insulation or good dielectric properties, good vibration damping properties, or low water absorption.

## COATING

### Surface Coatings

A very large field of use for polymers and resins is as components of surface coatings. If the term processing is generalized to include the preparation of a material in a form ready for use, then a discussion of the treatment given to various resins and polymers to prepare them for use as a surface coating is appropriate. The *application* of the coatings made from these substances is, of course, another matter and will not be included herein.

As is well known, the field of surface coatings is a very broad one and is generally considered to include any type of coating that is applied to any type of substrate in order to protect, identify, or decorate the surface. In other words, the purpose in applying a coating is considered either functional or decorative or both.

The fundamental principles involved in the formulation of protective coatings are relatively simple, but their reduction to practice is another matter, requiring a background of both theoretical knowledge and practical experience. The goal in the formulation of a protective coating is to obtain a solution of a material which, upon drying, will form a coherent and adherent film over the substrate to which it is applied. The film-forming ingredients may be either thermosetting or thermoplastic polymers and resins. To modify their properties, plasticizers, pigments, dyes, and extenders may be added. Among the considerations which must be taken into account for a satisfactory formulation are the molecular weight (solution viscosity) and the related property, solubility, of the film-forming resin, the application properties and intended method of application of the product, and the solvent combination necessary to obtain proper deposition of a continuous film.

It is a matter of interest that almost every known natural, modified natural, and synthetic polymer and resin has been considered for use as an ingredient of surface coatings. As has been mentioned in previous chapters under the appropriate heading, certain substances are more peculiarly adapted for use as coating ingredients than others. Suffice it to say in this brief discussion of a very large and complex field that it has been a general practice to divide the types of coatings into two general classes: those that "dry" (i.e., form a uniform, continuous, and adherent film which is sufficiently hard for the use intended) by evaporation of solvents alone, and those which dry by an oxidative or polymerization process or both, upon exposure in thin films to the atmosphere. The latter class may also contain solvents added for ease of application, and the solvents, of course, must evaporate after application of the coating. The essential difference between the two types is that, in the former, little or no chemical reaction takes place after deposition of the coating, whereas, in the latter process, one or more distinct types of chemical reaction take place in addition to loss of solvent.

Inasmuch as there are many classes of coatings which may dry principally by evaporation of the solvent and yet which may contain a minor proportion of ingredients which do undergo a chemical reaction, the above classification cannot be hard and fast. There are always, as so commonly occurs in making arbitrary classifications, a large class of substances which does not fit neatly into any of the categories outlined.

In the coatings industry, the following classification is also commonly made:

*Spirit Varnish.* This is a coating made by simply dissolving a hard resin in a suitable solvent or mixture of solvents. The most common example is shellac in alcohol. This type is more properly classified as a lacquer. The term is a carry-over from the days before true lacquers were known. There are very few spirit varnishes now made, one large use being that of coating label stock.

*Lacquer.* A lacquer consists essentially of a film-forming resin and a volatile solvent. Most lacquers are based upon cellulose nitrate as the principal film-forming ingredient; to a lesser extent, ethyl cellulose, cellulose acetate (and acetate-butyrate), chlorinated rubber, and the vinyl resins are used. In addition, lacquers usually contain a small amount of a hard resin, permanent external plasticizers (often an alkyd resin), active solvents, and diluents. Since the drying of a lacquer is not a chemical reaction, a catalyst is not required.

*Oil Varnish.* This type of coating is prepared by the reaction at an elevated temperature of oils and hard resins. Accordingly, they are often referred to as oleoresinous varnishes. These cure or dry by oxidation and probably polymerization mechanisms. An oleoresinous varnish contains, in addition to drying oils and resins, both driers and solvents. Coatings can be made from drying oils alone; they are tough, flexible, and weather resistant but lack hardness and gloss retention and require a relatively long time to dry. To increase the hardness and gloss retention, the addition of a hard resin is necessary, which may be a natural resin, like rosin or copal; a modified natural resin, like a rosin or copal ester; or a synthetic product, such as a phenolic resin. A "drier" (a catalyst) is almost always added to increase the rate of drying. The commonly used driers are the resinates, tallates, naphthenates, and "hexoates" of cobalt, lead, and manganese.

*"Synthetic" Varnish.* This term is loosely used to include alkyds and, more frequently, combinations of alkyds with urea or melamine resins, the latter two of which cure strictly by polymerization. Alkyds also usually require the addition of a metallic drier, while the latter resins are catalyzed by acids.

*Enamel.* An enamel is a pigmented varnish or lacquer. It is used to produce opaque films, usually of great hardness.

*Paint.* Specifically speaking, a paint is composed of pigments dispersed in drying oils. Hardening of films occurs, as with oil varnishes, by oxidation and polymerization of the oils, as well as by solvent evaporation. There is no sharp dividing line between paints and varnish enamels; however, in general, paint contains little, if any, hard resin while a varnish enamel contains an appreciable amount. The term "paint" is also used generically to include all types of surface coatings.

*Water-Based Paint.* In the 1940's, a new class of paints (used in the generic sense) was introduced and has grown rapidly in popularity. These are the water-based paints, known, often incorrectly, as latex or emulsion paints. They are made by emulsifying alkyd resins (of a special type) in water or by using directly emulsion-polymerized dispersions of vinyl chloride–vinylidene chloride and styrene-butadiene copolymers, as well as acrylic and vinyl acetate polymers and copolymers. Advantages of these dispersions over the usual solvent-based paints are fast dry, ease of application and clean up, and mild odor. (The latter desirable quality has been recently extended to solvent-based paints by using special, branched-chain, aliphatic hydrocarbons, known as "odorless" solvents.) The water-based paints are usually stabilized in a protein (casein) solution. When the paint is applied to a surface, the water evaporates, the latex breaks, and a continuous resinous coating forms.

Table 11-2 gives the approximate time of the commercial introduction of new resins and vehicles of significance to the *coatings* field.

TABLE 11-2. COMMERCIAL INTRODUCTION OF RESINS AND DISPERSIONS FOR COATINGS

| | |
|---|---|
| 1924 | Modified phenol-formaldehyde oil-soluble resins |
| 1927 | Oil-modified alkyd resins |
| 1928 | Pure phenol-formaldehyde oil-soluble resins |
| 1929 | Urea-formaldehyde resins |
| 1930 | Chlorinated rubber resins |
| 1933 | Vinyl copolymer resins |
| 1935 | Ethyl cellulose; cellulose acetate-butyrate resins |
| 1939 | Melamine-formaldehyde resins |
| 1944 | Silicone resins |
| 1947 | Polystyrene dispersions; epoxy resins |
| 1948 | Styrenated oils and alkyd resins |
| 1950 | Styrene-butadiene dispersions |
| 1952 | Poly(vinyl acetate) and acrylic copolymer dispersions |

The most important use of organic coatings is for the covering of wood, metal, cloth, and paper. The coatings impart to these materials some of the properties of the plastic materials and usually produce a more durable and more appealing article.

Vegetable oils and natural resins have been used for centuries in protective coatings. During the past thirty years, however, there has been a definite trend toward the use of synthetic resins and treated oils, and these materials are now used in almost all formulations of lacquers and varnishes for industrial and trade-sales uses. So great is the change that alkyd resins, used almost exclusively in products of the paint industry, are now one of the largest volume polymers manufactured.

Coatings are applied to produce a finished surface, as is done with paints, lacquers, and varnishes; when applied for further processing, as in the production of laminated materials, the coating is used as an adhesive and, in the case of porous materials, actually impregnates the material. Thus, adhesives and impregnating agents may be considered as special types of coatings but, since their function is that of bonding two surfaces together, rather than the modification of one surface, they are not considered here.

### Strippable Coatings

Temporary coatings, which are one type of strippable coating, have become extremely important, particularly during and since the last war, as a means of protecting surfaces during fabrication, shipping, handling, or storage. They are used to protect machined or polished surfaces of metal parts before assembly, to completely coat metal airplanes for ocean transportation, to protect guns during storage and metals during stamping operations. Unlike normal coatings, they are formulated to have good cohesion but relatively poor adhesion, so that while impervious to moisture or corrosive conditions so long as the film is unbroken, they will peel or strip readily from a substrate once a break is made.

*Dipping.* Thin films may be deposited from liquids on forms or molds by dipping. After the coating is "set," it is stripped from the mold. The form is often rotated during the drying period to insure even distribution of the coating.

Note that the purpose of the dipping operation differs from that of the usual type of temporary coating in that here it is the shaped coating which is desired. Actually, of course, once stripped, the artifact is no longer

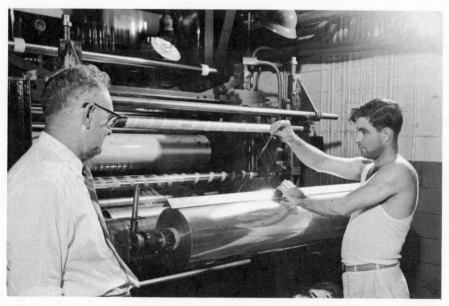

FIG. 11-48. "Casting" cellulose acetate film. (*Courtesy Celanese Corp. of America*)

considered a coating. This technique is useful in the manufacture of thin-walled, hollow, usually flexible objects.

*Film Casting.* Many varieties of films and sheets are now available. It has already been pointed out that such items may be obtained by extruding and calendering operations. A third method for obtaining films and sheets is that of coating or "casting" a solution of a film-forming resin onto a highly polished surface and stripping therefrom after drying. In practice, the solution of resin, plasticized and pigmented, if desired, is fed continuously from a reservoir through a slit onto a drum or continuous belt.   Alternatively, the solution may be doctored onto the surface by means of a knife blade or rod.   As the wet film travels over the drum or along the belt, the solvent evaporates, and the dried film is stripped from the surface and is wound up on a roll.

This operation, while relatively simple, requires solvent recovery in order to compete with hot-melt techniques.   Polymers used in this

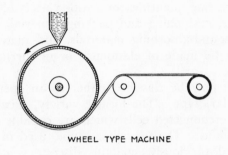

WHEEL TYPE MACHINE

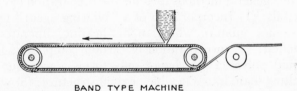

BAND TYPE MACHINE

Fig. 11-49.   Film "casting."   (Simonds, R. H., Weith, A. J., and Bigelow, M. H., *Handbook of Plastics*, 2nd ed., D. Van Nostrand Co., Princeton, N.J., 1949)

process include cellulose derivatives, vinyl chloride copolymers, and acrylic resins.   The process is only adaptable to resins of appreciable solvent solubility.

The application of the term "casting" to the above process is likely to be confusing, inasmuch as this term is more commonly used to describe the process of pouring a liquid resin into a mold and then allowing it to harden (see Casting).

*Electrodeposition.*   Electrodeposition is a method of making shaped articles by the process of depositing the material on a form (electrode) by the passage of an electric current through a liquid latex.   After deposition to the desired thickness, the article is stripped from the form.   This process is, of course, suitable only for use with charged, colloidal particles, such as rubber latex.   Since this technique is difficult to control, it is not widely used.   The manufacture of rubber gloves is probably the outstanding example of the commercial application of this process.

## EXPANDING

Cellular structural materials of low apparent density can be made in the form of "solid foams" from a large variety of plastics and elastomers. An expanded material may be defined as a solid whose volume contains an appreciable fraction of uniformly dispersed voids or cells.

The unique properties of these cellular compositions have caused them to be used in ever-increasing quantities for a wide variety of applications, which include sponges, cushioning and packing material, thermal and electrical insulation, sound-absorbing materials, and materials of construction.   They may be made of elastomers or of thermoplastic and thermosetting plastics.

Expanded materials may be classified either as an open-celled or a closed-celled (unicellular) type.   The former variety, exemplified by a sponge, consists of interconnected cells which are capable of absorbing large quantities of a fluid.   The unicellular type, used in most of the applications mentioned previously, contains discrete voids, each void being completely surround by a thin envelope of resin.

There are five general methods used for the preparation of expanded or foamed materials: (1) Incorporation of a "blowing agent" into a liquid resin or elastomer mixture which, upon heating, liberates a gas by chemical reaction; (2) incorporation of certain compounds into an unsaturated liquid polyester which not only forms a gas, but also crosslinks the resulting foam into a flexible or rigid structure; (3) whipping air into a colloidal suspension and subsequently setting the porous mass, as with foamed latex; (4) injection of a gas into a mix under high pressure in an autoclave; and (5) flash-vaporizing a solvent from a liquid mix.   All of the above methods are used commercially; however, only the first two use blowing agents.

Blowing agents are compounds which liberate an inert gas by decomposition or chemical reaction at room temperature or, more often, upon the application of heat.   Ammonium compounds and inorganic carbonates have been used for many years in the manufacture of sponge rubber. However, organic blowing agents are usually more advantageous in that gas evolution can be closely controlled by regulation of temperature, gas can be produced under pressure, and smaller amounts of agent are needed to produce equivalent volumes of gas.   Table 11-3 lists some of the representative commercial organic blowing agents available.   It may be noted that most of these compounds release nitrogen gas upon heating.

The common expanded materials are phenol-aldehyde and urea-aldehyde resins, polystyrene, polyethylene, polyurethanes, plasticized poly(vinyl chloride), cellulose acetate, and both natural and synthetic elastomers.   They all possess low densities and low thermal conductivities,

TABLE 11-3. COMMERCIAL ORGANIC BLOWING AGENTS

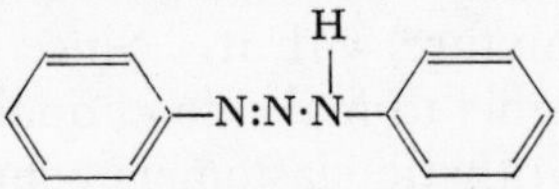

$$C_6H_5-N{:}N{\cdot}N(H)-C_6H_5$$

Unicel and Porofor DB

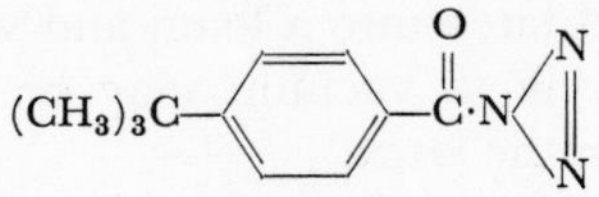

$$(CH_3)_3C-C_6H_4-\overset{O}{\overset{\|}{C}}{\cdot}N{<}\overset{N}{\underset{N}{|}}$$

Wingcel S

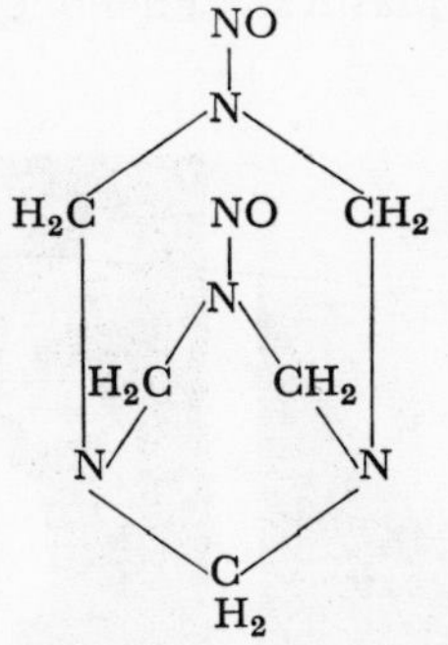

Unicel ND

$$H_2N{\cdot}HN{\cdot}O_2S-C_6H_4-O-C_6H_4-SO_2{\cdot}NH{\cdot}NH_2$$

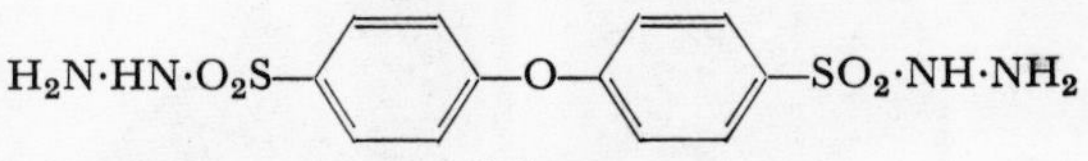

Celogen

$$(CH_3)_2C(CN){\cdot}N{:}N{\cdot}C(CN)(CH_3)_2$$

Porofor N

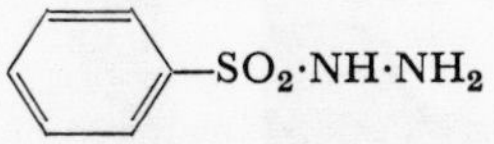

$$C_6H_5-SO_2{\cdot}NH{\cdot}NH_2$$

Porofor BSH

$$H_3C{\cdot}N(NO)({\cdot}\overset{O}{\overset{\|}{C}})-C_6H_4-\overset{O}{\overset{\|}{C}}({\cdot})N(NO){\cdot}CH_3$$

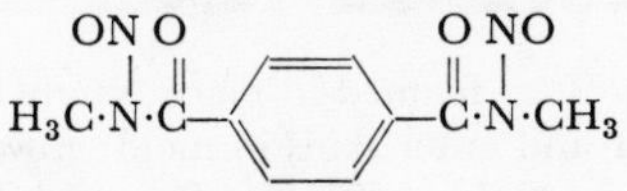

NTA

which confer outstanding insulating properties; the good moisture resistance and low flammability of many of the above make them particularly desirable for many structural applications.

Foamed, natural rubber latices were the earliest of the expanded materials to be commercially introduced. With the development of synthetic elastomers during the past fifteen years, many foamed structural materials have also been made from them. However, no foamed sponge was made from normal GR-S latex alone, 30 to 50 per cent natural rubber latex being used in admixture with it. Since the advent of cold GR-S latex, it has become possible to make good quality foamed material from blends of natural and synthetic elastomers containing much less natural rubber. The process in most general use for their preparation consists in beating the thickened latex into a foam and vulcanizing the stabilized latex foam. Alternatively, a vacuum may be applied to the mass to cause expansion of gas in the latex.

Low-density foam produced from special phenolic resins is probably the oldest of the expanded plastics. Phenolic foam is one of the lightest,

Fig. 11-50. Manufacture of a foamed-in-place sandwich radome: *Left:* Pouring foaming resin between inner and outer skins in mold; *Right:* Ultraviolet-cured radome being removed from mold. (*Courtesy Brunswick-Balke-Collender Co.*)

yet strongest, materials available. The density of highly expanded foam is approximately 0.3 to 0.4 pound per cubic foot. The material is so resilient that it will recover to approximately 80 to 90 per cent of its original volume when compressed less than 50 per cent. Although the production of a phenolic foam is relatively simple, the speed of reaction is such that automatic machinery and special-handling techniques are normally used. The foam is usually produced by beating a mixture of a liquid foaming-type phenolic resin, solvents, and a stabilizer so as to incorporate air, then adding an acid hardener, which also causes further foaming to take place.

A new method of producing foamed-in-place material is by the use of very small phenolic spheres (Microballoons), which may be bonded with a polyester, phenolic, or epoxy binder into a low-density material known as "syntactic" foam.   The spheres have an average diameter of 0.0013 inch and are filled with nitrogen.

Expanded cellulose acetate, known as cellular cellulose acetate (CCA) or Strux, is a unicellular product produced by a continuous extrusion process.   Flake cellulose acetate is converted into a rigid foam by the flash vaporization of a volatile solvent.   Density of the product is of the order of 6 to 7 pounds per cubic foot.

FIG. 11-51.   Hollow polyethylene spheres used to blanket a metal plating bath to control the escape of acid fumes and to minimize splashing.   (*Courtesy Bakelite Co.*)

Expanded polyethylene is made by the extrusion of a polyethylene compound containing a chemical blowing agent. The flexibility, toughness, low moisture absorption, abrasion and chemical resistance, and low electrical loss characteristics of polyethylene are retained in the cellular product with a reduction in density to half that of the unexpanded product. Expanded polyethylene is widely used in the electrical insulation field for such applications as television lead-in wire, telephone cable, and coaxial cable.

Unicellular poly(vinyl chloride) foams are used for insulation and flotation equipment. The open-celled type is used principally in upholstery and mattresses. The closed-cell type is usually made with chemical blowing agents, while open-celled foamed vinyl is made by mechanically mixing a gas into the resin. The former process resembles the one for sponge rubber, while the latter is like that for the manufacture of foam rubber. Both types can be made into a firm or a soft material, having, if desired, excellent fire resistance. Densities range from 3 to 20 pounds per cubic foot.

Vinyl resins foamed with blowing agents are produced in two ways. In one, the vinyl is blown in a closed mold to produce relatively thick sections of unicellular foam which may be used as made or sliced to the desired thickness. Articles molded in this way retain the details and proportions of the mold, even though the expansion may be completed outside the mold.

The other method consists in casting a vinyl dispersion mixed with a blowing agent in an open mold or coating a suitable web with the mixture, then allowing the mix to expand in a "free blow." Vinyl plastisols, for example, are blown in open molds by incorporating salts which evolve gas at the fusion temperature of the plastisol. Products blown in open molds generally contain some interconnected cells.

Silicone resins may also be blown. The products have a uniform pore pattern which is predominantly spherical and unicellular. The expanded products are nonflammable and exceptionally heat-stable, having heat distortion temperatures of over 375°C. They have good physical and electrical properties, low moisture absorption, exhibit excellent thermal insulating properties, but suffer from friability. Apparent densities vary between 10 and 20 pounds per cubic foot.

Polystyrene is offered commercially in the form of beads containing a blowing agent (Dylite). Upon heating with steam, the material expands readily to form unicellular, intricate shapes in molds. Densities from 1.5 to 15 pounds per cubic foot can be obtained. The products are used for low-temperature insulation, sandwich constructions, buoyant materials, packaging, toys, novelties, and displays, and in the electronics field. Pre-expanded polystyrene (Styrofoam) is also used extensively in the same fields of application. Weighing less than 2 pounds per cubic foot, Styrofoam exhibits low thermal conductivity, good moisture resistance and structural strength, and easy workability.

One of the newest developments is foamed plastics prepared from polyurethanes. The diisocyanate is unusual in that it provides the source of gas (carbon dioxide, in this case) as well as the cross-linking medium (see Polyurethanes, Chap. 8). Expanded polyurethanes may be either elastomeric or rigid. Both types are produced, however, by the chemical reaction between specific polyester resins, water, and polyisocyanates and obtain their cellular structure by internal carbon dioxide formation.

The largest volume of foamed polyurethane produced is of the elastomeric type. In addition to the polyisocyanate and the polyester resin, suitable accelerators (e.g., tertiary amines), water, and colorants are simultaneously combined in a high-pressure mixing head. The mixed components are forced out of a nozzle into a suitable container or mold in which the material foams and cures from its own heat of reaction. The density of the foam is controlled by the amount of water and excess polyisocyanate used.

Rigid foams are generally made by mixing two prepared components and pouring the product into a suitable mold. Two advantages of the two-component system are: (1) It is not necessary to install the expensive equipment required to pre-react the diisocyanate with the polyester under carefully measured and controlled conditions, and (2) it is simple for the user to merely mix the two components and "foam in place."

The polyurethane foams have some unique and desirable properties. They have high strength-to-weight ratios, high abrasion resistance, can be sewn, and can be fabricated with common wood-working tools. The foams not only have good resistance to oxidation, mildew, and vermin, but can be washed or dry-cleaned. They are odorless, nonallergenic, and oil- and solvent-resistant. One sometimes desirable characteristic of the rigid formulations is that they bond firmly to the walls of the container in which they are foamed.

## CASTING AND EMBEDDING

Casting differs from all of the preceding processes of shaping a plastic in that a *liquid* mix is poured into an open mold, where it is shaped without application of pressure.

It might seem that the simplest technique would be to melt a thermoplastic polymer and pour it into a mold. Unfortunately, most polymers exhibit appreciable decomposition when heated sufficiently to become fluid. Dissolving the polymer in a solvent also is unsatisfactory because excessive shrinkage would occur upon evaporation of the solvent. For these reasons, suitable liquids for many casting operations are obtained from monomers, both thermoplastic and thermosetting, which may, however, be partially polymerized prior to the casting operation.

Casting was introduced by Baekeland in the early part of this century as a process for making decorative phenolic items. It was useful for small volume production where the investment in expensive molds could not be justified. The early phenolic resins were not very satisfactory because they tended to crack and discolor with age. The formulations were subsequently improved and these resins have been one of the most widely used in casting operations. About 1934, the acrylic resins became available and, because of their optical clarity and good mechanical properties, have also become popular for cast applications. The technique of casting these thermoplastic resins, as well as styrene, in the form of sheets, rods, and tubes has already been described in Chapter 9.

Other cast plastics were developed during World War II, among the most important of which were the unsaturated polyester resins. Both the acrylics and the unsaturated polyester resins were used in large quantity during the war and subsequently for airplane cockpit enclosures and similar uses.

At about the same time, the class of casting resins known as hot-melt compounds began to be used in appreciable quantities. These include ethyl cellulose, cellulose acetate-butyrate, and, more recently, polyamide (Versamid) and polyethylene resins. The hot-melt compounds are the only class of casting materials which are already in the polymerized state before casting. Used either alone or in combination with waxes, their characteristics are such that they can be liquefied and cast satisfactorily.

The epoxy resins are the most recent members of the cast resins family. They produce a superior casting because they shrink very little during curing, and properly formulated castings are not subject to cracking, have excellent electrical characteristics, and are resistant to a wide variety of reagents.

Many types of molds are used in casting operations, the choice depending upon the type of resin being cast, the type of molding required, and the volume of production. Lead molds are common for phenol-formaldehyde castings. The molds are made by dipping a highly polished steel form into molten lead, removing, cooling in water, and stripping off the hardened lead sheath from the form in a knockout rack. The mold is used only once, after which it is remelted and the lead reused. For the casting of articles which, because of surface designs, cannot be removed from the straight-draw type of mold described above, a cored lead mold is used. For shapes which cannot be removed from either of the above types of mold, a split-lead mold is employed.

Rubber molds are sometimes used because complicated shapes can be produced rapidly. Since this mold has a relatively short life and is more costly to prepare, it is usually employed only when castings of unusual complexity are required. These molds are made by coating a wood, clay, or plaster model with several coats of rubber latex. The hardened rubber mold is split, removed from the model, and is supported in a female

FIG. 11-52. Preparation of a lead mold used in the casting of phenolic resins. Here, a steel mandrel is being dipped into a lead bath. (*Courtesy Marblette Corp.*)

plaster mold before the resin is poured in. The surface of a casting obtained from a rubber mold is not as good as that from a lead mold.

A more recent technique for the fabrication of large, hollow pieces is known as slush molding or, more properly, slush casting. A small quantity of resin is poured into a mold, which is similar to the molds described above, and the mold is rotated in a mechanical device until the resin hardens on the walls, whereupon the mold is opened and the hollow casting is removed.

It is desirable that casting resins be in the liquid form, yet be in a stage such that final polymerization or cross-linking is accomplished in a short time. Except for the hot-melt compounds, which are already polymerized, this is accomplished by partially polymerizing thin monomers to a syrupy consistency. They must not be so thick, however, that they fail to fill all recesses of the mold completely.

The thermosetting phenolic casting resins are poured at the syrupy A stage and the castings are cured in the molds at a temperature of 60°

Fig. 11-53.   Phenolic casting resin being poured into a mold.   (*Courtesy Marblette Corp.*)

to 80°C. This type of resin requires many days or even weeks for cure, depending upon the thickness of the casting. This slow cure is required to prevent occlusion of bubbles and to prevent cracking.

The final hardening of phenolic resins depends upon a relatively small amount of polymerization to form the requisite number of cross-links. In the case of the unsaturated monomers, such as the acrylic and allyl types, much more polymerization is required. It is for this reason, as well as to reduce the heat of reaction, that prepolymers are often made.

A specialized casting procedure is used in the field of dental plastics. Because of the convenience of the forming process and the quality of the restorations obtained, acrylic dentures have largely displaced cellulose nitrate, rubber derivatives, and other materials used prior to 1940. As a matter of fact, by 1946 approximately 98 per cent of all dentures produced in the United States were made from methyl methacrylate polymers and copolymers. A slurry is prepared from a mixture of approximately equal parts of monomer and finely divided polymer. Pigments, lubricants, and accelerators are incorporated. The mixture thickens as the polymer dissolves and, when the proper viscosity is attained, the slurry is poured into a plaster mold bearing the dental impression. Polymerization is usually completed by heating the mold for a few hours at about 80°C. The mold is lined with tin foil, cellophane, or an alginate for good release of the dental impression.

Although the unsaturated polyester resins can be cured by the use of the proper initiator at room temperature, most of them are heated in closed molds to prevent surface tackiness caused by the inhibiting effect of the oxygen in the air. Epoxy compounds, on the other hand, may be cured in open molds, since their cure is not subject to inhibition by oxygen.

The hot-melt compounds, consisting principally of ethyl cellulose or cellulose acetate-butyrate in combination with a wax, are merely poured into suitable molds as a hot, liquid melt. Upon cooling, they are ready for use, since no polymerization occurs during casting. These products, as well as many of the preceding types, are used in increasing amounts in the production of punches, blocks, jigs, fixtures, and other types of tooling.

In the production of such products, simple wood or plaster molds can be used. This method of tooling has been greatly advanced by the aircraft industry and, more recently, by the automobile industry, which have found that the production of items from steel and aluminum can be accomplished in much less time and at a great saving in cost over previously established methods. Among the types of tooling made from cast resins are dies, hammer forms, checking fixtures, mockups, assembly fixtures, prototypes, and various jigs and routing fixtures. Many of these items are also made by laminating and low-pressure procedures. These techniques, using both thermoplastic and thermosetting resins, but particularly reinforced unsaturated polyester and epoxy resins, are now generally known as *plastics tooling*.

A variation of the casting procedure is known as *embedding* or *embedment*. Many objects are embedded in transparent plastic for purposes of preservation, display, and study. For electrical and other industrial purposes, two other processes are used, known as *potting* and *encapsulation*. The latter is the covering of a device with an insulating or protective material, while potting involves the complete penetration of the voids in the device with a plastic substance.

Phenolic casting resins and, somewhat later, urea resins were among the

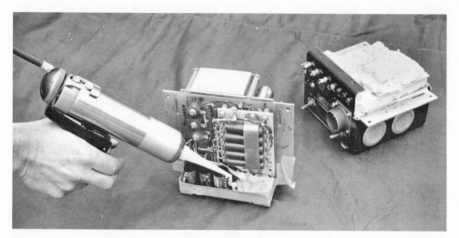

FIG. 11-54.   Potting an electronic unit with a room-temperature-vulcanizing silicone elastomer.   (*Dow-Corning Corp. photograph*)

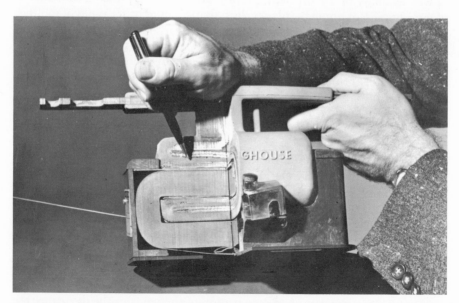

FIG. 11-55.   Encapsulation of a transformer with a silicone elastomer.   Good mechanical and dielectric protection is provided at temperatures of over 260°C.   (*Dow-Corning Corp. photograph*)

early materials used for embedding, but were not at first successful because of discoloration of the phenolic resins and cracking of both types. The methyl methacrylate resins were probably the first ones to be used successfully on a large scale. Subsequent improvements in phenolic resins have since led to their widespread adoption. More recently, other resins have come into use, among which the epoxy resins have been markedly successful.

For electrical potting and encapsulation uses, the phenolic, unsaturated polyester, silicone, polyurethane, and epoxy resins are of greatest value. Potting can be accomplished simply by heating the object in a mold above 105°C to drive off moisture, allowing the mold to cool, and then

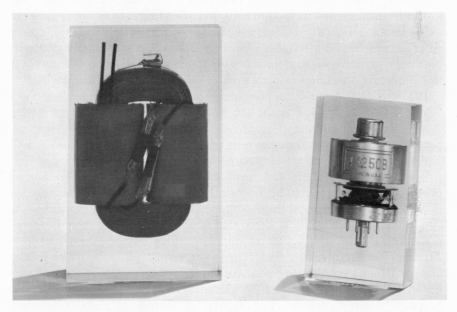

Fig. 11-56. Electrical components encapsulated in an epoxy resin. (*Courtesy Furane Plastics, Inc.*)

pouring in the liquid resin. After curing for about an hour, the casting is usually postcured outside the mold. In order to make sure that the liquid resin is forced into all voids in potting electrical devices, vacuum or pressure or centrifugal force is frequently utilized.

### SPINNING

The spinning of all modified natural and synthetic fibers is really an extrusion process. However, since the term is restricted to the production of fibers only, it will be desirable to discuss this operation separately so that the different methods may be compared. Spinning may be defined as the process whereby a polymer, temporarily fluid, is extruded from one or more small orifices and is then returned to the solid state in the form of a fiber. The fluid state is obtained: (1) By putting the polymer into solution in an ionized form, (2) by dissolving the polymer in a suitable solvent, or (3) by melting the dry polymer.

Each of the above three methods for extruding a polymer in the liquid state is of commercial importance, the choice depending upon whether or not a particular polymer can be conveniently put into solution or whether the polymer can be melted without decomposition. In all cases, spinning involves two fundamental operations: extrusion of monofilaments and a stretching of these filaments after extrusion. The latter step is necessary, as has been discussed in Chapter 10, in order to increase sufficiently the axial tensile strength of the monofilaments by molecular orientation. After extrusion and stretching, yarns or threads are normally made by twisting together a small number of coarse filaments or a large number of fine filaments, the latter having greater strength and pliability.

In *wet* or *solution spinning*, a polymer is first dissolved in a suitable solvent. Water is frequently used as the solvent if the polymer is of such a nature that it can be solubilized by reaction with an appropriate reagent. Examples are the solubilizing of cellulose with carbon disulfide and caustic and the solubilizing of proteins with caustic.

Water is a convenient and inexpensive solvent medium, but not all polymers can be made to be water-soluble. In this event, the polymer may be dissolved in a suitable organic solvent, if this is possible. In either case the solution is deaerated and filtered, and then is forced through the holes of a spinneret into a spinning bath. The bath either contains a reagent which reacts almost instantaneously with the solubilized polymer to convert it to the insoluble form or contains a nonsolvent liquid for the polymer which so dilutes the polymer solution that the polymer is precipitated. The former technique is more commonly employed. Derivatives of naturally occurring polymeric substances (e.g., cellulose nitrate) were first spun by this method.

In *dry spinning*, the polymer is dissolved in a suitable solvent and, after proper treatment, is also forced through a spinneret. This method differs from solution spinning in that the fibers are not passed into a spinning bath but are instead dried very rapidly by blowing a current of hot gas through the chamber into which the filaments are extruded. The evaporated solvent is recovered and reused. Note that, like the second method of wet spinning described above, no chemical change occurs. Examples of polymers spun by this process are cellulose acetate and vinyl chloride copolymers.

For fibers which have reasonably sharp softening temperatures, are sufficiently fluid above these temperatures, and are adequately heat-stable, the process of *melt spinning* may be employed. In this process, suitable fluidity is obtained by heat alone, no solvent being added to the polymer. Generally, fibers which are melt-spun are produced in the form of somewhat coarser monofilaments. Examples of melt-spun fibers are polyethylene, saran, nylon, Dacron (and glass). Note that the above polymers are either insoluble or are only slightly soluble in common or inexpensive solvents at room temperature, hence are not amenable to spinning by either of the other techniques.

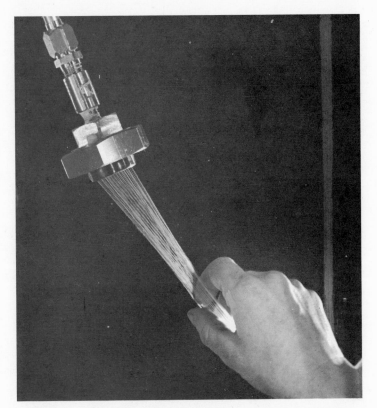

Fig. 11-57. Laboratory demonstration model of a wet-spinning operation. (*Courtesy Chemstrand Corp.*)

## FINISHING OF PLASTICS

The finishing of plastic materials involves operations performed on fabricated articles to impart smoothness to their surfaces, to remove fins and parting lines produced in molding operations, to drill and tap holes, to decorate the surfaces, and to otherwise bring the articles to the desired condition. In other words, the term "finishing" is used to cover those operations subsequent to the actual fabricating process.

A plastics fabricator always tries to produce a completely finished article from the molding or forming operation, but he rarely accomplishes this result. Regardless of the method used to fabricate an article, some finishing is generally required. Finishing operations are numerous and varied; in fact, every time a new application for a plastic material is found, a new method or technique of finishing usually must be developed. The finishing operations must be carefully studied in connection with the

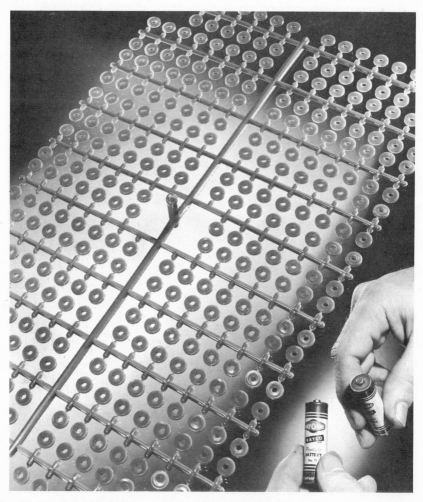

FIG. 11-58. Injection-molded polyethylene battery washers. Clearly shown are the sprue, gates, and runners which must be removed. (*Courtesy Eastman Chemical Products*)

product design to insure minimum cost. Frequently, the finishing labor may exceed the molding labor, and a poorly designed fabricating process may result in excessive over-all costs.

For molded articles, the process of finishing includes the removal of gates, sprues, runners, flash, and fins. Other operations which are common to the finishing of plastics are hand filing, sanding, cementing, carving, punching, trimming, piercing, tumbling, buffing, ashing, polishing, lapping, machining, grinding, reaming, threading, drilling, tapping, turning, milling, routing, sawing, stamping, embossing, metallizing, coating, and also annealing and postbaking.

Molded articles produced in flash and semipositive molds always have a fin, or flash, which is the excess material squeezed from the mold. In addition, moldings made in split-cavity molds have a parting line running around the article. Moldings made by the injection process will have gates and runners attached. All of these ridges or pieces of excess material must be removed. Probably the oldest and most commonly used method for removing fins from thermosetting articles is filing by hand. Another method employs a moving, flexible belt, coated with abrasive. Although belt sanding may be either a wet or dry process, the former method is usually preferable, as the water absorbs frictional heat, decreases abrasive loading, increases cutting speed, settles dust, and prolongs the life of the belt. A third method of removing flash is by tumbling. In this process, the articles are placed in an octagonal barrel which rotates, and the rubbing of the pieces over each other wears off the fins. Frequently other materials, known as breaking agents, are added to accelerate the definning operation. Wooden pegs, steel balls, jacks, or pieces of chain are some of the breaking agents used. In order to provide a cushioning effect for the pieces being tumbled, sawdust is often added.

Both gates and flash may be removed in a punch press, which consists of a shaped stamping plate to hold the article and a cutting blade. Parting lines are frequently removed by a process known as ashing, which is accomplished by use of a buffing wheel, made of muslin disks, to which fine, wet pumice is applied.

In addition to the techniques just described, several other methods are frequently used for removing flash and gates. A simple one is the use of ordinary hand shears, or snippers, for trimming thermoplastic materials. A band saw may be used for the same purpose. In other cases, gates may be cut off by the use of an electrically heated wire.

Cold-molded articles are usually finished by use of a carving spindle. A rapidly rotating cutter or burr on the end of the spindle quickly removes rough edges and fins.

Most plastic articles are subsequently polished to restore their inherent high surface luster. Both tumbling and buffing are employed. The tumbling operation is similar to the one mentioned previously for definning, except that polishing agents, such as pegs treated with waxes, are added, instead of breaking agents. Buffing is used for polishing large articles or small ones requiring unusually high surface gloss. Plastic articles are pressed against a rotating buffing wheel impregnated with such compounds as Tripoli, lime, pumice, rouge, and tallow.

Often a plastic piece must be cemented to another plastic or other material. The type of cement varies, depending upon the composition of the plastic. Thermoplastic compounds are easily joined by the use of a cement composed of the plastic dissolved in a suitable solvent; the cement attacks the plastic and becomes part of the assembly. Thermoset articles are usually joined by cements which harden by polymerization; the final assembly is sometimes given an after-bake to ensure complete polymerization and relieve stresses.

Articles made by processes other than that of molding are finished somewhat differently because they vary more widely in form and material used. Among the most commonly fabricated materials are the laminated and cast phenolics, laminated ureas, and sheets, rods, and tubes of the various thermoplastic resins. Operations frequently used include sawing, drilling, turning, punching, tapping and threading, and polishing. Laminated articles usually require less polishing than molded ones. Since many laminated articles are relatively large, tumbling is usually not feasible and buffing is resorted to. Simple sheet stock may also be finished by any of the above methods. Routing is frequently used to make such stock conform to a particular pattern. Square holes in sheet stock can be made by a technique known as chopping, using a steel cutting die in a power press.

Hot-gas welding has become an extremely useful technique for joining thermoplastic materials to form articles which would otherwise be difficult or impossible to make. Polyethylene and all varieties of vinyl chloride polymers are most commonly used for fabricating by this technique. Poly(methyl methacrylate), styrene copolymers, nylon, saran, and polychlorotrifluoroethylene can also be welded successfully.

Hot-gas plastic welding is similar in many respects to the gas welding of metals. The greatest difference lies in the application of the welding rod. In plastics welding, the rod, instead of becoming molten, is only softened sufficiently, together with the sheet, that the two will adhere to each other firmly and permanently. The actual process consists in heating both the rod and sheet by means of a stream of hot gas (usually air, except inert gas for polyethylene) at 200° to 300°C for most plastics until they reach their fusion temperatures, whereupon the rod is lightly pressed into the notch in the sheet and the two surfaces fused together. The mass production of plastic pails, filters, valves, and ducts utilizes this welding technique extensively. Plastic pipe is frequently joined by welded and flanged connectors, and plastic-covered cables are often spliced by means of the hot-gas welding technique.

Another operation performed on thermoplastic moldings is annealing, since strains are present in almost all molded pieces. Dimensional instability and susceptibility to crazing by solvents and thermal shock often occur in thermoplastic articles containing unrelieved stresses. Molded thermosetting resins may be postbaked in order to improve

FIG. 11-59. Hot-gas welding a polyethylene flange to a polyethylene-lined tank. (*Courtesy American Agile Corp.*)

dimensional stability by releasing strains and accelerating after-shrinkage and to reduce moisture content, thus improving their electrical characteristics.

Many plastics may be painted for decorative effects as a final step in the finishing operations. Since the various plastics differ in their physical and chemical properties, it is important to select the proper type of coating for the particular type of plastic material to be decorated. Both clear and pigmented lacquers are widely used to protect and decorate plastic surfaces; baking, which might be harmful to thermoplastics in particular, may thus be avoided. The choice of solvents must be carefully made, however, in order not to soften unduly the surface of the plastic article.

Coatings are applied by many different means, including spraying, silk screening, printing, dipping, rolling, and hot stamping. These are the same techniques used to decorate other types of surfaces and will not be discussed here further. Another method of applying a thin coating, known as metallizing, is sufficiently recent and interesting to warrant further discussion.

The process of metallizing plastics is often performed not for the purpose of imitating metals but rather to yield products that cannot be made of metals economically. More intricate shapes can be readily molded and plated from plastics than can be fabricated easily in metal and electroplated. Since the weight added by a thin metal coating is usually negligible, a metallized plastic article will have a decided weight advantage over a similar part made entirely of metal.

Further, metallic coatings of the proper type and thickness over plastic articles often eliminate or reduce such undesirable properties of some plastics as absorption of oils, solvents, and moisture, which may cause swelling or distortion, and the weatherability of the plastic is greatly increased. In addition, tensile, impact, and flexural strengths are increased, and resistance to abrasion and to distortion under heat is improved.

One of the outstanding advantages in metallizing plastics is the greater corrosion resistance offered by the metallic deposit, since it is applied to a plastic substrate rather than to the usual metallic base. This greatly increases resistance to salt water and corrosive atmospheres, since no electrolytic action can occur. The inert, plastic substrate, on the other hand, insures that the outer metal coating will last longer, and the combination provides a longer life for the entire plated article. The metallization of plastics has been widely applied in the field of electrical engineering and electronics, particularly for shielding electric insulators against metallic fields, high-frequency currents, or radioactive emanations. For such uses, articles molded of phenolic or styrene resins, which are excellent insulators, are plated with copper, cadmium, or lead. Solid metals, such as aluminum and magnesium, are being replaced, in part, by metallized plastics for electrical and radio shielding in aircraft.

Several methods are used for metallizing plastic products. The most widely used is vacuum plating, applied either by evaporation or by cathodic sputtering; next, chemical reduction, followed by electroplating; and, lastly, mirror spraying. Each technique has its particular fields of application.

A lustrous, adherent coating of metal can be deposited by vacuum evaporation on all types of plastic surfaces. Since sufficient metal may be deposited by this method to render the coating opaque, discolored or scrap plastic may be used for the article. Such items as

FIG. 11-60. A printed circuit used in a digital voltmeter. (*Courtesy Formica Corp.*)

costume jewelry, Christmas-tree ornaments, sequins, flashlight reflectors, children's toys and musical instruments are often coated by vacuum plating.

If the outer surface of a plastic article is plated, the process is known as "first-surface" coating. When a clear plastic article is metallized on the back surface, the process is known as "second-surface" coating. The latter exhibits a three-dimensional effect when viewed from the front, like that obtained by using true metallic inserts.   Automobile horn buttons and crests are examples of articles made by this technique.

Printed circuits are nowadays familiar examples of products requiring the use of metallizing for a functional purpose.   Such circuits require electroplating, since more metal must be applied than can ordinarily be obtained by metallizing.   Because the phenolic laminates usually used for these circuits are nonmetallic and, hence, cannot be directly electroplated, a thin film of copper is first applied by vacuum metallizing.   The surface can then be electroplated with copper to the desired thickness. Undesired metal areas are removed by photo-etching techniques, leaving the pattern desired.

Because aluminum looks like platinum or chromium when deposited in a thin film and because it is more easily vaporized than other metals, it is the metal most frequently used in vacuum metallizing operations. Like the rarer metals above, it does not tarnish, yet is much less expensive. However, aluminum is usually coated with lacquer as a protection against abrasion.   Uncoated metallized finishes are used only on expendable items or on items where abrasion resistance is not required.   Other metals less frequently used because of their cost and because they cannot be evaporated as readily are gold, silver, platinum, chromium, nickel, tantalum, and molybdenum.

Vacuum-metallizing with aluminum is accomplished by hanging small metal staples or crimped strips of the metal from coils of stranded tungsten wire filaments in a closed chamber.   The objects to be metallized are placed in the chamber on a rack, a vacuum (0.5 micron or less) is drawn, and the filaments are electrically heated to incandescence.   The aluminum evaporation and deposition take only a few seconds, producing an extremely thin coating approximately 0.000005 inch thick.   Metals other than aluminum are evaporated from "boats," which are troughs of tungsten or molybdenum sheet crimped on the ends to hold the molten metal.   The metal is vaporized in the boats, which are electrically heated in a manner similar to that employed for the tungsten wire in aluminum metallizing.

Cathode sputtering is another vacuum plating technique.   In this process, the metal to be deposited serves as an electrode (cathode) in an electrical system through which a high voltage of between 200 and 2,000 volts, depending upon the pressure, is passed.   Under the influence of this voltage, metal atoms leave the cathode and are deposited upon the plastic surfaces.   A vacuum of 1.0 to 0.01 mm Hg is usually employed in this process.   Since this is a lower vacuum than is necessary for vacuum metallizing, less expensive pumping equipment is required.   Disadvantages of this method are that the rate of deposition is slower than that of the previous method and some useful metals, such as aluminum, cannot be used; gold and silver are the usual metals employed.

The method of chemical reduction involves the formation of an electrically conductive film on a plastic surface by reacting an aqueous solution of a metallic salt with a suitable reducing agent. A silver film can be deposited on a plastic surface (after thorough cleaning and pre-treatment) by the reduction of an ammoniacal silver salt with formaldehyde. An intermediate layer of another metal, usually copper, is then electrodeposited over the silver, after which a third layer of the desired metal is electroplated over the copper. This technique is most often used when metallic coatings of greater than usual thickness are needed.

The mirror spray method, similar in chemical reaction to the first step of the chemical reduction method, involves the formation of a metallic film by the use of a spray gun. The gun is designed so that the metallic salt and reducing solutions are mixed within the gun before spraying or are sprayed individually through two concentric openings in the nozzle of the gun and are mixed after leaving the gun. In either case, the spray is deposited on the article as a reactive, film-forming mixture. This technique is used primarily for the application of brilliant silver films. The relatively low cost of this process is its principal advantage.

## REFERENCES AND RECOMMENDED READING

Barron, H., *Modern Plastics*, John Wiley and Sons, New York, 1945.

Billmeyer, F. W., Jr., *Textbook of Polymer Chemistry*, Interscience Publishers, New York, 1957.

Bjorksten, J., Tovey, H., Harker, B., and Henning, J., *Polyesters and Their Applications*, Reinhold Publishing Corp., New York, 1956.

Blom, A. V., *Organic Coatings*, Elsevier Publishing Co., Amsterdam (dist. by D. Van Nostrand Co., Princeton, N.J.), 1949.

Boundy, R. H. and Boyer, R. F., *Styrene*, Reinhold Publishing Corp., New York, 1952.

Delmonte, J., *Plastics in Engineering*, 3rd ed., Penton Publishing Co., Cleveland, 1949.

Dubois, J. H., *Plastics*, 3rd ed., American Technical Society, Chicago, 1945.

Dubois, J. H. and Pribble, W. I., *Plastics Mold Engineering*, American Technical Society, Chicago, 1946.

Ellis, C., *The Chemistry of Synthetic Resins*, Reinhold Publishing Corp., New York, 1935.

Encyclopedia Issue, *Modern Plastics*, Plastics Catalogue Corp., Bristol, Conn., 1956.

Fleck, H. R., *Plastics*, 2nd ed., Chemical Publishing Co., Brooklyn, N.Y., 1949.

Gordon, P. L. and Dolgin, G. J., *Surface Coatings and Finishes*, Chemical Publishing Co., Brooklyn, N.Y., 1954.

Haim, G. and Newmann, J. A., *Manual for Plastic Welding*, Vol. II, Crosby, Lockwood and Son, London, 1954.

Hicks, J. S., *Low-Pressure Laminating of Plastics*, Reinhold Publishing Corp., New York, 1947.

Hill, R., ed., *Fibres from Synthetic Polymers*, Elsevier Publishing Co., Amsterdam (dist. by D. Van Nostrand Co., Princeton, N.J.), 1953.

Holland, L., *Vacuum Deposition of Thin Films*, John Wiley and Sons, New York, 1956.

Houwink, R., ed., *Elastomers and Plastomers*, Vol. II, Elsevier Publishing Co., Amsterdam (dist. by D. Van Nostrand Co., Princeton, N.J.), 1949.

Kaye, S. L., *The Production and Properties of Plastics*, International Textbook Company, Scranton, Penn., 1947.

Kirk, R. E. and Othmer, D. F., eds., *Encyclopedia of Chemical Technology*, Interscience Publishers, New York, 1947–56.

Krumbhaar, W., *Coating and Ink Resins*, Reinhold Publishing Corp., New York, 1947.

Krumbhaar, W., *The Chemistry of Synthetic Surface Coatings*, Reinhold Publishing Corp., New York, 1937.

Langton, H. M., ed., *Synthetic Resins*, 3rd ed., Oxford University Press, London–New York, 1951.

Mansperger, D. E. and Pepper, C. W., *Plastics Problems and Processes*, 2nd ed., International Textbook Co., Scranton, Penn., 1942.

Marchionna, F., *Butalastic Polymers*, Reinhold Publishing Corp., New York, 1946.

Mason, J. P. and Manning, J. F., *The Technology of Plastics and Resins*, D. Van Nostrand Co., Princeton, N.J., 1945.

Mattiello, J. J., ed., *Protective and Decorative Coatings*, Vol. III, John Wiley and Sons, New York, 1941.

Moncrieff, R. W., *Artificial Fibres*, 2nd ed., John Wiley and Sons, New York, 1954.

Morgan, P., ed., *Glass Reinforced Plastics*, Philosophical Library, New York, 1954.

Nauth, R., *The Chemistry and Technology of Plastics*, Reinhold Publishing Corp., New York, 1947.

Payne, H. F., *Organic Coating Technology*, John Wiley and Sons, New York, 1954.

Rahm, L. F., *Plastics Molding*, McGraw-Hill Book Co., New York, 1933.

Richardson, H. M. and Wilson, J. W., eds., *Fundamentals of Plastics*, McGraw-Hill Book Co., New York, 1946.

Riley, M. W., *Plastics Tooling*, Reinhold Publishing Corp., New York, 1955.

Sasso, J., ed., *Plastics Handbook for Product Engineers*, McGraw-Hill Book Co., New York, 1946.

Schildknecht, C. E., ed., *Polymer Processes*, Interscience Publishers, New York, 1956.

Schmidt, A. X. and Marlies, C. A., *Principles of High-Polymer Theory and Practice*, McGraw-Hill Book Co., New York, 1948.

Seymour, R. B. and Steiner, R. H., *Plastics for Corrosion Resistant Applications*, Reinhold Publishing Corp., New York, 1955.

Simonds, H. R., *Industrial Plastics*, 3rd ed., Pitman Publishing Co., New York, 1955.

Simonds, H. R., Bigelow, M. H., and Sherman, J. V., *The New Plastics*, D. Van Nostrand Co., Princeton, N.J., 1945.

Simonds, H. R., Weith, A. J., and Bigelow, M. H., *Handbook of Plastics*, 2nd ed., D. Van Nostrand Co., Princeton, N.J., 1949.

Simonds, H. R., Weith, A. J., and Schack, W., *Extrusion of Plastics, Rubber and Metals*, Reinhold Publishing Corp., New York, 1952.

Society of the Plastics Industry, *Plastics Engineering Handbook*, 2nd ed., Reinhold Publishing Corp., New York, 1954.

Sonneborn, R. H., Dietz, A. G. H., and Heyser, A. S., *Fiberglas Reinforced Plastics*, Reinhold Publishing Corp., New York, 1954.

von Fischer, W., ed., *Paint and Varnish Technology*, Reinhold Publishing Corp., New York, 1948.

von Fischer, W. and Bobalek, E. G., eds., *Organic Protective Coatings*, Reinhold Publishing Corp., New York, 1953.

Wakeman, R. L., *The Chemistry of Commercial Plastics*, Reinhold Publishing Corp., New York, 1947.

Winding, C. C. and Hasche, R. L., *Plastics Theory and Practice*, McGraw-Hill Book Co., New York, 1947.

*Chapter 12*

# APPLICATIONS

It seems appropriate, after discussing the processing and fabrication of polymers, to close this book with a chapter on their applications. It will be obvious by now that any attempt to present a complete discussion of all applications—past, present, and future—is out of the question. In Chapters 6 through 9, the preparation, properties, and individual uses of the many commercial products have been covered. In this chapter an attempt will be made to cover broadly the applications of the more important polymers by end-use, rather than by discussing each one individually. Emphasis and greater detail will be given to applications which are recent or which have not been discussed previously. This does not, of course, imply that these uses are necessarily more important than the others.

In an effort to cover the field systematically, fibers will be discussed first, followed by plastics and elastomers.

### FIBERS

Fibers are utilized in a manner sufficiently different from plastics and elastomers that a whole field of terminology and specific tests has grown up that is devoted almost exclusively to the textile and related industries. Terms used in previous chapters to describe the properties of fibers may not be completely familiar to the reader working in another field. Hence, the terminology and some specific tests most frequently encountered in the textile field will be discussed briefly here.

A textile raw material is any substance which can be converted into a yarn and thence into a fabric of some kind. A textile *fiber* or monofilament is a single, fine strand of sufficient length, pliability, and strength to be spun into yarn and woven into cloth. Only its high length-to-breadth ratio is the essential characteristic of a fiber. By ASTM definition, the ratio of length to diameter is at least 100. The composition of the material does not determine that it will be a fiber; nylon, cellulose acetate, and acrylonitrile copolymers, for example, are used in the form of molded plastics as well as in the fiber form. It is merely the *shape* that is the determining characteristic of a fiber.

A real silk fiber, which is considered to be a continuous filament, may have a length of about 1,500 feet and a diameter of about 0.0006 inch, so that its length-to-breadth ratio may well be over $10^7:1$. For other natural fibers, average values of length-to-diameter ratios are much less—about 1,200 for flax, 1,400 for cotton, and 3,000 for wool. A high length-to-thickness ratio is equally characteristic of the modified natural and synthetic fibers also, particularly since they may be manufactured in continuous filament form.

For some special purposes, monofilaments are used directly, particularly in the form of thick monofilaments. A familiar application is their use for bristles, as in clothes, tooth, and paint brushes. Other applications depend upon certain decorative or novelty effects of thick monofilaments; however, most filaments spun are relatively thin and are formed into yarns.

*Yarn* is the generic term for an assemblage of fibers twisted or laid together to form a continuous strand used in weaving and knitting operations. In the case of man-made fibers, most yarns are composed of between 15 and 100 filaments. The advantage in multifilament construction is that it confers pliability on a yarn; one composed of a number of fine filaments is much more flexible than a single, thick filament of the same total diameter.

A *thread* is formed from three or more yarns tightly twisted together. Such items as strings, cords, and ropes are usually made like threads, by first assembling fibers into yarns and then assembling the latter into much larger units.

A *cloth* is a pliable fabric made by weaving, knitting, or felting. *Weaving* is the process of interlacing two sets of yarns, the warp and the filling, usually at right angles to each other. Strictly speaking, only woven goods are properly called textiles. *Knitting* is the formation of a fabric by the interlooping of successive single yarns or threads, each row of loops being caught into the previous row. *Felting* is a process in which fibers are massed, without weaving or knitting, into a continuous, dense mat. Thus, woven and knitted goods are based upon yarns or threads arranged in an orderly fashion, while a true felt, on the other hand, is based upon the fiber, a large number of which are arranged in an entirely random manner.

Fibers differ appreciably in cross-sectional area and shape. The fineness of a fiber or yarn is given as its mass per unit length. A common unit of measurement is the *denier*, which is the weight in grams of 9,000 meters of a fiber or yarn. (The denier, a coin, was used as a weight, long before the modified natural and synthetic fibers were made, to determine the size of the silk yarn.) Thus, two fibers may have the same denier yet have different cross-sectional areas if their specific gravities differ. One denier equals 4,464,528 yards per pound. The unit is used now for most of the man-made fibers. Other systems are usually used for wool and cotton.

The term *full-fashioned* is used to refer to hosiery that has been knit on a flat frame and shaped without varying the loop size significantly. The *gauge* of a full-fashioned machine indicates the degree of knitting fineness and is the number of needles per one and one-half inches of the

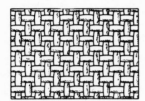 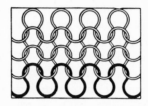 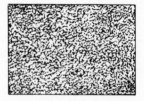

FIG. 12-1.    Examples of woven, knitted, and felted goods [1]

needle bar.    For example, 30-gauge means that 20 needles per inch have been used.    In recent years, higher gauges and finer deniers have been favored in knitting full-fashioned hosiery.    The first nylon hosiery made contained 40 denier 13 filament yarn for the boot (leg) and 70 denier 23 filament yarn for the rest of the stocking.    As knitting technology improved, 30 denier yarn was used for the boot, and more recently 15 denier monofilament yarn for the boot and 40 to 60 denier for the rest of the stocking have become common.

Yarns having the same denier may be composed of different numbers of filaments.    A 100 denier yarn, for example, may be produced with 20 filaments and also with 50 filaments.    The former would have a filament denier of 100/20 or 5, which is relatively coarse; the latter would have a filament denier of 100/50 or 2 and would be a fine yarn.    Thus, the more filaments present in a yarn of a given denier, the softer and more flexible it is.    Fine filament yarns are used in fabrics where good draping, noncreasing properties, and good hand are desired.    Such yarns, however, abrade more easily.    There are, of course, uses for both fine and coarse filament yarns.

Nearly all yarns are twisted, since untwisted yarn is difficult to weave or knit without damage.    The twist is expressed in turns per inch. Sometimes yarns are also doubled or folded; this should be done in such a way that the yarn is balanced.    Twisting always increases the denier of a fiber, low twists increasing the denier only slightly; continued

[1] By permission from Schmidt, A. X. and Marlies, C. A., *Principles of High-Polymer Theory and Practice*, Fig. 11-1, p. 466, McGraw-Hill Book Co., New York, 1948.

twisting causes a secondary twist to develop (the twisted fiber begins to "corkscrew") and then the denier increases rapidly.

*Tenacity* is the breaking strength of a yarn expressed in force per unit yarn number, as grams per denier. If a load of 450 grams will just break a 100 denier yarn, the tenacity is said to be 4.5 grams per denier. Some fibers, such as the regenerated proteins, have tenacities of about one gram per denier, which is quite low; others, like nylon and Fortisan, have tenacities of 6 to 7 grams per denier, which is high. *Tensile strength* is the breaking strength of a material expressed as force per unit cross-sectional area, as pounds per square inch. Since denier is a function of specific gravity, the tensile strength is not necessarily proportional to the tenacity and one may be calculated from the other only when the specific gravity is known.

It is of interest to note that silk is a very strong fiber. It has a tensile strength of about 64,000 psi. Only five other fibers are stronger: glass, flax, Fortisan, asbestos, and nylon, in that order. Weaker than silk are cotton, steel wire, viscose rayon, acetate, and wool. Silk and nylon are the toughest of the fibers, where toughness refers to the amount of energy which must be expended per unit mass in order to rupture the fiber. In fact, these two fibers are more than twice as tough as any of the other fibers.

The strength of a fiber may also be expressed in terms of its *breaking length*. This is the length of a fiber which will just break under its own weight. The breaking length of two yarns of the same material but of different deniers will be the same because, although one yarn is stronger, it is proportionally heavier. Other measurements which are of importance include the *elongation at break*, which describes the percentage of stretch which can be given to a yarn before it breaks, and the *elasticity* of a fiber, which is a measure of its ability to recover from strain and is given as the percentage of the original length a stretched fiber will return to after an applied tension has been released. Usually fibers have high elasticity for low stretches but have relatively low elasticity for high stretches.

Another term which is frequently used is *regain*. All fibers exposed to the atmosphere absorb moisture, the amount varying with the relative humidity and temperature. The regain of a fiber or yarn is the percentage weight of moisture present, based on the oven-dry weight of the material. Some fibers absorb moisture more readily than others under similar conditions; those that do are said to be more hygroscopic and have higher regain than less hygroscopic fibers. The molecular composition of a fiber determines its degree of hygroscopicity.

Both modified natural and synthetic fibers may be spun in the form of a continuous filament, whereas natural fibers, except for silk, grow in comparatively short *staple* lengths. The former types are made into staple fibers by gathering a large number of continuous filaments into a *tow* and chopping them to the desired length. This is most conveniently done immediately after the spinning and stretching operations. Yarn is easily made from continuous filaments by gathering the desired number of filaments side by side and giving them sufficient twist to hold them together. The production of yarn from short staple fibers is a much more difficult process mechanically and was not seriously considered as a source of yarn until about 1920, when large quantities of viscose rayon, remaining as torn and shredded waste from the continuous filament

FIG. 12-2.  Dacron staple fiber passing through a carding machine where it is changed to sliver.  (*Courtesy E. I. duPont de Nemours and Co.*)

spinning process, had to be disposed of. It was not, however, until some fifteen years later that the use of staple fiber really expanded rapidly— so rapidly that in a very few years more yarn was being made from staple fibers than from continuous filaments.

The process of making yarn from staple involves the following steps. The tangled mass of staple fibers must first be freed of trash and *carded* to a suitable preliminary degree of parallelism and uniformity. The product of this operation is a fluffy, continuous, untwisted strand of uniform density called the *sliver*. Greater uniformity and parallelism among the fibers are obtained by subjecting the sliver to tension by drawing, or *drafting*, an operation which yields a uniform, continuous, slightly twisted strand known as *roving*. Short, less desirable fibers may then be removed from the sliver by *combing*. The resulting yarns are cleaner and more uniform in texture and have a narrower fiber-length distribution. Finally, the roving is spun and is simultaneously drafted and twisted into a finished yarn of the desired weight and strength. Note that the meaning of the word "spun" has a different meaning here than when used to describe the process of extrusion of filaments.

The cross-sectional shapes of the various man-made fibers differ appreciably. Some fibers, such as nylon, are almost circular; others, like Orlon, have dumbbell or dog-bone cross-sections; those of viscose rayon are highly serrated; and those of cellulose acetate are lobed.

These differences in cross-sectional shape have great influence upon the physical properties of the product. In general, flat cross-sections impart high luster and excellent covering power, but have a harsh, unpleasant hand. Circular cross-sections produce a pleasant hand but poor covering power; the latter property might be expected, in view of the fact that a circular cross-section has the minimum surface for a given volume. Thus, wool and goat fibers have circular cross-sections and good hand, whereas cotton has a flat cross-section and feels harsher.

*Hand* (or handle) is the term used to describe the composite reaction incurred when a fabric is examined tactually; it is the "feel" of a fabric. Included in this term are such factors as whether the fabric is resilient or limp, warm or cold, pliable or stiff, rough or smooth, and thick or sheer. Good hand is not necessarily synonymous with good quality.

As Schmidt and Marlies[2] have pointed out, a fabric, during laundering, is exposed to the plasticizing action of a hot electrolyte solution (soap and alkali). Unless proper precautions are taken, excessive permanent shrinkage may occur. In the ordinary spinning, weaving, and finishing operations, yarns and fabrics are worked under tension and, as a result, finished goods are in a strained condition. The extended yarns will tend

[2] Schmidt, A. X. and Marlies, C. A., *Principles of High-Polymer Theory and Practice*, p. 483, McGraw-Hill Book Co., New York, 1948.

to contract somewhat the first time the fabric is laundered, causing shrinkage. (As a matter of fact, one method of producing crepe is to weave a fabric from yarns that shrink to different extents.) Various techniques have been used to treat cotton and other cellulosic yarns in

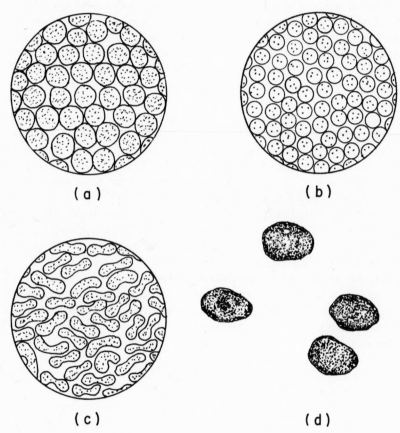

FIG. 12-3.   Cross-sections of (a) nylon; (b) Dacron; (c) Orlon; (d) Teflon.   500×.
(*Courtesy E. I. duPont de Nemours and Co.*)

order to minimize this type of shrinkage.   Probably the most effective method is the one known as *Sanforizing*.   In this process, the amount of shrinkage that the fabric will undergo during laundering is determined by actual test.   The cloth is then subjected to the proper amount of mechanical crimp along both the warp and the filling such that, upon subsequent laundering, the shrinkage occurring is compensated for by the loss of the mechanical crimp.

Stresses are partially released in woolen goods by pretreatment with steam or boiling water while under slight tension ("crabbing"). As a result, most shrinkage of wool is due to felting during laundering. Since dry cleaning employs nonpolar liquids at room temperature, it is a much safer method of cleaning woolen garments. The production of shrink-resistant woolens has been greatly increased by military demands for shrink-resistant clothing. Chlorination processes are used to the largest extent, but improvements are constantly being made on resin and rubber treatment processes.

Schmidt and Marlies[3] have also pointed out that, when a fabric is ironed, some of the techniques used in plastics molding are utilized. Wrinkles are removed and a crease may be imparted to a pair of trousers by first moistening (temporary external plasticizer), then ironing (using heat and pressure) until the fabric has been "molded" to the desired shape; the same technique is involved in the blocking of hats. This is the reason why, on warm, humid days, creases soon disappear.

Felt is defined as a fabric built up by the interlocking of fibers by a combination of mechanical work, chemical action, moisture, and heat. The word "felt" is applied to goods made without spinning, knitting, or weaving. Nonwoven, pressed felt is one of the oldest forms of fabric.

Only two major fibers have been used to make felt, namely, sheep's wool and the fur of other animals. Nylon, rayon, and protein fibers have each been added to wool or fur felts in recent years, but have served mainly as additives, imparting to the product some of their functional advantages or a cost advantage. Felt from man-made fibers is expected to supplement wool felt and even to replace it in applications where its properties are unique. Some of these are stability to further felting; resistance to heat, chemicals, mildew, and fungi; exceptional strength; and higher abrasion resistance.

Felt is of great industrial importance because it can be made in many densities, thicknesses, and qualities, and is easily designed into products. It cuts without fraying and can be die-cut, punched, turned, molded, or otherwise simply processed. It has a high degree of resiliency, an unusually high breaking strength, and a high coefficient of friction against wood, glass, and metal. Also, it is but slightly affected by such atmospheric conditions as moisture, sun, heat, and cold. Felt has a high capillary value (excellent wicking properties) and serves as a good filter medium. It dampens machine vibrations and deadens noise very effectively.

Although the term "felt" usually brings to mind men's and women's hats and similar materials, it should be pointed out that paper making, a tremendously large operation, is also a felting operation in which

3 Schmidt, A. X. and Marlies, C. A., *Principles of High-Polymer Theory and Practice*, p. 484, McGraw-Hill Book Co., New York, 1948.

cellulosic fibers are suspended in a liquid, the liquid is drained off through a screen, and a layer of randomly disposed intermeshed fibers is left behind. It is also of interest to point out that animal skins are natural felts, composed of intermeshed protein fibers, which are converted into leather by tanning operations.

Without question, by far the largest use of fibers is in the manufacture of textiles. In 1800, excluding silk, only 4 per cent of the world's textile fibers consisted of cotton, 18 per cent being flax, and 78 per cent being wool. Even one hundred years later, only these four fibers, all obtained from natural sources, competed for use in the world market. As a result of the industrial revolution of the last century, however, the use of cotton grew rapidly and the share of wool on the market dropped to less than 15 per cent. Yet, in spite of this, the consumption of wool has not decreased in amount but only in percentage. Today, in the United States, silk has almost succumbed to the inroads of the many modified natural and synthetic fibers, while cotton, although still far in the lead, has accounted for a slowly decreasing portion of the textile market.

Regenerated cellulose or rayon (principally viscose) and cellulose esters (principally cellulose acetate) account for most of the present modified natural fiber production and consumption. In the field of synthetic fibers, the variety and competition are much greater. Although all synthetic fibers account for only about 5 per cent of the total fiber consumption in the United States at present, their rate of growth is some thirty times that of the natural fibers. Among the more important synthetic fibers are the nylons, Acrilan, Dacron, dynel, Orlon, saran, polyethylene, and Teflon. Of these, the nylons undoubtedly account for a greater share of the market than any other fiber.

It has been estimated that almost 40 per cent of all man-made fibers were used for industrial purposes in 1955 in the United States. In addition to their uses in fabrics, the fibers have several specialty uses. Since nylon was the first wholly synthetic fiber, it is natural, aside from its unique properties, that its uses should have been extended earlier than the others. Ropes and threads, particularly of nylon, have become common. Nylon is being used experimentally in the manufacture of paper; the product is, to be sure, more expensive, but its superior properties, as compared to cellulose, will doubtless provide a small but significant market.

Nylon is now finding limited use in the bed-linen field. Although considerably more expensive than cotton, its lower density, longer wearing qualities, and ease of laundering may make it a successful competitor. Its low regain, however, makes it cold to the touch. Other synthetic fibers will doubtless be used for the same and similar applications.

In the manufacture of tire cord and fabric, the use of nylon has grown rapidly, displacing a significant quantity of the cotton and rayon heretofore used almost exclusively in this field. The rayon manufacturers are fighting this trend by improving the properties, especially the tensile strength, of their products.

Coarse monofilaments of vinylidene chloride copolymers (saran) are used in increasing amounts in the manufacture of screening. The screens are tough, sufficiently elastic to absorb moderate impact, are nonrusting, and never require painting.

A specialty use of certain fibers is as flock. Flock is made of very short fibers, usually 1/32 to 1/8 inch long. It is applied by sifting or spraying onto surfaces moistened with an adhesive; the resulting surface is soft and fuzzy to the touch. Record player turntables, some wallpapers and greeting cards, children's books, lamp bases, and novelty fabric decorations use considerable quantities of flock. Cellulose acetate and rayon are the fibers most commonly used.

In the unsaturated polyester laminating field, although glass fibers are most commonly used as the reinforcement, cotton, and to a lesser extent, synthetic fibers are used where maximum strength is not required.

Since the cost of wool has risen steeply in the past few years, rugs and carpeting are being made of cotton, rayon, nylon, and the newer fibers in increasing quantity. How much of the market the latter fibers will capture will probably depend primarily upon the price of wool, since all of its desirable properties are still unequaled by any other fiber.

In coats and jackets, linings are usually made of rayon and acetate. Many of the new pile fabrics used to insulate coats and jackets are now made of nylon, Orlon, Dacron, and dynel blends in place of cotton and wool. The synthetic piles are lighter, mat less, especially upon cleaning or laundering, and absorb less moisture, while retaining their excellent insulating qualities.

Synthetic furs have been made using dynel, Vicara, Acrilan, and Orlon, individually and in blends. By selection of proper denier size, fabrics can be produced to give almost any degree of softness, thus simulating the natural furs. The low regain of the new synthetics results in fabrics that dry rapidly and return to their fluffy state after drying. Synthetics offer relief to persons allergic to natural fibers. Blends of Vicara and dynel have found wide acceptance when made into mouton-type fabrics. These are being used as collar material on storm coats and children's snowsuits.

These recent developments are merely illustrative of a few of the changes taking place in the textile industry. It appears inevitable that these will in time be superseded or augmented by still newer discoveries and applications. It is safe to say that at no time in the history of the textile industry has such a revolution in the use of raw materials taken place as in the past twenty years.

## PLASTICS

The most diversified use of polymers and resins is in the field of plastics. Since plastics have physical properties between and often overlapping those of fibers and elastomers, almost every known polymer can be included in the plastics field.    By far the largest outlet is for constructional uses; i.e., applications of molded, formed, cast, extruded, and other fabrications.

### Constructional Uses

Although the plastics industry has justly claimed that its products are materials of construction in their own right, rather than mere substitutes for other materials, the plastics are now vigorously competing against such commonly used substances as ceramics, wood, leather, and many metals.

The applications of polymers for constructional uses have been covered in previous discussions of the specific polymers.    Further, many of the applications will already be familiar to the reader.    Hence, only some of the more recent developments will be stressed herein, while the more obvious and older uses will be only mentioned in passing.

One of the most rapidly growing fields of use for several of the plastics is that of pipe.    Although the sales volume of plastic pipe represented only about 1 per cent of the entire plastics industry as recently as 1953, it is anticipated that this figure will rise to about 10 per cent by 1960.

Fig. 12-4.   Polyethylene pipes used for syphoning irrigation water from ditch.   Black pigmentation is used to improve resistance to sunlight.   (*Courtesy Bakelite Co.*)

A large number of polymers has been found suitable for use in piping, tubing, and associated fittings. They are preferable to metals in many cases because of their ease of fabrication, light weight, and chemical inertness. Phenolic resins were one of the first to be used but have been displaced in large measure by polyethylene, styrene-butadiene-acrylonitrile copolymer mixtures, cellulose acetate-butyrate, poly(vinyl chloride), and vinyl chloride–vinylidene chloride copolymers. Of the approximately 30 million pounds of plastics used in pipe in 1954, about 60 per cent was polyethylene, 15 per cent was styrene-butadiene-acrylonitrile copolymer mixture, another 15 per cent was cellulose acetate-butyrate, and 3 per cent was poly(vinyl chloride).

Polyethylene pipe weighs only about one ninth as much as steel. Its flexibility, light weight, and ease of coupling make this pipe particularly

Fig. 12-5.   Extruded flexible polyethylene pipe.   (*Courtesy Eastman Chemical Products*)

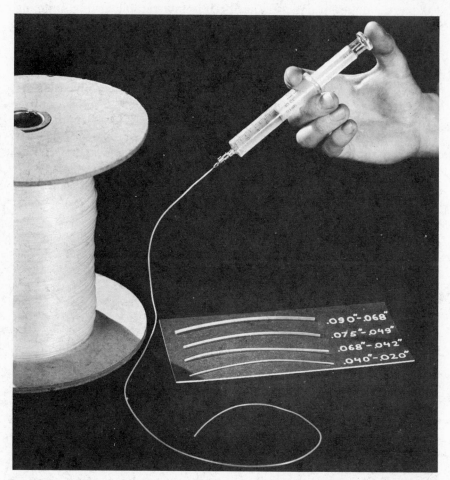

FIG. 12-6.    Precision extruded polyethylene tubing in very small diameters for medical
and industrial applications.    (*Courtesy Anchor Plastics Co.*)

useful for an important nonindustrial use, ranch and livestock watering.
One of the most attractive applications of flexible polyethylene piping for
water use is with jet pumping wells, where the piping can be coupled to
the jet unit and fed manually into the well, regardless of the depth.
This flexible piping also finds applications in food industries for handling
beverages, juices, and pulps.    Flexible polyethylene tubing is finding
use in telephone conduits.    Another very recent application is in radiant
heating.    Tubing is laid on rough flooring, held in position with hooks
while return bends are made, and covered with wire mesh.    The concrete
flooring is then laid, while water pressure is maintained in the tubing to
prevent its collapse during pouring and hardening of the concrete.

A mixture of copolymers of styrene and butadiene with acrylonitrile has found wide application in chemical plants. It has been used to replace monel metal completely in hydrochloric fume disposal systems in plating plants. The rigid type of this copolymer mixture resembles hard rubber but has somewhat greater resistance to dilute nitric and other oxidizing acids. It is also much tougher and shows good moisture and abrasion resistance. Probably its greatest weaknesses are its low resistance to many organic solvents and its rather limited outdoor durability. The polymer is an ideal replacement for alloys for small metal parts, and for pipes, valves, and sheeting for corrosive surfaces where solvents are absent.

Cellulose acetate-butyrate piping is being used successfully in low-pressure, low-temperature lines in the oil fields. In the production of oil, the four major sources of corrosion are salt water, sour crude oil,

Fig. 12-7.   Globe valve and piping fabricated from cellulose acetate-butyrate.   (*Courtesy Eastman Chemical Products*)

corrosive earth, and electrolytic action. Cellulose acetate-butyrate resists all of these. Typical uses include disposal well lines, vent lines, slurry lines, natural-gas lines, and even city water lines. However, this resin is degraded in the presence of certain solvents and strong alkalies.

One of the newer materials to be used in pipe manufacture is unplasticized poly(vinyl chloride), extruded in standard pipe and tubing sizes. The material has been used widely in Europe since early in World War II and has been found satisfactory as a replacement for copper and steel. It is resistant to acids, alkalies, and many solvents, is rigid but has a high impact strength, and weighs only about one fourth as much as steel. It has good resistance to chlorine and to certain oxidizing agents, such as sodium hypochlorite, and outstanding resistance to acids. As a result, many plants are using the plastic in valves and piping for chlorine, sodium hypochlorite, and hydrochloric acid. However, it is affected by certain solvents, especially halogenated compounds and ketones. The unplasticized polymer can be welded by the use of a hot-air torch to form

Fig. 12-8.   Rigid poly(vinyl chloride) ducts on right are in good condition after three years; metal duct on left failed in three weeks. (*Courtesy Atlas Mineral Products Co.*)

fume ducts, tank linings, and other equipment. It is now widely used for plumbing, irrigation, and oil-well lines. In viscose rayon plants, which handle a large amount of dilute sulfuric acid–sodium sulfate solutions, poly(vinyl chloride) in the form of spinning machine parts, sheeting, duct work, pipes, and valves is frequently specified.

Glass-fiber-reinforced plastic pipe is still in its infancy from a large-scale production standpoint in the industrial piping field. Advantages claimed for this type of pipe are high strength and light weight, impact resistance greater than that of most metals, a wide operating temperature range, high working pressure, and good insulating properties. These resins are resistant to a wide range of corrosive materials but not to strong alkalies or aromatic and halogenated hydrocarbons. This type of pipe is serving very satisfactorily in brine operations, where extremely corrosive conditions are encountered, and provides high impact strength and resistance to vibration. Tanks made of these reinforced plastics are used to transport fuel and water across the Arabian Desert. It is claimed that they will last ten to fifty times as long as steel tanks. Since the plastic is stronger than steel on an equal weight basis, pay loads have increased as much as 50 per cent. The resins also are being used in increasing amounts for many other products—hot and cold water lines, salt water lines on ships, oil-well piping, plating tanks, bathtubs, washing machines, aircraft, and boats.

Poly(vinyl alcohol) compounds are used in the chemical and petroleum industries as solvent- and gasproof hose, tubing, gaskets, packing, and gloves. The same material has been used to make a flexible hose for the air-conditioning and refrigeration industries to withstand attack by Freon and methyl chloride refrigerants. A specially compounded product has found an important application as a valve diaphragm resistant to chlorinated and aromatic hydrocarbons. Certain types are completely resistant to cold water up to a temperature of $15°C$.

Polystyrene exhibits good resistance to dilute acids and bases; hence it is used for water- and jet-well lines. Fittings of polystyrene are frequently used with polyethylene pipe. Polystyrene is rather brittle, however, and is subject to attack by most organic solvents.

Furan resins, which are dark, thermosetting resins, have good resistance to most acids, except the oxidizing ones, and to alkalies and many solvents. Although they have good rigidity and fair temperature resistance, they tend to cure and crack in service. Furan resin cements are commonly used in the construction of large pickling tanks. Probably the most useful furan resin is the asbestos-filled product, widely used for pipes, valves, tanks, towers, and almost every conceivable type of chemical structure.

Hard rubber, which exhibits good resistance to a number of acids and inorganic salt solutions, is easily machined, molded, extruded, and cemented. Unfortunately, its disadvantages include a low impact strength and limited resistance to oxidizing agents and to many solvents. Except where these limitations preclude its suitability, its uses are similar to those for the newer rigid and unplasticized poly(vinyl chloride) resins.

Probably as significant as their growing application as conduits of all kinds is the use of plastics in heavy-chemical plants as linings and coatings for vessels and pipes. They are applied as sheets, cements, molten sprays, and a variety of coating compositions. Rigid poly(vinyl chloride), for example, is widely used as a sheet lining material. The applications of phenolic resins are familiar and have been utilized for some time as baked coatings, built-up cement linings, and as binders for asbestos and graphite in the fabrication of a variety of equipment, such as piping, pumps, tanks, and ducts. Alkali resistance is improved by modification of the phenolics or by use of furan and furfuryl alcohol resins. Phenolic cements also serve as binders for brick chips, coke, quartz, or silica in the fabrication of porous media which are used as filter leaves, gas spargers, and supports for charcoal adsorption beds and ion exchange resins.

The chemical resistance of vinylidene chloride–vinyl chloride copolymers has resulted in their wide application in the handling of corrosive liquids and gases in the chemical industry. The successful use of saran in the form of pipe and tubing led to the development of saran-lined steel pipe, fittings, and valves. The saran is molded or extruded to a diameter slightly less than the inside diameter of the pipe it is to fit and is then mandrel-fitted into it. (Extruded cellulose acetate-butyrate tubing or pipe is also being used for lining steel pipe. The tubing is placed in the pipe and blown to size by means of steam.) Unlike plain steel or iron pipe, saran-lined pipe has an extremely low coefficient of heat transfer, a highly desirable property when insulating qualities are required. Successful applications include the handling of hydrochloric acid and organic chemicals containing hydrochloric acid. Another important use is in the demineralization of water, where saran-lined pipe is useful for handling, without contamination, the chemical supply for regenerating the ion exchange units and conveying the treated water to the point of use.

A useful form of saran is film which is transparent, flexible, and highly impermeable to water vapor and most gases. The shrinkage property of regular saran wrap can be used to advantage in over-wrap applications; for example, in the protection of underground steel pipelines, where a coating of hot wax is applied to the pipe and then saran film is wrapped spirally around the pipe. The heat of the wax causes the film to shrink tightly around the pipe, forming a moistureproof barrier against corrosion.

As plastics tooling continues to revolutionize production methods, many new products are appearing. In 1954, industrial tooling consumed more than 7 million pounds of plastics (mostly phenol-formaldehyde, unsaturated polyester, and epoxy resins). Approximately 25 per cent of all tooling for the automotive industries (not dies alone) is now manufactured with plastics, whereas in 1953 it was but 5 per cent. Similar percentages hold true for the aircraft and allied fields.

Some advantages of plastic over metal tools are handling ease and savings in time, cost, and manpower. Other advantages include simplicity in manufacture, resulting in lower tool room investment; ease of repair and alterations, in sharp contrast to expensive operations required for metal tool repair; savings in handling costs, resulting from the lighter weight of plastic parts; greater freedom of design, since intricate shapes and curves can be produced at a fraction of the cost required for metal counterparts; and small production runs, enabling manufacturers to carry out desirable alterations in product design made necessary by market studies.

Because of their high strength-to-weight ratios, many plastics are used in airplane construction. Resin-bonded plywood has probably contributed more to the realization of the value of plastics in aircraft than any other single factor. It has also become an important factor in marine construction. In addition to plywood, the glass-laminated, unsaturated polyester resins are becoming more widely used. The expanded resins are also finding wide use in aircraft and marine applications as structural, insulating, and reinforcing materials. In automobile construction the use of plastics began a long time ago and the amount has increased steadily. Distributor caps and rotors, steering wheels, instrument knobs, and floor mats are a few of the obvious applications.

The use of plastics in household appliances is almost unlimited. Appliance motor housings and fittings; bowls, dishes, and tableware; curtains and upholstery; lamp shades and reflectors; wall and floor tile; radio and television cabinets; and the many kitchen gadgets are a few examples.

Plastics are very popular for advertising and display purposes; resins frequently used are the cast and molded phenolic and urea resins, cellulose acetate, acrylic, and styrene resins, and various types of vinyl resins.

Plastics are used in large quantities in athletic and sports equipment, for plywood skis and toboggans, game boards and equipment, surf boards, canoes, and playground apparatus. They are used extensively in handicrafts, as materials of construction in home workshops, and for cameras, developing tanks, exposure meter housings, and movie film.

Many of the plastics are very satisfactory for musical instrument structural parts and for children's toys. As a result, modern toys are safer and more sanitary. Infant's toys are now made almost exclusively of plastics and rubberlike materials. Beach toys, rafts, boats, and backyard pools are plastic products. Even soap bubbles have been replaced by bouncing bubbles made of synthetic compositions, among them a partially polymerized methyl methacrylate resin.

Plastics are of use in the architectural field for decoration and functional finishing, as well as for structural purposes. Plastics, plywood, and laminates are extensively used in interiors of hotels, restaurants, offices, libraries, schools, theaters, hospitals, stores, and banks. Their use in furniture is wide. For decorative illumination, some plastics are superior to some of the materials previously used, particularly since the advent of low-temperature fluorescent lights. Many have good light transmission qualities and may be tinted, embossed, or louvered. Molded plastics are popular for decorative accessories, such as curtain rings, clock housings, and closet fittings. Phenolic and urea laminates cover wall and table surfaces, showers and bathrooms, bar fronts and tops, and restaurant interiors. The sandwich type of construction has been used in pre-fabricated houses.

Plastic articles are used for scientific, including medical, uses. Many medical instrument housings are made from plastics. They are also becoming more widely used in surgery for piping, hose lining, skin coverings, and as components of prosthetic devices.

A specialized field for only a few plastics but one which is of large volume is that of phonograph records. Early records were molded from

FIG. 12-9. This 7,000 gallon family swimming pool is made of vinyl-coated nylon.
(*Courtesy B. F. Goodrich Chemical Co.*)

hard rubber, but noisy reproduction and the expense of their fabrication led to the development of filled shellac records in 1888. After the discovery of phenol-formaldehyde resins, phenolic surfaced records were tried. These were much thicker than the records of today and frequently peeled in the sound grooves. Cellulose nitrate was subsequently tried, but its high flammability was a hazard. Normal cellulose acetate compositions have also been tried but have not had wide commercial acceptance. In the early 1930's, an excellent material was found to be the vinyl chloride resins. They have since come into general use for the more expensive disks and are, in fact, to a great extent responsible for the high-fidelity craze at the present time. More recently, polystyrene compositions have been used, particularly for the less expensive requirements of popular recordings, and cellulose triacetate is now just gaining a foothold in children's records. Because of its desirable physical characteristics, the latter product may well displace some of the vinyl chloride polymers in the near future.

The foregoing fields for the plastics are but a few of the many, but they serve to illustrate the fact that, except for the obvious physical limitations of the organic polymers, the applications appear to be limited only by man's imagination and ingenuity.

### THERMAL, ELECTRICAL, AND OPTICAL USES

Organic, high-molecular-weight polymers are unique in that, as a class, they exhibit less variation in thermal, electrical, and optical properties than do all other classes of substances, even though variations among themselves may be appreciable. Because of their organic nature, they are all relatively poor conductors of heat and electricity and, when pure, exhibit relatively good light-transmitting properties. The only close competitors in these respects are the inorganic glasses which, while generally harder, are also much more brittle.

The low thermal conductivities of polymers have made them especially useful as handles and knobs for household and industrial appliances which operate at elevated temperatures. This application is limited only by their softening or decomposition temperatures. Most unfilled plastics have thermal conductivities in the range of 20 to 200 Btu/hr/ft$^2$/°F/ft. Probably the most widely used heat-resistant plastics are the filled phenolic resin types and the silicones. These can withstand continuous temperatures of up to 250°C. Specially formulated types of plastics are even available for the rapid conduction of heat. Of course, for very high service temperatures and where heat must be dissipated very rapidly, metals must be used.

The extremely low thermal conductivities of the expanded polymers (0.02 to 0.03 Btu/hr/ft$^2$/°F/ft) have created a wide market for them in such insulating applications as walls or liners in homes, frozen-food and dry-ice truck bodies, and refrigerator cars. Within the limits of their softening temperatures, they are also widely used for the insulation of chemicals transported by truck and tank car which must be kept in a hot or molten condition. The usual expanded plastics are made from poly-styrene, cellulose acetate, poly(vinyl chloride), polyurethanes, and phenolic and urea resins.

With regard to electrical uses, all of the polymers are characterized by high electrical resistivities. Their limitations are those imposed by high ambient or operating temperatures and lack of sufficient strength and dimensional stability for certain applications; in such cases, ceramics are generally superior.

Most high-molecular-weight polymers are suitable for such direct-current and low-frequency alternating-current insulators as molded plug and switch bodies, and housings. The selection of the proper plastic depends upon the service conditions, cost, and mechanical shock resistance necessary. For high-voltage service, the dielectric strength must be considered and the choice becomes more limited. When flexibility is required, elastomeric materials must be used. Until comparatively recently rubber was almost the only material used for wire and cable insulation.

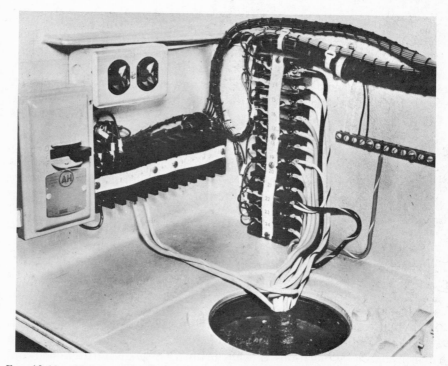

FIG. 12-10. Multi-conductor signal cable insulated with polyethylene and jacketed with vinyl resin. (*Courtesy Bakelite Co.*)

Now, such synthetic polymers as poly(vinyl formal), plasticized poly(vinyl chloride), and silicones are often preferred because they are better than rubber in one or more respects, such as arc resistance, temperature stability, abrasion resistance, solvent resistance, and aging properties. For applications where flexibility is not required, among the materials most widely used are hard rubber, polystyrene, phenolic laminates, aniline-formaldehyde resins, mica-filled phenolics, epoxy resins, and mineral-filled melamine resins. Each has its specific advantages and disadvantages.

Organic polymers are generally superior to inorganic materials in that they have inherently lower dielectric constants and loss factors. Furthermore, like glass and porcelain, they are less affected by moisture which increases the dielectric constant and loss factor and lowers the resistivity. At high (radio) frequencies, hydrocarbon polymers without polar groups are superior to those of higher polarity. Particularly useful polymers having very low dielectric constants and power factors are polystyrene, polyethylene, polytetrafluoroethylene, and some silicone oils. They are closely comparable to fused quartz in effectiveness, insofar as most electrical properties are concerned. However, any fillers, plasticizers, or lubricants added must be carefully selected, for they will detract from the optimum electrical properties obtainable with the resins alone.

In rare cases, it is necessary to combine other desirable properties of plastics (and elastomers) with good electrical conductivity. This can be accomplished by the addition of carbon. Conduction is desirable for the dissipation of static electricity in flooring in rooms containing volatile solvents (hospital operating rooms and dry-cleaning establishments), in gasoline-truck tires, and in heating pads and aviators' suits.

The superior optical properties of certain polymers has caused them to become widely accepted for a multitude of applications. For such items as windows and instrument dial faces, the transparent plastics compete with glass. Some advantages of such polymeric materials are that they have low specific gravities, are essentially nonshattering, have high mechanical shock resistance, have high light transmission and low haze values, and are relatively easy to fabricate. Their disadvantages as compared to glass are their lower scratch resistance, comparatively low optical stability, and their relatively high ultraviolet light transmission (unless specially compounded). The latter may, in some cases, be an advantage rather than a disadvantage (as in greenhouses).

Probably the acrylics, polystyrene, urea resins, poly(vinyl butyral), and poly(vinyl alcohol) are the only ones commonly used because of their individual and distinctive optical properties. The polymers of acrylic and methacrylic esters are characterized by colorless transparency, good adhesive qualities, elasticity, and good stability to light, moderate heat, and weathering. The aircraft industry has found cast and formed methacrylate sheets to be valuable in airplane construction, particularly in windows and windshields. Their optical properties also make them suitable for spectacle, watch, and camera lenses, goggles, edge-lighted signs, molded reflectors for indirect highway lighting, and illuminated advertising signs. Polystyrene, the only other organic polymer which has color and light-transmission properties comparable to the acrylics, is used in many of the same applications.

Many interior lights of automobiles and reflectors in home and office lighting fixtures are made of urea-formaldehyde plastics. The extensive use of urea plastics in the illuminating industry is due to their lightness of weight and shock resistance and their efficiency in providing a diffused light.

One other optical characteristic of certain polymers should be mentioned. In all crystals, other than those belonging to the regular or cubic systems, the optical density differs for different axes. They will thus exhibit the phenomenon of *double refraction* or *birefringence*. This means that when a beam of unpolarized light is passed through such a crystal, two refracted beams, polarized at right angles to each other, emerge instead of one. Thus, oriented, crystalline polymers will exhibit birefringence and the ability to polarize light. Unoriented, amorphous polymers and liquids are nonbirefringent.

(Substances exhibiting birefringence, when dissolved in a solvent, yield solutions which are nonbirefringent; if, however, the solutions are allowed to flow at such velocities that turbulence is avoided, they often become birefringent. This phenomenon is known as *streaming birefringence* and appears to be the result of flow-induced alignment of the solute.)

It has been found that films of certain polymeric materials, particularly poly(vinyl alcohol), in which the molecules have been highly oriented by drawing, may be used to polarize light. Spectacles and other optical lenses have been made by interleaving a layer of this oriented film between two layers of glass, cellulose acetate, or cellulose acetate-butyrate (Polaroid).

## Ion Exchange

The term "ion exchange" is used to describe the process in which positively or negatively charged ions are replaced by other similarly charged ions which are attached to an insoluble material. Ion exchange properties occur naturally in such widely diversified substances as humus, cellulose, wool and other proteins, resins, lignin, living cells, silicates, phosphates, fluorides, barium sulfate, silver chloride, alumina, and other inorganic substances.

The recognition of ion exchange dates back to the middle of the nineteenth century; for about the next fifty years, ion exchange studies were confined to the field of geochemistry. The process did not become useful industrially until the beginning of the twentieth century. Even then, its use was limited to water softening until about 1935 because of the unavailability of proper exchangers, in spite of the fact that the nature of ion exchange was understood.

In 1935, Adams and Holmes[4] in England discovered that certain synthetic resins then available were capable of exchanging ions quite readily. This discovery was soon followed by studies in both the United States and Germany, and rapid commercial development of these new resins was soon underway. The early resins were primarily phenolic types, typical cation exchange resins being reaction products of phenol, formaldehyde, and sodium sulfite, and typical anion resins being derived from a phenol, formaldehyde, and polyamines. These early products were not very satisfactory because of their low capacities and poor chemical and physical stabilities.

Shortly after World War II, considerable research in this field led to the commercial availability of higher capacity, more versatile, and more durable ion exchange resins. More recent studies have shown that resinous ion exchange substances may be synthesized having the physical properties and chemical characteristics desired for specific applications.

The only commercial inorganic exchangers used in any appreciable quantity are the natural and synthetic aluminosilicate cation exchanger gels. The original greensands and zeolites can be used only to soften water by exchanging sodium for the hardness-forming calcium and magnesium ions in the water. They lose some of their capacity in acid or alkaline waters and are objectionable because, in waters of low desired silica content, the effluent from them contains silica. These substances are inorganic and will not be discussed further.

From the point of view of its synthesis, there are two methods of forming an organic ion exchange resin. One consists in building the ionic groups into a resin structure prior to polymerization; i.e., the ionic groups are integral parts of the monomer. The second method consists in first forming a polymer and subsequently introducing the ionic groups into the polymer structure. The first method has the advantage that the resulting product is a homogeneous mass of good mechanical strength. In either case, the ionic groups cause the linear polymers to which they are attached to be soluble and chemically unstable. These undesirable properties are overcome by cross-linking the polymers. The higher the degree of cross-linking, the less the solubility, the less the amount of swelling in solution, and the more impermeable the gel formed. In practice, the resins are made to have the densest structure compatible with a satisfactory rate of ionic diffusion.

It may thus be seen that ion exchange resins are a special type of polyelectrolyte; i.e., a cross-linked polyelectrolyte. Their properties are determined to a great extent by the nature and number of the fixed and mobile charges and of the cross-linking bonds. The fixed charges or ionic groups determine the acidity or basicity of the resins, their capacity

4 Adams, B. A. and Holmes, E. L., *J. Soc. Chem. Ind.*, **54**, 1 (1935).

to exchange ions, and the amount of hydration of the resins. The mobile or exchangeable ions determine the type of exchange and also the amount of hydration of the resins. The degree of cross-linking determines the degree of swelling of the resin, the rate of diffusion of ions through the resin, and, to some extent, the exchange equilibrium constant. The degree of porosity of the vinyl-type polymers is controlled by regulating the amount of cross-linking (polyfunctional) agent used; with the (usually phenolic) condensation polymers, the amount of formaldehyde used controls the degree of cross-linking. The skeletal structure, although inert with respect to ion exchange behavior, determines the stability and life of the resin in actual use.

The earliest sulfonic acid cation exchangers were prepared from coal, lignite, peat, and other waste carbonaceous materials by sulfonating with sulfur trioxide, sulfuric acid, or chlorosulfonic acid. More recently, improved products have been prepared by sulfonating synthetic organic materials. The most commonly used cation exchangers are made by sulfonating a copolymer of styrene, ethyl vinyl benzene, and divinyl benzene. Other sulfonic cation exchangers may be prepared by the reaction of an aldehyde, a phenol, and a sulfonic acid or a sulfite. Exchange resins are known commercially by such trade names as Chempro, Amberlite, Dowex, and Permutit.

Carboxylic-type cation exchangers have been made by the oxidation of coal with nitric acid; by the reaction of phenol, acrolein, and the half-amide of oxamic acid; by the reaction of resorcylic acid with formaldehyde; and by the formation of carboxylic divinyl benzene copolymers. Other examples are the products formed by copolymerization of methacrylic acid with divinyl benzene and of maleic anhydride with styrene and divinyl benzene. Since they are less strongly acidic than the sulfonated resins, the carboxylic types are easily regenerated with acids but will not split salts of strong acids. Carboxylic resins are used principally in the exchange of large organic ions like streptomycin and for reducing excess alkalinity. Their exchange capacities are the highest among the cation exchangers.

The phosphonic acid resins are intermediate in strength between the sulfonated and carboxylic types. They have excellent exchange capacities at high pH's and can be regenerated efficiently with acid.

All anionic exchangers are synthetic resin amines. The early weakly basic resins were prepared by the polymerization of an aromatic amine and formaldehyde or by the reaction of a polyamine, phenol, and formaldehyde. Nitration and subsequent reduction of styrene-divinyl benzene copolymers also yield a weakly basic anion exchange resin. More basic anion resins have been prepared from formaldehyde and heterocyclic nitrogen bases, such as guanidine. Phenols are sometimes added to such compositions to improve their physical properties.

Current methods for the synthesis of more strongly basic exchange resins are those which incorporate the quaternary ammonium group. These include polymerization by quaternation, introduction of quaternary ammonium groups into preformed resins, and polymerization of monomers containing quaternary ammonium groups. The second technique is at present the most suitable and is utilized commercially for the preparation of strongly basic resins. In this method, a chemically inert matrix is first prepared, then functional groups are introduced by successive chloromethylation and quaternation. Examples are the resins obtained by the chloromethylation of styrene-divinyl benzene copolymers in chloromethyl ether solution followed by amination with *tert*-amines.

A new anionic resin series has recently been reported. Although based upon styrene, the highly porous and strongly basic series is cross-linked without using a polyvinyl compound. A chemical group which aminates readily is attached to the resin matrix, eliminating the need for chloromethylation prior to amination. The usual anion resins, normally regenerated with sodium chloride, require restoration with sodium hypochlorite after about ten cycles of use. These newer resins are expected to need less frequent restoration.

Another new class of polymers, based upon hydroquinone, will exchange *electrons* and can be used to conduct oxidation and reduction reactions by the same methods employed with the usual ion exchange resins. This type of polymer has a substituent group which can be reversibly oxidized under a wide range of conditions. The quinone-hydroquinone system was the first to be investigated because this reaction had already been studied intensively, the oxidation was known to be truly reversible, and the compounds were suitable for a wide range of mechanical manipulations. To make the polymer, vinyl groups are attached to hydroquinone molecules. The hydroxyl groups, which are polymerization inhibitors, are masked by esterifying with benzoic acid. The product is polymerized to a molecular weight of between 50,000 and 60,000. The benzoyl groups are then removed by saponification. The product has the advantage in oxidation or reduction reactions that no contaminant is introduced into the product.

Considerable effort is now being devoted to the synthesis of resins showing high specificity for particular ionic species and to the synthesis of resins of special physical form and shape. Most attempts to synthesize highly selective resins have been based upon the incorporation of functional groups usually found in the selective organic analytical reagents. The results have not been too successful to date.

Idealized structures of some cation and anion exchangers are given in Figure 12-11.

The important industrial applications of ion exchange at present

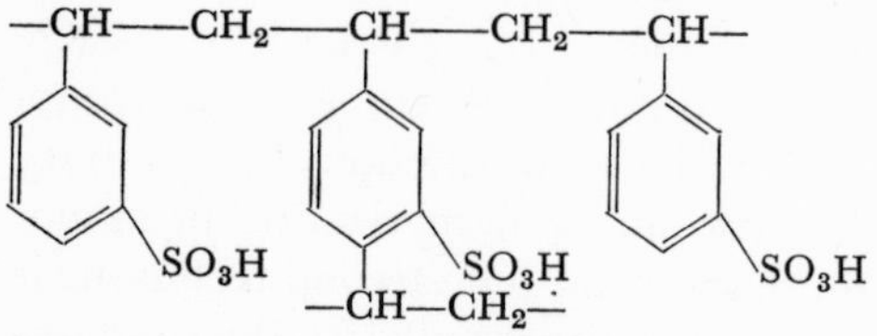

$$-CH-CH_2-CH-CH_2-CH-$$

Sulfonic Acid Cation Exchange Resin

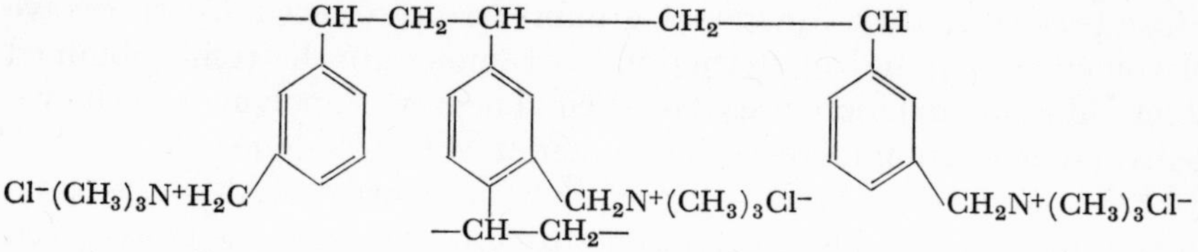

Strong Base Anion Exchange Resin

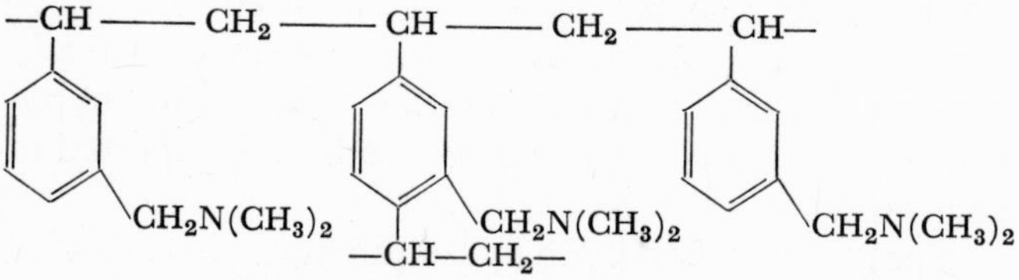

Weak Base Anion Exchange Resin

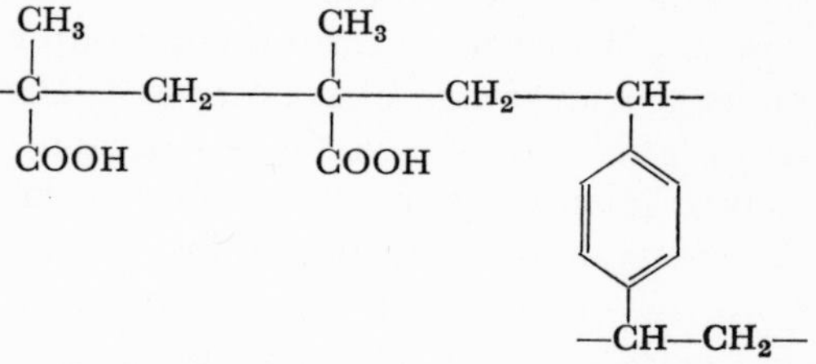

Carboxylic Acid Cation Exchange Resin

FIG. 12-11.   Typical ion exchange resins

include the transformation, fractionation, concentration, or removal of ionic substances from solutions, and the catalysis of chemical reactions.

The softening of water is still one of the major uses of ion exchange. In this application, the hardness-producing ions in water are removed and replaced by sodium ions by passage through a column of a cation exchanger, which is periodically regenerated with brine.  The organic ion exchange resins are rapidly replacing the older inorganic synthetic alumino-silicate gels and the naturally occurring silicate, glauconite (greensand).

The removal of all electrolytes from water is an extremely interesting and important ion exchange application. In one method, the electrolyte solution is passed through a cation exchanger in the hydrogen form in order to remove the cations, replacing them with hydrogen ions; the acid solution is then passed through an anion exchange resin in the hydroxyl form. In another method (reverse deionization), the electrolytes are converted into their hydroxides by passage through the hydroxyl form of a strong anion exchange resin; the basic solution is then passed through the hydrogen form of a cation exchange resin.

In demineralization applications, a weak base exchanger is used to process the effluent from a strong cation resin bed, since the weak anion resins will not split salts. The latter have high capacities, however, and can be regenerated with medium strength alkalies. Strong base exchangers, on the other hand, will remove acids as weak as silicic and can be used for salt-splitting but require caustic regeneration.

The most recent method of complete deionization involves the passage of an electrolyte solution through a mixture of the hydroxyl and hydrogen forms of an anion- and a cation-exchange resin (mixed-bed technique). In order to regenerate this system, hydraulic separation of the two resins is accomplished by backwashing the resin bed with water, enabling the two resin components to separate according to their respective densities. The anion exchange resin (the lighter component) forms a layer above the cation exchange resin.

The use of a single mixture for removing the electrolytes from a solution has been of value in special situations. Because of the high electrolyte content of sea water, the use of the mixed bed or other conventional techniques is not feasible. During World War II, a special mixture was devised for the emergency preparation of a potable water from sea water. Silver zeolite, together with a small quantity of barium hydroxide, was compressed to form a briquette which rendered ten times its volume of sea water potable. The exchange reactions were:

$$AgZ + NaCl \rightarrow NaZ + AgCl$$
$$Ba(OH)_2 + MgSO_4 \rightarrow Mg(OH)_2 + BaSO_4$$

The contaminants were filtered off as insoluble salts.

Due largely to the availability of new exchange materials, ion exchange now performs service in many diverse fields. In industrial water treatment alone, ion exchange is used for demineralization, alkalinity reduction, and silica removal. Removal and recovery of metals, acids and bases, separation of ions, and de-ashing of organics are other processes in which ion exchange plays an important role.

Additional applications include pharmaceutical uses, such as the separation and purification of amino acids, alkaloids, complex alcohols, enzymes, vitamins, and hormones; food processing uses, particularly in beverage manufacture, for the removal of hardness in waters and for the recovery of organic acids from food waste; and miscellaneous uses, such as the preparation of pure sols of various acids and hydrous oxides and the refining of uranium from its ores. An interesting use of ion exchange beds is to recover the sugar from waste mill juices pressed from pineapple trimmings and shells. More than 5,000 tons of sugar can be recovered yearly from these juices. They are treated with lime to precipitate and recover the citric acid present. The juice is then sent on to ion exchange cells for purification, after which it is concentrated in evaporators into syrup.

Another recent application of ion exchange materials is as catalysts for many homogeneous and heterogeneous reactions. Advantages in the use of ion exchange resins in place of the conventional soluble acids and bases are that the resulting products are not contaminated by the catalyst, the catalyst can be used repeatedly, and it may frequently cause fewer side reactions.

Ion exchange can also be utilized to remove impurities from nonaqueous systems, such as liquid ammonia, acetone, or benzene. The rates of exchange are generally slower than in aqueous media; exchange occurs to a greater extent, or more rapidly, in polar solvents than in nonpolar solvents.

Three general techniques are employed to bring about contact between exchange materials and solutions: batch, fixed bed, and continuous. Because of its simplicity and effectiveness, the fixed bed technique has been most widely used. The most recent of the methods, continuous ion exchange, using conventional resins, is now in limited operation and is preferred where high throughputs are desired.

Commercial applications of batch exchange include the production of pectin from grapefruit peel, calcium removal from milk, and catalysis. Some applications of fixed bed exchange are water conditioning of all kinds (including complete deionization), metals recovery, purification of organic compounds, and the removal of minerals from nonionized organic materials (ion exclusion). Because continuous ion exchange is so recent and the cost and complexity of the equipment are greater than those of the earlier processes, commercial uses are few. Potential applications include water softening and demineralization; metals recovery, de-ashing of glycerol, sugar syrups, and other organics; and all other applications where large-scale ion removal is necessary.

One very recent development must be mentioned: electromembrane ion exchange. In many areas of the world, such a shortage of potable water exists that various means for recovering such water from brackish and sea waters are being studied. Use of distillation methods, ion exchange resins, and electrodialysis have received the most attention. The recent development of synthetic ion exchange membranes has greatly stimulated interest in the deionization of saline and brackish waters by the latter method.   The principal defect of earlier membranes was their lack of permselectivity—i.e., their failure to possess, over a wide concentration range of the surrounding solution, properties which would cause the transport numbers of the ions within them to differ from those of the same ions in the free solutions surrounding the membrane and in equilibrium with it.   The newer synthetic membranes possess such properties, due principally to the high concentration of fixed-charge groups in the membranes.

In use, exchange membranes divide an electrolytic cell into two, three, or more compartments and act as barriers to control ionic movement. If the anode compartment of a cell is separated from a cathode compartment by a cation-permeable membrane, cations in the anode compartment can move freely through the membrane into the cathode compartment without allowing many anions to pass in the opposite direction.   Conversely, use of an anion-permeable membrane permits transfer of anions between compartments while allowing passage of only a few cations.   Only two electrodes are required and any number of alternate chambers can be connected in either a series-flow connection or a parallel-flow arrangement.   Possible applications, some of which have been experimentally tried, include the treatment of brackish or saline waters, desalting of aqueous organic solutions, recovery of sulfuric acid and iron from spent pickle liquors, production of salt-free caustic and chlorine by electrolysis, and recovery of chlorine or hydrochloric acid from spent hydrochloric acid pickle liquor.   So far, the initial large capital investment and certain operational difficulties have delayed rapid progress in the utilization of this promising process.

### Adhesives, Coatings, and Films

These three general applications of polymers and resinous substances are grouped together because they are all used in the form of relatively thin layers.  Surface coatings are thin layers that must adhere to one surface, whereas adhesives must join two; films are thin, unsupported layers of a substance.  Greater attention will be devoted to adhesives, since the theory and applications have not been covered in previous chapters.

**Adhesives**

A common and nontechnical definition of an adhesive is that it is a substance capable of holding materials together by surface attachment.

More specifically, adhesion, as defined by Boyd and Harkins,[5] is the process occurring when: (1) A solid and a liquid are brought together to form an interface, (2) the surface energies of the two substances are transformed into the energy of the interface, and (3) heat is evolved. Stated in another way, *adhesion* may be defined as the attraction existing among molecules of unlike substances at their interface. Similarly, *cohesion* is the attraction existing among like molecules. Since molecular forces are responsible for adhesion and cohesion, it is clear that the intrinsic strength of an adhesive bond is no stronger than the sum of the molecular forces present.

Adhesion has been attributed to both specific adhesion and mechanical adhesion. *Specific adhesion* is defined[6] as "adhesion between surfaces which are held together by valence forces of the same types as those which give rise to cohesion." *Mechanical adhesion* is defined[6] as "adhesion between surfaces in which the adhesive holds the parts together by interlocking action." Most experimental evidence indicates that the phenomenon of adhesion is specific. Contrary to popular belief, purely mechanical adhesion seldom, if ever, occurs.

The types of chemical forces involved in adhesion and cohesion are the same ones responsible for the usual intra- and intermolecular forces; namely, electrostatic, covalent, and metallic (primary bonds), and residual bonding forces (van der Waals or secondary bonds).

The adhesion of most adhesives, either in solution or as solid films, to other nonmetallic surfaces appears to be due, in large measure, to secondary valence forces. These forces have been discussed in Chapter 10. In the case of thermosetting polymers, primary valence forces may also be involved. Ion-ion and ion-dipole forces are reported to be important for the adhesion of animal glue and urea-formaldehyde resins to solid surfaces.

"Adhesive" and "cement" are general terms and include both the synthetic resin adhesives and the vegetable and animal adhesives, such as glues, gums, mucilages, and pastes. These latter terms are often used loosely and interchangeably, but they do have rather specific meanings. As pointed out in Chapter 8, glues are animal products; gums, mucilages, and pastes are vegetable products. Gums are colloidal substances containing complex organic acids or their salts and are usually soluble in water; mucilages are (1) aqueous solutions of gums, and (2) mixtures of gelatinous substances found in certain plants (e.g., seaweeds) containing complex carbohydrates; pastes are usually preparations of such substances as starch and flour with water.

An adhesive must be physically in such a state that its molecules can

[5] Boyd, G. E. and Harkins, W. D., *J. Am. Chem. Soc.*, **64**, 1190, 1195 (1942).
[6] ASTM, D907–49T.

come into sufficiently close contact with the surface of the adherend that molecular forces can become operative. Thus, adhesives are generally in a liquid or semiliquid state at some stage of the bonding operation. An adhesive can be synthesized in contact with the adherend, as in the case of monomers which polymerize or otherwise react to form a solid adhesive *in situ*; a solid material can be applied in solution in a volatile solvent; a solid adhesive can be liquefied by heating; or a solid material can be liquefied by applied pressure, becoming solid again when the pressure is removed. In order to convert the adhesive into a hardened state, chemical or physical changes are necessary; these include polymerization, oxidation, vulcanization, gelation, hydration, evaporation of volatile constituents, reduction of pressure, or cooling below the softening range. These techniques are summarized in Table 12-1.

TABLE 12-1.   CLASSIFICATION OF ADHESIVES ACCORDING TO METHOD OF OBTAINING FLOW AND SOLIDIFICATION[7]

| Class of Adhesive | Means of Obtaining Flow | Cause of Solidification |
|---|---|---|
| Solvent sensitive | Dissolve in solvents | Evaporation of solvents |
| Pressure sensitive | Increase pressure | Release of pressure |
| Temperature sensitive | Increase temperature | Decrease of temperature |
| Reaction sensitive | Use of low-molecular-weight reactants | Chemical reaction, including polymerization |

Adhesives are almost always mixtures of natural or synthetic polymers or of polymers admixed with low-molecular-weight liquids. This is partly so because polymers or their solutions and dispersions have highly desirable rheological properties for attaining ease of application and intimate and long lasting contact with the adherend.

In order for a substance to adhere to a surface it must first adapt itself to the surface; i.e., wet the surface. This step involves an orientation of dipole, polar, and/or hydrogen-bonding groups at the interface. The second step may be regarded as an equilibrium-adsorption phenomenon; i.e., adhesion and adsorption are manifestations of the same phenomena and may be regarded as equivalent.

The strong unbalanced forces existing at free surfaces account for the high adsorptive capacity of clean surfaces. When surface contaminants are removed by mechanical action or by heating in a vacuum, these forces become very effective in bonding solids together. Such cleaning occurs naturally by mechanical action (for example, in automotive brakes) but is otherwise achieved only with difficulty. However, when surface cleanliness is obtained, the interfacial bonds formed by the

[7] Clark, Rutzler, J. E., Jr., and Savage, R. L., eds., *Adhesion and Adhesives Fundamentals and Practice*, Table I, p. 11, Society of Chemical Industry, London (John Wiley and Sons, New York), 1954.

application of small pressures have strengths comparable to that of the cohesive strength of the parent substance.

Since a clean surface is necessary to obtain adhesive bonds of maximum strength, adhesion must be largely specific. Unfortunately, certain types of foreign materials, such as adsorbed liquids and gases, are very difficult to detect and to remove. The presence of such materials on the surface of an adherend determines, to a great extent, whether or not a particular adhesive will bond to a particular adherend.

Since the total adhesive force is proportional to the area of the interface, several methods are employed to increase the area of solid surface available for participating in the bonding operation. Physical means include sandblasting and sandpapering, and chemical means, acid etching and solvent attack. A smooth surface produces a stronger joint than a roughened one of the same area, since the depressions in the rough surface, in addition to the gap between the two surfaces, must be filled. Furthermore, if the surface is very rough, air bubbles may be trapped in the bond line. Such areas of interfacial discontinuity will cause local high concentrations of stress and may cause premature failure of the entire bond upon the application of an external force. Thus, fine sanding of wood surfaces immediately prior to bonding yields a much better bond than that obtained when the surfaces are planed or roughly sanded, since the fine sanding operation both cleans the surface and increases its surface area without roughening it unduly.

In addition to the classification given in Table 12-1, adhesives may be classified according to composition. Such a classification is difficult to make because of the complexity of modern adhesive formulations. Very frequently, adhesive formulations contain several components from more than one of the above groups. Excluding mixtures, however, a classification of adhesives based on composition is given in Table 12-2.

Vegetable and animal adhesives have been used since the beginning of history. They are capable of forming a good bond under dry conditions but usually fail if the joints become damp. Included among the vegetable adhesives are flour pastes, starch and dextrin adhesives, and gums.

The starch-based adhesives are the most important of all paper adhesives and are used in this field in greater quantity than all the rest. Starch may be varied chemically in many ways (see Starch, Chap. 6), so that adhesives from starch can be made to accommodate a wide variety of paper packaging operations. The starches most commonly used are obtained from potato, corn, and tapioca. Rice and wheat starches are also used to a limited extent. Potato starch yields a dextrin with good adhesive qualities but of undesirable taste and odor. Tapioca starch, which does not have these disadvantages, is often used for the preparation

TABLE 12-2.   CLASSIFICATION OF ADHESIVES BASED ON COMPOSITION[8]

Naturally occurring materials
    Starch and dextrins (from vegetable sources)
    Proteins (from both vegetable and animal sources)
        Animal (bones, hides, sinews)
        Blood (whole blood or albumin)
        Casein (from milk)
        Alpha protein (from soya beans)
    Other materials
        Asphalt
        Shellac
        Natural rubber (including reclaimed rubber)
        Sodium silicate (inorganic)
Synthetic materials
    Thermoplastic resins (cellulose esters and ethers, acrylic esters, polyamides, polystyrene, synthetic elastomers, poly(vinyl alcohol) and derivatives)
    Thermosetting resins (urea, melamine, phenol, resorcinol, furan, epoxy, and unsaturated polyester resins)

of adhesives for envelopes, postage stamps, and similar materials. Dextrins from corn starch are very satisfactory and probably account for the greatest tonnage of dextrin adhesives.

Adhesives from natural gums include gum tragacanth and particularly gum arabic. Also used are rosin-based adhesives, consisting of rosin melted with plasticizers, and rubber-based adhesives, which form the base of many of the permanently tacky adhesives used on surgical tapes, flypapers, and pressure-sensitive tapes. Rubber is also widely used in latex form as a paper adhesive. When compounded with casein, it is used in the manufacture of stationery pads; when uncompounded and purified, it is the usual adhesive on self-sealing envelopes.

Animal glues are made from the bones and skins of animals. Glycerol is often added to glue to plasticize it so as to form adhesives which must form flexible films upon drying; the binding of books requires such a product. The largest single use of glue in the paper trade is in the production of gummed sealing tape. Its value here is due to its ability to absorb sufficient water to liquefy long enough to present a wet adhesive surface while the tape is being applied, then quickly to absorb the water until the liquid gels and a firm bond is created. Hide glues are widely used in the manufacture of printers' rollers and padding glues. The strength of their bonds also makes them useful for wood joining, for the manufacture of abrasives and abrasive wheels, and for textile and paper sizing. Hide glues also find wide application, either alone or compounded, as a general adhesive. Bone glues are used where the greater strength of hide glues is not required; for example, in adhesives for laminations, in sizes for the coating of paper and textiles, and in gummed labels and tapes for remoistening purposes. Note that glues

[8] Clark, Rutzler, J. E., Jr., and Savage, R. L., eds., *Adhesion and Adhesives Fundamentals and Practice*, p. 74, Society of Chemical Industry, London (John Wiley and Sons, New York), 1954.

form good bonds only with certain materials, particularly with cellulosics, such as wood and paper.

The introduction of other protein (casein, soya bean, and blood) adhesives has resulted in a marked improvement over animal glues with respect to water resistance. However, they are also subject to fungus attack and are not completely water-resistant.

With the advent of synthetic resin adhesives, great improvements have been attained. It has become possible to bond materials so tenaciously that in many cases the bond is the strongest part of the structure. However, no single substance embodies all of the desirable properties of a universal adhesive, particularly since the requirements may vary over a wide range of properties. The property that makes the newer adhesives important is their versatility. In addition to the fact that most of the many synthetic resins exhibit adhesive properties in varying degrees, these properties can be widely altered by varying their method of synthesis, formulation, and application.

Both thermoplastic and thermosetting synthetic resins are used as adhesives. The commonly used synthetic resins are the phenolic, urea, melamine, resorcinol, furan, and unsaturated polyester resins, emulsion polymers, synthetic proteins, and mixtures of elastomers and resins. The lacquer types include all adhesives which consist of resins dissolved in organic solvents. The most familiar are those containing cellulose nitrate mixed with a variety of other resins, plasticizers, and solvents. The hot-melt adhesives consist of mixtures of thermoplastic resins, plasticizers, and often fillers. The so-called emulsion types include acrylic and poly(vinyl acetate) as well as the synthetic elastomer suspensions. The thermosetting types include the phenolic, urea, melamine, resorcinol, furan, and unsaturated polyester resins. Thermoplastic resins, of course, cannot be used at high service temperatures. Thermosetting resins are more versatile in this respect and also produce the more impervious adhesives. Joints bonded with the latter type can be completely waterproofed, resist high temperatures, and are unattacked by fungi. The use of plywood construction in boats and airplanes demonstrates the strength and durability of this type of adhesive.

As a matter of fact, the bonding of wood is the largest use for adhesives, and their greatest single application is in the manufacture of plywood. The types of adhesives used for the bonding of wood are many and include the natural resin as well as numerous synthetic resin types. For general woodworking and furniture construction, the protein (animal glues, casein and albumin) adhesives have been used for many years. These are generally quite satisfactory except, as pointed out earlier, under conditions of very high or low humidities, where the more durable synthetics are now preferred. Soya bean protein finds its greatest use in the manufacture of Douglas fir plywood, although for outdoor weather exposure (exterior grades), the phenol- or urea-formaldehyde adhesives are preferred. The phenolic resin adhesives are also widely used in the fabrication of solid woods, laminated wood, and fiber and paper laminates.

Cellulose nitrate cements are sold in collapsible tubes for household repairs which require the joining of broken ceramic surfaces, wood, paper, leather, cloth, and metal. Although an excellent bonding agent for wood, this type of adhesive is seldom used for plywood or furniture manufacture, principally because of its relatively high cost. Cellulose acetate cements have an even more limited use than the nitrate cements but can also be used for wood, paper, and leather.

The urea resin adhesives have largely displaced glues and casein adhesives, not only because their quality is better but also because they require less water in their formulation. Further, urea resins are colorless, while the natural protein adhesives often produce undesirable dark stains. Like the phenolics, urea resin adhesives are widely used for making assemblies of wood and of plywood, although their use in bonding fabric and paper to each other and to wood is growing.

Melamine-formaldehyde resins are also employed as adhesives for wood. Their superior water resistance and hardening capacity results in joints which are resistant to boiling water. Although straight melamine adhesives have outstanding outdoor durability, they are usually too expensive for all but special applications.

The resorcinol-formaldehyde adhesives, when properly cured at room temperature, are as durable as are the hot-pressed phenolic resins. The outstanding characteristic of the resorcinol resins is their neutral character, which avoids damage to cellulosic fibers. Since resorcinol is a relatively costly raw material, mixed phenol-resorcinol adhesives have been developed in which the major properties of the resorcinol adhesives have been retained.

As with the resorcinol adhesives, furan resins are practically neutral and, uncatalyzed, have good storage and pot life. Similarly, they are dark in color. They form bonds of high strength without the extreme brittleness of the resorcinol resins and thus are preferable in applications where thick bond lines are unavoidable. Their cost is slightly lower than that of the phenol-resorcinol adhesives.

The unsaturated polyester resins, used principally in low-pressure fabrication, are liquids or pastes containing little or no solvent, and upon curing yield infusible, insoluble solids having great strength. They can be cured under a wide range of pressures and even at no pressure at all (contact adhesive). Their cost is comparable to that of the resorcinol and polyamide resins. They do not form a good bond to hydrophilic surfaces, such as wood, paper, or cotton fabrics, without the use of special techniques, and only recently have they been successfully cured at room temperature. Thus far, their use as assembly adhesives has been concentrated in certain special fields, particularly the bonding of cured, unsaturated polyester resin laminates to each other and to metals.

The epoxy resins are a very recent development. Although thermoplastic when unmodified, they can be cross-linked by polyamines, anhydrides, and other di- or polyfunctional agents. They exhibit outstanding adhesion to a wide variety of substances, including glass and ceramics, and are characterized by low shrinkage and high mechanical strength.

Industry has developed to high degree the technique of producing emulsions and dispersions of resins in liquids containing little or no organic solvent. Many resins, known to be excellent adhesives but of previously limited use because of their low solubility in expensive and generally flammable organic solvents, have been successfully used in the form of emulsions or dispersions. This type of formulation eliminates the need for undesirable solvents and permits the application of mixtures of high solids content, comparable to those of the older water-soluble adhesives. Simple dispersions of some resins can be used, but better results are usually obtained by emulsifying together a latex and a tacky base, the latter of which increases the viscosity and adhesiveness of the mixture. These products are used for laminating aluminum foil to paper, for the labeling of aluminum containers, for sticking wood to metal, and for adhesion to many difficult surfaces in the manufacture of such items as cosmetics, electrical components, and lamp shades. They are neutral or slightly alkaline, have practically no odor, have good keeping qualities if not frozen, and are flexible and almost colorless. They generally are set by evaporation of the water.

Since natural proteins have long been employed as adhesives, the modified natural (Versamid-type) and synthetic (nylon-type) polyamides have been examined for their adhesive properties. The former type has been particularly successful, but these resins, particularly the latter type, have not yet been widely adopted because of their lack of advantage over the better known and less expensive phenol- and urea-formaldehyde resins.

In the bonding of metals, special problems arise. A metal consists of a crystalline arrangement of metallic cations having free electrons moving in the interstices in a continuous set of energy levels. Such a metallic structure is relatively homogeneous and nonpolar; however, because of the mobility of the free electrons, a metal has forces induced at its surfaces which are equal and opposite to the polar forces of an adhesive in contact with it. An adhesive, therefore, will have as great an affinity for a metal as it will have for any other substance which has a permanent but opposite polarity of the same magnitude as its own.

As a result, adhesion to metals appears to depend upon the formation of a two-dimensional metal compound at the interface. For bonds of high strength, these primary valence bonds are desirable. Thus, good adhesives for metals contain groups which readily form metallic compounds. Supplementary strength can, of course, be obtained from secondary valence forces.

Because of the dissimilarity between metallic and other types of bonds, the development of good organic adhesives for metals is relatively recent. The first success was the bonding of elastomers to metals; now satisfactory adhesives are available for bonding metals to one another. Examples of metal adhesives include poly(vinyl esters and acetals), polyesters, neoprene, chlorinated rubber, acrylonitrile elastomers, vulcanized rubber, Thiokol, and particularly the newer epoxy compounds.

Because of the difference in the coefficients of expansion between metals and organic compounds, metal adhesives must also be somewhat elastic. Thus, phenolic resins alone make unsatisfactory metal adhesives, even though they contain hydroxyl groups which have good metal-combining properties; however, by combining elastomeric compounds (e.g., nitrile rubber) with phenolic resins, excellent metal adhesives are obtained.

In bonding a metal to a nonmetal, it is not always possible to satisfy the bonding requirements of both adherends with one adhesive, sometimes because the nonmetallic substance cannot withstand high temperature curing, which may be necessary for the development of good adhesion to the metal. In order to compensate for the inequalities between different metals and variations within one metal, primers are often applied to provide an anchor coat. In many cases, the primer serves as a substitute for more expensive operations, such as sand blasting, wire brushing, or other metal treatment. A primer may also be used principally to prevent under-film corrosion, thus prolonging adhesion rather than improving initial adhesion. The primer coat is usually baked and thus gives excellent primary-valence adhesion to the metal.

A large field of use for adhesives is in the safety-glass industry. A résumé of the development of adhesives for this use may be of interest. Cellulose nitrate was cemented between pieces of glass with Canada balsam as early as 1906. In 1911, an adhesive for bonding glass was composed of gelatin moistened with alcohol. However, cellulose nitrate was used for twenty years as the principal impact-resisting interlayer for safety glass despite its yellowing characteristics, temperature sensitivity, and tendency to separate from the glass. About 1930, other cellulosic derivatives, particularly the acetates, were under examination. In 1935, the coating of glass and the interlayer sheet with an organic ester of silicic acid to promote adhesion was claimed. Shortly thereafter, flexible poly(acrylic esters) were tried as safety-glass interlayers. About 1936, poly(vinyl butyral), which was specifically made for use as safety-glass interlayer, came into use. It rapidly supplanted the previous adhesives because of its high clarity, low temperature sensitivity, high impact strength, good weatherability, and good bonding to glass without requiring the use of intermediate adhesives.

In connection with the subject of glass, it is of interest to point out that the weakness of a freshly formed glass surface is caused by its sensitivity to contact with other glass surfaces. These uncontaminated surfaces combine chemically (adhere) on contact and their separation produces a scratch. This process can be prevented by artificially contaminating the active glass surfaces. A coating of starch, oil, or, more recently, silicone emulsions (see p. 345) prevents the seizure and scratching and greatly reduces subsequent breakage.

Another most interesting application of adhesives is in the formation of pressure-sensitive adhesives. Pressure-sensitive adhesion may be defined[9] as the adhesion of a deformable solid to a surface, effected by the application of moderate pressure. It differs from conventional adhesion in that no increase in the original cohesive strength is necessary. The adhesive must require no heat, solvent, water, or any other preparation before application to the surface to which it will adhere. Two conditions must always be met: the adhesive must have a permanent tackiness which produces a satisfactory bond between dissimilar surfaces, and it must be sufficiently cohesive that it can be unwound from a roll or removed from a suitable surface without splitting the adhesive layer or leaving a residue on the adherend.

The development of pressure-sensitive adhesive tapes is generally considered to have begun about 1925. Prior to that time, surgical tapes and electricians' (friction) tapes were available. The pressure-sensitive adhesives were developed to fill a need in the automotive industry for a masking tape which would allow the temporary protection of surfaces which were coated with more than one color of paint. Since that time, the growth of this type of adhesive has been phenomenal. These tapes are now universally used for masking, holding, reinforcing, sealing, protecting, splicing, and identifying applications.

Most of the pressure-sensitive adhesives contain an elastomer and a plasticizer, the latter usually consisting of a hard resin and an oil; the resin and oil together give tack and the elastomer and the resin produce adhesive strength. In some cases, a pressure-sensitive adhesive may contain only a high-molecular-weight elastomer plasticized with a low-molecular-weight fraction of the same material; e.g., polyisobutylene.

[9] Clark, Rutzler, J. E., Jr., and Savage, R. L., eds., *Adhesion and Adhesives Fundamentals and Practice*, p. 127, Society of Chemical Industry, London (John Wiley and Sons, New York), 1954.

The adhesive is applied to sheeting, such as cloth, paper, or cellophane, and is then cut into tape and rolled.

Even from this brief review of the applications of adhesives, it will be clear that their use and importance are increasing steadily. The techniques of fabricating almost all materials have been profoundly influenced by the growing versatility of adhesives. Their use in the low-pressure fabrication of aircraft structures is merely one example of this relatively recent method of fabrication, and the gradual replacement of mechanically riveted, bolted, screwed, and nailed joints with chemically bonded joints indicates the value of adhesive bonding as a method of fabrication. Some advantages of cemented parts in aircraft construction are that rivets and rivet holes with their resulting stress concentrations are eliminated; the strength-weight ratio is often increased; sandwich construction, which is lightweight and strong, is made possible; smoother surfaces are obtained; metal-to-metal, completely sealed joints are possible; and the adhesive may also act as an electrical insulator, allowing the joining of dissimilar metals without the occurrence of the frequently encountered corrosive contact-potential effect.

It may thus be seen that adhesive bonding is so varied in its applications that it cannot be discussed here in complete detail. The radical expansion of the types of assembly adhesives available has in large measure been brought about by the desire to bond materials of construction other than wood, plywood, and paper, and, as a result, the new adhesives have vastly broadened the art of assembly bonding. Even though new applications of adhesive bonding are constantly being developed, it has been for some time the most generally used method of joining materials.

## Coatings

Organic, polymeric coatings are applied to various substrates, principally wood, metal, and paper, for decorative effects or for some functional purpose, such as to provide corrosion resistance, protect printing, provide a barrier to moisture, provide abrasion resistance, change the appearance, or identify the object. Such coating may be either clear or opaque.

As pointed out in the previous chapter, nearly all of the many different polymers and resins may be put into solution and then applied to surfaces by spraying, dipping, brushing, roller coating, and printing. The commonly used film-forming materials are the acrylics, alkyds, chlorinated rubber, coumarone-indene, phenolic, maleic, polyterpene, and urea resins. Also used are natural rubber, GR-S, neoprene, furan, vinyls, saran, polyethylene, greases and waxes, and bitumens. Some of the newer coatings are made from silicones, allyl compounds, epoxy resins, polyurethanes, and styrene copolymers. In addition, isomerized and chemically processed oils, including tall oil and its derivatives, are used in large amounts.

Some of the typical applications are as house paints; furniture finishes; architectural finishes; automobile and truck primers and finishes; refrigerator, stove and washing machine finishes; marine finishes; leather finishes; cable lacquer coatings; masonry coatings; and textile and rubber cloth coatings.

Coatings are applied to wood and metal to decorate the surfaces, change the colors, make a more pleasing appearance, provide a smoother surface, and particularly to protect the surfaces from the action of light, air, moisture, and other chemical agents. Wooden furniture finishes, once almost completely oleoresinous, are now usually made of cellulose nitrate lacquers, chiefly because of the latter's fast drying property. This has been occasioned by the trend to rapid assembly line manufacture and finishing methods. Some "synthetic" varnishes are used for furniture finishes because of their greater resistance to solvents and other chemicals.

In the field of exterior house paints, the old oil and pigment combinations are still in wide use. The use of alkyd and styrene-butadiene resins as a partial or total replacement for the oils is recent. The most significant improvements in such paints have been in the pigments used and in the replacement of older turpentine-type thinners with better or less expensive petroleum solvents.

Indoors, considerable changes have taken place in enamels and wall paints. Most enamels now contain the less yellowing alkyd resins instead of the oleoresinous vehicles formerly employed. Wall paints have split into two general classes: the organic solvent type and the aqueous dispersion type. Whereas alkyd resins are usually contained in the former class of coatings, the latter is generally composed of styrene-butadiene, poly(vinyl acetate), or acrylic latices. In the automotive field, both cellulose nitrate lacquer enamels and the "synthetic" enamels are used. The latter are composed chiefly of alkyd resins in combination with an aminoplast. Quite recently, certain polyfunctional acrylic monomers have been developed for use in acrylic coatings for automobiles. Another large but specialized field of metal decorating is that of cans and closures of all types. Alkyds, phenolics, and the vinyl resins are most frequently used.

Coatings are applied to paper for decorative and functional purposes— to increase the gloss and smoothness, to increase the moisture-vapor-transmission resistance and to protect the surface from abrasion, heat, and chemical action. Cellulose nitrate and vinyl lacquers and oleoresinous varnishes are commonly used. Printing inks are special types of opaque and variously colored coatings, widely used on paper, as well as on metal and cloth. They are used not only to impart visual information but also for decorative (design) purposes.

Certain resins have been used with varying degrees of success in coatings to improve the wearing qualities of leather; included are the phenolic, urea, alkyd, cellulose nitrate, acrylic, vinyl, and silicone resins.

Organic coatings are applied to fibers and cloth to reduce their permeability, to improve their resistance to water, to increase their stiffness or

FIG. 12-12. Vinyl-based protective coating used on off-shore oil-drilling rigs in the Gulf of Mexico. Six coats have been applied, which are expected to protect the metal for up to 30 or 40 years. (*Courtesy Bakelite Co.*)

help them retain their shape, and to aid in weaving operations. A recent development in the textile finishing field has been the application of thermosetting resins to impart crease or wrinkle resistance to cellulosic fibers, particularly rayon. Commonly used products for this purpose are the urea- and melamine-formaldehyde resins. The fabric is treated with

water-soluble precondensates and a catalyst. The treated fabric is dried
and heated at an elevated temperature to polymerize further the resin
within the fiber structure. These resins impart wrinkle resistance,
improved fabric draping qualities, and increased weight, together with a
desirable degree of fabric firmness. Such finishes maintain good dimensional stability in certain fabrics through repeated laundering and dry
cleaning.

Another recent advance in durable finishes for improvement of fabric
appearance is the application of similar thermosetting resins to obtain
embossed effects on cotton and rayon. The resins are applied as precondensates and the embossing is carried out before the curing operation.
The embossing resists laundering and dry-cleaning operations.

### Films

The use of plastics in the form of films and sheeting for functional and
decorative uses has become one of the largest outlets for polymers. The
common plastics for this use include poly(vinyl chloride) and its copolymers, vinylidene chloride–vinyl chloride copolymers (saran), regenerated
cellulose (cellophane), the cellulosic derivatives (cellulose acetate,
acetate-butyrate, nitrate, and ethyl cellulose), poly(vinyl alcohol), the
fluorinated ethylene compounds, polystyrene, nylon, poly(ethylene terephthalate) (Mylar and Melinex), polyethylene, and rubber hydrochloride
(Pliofilm).

Probably the largest use of unsupported film is in packaging applica-

Fig. 12-13.    Polyethylene film used as a strawberry mulch reduces mold rot on straw-
berries. (*Courtesy Bakelite Co.*)

tions, not only for food and household commodities but also for industrial chemicals, both solid and liquid. In the former field, saran, cellophane, the cellulosic derivatives, polyethylene, and Pliofilm are competitive, not only among themselves but also with their precursor, paper. The greater resistance to tearing, greater transparency, and better moisture-vapor-transmission resistance of the modified natural and synthetic films have, in a great many instances, compensated for their inherently greater cost.

The property of good resistance to the transmission of water vapor (in

Fig. 12-14. Polyethylene film placed between floor beams and subflooring serves as a moisture barrier in home construction. (*Courtesy Bakelite Co.*)

addition to that of other gases) is of great importance in the packaging of hygroscopic materials as well as of those which must remain moist. Relatively few polymers have this property; of more than 100 materials evaluated, only the following have been found to have a low moisture permeability: vinylidene chloride copolymers with vinyl chloride, acrylonitrile, and isobutylene; polyethylene, fluorinated ethylene polymers, polyisobutylene, butyl rubber, and rubber hydrochloride. It appears that structural requirements for low permeability include: (1) A saturated or nearly saturated carbon chain, (2) little or no chain branching, (3) high lateral and fair longitudinal symmetry, and (4) a high proportion of small, hydrophobic substituents. The above polymers fulfill these requirements to a fair degree.

The use of unsupported films for packaging in industrial applications is much more recent. The growing importance of quality standards in the sale of chemical products has resulted in increased emphasis on the prevention of contamination in storage and shipping containers. This has caused a trend toward the wider use of loose plastic linings, plastic packaging, and plastic coatings. The most widely used plastic in this field is polyethylene.

Poly(ethylene terephthalate) film, a newcomer to the field, has a combination of physical, electrical, and chemical properties which makes it particularly suitable for many electrical and other industrial uses. Among its outstanding characteristics are its high mechanical, dielectric,

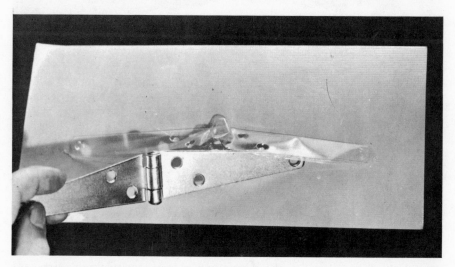

FIG. 12-15. "Cast" vinyl film used for skin-packaging. This technique is used for displaying a solid product against an adhesive-coated backing by covering it with a preheated plastic film which settles tightly around the contours of the product when air is evacuated from beneath it. (*Courtesy Bakelite Co.*)

and impact strengths over a wide range of temperatures and humidities. Its moisture absorption is very low—about 0.3 per cent. Its high dielectric constant, high dielectric strength, and low power factor make the film valuable as a condenser dielectric and for cable and wire insulation. Poly(ethylene terephthalate) film resists attack by many chemicals, oils, and solvents. It also shows good resistance to most of the common electrical varnishes and impregnants. While the electrical field will be one of the largest single markets for the new film, such applications as

FIG. 12-16.   Bag and drum liners of polyethylene film.   (*Courtesy Catalin Corp. of America*)

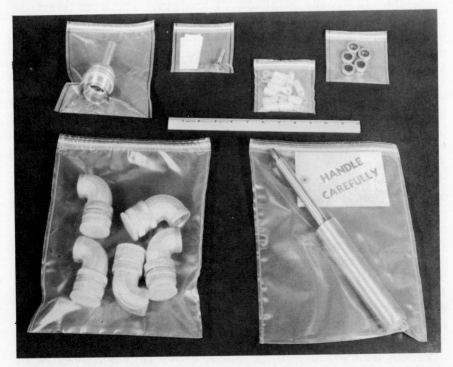

FIG. 12-17.   Industrial parts are protected against moisture, air, and dirt in these reusable polyethylene bags fitted with a self-locking closure.   (*Courtesy Bakelite Co.*)

magnetic sound-recording tapes, electrical tapes, pressure-sensitive tapes, printed covering for acoustical tile, metallic yarn for drapes and clothing, lightweight storm windows, agricultural glazing, and many others are growing rapidly.

In addition to poly(ethylene terephthalate), plasticized poly(vinyl chloride), polytetrafluoroethylene, polychlorotrifluoroethylene, cellophane, and certain of the cellulosic derivatives are widely used in the form of tapes for electrical and thermal insulation and in both tape and sheet forms for the wrapping and lining of metal containers and pipe for protection against corrosion.

### ELASTOMERS

Elastomers are indispensable to our modern civilization. Without them, two of our largest industries, transportation and electrical, would never have attained their present state of development, and many other industries would never have arisen or would have been severely handicapped.

By far the greatest single field of use for elastomers is in the transportation industry for tires and tubes. In tires, GR-S and natural rubber blends account for almost all products. The more severe the requirement, the more natural rubber is used. For example, airplane tires are composed almost entirely of natural rubber, truck tires generally contain more natural rubber than GR-S, automobile tires contain more GR-S than natural rubber, and bicycle tires are made of almost all GR-S. More than half of all GR-S and natural rubber production is consumed by these four items. As has been mentioned in earlier chapters, both butyl rubber and polyurethane elastomers are now being aggressively investigated for use in tire manufacture.

In the manufacture of inner tubes for tires, except for airplane tubes and very large truck tire tubes, which are principally of natural rubber, the superior gas impermeability of Butyl has caused its almost universal adoption. An appreciable amount of natural rubber, GR-S, and neoprene is consumed in related transportation items, including tube valves, retread materials, tire and tube repair materials, and tank treads.

The remainder of the elastomer consumption is in the field of mechanical goods. Here, a very diverse line of products is made. For the manufacture of light, resilient goods, latex foams are very popular. Most of the elastomers may be foamed, but natural rubber, GR-S, neoprene, plasticized poly(vinyl chloride), and polyurethanes account for almost all production. More than half of the natural rubber latex available is converted into foam.

Various natural and synthetic latices, whose particles are electrically charged, are used in the manufacture of rubber labels, gloves, and various coated metal articles. Commonly used latices are those of natural rubber, GR-S, neoprene, and nitrile rubber. Both the older electrical deposition and the more recent "wireless" Anode processes are used to neutralize the charged particles so that they coalesce and adhere to a metal form.

Flexible hose accounts for another large share of elastomer consumption. The variety of hose made is very large, since hose is specially

FIG. 12-18. Cured tire being removed from the mold. (*Courtesy Goodyear Tire & Rubber Co.*)

made for each application. A partial list of types includes air, acid, beverage, chemical, creamery, driller's, fire, gasoline, oil, hydraulic, welding, sandblasting, paint spray, steam, suction, and water hose, as well as tubing of all kinds. In this field, GR-S, natural rubber, neoprene, Thiokol, and nitrile rubber are used in greatest amount, the latter three particularly for oil- and solvent-resistant applications.

The electrical industry requires large quantities of elastomers for wire insulation and cable covering purposes. GR-S and neoprene account for most of the material used in this industry, although butyl rubber, plasticized poly(vinyl chloride), silicone elastomers, and some nitrile rubber are used in specialty applications. Of course, at the higher frequencies and voltages, the less polar materials are preferred. More than one fourth of the neoprene made is consumed by the electrical industry.

Almost all of the elastomeric substances have been used in gaskets, packings, and seals for mechanical apparatus. GR-S accounts for perhaps half of the applications, but nitrile rubber, acrylic elastomers, polyisobutylene and filler combinations, silicone elastomers, neoprene, chlorosulfonated polyethylene, butyl rubber, Thiokol, and, of course, natural rubber are used. As in other applications, each elastomer has its particular desirable and undesirable properties, and selection of the proper product requires an intimate knowledge of the characteristics of each elastomer.

Flat and V belting for power transmission, conveyors, and elevators (inclined conveyors with buckets) are compounded principally from natural rubber, GR-S, and neoprene. Conveyors and elevators transport such items as sand, grain, ore, coal, slag, ice, and packaged goods from one point to another. Many have special surfaces to accommodate a particular operating condition; for example, smooth surfaces to resist cutting, tearing, or abrasion; oil-resistant surfaces; and textured surfaces for gripping are common.

"Rubber" footwear, such as gym shoes and wading boots, in addition to being made of natural rubber, also are composed of GR-S in lesser quantities. On the other hand, heels and soles of shoes not made of real leather are usually made of GR-S. Neoprene is used where greater abrasion and oil resistance is desired.

As was discussed in the earlier section on adhesives, elastomeric compounds are widely used in adhesive formulations where flexibility of the bond or good tack is required. Most often used are natural rubber (and its latices), GR-S, nitrile rubber (often combined with phenolic resins), neoprene, and some reclaimed natural and synthetic elastomers. Some applications are upholstery and fabric cements, nonslip rug backing, tire cord adhesives, fruit-jar lid seals, and general-purpose adhesives for bonding wood, metal, plastic, paper, fabric, glass, and ceramics. Adhesive tapes of all kinds—electrical splicing, surgical, masking, pressure sensitive, and friction—use elastomeric products.

For high-temperature applications, few elastomers are suitable. Only two, silicone and acrylic elastomers, can operate above about 200°C for any appreciable length of time without decomposing or losing their desirable properties. At the present time, the high-temperature limits of some of the commercial elastomers are given in Table 12-3.

The manufacture of flooring and floor tile is conducted on a large scale.

TABLE 12-3.   HIGH-TEMPERATURE LIMITS OF SOME COMMERCIAL
ELASTOMERS, °C[10]

| Silicones | . | . | 275 |
|-----------|---|---|-----|
| Acrylics | . | . | 200 |
| Nitrile | . | . | 175 |
| Neoprene | . | . | 160 |
| Butyl | . | . | 150 |
| GR-S | . | . | 140 |
| Natural | . | . | 130 |
| Thiokol | . | . | 120 |

The so-called "rubber" flooring and tile are almost always composed of GR-S elastomer. This material wears very well and retains its slight resilience indefinitely.

Chemical storage and reaction tanks, railway tank cars, pickling and plating tanks, pipes and valves are often lined with an inert elastomer to prevent metal corrosion or product contamination. Materials used for this purpose include natural rubber, GR-S, neoprene, butyl rubber, nitrile rubber, and plasticized poly(vinyl chloride). Natural and synthetic hard rubbers are also widely used, but these are not considered elastomers.

In the printing industry, molded plates and dies, stamps, printing type (e.g., Flexographic), daters, sign markers, lithographic and rotogravure offset blankets, and printing-press rollers are made of elastomeric compositions. Generally speaking, the oil- and solvent-resistant types are used in most applications for obvious reasons.

Elastic threads and tapes are almost always made from pure gum natural rubber. They are used in clothing for such articles as suspenders, sock tops, garters, and girdles, and also for such miscellaneous applications as goggle and mask straps and golf balls.

A very interesting development in the use of elastomers has been the production of torsion rod springs (Torsilastic) as a replacement for metal coil and leaf springs for vehicles and for industrial applications. Composed of a solid or tubular shaft, a cylindrical shell, and an elastic compound permanently bonded to both, the spring does not squeak, never needs lubrication, is unaffected by mud, dirt, and water, eliminates friction, reduces noise level, absorbs shock from all directions, and provides a rubber cushion between the suspended mass and its foundation. The successful development of this type of spring was due in large measure to the development of a suitable elastomeric adhesive that would permanently bond elastomers to metal.

In addition to the aforementioned applications, elastomeric substances are used in a variety of miscellaneous applications which include such diverse products as grommets, boots, packing rings, mountings for

[10] Fisher, H. L., *Ind. Eng. Chem.*, **46**, 2067 (1954).

vibrating machinery, laboratory stoppers, pump valves and diaphragms, toys and balloons, athletic goods, and sponge rubber products.

The list of applications for elastomers is by no means exhausted by the foregoing enumeration, but most principal uses have been mentioned. It should be clear, at any rate, that little fault can be found with the opening sentence of this section. As both new and improved elastomeric polymers are developed, there can be little doubt that the scope of their uses will grow ever wider.

## REFERENCES AND RECOMMENDED READING

Alexander, J., ed., *Colloid Chemistry Theoretical and Applied*, Vol. VI, Reinhold Publishing Corp., New York, 1946.

American Viscose Corporation, *Rayon Technology (Including Acetate)*, McGraw-Hill Book Co., New York, 1953.

Barron, H., *Modern Synthetic Rubbers*, 2nd ed., D. Van Nostrand Co., Princeton, N.J., 1943.

Bjorksten, J., Tovey, H., Harker, B., and Henning, J., *Polyesters and Their Applications*, Reinhold Publishing Corp., New York, 1956.

Burk, R. E. and Grummitt, O., eds., *Frontiers in Colloid Chemistry*, Interscience Publishers, New York, 1950.

Burton, W. E., ed., *Engineering with Rubber*, McGraw-Hill Book Co., New York, 1949.

Clark, Rutzler, J. E., Jr. and Savage, R. L., *Adhesion and Adhesives*, Society of Chemical Industry, London (dist. by John Wiley and Sons, New York), 1954.

deBruyne, N. A. and Houwink, R., eds., *Adhesion and Adhesives*, Elsevier Publishing Co., Amsterdam (dist. by D. Van Nostrand Co., Princeton, N.J.), 1951.

Delmonte, J., *Plastics in Engineering*, 3rd ed., Penton Publishing Co., Cleveland, 1949.

Delmonte, J., *The Technology of Adhesives*, Reinhold Publishing Corp., New York, 1947.

Encyclopedia Issue, *Modern Plastics*, Plastics Catalogue Corp., Bristol, Conn., 1956.

Fleck, H. R., *Plastics*, 2nd ed., Chemical Publishing Co., Brooklyn, N.Y., 1949.

Hall, A. J., *The Standard Handbook of Textiles*, D. Van Nostrand Co., Princeton, N.J., 1946.

Hill, R., ed., *Fibres from Synthetic Polymers*, Elsevier Publishing Co., Amsterdam (dist. by D. Van Nostrand Co., Princeton, N.J.), 1953.

Houwink, R., ed., *Elastomers and Plastomers*, Vol. II, Elsevier Publishing Co., Amsterdam (dist. by D. Van Nostrand Co., Princeton, N.J.), 1949.

Inderfurth, K. H., *Nylon Technology*, McGraw-Hill Book Co., New York, 1953.

Kaye, S. L., *The Production and Properties of Plastics*, International Textbook Company, Scranton, Penn., 1947.

Kirk, R. E. and Othmer, D. F., eds., *Encyclopedia of Chemical Technology*, Interscience Publishers, New York, 1947–56.

Kraemer, E. O., ed., *Advances in Colloid Science*, Vol. I, Interscience Publishers, New York, 1942.

Kunin, R. and Meyers, R. J., *Ion Exchange Resins*, 2nd ed., John Wiley and Sons, New York, 1952.

Marchionna, F., *Butalastic Polymers*, Reinhold Publishing Corp., New York, 1946.

Mason, J. P. and Manning, J. F., *The Technology of Plastics and Resins*, D. Van Nostrand Co., Princeton, N.J., 1945.

Mattiello, J. J., ed., *Protective and Decorative Coatings*, Vol. III, John Wiley and Sons, New York, 1943.

Mauer, L. and Wechsler, H., *Man-Made Fibers*, Rayon Publishing Corp., New York, 1953.

Mauersberger, H. R., ed., *Matthew's Textile Fibers*, 6th ed., John Wiley and Sons, New York, 1954.

McGregor, R. R., *Silicones and Their Uses*, McGraw-Hill Book Co., New York, 1954.

McPherson, A. T. and Klemin, A., eds., *Engineering Uses of Rubber*, Reinhold Publishing Corp., New York, 1956.

Moakes, R. C. W. and Wake, W. C., eds., *Rubber Technology*, Academic Press, New York, 1951.

Moncrieff, R. W., *Artificial Fibres*, 2nd ed., John Wiley and Sons, New York, 1954.

Nachod, F. C. and Schubert, J., *Ion Exchange Technology*, Academic Press, New York, 1956.

Nauth, R., *The Chemistry and Technology of Plastics*, Reinhold Publishing Corp., New York, 1947.

Osborn, G. H., *Synthetic Ion-Exchangers*, Macmillan Co., New York, 1956.

Riley, M. W., *Plastics Tooling*, Reinhold Publishing Corp., New York, 1955.

Sasso, J. and Brown, M. A., Jr., *Plastics in Practice*, McGraw-Hill Book Co., New York, 1945.

Schildknecht, C. E., ed., *Polymer Processes*, Interscience Publishers, New York, 1956.

Schmidt, A. X. and Marlies, C. A., *Principles of High-Polymer Theory and Practice*, McGraw-Hill Book Co., New York, 1948.

Seymour, R. B. and Steiner, R. H., *Plastics for Corrosion Resistant Applications*, Reinhold Publishing Corp., New York, 1955.

Simonds, H. R., *Industrial Plastics*, 3rd ed., Pitman Publishing Co., New York, 1945.

Simonds, H. R., Weith, A. J., and Bigelow, M. H., *Handbook of Plastics*, 2nd ed., D. Van Nostrand Co., Princeton, N.J., 1949.

Society of the Plastics Industry, *Plastics Engineering Handbook*, 2nd ed., Reinhold Publishing Corp., New York, 1954.

Sonneborn, R. H., Dietz, A. G. H., and Heyser, A. S., *Fiberglas Reinforced Plastics*, Reinhold Publishing Corp., New York, 1954.

Wakeman, R. L., *The Chemistry of Commercial Plastics*, Reinhold Publishing Corp., New York, 1947.

Whitby, G. S., ed., *Synthetic Rubber*, John Wiley and Sons, New York, 1954.

# SUBJECT INDEX

# NAME INDEX